EXPLORING
SOCIAL
PSYCHOLOGY

CANADIAN EDITION

EXPLORING

SOCIAL PSYCHOLOGY

CANADIAN EDITION

ROBERT A. BARON
Rensselaer Polytechnic Institute

DONN BYRNE
State University of New York at Albany

GILLIAN WATSON
University of British Columbia

Allyn & Bacon Canada
Scarborough, Ontario

Canadian Cataloguing in Publication Data

Baron, Robert A.
   Exploring social psychology

Includes bibliographical references and index.
ISBN 0–205–17228–8

1. Social psychology. I. Byrne, Donn.
II. Watson, Gillian. III. Title.

HM251.B37   1994   302   C94–932688–7

© 1995 Allyn & Bacon Canada
A Division of the Simon & Schuster Publishing Higher Education Group
1870 Birchmount Road
Scarborough, Ontario, M1P 2J7

Executive Editor: Cliff Newman
Managing Editor: Marta Tomins
Production Editor: Imogen Brian
Copy Editor: Deborah Burrett
Photo Research: Angelika Baur
Cover/Interior Design: Alex Li
Cover Image: Diana Ong/SuperStock
Page Layout: Zena Denchik

Printed and bound in the United States

CONTENTS

CHAPTER 2

Social Perception and Social Cognition: Internalizing our Social World 36

CHAPTER 3
Attitudes: Evaluating the Social World   76

CHAPTER 4

Identity and Culture: The Self in a Multicultural Context   108

CHAPTER 7
Social Influence: Changing Others' Behavior   235

CHAPTER 8
Helping and Harming: Prosocial Behavior and Aggression   266

CHAPTER 9
Groups and Individuals: The Consequences of Belonging 312

CHAPTER 10

Applied Social Psychology: Health, Environmental, and Legal Applications   350

PREFACE

We are pleased to introduce the first Canadian edition of *Exploring Social Psychology*. It has been a popular text in North America for fifteen years through three editions. But the present edition is the first specifically designed to introduce Canadian students to the fascinating study of social psychology.

Before describing the original features of this edition, we should explain why we felt a Canadian edition was necessary. First, even the best American textbooks do not tackle many issues unique to Canadian society, as teachers of social psychology soon become acutely aware, nor do they fully represent the experience of Canadian students coping in a diverse multicultural context. Second, Canadian social psychology has developed tremendously in recent decades, contributing significantly to mainstream social psychology, in addition to broadening our understanding of specifically Canadian issues and social behavior. From a Canadian perspective, this contribution has been under-represented in most textbooks. We hope that this book achieves a balance in representing some of the issues unique to Canada, and providing an introduction to the work of Canadian social psychologists, as well as to the extensive international literature of social psychology.

FEATURES OF THE CANADIAN EDITION

While the backbone (and most of the meat) of this book remains the excellent writing and scholarship of Robert Baron and Donn Byrne, extensive additions and changes have been made for this Canadian edition. The aim of this new material is to stimulate students into thinking about social psychology issues in Canada, as well as their own part in Canadian society, and to increase the relevance of social psychology ideas to them.

First, a major theme of this book—the importance of culture to social behavior—reflects the multicultural nature of Canadian society itself. Accordingly we have introduced cross-cultural research in many chapters. In addition, this theme is particularly evident in Chapter 4: Identity and Culture: The Self in a Multicultural Context. This new chapter presents research on the self from the traditional perspective (self-schemas, self-esteem, self-focusing etc.), but it also takes a more cultural and group-based look at the self from the perspective of social identity theory and cross-cultural psychology. Finally, it contains a section introducing some important concepts and additional recent research from cross-cultural psychology.

Second, Canadian material has been introduced throughout the book in two major ways: 1) by featuring Canadian research in the body of the text and in the Special Sections mentioned below; and 2) by providing Canadian examples and issues relevant to the theoretical concepts presented. A few examples are given on the following page.

1) A SELECTION OF THE CANADIAN RESEARCH:

"Attraction on the Capilano Bridge"—Dutton & Aron's classic (1974) field study of attraction at Vancouver's Capilano Brigde. (Chapter1).

"Attribution in Intergroup Relations: The Ultimate Attribution Error and Beyond"—featuring the work of Don Taylor and of Serge Guimond and colleagues in Quebec. (Chapter 2)

"Dissonance Reduction at the Race Track: Does Confidence Increase after We Place a Bet"—Knox & Inkster's (1968) classic study of bettors at Vancouver race tracks. (Chapter 3)

"The Independent and Interdependent Self"—featuring Heine's recent cross-cultural studies of the Canadian and Japanese self-concept. (Chapter 4)

"Acculturation: The Immigrant Experience"—John Berry's model and long-term research on acculturative stress among Canada's Native and ethnic groups. (Chapter 4)

"Authoritarian Personality Revisited"—the prize-winning work of Bob Altemeyer on right-wing authoritarianism. (Chapter 5)

"Responses of the Victims of Prejudice"—featuring Dion's work on self-presentation and emotion, as well as Canadian research on the personal/group discrimination discrepancy. (Chapter 5)

"Loneliness: the Absence of Close Relationships"—featuring Perlman & Peplau's model of loneliness. (Chapter 6)

"Rural versus Urban Helping: The Importance of Context"—Using Rushton's (1978) study of helping in and around Toronto as the center for discussion of rural versus urban differences. (Chapter 8)

"Second Language Learning and Bilingualism: The Contribution of Wallace Lambert."—classic Canadian applied research. (Chapter 10)

2) A SELECTION OF THE CANADIAN EXAMPLES AND ISSUES:

What is the nature of Canadian society and how does it differ from the United States? (Chapter 1)

Causal attributions during the Dubin Inquiry for the Ben Johnson affair/Augmenting the success of Silken Laumann at the last Olympics. (Chapter 2)

Do the values of English and French Canadians and Americans differ? (Chapter 3)

Racism in Canadian history: The institutional origins of prejudice and discrimination. (Chapter 5)

Is the typical family in Canada changing? (Chapter 6)

Levels of violence in Canada: Can spousal abusers be treated? (Chapter 8)

Has the level of criminal victimization increased? (Chapter 10)

Was the signing of the Meech Lake Accord an example of groupthink? (Chapter 9)

CONTINUITY IN THE FACE OF CHANGE:
WHAT—FOR GOOD REASONS—REMAINS THE SAME

As the preceding comments suggest, change has indeed been a dominant theme of this revision: Canadian examples, topics, and research are sprinkled liberally throughout the book. This does not imply, however, that everything is new. On the contrary, the same basic vision of what a useful social psychology text should be like is maintained in this new edition. Key aspects of this perspective, which lies at the very heart of the book, include:

Updating the coverage: The coverage of basic topics in social psychology continues to be a priority but this has, as always, been updated to reflect current perspectives and directions.

A Reader-Friendly Approach: As in the past, we have made vigorous efforts to make the book as interesting and appealing to students as possible. To us, this implies many concrete steps, such as writing in language students can understand, including a wide variety of reader aids (chapter outlines, detailed summaries, glossaries), and carefully selecting and designing illustrations. We have retained the approach and features students have liked in *Exploring Social Psychology.*

Several Special Sections: In addition to the new Canadian material described above, this edition retains several features present in previous editions:

FOCUS ON RESEARCH: CLASSIC CONTRIBUTIONS or CLASSIC CANADIAN CONTRIBUTIONS. These sections describe classic studies in social psychology from Canada or the international arena. They help illustrate the foundations of modern social psychology, and call attention to the fact that even what is newest has important roots in past research and theory.

FOCUS ON RESEARCH: THE CUTTING EDGE. These sections describe recently published research in social psychology—research that, in our view, is especially interesting or important.

SOCIAL PSYCHOLOGY: ON THE APPLIED SIDE. These sections describe applications of the findings of principles of social psychology to practical problems and issues.

(Please note, however, that *virtually all of these sections are new;* they are not merely repeats from the previous edition.)

A Broad Eclectic Approach to the Field: As in past editions, we have adopted a "Let 1000 Flowers Bloom!" approach to presenting social psychology. In essence, we let the field speak for itself, rather than attempting to impose our own views or preferences on it.

In sum, while this new edition does indeed constitute a major revision with increased relevance for Canadian students, it retains the approach and features that have made this text so popular.

ACKNOWLEDGMENTS

SOME WORDS OF THANKS FROM THE CANADIAN AUTHOR

Preparing this text has been a truly social experience—that is, many people have co-operated and cajoled to complete it. I have also needed, and greatly appreciated, the social support of my friends and colleagues to weather the deadlines.

First, I want to thank Chris Davis who acted as the researcher and first reader for the manuscript. More than that, however, he made this a joint venture, contributing his ideas, suggestions for Canadian material, incisive critique, and cheerful presence.

Second, at Allyn and Bacon, my sincere thanks to Cliff Newman for initiating this project, to Managing Editor Marta Tomins for her advice and encouragement through-out, to Production Editor Imogen Brian for pleasantly ensuring we met those deadlines (almost), to Deborah Burrett for her very careful and constructive copy-editing, and to Tim Collins who first suggested the idea to me. This must be a very pleasant orga-nization to work in, if my experience is any measure.

I would like also to thank Shelagh Towson for her very helpful comments on the first part of this book.

Finally, I am indebted to Dan Perlman and Susan Butt of the University of British Columbia for the benefit of their experience, advice, and time at the beginning of this project.

ROBERT A. BARON is currently Professor of Psychology and Professor of Management at Rensselaer Polytechnic Institute. A Fellow of the APA since 1978, he received his Ph.D. from the University of Iowa (1968). Professor Baron has held faculty appointments at the University of South Carolina, Purdue University, the University of Minnesota, University of Texas, University of Washington, and Princeton University. He has received numerous awards for teaching excellence at these institutions. Professor Baron has also been a visiting Fellow at the University of Oxford (England). He served as a Program Director at the National Science Foundation from 1979 to 1981. Professor Baron has published more than ninety articles in professional journals and twenty-three invited chapters. He has served on the editorial boards of numerous journals (e.g., *Journal of Personality and Social Psychology, Journal of Applied Social Psychology*), and is currently an associate editor for *Aggressive Behavior*. He is the author or co-author of twenty-five books, including *Human Aggression, Psychology,* and *Behavior in Organizations*. He holds a U.S. patent for an invention designed to improve the physical environment of living and working spaces through air filtration and noise control. At present, Professor Baron's major research interests focus on applying the principles and findings of social psychology to behavior in work settings (e.g., the causes and management of organizational conflict; impact of the physical environment on task performance and productivity). Professor Baron is a long-time runner; his hobbies include woodworking, music, and enjoying fine food.

DONN BYRNE holds the rank of Distinguished Professor of Psychology and is the Director of the Social-Personality Program at the University at Albany, State University of New York. He received the Ph.D. degree in 1958 from Stanford University and has held academic positions at the California State University at San Francisco, the University of Texas, and Purdue University as well as visiting professorships at the University of Hawaii and Stanford University. A past president of the Midwestern Psychological Association and of the Society for the Scientific Study of Sex, he is a Fellow of the Society for Personality and Social Psychology, Society for the Psychological Study of Social Issues, and the Society for the Scientific Study of Sex; he is a Charter Fellow of the American Psychological Society. He has authored fifteen books, thirty-one invited chapters, one hundred and thirty-seven articles in professional journals, plus twenty-two additional publications such as book reviews and brief notes. He directed the doctoral work of forty-two Ph.D.s as well as that of several current graduate students at Albany. He has served on the Editorial Boards of *Experimental Social Psychology, Journal of Applied Social Psychology, Sociometry, Journal of Sex Research, Journal of Personality, Interamerican Journal of Psychology, Journal of Research in Personality, Psychological Monographs, Social Behavior and Personality: An International Journal,* and *Review of Personality and Social Psychology*. He was invited to deliver a G. Stanley Hall lecture at the 1981 meeting of the American Psychological Association in Los Angeles and a State of the Science address at the 1981 meeting of the Society for the Scientific

Study of Sex in New York City. He was an invited participant in Surgeon General Koop's Workshop on Pornography and Health in 1986, and received the Excellence in Research Award from the University at Albany in 1987 and the Distinguished Scientific Achievement Award from the Society for the Scientific Study of Sex in 1989. His current research interests include interpersonal attraction and the prediction of sexually coercive behavior. In his leisure time he enjoys fiction, the theatre, and working on landscaping projects such as the construction of a walkway at his home.

GILLIAN WATSON was an immigrant to Canada from Britain in the 1970s and has been interested in the cross-cultural experience ever since. Maintaining that theme, she received her first degree from McGill University in Quebec (1980), doctorate (or D. Phil. as it's called) from Oxford University in England (1985), and spent a post-doctoral year with the Department of Communication in Ottawa. Her research interests include justice, intergroup relations, and cross-cultural psychology. She has been lecturing at the University of British Columbia since 1987.

Chapter ONE

The Field of Social Psychology: How We Think about and Interact with Others

SPECIAL SECTIONS

The essence of this book is *people*. More specifically, it is a text about people interacting with, and thinking about, others—the *social side* of our existence as human beings. In our opinion, this is truly a fascinating topic, partly for the following reason: *other people often play a crucial role in our lives*. At different times and in different contexts, other people are the source of many of our most satisfying forms of pleasure (love, praise, help) and many of our most important forms of pain (rejection, criticism, embarrassment). So it is not at all surprising that we spend a great deal of our time interacting with others, thinking about them, and trying to understand them (see Figure 1.1). Although the cartoon shown in Figure 1.1 is intended to be humorous, it illustrates a central aspect of social interaction: the difficulty we have when we attempt to understand other people. Its humor is based upon the fact that judges are obliged to be unbiased and objective in their evaluation of others—we don't expect such superficiality from a judge! In our everyday contact with others, we also make such instant judgments and there is no obligation on us to be unbiased.

For example, most people have been in the position where they have had to ask directions of someone on a city street. Usually you are faced with a random assortment of individuals, and you have instantly to judge who is most likely to be of help: who will understand your request, who will have the knowledge you need, who will be pleasant to interact with, and so on. You make this kind of judgment amazingly rapidly, apparently with little effort. And almost certainly, you would not approach a person similar to the man with the "beady" eyes and grim expression in the cartoon. Of course, this may be very unfair to someone who merely has an unfortunate face, but you probably wouldn't have time to consider whether you were being prejudiced.

This simple example of social contact can illustrate a number of important facets of social behavior—it is seldom simple! First, social contact often involves making decisions and judgments about others. The kind of rapid assessment shown in our example is often a necessity in today's fast-paced world. Second, we bring to any such judgments a large amount of social knowledge gained through our prior experiences with others. Third, even though our social knowledge is abundant, this does not prevent misjudgment and bias. In the example above, another person is judged solely on the basis of his appearance, a common aspect of *prejudice and discrimination* (in chapter 5). Finally, contact with others is a constant factor in our lives. Most Canadians live in an urban setting, cheek-by-jowl with hundreds or thousands of others. In order to meet most of our

FIGURE 1.1 We spend much of our time interacting with others, thinking about them, or trying to understand them.

Source: The Wall Street Journal, 8 March 1988.

You're innocent until proved guilty, Mr. Throgmorton … although I don't think I've ever seen beadier eyes.

daily goals and needs, contact with many people, known and unknown, is inevitable. But beyond that, we often actively seek out others just for their company—we are truly "social animals" as one writer has put it (Aronson, 1994).

In sum, it is not an exaggeration to say that *our social relations with others constitute one of the most important parts of our lives.* Consequently, we spend a lot of time and effort thinking about others, trying to understand them, and trying to extract basic principles concerning social behavior—principles that can help us predict others' actions in our future dealings with them. In these efforts we are often guided by what many people call "common sense"—the collective knowledge of our own society concerning social relations. Such knowledge is informal in nature and is based partly upon casual observation of human behavior in social situations, and partly on the writings of poets, philosophers, novelists, and playwrights who have written about human social relations for thousands of years. "Commonsense" knowledge is highly appealing and often seems to capture essential truths about social behavior. Consider the following well-known sayings: "Love looks with the heart, not with the eyes"; "Misery loves company"; "Birds of a feather flock together."

Yet, in many respects, such *informal knowledge* offers a somewhat confusing picture of human social behavior. For example, common sense suggests that prolonged separation can strengthen bonds of affection: "Absence makes the heart grow fonder." At the same time, though, it warns us that separation can weaken such bonds: "Out of sight, out of mind." Which is correct? Can both be right? The "wisdom of the ages" offers no clear-cut answers.

How, then, can we obtain more conclusive—and accurate—information about this topic? How, in short, can we replace speculation, intuition, and insightful guesses with something more definitive? One compelling answer is provided by the field of **social psychology**. And the answer is as follows: *Accurate and useful information about even the most complex aspects of social behavior and social thought can be acquired through the use of basic methods of science.* In short, social psychologists suggest that our understanding of the ways in which we think about and interact with others can be greatly enhanced if we replace the informal methods used by poets, philosophers, playwrights, and novelists with the more systematic methods that have proved invaluable in other fields of science.

Though this suggestion might seem both reasonable and obvious, you may be surprised to learn that a science-oriented approach to the study of social relations is quite new. Only at the end of the last century were social psychological methods initially developed, and the field has been an active one primarily in the decades since World War II. Despite its recent arrival on the scene, however, social psychology has provided some very valuable knowledge about behavior. Perhaps the breadth and potential value of the information it yields are best suggested by a list like the one in Table 1.1. Please note that the questions in the table represent only a small sample of the many topics currently being studied by social psychologists. The field is currently so diverse and so far-ranging in scope that no single list could possibly represent all of the topics it considers.

Before we turn to these intriguing topics, however, we believe it will be useful to pause briefly in order to provide you with certain background information. In the remainder of this chapter, then, we will focus on completing three preliminary tasks. First, we will present a formal *definition* of social psychology—our view of what it is and what it seeks to accomplish. Second, we will offer a capsule summary of social psychology's *history*—how it began, how it developed, and where it is today. Finally, we will examine some of the basic methods used by social psychologists in their *research*. Our goal here is simple: helping you to understand just how the facts and principles presented throughout this text were obtained. Before proceeding, you may find it useful to read the section, "On the Applied Side." This indicates why the systematic study of social behavior is an important task and a timely one.

■ **This is a small sample of the questions that are currently being studied by social psychologists, and that we'll address in this text.**

TABLE 1.1 The Breadth of Social Psychology

Question	Chapter in Which It Is Covered
What techniques do individuals use to "look good" to others—to manage the impressions they make upon them?	Chapter 2
Do we pay more attention to negative information about others than to positive information about them? And if so, why?	Chapter 2
Can our attitudes be changed by stimuli we don't consciously notice?	Chapter 3
Why do some individuals have positive self-evaluations (high self-esteem) while others are much lower in this regard?	Chapter 4
Do people from Western and Eastern cultures differ in their understanding of fairness in relationships?	Chapter 4
How do people respond when they believe that someone has discriminated against them personally or their group?	Chapter 5
What is jealousy? What are its major causes? Effects?	Chapter 6
What tactics do people use in order to get their own way?	Chapter 7
Are people less likely or more likely to offer help to others when they are part of a crowd than when they are alone?	Chapter 8
What are charismatic leaders? What characteristics make them so successful in influencing their followers?	Chapter 9
Are eye-witnesses to a crime accurate? Should we base a conviction on their evidence?	Chapter 10

Solving Society's Problems: Technology is not Enough

Think for a moment about what you consider to be the most serious social problems we face as human beings, problems that threaten our very survival. Each of us might provide slightly different lists, but many would agree with respect to the AIDS epidemic, the incidence of violent crime, air pollution, the consequences of a steadily increasing world population, ethnic conflict, and many more (see Figure 1.2). Though we might agree on identifying such problems and about the desirability of solving them, *how* do we do so?

One possibility is to develop improved technology that will enable us to eliminate these pressing problems. Thus, distribution of effective contraceptives, an AIDS vaccine, the use of improved crime fighting devices or air cleansing equipment in factories and cars might be expected to yield a safer, healthier, and cleaner world. Yet, there are two major difficulties in pursuing purely technological solutions. One is that the appropriate technology needed to solve some problems simply may not be available in the foreseeable future. The other difficulty is that human beings are involved at each step of the process. People must decide to spend the time, money, and effort to create and to use the necessary products. Beyond that, it is obvious that wars are instigated or not, contraceptives are used or not, and antipollution equipment is installed or not *by people*.

We have already discussed the fact that reliance on common sense as a guide to predicting or explaining behavior can be both confusing and inaccurate. Because social psychology uses scientific procedures to study people's behavior, it might be assumed that it has already discovered solutions to the "people-management" side of society's problems. Is this true?

The answer, of course, is "no," but the situation is far from hopeless. As you will learn in the following chapters, social psychology can tell us more about controlling violent behavior, encouraging preventive health practices or environmentally responsible behavior than was possible 20, or even 10, years ago. We believe that continued advances in such knowledge may be as essential as advances in technology in assuring the survival of our species and our planet.

■ Needed for survival: A marriage of psychology and technology

FIGURE 1.2 Problems such as the AIDS epidemic, violent crime, or preserving the environment cannot be solved by technological advances alone. Effective solutions will also require the ability to understand the behavior of individuals and devise means to change that behavior in desired ways.

SOCIAL PSYCHOLOGY: A WORKING DEFINITION

Offering a formal definition of almost any field is a complex task. In the case of social psychology, this complexity is increased by two factors: (1) the field's great diversity, and (2) its rapid rate of change. Despite the broad sweep of topics they choose to study, though, most social psychologists seem to focus the bulk of their attention on one central task: Understanding how and why individuals behave, think, and feel as they do in situations involving other persons. Taking this central focus into account, our working definition of social psychology is as follows: *Social psychology is the scientific field that seeks to understand the nature and causes of individual behavior and thought in social situations.* In other words, social psychology seeks to understand how we think about and interact with others. We will now clarify several aspects and implications of this definition.

SOCIAL PSYCHOLOGY IS SCIENTIFIC IN NATURE

In the minds of many persons, the term *science* refers primarily to fields such as chemistry, physics, and biology. Such persons may find somewhat puzzling our view that social psychology, too, is scientific. How can a field that seeks to investigate the nature of love, the causes of aggression, and everything in between be scientific in the same sense as astronomy, biochemistry, or geophysics? The answer is surprisingly simple. In reality, the term *science* does not refer to a select group of highly advanced fields. Rather, it refers to a general set of methods—techniques that can be used to study a wide range of topics. In deciding whether a given field is or is not scientific, therefore, the crucial question is: *Does it make use of scientific procedures?* To the extent that it does, it can be viewed as scientific in orientation. To the extent that it does not, it can be identified as falling outside the realm of science.

What are these techniques and procedures? We'll describe them in detail in a later section. Here, we'll merely note that they involve efforts to gather systematic information about issues or processes of interest, plus an attitude of skepticism. It is a basic premise of science that all assertions about the natural world should be tested, retested, and tested again before they are accepted as accurate. For example, consider the assertion by Ralph Waldo Emerson that "Beauty is the mark God sets on virtue"—the suggestion, in essence, is that people who are beautiful possess other virtues as well. Is this true? According to basic rules of science, we can tell only by subjecting this idea to careful, systematic research. (In fact, such research has been conducted, and we'll examine it in chapter 6.) In contrast, fields that are not generally regarded as scientific in nature make assertions about the natural world and about people that are not subjected to careful tests. In such fields the intuition, beliefs, and special skills of practitioners are considered to be sufficient (see Figure 1.3).

So, is social psychology scientific? Our reply is, definitely yes. Although the topics that social psychologists study are very different from those in the physical or biological sciences, the methods they employ are similar in nature and orientation. For this reason, it makes good sense to describe social psychology as basically scientific in nature.

SOCIAL PSYCHOLOGY FOCUSES ON THE BEHAVIOR OF INDIVIDUALS

Societies differ widely in terms of their expectations concerning courtship and marriage; yet it is still individuals who fall in—and out of—love. Similarly, societies vary greatly in terms of their overall level of bigotry; but it is still individuals who hold stereotypes about specific groups, experience negative feelings toward them, or seek to exclude them from jobs, neighborhoods, or schools. In short, social behavior and

■ Science versus nonscience: Different methods, different values

FIGURE 1.3 In fields such as social psychology, data are gathered systematically and all hypotheses are carefully tested before being accepted as accurate. In nonscientific fields, in contrast, hypotheses and assertions are accepted at face value in the absence of any systematic tests of their accuracy.

social thought rest, ultimately, with individuals. Given this basic fact, social psychologists have chosen to focus most of their attention on the actions and thoughts of individuals in social situations. They realize, of course, that such behaviors always occur against a backdrop of, and are influenced by, sociocultural factors. Social psychologists' major interest, however, lies in understanding the factors that shape the actions and thoughts of individual human beings within social settings.

SOCIAL PSYCHOLOGY SEEKS TO UNDERSTAND THE CAUSES OF SOCIAL BEHAVIOR AND THOUGHT

In a key sense, the heading of this section states the most central aspect of our definition, the very core of our field. What it means is that social psychologists are principally concerned with understanding the wide range of conditions that shape the social behavior and thought of individuals—their actions, feelings, beliefs, memories, and inferences—with respect to other persons. Obviously, a huge number of different factors play a role in this regard. It is also clear, however, that most factors affecting social interaction fall into five major categories: (1) *the actions and characteristics of others*; (2) basic *cognitive processes* such as memory and reasoning—processes that underlie our thoughts, beliefs, ideas, and judgments about others; (3) *ecological variables*—direct and indirect influences of the physical environment; (4) the *cultural context* in which social behavior and thought occur; and (5) *biological aspects* of our nature and genetic inheritance that are relevant to social behavior. These categories are summarized in Figure 1.4, but a few words about each one will help clarify their essential nature.

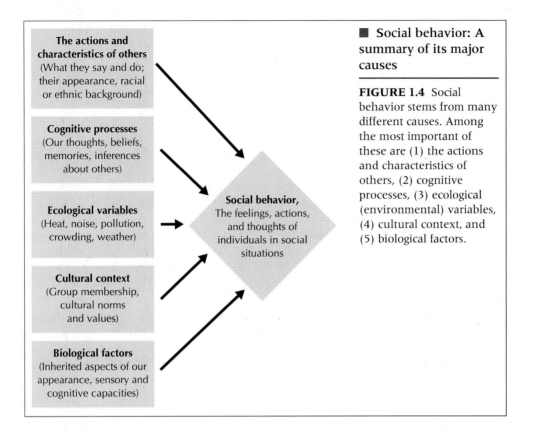

The actions and characteristics of others
(What they say and do; their appearance, racial or ethnic background)

Cognitive processes
(Our thoughts, beliefs, memories, inferences about others)

Ecological variables
(Heat, noise, pollution, crowding, weather)

Cultural context
(Group membership, cultural norms and values)

Biological factors
(Inherited aspects of our appearance, sensory and cognitive capacities)

Social behavior,
The feelings, actions, and thoughts of individuals in social situations

■ Social behavior: A summary of its major causes

FIGURE 1.4 Social behavior stems from many different causes. Among the most important of these are (1) the actions and characteristics of others, (2) cognitive processes, (3) ecological (environmental) variables, (4) cultural context, and (5) biological factors.

The actions and characteristics of others

Consider the following incidents:

> One second after the traffic light turns green, the driver behind you begins to honk her horn angrily.

> Your professor praises a paper you wrote, describing it to the entire class as the best one he's read in several years.

> At the beach, a very attractive person on a nearby blanket catches your eye and smiles at you in a very enticing manner.

Will these actions by others have any impact upon your behavior and thought? Absolutely! So it is clear that often we are strongly affected by the actions of other persons.

Now, be honest: Have you ever felt uneasy in the presence of a handicapped person? Do you ever behave differently toward elderly people than toward young ones? Toward persons belonging to various racial and ethnic groups? Toward persons higher in status than yourself (e.g., your boss) than toward persons lower in status (e.g., children)? Your answer to some of these questions is probably yes, for we are often strongly affected by the visible characteristics and appearance of others.

Cognitive processes

Do you remember the example used at the beginning of this chapter about asking for directions on the street? You will recall the list of characteristics of others you had to evaluate before you approached someone. You might weigh the appearance, ethnicity, gender and pleasantness of potential direction-givers. The way in which you use the social information at hand, as well as your existing knowledge of others, will determine your final decision about who to approach. This use of our own memories and knowledge, our thoughts and attitudes about those around us is the process of *social cognition*. Whatever precise thoughts go through your mind, it is clear that basic cognitive processes such as memory, reasoning, and judgment all play a role. Social psychologists are well aware of the importance of such cognitive processes and realize that they must be taken into careful account in our efforts to understand many aspects of human social behavior (Fiske & Taylor, 1991).

Ecological variables: Impact of the physical environment

Are people more prone to wild, impulsive behavior during the full moon than at other times (Rotton & Kelly, 1985)? Do we become more irritable and aggressive when the weather is hot and steamy than when it is cool and comfortable? Does exposure to high levels of noise, polluted air, or excessive levels of crowding have any impact on our social behavior or performance of various tasks? Research findings indicate that the physical environment does indeed influence our feelings, thoughts, and behavior, so ecological variables certainly fall within the realm of modern social psychology (Baron, In Press; Bell, et al., 1990). And indeed, we'll consider their impact in chapter 10.

Cultural context

Social behavior, it is important to note, does *not* occur in a cultural vacuum. On the contrary, it is often strongly affected by cultural norms (social rules concerning how people should behave in specific situations), membership in various groups, and shifting societal values. Whom should people marry? How many children should they have? Should they keep their emotional reactions to themselves or demonstrate them openly? How close should they stand to others when talking to them? (See Figure 1.5.) Is it appropriate to offer gifts to public officials in order to obtain their favorable action on various requests? These are only a small sampling of the aspects of social behavior that can be—and regularly are—influenced by cultural factors. By **culture** we simply mean the organized system of shared meanings, perceptions, and beliefs held by persons belonging to a particular group (Smith & Bond, 1993).

■ Cultural factors influence social behavior

FIGURE 1.5 The distance between two people holding a conversation varies across different cultures. In some (left photo), a distance of four to five feet is considered appropriate. In others (right photo), a much smaller distance is preferred.

Every day in Canadian cities we encounter people who come from diverse cultural backgrounds. It would be difficult for most Canadians not to be aware of the importance of cultural differences in their interactions with others and the problems that this can sometimes create. Indeed, the Canadian government officially recognizes and encourages this cultural diversity, a fact that will be discussed further in the section, "The Nature of Canadian Society and Social Behavior." Clearly, then, efforts to understand social behavior must take careful account of cultural factors. If they do not, they stand the very real chance of being what one prominent researcher described as *experiments in a vacuum* (Tajfel, 1982)—studies that tell us little about social behavior under real-life conditions and in real-life settings. As we'll discuss below, attention to the effects of cultural factors is an increasingly important trend in modern social psychology, one in which Canadian researchers are on the forefront. The field of social psychology is endeavoring to take account of the increasing cultural diversity that is a hallmark of the late twentieth century. In fact, diversity will be a major theme of this book, and one to which we will return in every chapter.

THE NATURE OF CANADIAN SOCIETY AND SOCIAL BEHAVIOR

"Americans and Canadians are not the same; they are products of two very different histories, two very different situations." (Margaret Atwood , 1982, p. 392)

"[Canada] began as the part of British North America that did not support the [American] Revolution, and Canadians have continued to define themselves by reference to what they are not—American—rather than in terms of their own national history and tradition." (Seymour Lipset, 1990, p. 3)

"The concern of Canada's Fathers of Confederation with 'Peace, Order, and Good Government' implies control of, and protection for the society. The parallel stress of America's Founding Fathers on 'Life, Liberty, and the Pursuit of Happiness' suggests upholding the rights of the individual." (Lipset, 1990, p. 13–14)

As these quotes (the first from a Canadian author and the others from an American social scientist) suggest, Canada has struggled to achieve a separate identity—one that is different from its British roots and, perhaps more importantly, distinct from its neighbor to the south, the United States.

Social psychologists living and working in Canada have had the same problem in attempting to define a Canadian social psychology (Earn & Towson, 1986). On the one hand, historically the United States has been the dominant force in the world of psychology (Moghaddam, 1987, 1990), and the bulk of the material in this book reflects that fact. On the other hand, many Canadian social psychologists are aware, as are many of the readers, that Canadian society and the behavior of Canadians, is somehow different. But what are these differences? And are they extensive or fundamental enough to define a Canadian character or a distinctly Canadian social psychology? We wanted, in this first chapter, to discuss some of these Canadian societal differences and to suggest the ways in which they might relate to research on social behavior. Below we will attempt to outline some of the things that make Canada different.

MULTICULTURALISM: CANADIAN CULTURAL DIVERSITY

Possibly the most important factor distinguishing Canada as a society from the United States is its policy and attitude towards the many groups that make up its population. Canada has an official policy of multiculturalism that stresses the value of cultural differences to our society and encourages groups to maintain their cultural identities. Within that cultural

▶

context, Canada is a bilingual country: French and English being the two official languages. The idea behind multiculturalism is that the fabric of Canadian society should represent a *cultural mosaic*: that is, separate cultural groups, secure in their own identities, should come together and form a strong unified whole. The United States, in contrast, has historically emphasized assimilation of immigrant groups. The idea has been that the U.S. should be a *melting pot* where immigrants, within one or two generations, could assimilate (or "melt") into the American way of life.

■ Canada today

FIGURE 1.6 Some of the characteristics that make Canada different (from the U.S.A.) are its multiculturalism, its relative stability and lack of violence and its sense of community.

Of course, in both countries the ideal and the reality are often quite far apart! In the United States many groups have not "melted." They continue to have separate customs, residential areas and social relationships. For example, assimilation has not occurred in areas such as Chinatown in San Francisco or in the "ghettos" of many American cities, and this can sometimes lead to conflict between groups (e.g., the 1993 Los Angeles riots). In Canada, respect for cultural diversity has often been found wanting and the policy of multiculturalism is not without its critics. We too have had our ethnic conflicts (e.g., the Oka crisis in Quebec or the issue of turbans in the Legion halls), and continuing regional disputes threaten to tear holes in Canada's mosaic. Nonetheless, Canada has a reputation as one of the most livable and ethnically tolerant of Western societies.

How does multiculturalism relate to social psychology in Canada? Simply stated, awareness of the importance of cultural diversity has led Canadian researchers and theorists to focus more on cultural differences and relations between groups. They have been on the forefront internationally in the areas of *bilingualism* and *cross-cultural psychology* (see chapter 4) and *intergroup relations* (see chapter 5; e.g., Berry, Poortina, Segal & Dasen, 1992; Lambert, 1967; Taylor & Moghaddam, 1987).

A KINDER, GENTLER SOCIETY: STABILITY AND VIOLENCE IN CANADA
A second major factor that distinguishes Canada from the United States is its relative lack of violence and its greater social stability. One indicator is the rates of violent crime, which are considerably lower in Canada. For example, in 1987 the murder rate in Canada was 2.5 per 100 000 population, and for the United States it was 8.3 per 100 000 population (Lipset, 1990)—more than three times greater. Given that we are such close neighbors, the size of this gap suggests a fundamental difference between the Canadian and U.S. societies.

The Canadian self-image is of a peace-loving society, and our values reflect this (as we will discuss further in chapter 3). Canadians

▶

show greater respect for, and confidence in, their legal institutions compared to Americans (Lipset, 1990a). In the international arena, Canada's role has traditionally been one of conciliation and peace-keeping. But we cannot become complacent. All Canadians have been aware of a number of incidents of shocking violence in recent years, from the "Just Desserts" killing in Toronto to the sports-related riots in Montreal and Vancouver. Such incidents are often seen as signs of an escalation of violence in this society. However, this impression is not supported by recent crime statistics (Gartner & Doob, 1994), which continue to attest to Canada's relative stability.

Although we have a less violent society, Canadian social psychologists have still made significant contributions in the areas of aggression (e.g., Rule, 1976, 1986) and in *forensic psychology* (the intersection of psychology and the law; e.g., Doob, 1976, 1984; Wells, 1984; Dutton,1992). These topics will be further discussed in chapter 8, "Helping and Harming," and in chapter 10, "Applied Social Psychology."

COMMUNITARIAN VALUES: CANADA'S SENSE OF COMMUNITY

Seymour Lipset has suggested that the differences between Canada and the United States can be traced back, in part, to the historical beginnings of both countries. As the last quote above suggests, the United States has emphasized *individual* rights and freedoms since its beginning, while in Canada there has been a relatively greater emphasis on the maintenance of peace and order in *society*. We have seen this reflected in Canadian values with respect to the law. But this historical difference may also have led Canadian society to be more *communitarian*; that is, it focuses "upon the cooperation of its citizens and the need to protect their welfare" (Lipset, 1990). Canadian federal government has a greater role in the lives of its citizens. It has assumed a larger role in the economy (Mercer & Goldberg, 1982) and provided more extensive social and welfare programs (Kudrle & Marmor, 1981). Public opinion polls suggest that, relative to Americans, Canadians give greater support to this governmental involvement and give more weight to the importance of *equality* between groups in society (Lipset, 1990). Broadly, we can say that Canadian society appears to be more *communal* (focused on the community) and less *individualistic* (focused on the individual) than the United States. We should emphasize, however, that this is only *relative* to the United States. According to one researcher, Canada is one of the more individualistic countries when compared with fifty others around the world (Hofstede, 1983).

In social psychology, the interest of Canadian researchers in group processes, as mentioned above, may be a result of this greater sense of community and greater group-orientation. Perhaps there has also been more emphasis on the constructive role of group relations in people's lives (Taylor & Moghaddam, 1987) and the impact of society upon the individual (Berry, Kim, Minde & Mok, 1987; Taylor & McKirnan, 1984).

In summary, we have suggested that Canadian society is more *multicultural, less violent and unstable,* and *more communitarian* relative to the United States. However, a word of warning may be necessary: Do not make the mistake of assuming that every Canadian is more supportive of cultural diversity, less violent and more community-minded than every American. This is simply not the case. The differences we outlined are *average* ones and there is considerable overlap in the behavior and responses of the populations of both countries. Compared to other nations and cultures, the two countries and their citizens have a great deal in common.

Similarly, Canadian social psychology is not completely distinct from American, as most Canadian social psychologists agree (Rule & Wells, 1981; Earn & Towson, 1986). However, recognition of these differences has produced an interest in Canadian issues and a particularly Canadian perspective in the areas of language, culture and group relations. Canadians have also made significant contributions to most of the topic-areas of social psychology and we will endeavor to point out these contributions throughout this book.

Biological factors

Is social behavior influenced by biological processes and by genetic factors? Ten years ago most social psychologists would have answered no, at least with regard to genetic factors. Now, however, the pendulum of scientific opinion has swung in the other direction, and many believe that our preferences, behaviors, emotional reactions, and even cognitive abilities are affected to some extent by our biological inheritance (Buss, 1990; Nisbett, 1990). The view that biological and genetic factors play an important role in social behavior has, perhaps, been most dramatically stated by the field of **sociobiology**, a discipline suggesting that many aspects of social behavior are the result of evolutionary processes. From the sociobiological perspective, in essence, we all exist primarily to serve our genes—to ensure that our genetic material is passed on to as many offspring as possible (Barkow, 1989; Wilson, 1975). And this basic assumption is used to explain many aspects of social behavior. For example, sociobiologists would argue that if we find specific physical features attractive in potential romantic partners (e.g., a smooth skin, lustrous hair), this is because such features are associated with good health and thus with high reproductive capacity. In short, we like them because doing so increases our chances of passing our genes to future children.

While many social psychologists accept the view that biological and genetic factors can play some role in social behavior, they seriously question several of the basic assumptions of sociobiology (Brewer, 1990; Cantor, 1990). For example, they reject the view that behaviors or characteristics that are affected by genetic factors cannot be altered. Similarly, social psychologists reject the implicit assumption that because they are the result of a long evolutionary process, tendencies in social behavior that currently exist *should* exist because they are *natural*. On the contrary, they argue, even strong genetic predispositions or preferences can be changed. For example, no one would argue that we should not attempt to correct vision defects—which are in large part genetically determined—by means of corrective lenses. In short, the fact that biological factors may play a role in social behavior in no way implies that such tendencies cannot, and should not, be altered.

These and other objections to the basic assumptions of sociobiology have led social psychologists who wish to study the role of biological and genetic factors in social behavior to propose another name for their field: **evolutionary social psychology** (Buss, 1990). This term suggests that social behavior is indeed affected by natural selection; tendencies toward behaviors that are most adaptive from the point of view of survival often increase in strength over time within a given population. But it also recognizes the fact that such tendencies are definitely not set in stone. On the contrary, they can—and do—change in response to shifting environmental and social conditions, and they can even be altered or overridden by cognitive processes. We will comment on the role of genetic factors in various forms of social behavior at several points in later chapters.

SOCIAL PSYCHOLOGY: SUMMING UP

To conclude: Social psychology focuses mainly on understanding the causes of social behavior and social thought—on identifying factors that shape our feelings, behavior, and thought in social situations. It seeks to accomplish this goal through the use of scientific methods, and it takes careful note of the fact that social behavior and thought are influenced by a wide range of social, cognitive, environmental, cultural, and biological factors. While the bulk of social psychology has originated in the United States, Canadian social psychologists have made major contributions to this literature, and the nature of Canadian society has led them to address many issues particularly relevant to Canadians.

The remainder of this text is devoted to summarizing some of the key findings of social psychology. This information is fascinating and we're certain you will find it of interest. But please be warned: It is also full of surprises and will challenge many of your current ideas about people and relations between them. It is probably safe to predict that after exposure to our field, you'll never think about social relations in quite the same way as before. If you value such change and look forward to gaining new insights—as we're confident you do—please read on.

SOCIAL PSYCHOLOGY: A CAPSULE MEMOIR

When, precisely, did social psychology begin? This question is difficult to answer, for speculation about social behavior stretches back to ancient times (Allport, 1985). Any attempt to present a complete survey of the historical roots of social psychology would quickly bog us down in endless lists of names and dates. Because we definitely wish to avoid that pitfall, this discussion will be quite limited in scope. We will focus mainly on the emergence of social psychology as an independent field, its growth in recent decades, where it stands now, and where we believe it will move next.

THE EARLY YEARS: SOCIAL PSYCHOLOGY EMERGES

Few fields of science mark their beginnings with formal ribbon-cutting ceremonies. Instead they develop gradually, as growing numbers of scientists become interested in specific topics or develop new methods for studying existing ones. This pattern certainly applies to social psychology. No bottles of champagne were uncorked to mark its entry on the scene, so it is difficult to choose a specific date for its official launching. Perhaps the years between 1908 and 1924 qualify as the period during which social psychology first appeared as an independent entity. In each of these years, an important text containing the words *social psychology* in its title was published in North America. The first, by William McDougall (1908), was based largely on the view that social behavior stems from innate tendencies or *instincts*. As we have just seen, many modern social psychologists are willing to entertain the notion that genetic factors play a role in some aspects of social behavior. Most, however, reject the idea of fixed, unchanging instincts as an important cause of social behavior. Thus, it is clear that the field had not assumed its modern perspective with McDougall's book.

The second volume, by Floyd Allport (1924), is a different story. That book is much closer—surprisingly close, given the date of its publication—to the modern orientation of the field. Allport argued that social behavior stems from many different factors, including the presence of other persons and their specific actions. Further, his book emphasized the value of experimentation and contained discussions of actual research that had already been conducted on such topics as conformity, the ability to recognize the emotions of others from their facial expressions, and the impact of audiences on task performance. Because all these topics have been studied by social psychologists in recent years, the following conclusion seems justified: by the middle of the Roaring Twenties, social psychology had appeared and had begun to focus on many of the issues and topics it still studies today. It was during these years that the first courses in social psychology were taught at Canadian institutions—as early as 1913 in Manitoba and 1926 in British Columbia, though at that time the topic was seen as part of "moral" philosophy or "mental science" (Alcock, Carment & Sadava, 1994; Hoff, 1992; Wright & Myers, 1982).

The two decades following publication of Allport's text were marked by rapid growth, particularly in the United States. New issues were studied, and systematic methods for investigating them were devised and polished. Important milestones in the development of the field during this period include research by two of its founders—Muzafer Sherif and Kurt Lewin. Sherif (1935) studied the nature and impact of *social norms*—rules indicating how individuals ought to behave—and so contributed many insights to our understanding of pressures toward *conformity*. Lewin and his colleagues (Lewin, Lippitt, & White, 1939) carried out revealing research on the nature of leadership and related group processes. Quite apart from this research, Lewin's influence on social psychology was profound, since many of his students went on to become very prominent in the field. Their names (e.g., Leon Festinger, Harold Kelley, Morton Deutsch, Stanley Schachter, John Thibaut) will feature prominently in later sections of this text.

Between the two world wars (1918–1939) Canadian psychologists were mostly involved in applied research. They were instrumental in developing methods for selection and classification of military personnel in wartime. This concern with applied research also produced some of the first truly social psychological research in Canada—at McGill, into the psychological effects of unemployment during the depression years, and in Toronto, into family relationships (Wright & Myers, 1982).

In short, by the close of the 1930s, social psychology was an active, growing field in the United States and was just beginning to have an impact in Canada. Its literature had already contributed much to our knowledge of human social behavior.

SOCIAL PSYCHOLOGY'S YOUTH: THE 1940s, 1950s, AND 1960s

After a pause resulting from World War II, social psychology continued its growth during the late 1940s and the 1950s. During this period, the field expanded its scope in several directions. Social psychologists focused attention on the influence that groups and group membership exert on individual behavior (Forsyth, 1991). And they examined the link between various personality traits and social behavior, in, for example, noted research on the *authoritarian personality*—a cluster of traits that predispose individuals toward acceptance of extreme political ideologies such as Nazism (Adorno, et al., 1959; see Figure 1.7). This research has continued to the present day in Canada, although the phenomenon is now termed *right-wing* authoritarianism (Altemeyer, 1981, 1988).

■ **Extremists: Do they share certain traits?**

FIGURE 1.7 Research conducted by social psychologists identified a number of characteristics that appear to be shared by members of a wide variety of extremist hate groups.

One of the significant events of this period was the development of the theory of **cognitive dissonance** (Festinger, 1957). This theory proposed that human beings dislike, and will strive to eliminate, inconsistency between their attitudes or inconsistency between their attitudes and their behavior. While this theory may strike you as being quite sensible, it actually leads to many unexpected predictions. (We will examine it in detail in chapter 3.)

In an important sense, the 1960s can be viewed as the time when social psychology fully came of age in the United States. Canadian social psychology began to expand towards the end of the 1960s. (Table 1.2 shows many of those Canadian developments placed in their historical context.) Wallace Lambert produced his groundbreaking research on bilingualism and French immersion during this decade (Lambert, 1967; Lambert, Gardner, Barik & Tunstall, 1963). Other Canadian social psychologists were also beginning to publish research that would later develop a distinctly Canadian flavor (e.g., Berry, 1967; Taylor & Gardner,1969). During this turbulent decade of rapid social change, the number of social psychologists rose dramatically in Canada, Europe and the United States. The field expanded to include practically every aspect of social interaction you might imagine. So many lines of research either began or developed during these years that it would be impossible to list them all here. Suffice it to say that the scope of social psychology virtually exploded during this period.

THE 1970s AND 1980s: A MATURING FIELD

The rapid pace of change did not slacken during the 1970s; if anything, it accelerated. Certainly, it was in the 1970s that Canadian social psychology came into its own as researchers began to examine issues relevant to the Canadian society and began to have an impact internationally. Table 1.2 shows just a few of the interesting lines of research that were being developed. You can see the relevance of such topics as cross-cultural psychology and second-language learning to a Canadian context. On the international front, many lines of study begun during the 1960s were expanded. Several new topics rose to prominence or were studied from a new perspective. Among the most important of these were *attribution* (How do we infer the causes behind others' behavior?); *gender differences* and *sex discrimination* (To what extent does the behavior of women and men actually differ in various situations? What are the adverse effects on women of negative stereotypes concerning their supposed traits?); *intergroup relations* and *cross-cultural social psychology* (How do the differences and the relations between social groups influence the lives of individual group members?); and *environmental psychology* (What is the impact of the physical environment—factors such as noise, heat, crowding, and air pollution—on social behavior?).

Crisis in social psychology

An important event for social psychology, beginning in the 1970s and extending into the 1980s, was a "crisis" that raised basic questions about the direction of both theory and research. This crisis originated from within the social psychological community (Elms, 1975; Gergen, 1973), but was particularly strongly pursued in Europe and Canada (Israel & Tajfel, 1972; Moghaddam, 1990; Moscovici,1972; Strickland, Aboud & Gergen, 1974; Taylor & Brown, 1979). It has been suggested that social psychology might have been responding to the social and political upheavals of the late '60s (Steiner, 1974) with an ideological revolution of its own, as well as attempting to counter the United States' domination of the field (Moghaddam, 1990).

Whatever its origins, the questions raised by this crisis alerted social psychologists to some issues of continuing importance. For example, questions were raised about whether social psychological findings were *culture-biased* because they had been largely produced in one culture—the United States (Berry, 1978). A second, and related,

■ **Social psychology's development related to recent history of Canada and the world**

TABLE1.2 The development of social psychology since the 1950s is set in its historical context, with a (small) selection of Canadian contributions highlighted.

(Note: Canadian events are shown in **Bold**)

Social Psychology's Development		Historical Events
Development of Founding Theories in U.S.A.	**1950s**	Korean War (1950-52): **Canada sends troops**
		The Cold War begins
Adorno: Authoritarian personality (1950)		Television age begins
Allport: Nature of prejudice (1954)	1956	**Lester Pearson's part in Suez Crisis earns**
Festinger: Cognitive dissonance theory (1957)		**Nobel Peace Prize**
Heider: Attribution theory (1958)		
Thibaut & Kelly: Social exchange theory (1959)		
Expansion of research in U.S.A. and Canada	**1960s**	**The 'Quiet Revolution' begins in Quebec**
		The Cuban Missile Crisis
Newcomb: Attraction (1961)	1963	Assassination of John F. Kennedy
Milgram Obedience experiments (1963)		Vietnam War (1966-74): **Canada accepts U.S.**
Lambert: Bilingualism and French		**draft dodgers**
Immersion (1960s)	mid '60s	Political & social movements and countercul-
Latané & Darley: Bystander effect (1967)		ture in North America and Europe
Kelley: Attribution theory (1967)	1968	**'Trudeaumania': Trudeau Government**
		elected
Research expansion continues.	**1970s**	**October Crisis in Quebec: War Measures**
'Crisis' in social psychology		**Act enacted**
	1971	**Policy of Multiculturalism formally**
Gardner: Second language learning (1972)		**adopted**
Berry: Cross-cultural psychology (1976)	1974	Watergate crisis in U.S.A.
Doob: Forensic psychology(1976)		
Tajfel: Social identity theory (1979)		
Love and relationships		
Social cognition expands		
Applications of Social Psychology expand		
Maturity of social psychology	**1980s**	
	1981	**Patriation of the British North America**
Perlman: Relationships & loneliness (1981)		**Act & Charter of Rights**
Wells: Eyewitness Testimony	1984	**Mulroney Era begins: Mulroney**
Petty & Cacioppo: Persuasion & cognition		**Government elected**
Taylor: Intergroup relations (1987)		Conflict in Central America
Bouhris: Social psychology of language	1987	**Meech Lake Accord signed**
Rusbult; Sternberg: Commitment & love	1988	**Free Trade Agreement with U.S.**
Present and Future Trends	**1990s**	Berlin Wall falls — End of Cold War
		Meech Lake Accord fails to be ratified
Importance of cognition and applications continues	1991	Persian Gulf War
Adoption of a multicultural perspective	1992	**Charlottetown Accord referendum**
	1993	**Chrétien Government elected**
	1994	End of Apartheid in South Africa

criticism pointed out that social psychology had tended to neglect the importance of *societal level processes* such as cultural differences and intergroup relations (Israel & Tajfel, 1972; Taylor & Brown, 1979). A third major area of questioning involved a methodological issue: the *context of research*. Research had predominantly taken place in university laboratories using students as subjects, and critics questioned whether the artificial setting of a laboratory and the over-use of student subjects could produce findings that reflected the scope of real-world social behavior (Harré & Secord, 1972; Sears, 1986). The implications of these issues continue to be debated to the present day. However, the effects of the crisis can be seen in the development of topics such as cross-cultural psychology and intergroup relations and the taking of a more multi-cultural perspective generally in social psychology. Researchers began to recognize that there was a need to increase the amount of field research, to study the behavior of people in real-life situations as well as in the laboratory. It should be noted, how-ever, that laboratory research is still the dominant methodology in social psychology (Sears, 1986) and the reason for its continued popularity will become obvious in the next section, which is on research methods.

Finally, in addition to the topics mentioned earlier, two larger-scale trends took shape in and expanded during the 1980s. Since these trends are of great significance to our understanding of modern social psychology, we will describe them here.

Growing influence of a cognitive perspective

As noted earlier, social psychologists have long realized that cognitive factors—atti-tudes, beliefs, values, inferences—play a key role in social behavior. Starting in the late 1970s, however, interest in such topics took an important new form. At this time many social psychologists concluded that our understanding of virtually all aspects of social be-havior could be greatly enhanced by attention to the cognitive processes that underlie them (e.g., Wyer & Srull, 1988). This approach involves, briefly, efforts to apply to many aspects of social thought and social behavior basic knowledge about such issues as (1) how memory operates, (2) how reasoning occurs, and (3) how new informa-tion is integrated into existing mental frameworks. Major insights into many aspects of social behavior have been gained, and new issues previously overlooked (e.g., The im-pact of current moods on social thought and vice versa; Stroessner, Hamilton, & Mackie, 1992) have been brought into sharp focus. We will discuss such research in chapter 2.

Growing emphasis on application: Exporting social knowledge

The 1970s and 1980s were also marked by a second major trend in social psychology: growing concern with the *application* of social knowledge. An increasing number of so-cial psychologists have turned their attention to questions concerning *personal health* (e.g., What factors help individuals resist the adverse impact of stress? Are certain life-styles or personal characteristics linked to coronary disease?); the *legal process* or *forensic psychology* (e.g., How valid is eyewitness testimony? What information is most influential in shaping the decisions of jurors?); and the *physical environment* (e.g., How does the architecture of student housing affect the social behavior of residents? How can we persuade people to recycle?). Whatever its specific focus, such research at-tempts to apply the findings and principles of social psychology to the solution of practical problems. This theme is certainly not new in our field; Kurt Lewin, one of its founders, once remarked, "there's nothing as practical as a good theory," by which he meant that theories of social behavior and thought developed through systematic re-search often turn out to be extremely useful in solving practical problems. There seems little doubt, however, that interest in applying the knowledge of social psy-chology to practical issues has increased in recent years, with many beneficial results. We will examine this work in detail in chapter 10.

WHERE DO WE GO FROM HERE?
THE 1990s AND BEYOND

Earlier we noted that *diversity* is a prime characteristic of social psychology. Given this fact, predictions about the future of the field are uncertain to say the least. Still, at the risk of being proven wrong by future events, we wish to offer the following guesses about how social psychology will change in the coming decades.

Cognition and application:
Growing knowledge, growing sophistication

The first of our predictions is the one on firmest ground: the two major trends described above—growing influence of a cognitive perspective and increasing interest in application—will continue. Knowledge about cognitive processes (memory, reasoning, inference) is accumulating very quickly. It seems only natural that social psychologists will use that knowledge in their efforts to understand social behavior and, especially, social thought. Such work has already yielded valuable results, and we are confident it will continue to do so in the decades ahead.

Similarly, we predict that interest in applying the principles and findings of social psychology will also continue. Increased concern with application appears to be a natural outgrowth of increasing maturity in almost any field. Thus, as social psychology advances, efforts to apply its growing knowledge to practical issues will continue and perhaps expand.

The role of affect: Realizing that feelings count, too

It is a basic law of physics that actions produce opposite reactions of comparable scope. In a sense, the same principle seems to apply to the growing emphasis on cognition in social psychology. Partly in response to the increasing interest in various aspects of social thought, many researchers have called for renewed focus on the impact of the emotional side of our existence (Schwarz, 1990). As a result, much recent research has sought to examine the impact of *affective states*—relatively mild and short-lived changes in our current moods or feelings (Forgas, 1991; Isen & Baron, 1991; Schwarz, 1991). In addition, a growing volume of research has focused on complex interactions between affect and cognition—how feelings shape thought and how thought shapes feelings (Schwarz, 1990). We'll examine this relationship in detail in chapter 2. For the moment, we'll merely note that, in our opinion, research on the role of affect in social behavior and social thought will continue, and perhaps accelerate, during the next decade.

Adoption of a multicultural perspective:
Taking full account of social diversity

Statistics indicate that in the late twentieth century cultural diversity is a fact of life in many western countries, including Canada and the United States. When I (Bob Baron) was in high school, I received an unusual present from my uncle: a book that provided an introduction to the United States for Europeans planning to visit this country for the first time. In retrospect, one section was of special interest. It stated that the population of the United States was "about 90 percent of European descent." How the world has changed since the late 1950s when the book was written! At the present time, the population of the United States is far more diverse than this book suggested. Consider California, the most populous state. At present, only 57 percent of its population is of European descent, and projections indicate that by the year 2000 no single group will be in the majority. And for the United States as a whole, it is projected that by the year 2050 merely 53 percent of the population will be of European descent.

■ **Multicultural diversity: A fact of life in the late twentieth century**

FIGURE 1.8 In Canada and many other countries, cultural diversity is a key national characteristic. Social psychology is currently studying this diversity and the impact of cultural and ethnic factors upon social behavior.

As a Canadian immigrant in the 1970s, I (Gillian Watson) was struck by the diversity of Canada's population compared to that of Britain, from which I'd come. I saw this as one of the attractions and strengths of Canada, though I remember wondering how I would pronounce the varied names on my first class list. The changes in population descent in Canada have been fairly gradual (see Table 1.3). People of European origin still make up the majority of the population as of 1991. The proportion of those from the two founding European cultures, British and French, has remained fairly constant. There has, however, been an increase in people from other parts of Europe and from Asia. People of aboriginal descent are a larger proportion of the population in 1991, probably because of changes in regulations governing their status. Of course, the five groups in Table 1.3 could be broken down into many more separate cultural groups (e.g, Italians, Greeks, Vietnamese, Japanese, etc.). This might more realistically represent Canada's multicultural diversity, which is one of the nation's key qualities. Internationally, large-scale migration is occurring in many areas, and international trade and travel are certainly on the rise. The result: the days of relative cultural isolation are fast coming to a close.

■ **Canada's Changing Multiculturalism: Ethnic descent of Canadians since 1951**

TABLE 1.3 Changes in the ethnic origin of Canada's population include a slight decrease in the proportion who are of British origin and a small increase in the proportion whose origin is other parts of Europe and Asia.

	1951	1971	1991*
British	47.9%	44.6%	44.6%
French	30.8%	28.7%	31.1%
Other European	18.2%	23.0%	33.7%
Asian	0.5%	1.3%	6.1%
Aboriginal	1.2%	1.4%	3.7%
Total Population in millions	(14.0 M)	(21.6 M)	(27.0 M)

*In 1991, respondents were given the option of listing a second ethnicity. 29% of the population listed more than one ethnicity, thus percentages add to more than 100%.

Sources: Statistics Canada Census Reports, 1951, 1971, 1991.

What is the impact of such diversity on social psychology? In our view the effects are both pronounced and far-reaching. Many social psychologists now believe that cultural factors and forces are so powerful that they can influence even the most basic aspects of social behavior (Smith & Bond, 1993). Why do persons from different cultures react in contrasting ways to various situations? What factors in their cultures are responsible for these differences? A growing number of social psychologists believe that studying such issues may help clarify which aspects of social behavior are universal among human beings and which are products of cultural factors. For all these reasons social psychology has moved toward a **multicultural perspective**—a focus on multicultural diversity—in recent years; and it is our prediction that this trend will continue in the years ahead.

Those, then, are our predictions. Will they prove to be accurate? Only time and the course of future events will tell. Regardless of their fate, however, there is one additional prediction we are willing to make with great confidence: No matter how social psychology changes in the years ahead, it will remain an active, vital field—one with an impressive potential for contributing to human welfare.

ANSWERING QUESTIONS ABOUT SOCIAL BEHAVIOR AND SOCIAL THOUGHT: RESEARCH METHODS IN SOCIAL PSYCHOLOGY

By now you should have a basic grasp of (1) what social psychology is; (2) how it developed; and (3) where, perhaps, it is headed. With that information in place, it is appropriate for us to turn to another essential issue: How do social psychologists attempt to answer questions about social behavior and social thought? How, in short, do they seek to expand our knowledge of these basic topics? To provide you with a useful overview of this process, we will touch on three related issues. First, we will describe two key *methods of research in social psychology*. Next, we will examine the role of *theory* in such research. Finally, we will consider some of the complex *ethical issues* that arise in social psychological research and that, to a degree, are unique to such research.

THE EXPERIMENTAL METHOD: KNOWLEDGE THROUGH INTERVENTION

If a large sample of social psychologists were asked to name the method of research they most prefer, most would probably reply with the term **experimentation**. Unfortunately, our past experience suggests that many persons view experimentation as being somewhat mysterious and complex. In fact, that is far from the case. In its essential logic experimentation is surprisingly simple. To help you understand its use in social psychological research, we will first describe the basic nature of experimentation and then comment on two conditions that are essential for its successful use.

Experimentation: Its basic nature

A researcher who decides to employ the experimental method generally begins with a clear-cut goal: to determine whether (and to what extent) a specific factor (*variable*) influences some aspect of social behavior. To find out, the researcher then (1) systematically varies the presence or strength of this factor, and (2) tries to determine whether those variations have any impact on the aspect of social behavior or social thought under investigation. The central idea behind these procedures is this: if the factor varied does exert such effects, individuals exposed to different amounts (levels) of the factor should show different patterns of behavior. Exposure to a small amount of the factor should result in one level or pattern of behavior, exposure to a larger amount should result in another pattern, and so on.

Generally, the factor systematically varied by the researcher is termed the **independent variable**, while the aspect of behavior studied is termed the **dependent variable**. In a simple experiment, then, subjects in different groups are exposed to contrasting levels of the independent variable (e.g., low, moderate, high). The researcher then carefully examines and compares the behavior of these persons to determine whether it does in fact vary with different levels of the independent variable. If it does—and if two other conditions described below are also met—the researcher can tentatively conclude that the independent variable does indeed affect the aspect of behavior or cognition being studied.

Perhaps a concrete example will help you to form a clearer picture of this process. Let's consider an experiment designed to examine the *hypothesis* (an as yet unverified suggestion) that the faster people talk (at least up to a point), the more persuasive they are. In such research, the independent variable would be the speed at which would-be persuaders speak and the dependent variable would be some measure of the attitudes or preferences held by the persons the persuaders are trying to influence. For example, such a study might involve delivery of a speech designed to alter the attitudes of audience members toward a particular issue—let's say, attitudes toward legislation that will place strict controls on the release of chemicals that deplete the earth's ozone layer. For argument's sake, imagine that the audience consists of executives from air-conditioning companies—businesses that use vast amounts of the chemicals to be regulated. It is probably safe to assume, therefore, that they will be initially opposed to the legislation. How would the experiment proceed? A basic strategy would be to expose several different groups of participants to the same persuasive message while systematically varying the speed at which it is delivered. Thus, one group of subjects would be exposed to the message presented at a slow rate of speech (about 150 words per minute). A second group would hear the same message presented at an average rate of speech (about 170 words per minute). A third group would hear the message delivered at a very fast pace (190 words per minute).

After all groups heard the speech, the dependent variable—some measure of the audience members' attitudes toward the legislation—would be collected. For example, participants might be asked to indicate the extent to which they favored the proposed law by circling one number on a scale such as the one shown in the top part of Table 1.4. Alternatively, they might be asked to indicate the extent to which they agreed or disagreed with the speaker (see Table 1.4).

If rate of speech does affect persuasion, then we might obtain a pattern of results such as those shown in Figure 1.9. As this figure indicates, the faster the persuader speaks, the more favorable are the attitudes of audience members toward the legislation. We must assume, by the way, that subjects in the three groups do not differ with respect to their attitudes prior to hearing the persuasive message. If they do, serious complications can occur in terms of interpreting any results that are obtained. (Actually, several studies have been conducted to investigate the relationship between speed of speech and persuasion. Some have yielded a pattern of findings precisely like those in Figure 1.9; Miller et al., 1976; Woodall & Burgoon, 1984. However, other research—to which we'll return in chapter 3—indicates that fast talkers are not always more persuasive than slower ones; Smith & Shaffer, 1991.)

Successful experimentation: Two basic requirements

Earlier it was noted that before we can conclude that an independent variable has affected some form of behavior, two important conditions must be met. And a basic understanding of these conditions is essential for evaluating the usefulness of any experiment.

TABLE 1.4 Measuring reactions to a persuasive message

To what extent do you favor legislation designed to limit the release into the atmosphere of chemicals that damage the earth's protective ozone layer? (Please circle one number.)

Strongly Opposed   **Favor**

| 1 | 2 | 3 | 4 | 5 | 6 | 7 |

To what extent do you agree with the views expressed by the speaker? (Check one.)

  Strongly disagree

  Disagree

  Neither agree nor disagree

  Agree

  Strongly agree

■ Experimentation: A simple example

FIGURE 1.9 In the experiment illustrated here, groups listen to persuasive appeals delivered by a communicator who speaks at a slow, moderate, or fast rate. Results indicate that the faster the communicator speaks, the more favorable are listeners' attitudes toward the speaker's message. These findings suggest that speed of speech is one factor affecting persuasion.

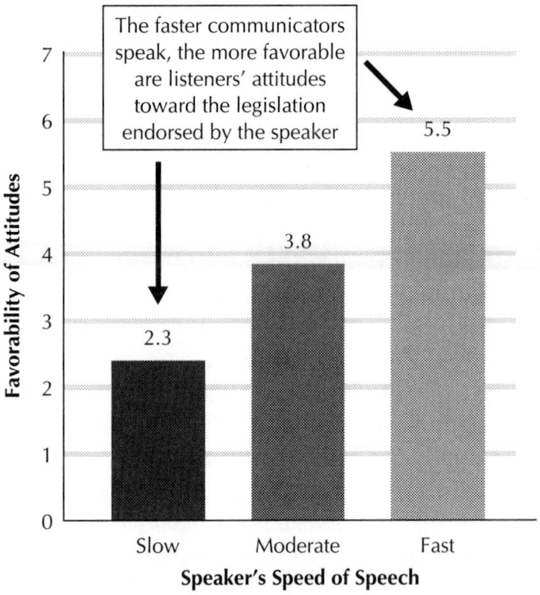

The faster communicators speak, the more favorable are listeners' attitudes toward the legislation endorsed by the speaker

Slow: 2.3 Moderate: 3.8 Fast: 5.5

Favorability of Attitudes

Speaker's Speed of Speech

The first condition involves what is usually termed the **random assignment of subjects to groups**. According to this principle, each person taking part in a study must have an equal chance of being exposed to each level of the independent variable. The reason for this rule is simple: If subjects are *not* randomly assigned to each group, it may prove impossible to determine whether differences in their behavior in the study stem from differences they brought with them, from the impact of the independent variable, or from both. For instance, continuing with our study of speed of speech and persuasion, imagine participants in the study are drawn from two different sources: first-year law students and a group of high school dropouts enrolled in a special course designed to equip them with basic vocational skills. Now imagine that because of purely logistical factors (such as differences in the two groups' schedules), most of the participants exposed to the slow talker are law students, while most of the people exposed to the fast talker are high school dropouts. Suppose that results indicate that participants exposed to the fast talker show much more agreement with the views expressed than participants exposed to the slow talker. What can we conclude? Not much, because it is entirely possible that this difference stems from the different mixes of participants in the two experimental conditions: In the slow-talker condition, 75 percent of the participants are law students and 25 percent are high school dropouts, while in the fast-talker condition the opposite is true. Since law students may be somewhat harder to persuade than high school dropouts, we can't really tell why these results occurred. To avoid such problems, it is crucial that all subjects have an equal chance of being assigned to different experimental groups (treatment).

The second condition referred to above may be stated as follows: Insofar as possible, all other factors that might also affect participants' behavior, aside from the independent variable, must be held constant. To see why this is so, consider what would happen if, in the study on speed of speech and persuasion, different speakers were used in each condition. Further, imagine that one of these speakers—the fast talker—had a beautiful English accent (an accent many Americans find very pleasant). Now assume that participants express greatest agreement with this speaker. What is the cause of this result? The fact that the speaker talked rapidly? Her accent? Both factors? Obviously, it is impossible to tell. In this situation, the independent variable of interest (speed of speech) is "confounded" with another variable—whether the speakers have an accent—that is not really part of the research. When such **confounding** occurs, it is impossible to determine the precise cause of any differences among the various groups in an experiment. The result: The findings are largely uninterpretable.

In the case we have just described, confounding between variables is relatively easy to spot. Often, though, it enters in more subtle ways. For this reason, researchers wishing to conduct successful experiments must always be on guard against it. Only when confounding is prevented can the results of an experiment be interpreted with confidence. The field research described in the section, "Classic Canadian Contributions: Attraction on the Capilano Bridge," illustrates the difficulty of controlling possible confounds outside the laboratory.

THE CORRELATIONAL METHOD: KNOWLEDGE THROUGH SYSTEMATIC OBSERVATION

Earlier we noted that experimentation is usually the preferred method of research in social psychology. (We'll see why below.) Sometimes, though, experimentation simply cannot be used. There are two reasons why this may be so. First, systematic variation in some factor of interest may be beyond an experimenter's control. Imagine, for example, that a researcher believes that panic in the stock market often stems from certain kinds of statements by the prime minister and by the head of the Bank of Canada. Obviously, the researcher cannot arrange for these persons to make such statements in order to observe the effects. The actions of the president and other high government officials are outside her or his control.

Second, ethical constraints may prevent a researcher from conducting what might otherwise be a feasible experiment. In other words, it might be possible to vary some factor of interest, but doing so would violate ethical standards accepted by scientists or society generally. For example, imagine that somehow a researcher *could* induce the prime minister and the head of the Bank of Canada to make statements calculated to trigger a wild panic on Bay Street. Clearly, doing so would be unethical. After all, what gives this researcher the right to expose millions of persons to financial or psychological harm? Similarly, and perhaps a bit more realistically, suppose that a social psychologist had reason to suspect that certain kinds of beliefs about one's romantic partner are especially damaging to long-term relationships. Could this researcher try to induce such beliefs among one group of couples but not among another in order to determine whether divorces and other breakups were more common in the first group than in the second? Obviously not, for in conducting such a study, the researcher would endanger the happiness and well-being of the unknowing participants.

Faced with such difficulties, social psychologists often adopt an alternative research technique known as the **correlational method**. In this approach, researchers make no efforts to change one or more variables in order to observe the effects of these changes on some other variable. Instead, they merely observe naturally occurring changes in the variables of interest to learn if changes in one are associated with changes in the other. Such associations are known as *correlations*, and the stronger the association, the higher the correlation. (Correlations range from −1.00 to +1.00, and the greater the departure from 0.00, the stronger the relationship between the variables in question. Thus, a correlation of −.80 indicates a stronger relationship between two variables than a correlation of +.40.)

To illustrate the correlational method, let's return, once again, to our study of speed of speech and persuasion. A researcher wishing to examine this issue by means of the correlational method might proceed as follows. First, she or he would measure the speed of speech of many would-be persuaders in a wide range of contexts (politics, sales, and so on). In each of these contexts, the researcher would also obtain some measure of the success of the would-be persuaders—for example, the percentage of votes each candidate receives, the amount of merchandise each salesperson moves. If fast talkers are more persuasive than slow talkers, results might indicate that these two variables are positively correlated: The faster candidates and salespersons speak, the greater their success.

The correlational method offers several useful advantages. For one thing, it can be used to study behavior in many real-life settings. For another, it is often highly efficient and can yield a large amount of interesting data in a short time. Moreover, it can be extended to include many different variables at once. Thus, in the study described above, information on the physical attractiveness, age, height, and gender of the political candidates and salespersons might be obtained. Through a statistical procedure known as *regression analysis*, the extent to which each of these variables is related to—and therefore predicts—success in politics and sales could then be determined.

Unfortunately, however, the correlational method suffers from one major drawback that greatly lessens its appeal to social psychologists. *In contrast to experimentation, the findings it yields are often somewhat uncertain with respect to cause-and-effect relationships.* The fact that changes in one variable are accompanied by changes in another in no way guarantees that a causal link exists between them—that changes in the first caused changes in the second. Rather, in many cases, the fact that two variables tend to rise or fall together simply reflects the fact that both are caused by a third variable. For example, suppose that a researcher finds that the faster politicians talk, the higher the percentage of votes they receive. Does this mean that speed of speech causes voters to prefer certain candidates? Perhaps. But it may also be that fast-talking candidates know more about the issues than slower-talking ones. If this is the case, then the relationship between speed of speech and the outcome of elections is somewhat spurious. In fact both speed and success as a candidate are related to a third factor—knowledge of the issues. Perhaps this key point can be clarified by a few additional examples of correlations that do not indicate causation. These are listed in Table 1.5. Can you identify the third factors that may underlie the relationships shown in the table?

By now the main point should be clear. The existence of even a strong correlation between two factors should not be interpreted as a definite indication that they are causally linked. Such conclusions are justified only in the presence of additional, confirming evidence.

■ All of the correlations listed here have actually been observed. However, none indicates that the two factors involved are causally linked. Can you determine what third factor makes each pair of factors seem to be related to one another? (Answers appear below.)

TABLE 1.5 Examples of correlations that don't imply causation

Observed Correlation	Possible Underlying Cause
1. The more people weigh, the higher their salaries.	1.
2. The greater the number of storks nesting on roofs in Northern Europe, the greater the number of births nine months later.	2.
3. The greater the degree of crowding in cities, the higher their crime rates.	3.

Answers
1. Weight and earnings both increase with age and experience.
2. Cold weather makes roofs an attractive place to nest and also causes people to remain indoors—where they engage in activities that increase births!
3. Crowding and crime are both related to poverty.

Attraction on the Capilano Bridge: A Natural Experiment

In the early 1970s, Don Dutton and Arthur Aron, working at the University of British Columbia, were interested in a fundamental mechanism of attraction—the fact that it is often associated with intense emotional arousal. In fact, their hypothesis suggested that being in a state of emotional arousal *before* meeting an attractive potential partner would increase the likelihood of sexual attraction. The *independent variable* in this hypothesis was emotional arousal, and they were able to take advantage of a field setting nearby where arousal was naturally varied (see Figure 1.10). The Capilano Gorge, a popular tourist attraction, contained two types of bridge: one a suspension bridge, one-and-a-half metres wide, swaying 70 metres above a rocky canyon, and the other a broader bridge only 3 metres above a

■ Attraction on the Capilano Bridge

FIGURE 1.10 Dutton and Aron's classic research might suggest that people crossing this bridge have an increased likelihood of being attracted to others because of the increased emotional arousal that its great height induces.

▶

calm and shallow stream. They could be assured that people crossing the Capilano suspension bridge would feel considerably more arousal (fear) than those on the lower bridge. This type of research is termed a **natural** or **quasi-experiment**; that is, an experiment in which the natural environment, rather than the experimenter, sets the different levels of the independent variable.

An attractive female interviewer asked males coming off both bridges if they would fill out a questionnaire supposedly for her class psychology project concerned with the effects of scenic beauty on creativity. They were asked to write a small passage about an ambiguous picture presented to them, and then the interviewer offered each subject her telephone number in case they wanted more information about the study. *Dependent variables* measuring attraction were the amount of sexual imagery in the written passages and the number of phone calls subjects made to the interviewer. We should also mention that the experiment was repeated with a male interviewer questioning male subjects.

Results supported the hypothesis: Men who had crossed the suspension bridge (high arousal group) showed greater sexual imagery in their written passages and were more than three times as likely to call the female interviewer than men who had crossed the low, nonsuspension bridge (low arousal group). Results for the male interviewer showed no significant difference between the high and low arousal conditions: the presence of a potential partner was necessary before arousal was interpreted as sexual attraction.

This is a classic study in the attraction literature and provides support for the three-factor theory of passionate love (Hatfield & Walster, 1981), as you will see later in chapter 6. However, for our purposes it also highlights some potential problems in conducting field research. While the setting of this study was a more realistic one for investigating attraction than a research laboratory might have been, it was also more difficult to control for possible *confounding* of variables. You may have already noticed that this study violated the two basic requirements for successful experimentation: *random assignment of subjects to groups* and *holding other factors constant*. This is why such studies are sometimes given the name *quasi-experiments*, i.e., because they are not truly experimental. Subjects were not randomly assigned to the high and low arousal conditions of this experiment—they assigned themselves! And further, it is more difficult when you are out in the field to hold constant other factors that might influence subjects' behavior. Two of these potential problems in interpreting results were recognized by these researchers. Personality differences between those who crossed the suspension bridge and those who did not might explain their greater levels of attraction to the female interviewer. For example, perhaps the suspension bridge group were more daring and would be more likely to consider calling an attractive woman—emotional arousal from the crossing would have nothing to do with results in that case. Second, the female interviewer may have acted differently towards one group than the other. She might, for example, have smiled more at the suspension bridge group because of the greater beauty of the setting. She had been trained to be constant in her behavior, but the success of this training would be much more difficult to monitor in the field. Each of these factors was controlled in subsequent *laboratory* experiments, and results still showed the effect of prior arousal in increasing attraction.

This research also illustrates the use of both field and laboratory settings to examine an hypothesis. This combination is a common one and derives from two important aspects of research in social psychology. First, each setting has its advantages and disadvantages. The laboratory is the context in which a researcher can have most control of variables and can most avoid their confounding. Therefore, a researcher can have more confidence in any cause-effect relationships between variables that are demonstrated. But on the down side, the laboratory tends to be an artificial setting for the study of social behavior, as noted previously. In contrast, field experiments, have much greater realism but provide less control of variables, as we have seen above. The second reason for use

➤

of both settings is that this provides *replication*. Science requires that hypotheses should be confirmed over and over again before they are accepted as fully valid. Further, in social psychology such confirmations should employ as wide a range of methods and settings as possible. One supporting experiment might contain unseen errors, but, with each additional supporting study in differing settings, we can begin to have greater confidence in our hypothesis.

Finally, this study has implications for your own romantic life even if you live miles from the Capilano Suspension Bridge. For instance, it is no wonder that people become attracted to each other at clubs: the noise, the lights, the dancing are all guaranteed to raise arousal levels even before you set eyes on that attractive person...!

THE ROLE OF THEORY IN SOCIAL PSYCHOLOGY

Over the years, the students in our classes have often asked: "How do social psychologists come up with such interesting ideas for their research?" As you can probably guess, there is no simple answer. Some research projects are suggested by informal observation of the social world around us. Social psychologists take note of some puzzling aspect of social behavior or social thought and plan investigations to increase their understanding of that aspect. On other occasions, the idea for a research project is suggested by the findings of an earlier study. Successful experiments in social psychology do not simply answer questions; they often raise new ones as well. Perhaps the most important basis for research in social psychology, however, is formal **theories**.

In simple terms, theories represent efforts by scientists in any field to answer the question *Why?* Theories involve attempts to understand precisely why certain events or processes occur as they do. Thus, theories go beyond mere observation or description of aspects of social behavior; they seek to *explain* them as well. The development of comprehensive, accurate theories is a primary goal of all science (Howard, 1985; Popper, 1959), and social psychology is no exception. Accordingly, a great deal of research in our field is concerned with efforts to construct, test, and refine theoretical frameworks. But what, precisely, are theories, and how are they used in social psychological research? Perhaps the best way to answer is through a concrete example.

Imagine that we observe the following: when people work together in a group, each member exerts less effort on the joint task than when they work alone. (This is known as *social loafing*, and is discussed in chapter 9.) The observation just described is certainly useful by itself. After all, it allows us to predict what will happen when individuals work together, and it also suggests the possibility of intervening in some manner to prevent such outcomes. These two accomplishments—*prediction* and *intervention* (sometimes known as *control*)—are major goals of science. Yet, the fact that social loafing occurs does not explain *why* it takes place. It is at this point that theory enters the picture.

In older fields of science such as physics or chemistry, theories are often stated as mathematical equations. In social psychology, however, they are usually phrased as verbal statements or assertions. For example, a theory designed to account for social loafing might read as follows: When people work together, they realize that their outputs will not be individually identifiable and that all participants will share in the responsibility for the final outcome. As a result, they conclude that they can get away with "taking it easy" and so exert less effort on the task. Regardless of how they are expressed, theories consist of two main parts: (1) several basic concepts (e.g., social loafing, identifiability of individual outputs, and shared responsibility); and (2) statements concerning relationships among these concepts (e.g., as the identifiability of individual outputs decreases, social loafing will increase).

Formulation of a theory is just the first step in a continuing process, however. Only theories that have been carefully tested and confirmed are useful; so in social psychology, as in all other fields of science, after a theory is proposed, several procedures normally follow. First, predictions are derived from the theory. These predictions are formulated in accordance with basic principles of logic and are known as *hypotheses*. For example, one hypothesis that might be derived from a theory of social loafing as described above is as follows: To the extent that members of a group believe their work will be identifiable, social loafing will decrease.

Next, hypotheses are tested in actual research. If they are confirmed, confidence in the accuracy of the theory is increased. If, instead, such predictions are disconfirmed, confidence in the theory is weakened. Then the theory may be altered so as to generate new predictions. These are subjected to test, and the process continues. If the modified predictions are confirmed, confidence in the revised theory is increased; if they are disconfirmed, the theory may be modified again or, ultimately, rejected. Figure 1.11 summarizes this process.

Please note, by the way, that theories are useful from a scientific point of view only to the extent that they lead to *testable* predictions. If a theory fails to generate hypotheses that can be examined in actual research, it cannot be viewed as scientific in nature.

THE QUEST FOR KNOWLEDGE AND THE RIGHTS OF INDIVIDUALS: SEEKING A DEFENSIBLE BALANCE

In their use of experimentation and systematic observation, and in their reliance on comprehensive theories, social psychologists do not differ from researchers in many other fields. One technique, however, does seem to be unique to research in social psychology: **deception**. Basically, this technique involves efforts by researchers to withhold or conceal information about the purposes of a study from the persons who participate

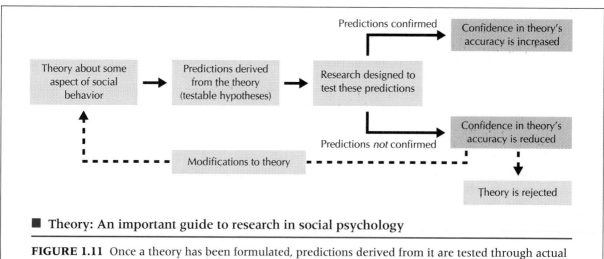

■ **Theory: An important guide to research in social psychology**

FIGURE 1.11 Once a theory has been formulated, predictions derived from it are tested through actual research. If these are confirmed, confidence in the theory's accuracy is increased. If they are disconfirmed, confidence in the theory's accuracy is reduced. The theory may then be modified so as to generate new predictions, or it may ultimately be rejected.

in it. The reason for using this procedure is simple: Many social psychologists believe that if participants know the true purposes of an investigation, their behavior will be changed by that knowledge. The research itself will then have little chance of providing useful information.

On the face of it, this is a reasonable belief. For example, imagine that in a study designed to examine the effects of physical attractiveness on first impressions, participants are informed of this purpose. Will they now react differently to a highly attractive stranger than they would have in the absence of this information? Perhaps, for now, they may lean over backwards to avoid evaluating the attractive person in a favorable manner, to prove that *they* are not affected by a stranger's outward appearance.

Because of such considerations, many social psychologists feel that deception—at least on a temporary basis—is essential for their research (Suls & Rosnow, 1988). The adoption of this technique is not, however, without its costs. Deceiving research participants or withholding information from them, no matter how justified, raises important ethical issues.

First, it is possible that at least some persons exposed to deception will resent having been led astray. They may then adopt a negative attitude toward social research generally. Second, deception, even when temporary, may result in some type of harm to the persons exposed to it (Kelman, 1967). They may experience discomfort, stress, or negative shifts in self-esteem. Finally, there is the very real question of whether scientists committed to the search for knowledge should place themselves in the position of deceiving persons kind enough to assist them in this undertaking.

In short, the use of deception does pose something of a dilemma to social psychologists. On the one hand, it seems essential to their research. On the other, its use raises serious problems. How can this issue be resolved? At present, opinion remains divided. Some of our colleagues feel that deception, no matter how useful, is inappropriate and should be abandoned. Yet many others (perhaps a large majority) believe that temporary deception is acceptable, provided that certain safeguards are adopted (Baron, 1981). The most important of these are **informed consent** and thorough **debriefing**. (Both procedures, by the way, are required by ethical standards published by the American Psychological Association.)

Informed consent involves providing research participants with as full as possible a description of the procedures to be followed *prior* to their decision to take part in a study. By following this principle, researchers ensure that subjects know what they are getting into and what they will be asked to do before making a commitment to participate. In contrast, debriefing *follows* each experimental session. It consists of providing participants with a full explanation of all major aspects of a study, including its true goals and an explanation of the need for temporary deception. The guiding principle is that research participants should leave in at least as favorable or positive a state as when they arrived.

Fortunately, a growing body of evidence indicates that, together, informed consent and thorough debriefing can eliminate—or at least substantially reduce—the potential dangers of deception (Smith & Richardson, 1985). For example, most subjects report that they view temporary deception as acceptable and do not resent its use (Rogers, 1980). And thorough debriefing does appear to eliminate many negative effects experienced by subjects as a result of temporary deception (Smith & Richardson, 1985). Still, it is unwise to take the safety or appropriateness of deception for granted (Rubin, 1985). Rather, it appears that the guiding principles for all researchers planning to use this procedure in their studies should be these: (1) Use deception only when it is absolutely essential to do so—when no other means for conducting a study exist; (2) always proceed with great caution; and (3) make certain that the rights, safety, and welfare of research participants come first, ahead of all other considerations.

USING THIS BOOK: A READERS' ROAD MAP

Before concluding this introduction to the field of social psychology, we'd like to comment briefly on several features of this text. First, please note that we've taken several steps to make our text easier and more convenient for you to use. Each chapter begins with an outline of the major topics covered and ends with a detailed summary. Key terms are printed in **boldface type** and are defined in a glossary at the end of the chapter. Because figures and charts contained in original research reports are often quite complex, every graph and table in this text has been specially created for it. In addition, all graphs contain special labels designed to call your attention to the key findings presented (see Figure 1.12 for an example). We think that you'll find all of these illustrations easy to read and—more importantly—that they'll contribute to your understanding of social psychology.

Second, we want to note that we've included several special sections throughout the text. These do not interrupt the flow of text materials; rather, they are presented at natural breaks in content. All are designed to highlight information we feel is especially important and interesting.

The first type of special insert is called **Focus on Research** and describes specific studies performed by social psychologists. These sections appear in two forms: (1) those subtitled *Classic Contributions* or *Classic Canadian Contributions*, which describe studies now widely viewed as classics in the field, and (2) those subtitled *The Cutting Edge,* which focus on projects carried out at what we feel are the frontiers of knowledge in social psychology.

The second type of special section is titled **Social Psychology: On the Applied Side**. These sections highlight the practical implications of social psychology—ways in which its knowledge and principles can contribute to the solution of a wide range of practical problems.

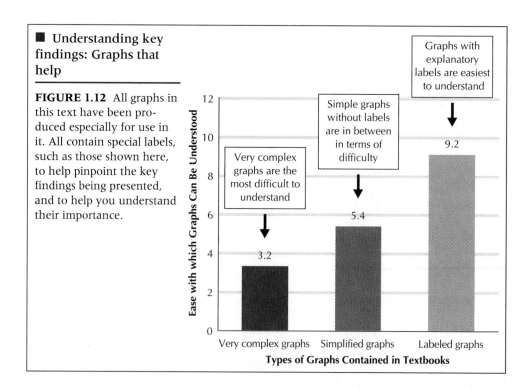

■ Understanding key findings: Graphs that help

FIGURE 1.12 All graphs in this text have been produced especially for use in it. All contain special labels, such as those shown here, to help pinpoint the key findings being presented, and to help you understand their importance.

Finally, from time to time, we present special sections labeled **Work in Progress.** These are included for two reasons: (1) to report very recent follow-ups to specific studies, and (2) to illustrate the fact that research in social psychology is never complete. On the contrary, it is an ongoing process in which each investigation leads naturally to others and in which the number of intriguing questions remaining to be answered *increases* rather than decreases over time.

To sum up:

It is our hope that together, these features of our text will help to enhance your first encounter with social psychology. We also hope that they will help us to communicate to you our own excitement with the field, for despite the fact that between us we have more than sixty-five years of combined teaching and research experience in social psychology, we still find it as fascinating as—perhaps even *more* fascinating than—ever. To the extent we succeed in these tasks, and only to that extent, will we conclude that as authors, teachers, and representatives of social psychology, we have succeeded.

SUMMARY AND REVIEW

THE NATURE OF SOCIAL PSYCHOLOGY

Social psychology is the scientific field that seeks to understand the nature and causes of individual behavior in social situations. It uses scientific methods to obtain new information about how we interact with and think about other persons.

THE DEVELOPMENT OF SOCIAL PSYCHOLOGY

Speculation about social behavior and thought has continued since antiquity; a science-oriented field of social psychology, however, emerged only during the present century. Once established, it grew rapidly and currently investigates every conceivable aspect of social behavior and social thought.

Two recent trends in the field have involved the growing influence of a cognitive perspective—efforts to apply knowledge about cognitive processes to the task of understanding social behavior—and an increasing emphasis on *applying* the principles and findings of social psychology to a wide range of practical problems.

We predict that these trends will continue in the future. In addition, social psychology has also adopted a *multicultural perspective*, particularly important to Canadian society. It both studies and takes careful account of ethnic and cultural factors as determinants of social behavior.

RESEARCH METHODS IN SOCIAL PSYCHOLOGY

In conducting their research, social psychologists often employ *experimentation* and the *correlational method*. Experimentation involves procedures in which researchers systematically vary one or more factors (variables) to examine the impact of such changes on one or more aspects of social behavior or thought. The correlational method involves careful observation and measurement of two or more variables to determine whether changes in one are accompanied by changes in the other.

In choosing the topics of their research and in planning specific studies, social psychologists are often guided by formal *theories*. These are logical frameworks that seek to explain various aspects of social behavior and thought. Predictions from a theory are tested in research. If they are confirmed, confidence in the accuracy of the theory is increased. If they are disconfirmed, such confidence is reduced.

Social psychologists often withhold information about the purpose of their studies from the persons participating in them. Such temporary *deception* is deemed necessary because knowledge of the hypotheses behind an experiment may alter participants' behavior. Although the use of deception raises important ethical issues, most social psychologists believe that it is permissible, provided that proper safeguards such as *informed consent* and *thorough debriefing* are adopted.

Cognitive Dissonance An unpleasant state that occurs when individuals discover inconsistencies between two of their attitudes or between their attitudes and their behavior.

Confounding Confusion that occurs when factors other than the independent variable in an experiment vary across the experimental conditions. When confounding occurs, it is impossible to determine whether results stem from the effects of the independent variable or from the other variables.

Correlational Method A method of research in which a scientist systematically observes and measures two or more variables to determine whether changes in one are accompanied by changes in the other.

Culture The organized system of shared meaning, perceptions and beliefs held by persons belonging to a particular group. This often includes a particular language or system of communication, social customs and organizations, as well as artifacts and artistic products of that group.

Debriefing Procedures at the conclusion of a research session in which participants are given full information about the nature of the research and the hypothesis or hypotheses under investigation.

Deception A technique whereby researchers withhold information about the purposes or procedures of a study from persons participating in it. Deception is used in situations in which information about such matters might be expected to change subjects' behavior, thus invalidating the results of the research.

Dependent Variable The variable that is measured in an experiment. In social psychology, the dependent variable is some aspect of social behavior or social thought.

Evolutionary Social Psychology A newly emerging area of research that seeks to understand the potential role of genetic factors in various aspects of social behavior.

Experimentation A method of research in which one factor (the independent variable) is systematically changed to determine whether such variations affect a second factor (the dependent variable).

Independent Variable The variable that is systematically varied by the researcher in an experiment.

Informed Consent A procedure by which subjects are told in advance about the activities they will perform during an experiment. The subjects then take part in the study only if they are willing to engage in such activities.

Multicultural Perspective Focus on understanding the cultural and ethnic factors that influence social behavior and which contribute to differences in social behavior or social thought between various ethnic and cultural groups.

Natural or Quasi-experiment A field study in which the natural environment, rather than the researcher, varies the independent variable. This is not a true experiment because it violates the basic requirements of random assignment of subjects and holding other factors constant.

Random Assignment of Subjects to Groups A basic requirement for conducting valid experiments. According to this principle, research participants must have an equal chance of being exposed to each level of the independent variable.

Social Psychology The scientific field that seeks to understand the nature and causes of individual behavior and thought in social situations.

Sociobiology A field that contends that many forms of behavior can be understood within the context of efforts by organisms to pass their genes on to the next generation.

Theories Efforts by scientists in any field to answer the question *Why?* Theories involve attempts to understand precisely why certain events or processes occur as they do.

Jackson, J. M. (1988). *Social psychology, past and present: An integrative orientation.* Hillsdale, NJ: Erlbaum.

A thoughtful overview of the roots and development of social psychology. The book is organized around major themes in social psychological research and emphasizes the fact that modern social psychology has important intellectual roots in several different fields.

Jones, E. E. (1985). Major developments in social psychology during the past five decades. In G. Lindzey & E. Aronson (Eds.), *Handbook of social psychology* (Vol. 1). New York: Random House.

In this chapter an eminent social psychologist describes what he perceives to be the major trends in theory and research in social psychology during the past fifty years. After reading this summary, you'll have a very good idea of how social psychology emerged as an independent field and how it then developed.

TWO

Social Perception and Social Cognition: Internalizing our Social World

....

Nonverbal Communication: The Unspoken Language
Nonverbal Communication: The Basic Channels

Impression Formation and Impression Management: Combining—and Managing—Social Information
Impression Formation: The Primacy of First Impressions/Impression Management: The Fine Art of Looking Good

Attribution: Understanding the Causes of Others' Behavior
Theories of Attribution: Frameworks for Understanding How We Attempt to Make Sense out of the Social World/Attribution: Some Basic Sources of Bias/Attribution in Intergroup Relations: the Ultimate Attribution Error and Beyond

Schemas, Heuristics and Biases: Coping with Information Overload
Schemas: Organizing Social Information/Heuristics: Cognitive Shortcuts

The Role of Affect: How Feelings Influence our View of the World
The Nature of Emotion: Contrasting Views/How Affect Influences Cognition

SPECIAL SECTIONS

SOCIAL PSYCHOLOGY: ON THE APPLIED SIDE
   Multicultural Mistakes: Cultural Differences in Nonverbal Communication.

You have just moved into a student residence and are pleased to be getting to know Tom, another newcomer just like you. He seemed a friendly guy, until this morning. When you met in the hall this time, the smile he gave you was slightly tense; the remarks you exchanged seemed mechanical and awkward. Perhaps your previous impressions of Tom were wrong—he isn't really a friendly person or he never really liked *you*. But did you really see his behavior correctly this time? Maybe the fact that you are feeling a bit down today colored your interpretation of his behavior. Perhaps the smile was just as friendly as before—you just couldn't see it that way. If he *was* colder, why? Was it something you did? Or was he feeling low today too and it had nothing to do with you? …And you were just going to invite him to a barbeque on the weekend!— Is that a good idea now? Admit it. Other persons are often something of a mystery (see figure 2.1). They say and do things we don't expect, have motives we don't understand, and seem to see the world through eyes very different from our own. Yet, because they play such a key role in our lives, the mystery of other people is one we can't afford to leave unsolved. Accordingly, we often engage in efforts to understand others—to gain insight into their intentions, traits, and motives. We try to figure out what other persons are really like, why they do and say the things they do. Then, on the basis of that knowledge, we make judgments about them, sort out what we know and add it to previous information, and we try to determine the best way of interacting with them.

In Chapter 1 we emphasized that the way in which we perceive, understand, and interpret the social world forms the basis of all social behavior. Traditionally, these processes have been split into two parts: **social perception**, the process through which we seek social information, form impressions of others, and register or encode that information in our minds; and **social cognition**, the process through which we recall, interpret, reason, and make judgments about others. Whereas *social perception* is concerned with the *intake* of social information, *social cognition* is concerned with *the use and manipulation* of social information.

Although we may think of social perception and social cognition as distinct processes, they are clearly linked and, at times, inseparable. In the example above, when you made judgments about the reasons for Tom's behavior (a cognitive process) this was influenced by the way you had seen him previously (a perceptual process). Thus,

■ **People are often something of a mystery.**

FIGURE 2.1 We often engage in efforts to understand other people.
Source: Universal Press Syndicate

"You're quite a puzzle, aren't you?"

our cognitions are influenced by our perceptions. Similarly, what we perceive is influenced by our cognitions—our already existing knowledge and beliefs about the social world. Often we see what we expect to see; not necessarily what is there. So you may have *perceived* Tom as colder because, feeling down on yourself, you did not believe (a *cognition*) that he would be friendly to you. The point is that social perception and social cognition are *interdependent* processes; that is, they both influence each other. While perception is concerned with the intake of information, that process is influenced by the way we organize and think about our experiences. Similarly, social cognition is concerned with the use and manipulation of social information, but this information has been filtered through our selective perceptions.

While our efforts to understand the persons around us take many different forms, one of the first aspects of another person from which we can gather information is their *nonverbal communications*—what is sometimes called their "body language." Facial expressions, eye contact, body posture, and movements can provide an initial clue to someone's current feelings and mood. In an initial interaction with another, we will try to form an overall *impression* of them: combining the information we have gathered. Common sense suggests that such *first impressions* are very important; and, as we'll soon see, research findings tend to confirm this widespread belief. The other side of the coin, of course, involves efforts on *our* part to make favorable impressions on others—a process known as *impression management*. We often go beyond this, though, and attempt to understand the more lasting causes behind others' actions—their traits, motives, and intentions. Information relating to this second task is acquired through *attribution*—a complex process in which we observe others' behavior and then attempt to *infer* the causes behind it from various clues (Kelley, 1972). This process was evident in the puzzlement over Tom's behavior: Why was he less friendly? Was it something that you had done? These are the kinds of questions that often cross our minds when faced with the puzzle of other people's behavior. Finally, we are called upon to make diverse judgments about the social world and other people, often very quickly. The use of simple decision-making strategies or *heuristics*, while it can save us time, can also lead to misjudgments. And as indicated above, we are sometimes motivated to perceive and think about the world in ways that maintain our self-esteem.

For example, it would be nice if you could blame Tom's unfriendliness on his own mood. If it was something you had done, then you would immediately begin to feel uncomfortable about yourself—to worry about whether he liked you. Both our cognitive shortcuts and our motivations can lead to *biases*—systematic distortions in the way we perceive and think about the world.

NONVERBAL COMMUNICATION: THE UNSPOKEN LANGUAGE

In many cases, social behavior is strongly affected by temporary factors or causes. Shifting moods, fleeting emotions, fatigue, illness, various drugs—all can influence the ways in which we think and behave. Most persons, for example, are more willing to do favors for others when in a good mood than when in a bad mood (George, 1991; Isen, 1987). Similarly, many people are more likely to lose their tempers and lash out at others in some manner when feeling irritable than when feeling mellow (Anderson, 1989; Bell, 1992).

Because such temporary factors often exert important effects on social behavior and thought, it is useful to know something about them. But how can we obtain such knowledge? How can we know whether others are in a good or a bad mood; whether they are experiencing anger, joy, or sorrow; or whether they are under the influence of some drug that might affect their judgment? One answer is obvious: We can ask them directly. Unfortunately, this strategy sometimes fails, for the simple reason that others are often unwilling to reveal their inner feelings and reactions to us. Indeed, they may actively seek to conceal such information or to mislead us with respect to their current emotions (DePaulo, 1992). Their reasons for doing so are often good ones. For example, a saleswoman who reveals her own aversion to products favored by potential customers will probably obtain few orders. A diplomat who reveals his or her true feelings to opponents may be less effective as a negotiator than one who conceals such reactions.

In situations such as these, when others actively attempt to conceal their true feelings or preferences from us, it is not necessary to give up in despair. On the contrary, we can often still obtain revealing information about their inner feelings and reactions by paying careful attention to their *nonverbal behaviors*—changes in facial expressions, eye contact, posture, body movements, and other expressive actions. As noted by DePaulo (1992), such behavior is relatively *irrepressible*—that is, difficult to control—so even when others *try* to conceal their inner feelings, these often leak out in many ways through nonverbal cues. So, in an important sense, nonverbal behaviors constitute a silent but eloquent language. For this reason, the meanings they convey and our efforts to interpret these, are often described by the term **nonverbal communication**. Such communication is very complex, and it has been studied from many different perspectives. Here, however, we will focus on two major issues: (1) What are the basic channels through which nonverbal communication takes place? and (2) what is the role of nonverbal communication in social perception and ongoing social interaction?

NONVERBAL COMMUNICATION: THE BASIC CHANNELS

How do we communicate nonverbally ? This question has been the subject of careful research attention for several decades. The findings of that research have identified the *basic channels* of nonverbal communication—those aspects of our behavior that transmit key information about our inner emotional and affective states. These seem to involve *facial expressions, eye contact, body movements* and *posture*, and *touching*.

Unmasking the face:
Facial expressions as clues to others' emotions

More than two thousand years ago, the Roman orator Cicero stated: "the face is the image of the soul." By this he meant that human feelings and emotions are often reflected on the face and can be read there in specific expressions. Modern research suggests that Cicero—and many other observers of human behavior—were correct in this belief: it is possible to learn much about others' current moods and feelings from their facial expressions. In fact, it appears that six different basic emotions are represented clearly, and from a very early age, on the human face: anger, fear, sadness, disgust, happiness, and surprise (Ekman, in press; Izard, 1991; see figure 2.2). Please note: this in no way implies that human beings are capable of demonstrating only six different facial expressions. On the contrary, emotions occur in many combinations (for example, anger along with fear, surprise with happiness). Further, each of these reactions can vary greatly in strength. Thus, while there seem to be only a small number of basic themes in facial expressions, the number of variations on these themes is large.

But do facial expressions really reflect individuals' underlying emotions? After all, as we'll note in more detail later, most persons learn to regulate their facial expressions so that they smile, frown, or show surprise only in situations defined by

■ Basic facial expressions

FIGURE 2.2 Facial expressions such as these provide valuable information about others' emotional states. Can you identify the emotion shown on each face?

Answers are: The emotions shown, top, left to right are anger; fear; sadness; at bottom, left to right are disgust; happiness; and surprise.

their particular culture as appropriate for such expressions (DePaulo, 1992). What evidence indicates that facial expressions are closely linked to underlying emotional states and so can serve—at least part of the time—as accurate guides to these reactions? Many lines of research address this issue, but two seem to be most revealing.

In the first, researchers record electrical activity in various facial muscles associated with distinct facial expressions—while participants describe experiences associated with a wide range of emotions (e.g., Cacioppo et al., 1988). The same persons are then shown videotapes of their own faces and asked to indicate what they were thinking, feeling, or imagining at various times. When these self-reports are related to electrical activity in facial muscles at those times, revealing patterns emerge. For example, certain muscles show maximal electrical activity at times when participants report feeling sad, while different muscles show maximal electrical activity at times when participants report feeling happy. So underlying emotional experiences do seem to be closely linked to facial expressions.

A second line of research on the relationship between facial expressions and underlying emotional experiences adopts a different approach (e.g., Levenson, Ekman, & Friesen, 1990; Levenson et al., 1992). In these studies individuals are asked to move various parts of their faces so as to produce configurations resembling certain facial expressions. For example, they may be asked to wrinkle their nose while letting their mouth open (an expression resembling that of disgust). Note that participants are *not* told to demonstrate happiness, anger, fear, and so on; they are merely asked to move parts of their faces in very specific ways. While they move various facial muscles, a wide range of physiological reactions, such as heart rate, finger temperature, respiration, and skin conductance, are recorded. Finally, participants also report on any emotional experiences, thoughts, or memories they experience while moving their facial muscles. Results indicate that different posed facial expressions are accompanied by changes in patterns of physiological activity. For example, the facial expression of fear is associated with high heart rate and short respiratory periods (short intervals between breaths). In addition—and this is a key finding—the more closely the facial expressions shown by participants resemble those associated with specific emotions, the greater the tendency of participants to report experiencing those same emotions. From these two lines of research we have strong evidence for a fundamental connection between facial expression and emotion that appears to be innate.

However, as additional confirmation of this, reseach has also investigated the question of the extent to which facial expressions are universal. Do people living in widely separated geographic areas demonstrate similar facial expressions in similar emotion-provoking situations, and can these be readily—and accurately—recognized by persons from outside their own ethnic or cultural group (Ekman, 1989)? Perhaps the most convincing confirming evidence is provided by a series of studies conducted by Ekman and Friesen (1975).

These researchers traveled to isolated areas of New Guinea and asked persons living there to imagine various emotion-provoking events—for example, your friend has come for a visit and you are happy; you find a dead animal that has been lying in the hot sun for several days, and it smells very bad. Then these subjects were asked to show by facial expressions how they would feel in each case. Their expressions were very similar to ones a North American might show in those situations (see Figure 2.3). It appears that when experiencing basic emotions, human beings all over the world tend to show highly similar facial expressions. Further, when individuals living in widely separated countries are shown photos of strangers from other cultures demonstrating anger, fear, happiness, sadness, surprise, and disgust, they are quite accurate in identifying these emotions (e.g., Ekman, 1973). Thus, it appears that facial expressions do communicate the same basic messages across diverse cultures around the world.

In sum, it appears that the link between emotional experiences and certain aspects of facial expressions is a basic and instinctive one. When individuals experience various emotions, electrical activity in specific facial muscles increases, and when they move these muscles into the patterns of specific facial expressions, they show distinctive shifts in physiological reactions *and* report experiencing the emotions in question. Also, individuals all over the world show and recognize similar facial expressions as associated with particular emotions. On the basis of such findings, it seems reasonable to conclude that unless individuals deliberately seek to override the links between emotions and facial expressions, they will, as DePaulo notes, usually "...wear their emotions on their faces" (1992, p. 205). We will return to efforts to control or manage facial expressions in the discussion below of the role of nonverbal cues in efforts at self-presentation and deception.

Gazes and stares: The language of the eyes

Have you ever had a conversation with someone wearing mirror-lensed glasses? If so, you know that this can be an uncomfortable situation. Since you can't see the other person's eyes, you are uncertain about how she or he is reacting. Taking note of the

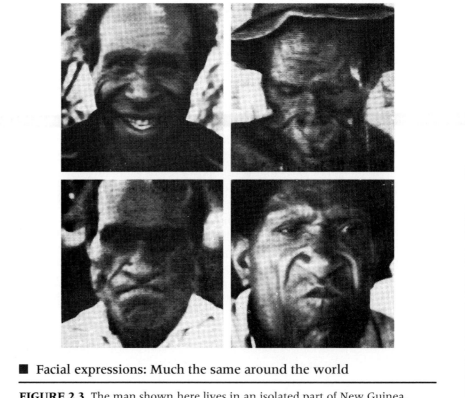

■ Facial expressions: Much the same around the world

FIGURE 2.3 The man shown here lives in an isolated part of New Guinea. When asked to imagine various emotion-provoking events and show how he would feel, he demonstrated these facial expressions. The fact that these are very similar to facial expressions you would show when performing the same task provides evidence for the view that there is a universal element to facial expressions. (The emotions shown are—in clockwise order—happiness, sadness, anger, and disgust.)

Source: From Ekman & Friesen, 1975, p. 27; by permission of the authors.

importance of cues provided by others' eyes, ancient poets often described the eyes as "windows to the soul." In one important sense, they were right: we do often learn much about others' feelings from their eyes. For example, we interpret a high level of gazing from another as a sign of liking or friendliness (Kleinke, 1986). In contrast, if others avoid eye contact with us, we may conclude that they are unfriendly, don't like us, or are simply shy (Zimbardo, 1977).

While a high level of eye contact from others is usually interpreted as a sign of liking or positive feelings, there is one important exception to this general rule. If another person gazes at us continuously and maintains such contact regardless of any actions we perform, she or he can be said to be **staring**. A stare is often interpreted as a sign of anger or hostility—consider the phrase *a cold stare*—and most people attempt to minimize their exposure to this particular kind of nonverbal communication when possible (Ellsworth & Carlsmith, 1973). Thus, they may quickly terminate social interaction with someone who stares at them; they may even leave the scene (Greenbaum & Rosenfield, 1978). Given these facts, it is clear that staring is one form of nonverbal behavior that should be used with great caution in most situations.

Body language: Gestures, posture, and movements

Try this simple demonstration:

> First, try to remember some incident that made you angry—the angrier the better. Think about it for about a minute.

> Now try to remember another incident—one that made you feel sad—again, the sadder the better.

Compare your behavior in the two contexts. Did you change your posture or move your hands, arms, or legs as your thoughts shifted from the first event to the second? The chances are good that you did, for our current moods or emotions are often reflected in the position, posture, and movement of our bodies. Together, such nonverbal behaviors are termed **body language**, and they too can provide us with several useful kinds of information about others.

First, as just noted, body language often reveals much about others' emotional states. Large numbers of movements—especially ones in which one part of the body does something to another part (e.g., touching, scratching, rubbing)—suggest emotional arousal. The greater the frequency of such behavior, the higher the level of arousal or nervousness seems to be (Harrigan, 1985; Knapp, 1978). A study by Harrigan and her colleagues (Harrigan, et al., 1991) is especially revealing. In this experiment participants watched videotapes in which one person interviewed another. The persons being interviewed showed either no body movements involving self-touching, or various patterns of self-touching with the hands. Results indicated that the specific hand movements made affected the extent to which interviewees were seen as calm or expressive. For example, an interviewee was rated as most calm and least expressive when he or she engaged in no self-touching movements. Ratings of least calm were associated with arm self-touching, and greatest expressiveness was associated with nose touching. These and related findings indicate that both the total amount of movement and the pattern and nature of such movement provides information on others' feelings or traits.

Larger patterns of movement, involving the whole body, can also be informative. Such phrases as "he adopted a *threatening posture*" and "she greeted him with *open arms*" suggest that different body orientations or postures can be suggestive of contrasting emotional reactions; and, in fact, recent research by Aronoff, Woike, and Hyman (1992) confirms this possibility. Researchers examined samples of choreographed dancing for ballet characters who are threatening (e.g., Macbeth) or warm (e.g. Romeo and Juliet) to see if they adopted different kinds of postures. Results show

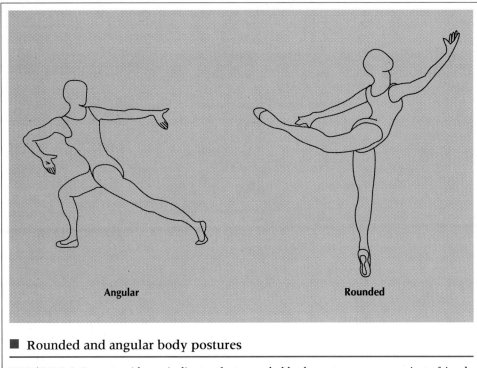

■ **Rounded and angular body postures**

FIGURE 2.4 Recent evidence indicates that rounded body postures communicate friendliness and warmth while angular body postures communicate threat or hostility.

Source: Based on information in Aronoff, Woike, & Hyman, 1992.

that the threatening characters used angular poses nearly three times as often as the warm characters. In contrast, the warm characters engaged in rounded poses almost four times as often as the threatening characters (see Figure 2.4). Of course, the postures shown by these dancers were carefully posed ones; thus, there is no guarantee that the same results would be obtained with respect to real-life (nonposed) postures. Still, when combined with other research conducted by Aronoff et al. (1992), these findings suggest that large-scale body movements or postures can sometimes serve as an important source of information about others' emotions and traits.

Finally, we should add that more specific information about others' feelings is often provided by gestures. These fall into several different categories, but perhaps the most important are *emblems*—body movements carrying highly specific meanings in specific cultures. For example, in several countries, holding one's hand with the thumb pointing up is a sign of "Okay." Similarly, seizing one's nose between the thumb and index finger is a sign of displeasure or disgust. Emblems vary greatly from culture to culture, but every human society seems to have at least some signals of this type for greetings, departures, insults, and the description of various physical states.

Another category of gestures important in nonverbal communication are the *hand gestures* that accompany conversational speech. Such gestures are used for emphasis or clarification and occur quite frequently during face-to-face conversations. Existing evidence indicates that they can aid comprehension of spoken messages, although only to a relatively minor degree (Graham & Argyle, 1975; Krauss, Morrel-Samuels, & Colasante, 1991).

In sum, there does appear to be a language of the body—a set of nonverbal cues that communicate much about others' feelings, reactions, and traits. And we draw upon such body language frequently in our efforts to understand the people around us. One complication arises when the body language of people interacting derives from differing cultures. The kind of "multicultural mistakes" that can occur are discussed below in the section, "Social Psychology: On the Applied Side."

Touching: The most intimate nonverbal cue

Suppose that during a conversation with another person, she or he touched you briefly. How would you react? what information would this behavior convey? The answer to both questions is, it depends. And what it depends upon is several factors relating to who does the touching (a friend or a stranger, a member of your own or of the other gender); the nature of this physical contact (brief or prolonged, gentle or rough); and the context in which it takes place (a business or social setting, a doctor's office). Depending on such factors, touch can suggest affection, sexual interest, dominance, caring, or even aggression. Despite such complexities, a growing body of evidence indicates that when one person touches another in a manner that is considered acceptable in the current context, positive reactions generally result (Alagna, Whitcher, & Fisher, 1979; Smith, Gier, & Willis, 1982). This fact is clearly illustrated by an ingenious study carried out by Crusco and Wetzel (1984). These investigators enlisted the aid of waitresses working in two restaurants, who agreed to treat customers in one of three distinct ways when giving them their change: they either refrained from touching these persons in any manner, touched them briefly on the hand, or touched them for a longer period of time on the shoulder. The investigators assessed the effects of these treatments by examining the size of the tips left by the patrons. Results were clear: both a brief touch on the hand (about one-half second) and a longer touch on the shoulder (one to one and a half seconds) significantly increased tipping over the no-touch control condition. Thus, consistent with previous findings, being touched in an innocuous, nonthreatening way seemed to generate positive rather than negative reactions among recipients. Please note: touching does not always produce such effects. If it is perceived as a status or power play, or if it is too prolonged, or too intimate in a context where such intimacy is not warranted, touching may evoke anxiety, anger, and other negative reactions.

Gender differences in touching: Who touches whom, and when? While touching is strongly affected by social context and by cultural rules dictating who can touch whom and when, another aspect to physical touching deserves careful attention: gender differences in this form of nonverbal activity. An early and frequently cited study on this issue by Henley (1973) reported that in public places males are more likely to touch females than vice versa. More recent research, however, suggests that the relationship between gender and touching is more complex than this (e.g., Stier & Hall, 1984). In greetings and leave-takings, gender differences in touching do not seem to occur (Major, Schmidlin, & Williams, 1990). And age appears to be an important determinant of who touches whom.

The clearest evidence to date on the effects of age on touching is that reported by Hall and Veccia (1991). These researchers observed touching between thousands of persons in a wide range of public places—shopping malls, movie lines, hotel lobbies, airports. The researchers recorded instances of touching with the hand and with other body parts, as well as the age of the people involved. (This ranged from the teens through middle age.) They observed several interesting sex differences. For example, across all ages, males tended to use "arm-around" touching more frequently than females, while females more often used "arms-linked" touching. Overall, however, there was no difference between the sexes in frequency of touching: females touched males about as frequently as males touched females. Striking gender differences *were* observed, however, when age was taken into account. Among young couples, males touched females far more often than females touched males. This disparity decreased with age, however, until, among older couples, females touched males far more often than males touched females (see Figure 2.5).

What is the reason for this reversal with increasing age? One possibility mentioned by Hall and Veccia (1991) is that among younger persons (especially teenagers) relationships are not yet well established; and in such relationships, sex roles encourage visible gestures of possessiveness by males. As relationships develop, however, sex roles may require more gestures of possessiveness by females. Whatever the explanation for the age reversal observed by Hall and Veccia, it is interesting to note that across all ages there is no overall difference in touching between males and females. This is just one example of a supposed gender difference that tends to disappear on systematic closer observation; we'll meet many others in this book.

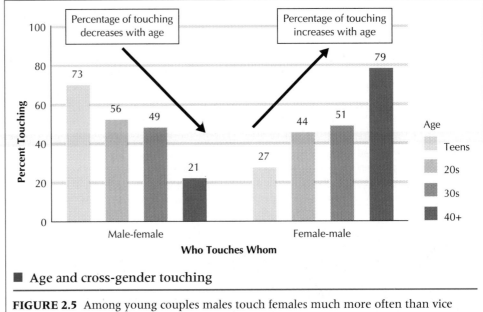

■ Age and cross-gender touching

FIGURE 2.5 Among young couples males touch females much more often than vice versa. This difference fades with increasing age and is ultimately replaced by an opposite pattern among older couples.

Source: Based on data from Hall & Veccia, 1991.

Multicultural Mistakes: Cultural Differences in Nonverbal Communication

In chapter 1 we noted that social psychologists in the United States have generally assumed that the findings of their research are universal—that they apply to all human beings in all cultures and perhaps across time (Smith & Bond, 1993). Findings such as those of Ekman and Friesen (1975), described earlier, encouraged the belief that findings in one culture could be generalized to another and would apply equally well. But can we assume, then, that nonverbal communications are similar across all cultures—that cross-cultural mistakes are rarely made? This is an important question for Canadians, who frequently communicate in a multicultural context. As you can see from Figure 2.6, one Canadian politician suggested that we could not make that assumption in the context of communication between Western Canadians and the Québecois.

When we attempt to understand the nonverbal behavior of those from other cultures, social perceptions might create difficulties for us if the meaning we impose upon others' nonverbal behavior derives from our *own* culture and not theirs. Does the fact that the connection between emotion and facial expression has been confirmed in many cultures mean that nonverbal cues never require an interpeter: that cultural differences in facial expressions do not exist?

A recent cross-cultural study conducted by Levenson et al. (1992) provides intriguing evidence for the existence of such differences. These researchers investigated the facial expressions and underlying emotional experiences of a cultural group named the Minangkabau who live in West Sumatra (part of Indonesia). In the Minangkabau culture the internal aspects of emotion—the subjective feelings we experience as individuals—are viewed as less important than is true in many other cultures. Instead, the Minangkabau emphasize the external aspects of emotion, such as the effects of emotional expression on interpersonal relations. Thus, members of this culture are trained as children to mask

■ **Multicultural mistakes in nonverbal communication: A politician's hypothesis**

FIGURE 2.6 Reform Party leader Preston Manning was recently reported as saying that "when a Western Canadian is feeling deeply about something they become more and more silent" (*Vancouver Sun*, 22/04/1994, p. A1). In contrast, he suggested the Québecois tend to wave their hands and raise their voices when they feel strongly. And this can lead to the "danger of people interpreting silence (from Westerners with regard to Quebec separation) as indifference or not understanding or not caring" (p. A1). Mr Manning is hypothesizing that there is a cultural difference in nonverbal behaviors of Francophones and Anglophones and, further, that this can lead to misinterpretation and miscommunication between these groups.

▶

strong negative emotions, especially anger, to a much greater degree than persons in Western cultures. This reflects the Minangkabau's belief that expression of such emotions is disturbing to normal social relations.

To study the role of these cultural factors in emotion and facial expressions, Levenson and his colleagues asked young Minangkabau males to show various facial expressions—ones usually identified as reflecting happiness, sadness, disgust, fear, and anger. The participants' physiological reactions were recorded as they showed each expression; and, in addition, participants reported on whether and to what extent they experienced various emotions as they produced these facial expressions. Results found that the Minangkabau were more constrained in demonstrating these emotions than Americans. In addition, they showed weaker physiological arousal and reported experiencing weaker emotions than Americans when showing each facial expression. However, it is important to note that the patterns of physiological reactions shown by members of both cultures when demonstrating various facial expressions were highly similar. Differences between the cultures were mainly ones of intensity, not ones reflecting different patterns of subjective or physiological reactions to various facial expressions.

In sum, although the connection between facial expressions and emotions appears to be inherent, important differences do exist between cultures with respect to *display rules*—beliefs about when, and to what degree, various emotions should be expressed. Moreover, these cultural differences are reflected in emotional reactions and subjective experiences as well as facial expressions.

It is important to look beyond the scientific findings to their implications for Canadians. How would such variation in the intensity of facial expression affect communication between cultures? You can imagine that the relatively animated facial expressions of North Americans would appear exaggerated to the Minangkabau, if not rude and imposing! Alternatively, a North American might interpret their restraint as rather unfriendly or cold. In Canada, where cultural groups range from the highly expressive to the highly reserved,

such miscommunication must occur frequently.

An extension of such cultural difference was found in one study comparing conversational norms of foreign students studying in the U.S.A. (Watson, 1970). Watson distinguished between cultures in terms of degree of "contact" during conversation. People from *contact cultures* (i.e., Arabic, Latin American and Southern European) tended to face each other more directly, speak more loudly, to have greater eye contact, to maintain a closer distance, and touch more often than those in *non-contact* cultures (i.e., Asian, Northern European, Indian and Pakistani). Again, we can speculate that when a person from a contact culture is conversing with a person from a non-contact culture neither of them may be very comfortable. If, for example, they maintain a distance that is comfortable for the contact person, the non-contact person will feel crowded and probably readjust his or her distance a step back or so. The contact person would respond by feeling as if the other person has just signalled less friendliness—was being "stand-offish," as we say— and perhaps he or she would also adjust position to be closer. You imagine an ongoing dance of retreat by one and advance by the other!

Watson's (1970) study also indicated that communication might falter over eye contact and touch. Students from Arabic cultures indicated that eye contact was very important and desirable during conversation. However high levels of eye contact are sometimes interpreted as disrespectful and imposing by someone from an Asian culture. Arabic men who were friends in Watson's sample would hold hands, whereas among adults in North America it is usually those who are sexually attracted or attached who hold hands. We do not need to spell out the potential difficulties here!

Finally differences in another channel of nonverbal communication have the potential for more serious problems—the exchange of unintentional insults! Hand gestures show a great deal of cultural variation. For example, the "thumbs-up" gesture means that something is fine in North America and Britain, and in both places the thumb is used to hitch-hike. However, this might not be advisable in Greece where the thumb is used for a sexual insult,

▶

similar in meaning to the "one-finger salute" of North America. For the same reasons, if you travel to Britain, never use the V-sign (commonly meaning "victory") with your palm turned towards the body...(Morris, Collett, Marsh & O'Shaughnessy, 1979).

At this point you may be wondering why we don't come to cross-cultural blows more often. The potential for miscommunication and for misjudgment seems limitless. To some extent, this may be because we make allowances for someone when we know they are from a very different background. It has been shown with verbal communication that we will sometimes accommodate or adapt our language to fit in with another person's (Giles, Mulac, Bradac, & Johnson, 1986). Similar adjustments can be made nonverbally. Nonetheless, miscommunication and misunderstanding between cultures is not infrequent. We spend many years training our children to communicate with precision verbally in their own and other languages. Yet nonverbal communication receives little attention in education, even though it can be as important as verbal (Mehrabian & Weiner, 1969).

Such "multicultural mistakes" might be reduced if both verbal and nonverbal channels were part of linguistic training.

Returning to the hypothesis in Figure 2.6, it does have partial support in the findings of LaCroix and Rioux (1978). Using French and English bilingual speakers in Quebec, they found that the use of hand gestures was more frequent among those for whom French was their mother-tongue. Further, observers had 71 percent success in identifying the mother-tongue of a speaker on the basis of their gestures alone. While this study provides evidence of nonverbal differences between French and English speakers, it does not provide any information about the extent to which such differences contribute to misunderstanding between French and English Canada at the national level.

In answer to the question with which we began, therefore, we cannot assume that nonverbal behavior will be the same across all cultures. Facial expression seems to be the exception among channels of nonverbal communication. The cultural diversity we have seen above is more frequently the rule.

IMPRESSION FORMATION AND IMPRESSION MANAGEMENT: COMBINING— AND MANAGING—SOCIAL INFORMATION

Impression formation and impression management are opposite sides of the same coin: a social interaction. When you interact with someone for the first time you are often attempting to *form an impression* of that person—to get an idea of the kind of individual you are dealing with. Meanwhile, that person is trying to make a particular kind of impression on you; in fact he or she is attempting to *manage* your impression formation. Whether either of you succeeds at your aim depends upon your social skills, and those vary considerably (Argyle, 1969). Nonetheless, your efforts are an important part of initial interaction.

IMPRESSION FORMATION: THE PRIMACY OF FIRST IMPRESSIONS

First impressions, it is widely held, are very important. Most of us assume that the initial impressions we make on others will shape the course of our future dealings with them in crucial ways. Further, we believe that such impressions may be quite resistant to change, even in the face of later contradictory information. It is for these reasons that most people prepare very carefully for first dates, job interviews, and other situations in which they will meet others for the first time (see Figure 2.7). Are these commonsense assumptions about the nature of first impressions accurate? The answer provided by several decades of research is at least a qualified yes (e.g., Anderson, 1981; Burnstein & Schul, 1982; Wyer, 1988).

The first systematic research on this issue was performed by Asch (1946). He used a straightforward procedure in which subjects in two different groups were given one of the following descriptions of a hypothetical person:

intelligent-industrious-impulsive-critical-stubborn-envious

envious-stubborn-critical-impulsive-industrious-intelligent

Obviously, the two lists are identical in content; they differ only in the order in which the adjectives are presented. In the first list, positive traits are followed by negative ones, while in the second list, the opposite is true. Subjects who read the first list rated the imaginary person as more sociable, humorous, and happy than those who read the second list: a *primacy effect* had occurred—subjects were most influenced by the first information they read.

Why did these differences occur? Asch suggested that the order was important because the first adjectives subjects read changed the meaning of the ones they read later. With the first list, having learned that someone was intelligent and industrious, they interpreted the later, more negative adjectives within this favorable context. Thus, the fact that the hypothetical person was *critical* implied that this person made good use of his or her intelligence. With the second list, in contrast, having learned that the imaginary person was envious and stubborn, subjects interpreted the fact that she or he was also intelligent as suggestive of calculating shrewdness.

A more modern interpretation of Asch's findings suggests that these primacy effects occur because once we have some initial information at our disposal, we just don't bother to pay a lot of attention to additional input. After all, we already have enough information to form an impression, so why deal with any more? This tendency to minimize the amount of cognitive work we do when thinking about others is a strong one and plays a key role in many forms of social thought and perception (Fiske & Taylor, 1991).

What are the factors that influence the relative weight we place on various pieces of information about others? Among the most important of these are: (1) the source of the input—information from sources we trust or admire is weighted more heavily than information from sources we distrust (Rosenbaum & Levin, 1969); (2) we tend to weight negative information and more untypical or unusual information

■ **Making a good first impression**

FIGURE 2.7 Many persons believe that first impressions are very important. Because of this assumption, they try to enhance their appearance before meeting others for the first time.

about others more heavily than positive or typical information, perhaps because it is more novel or distinctive (Fiske, 1980; Mellers, Richards & Birnbaum, 1992); (3) we often assign greater weight to information we receive first (information with primacy) than to information we receive later.

Perhaps a concrete example will help illustrate these points. Imagine that you accept a blind date. Prior to the date, you receive conflicting opinions of the person you are going to meet from a close friend and from someone you hardly know. Clearly, information from your friend will probably weigh more heavily in your developing impression. If the information provided by the casual acquaintance is negative, however, while that provided by your friend is positive, the negative information may have a stronger impact (e.g., Hansen & Hansen, 1988). When you meet your blind date, the first thing this person does is compliment you. Later your date says some annoying things. Still, she or he started out on the right foot, so your impression remains relatively favorable. During the course of the evening, you discover that your date likes pizza. This is a typical reaction, so it doesn't influence your developing impression very much. However, when you learn that your date carries a miniature camera and is taking clandestine photos of the night's events, *this* information does have a big impact on your impression; after all, this is highly unusual behavior among the persons you know.

In sum, impression formation is a complex cognitive process in which we combine information about others with existing cognitive frameworks to form unified, overall impressions. The task itself often seems effortless, but research by social psychologists indicates that there is a lot going on beneath the surface.

IMPRESSION MANAGEMENT: THE FINE ART OF LOOKING GOOD

The desire to make a favorable impression on others is a strong one. Few people would behave like the character shown in Figure 2.8; the stakes are simply too high. On the contrary, most of us engage in active efforts to regulate how we appear to others in order to appear in the best or most favorable light possible. This process is known as **impression management**, and considerable evidence indicates that persons who can perform it successfully gain important advantages in many social settings (Schlenker, 1980; Luginbuhl & Palmer, 1991). But what tactics do individuals use to create favorable impressions on others? And which of these are most successful? These are the issues we'll consider next.

■ Negative impression management

FIGURE 2.8 Very few of us would behave like this character when applying for a job.
Source: NEA, Inc., 1987.

Impression management: Basic tactics

As your own experience probably suggests, impression management takes many different forms and involves a wide range of specific tactics. First, and perhaps most obviously, individuals wishing to make a good impression on others often attempt to alter their own appearance in specific ways. For example, they dress in ways that they believe will be evaluated favorably by others. Such tactics appear to succeed. It has been found, for example, that when women dress in a professional manner (business suit or dress, subdued jewelry), they are evaluated more favorably for management positions than when they dress in a more traditionally feminine manner (dresses with patterns, large jewelry; Forsythe, Drake, & Cox, 1985). Many other aspects of personal appearance, too, are involved in efforts at impression management, including hair styles, cosmetics, and even eyeglasses (e.g., Baron, 1989; Harris, 1991).

Other tactics of impression management involve what are sometimes described as *other-enhancement*—efforts to induce favorable reactions in target persons by specific actions toward them. Among the most important of these tactics are *flattery*—heaping undeserved praise on target persons; expressing agreement with their views; showing a high degree of interest in them (hanging on their every word); and demonstrating high levels of liking or approval for them either verbally or nonverbally. An additional tactic involves doing favors—favors smaller than the ones the person engaging in impression management wants in return. Finally, recent evidence indicates that individuals sometimes ask for advice or feedback from others as a means of gaining their approval (Morrison & Bies, 1991). Many people find it flattering to be asked for such aid, and this can lead them to form favorable impressions of the person seeking the assistance.

ATTRIBUTION: UNDERSTANDING THE CAUSES OF OTHERS' BEHAVIOR

Nonverbal communication and impression formation can be useful in beginning to understand others. Yet eventually we will want to know more—to understand others' lasting traits and to know the causes behind their behavior—why they have acted as they have. The process through which we seek such information is known as **attribution**. More formally, attribution refers to our efforts to understand the causes behind others' behavior and, on some occasions, the causes behind *our* behavior, too. Attribution has been a topic of major interest in social psychology for several decades (e.g., Graham & Folkes, 1990; Heider, 1958; Jones, 1990).

THEORIES OF ATTRIBUTION: FRAMEWORKS FOR UNDERSTANDING HOW WE ATTEMPT TO MAKE SENSE OUT OF THE SOCIAL WORLD

Because attribution is complex, many theories have been proposed to explain its operation (e.g., Gilbert, Pelham, & Srull, 1988; Trope, 1986). Here, we will focus on two that have been especially influential.

From acts to dispositions: Using others' behavior as a guide to their lasting traits

The first of these theories—Jones and Davis's (1965) theory of correspondent inference—asks how we use information about others' behavior as a basis for inferring that they possess various traits or characteristics. In other words, the theory is concerned with how we decide, on the basis of others' overt actions, that they possess specific traits or dispositions that they carry with them from situation to situation and that remain fairly stable over time.

At first glance this might seem to be a trivially simple task. Others' behavior provides us with a rich source on which to draw, so if we observe it carefully, we should be able to learn a lot about them. Up to a point this is true. The task is complicated, however, by the following fact: Often, individuals act in certain ways not because doing so reflects their own traits or preferences, but rather because external factors leave them little choice. For example, imagine that you observe a clerk refusing to accept a customer's personal check. Does this mean that the clerk is suspicious of strangers? Not necessarily. She may merely be obeying strict company rules concerning payment for merchandise. She may actually be a very trusting person who experiences great embarrassment in such instances. In situations such as this—which are extremely common—using others' behavior as a guide to their lasting traits or motives can be quite misleading.

How do we cope with such complications? According to Jones and Davis's theory (Jones & Davis, 1965; Jones & McGillis, 1976), we accomplish this difficult task by focusing our attention on certain types of actions—those most likely to prove informative.

First, we consider only behaviors that seem to have been freely chosen. We tend to ignore or at least discount behaviors that were somehow forced on the person in question. Second, we pay careful attention to actions that produce what Jones and Davis term **noncommon effects**—outcomes that can be achieved by one specific action, but not by others. The advantage offered by focusing on noncommon effects can be readily demonstrated.

Imagine that one of your casual friends has just gotten engaged. Her future spouse is extremely handsome, has a great personality, is wildly in love with your friend, and is very rich. Why did she agree to marry him?

Obviously, it's difficult to tell. There are so many good reasons that you can't choose among them. Now, in contrast, imagine that your friend's fiance is very attractive but that he is known to be painfully boring and irritating and treats your friend with great indifference; also, that he has no visible means of support and intends to live on your friend's savings. Does your friend's decision to marry this person tell you anything about her personal characteristics? Now, it does; in fact, you can probably assume that she places great weight on physical attractiveness in potential lovers. So, as you can see, we can usually learn more about others from actions or decisions on their part that yield noncommon effects than from ones that do not.

Finally, Jones and Davis suggest that we also pay greater attention to actions by others that are low in *social desirability* than to actions that are high on this dimension. In other words, we learn more about others' traits or characteristics from actions they perform that are somehow out of the ordinary than from actions that are very much like those performed by most other persons. For example, if you watched the sales clerk mentioned above operate the register or wrap customers' packages, you would not learn much about her as a unique individual. These actions are basically part of her job. But if you saw her urging a customer to visit another store where some item was cheaper, you would learn something of interest: Such behavior is definitely not part of her regular duties.

In sum, according to the theory proposed by Jones and Davis, we are most likely to conclude that others' behavior reflects their stable traits (i.e., we are likely to reach accurate or *correspondent inferences* about them) when that behavior (1) occurs by choice; (2) yields distinctive, noncommon effects; and (3) is low in social desirability.

Kelley's theory of causal attributions:
How we answer the question *Why?*

Consider the following events:

> You receive a much lower grade on an exam than you were expecting.

> Your roommate refuses to lend you a small amount of money, even though he has often done so in the past.

> You phone one of your friends repeatedly and leave messages on her answering machine, but she never returns your call.

What question would arise in your mind in each of these situations? The answer is clear: *Why?* You would want to know *why* your grade was so low, *why* your roommate refused to lend you the money, and *why* your friend wouldn't return your calls. In countless life situations, this is the central attributional task we face. We want to know why other people have acted as they have, or why events have turned out in a particular way. Such knowledge is crucial, for only if we understand the causes behind others' actions can we adjust our own actions accordingly and hope to make sense out of the social world. Obviously, the number of specific causes behind others' behavior is large. To make the task more manageable, therefore, we often begin with a preliminary question: Did others' behavior stem mainly from *internal* causes (their own characteristics, motives, intentions); mainly from *external* causes (some aspect of the social or physical world); or from a combination of the two? For example, you might wonder whether you received a lower grade than expected because you didn't study enough (an internal cause), because the questions were difficult and tricky (an external cause), or, perhaps, because of both factors. Similarly, you might wonder whether your friend hasn't returned your calls because her machine is malfunctioning (an external cause), or because she is upset with you for some reason (an internal cause). Revealing insights into how we carry out this initial attributional task are provided by a theory proposed by Kelley (Kelley, 1972; Kelley & Michela, 1980).

According to Kelley, in our attempts to answer the question *Why* about others' behavior, we focus on information relating to three major dimensions. First, we consider **consensus**—the extent to which others react to some stimulus or event in the same manner as the person we are considering. The higher the proportion of other people who react in the same way, the higher the consensus. Second, we consider **consistency**—the extent to which the person in whose behavior we are interested reacts to the stimulus or event in the same way on other occasions. In other words, consistency relates to the extent to which the person's behavior is unvarying over time. And third, we examine **distinctiveness**—the extent to which the person reacts in the same manner to other, different stimuli or events. (Please don't confuse consistency and distinctiveness. Consistency refers to similar reactions to a given stimulus or event at *different times*. Distinctiveness refers to similar reactions to *different stimuli or events*. If an individual reacts in the same way to a wide range of stimuli, distinctiveness is said be *low*.)

Kelley's theory suggests that we are most likely to attribute another's behavior to *external* causes under conditions in which consensus, consistency, and distinctiveness are all high. In contrast, we are most likely to attribute another's behavior to *internal* causes under conditions in which consensus and distinctiveness are low, but consistency is high. Finally, we usually attribute behavior to a combination of internal and external factors when other combinations of information apply. Perhaps a concrete example will help illustrate the reasonable nature of these suggestions.

You may well remember the dismay Canadians felt when Ben Johnson was stripped of his gold medal in the 1988 Olympics because he tested positive for the use of steroids. An official investigation was launched in Canada (the Dubin Inquiry) to answer the question *why* had this happened? According to Kelley's theory, the answer would depend on information relating to the three factors mentioned above. And certainly the Dubin Inquiry was interested in whether other athletes had taken steroids at the Olympics (consensus information), whether Ben Johnson had taken steroids before other athletic events (consistency information), and his honesty in general (distinctiveness information). Let's use a hypothetical example, imagine that the following conditions had prevailed at such an inquiry:

1.   No other Canadian athlete was found to have taken steroids at the Olympics (*consensus is low*).

2.   The athlete being investigated was found to have taken steroids before other international athletic events (*consistency is high*).

3.   The athlete was known to have cheated in other competitive situations (*distinctiveness is low*).

In this case Kelley's theory suggests that an internal attribution would have been made: the athlete would have caused his own downfall (see the upper portion of Figure 2.9).

To continue our hypothetical example, now imagine that these different conditions had prevailed:

1.   Many other Canadian athletes were found to have taken steroids at the Olympics (*consensus is high*).

2.   The athlete being investigated was found to have taken steroids before other international athletic events (*consistency is high*).

3.   The athlete was *not* known to act dishonestly in other competitive situations (*distinctiveness is high*).

Here, Kelley would predict that attribution would be made to external causes—the pressure of the Olympics or the context of international athletics, and, indeed, some commentators did draw this conclusion in the Ben Johnson case (refer to the lower portion of Figure 2.9).

You will recall that the Dubin Inquiry actually attributed blame to both Johnson and his coach Charlie Francis, as well as calling for tougher standards in Canadian athletics organizations. This may well be due to the fact that Johnson had initially lied when asked about his actions and his honesty was, therefore, in question (making distinctiveness lower). Also, only a few athletes came forward and admitted to taking steroids (making consensus only moderate). In this kind of situation, Kelley's theory suggests that attribution would be made to a combination of internal and external causes—which is exactly what happened.

As we noted earlier, Kelley's theory is reasonable; and it seems applicable to a wide range of social situations. Further, basic aspects of the theory have been confirmed by the results of many different studies (e.g., Harvey & Weary, 1989; McArthur, 1972). We should note, though, that research on the theory also suggests the need for certain modifications. Some of these are described below.

When do we engage in causal attribution?
The path of least resistance strikes again

The kind of causal analysis described by Kelley requires considerable effort. Paying close enough attention to others' behavior to gather information about consensus, consistency, and distinctiveness can be quite difficult. Given this fact, it is not surprising to learn that people tend to avoid such cognitive work whenever they can. Often, they

■ **Kelley's theory of causal attribution: some concrete examples**

FIGURE 2.9 Under the conditions shown in the top portion of this figure, we would attribute an athlete's behavior to internal causes (e.g., his or her dishonesty or desire to win at any cost). Under the conditions shown in the lower portion, we would attribute the behavior to external causes (e.g., influence of a coach, pressure of the Olymics, etc.).

are all too ready to jump to quick and easy conclusions about the causes behind others' actions (Lupfer, Clark, & Hutcherson, 1990). They can do this because they know from past experience that certain kinds of behavior generally stem from internal factors, while other kinds usually derive from external ones (Hansen, 1980).

So, precisely when does the kind of careful analysis described by Kelley occur? Primarily under three conditions: (1) when people are confronted with unexpected events (ones they cannot readily explain in terms of what they already know about a specific situation or person, or about people generally); (2) when they encounter unpleasant outcomes or events; and (3) when the events are important enough to them that the effort seems necessary. In sum, Kelley's theory appears to be an accurate description of causal attribution *when such attribution occurs*. It may not describe people's behavior in many situations, though, because they simply don't want to bother.

Augmenting and discounting: Multiple potential causes

We return to the Dubin Inquiry example to illustrate an added complexity of Kelley's attribution model. The Inquiry was faced with a situation in which many causal factors had to be taken into account: Johnson's own knowledge that he was breaking the rules; his coach and his doctor's powerful part in the planning and administering of the drug; the context of international athletics where, some claimed, most winning athletes used artificial performance-enhancers. In this context, how could the blame be placed upon only one of those factors? The more the daily evidence before the inquiry added weight to each of these potential causes, the less it became possible to see only Ben Johnson as the cause. This example illustrates the **discounting principle** (sometimes called the *subtraction rule*), which suggests that we reduce (discount) the importance of any potential cause of a person's behavior to the extent that other potential causes also exist (Kelley, 1972).

Now imagine a somewhat different situation: A Canadian rower comes third in the Olympics. You think this is a fairly good performance until you learn that this athlete had her right leg shattered in an accident just weeks before the games. Now what do you think of her efforts? Almost certainly, you think this is a great performance—she succeeded against all odds! This example refers to Silken Laumann (See Figure 2.10) and illustrates a second attributional principle—the **augmenting principle**. It suggests that when a factor that might facilitate a given behavior (i.e., her determination and skill) and a factor that might inhibit it (i.e., the injury) are both present and the behavior actually occurs, we assign added weight to the facilitative factor (i.e., her determination and skill become heroic). We do so because that factor has succeeded in producing the behavior even in the face of an important inhibitory barrier.

A growing body of evidence suggests that both augmenting and discounting play an important role in attribution, especially when we can't observe others' actions over extended periods of time or in several situations (i.e., when information about consistency and distinctiveness is lacking). Thus, both augmenting and discounting should be taken into account when we apply Kelley's theory.

■ The augmenting principle in action

FIGURE 2.10 Silken Laumann won a bronze medal in the 1992 Olympics. Her performance was seen as heroic because of the incredible odds against which she battled to achieve that end. Only weeks before the competition, her right leg was splintered in a rowing collision. Doctors initially questioned whether she would walk properly again and dismissed the possibility of her actually competing.

ATTRIBUTION: SOME BASIC SOURCES OF BIAS

Our discussion of attribution so far seems to imply that it is a highly rational process in which individuals seeking to identify the causes of others' behavior follow orderly cognitive steps. In general, this is so. We should note, however, that attribution is also subject to several forms of bias—tendencies that can lead us into serious errors concerning the causes of others' behavior. Several of these errors are described below.

The fundamental attribution error:
Overestimating the role of dispositional causes

Imagine that you witness the following scene. A man arrives at a meeting forty minutes late. On entering, he drops his notes all over the floor. While he is trying to pick them up, his glasses fall off and break. Later he spills coffee all over the desk. How would you explain these events? The chances are good that you would reach conclusions such as these: this person is disorganized, clumsy, and generally incompetent. Are such attributions accurate? Perhaps. But it is also possible that the man was late because of unavoidable delays at the airport, dropped his notes because they were printed on very slick paper, and spilled the coffee because the cup was too hot to hold. That you would be less likely to consider such potential causes reflects what is often termed the **fundamental attribution error**—our strong tendency to explain others' actions in terms of dispositional (internal) rather than situational (external) causes. In short, we tend to perceive others as acting as they do because they are "that kind of person," rather than because of the many situational factors that may have affected their behavior.

This tendency to overemphasize dispositional causes while underestimating the impact of situational ones seems to arise from the fact that when we observe another person's behavior, we tend to focus on his or her actions; the context in which these occur often fades into the background. As a result, the potential impact of situational causes receives less attention. A second possibility is that we do notice such situational factors but tend to assign them insufficient weight (Gilbert & Jones, 1986).

Whatever the basis for the fundamental attribution error, it has important implications. For example, it suggests that even if individuals are made aware of the situational forces that adversely affect disadvantaged groups in a society (e.g., poor diet, shattered family life), they may still perceive these persons as "bad" and responsible for their own plight. In such cases, the fundamental attribution error can have serious social consequences.

Interestingly, growing evidence suggests that while our tendency to attribute others' actions to dispositional causes is robust, it weakens over time (e.g., Burger, 1986; Frank & Gilovich, 1989). In other words, while we tend to attribute others' actions to internal causes soon after it has occurred, we take greater and greater account of situational (external) causes as time passes. This kind of shift in attributions is illustrated very clearly in research conducted by Burger (1991). In several studies, he asked participants to listen to a speech given by a stranger. Participants were told that the person had no choice but to take the position he had—this was required. Despite this fact, however, when participants were asked to rate the speaker's true attitude immediately after hearing the speech, they tended to believe that what the speaker said reflected his actual views; in other words, they ignored the situational causes and made internal attributions ("If he said it, that's what he believes"). Other participants, however, asked to rate the speaker's true attitudes one week *after* hearing the speech, did not show the same pattern—they did not attribute the speaker's comments to his true attitudes. Apparently the fundamental attribution error decreases over time because the accessibility of personal information diminishes more rapidly than the accessibility of situational information (Burger, 1991).

The actor-observer effect: You fell; I was pushed

Another and closely related type of attributional bias can be readily illustrated. Imagine that while walking along the street, you see someone stumble and fall down. How would you explain this behavior? Probably in terms of internal characteristics. You might assume that the person is clumsy. Now, suppose the same thing happens to you; would you explain your own behavior in the same terms? Probably not. Instead, you might well assume that you tripped because of situational causes—wet pavement, slippery shoes, and so on.

This tendency to attribute our own behavior to external or situational causes, but that of others to internal ones, is known as the **actor-observer effect** (Jones & Nisbett, 1971) and has been observed in many different studies (e.g., Frank & Gilovich, 1989). It seems to stem in part from the fact that we are quite aware of the situational factors affecting our own actions but, as outside observers, are less aware of such factors when we turn our attention to the actions of others. Thus, we tend to perceive our own behavior as arising largely from situational causes but the behavior of others as deriving mainly from their traits or dispositions.

The self-serving bias:
"I can do no wrong, but you can do no right"

Suppose that you write a term paper for one of your courses. When you get it back you find the following comment on the first page: "An *excellent* paper—one of the best I've read in years. A++." To what will you attribute this success? If you are like most people, the chances are good that you will explain your success in terms of internal causes—your high level of talent, the tremendous amount of effort you invested in writing the paper, and so on.

Now, in contrast, imagine that when you get your paper back, this comment is written on it: "Horrible paper—one of the worst I've read in years. D–." How will you interpret this outcome? In all likelihood, you will be sorely tempted to focus mainly on external (situational) factors—the difficulty of the task, your professor's unreasonable standards, and so on.

This tendency to attribute positive outcomes to internal causes but negative ones to external factors is known as the **self-serving bias**, and it can have a powerful effect on social relations (Brown & Rogers, 1991; Miller & Ross, 1975).

Why does this "tilt" in our attributions occur? Several possibilities have been suggested, but most of these can be classified into two categories: cognitive and motivational explanations. The cognitive model suggests that the self-serving bias stems primarily from certain tendencies in the way we process social information (Ross, 1977). Specifically, it suggests that we attribute positive outcomes to internal causes but negative ones to external causes because we expect to succeed, and we have a stronger tendency to attribute expected outcomes to internal causes than to external causes. In contrast, the motivational explanation suggests that the self-serving bias stems from our need to protect and enhance our self-esteem, or the related desire to look good in the eyes of others (Greenberg, Pyszczynski, & Solomon, 1982). Both cognitive and motivational factors may well play a role in this type of attributional error, though recent evidence has shown support for the latter (Brown and Rogers, 1991). There is also recent evidence from cross-cultural psychology that this bias may be specific to Western cultures, rather than the general tendency it was thought to be (e.g., Hau & Salili, 1991; see chapter 4 for a discussion of this research).

Whatever the precise origins of the self-serving bias, it can be the cause of much interpersonal friction. For example, it often leads persons who work together on a joint task to perceive that *they*, not their partners, have made the major contributions. Similarly, it leads individuals to perceive that while their own successes stem from internal causes and are well deserved, the successes of others stem from external factors and are less appropriate. Also, because of the self-serving bias, many persons tend to perceive negative actions on their part as reasonable and excusable, but identical actions on the part of others as irrational and inexcusable (Baumeister, Stillwell, & Wotman, 1990). Thus, the self-serving bias is clearly one type of attributional error with serious implications for interpersonal relations.

ATTRIBUTION IN INTERGROUP RELATIONS: THE ULTIMATE ATTRIBUTION ERROR AND BEYOND

When our identity is bound to a particular group, the self-serving bias can extend beyond the self. If my team wins the Stanley Cup it's because we deserved it, we were simply the better team! But, of course, if we lose, our opponents were playing "dirty" and the referee was "blind" or biased—it definitely wasn't our fault (see Figure 2.11). This phenomenon which has been shown to occur in relation to many types of groups (Hewstone, Bond, & Wan, 1983; Taylor & Jaggi, 1974), can have a disastrous effect upon intergroup relations (see chapters 4 and 5). For this reason, it was termed by one of its earliest researchers (Pettigrew, 1979) *the ultimate attribution error*—our

■ The ultimate attribution error

FIGURE 2.11 When our identity is tied to the fate of a group, such as a sports team, we show biased attributions: When we win we deserve the best; but if the opposing team wins, they were lucky. If we lose we were "robbed" by the referee; if they lose it's because they stink.

tendency to attribute negative outcomes of our own group (the ingroup) to external causes and positive outcomes of our own group to internal causes. Conversely, we will tend to attribute negative outcomes of outgroups (ones to which we don't belong) to their characteristics (internal causes) and positive outcomes to external factors ("they" had help or were lucky). This pattern of attributional bias can protect the individual's identity and sense of self-esteem if they are bound to the group. It can also maintain morale within a group. For example, when asked to explain why students from one university in Hong Kong tend to receive better starting jobs than those from another university, students at the favored school attributed their success to better preparation. Those at the school whose graduates received less desirable jobs attributed this outcome to better personal connections on the part of students at the other school (Hewstone, Bond, & Wan, 1983). Similar results have been observed in many other contexts (e.g., Hewstone & Jaspars, 1982): In each instance, individuals made more favorable and flattering attributions about members of their ingroup than about members of various outgroups.

Researchers in Canada have extended our understanding of attribution at the group level. For example, Don Taylor and colleagues at McGill (Taylor, Doria & Tyler, 1983) followed a university sports team throughout one extremely poor season. Analysis of attributions by team members showed that their explanations did indeed protect the morale of the team, as the ultimate attribution error would lead us to expect. However, simple external attribution for failure was uncommon. Team members tended to take individual responsibility, making internal attributions to themselves (e.g., "I could have improved my play"), thus, relieving the team as a whole of blame. The few successes this team achieved were, in contrast, attributed to the team as a whole. Taylor, et al. suggest that there are three possible levels of attribution in this situation: (1) *internal to the individual* group member; (2) *internal to the group* as a whole; and (3) *external to the group*. The pattern of attribution they found (level 1 was applied to self for failure and level 2 was used for success) was termed *group-serving* by Taylor et al. It effectively maintained group cohesiveness by not blaming failures on other team members, and, further, it maintained morale by implying that improvements in team performance were possible. A simple external attribution (e.g., to stupid or corrupt officials or the other teams' tactics) would have left the team with very little possibility of changing future outcomes.

A second series of studies by Guimond and colleagues (Guimond & Dubé, 1989; Guimond, Begin, & Palmer, 1989) examined explanations for economic disadvantage by groups in Quebec. Research has shown (Shapiro & Stelcner, 1987) that French-speakers on average have a lower annual income than English-speakers and this is true even within Quebec. Guimond and Dubé (1989) compared the attributions of Francophones and Anglophones for the relative disadvantage of Francophones. As the ultimate attribution error would predict, Anglophones tended to make internal attributions for Francophone disadvantage, for example, blaming their lack of initiative or their failure to pursue education. Francophones put greater blame on external factors, mentioning problems with the economic system in Quebec and Canada, or discrimination against Francophone employees.

However, these researchers pointed out that there might be additional explanations for such results beyond the group-serving one of the ultimate attribution error. They speculated that the difference in attribution between groups might stem from cultural socialization. It is possible that French-Canadian culture tends to focus more on situational causes than English-Canadian culture, and that members of each group learn the culturally appropriate way to interpret the world. A subsequent study supported this second explanation. Guimond, Begin, & Palmer (1989) reasoned that if attributional styles were learned, then the education system might impart them.

In particular, those who majored in topics with an *external* focus of explanation (e.g., the social sciences) should make more external attributions. This is exactly what they found. Social science students made more situational attributions for economic disadvantage compared to students in the natural sciences and commerce. They even made more situational attibutions than the poor and unemployed themselves, as a second study showed! But more important, this difference between student groups tended to be more marked the longer students had been involved in education, suggesting that attributional styles were being learned as part of the topic of study. Other recent studies comparing attributional styles of different cultural groups provide further confirmation. Forgas, Furnham, and Frey (1989) found that subjects from the United Kingdom, Germany, and Australia had different explanations for wealth and economic success. Subjects from the two European countries, where a traditional class-system has survived, considered external factors (specifically, family background) as most important in determining levels of wealth, whereas Australian subjects, living in a newer and less class-ridden society, saw individual qualities as the most important determinants of wealth.

In sum, these intriguing recent results imply that when examining attribution at the intergroup or international level, we cannot simply transfer the *self*-serving bias to attributions between *groups*. There is evidence for the existence of an ultimate attribution error. Of course we love to stand in the reflected glory of our group's successes and feel shamed by their failures. However, group attributions tend to be somewhat more complex than individual attributions. The Canadian research above suggests that individuals can show self-sacrificing attributional patterns (blaming themselves for group failure) if this aids group cohesiveness and morale during difficult times. Further, accumulating cross-cultural research in Canada and elsewhere points to the importance of culture in influencing the attributions we make: the belief systems and historical experiences of groups may produce a *cultural style of attribution* which members share (Miller, 1984). The impact of group-membership and culture on our sense of identity and our attributions will be explored further in chapter 4.

SCHEMAS, HEURISTICS AND BIASES: COPING WITH INFORMATION OVERLOAD

We are not always the rational and efficient thinkers that we would like to be. Three key characteristics of social cognition contribute to this. First, people often prefer the path of least resistance, and this preference applies to cognitive, as well as to physical, efforts. In fact, it is a guiding principle of social cognition: All things being equal, most of us will do the least amount of mental work we can get away with in most situations (e.g., Fiske & Taylor, 1991). Of course, this is not always true. There are situations in which individuals willingly engage in complex and effortful forms of social thought (e.g., Tetlock & Boettger, 1989). For example, processes of attribution are often complex and cognitively time-consuming. However, *we seek to minimize such cognitive effort* whenever we can. Second, we are often faced with excessive amounts of social information—this is termed **information overload**—and this forces us to be *selective in our processing*. We impose organization upon information (e.g., we use schemas and social categorization), and we use mental shorcuts in evaluating this information. Third, human beings are definitely not computers. While we can imagine a person who reasons in a perfectly logical manner and rarely (if ever) makes errors, we are unlikely ever to meet one— unless it is Mr. Spock of "Star Trek" fame (see Figure 2.12). Being human, *we are fallible*—highly fallible—where the cognitive side of life is concerned. Social thought is certainly no exception to this rule.

FIGURE 2.12 While Mr. Spock (of "Star Trek") appears to be totally logical, the rest of us, as mere human beings, can't hope to match his performance where social thought is concerned.

In sum, our attempts to understand others and make sense out of the social world sometimes involve little effort and are selective and fallible. It is not surprising that we suffer from a range of cognitive limitations and biases that together can, and sometimes do, lead us into serious error. In this section we'll consider several of these imperfections of social cognition (e.g., Fiske & Taylor, 1991; Srull & Wyer, 1989). As you'll soon see, these tendencies are as intriguing as they are potentially disturbing. Before turning to specific examples of these limitations, however, we should carefully emphasize the following point: While such aspects of social thought sometimes result in errors, they are also, in key respects, quite adaptive. They help us to focus on the kinds of information that are usually most informative, and they reduce the overall effort required for understanding our social world. Further, they sometimes help us to feel good about our world or ourselves and to maintain a consistent worldview. So, as is true of virtually every important aspect of human behavior, these tendencies cut both ways and can be beneficial as well as detrimental. Having said that, we'll turn without further delay to a major cogntive short cut.

SCHEMAS: ORGANIZING SOCIAL INFORMATION

One key finding of research on social cognition is this: Our thoughts about the social world are definitely not a mixture of random ideas and knowledge. On the contrary, information we have acquired through experience is organized into cognitive structures known as **schemas** (e.g., Fiske & Taylor, 1991; Wyer & Srull, 1984). In a sense, schemas can be thought of as "mental scaffolds"—cognitive structures that hold and organize information. Schemas are important because once they are formed, they exert powerful effects on the processing of information related to them. For example, they influence which aspects of the social world get selected for attention, what information gets entered into memory (usually, information consistent with schemas), what is later retrieved from memory storage, and how it is interpreted (Greenwald & Pratkanis, 1984; Higgins & Bargh, 1987).

In these respects they play a key role in our understanding of other persons, ourselves, and the social world generally. Their main function is to help us cope with information overload by speeding up the processes of social cognition. However, on the down side, because they focus our attention on particular aspects of incoming information, some information about the social world is lost through use of schemas. Similar problems occur when we use shortcuts in making social judgments.

HEURISTICS: COGNITIVE SHORTCUTS

In many cases, people adopt strategies to help them make social judgments in the face of information overload. To be successful, such strategies must have two properties. First, they must provide a quick and simple way of dealing with large amounts of social information. Second, they must *work*—they must be reasonably accurate much of the time.

While many potential shortcuts for reducing mental effort exist, the ones that have received most attention with respect to social cognition are **heuristics**—simple decision-making rules we often use to make inferences or draw conclusions quickly and easily. To understand how heuristics work, consider an analogy. Suppose you want to estimate the dimensions of a room but don't have a tape measure. What will you do? One possibility is to pace off its length and width by placing one foot almost exactly in front of the other. Since the distance from the heel to the toe of an adult's foot is approximately twelve inches, you will be able to get rough estimates of the room's dimensions through this "quick-and-dirty" method.

In a similar manner, we make use of many different mental heuristics in our efforts to think about and use social information. Two of these that are used frequently in everyday life are known as *representativeness* and *availability*. These heuristics can also lead to a number of biases or *fallacies* (false reasoning or conclusions).

Representativeness: Judging by resemblance

Imagine that you have just met your next-door neighbor for the first time. On the basis of a brief conversation with her, you determine that she is very neat in her habits, has a good vocabulary, reads many books, is somewhat shy, and dresses conservatively. Later you realize that she never mentioned what she does for a living. Is she a business executive, a librarian, a waitress, an attorney, or a dancer? One quick way of making a guess is to compare her with other members of each of these occupations; simply ask yourself how well she resembles persons you have met in each of these fields. If you proceed in this fashion, you may well conclude that she is a librarian. After all, her traits seem to resemble the traits many people associate with librarians more closely than the traits of dancers, attorneys, or waitresses. In this instance, you would be using the **representativeness heuristic**. In other words, you would make your judgment on the basis of a relatively simple rule: *The more similar an individual is to "typical" members of a given group, the more likely he or she is to also belong to that group.*

Such judgment rules are developed because of their utility, so the representativeness heuristic often leads to accurate conclusions. As you probably know from your experience, however, there are exceptions to this general rule. Some librarians are extroverted and lead exciting social lives; some dancers are shy and read lots of books. And some professors (believe it or not) climb mountains, practice sky-diving, and even run for political office in their spare time (see Figure 2.13). Because of such exceptions, the representativeness heuristic, although useful, can lead to serious errors in at least some instances. In addition, and perhaps more importantly, reliance on this heuristic can lead us to overlook other types of information that could potentially be very useful. The most important type is information relating to *base rates*—the frequency with which some event or pattern occurs in the general population. The tendency to overlook such information when relying on the representativeness heuristic was illustrated some years ago by a famous study carried out by Tversky and Kahneman (1973).

■ **The representative heuristic in action**

FIGURE 2.13 Do you find it surprising that the persons shown here are Hewlett–Packard employees? If so, this may result in part from the operation of the representativeness heuristic—our tendency to assume that the more similar an individual is to "typical" members of a given group, the more likely it is that she or he belongs to that group.

Participants in this study were told that an imaginary person named Jack had been selected from a group of one hundred men. They were then asked to guess the probability that Jack was an engineer. Some participants were told that thirty of the one hundred men were engineers (thus, the base rate for engineers was 30 percent). Others were told that seventy of the men were engineers. Half of the subjects received no further information. The other half, however, also received a personal description of Jack that either resembled the common stereotype of engineers (e.g., they are practical, like to work with numbers, etc.) or did not. When participants in the study received only information relating to base rates, their estimates of the likelihood that Jack was an engineer reflected this information: They thought it more likely that Jack was an engineer when the base rate was 70 percent than when it was 30 percent. However, when they received personal information about Jack, they tended to ignore this important information. They made their estimates primarily on the basis of whether Jack seemed to resemble their stereotype of an engineer. In sum, subjects tended to overlook a valuable form of information and to operate in terms of representativeness alone. This tendency to ignore useful base rate information is known as the **base rate fallacy**.

Availability: What comes to mind first?

Which is more common—words that start with the letter *k* (e.g., king) or words with *k* as the third letter (e.g., awkward)? Tversky and Kahneman (1982) put this question to more than one hundred people. Their findings were revealing. In English there are more than twice as many words with *k* in third place as there are with k in first place. Yet despite this fact, a majority of the subjects guessed incorrectly: They assumed that there were more words beginning with *k*. Why was this the case? In part, because of their use of another heuristic—**availability**. According to this heuristic, the easier it is to bring instances of some group or category to mind, the more prevalent or important these are judged to be. This heuristic, too, makes good sense: After all, events or objects that are common *are* usually easier to think of than ones that are less common, because we have had more experience with them. But relying on availability in making such judgments can also lead to errors, such as the one involving words with the letter *k*. As another example, consider the case of a professor who is grading students on the basis of class participation. As she assigns grades, she thinks: "Hm … let's see … how often did Jose participate? Did he speak up more than Laurel?" Does the ease with which she can recall each student's comments reflect the actual frequency with which the students contributed? Not necessarily. Perhaps she is more likely to remember comments that were made very forcefully, with lots of conviction. To the extent this is so, she may assign higher grades to those students who express themselves with greatest conviction—not necessarily to those who have participated most.

The false consensus effect: Availability and the tendency to assume that others think as we do

Be honest: on a scale ranging from 1 (strongly opposed) to 7 (strongly in favor), what is your view about permitting persons with an openly homosexual life-style to join the nation's military forces? Now, out of one hundred other students, how many do you think share your view, whatever it is? (that is, how many are on the same side of the neutral point on this scale [4] as yourself?) If you are like most people, the number you indicated is higher than what would be revealed by an actual survey. In other words, you assume that people agree with you to a greater extent than they actually do. This is known as the **false consensus effect**, and it has been observed in many different contexts. For example, in one study high school boys who smoked estimated that 51 percent of their fellow male students smoked, but nonsmoking boys estimated that only 38 percent smoked (Sherman, Presson, & Chassin, 1984). In a similar manner, students tend to overestimate the proportion of other students who agree with their attitudes about drugs, abortion, seat belt use, university policies, politics, and even Ritz crackers (Nisbett & Kunda, 1985; Suls, Wan, & Sanders, 1988). In short, the false consensus effect is quite common (although in an absolute sense, it is not very large).

What is the basis for this tendency to assume that others think as we do? Two factors seem to play a role. First, most people want to believe that others agree with them, because this enhances their confidence that their own actions, judgments, or lifestyles are normal or appropriate (Marks & Miller, 1987; Sherman, Presson, & Chassin, 1984). In other words, the false consensus effect serves a self-enhancing function.

Second, this tendency seems to stem, at least in part, from reliance on the availability heuristic. This can occur two distinct ways. Some people, at least, find it easier to notice and later remember instances in which others agreed with them than instances in which they disagreed. As a result of such distortion in processing social information, people find it easier to bring instances of agreement to mind. Then they perceive these instances as more frequent than instances of disagreement. Alternatively, since most of us tend to choose as friends and associates others who share our views (see our discussion of attraction in chapter 6), we are actually exposed to many instances of agreement. This, too, leads to higher availability for agreement than disagreement and contributes to the occurrence of the false consensus effect.

We should note, by the way, that while the false consensus effect is common, it is far from universal. A researcher in Canada demonstrated that when the desire to stand out from the crowd in some positive way is stronger than the desire to be similar to others, the false consensus effect may fail to occur (Campbell, 1986). It may be comforting to assume that others share our attitudes and, perhaps, even our undesirable attributes (such as the inability to resist rich desserts). However, for highly desirable attributes, people are often motivated to perceive themselves as unique (e.g., Goethals, 1986; Suls & Wan, 1987).

Priming: Some effects of increased availability

During the first year of medical school, many students experience what is known as the "medical student syndrome." They begin to suspect that they (or their friends or families) are suffering from serious illnesses. An ordinary headache, for example, may cause such students to wonder if they have a brain tumor. A mild sore throat may result in anxiety over the possibility that some rare but fatal type of infection has begun. What accounts for these effects? One factor seems crucial. The students are exposed to descriptions of diseases day after day in their classes and assigned readings. As a result, such information is high in availability. Thus, when a mild symptom occurs, it is readily brought to mind, with the result that the students tend to imagine the worst about their current health!

Such effects are termed **priming**. Specifically, priming involves any stimuli that heighten the availability of certain types or categories of information so that they can be readily brought to mind. Many instances of priming occur in everyday life. For example, after watching an especially frightening horror movie, many persons react strongly to stimuli that would previously have had little impact upon them ("What's that dark shape at the end of the driveway?" "What's that creak on the stairs?"; see Figure 2.14).

Similarly, after viewing a television show filled with sexual remarks and content, some persons, at least, are more likely to perceive innocuous remarks or gestures by others as come-ons than might otherwise be true.

The occurrence of priming effects has been demonstrated in many different studies (e.g., Higgins & King, 1981; Wyer & Srull, 1980). For example, in one of the earliest experiments on this topic (Higgins, Rohles, & Jones, 1977), participants were shown lists of positive traits (e.g., adventurous, independent) or negative traits (e.g., reckless). Then, in what they thought was a separate task, they were asked to form an impression of an imaginary person. They formed these impressions on the basis of descriptions of his behavior that were either relevant to the previously viewed traits (e.g., sailing across the Atlantic, climbing mountains) or unrelated to them. Results indicated that subjects'

■ Priming in action

FIGURE 2.14 After seeing a frightening horror movie, many persons react with fear to stimuli that might fail to evoke such reactions in the absence of such priming (i.e., at times when they have not recently seen such a scary film).

impressions of the imaginary character were indeed affected by the trait words, but only when these were relevant to the descriptions of his behavior. Thus, participants' impressions were more favorable if they had previously seen relevant positive traits (e.g., adventurous) than if they had previously seen relevant negative ones (e.g., reckless). In short, their social judgments were affected by priming—by words that had activated different aspects or categories of their memories.

Counterfactual thinking: When alternatives are available

Imagine the following events:

> Ms. Caution never picks up hitchhikers. Yesterday, however, she gave a stranger a ride. He repaid her kindness by robbing her.

Now, in contrast, consider the following events:

> Ms. Risk frequently picks up hitchhikers. Yesterday, she gave a stranger a ride. He repaid her kindness by robbing her.

Which of these two persons will experience greater regret? If you answered "Ms. Caution, of course," your thinking in this instance is very much like that of other persons. An overwhelming majority of respondents identify Ms. Caution as feeling more regretful (Kahneman & Miller, 1986). Why is this the case? Both individuals have suffered precisely the same negative outcome: They have been robbed. Why, then, do we perceive Ms. Caution as experiencing more regret? In most general terms, it appears that our reactions to events depend not only on the events themselves but on what these events bring to mind (Miller & McFarland, 1990). When we have some experience, we do not think only about the experience itself. We also engage in *mental simulation* with respect to it. This often results in **counterfactual thinking**—bringing alternative events and outcomes to mind. In this particular instance, we may think, "If only Ms. Caution had not broken her usual rule against picking up hitchhikers, she'd be okay."

But why, precisely, does such counterfactual thinking lead us to believe that Ms. Caution will experience more regret? In part, because it is easier to imagine alternatives to unusual behavior, such as Ms. Caution's picking up the hitchhiker, than it is to imagine alternatives to usual, normal behavior (e.g., Ms. Risk's picking up the hitchhiker). So, we conclude that Ms. Caution experienced more regret because it is easier to imagine her acting in a different way—sticking to her rule—than it is to imagine Ms. Risk acting differently. This is not to suggest that Ms Risk would *not* feel regret in a real life situation (see Davis, Lehman, Wortman, Silver, & Thompson, 1994). Rather, it suggests that we, as observers, find it easier to generate counterfactual alternatives to Ms. Caution's behavior because it is unusual for her.

This reasoning leads to the interesting prediction that negative outcomes that follow unusual behavior will generate more sympathy than ones that follow usual behavior. Precisely such effects have been demonstrated in many recent studies (Kahneman & Tversky, 1982). For example, in one Canadian investigation, Miller and McFarland (1986) asked subjects to read a description of a victim of a crime to determine how much money he should receive as compensation for his injuries. All subjects read about a male victim who lost the use of his right arm as the result of a gunshot wound that occurred when he walked in on a robbery in a neighborhood convenience store. One group of subjects (the *normal behavior* condition) learned that on the night he was shot, the victim had gone to a store he visited frequently. Another group (the *abnormal behavior* condition) learned that he had gone, for a change of pace, to a store he rarely visited. (Please note: In this context "abnormal" merely means unusual.) Confirming predictions, subjects assigned greater compensation to the victim when his wound occurred at a store he rarely visited than when it occurred at a store he visited frequently. In other words, when subjects could readily imagine an alternative outcome (e.g., the man did not visit this store and was not wounded), they felt more sympathy for him and awarded him larger compensation.

As you can see, counterfactual thinking is closely related to the availability heuristic. The ease with which individuals can imagine alternative events ("What might have been") depends, to some extent, on how available alternative outcomes are. The more readily such alternatives can be brought to mind, the stronger our reactions to the present situation. Whatever the precise mechanisms involved, it is clear that our reasoning about the causes of various events, and our judgments or decisions about these events, can be strongly influenced by counterfactual thinking—by our thoughts about "what might have been."

In sum, the availability heuristic appears to play a part in many cognitive processes. We often make judgments based on the first information that comes to mind. And sometimes this can lead to a bias in our judgments such as the *false consensus effect. Priming* from external events and conditions can increase the availability in memory of specific types of information and this can strongly influence our social judgments. The intensity with which we respond to events is partly determined by how easily we can imagine alternative outcomes, and such *counterfactual thinking* depends upon the availability of these alternatives.

THE ROLE OF AFFECT: HOW FEELINGS INFLUENCE OUR VIEW OF THE WORLD

Imagine the following situation: You are sitting in your room studying when your thoughts turn to something that happened earlier in the week. You have a lab partner in one of your courses, and the two of you are working together on an important project. You made an appointment to meet at the library to go over your plans for the project, but your partner wasn't there at the agreed-upon time. You waited for him with mounting impatience for almost thirty minutes. Just when you were about to give up, he finally showed up. When you expressed your annoyance at his being so late, he muttered a weak excuse about losing track of the time. When you stated that that was no reason to be so late, he actually got mad at you and threatened to leave. Since the project is very important, you bit your tongue and went on with the meeting. But now, as you think about this incident, you feel yourself getting angry all over again. Just who the heck does he think he is, anyway? What colossal nerve!

Situations such as this one suggest that emotional states frequently exert strong effects upon our cognitive processes—our current thoughts as well as memories we bring to mind (e.g., Forgas, 1991). Since much of this work has dealt with the effects of mild, temporary shifts in feelings rather than with those of intense and long-lasting emotions, the term *affect* seems more suitable than the term emotion in describing such work (Isen, 1987). Thus, we'll use this term throughout most of this discussion.

Research on the influence of affect on cognition has yielded many intriguing results (e.g., Isen & Baron, 1991; Schwarz, 1991). It is now clear that even very mild shifts in individuals' current feelings can alter aspects of cognition. However, we'll first consider several contrasting views concerning the nature of emotion (e.g., Ekman, 1992) and one intriguing explanation for how even mild shifts in affect can influence social cognition.

THE NATURE OF EMOTION: CONTRASTING VIEWS

Feelings are a central part of everyday life, so over the centuries, many different views about the nature of emotions have been offered. Within psychology, however, three approaches have received most attention. The first, often known as the **Cannon-Bard theory**, is the common-sense perspective. It suggests that when we are exposed to emotion-provoking (emotion-eliciting) events or stimuli, we quickly experience *both* the physiological signs of emotion and the subjective experiences we label as fear, anger, joy, and so on. In other words, both types of reaction occur concurrently and stem from the same eliciting events. For example, imagine that one day, you switched on the radio and learned that you had just won the lottery. Your pulse and blood pressure would leap to high levels, and you would quickly be swept by waves of surprise and intense elation.

In contrast, the **James-Lange theory** proposes that our subjective emotional experiences are actually the result of our relatively automatic physiological reactions to various events. According to this view, we experience anger, fear, joy, or sorrow *because* we become aware of a racing heart, tears streaming down our face, and so on. Returning to the lottery example, the James-Lange theory suggests that you would experience elation *because* you quickly feel (and become aware of) all the physiological signs of this emotion. As James himself noted in another example, if you see a bear while in the woods, you begin to run. Then you experience fear because of the feelings of intense arousal produced by this activity.

A third view—Schachter's **two-factor theory**—suggests that any form of arousal, whatever its source, initiates a search for the causes of these feelings. The causes we then identify play a key role in determining the label we place on our arousal, and so on the emotion we experience. Thus, if we feel aroused in the presence of an attractive person, we may label our arousal as "love" or "attraction." If we feel aroused after a near miss in traffic, we label it as "fear" or perhaps "anger" (toward the other driver, who was clearly at fault!). In short, we perceive ourselves to be experiencing the emotion that external cues suggest we *should* be feeling (see Figure 2.15). This is an intriguing view, and one that is supported by the findings of many studies (e.g., Reisenzein, 1983). We should note, however, that the process described by Schachter and Singer seems to occur in cases where our level of arousal is relatively low. Intense feelings of arousal seem to be aversive (negative) in and of themselves, and are interpreted as such regardless of the situation (e.g., Marshall & Zimbardo, 1979).

Which of these views is most accurate? As we'll note in chapter 4, the results of many studies offer support for the view proposed by Schachter and Singer, so it is clear that cognitive and situational factors do play a role in our subjective emotional

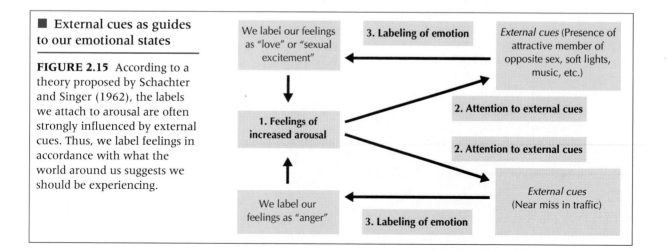

■ **External cues as guides to our emotional states**

FIGURE 2.15 According to a theory proposed by Schachter and Singer (1962), the labels we attach to arousal are often strongly influenced by external cues. Thus, we label feelings in accordance with what the world around us suggests we should be experiencing.

We label our feelings as "love" or "sexual excitement"

3. Labeling of emotion

External cues (Presence of attractive member of opposite sex, soft lights, music, etc.)

1. Feelings of increased arousal

2. Attention to external cues

2. Attention to external cues

We label our feelings as "anger"

3. Labeling of emotion

External cues (Near miss in traffic)

reactions (e.g., Olson & Ross, 1988). Over the years, however, even more attention has been directed to the task of determining whether the Cannon-Bard or the James-Lange view is more accurate. Until recently, the weight of existing evidence seemed to favor the common-sense Cannon-Bard approach: Emotion-provoking events produce both physiological arousal and the subjective experiences we label as emotions. More recently, however, the pendulum has swung in the opposite direction, with an increasing amount of evidence providing support for some form of the James-Lange theory. For example, research conducted with highly sophisticated equipment indicates that different emotions are indeed associated with different patterns of physiological activity. Not only do anger and sorrow *feel* different, they are reflected in somewhat different patterns of brain activity and in contrasting patterns of activity in various facial muscles (e.g., Ekman, Davidson, & Friesen, 1990; Izard, 1992). Research has investigated whether subtle changes in facial expression can produce changes in emotion—this idea is termed the **facial feedback hypothesis** and has generally received support (McCanne & Anderson, 1987), as we saw earlier in this chapter.

HOW AFFECT INFLUENCES COGNITION

Does being in a positive or negative mood influence the way we think? Informal observation suggests that this is indeed the case. As one old song puts it, when we are happy, "We see the world through rose-colored glasses"—everything takes on a positive tinge. And most people are aware of the fact that they think differently when feeling happy than when they are depressed. For example, when we are experiencing positive feelings (affect), difficult tasks or situations seem easier to perform or deal with than when we are experiencing negative feelings. Are these subjective impressions correct? Growing evidence suggests that they are—that our current affective states do indeed have important effects on how we process social information.

First, it has been found that affective states influence the perception of ambiguous stimuli. In general, a person perceives (and evaluates) these more favorably when he or she is experiencing positive affect than when experiencing negative affect (see Figure 2.16; Fiske & Neuberg, 1990; Isen & Shalker, 1982). For example, when asked to interview applicants whose qualifications for a job are ambiguous, research subjects assign higher ratings to these persons when they are in a positive mood (e.g.,

■ Moods and social judgment

FIGURE 2.16 Being in a good mood may lead to behavior and judgments inconsistent with the duties of a tax-collector!

Source: North America Syndicate. Inc. 1990.

"We're shorthanded this week, Sneedby. We've got three agents out with a good mood!"

they have just received favorable feedback or won a small prize) than when they are in a negative mood (e.g., they have just received negative feedback; Baron, 1987). Interestingly, such effects are strongest when the qualifications of the applicants are truly ambiguous: They are neither highly qualified nor clearly unqualified for the job. When qualifications are very good or very bad, the effects of mood on this kind of decision are greatly reduced (Baron, 1993).

Second, positive and negative affect exert a strong influence upon memory (Isen, 1987). In general, information consistent with our current mood is easier to remember than information that is inconsistent with it. Moreover, mood seems to exert such effects both at the time of *encoding* (when information is first entered into memory) and at the time of *retrieval* (when such information is recalled; e.g., Forgas, 1991; Forgas & Bower, 1988). Positive and negative affect have also been found to influence the way in which information is organized in memory. Persons experiencing positive affect seem to include a wider range of information within various memory categories than persons in a neutral or negative mood (Isen & Daubman, 1984). Those experiencing positive affect provide more unusual associates to neutral words and rate objects that are not very typical of a given category as more representative of it than persons who are not in a positive mood. (For example, they rate the word elevator as more representative of the category *vehicle* than persons in a negative mood; Baron, Rea, & Daniels, 1992; Isen et al., 1985).

Third, there is some indication that persons in a good mood are more creative. At least, they are more successful in performing tasks involving creative problem-solving (searching for novel approaches, exploring new uses for familiar objects) than persons in a neutral mood (Isen, Daubman, & Nowicki, 1987).

Fourth, the question arises: How do positive and negative moods exert such effects on social cognition? Research on this important issue has begun only recently, but one approach (Forgas, 1991a) suggests that mood influences the *strategies* we use when processing social information. Specifically, when we are in a positive mood, we are motivated to maintain these feelings. Thus, we may avoid any form of hard cognitive work, since this might interfere with our positive affect. In contrast, when we are in a negative mood, motivated processing designed to help eliminate these feelings may occur. In such cases, we will engage in a selective search for information designed to enhance our feelings and may recall such information more accurately. This is what Forgas describes as a *motivated processing strategy*. Forgas' own research (1991b) and that of other investigators (Schwartz & Bless, 1991) indicate that our current moods often influence the way in which we process social information. Since these processing strategies, in turn, shape the decisions we make and the judgments we reach, it is clear that affective states play a key role in social cognition and also in many aspects of our relations with other persons.

Finally, we should mention that the influence of affect on cognition is reciprocal: our thought processes also influence our feelings. Less research has focused on this area, but we will examine some important ways in which cognition can influence feeling in the emotionally charged contexts of aggression and helping behavior in chapter 8.

NONVERBAL COMMUNICATION

Social perception is the process through which we attempt to understand other persons. To obtain information about the temporary causes of behavior (e.g., others' emotions or feelings) we focus on *nonverbal cues*. These are provided by others' facial expressions, eye contact, body posture or movements, and touching. Nonverbal behavior plays an important role in social interaction. It is often used for purposes of *impression management*.

IMPRESSION FORMATION AND IMPRESSION MANAGEMENT

Common sense is correct in suggesting that first impressions are important. We form such impressions by combining available information about others, with each piece of information weighted in terms of its importance. Individuals engage in many tactics to make favorable impressions on others. Together, these are known as tactics of *impression management*. These include efforts to improve one's personal appearance and various forms of *other-enhancement*; for example, flattery and agreeing with others' views. Impression management often succeeds in its goals.

ATTRIBUTION: UNDERSTANDING THE CAUSES OF OTHERS' BEHAVIOR

Knowledge about the lasting causes of others' behavior is acquired through attribution. In this process, we infer others' traits, motives, and intentions from observation of their behavior; and we focus on the aspects of their behavior that are most likely to be revealing in this respect. In order to determine whether others' behavior stems mainly from internal or external causes, we focus on information relating to *consensus*, *consistency*, and *distinctiveness*. We engage in careful causal analysis only under certain circumstances, however—for example, when others behave in unexpected ways. Attributions are affected by *discounting*—a tendency to discount one potential cause of behavior when others are also present—and by *augmenting*—a tendency to emphasize the importance of factors that might cause a specific behavior when the behavior occurs despite the presence of factors that might inhibit it. Attribu-

tion is subject to several forms of bias or error, including the *fundamental attribution error*, the *actor-observer effect*, and the *self-serving bias*.

SCHEMAS, HEURISTICS, AND BIASES

Social Cognition consists of the processes through which we notice, interpret, remember, and later use information about the social world. In order to minimize the effort required for these complex tasks, or to cope with *information overload*, individuals often organize information or use mental shortcuts. The major cognitive structure that organizes information is termed a *schema*. Mental shortcuts often involve the use of *heuristics*—mental rules of thumb that permit rapid decisions about various stimuli. For example, people may judge the frequency of a stimulus in terms of *representativeness*—the extent to which it is similar to other, related stimuli. Another important heuristic is *availability*—the ease with which information can be brought to mind. Recent evidence indicates that the greater such ease, the stronger the impact of the information on our judgments. These heuristics can lead to biases such as the *base-rate fallacy* and the *false-consensus* effect. *Priming* involves procedures that increase the availability of specific information in consciousness. Our response to events is often determined by the availability of alternative outcomes. If we can imagine the opposite of what has actually happened—a process known as *counterfactual thinking*—this leads us to have more sympathy for persons who suffer negative outcomes after unusual behavior than after typical behavior. Similarly, we assign greater responsibility and blame to those who have caused negative outcomes if they occur under unusual circumstances—that is, we can readily imagine how such outcomes might *not* have occurred.

AFFECT AND COGNITION

Sharply contrasting views of the nature of emotions have been proposed. The *Cannon-Bard theory* suggests that emotion-provoking stimuli evoke both physiological reactions and subjective emotional states. In contrast, the *James-Lange theory* suggests that emotional experiences stem primarily from our recognition of changes in our bodily states. Schachter's *two-factor theory* proposes that it is the cognitive label we attach to physiological arousal that is crucial.

Mild shifts in affect have been found to influence interpretation of ambiguous stimuli, memory, creative problem-solving, risk-taking, and many other forms of behavior. In addition, current moods influence the specific strategies we adopt for processing social information. Cognition also influences our affective states.

KEY TERMS

Actor-observer-effect The tendency to attribute our own behavior mainly to situational causes but the behavior of others mainly to internal (dispositional) causes.

Affect Temporary and relatively mild feelings, or moods.

Attribution The process through which we seek to identify the causes of others' behavior and so gain knowledge of their stable traits and dispositions.

Augmenting Principle The tendency to attach greater importance to a potential cause of behavior if the behavior occurs despite the presence of other, inhibitory causes.

Automatic Vigilance The strong tendency to pay attention to undesirable or negative information.

Availability Heuristic A strategy for making judgments on the basis of how easily specific kinds of information can be brought to mind. Information that can be readily remembered is viewed as more prevalent or important than information that cannot be readily remembered.

Base Rate Fallacy The tendency to ignore or underuse information relating to base rates—the relative frequency with which conditions, events, or stimuli actually occur.

Body Language Cues provided by the position, posture, and movement of people's bodies or body parts.

Cannon-Bard Theory A theory of emotion suggesting that various stimuli elicit both physiological reactions and the subjective reactions we label as emotions.

Consensus The extent to which actions by one person are also shown by others.

Consistency The extent to which an individual responds to a given stimulus or situation in the same way on different occasions (i.e., across time).

Correspondent Inference (theory of) A theory describing how we use others' behavior as a basis for inferring their stable dispositions.

Counterfactual Thinking The tendency to evaluate events by thinking about alternatives to them (e.g., "What might have been"). The more readily such alternative events or outcomes come to mind, the stronger our reactions to the events that actually occurred.

Discounting Principle The tendency to attach less importance to one potential cause of some behavior when other potential causes are also present.

Distinctiveness The extent to which an individual responds in a similar manner to different stimuli or different situations.

Facial Feedback Hypothesis The suggestion that changes in facial expression can induce shifts in emotions or affective states.

False Consensus Effect The tendency to assume that others behave or think as we do to a greater extent than is actually true.

Fundamental Attribution Error The tendency to overestimate the impact of dispositional (internal) causes on others' behavior.

Heuristics Rules or principles that allow individuals to make social judgments rapidly and with reduced effort.

Impression Management Techniques designed to create a favorable impression of oneself in others (target persons).

Information Overload Instances in which our ability to process information is exceeded.

James-Lange Theory A theory of emotion contending that emotional experiences result from our perceptions of shifts in bodily states. For example, according to this theory, we become fearful because of awareness of such physiological reactions as increased heartbeat, shortness of breath, and so on.

Noncommon Effects Effects produced by a particular cause that could not be produced by any other apparent cause.

Nonverbal Communication Communication between individuals that does not involve the content of spoken words. It consists instead of an unspoken language of facial expressions, eye contact, and body language.

Priming Occurs when stimuli or events increase the availability of specific types of information in memory.

Representativeness Heuristic A strategy for making judgments based on the extent to which current stimuli or events resemble ones we view as being typical.

Schemas Organized collections of beliefs and feelings about some aspect of the world. Schemas operate like mental scaffolds, providing structure for the interpretation and organization of new information we encounter.

Self-serving Bias The tendency to attribute positive outcomes in one's own life to internal causes (e.g., one's own traits or characteristics) but negative outcomes or events to external causes (e.g., chance, task difficulty).

Social Cognition The process in which individuals use and manipulate social information. That is, they interpret, analyze, remember, and use information about the social world; a major area of research in social psychology.

Social Perception The process in which we take social information in through the senses.

Staring A form of eye contact in which one person continues to gaze steadily at another regardless of what the recipient does.

Two-factor Theory A theory of emotion suggesting that in many cases we interpret our emotional states in terms of external cues. That is, we sometimes experience the emotions that our inspection of the world around us suggests we should be experiencing.

Ultimate Attribution Error Our tendency to attribute negative outcomes of the ingroup to external causes and positive outcomes to internal causes. In contrast, we will tend to attribute negative outcomes of outgroups to internal causes and positive outcomes to external causes.

FOR MORE INFORMATION

Harvey, J. H., & Weary, G. (Eds.) (1985). *Attribution: Basic issues and applications*. San Diego: Academic Press.

   This collection of chapters, each prepared by an expert researcher, discusses major theories of attribution, recent research findings, and how knowledge about this key aspect of social perception has been applied to many practical problems.

Ross, M., & Fletcher, G. J. O. (1985). Attribution and social perception. IN G. Lindzey and E. Aronson (Eds.), *Handbook of social psychology*. New York: Random House.

   A comprehensive discussion of many aspects of social perception. While the chapter is intended mainly for professional social psychologists, it is clearly written and contains a great deal of interesting information.

Siegman, A. W., & Feldstein, S. (Eds.) (1987). *Nonverbal behavior and communication*. Hillsdale, NJ: Erlbaum.

   Contains chapters on various aspects of nonverbal communication prepared by experts on this

topic. Included are truly fascinating discussions of body movement and gestures, nonverbal aspects of speech, and the ways in which nonverbal cues regulate conversations and even group processes. This is an excellent source to consult if you'd like to know more about nonverbal communication.

Fiske, S. T., & Taylor, S. E. (1991). *Social cognition* (2nd ed.). New York: McGraw-Hill.

   A clear and thorough review of research on social cognition. Many basic aspects of our thinking about others (e.g., attribution, memory for social information) are examined in an insightful manner.

Kahneman, D., Slovic, P., & Tversky, A. (Eds.). (1982). *Judgment under uncertainty: Heuristics and biases*. Cambridge, England: Cambridge University Press.

   A collection of articles and chapters focused on heuristics, biases, and fallacies. If you want to learn more about the ways in which we make use of mental shortcuts and err in our efforts to understand the social world, this is must reading.

Chapter THREE

Attitudes:
Evaluating the Social World

....

SPECIAL SECTIONS

In Canada today issues such as Quebec separatism, abortion, preservation of the rain forest, and assisted suicide are hotly debated. For example, a person who supports the idea of legalizing assisted suicide might suggest that people should be able to have the choice of a dignified death in which they, instead of the medical profession, are in control. To the supporters of such legislation, their beliefs, feelings, and knowledge all line up to make this position the obvious one for them. On the other side of the debate, a person who rejects the idea of legislating assisted suicide might suggest that life and death are not ours to choose; the decision is God's. Thus, to endorse assisted suicide is to endorse killing or murder. For this person, their feelings, beliefs, and knowledge also point to one obvious conclusion—but the opposite one. Why do two people, who probably have equal knowledge and ability, reach such opposing conclusions? How could we persuade one of them to agree with the other? Many social psychologists would suggest that in order to answer these questions—and truly to understand why people hold the views they do—it would be necessary to consider the topic of *attitudes*.

Attitudes have long been a central topic in the field of social psychology, and for good reason: They shape both our social perceptions and our social behavior (Pratkanis, Breckler, & Greenwald, 1989). But what, precisely, are they? Many different definitions have been suggested, but recently there has been growing consensus among social psychologists that attitudes involve *associations between attitude objects (virtually any aspect of the social world) and evaluations of those objects* (Fazio, 1989). More simply, many researchers believe that attitudes can be viewed as *evaluations of various objects that are stored in memory* (Judd et al., 1991). Returning to the issue above, as an opponent of assisted suicide, a person's attitude would involve an evaluation of it—in this case, abhorrence—plus a link or association between the idea of assisted suicide and this evaluation. Whenever a discussion of the pros and cons in a newspaper or magazine was encountered, this evaluation would be retrieved from memory. And once present in consciousness, it would color further perceptions and exert a directing influence on that person's social behavior—in this case, a tendency to vote against the issue or work to quash any legislation.

The same basic principles apply to any other attitude object—any aspect of the social world that is the focus of an attitude. Thus, my negative attitude toward separatism would involve my evaluation of the issue (strongly negative) together with the tendency for this evaluation to be retrieved from memory and brought into conscious thought whenever it, or perhaps related topics, were mentioned (Judd & Krosnick, 1989). One additional, and important, point: Attitudes definitely do *not* exist in isolation. Rather, they are linked to one another in memory. Thus, activation of one attitude can—and often does—tend to activate related attitudes as well (Judd, Drake, Downing, & Krosnick, 1991). This is an important point, and one to which we'll return in later sections of this chapter.

Now that we've defined attitudes and described some of their basic features, we can turn to the wealth of information about them uncovered by social psychologists. In order to provide you with a useful overview of this intriguing body of knowledge, we'll proceed as follows. First, we'll examine the process through which attitudes are *formed* or *developed*. Next, we'll consider the relationship between attitudes and behavior. This link is more complex than you might expect, so be prepared for some surprises. Third, we'll examine how attitudes are sometimes *changed* through persuasion and related processes. The word *sometimes* should be emphasized, for as we'll note in another section, changing attitudes that are important to those who hold them is far from easy. Finally, we'll consider *cognitive dissonance*—an internal state with far-reaching implications for social behavior and social thought that, surprisingly, sometimes leads individuals to change their own attitudes in the absence of external pressure to do so.

FORMING ATTITUDES: LEARNING, EXPERIENCE, CULTURE AND ... GENES?

Do babies enter the world with political opinions, racial hatreds, and the diverse preferences they will express as adults fully formed? Few of us would say yes. On the contrary, most people believe that attitudes are acquired in a gradual manner through experience. In a word, most people believe that attitudes are primarily *learned*. Social psychologists, too, accept this position. But please take note: We would be remiss if we did not call your attention to a small but growing body of evidence suggesting that genetic factors, too, may play some role in our attitudes. So, after examining the major ways in which attitudes are acquired, we'll briefly describe some of the evidence pointing to this surprising conclusion.

SOCIAL LEARNING: ACQUIRING ATTITUDES FROM OTHERS

One source of our attitudes is obvious: We acquire them from other persons through the process of **social learning**. In other words, we acquire many of our views from situations in which we interact with others or merely observe their behavior. Such social learning occurs in diverse ways, but three are most important.

Classical conditioning: Learning based on association

It is a basic principle of psychology that when one stimulus regularly precedes another, the one that occurs first may soon become a signal for the one that occurs second. In other words, when the first stimulus is presented, individuals come to expect that the second will follow. As a result, they may gradually show the same kind of reactions to the first stimulus as they do to the second, especially if the second stimulus is one that induces fairly strong reactions when encountered. Consider, for example, someone whose shower emits a low hum just before the hot water runs out and turns into an icy stream. At first he may show little reaction to the hum. After it is followed by freezing water on several occasions, though, he may well experience strong emotional arousal (fear!) when it occurs. After all, it is a signal for what will soon follow—something quite unpleasant.

What does this process—known as **classical conditioning**—have to do with attitudes and their formation? Potentially, quite a bit. Many studies indicate that when initially neutral words are paired with stimuli that elicit strong negative reactions—electric shocks, harsh sounds—the neutral words acquire the capacity to elicit favorable or unfavorable reactions (e.g., Staats & Staats, 1958; Staats, Staats, & Crawford, 1962). Since evaluative reactions lie at the very core of attitudes, these findings suggest that attitudes toward initially neutral stimuli can be acquired through classical conditioning. To see how this process might work under real-life conditions, imagine the following situation. A young child sees her mother frown and show other signs of displeasure each time the mother encounters members of a particular minority group. At first the child is quite neutral toward members of this group and their identifiable characteristics (skin color, style of dress, accent). Repeated pairing of these characteristics with her mother's negative emotional reactions, however, produces classical conditioning: Gradually the child comes to react negatively to these visible stimuli and so to the minority group itself (see Figure 3.1). We'll consider such attitudes in more detail in chapter 5, in our discussion of *prejudice*.

Until recently, the primary evidence for the occurrence of this process was provided by the kind of studies described above—ones in which neutral words (for example, the names of imaginary groups of people) were paired with various emotion-provoking stimuli. Unfortunately, the results of such studies are far from conclusive, because it is possible that the persons who participated in them expressed favorable or unfavorable attitudes to these words because they guessed that this was what the experimenter hoped to find—an effect often termed **demand characteristics**. This interpretation is supported by the finding that in such studies, only individuals who were aware of the link

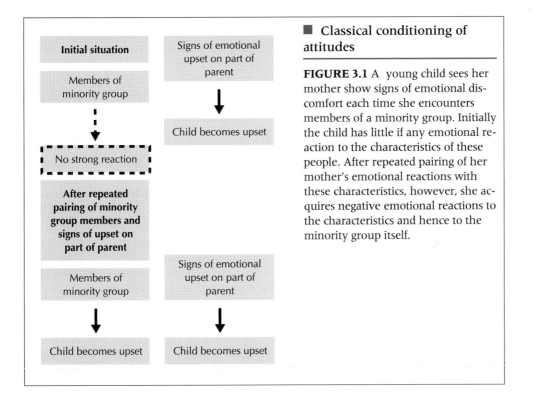

■ **Classical conditioning of attitudes**

FIGURE 3.1 A young child sees her mother show signs of emotional discomfort each time she encounters members of a minority group. Initially the child has little if any emotional reaction to the characteristics of these people. After repeated pairing of her mother's emotional reactions with these characteristics, however, she acquires negative emotional reactions to the characteristics and hence to the minority group itself.

■ Subliminal conditioning of attitudes

FIGURE 3.2 Individuals saw affect-inducing photos for very brief periods of time immediately before viewing photos of a stranger engaged in normal life activities. Although the affect-inducing photos were shown so briefly that participants in the study could not report their contents, exposure to these photos affected ratings of the stranger. These findings provide evidence for the subliminal conditioning of attitudes.

Source: Based on data from Krosnick et al., 1992.

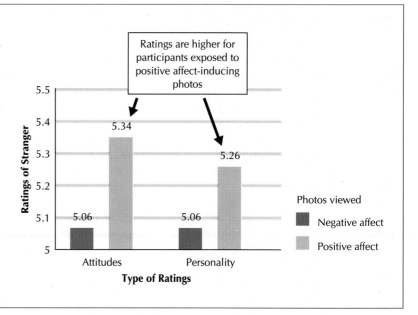

between neutral words and the occurrence of positive or negative events showed the conditioning effect (Page & Kahle, 1976). A recent line of research, however, provides more convincing evidence for the role of classical conditioning in the formation of attitudes. Krosnick, Betz, Jussim, and Lynn (1992) showed that attitudes can be developed through subliminal conditioning (conditioning that takes place below the threshold of awareness). Just before they were asked to indicate their attitudes to some photos of a stranger, subjects were exposed to photographs that induced positive or negative emotions . However, these emotion-inducing photos were presented subliminally, for less than a tenth of a second, and subjects were unaware of their content. Participants were then asked to indicate their attitudes toward the stranger in the second photo.

Krosnick and his colleagues reasoned that under these conditions, subjects would not be able to guess the purpose of the study, so demand characteristics would not operate. Thus, if subjects' attitudes were influenced by the affect-inducing slides, this would provide strong evidence for the classical conditioning of attitudes. As you can see from Figure 3.2, these effects were actually obtained. Subjects exposed to the positive affect-inducing scenes reported significantly more positive attitudes, and rated the target person more favorably on trait dimensions, than those exposed to the negative affect-inducing scenes. In short, findings provided evidence for the **subliminal conditioning** of attitudes.

These results help explain why some attitudes—including various forms of racial and ethnic prejudice—are so resistant to efforts to change them. If these attitudes are developed through classical conditioning in a largely unconscious manner (as in the example of the child and mother presented earlier), then it is not at all surprising that rational arguments against such views are unsuccessful in altering them. After all, they are based primarily on emotional reactions acquired through conditioning. To the extent this is so, then other approaches may be more effective in countering such attitudes.

Instrumental conditioning: Learning to state the "right" views

Have you ever heard a three-year-old state, with great conviction, that she is a Conservative or a Liberal? Or that Fords (Hondas) are superior to Chevrolets (Mazdas)? Children of this age have little comprehension of what these statements mean. Yet they make them all the same. Why? The answer is obvious: They have been praised or rewarded in various ways by their parents for stating such views. As we're sure you know, behaviors that are followed by positive outcomes are strengthened and tend to be repeated. In contrast, behaviors that are followed by negative outcomes are weakened, or at least suppressed. Thus, a second way in which attitudes are acquired from others is through the process of **instrumental conditioning.** By rewarding their children with smiles, agreement, or approval for stating the "right" views—the ones they themselves favor—parents and other adults play an active role in shaping their offspring's attitudes. It is for this reason that until they reach their teen years, most youngsters express political, religious, and social views highly similar to those held by their families. Given the power of positive reinforcement to influence behavior, it would be surprising if they did not.

Modeling: Learning by example

A third process through which attitudes are formed can operate even when parents have no desire to transmit specific views to their children. This third process involves **modeling**—in which individuals acquire new forms of behavior merely through observing the actions of others. It is often said that "little pitchers have big ears," and where attitude formation is concerned, this is certainly true. In many cases children hear their parents say things not intended for their ears or observe their parents engaging in actions the parents tell them not to perform. For example, mothers and fathers who smoke often warn their children against such behavior, even as they light up a cigarette. Similarly, parents may warn their children against the dangers of alcohol but then throw parties at which people drink until they become tipsy—or worse. What message do children acquire from such instances? The evidence is clear: that they should do as their parents *do*, not as they *say*.

DIRECT EXPERIENCE:
ACQUIRING ATTITUDES FROM LIFE

While we often acquire attitudes from others through social learning, we also form such reactions through direct personal experience. For example, how do you know that you like or dislike various foods? Probably because you have tasted them. How do you know that you like or dislike different kinds of music? Again, because you have heard them and found that you enjoyed some types but found others unappealing. Of course, this is not always the case. Sometimes people merely assume that they will react negatively to various experiences and so avoid actually having them. For example, many people recoil at the thought of eating squid or octopus without ever having tasted these foods. They assume that they won't like them, and they may be totally surprised if, gathering their courage, they do try them and find that such foods are delicious.

Interestingly, research findings suggest that attitudes formed through direct experience with attitude objects are stronger in several respects than the kind of "anticipated" attitudes just described or attitudes borrowed from others (Fazio & Zanna, 1981). For example, individuals who form their attitudes about an object through direct experience with it have been shown to respond more quickly when asked to express their reactions to the object than individuals who form such attitudes indirectly (by watching someone else eat some food or engage in other activities; Fazio et al., 1982). Quick responses of this type are usually interpreted as a sign of attitude strength. In addition, attitudes stemming from direct experience are held more confidently and are more resistant to change than attitudes formed through indirect experience (Wu & Shaffer, 1987).

In sum, attitudes resulting from direct experience tend to be stronger in several respects than ones resulting from vicarious experiences. One practical message in such findings is clear: If you hold strong attitudes about some aspect of the social world and want someone else to share them, you should arrange for this person to have direct experience with the attitude object. In the absence of such experience, his or her attitudes will probably be only pale reflections of your own more passionate views.

CULTURAL FACTORS: THE ROLE OF CULTURAL VALUES

Cultural background can also influence attitude formation (Davidson & Thompson, 1980). In the previous chapter we saw that our way of explaining economic disadvantage can be influenced by our cultural group or the "academic culture" in which we have been educated (Guimond & Palmer, 1990). Culture has been shown to play a part in many other forms of social cognition (Smith & Bond, 1993; Moghaddam, Taylor, & Wright,1993). At the cultural level, researchers have often examined broader *cultural values* rather than specific attitudes.

Values are broad and abstract principles of life. They contain our moral beliefs and our standards of conduct. Where they differ from attitudes is in their generality or abstractness (Schwartz, 1992). For example, the values of liberty or equality are non-specific—they do not relate to one particular type of event or object as an attitude does. Rather, they guide our thinking or actions over a broad range of situations. A value may guide your attitudes to many issues. For example a belief in equality could influence your attitudes to welfare, affirmative action programs and even whether professors should be called by their first names. There is evidence that values are translated into action via our attitudes. That is, values may determine attitudes, which in turn may determine behavior. Homer and Kahle (1988) found that internal values such as security and self-fulfillment were strongly related to specific attitudes towards nutrition, which in turn were related to food-shopping behavior.

Values can be culturally transmitted through processes of social learning in our homes, schools, and among our friends. We have mentioned research above that has demonstrated that cultural styles of reasoning will become more evident in children as they mature (Miller, 1984). Among adults, major studies comparing values of over 50 nations have found measurable differences between groups from different cultures (Hofstede, 1980; Schwartz, 1992). Findings of Hofstede's study (1980), for example, showed that Canadians and Americans had very similar rankings in three out of four values: They were similar in showing high individualism (focus on individual choice rather than group goals), low uncertainty avoidance (placed little value on stability and order) and low power distance (little value on hierarchical relationships). However, a difference occurred for one value related to achievement orientation, Americans showing a higher ranking for this value than Canadians. Furthermore, both countries' responses differed markedly from those of a number of others in South America, Africa, and Asia (e.g., Venezuela, Colombia, Pakistan, and West African region).

An extensive survey carried out by Gallup under the sponsorship of CARA (the Centre for Applied Research in the Apostolate) in the early 1980s (1983, cited in Lipset, 1990) compared values and attitudes of 1729 Americans and 1251 Canadians. Table 3.1 summarizes some of the value and attitude differences they found. The top part of this table shows differences in some fundamental values and the bottom part shows some related specific attitudes.

We have noted above that Canada and the U.S.A, when compared to other cultures around the world, are very similar. With that proviso, you can see that Canadian values, relative to American, put greater emphasis on the equality between groups and

TABLE 3.1 Differences in values and attitudes between Americans, Franco-Canadians and Anglo-Canadians.

	U.S.A.	CANADA	
		Anglo-Canadian	(both) Franco-Canadian

	U.S.A.	Anglo-Canadian	(both)	Franco-Canadian
VALUES:				
1. LIBERTY versus EQUALITY*				
A. Those choosing liberty	72%	64%		57%
B. Those choosing equality	20%	29%		38%
2. SOCIAL ORDER versus FREE SPEECH				
Those choosing social order	35%	45%		49%
3. INDEPENDENCE				
Those choosing independence as "especially important" for children to learn	32%	27%		15%
ATTITUDES:				
1. SUPPORT FOR LAW AND ORDER				
a) Support for banning civilian handgun ownership (Roper, 1976; CROP, 1977)	36%		(72%)	
b) Positive feelings towards the legal system	51%	59%		72%
2. TOLERANCE FOR NONCONFORMISTS AND DEVIANTS				
a) Opposed to having people with criminal records as neighbors	48%	40%		30%
b) Finding emotionally unstable people offensive as neighbors	47%	33%		13%
c) Disapproval of a woman who wants a child without a stable relationship with a man	58%	53%		34%
3. ATTITUDES TO RELIGION				
a) Belief in a personal God	65%	49%		56%
b) Accept fully each of the ten commandments	83%	76%		67%

*1. Questions for LIBERTY versus EQUALITY

Which of these two statements comes closest to your own opinions?
A. I find that both freedom and equality are important but if I were to make up my mind for one or the other, I would consider personal freedom more important, that is, everyone can live in freedom and develop without hindrance.

B. Certainly both freedom and equality are important but if I were to make up my mind for one of the two, I would consider equality more important, that is, that nobody is underprivileged and that social class differences are not so strong.

Source: Unless otherwise indicated, all percentages are based upon the CARA–Gallup Poll (1983) as presented in Lipset, 1989, 1990.

social order in society and are less likely to endorse the value of liberty or freedom and independence. This suggests, as Seymour Lipset argued, "that Canada has been a more class-aware, elitist, law-abiding, statist, collectivity-oriented and... group-oriented society than the United States" (1990b, p.2).

A glance at specific attitudes in the bottom part of Table 3.1 shows some interesting patterns. Canadians show greater support for law and order (perhaps reflecting the value of social order), somewhat more personal tolerance and stricter religious attitudes than Americans, with Francophones showing the greatest tolerance of nonconformity and deviance.

One interesting pattern that emerged consistently from this survey is that Anglo-Canadians were closer to Americans in their values and attitudes (though differences were generally statistically significant) while Franco-Canadians were consistently furthest from Americans in their responses. It should be noted, however, that researchers analyzing results of a large Canadian 1977 survey, found no difference between Anglophones and Francophones in the importance they gave to values of achievement, prosperity, independence, and family security (Baer & Curtis, 1984).

To end on a more cautionary note, the findings presented above do not tell us anything about the behavior of individual Canadians or Americans. They are average figures and do not show a very large gap compared to many cultural differences. They also do not begin to address the extensive subcultural differences in Canada's multicultural mosaic. Schwartz (1992) has pointed out the difficulty inherent in comparing the values of very different cultures while using value dimensions defined in a Western context. We are in danger of completely neglecting important value dimensions of Eastern cultures. These issues will be further discussed in chapter 4, "Identity and Culture."

GENETIC FACTORS: SOME SURPRISING RECENT FINDINGS

Can we inherit our attitudes—or, at least, a propensity to develop certain attitudes about various topics or issues? At first glance, most people—and most social psychologists—would answer with an emphatic *no*. While we readily believe that genetic factors can shape our height, eye color, and other physical characteristics, the idea that such factors might also influence our thinking—including our preferences and our views— seems strange to say the least. Yet if we remember that thought occurs within the brain and that brain structure, like every other part of our physical being, is certainly influenced by genetic factors, the idea of genetic influences on attitudes becomes, perhaps, a little easier to imagine. And in fact, direct empirical evidence for such influences has been obtained in several recent studies (Arvey et al., 1989; Keller et al., 1992).

Most of this evidence involves comparisons between identical (monozygotic) and nonidentical (dizygotic) twins. Since identical twins share the same genetic inheritance, while nonidentical twins do not, higher correlations between the attitudes of the identical twins would suggest that genetic factors play a role in shaping such attitudes. This is precisely what has been found: The attitudes of identical twins *do* correlate more highly than those of nonidentical twins (e.g., Waller et al., 1990). Additional studies have examined the attitudes of twin pairs (both identical and nonidentical) who were separated very early in life. Even though such twins were raised in very different environments, their attitudes still correlate more highly than the attitudes of nonidentical twins or unrelated persons (Waller et al., 1990). It is also important to note that such findings have been obtained for several different kinds of attitudes, ranging from interest in religious occupations and religious activities through job satisfaction (Arvey et al., 1989).

Needless to add, twin research, like research employing any methodology, can be questioned on several grounds. For example, twins are an unusual group, so results obtained with them may not generalize to other groups of people. Similarly, even when separated early in life, twins may be assigned by adoption agencies to similar environments; this could falsely inflate the apparent role of genetic factors in social attitudes.

Still, given the many safeguards and controls built into these studies, it is hard to ignore their findings. To the extent the results they report are confirmed in additional research, we will be left with the rather startling conclusion that some of our attitudes, like many aspects of our physical appearance, are influenced—at least to a degree—by propensities inherited from our parents.

ATTITUDES AND BEHAVIOR: THE ESSENTIAL LINK

Do attitudes shape behavior? Your first answer is likely to be, "Of course." After all, you can remember many incidents in which your own actions were strongly shaped by your opinions. You may be surprised to learn, therefore, that until quite recently, evidence concerning the strength of the link between attitudes and behavior was far from conclusive. Many studies seemed to suggest that this relationship was sometimes more apparent than real. For example, in a classic study on this topic, LaPiere (1934) toured the United States with a young Chinese couple, stopping at more than 250 hotels, motels, and restaurants. In all that time, he and his friends were refused service only once. When LaPiere wrote to the same businesses several months later and asked whether they would serve Chinese patrons, however, *fully 92 percent reported that they would not!* (Remember, this was 1934—a time when it was not unusual for people to admit openly to strong racial or ethnic prejudice.)

To make matters worse, about twenty-five years ago, one social psychologist (Wicker, 1969) reviewed all the evidence existing at that time on the link between attitudes and behavior and came to an unsettling conclusion: Attitudes and behavior are at best only weakly related, and often there is virtually no relationship between them. Social psychologists were stunned. Had they been wasting their time by studying the nature of attitudes and various means of changing them?

The answer that has emerged from systematic research conducted during the past two decades is a definite *no*. Attitudes and behavior, it appears, are often closely linked. This is not always the case, and the relationship between them is far more complex than common sense would suggest. In general, though, attitudes do predict many forms of social behavior across a wide range of contexts. In the remainder of this discussion, we will focus on various factors that determine the strength of the crucial attitude-to-behavior link.

ATTITUDE SPECIFICITY

Consider two of your own attitudes. Suppose, for example, that you approve of newspaper recycling (a specific attitude) and that you oppose racial discrimination (a more general attitude). Which attitude will be more strongly related to your actual behavior? If you endorse newspaper recycling, the odds are very high that you will recycle virtually every newspaper you read. Thus, your behavior in such situations is highly predictable from your attitude. But now consider your opposition to racial discrimination. Probably you don't take every opportunity to protest such discrimination—you don't participate in every demonstration or sign every petition relating to this important issue. As a result, your actions can't be predicted very accurately from your general attitude about discrimination, or at least, not as accurately as your recycling of newspapers. So, while you probably feel that opposing racial discrimination is as important an issue as recycling, your specific attitude towards newspaper recycling may well be a better predictor of your overt actions than your more general attitude about racial discrimination.

A concrete, and persuasive, illustration of the greater power of specific than general attitudes to predict behavior is provided by a study conducted by Newcomb,

Rabow, and Hernandez (1992). They asked students in three different countries (the United States, Britain, and Sweden) to express both general and specific attitudes about nuclear war. General attitudes related to the view that war is unacceptable, while specific attitudes involved more specific reactions to nuclear weapons, nuclear war, and even nuclear power plants. Participants also reported on the extent to which they had engaged in activist behaviors relating to nuclear issues—whether they had joined a group, given money, written a letter to a newspaper, or signed a petition relating to these issues. As predicted, specific attitudes concerning nuclear war and nuclear issues were much better predictors of activist behaviors than more general attitudes; this was true in all three countries. These findings, and those of many other studies, indicate that specific attitudes are indeed better predictors of overt behavior than more general attitudes.

ATTITUDE COMPONENTS

You love pizza. Just the thought of one—hot, bubbling, crusty—brings a smile to your lips. You also have several thoughts about why you love it so much: You know that it tastes good, is really quite nourishing, and is both filling and inexpensive. In short, your attitude toward pizza involves both feelings (an affective or evaluative component) and various forms of knowledge (a cognitive component). Which of these components exerts a stronger impact on your behavior and is a better predictor of it? Probably your feelings—especially when you are hungry.

Now consider a situation in which you must choose between two college courses. One sounds more interesting than the other, but you know that the duller-sounding course will count toward your degree requirements. Again, your attitude toward these courses involves both affective and cognitive components. Which component will play a more important role in your choice? Here, it seems reasonable to predict that the cognitive component will predominate.

These examples help illustrate another key point about the attitude-behavior relationship: The various components of attitudes are not always highly consistent. For example, the affective component may be very positive—you are in love!—while the cognitive component is not so favorable—you have doubts about the future of the relationship. More to the point, when the components are inconsistent, one of them may be more closely related to specific forms of behavior than the other (Millar & Tesser, 1989); and it is this more closely related component that is the best predictor of behavior. Thus, when you are in the presence of the object of your affections, being in love (the affective or evaluative component) may predict your actions to a greater degree than the doubts about the future of your relationship (the cognitive component). In contrast, when you are apart from this person, the cognitive component may be a better predictor of your behavior.

ATTITUDE STRENGTH, VESTED INTEREST, AND THE ROLE OF SELF-AWARENESS

Obviously, strong attitudes predict behavior better than weak ones. There are several less-obvious factors related to attitude strength, however. One of these is direct experience. Earlier, we noted that attitudes formed through direct personal experience are often stronger than ones acquired through observation. It is not surprising, then, that attitudes of the first type are generally stronger predictors of behavior than attitudes of the latter type (Fazio et al., 1982).

A second factor is the extent to which individuals have a **vested interest** in the attitude object. When we say that someone has a vested interest, we mean that the event or issue in question has a strong effect on the person's life. Having a vested interest increases the strength of the attitude-behavior link. This fact is demonstrated quite clearly in a study conducted by Sivacek and Crano (1982). They contacted students and pretended to solicit their help in campaigning against a proposed state law that would raise the legal drinking age from eighteen to twenty. Nearly all students were opposed to the law, regardless of their own age. Some of them, however, had a vested interest—the ones young enough so that passage of the law would prevent them from drinking legally in the years immediately ahead. Students who were a little older had no vested interest; even if the law passed, they would already be over twenty by the time it took effect. Which group do you think agreed to campaign against the law? The younger students, of course. The older ones, while equally opposed to it in principle, lacked any vested interest. Thus, their attitudes were not as accurate a predictor of their overt behavior.

A third factor determining the strength of the attitude-behavior link involves *self-awareness*. This refers to the extent to which individuals focus on their own attitudes and actions—a state that can be induced even by such simple actions as gazing into a mirror (see Figure 3.3). Growing evidence indicates that heightened self-awareness increases the degree of consistency between privately held attitudes and overt behavior (e.g. Hutton, & Baumeister, 1992; Pryor et al., 1977). There are two reasons why this is so: (1) Self-awareness increases our access to our own attitudes—we can report them more accurately when our self-awareness is heightened than when it is not. Obviously, the more readily we can bring attitudes to mind, the greater the possibility that they will affect our behavior. (2) In situations where overt behaviors are required, self-awareness can bring specific attitudes more sharply into focus, thus enabling them to guide the actions that follow. Enhancing self-awareness, it appears, is akin to saying to someone: "Before you act, stop for a moment and think about who you are and what you believe to be true. In light of these thoughts, what course of action should you take?" Such reflection makes it more likely that behavior will follow from existing attitudes and less likely that it will be determined by situational factors. The result? The link between attitudes and overt behavior is strengthened.

■ **Heightened self-awareness and the attitude-behavior link**

FIGURE 3.3 Growing evidence suggests that when individuals experience heightened self-awareness, the link between their attitudes and their overt behavior is strengthened.

ATTITUDE ACCESSIBILITY: THE FORCE THAT BINDS

In our discussion of social cognition (chapter 2), we called attention to the concept of *availability*—the ease with which specific information can be brought to mind. A similar concept is useful in understanding the relationship between attitudes and behavior: **attitude accessibility**. This refers to the ease with which specific attitudes can be recalled from memory and brought into consciousness, where they can influence and guide behavior. According to the *attitude accessibility model* proposed by Fazio (1989), such accessibility plays a key role in the attitude-to-behavior link. This model suggests that in an initial step attitudes are *activated*—retrieved from memory by presentation of the attitude object or some other stimulus. Once activated, attitudes influence perception of the attitude object and of the situation in which it is encountered. These perceptions, in turn, then influence subsequent behavior toward the attitude object (see Figure 3.4 for an overview of the model).

But what determines whether specific attitudes are activated? The attitude accessibility model proposes that *associative strength*—the strength of the association in memory between an attitude object and its evaluation—is crucial. The stronger this association, the more readily is an attitude activated and the stronger its effects on subsequent behavior. Having said this, we should note that recent evidence indicates that in fact many attitudes are activated in a seemingly automatic manner by the attitude objects to which they refer. This *automatic attitude activation effect* is compellingly illustrated by research performed by Bargh et al. (1992).

These researchers presented to participants the names of various attitude objects (e.g., beer, cake, crime, divorce, gift, recession, taxes) on a computer screen for a brief period of time. Soon afterward, an adjective appeared on the screen. Participants' task was to indicate whether the adjective was good or bad in meaning by pushing one of two buttons labeled *good* or *bad*. Some of these adjectives had a positive meaning (beautiful, excellent, magnificent), while others had a negative meaning (dreadful, painful, miserable, hideous). The researchers reasoned that presentation of each attitude object would automatically elicit the matching attitude. If this was of the same valence as the adjective shown (for example, both were positive), then they predicted that subjects' speed in reporting whether the adjective was good or bad would be enhanced. If the attitude was different in valence from the adjective, however, the opposite effect would occur: Speed

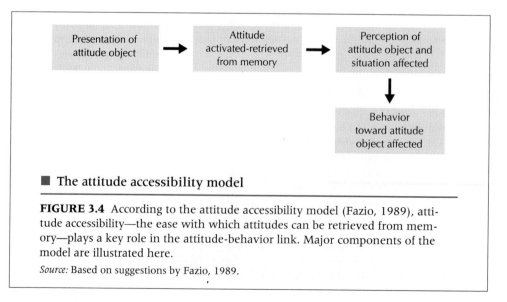

■ The attitude accessibility model

FIGURE 3.4 According to the attitude accessibility model (Fazio, 1989), attitude accessibility—the ease with which attitudes can be retrieved from memory—plays a key role in the attitude-behavior link. Major components of the model are illustrated here.

Source: Based on suggestions by Fazio, 1989.

would be reduced. This is precisely what occurred. Moreover, in contrast to findings of earlier research (e.g., Fazio et al., 1986), this was true for relatively weak attitudes (ones relatively low in accessibility) as well as for relatively strong ones (attitudes high in accessibility). So, in short, it appears that many attitudes are activated in a seemingly automatic manner by the attitude objects to which they refer. And once activated, of course, they are present in consciousness to guide overt actions. Why, then, are some attitudes better predictors of behavior than others? The answer may involve the fact that although many attitudes are activated in an automatic fashion, the intensity of such activation may vary greatly. Thus, the presence of a hot, bubbling pizza may activate your attitude toward pizza in a powerful fashion; coming across a newspaper article about the budget deficit may activate your attitude toward the deficit to a much weaker degree.

Regardless of the precise mechanisms involved, one key point seems clear: Attitude accessibility plays an important role in the attitude-to-behavior link. Moreover, this concept allows us to tie together seemingly diverse factors and findings about this crucial link. Attitude strength, specificity, vested interest, and even self-awareness can all be understood in terms of their relationship to attitude accessibility. In each case, the kinds of attitudes that have been found to be closely related to behavior are the ones that would probably be most accessible—for example, strong, specific, and personally relevant ones (Krosnick, 1989). Thus, as the attitude accessibility model suggests (Fazio, 1989), attitude accessibility may indeed be crucial to understanding why attitudes sometimes predict behavior accurately and why sometimes they do not.

PERSUASION:
THE PROCESS OF CHANGING ATTITUDES

How many times during the past twenty-four hours has someone, or some organization, tried to change your attitudes? If you stop and think for a moment you may be surprised at the result, for it is clear that every day we are bombarded with countless efforts of this type. Newspaper and magazine ads, radio and television commercials, political speeches, appeals from charitable organizations—the list seems almost endless. To what extent are such attempts at **persuasion** successful? And what factors determine whether they succeed or fail? It is to these issues that we turn next.

PERSUASION: THE TRADITIONAL APPROACH

In most cases, efforts at persuasion involve the following elements: Some *source* directs some type of message (*communication*) to those whose attitudes she or he wishes to change (the *audience*). Taking note of this fact, much early research on persuasion focused on these key elements, addressing various aspects of the question: *Who* says *what* to *whom* and with what effect? This traditional approach to persuasion is sometimes known as the *Yale Approach*, since much early research within this framework was conducted at Yale University. Such research sought to identify those characteristics of communicators (sources), communications (persuasive messages), and audiences that, together, would serve to maximize the impact of efforts at persuasion (Hovland, Janis, & Kelley, 1953). The findings of this early research were complex and not always entirely consistent. Among the most notable, however, were the following (summarized in Table 3.2):

1. Experts are more persuasive than nonexperts (Hovland & Weiss, 1951). The same arguments carry more weight when delivered by people who seem to know what they are talking about and to have all the facts than when they are made by people lacking such expertise.

TABLE 3.2 A summary of some of the major findings

Persuasion: Some key results

Factor	More Attitude Change (successful persuasion)	Less Attitude Change	Comment
Source (Characteristics of the person who is trying to persuade someone)	Expert Popular Attractive Speaks rapidly	Nonexpert Unpopular Unattractive Speaks slowly	Rapid speech suggests expertise
Communication (Characteristics of the persuasive message)	Persuasive intent is not obvious Considers both sides of the issue Fear arousing Distraction	Obviously trying to persuade Presents only one side No fear Not distracted	When audience is initially opposed Distraction may determine whether persuasion occurs via central or peripheral routes
Audience (Characteristics of the person who is being persuaded)	Low self-esteem	High self-esteem	High self-esteem persons may be persuaded, but don't want to admit it

2. Messages that do not appear to be designed to change our attitudes are often more successful than ones that seem intended to manipulate us in this fashion (Walster & Festinger, 1962). In other words, we usually don't trust—and generally refuse to be influenced by—persons who deliberately set out to persuade us.

3. Attractive and popular communicators (sources) are more effective in changing attitudes than unattractive and unpopular ones (Kiesler & Kiesler, 1969). This is one reason why politicians devote so much effort to the task of enhancing their personal appeal to voters. (Please refer to our discussion of *impression management* in chapter 2.)

4. People are sometimes more susceptible to persuasion when they are distracted by some extraneous event than when they are paying full attention to what is being said (Allyn & Festinger, 1961). This is one reason why political candidates often arrange for "spontaneous" demonstrations during their speeches: The distraction generated among audience members may enhance their acceptance of the speaker's points.

5. Individuals relatively low in self-esteem are often easier to persuade than those high in self-esteem (Janis, 1954). Lacking in self-confidence, low-self-esteem persons are more susceptible to social influence from others.

6. When an audience holds attitudes contrary to those of a would-be persuader, it is often more effective for the communicator to adopt a *two-sided approach*, in which both sides of the argument are presented, than a *one-sided approach*. Apparently, strongly supporting one side of an issue while acknowledging that the other side has a few good points in its favor serves to disarm audiences and makes it harder for them to resist the source's major conclusions.

7. People who speak rapidly are generally more persuasive than persons who speak more slowly (Miller et al., 1976). This idea is contrary to the popular

view that people distrust fast-talking salespersons and politicians. One reason rapid speech is more persuasive is that it seems to convey the impression that the communicator knows what she or he is talking about.

8. Persuasion can be enhanced by messages that arouse strong emotions (especially fear) in the audience, particularly when the message provides specific recommendations about how a change in attitudes or behavior will prevent the negative consequences described in the fear-provoking message (Leventhal, Singer, & Jones, 1965). Such fear-based appeals seem to be especially effective in changing health-related attitudes and behavior (Robberson & Rogers, 1988).

At this point we should insert a note of caution: While most of these findings have withstood the test of time and appear to be accurate, some have been modified, to a degree, by more recent evidence. For example, while fast talkers are often more persuasive than slow ones, recent findings indicate that this is true only when the speakers present views different from those held by their audience (Smith & Shaffer, 1991). When they present views consistent with those of their audience, fast talkers may actually be less persuasive, in part because the speed of their speech prevents listeners from thinking about and elaborating the message while it is being presented. Similarly, persons low in self-esteem are not always easier to persuade than those high in self-esteem (Baumeister & Covington, 1985). Indeed, it appears that people high in self-esteem are often persuaded, but simply don't want to admit it! Such exceptions aside, the findings reported above represent useful generalizations about persuasion, and form an important part of our knowledge about this process.

PERSUASION: THE COGNITIVE APPROACH

The traditional approach to understanding persuasion has certainly been useful; it provided a wealth of information about the "when" and "how" of persuasion—when such attitude change is most likely to occur and how, in practical terms, it can be produced. This approach was less helpful, however, with respect to the *why* of persuasion: it did not provide an equal number of insights into the question of why people change their attitudes in response to persuasive messages.

This issue has been brought into sharp focus in a more modern approach to understanding the nature of persuasion known as the **cognitive perspective** (Petty & Cacioppo, 1986; Chaiken, 1987). The cognitive perspective asks not *Who says what to whom and with what effect?* but *What cognitive processes determine when someone is actually persuaded?* In other words, this newer perspective focuses on what many researchers term a *cognitive response analysis*—efforts to understand (1) what people think about when they are exposed to persuasive appeals; and (2) how these thoughts and relevant cognitive processes determine whether, and to what extent, people experience attitude change (Petty, Ostrom, & Brock, 1981). The major theory taking this perspective is the *elaboration likelihood model* (Petty & Cacioppo, 1986).

The elaboration likelihood model: Two routes to persuasion

What happens when individuals receive a persuasive message? According to Petty and Cacioppo (1986), they think about it, the arguments it makes, and (perhaps) the arguments it has left out. It is these thoughts—not the message itself—that then lead either to attitude change or to resistance.

But how does persuasion actually occur? According to the *elaboration likelihood model* (ELM), two different routes are possible, reflecting contrasting amounts of cognitive effort on the part of message recipients. When persuasive messages deal with issues that are important or personally relevant to recipients, the recipients are likely to devote careful attention to the message and the arguments it contains. In that case, persuasion occurs through what is known as the **central route**. Here, such activities as evaluating the strength or rationality of the argument and deciding whether its content agrees or disagrees with current beliefs tend to occur. When messages are processed via this central route, attitude change will occur only to the extent that the arguments presented are convincing and the facts marshaled on their behalf are strong ones.

In contrast, when messages deal with issues that are relatively unimportant and not personally relevant to recipients, persuasion occurs through what is known as the **peripheral route**. Here, little cognitive work is performed, and attitude change, when it occurs, involves a seemingly automatic response to *persuasion cues*—information relating to the source's prestige, credibility, or likability, or to the style and form of the message she or he presents. Attitude change is more likely to occur through the peripheral route when audience members are distracted and can't engage in a careful analysis of the speaker's message (e.g., Petty, Wells, & Brock, 1976). Figure 3.5 presents an overview of the ELM model and the two routes to persuasion it describes.

At this point, it is important to note that a persuasive message may be relevant or important to us for several reasons. As Johnson and Eagly (1989) state, we may find such messages personally involving because they are relevant to our basic values or because they are related to important outcomes. Research findings suggest that in the former case, involving persuasive messages will indeed activate careful cognitive processing; but we will engage in this processing primarily to bolster and support our current attitudes—*not* to weigh or evaluate carefully the information the messages contain. Thus, even when we find a message important or personally involving, we will not necessarily enter the central route and think systematically about its content.

The elaboration likelihood model appears to be of considerable value in several respects. Perhaps most important, it helps explain, in modern cognitive terms, the impact of many variables found, in earlier research, to affect persuasion. For example, it helps explain why individuals who are distracted by events or stimuli unrelated to a persuasive message may be influenced by the message to a greater degree than

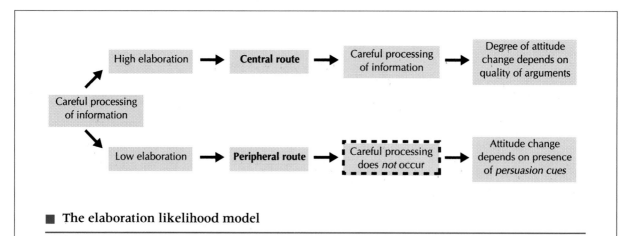

■ The elaboration likelihood model

FIGURE 3.5 According to the elaboration likelihood model, persuasion can occur in either of two distinct ways. Individuals can engage in careful, systematic processing of the information contained in persuasive messages, in which case persuasion occurs through the central route (upper pathway). Alternatively, individuals may respond largely to persuasion cues (such as information about the source's credibility, status, or likability). In this case persuasion occurs through the peripheral route (lower pathway).

Source: Based on suggestions by Petty & Cacioppo, 1986.

those who are not. Such distraction may prevent individuals from engaging in careful analysis of the communication—from entering the central route. Thus, they may be more readily persuaded by relatively weak arguments or may respond to persuasion cues such as the communicator's attractiveness (DeBono, 1992). Similarly, consider the effect of likability of the source. Many studies indicate that persuasive messages from sources we like are more effective in producing persuasion than identical messages from sources we dislike, or even from those toward whom we have neutral feelings (Kiesler & Kiesler, 1969). The ELM model explains this finding in the following manner: The greater our liking for the sources of persuasive messages, the stronger our motivation to process this information. And then, assuming the message contains convincing arguments, the greater the extent to which we will be persuaded by it. Direct evidence for this reasoning has recently been provided by a study conducted by Roskos-Ewoldsen and Fazio (1992).

These researchers exposed participants to a persuasive message that advocated the banning of aerosol cans. This message contained several convincing arguments (the chemical propellant in aerosol cans is destructive to the earth's ozone layer; aerosol spray cans are dangerous because they can explode if they become too hot). In a control condition, this message was not attributed to any particular source. In two other conditions, in contrast, it was attributed to Jacques Cousteau—an individual toward whom most people report relatively positive attitudes. Instead of attempting to vary participants' liking toward Jacques Cousteau, the researchers adopted a different strategy: They varied the number of times the participants rated him on various dimensions. In a *low accessibility* condition, participants rated Cousteau on only one dimension: unlikable/likable. In a high accessibility condition, in contrast, they rated him on five different dimensions (e.g., deceptive/trustworthy, unpleasant/pleasant, unlikable/likable). The researchers reasoned that liking for Jacques Cousteau would be more accessible in the high accessibility group than in the low accessibility group. Thus, participants would express greater agreement with his persuasive message in this condition. As shown in Figure 3.6, results offered clear support for this prediction.

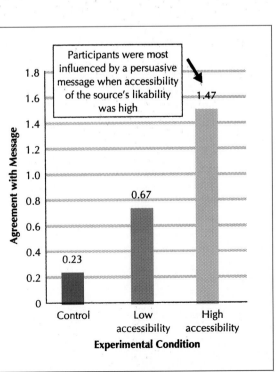

■ **Source likability and persuasion: A cognitive perspective**

FIGURE 3.6 When the accessibility of information concerning Jacques Cousteau's likability was increased, participants were readily persuaded by a message attributed to him. When the accessibility of information concerning Cousteau's likability was low, in contrast, participants showed less susceptibility to persuasion in response to the same message.

Source: Based on data from Roskos-Ewoldsen & Fazio, 1992.

These findings are consistent with the elaboration likelihood model, which would suggest that individuals will exert more cognitive effort in processing messages from liked than from disliked sources or, as in this study, from liked sources for whom such liking has been made more accessible.

This model has also provided clues to the characteristics of the recipient of persuasion that influence effectiveness of the central and peripheral routes. For example, studies that have varied subjects' involvement with the attitudinal issue (e.g., students' involvement with raises in student fees) have demonstrated that those for whom an issue is relevant will be persuaded through central route arguments of good quality. In contrast, those who are not involved in the attitudinal issue will be more persuaded by peripheral cues such as the quantity of arguments, regardless of their quality (Petty & Cacioppo, 1986). Recent research suggests that variations in self-awareness (Hutton & Baumeister, 1992) may be related to whether one is persuaded through central or peripheral routes. For example, when people are made more self-aware by being placed in front of a mirror, they tend to be more influenced by persuasive messages that use the central route (i.e., have convincing arguments) than those who are not made self-aware.

In sum, the ELM offers important insights into persuasion. It explains *how* persuasive messages induce attitude change, and calls attention to the fact that persuasion can occur along either of two distinctly different routes. Further, the model has been related to individual characteristics and differences that affect cognitive processing of information. Clearly, such models constitute a marked advance in our understanding of this important process.

Attitude function, attitude object, and persuasion

At several points in this chapter, we have noted that attitudes can serve any of several different functions for the persons who hold them. Often, attitudes help the attitude-holders to organize and interpret diverse sets of information (*knowledge function*). They also permit individuals to express their central values or beliefs (*self-expression* or *self-identity function*). And attitudes sometimes help their holders to maintain or enhance their self-esteem (*self-esteem function*) by, for example, comparing themselves favorably with other persons or groups.

The functions served by attitudes are important from the point of view of a cognitive analysis of persuasion. Persuasive messages containing information relevant to specific attitudes—and, especially, information relevant to the functions served by those attitudes—will be processed differently (perhaps more carefully) from persuasive messages that do not contain such information. To the extent this is true, the precise conditions required for successful persuasion should vary with the functions served by various attitudes.

Convincing evidence for a relationship between attitude function and persuasion has been gathered in several different studies (Shavitt, 1989). For example, in one carefully conducted experiment on this issue, Shavitt (1990) noted that because of their basic nature, certain objects are associated with attitudes serving primarily one kind of function. For example, some objects (e.g., air conditioners) serve primarily a *utilitarian function*—people buy and use them because of the rewards they provide. Thus, attitudes about them can be expected to focus on this function. In contrast, other objects (e.g., perfume) serve a *self-identity function*—they permit individuals to express their identity, their values, or the reference groups to which they would like to belong. To put it more concretely, people buy some products, like air conditioners, because they enjoy the comfort these provide. They buy other products, like perfume, at least in part because these allow them to transmit a particular kind of personal image.

Given such differences, Shavitt reasoned that persuasive appeals that focus on the appropriate attitude function for a given object will be more successful than those that focus on other attitude functions. Specifically, persuasive messages that emphasize the features of a product should be more successful in changing attitudes about air conditioners and coffee than about perfume or greeting cards. In contrast, persuasive messages that emphasize the image various products yield should be more persuasive for perfume and greeting cards.

To test these predictions, Shavitt exposed female participants to four pairs of ads—one ad about each of two brands of each of four products. In each ad pair, one focused on features (e.g., the flavor and aroma of a brand of coffee), while the other focused on what the product indicated about the purchaser's taste and values (e.g., how use of a brand of coffee would indicate to others one's good judgment). Results offered strong support for the major hypothesis. For the utilitarian products (air conditioners, coffee), participants strongly preferred the brands that had been promoted by ads that focused on their features. For the self-identity products (perfume, greeting cards), however, participants strongly preferred the brands that had been promoted on the basis of their snob appeal. In short, the persuasive appeals whose content matched the function of the product (and hence attitudes about it) were more effective than those whose content did not. These findings indicate that where persuasion is concerned, the functions served by attitudes are an important factor to consider. Messages that draw a bead on these functions may be processed more carefully, and so exert greater impact, than ones that do not.

WHEN ATTITUDE CHANGE FAILS: RESISTANCE TO PERSUASION

Given the frequency with which we are exposed to persuasive messages, one point is clear: If we changed our attitudes in response to even a small fraction of these messages, we would soon be in a sorrowful state. Our views on a wide range of issues would change from day to day or even from hour to hour; and, reflecting this fact, our behavior too would show a strange pattern of shifts and reversals. Obviously, this does not happen. Despite all the charm, charisma, and expertise would-be persuaders can muster, our attitudes remain remarkably stable. Rather than being pushovers where persuasion is concerned, we are a tough sell and can withstand even powerful efforts to change our attitudes. Why? What factors provide us with such impressive ability to resist? We will now describe several of these.

■ **Resistance to persuasion: One reason why it's high**

FIGURE 3.7 Despite all the charm, charisma, and expertise would-be persuaders can muster, our attitudes remain remarkably stable.

REACTANCE: PROTECTING OUR PERSONAL FREEDOM

Have you ever found yourself becoming irritated at one of the "motivational" speakers on television or a salesperson who tries too hard? You begin to feel "brow-beaten" and feel that you want to find holes in their every argument. You may, in fact, turn off your TV or escape from the sales person. This is an example of what social psychologists term **reactance**—the negative reactions we experience when we conclude that someone is trying to limit our personal freedom by getting us to do what *they* want us to do. Research findings suggest that in such situations we often change our attitudes (or behavior) in a direction exactly *opposite* to that being urged on us—an effect known as **negative attitude change** (Brehm, 1966; Rhodewalt & Davison, 1983). Indeed, so strong is the desire to resist excessive influence that in some cases individuals shift away from a view someone is advocating even if it is one they would otherwise normally accept!

The existence of reactance is one principal reason why hard-sell attempts at persuasion often fail. When individuals perceive such appeals as direct threats to their personal freedom (or to their image of being a free and independent human being), they are strongly motivated to resist. And such resistance, in turn, virtually guarantees that many would-be persuaders are doomed to fail.

FOREWARNING: PRIOR KNOWLEDGE OF PERSUASIVE INTENT

On many occasions when we receive a persuasive message, we know full well that it is designed to change our views. Indeed, situations in which a communicator manages to catch us completely unprepared are quite rare. Does such advance knowledge or **forewarning** of persuasive intent help us to resist? Research evidence suggests that it does (e.g., Cialdini & Petty, 1979; Petty & Cacioppo, 1981). When we know that a speech, taped message, or written appeal is designed to alter our views, we are often less likely to be affected by it than if we do not possess such knowledge. The basis for such beneficial effects seems to lie in the impact that forewarning has on key cognitive processes. When we receive a persuasive message, especially one contrary to our current views, we often formulate *counterarguments* against it. Knowing about the content of such a message in advance provides us with extra time in which to prepare our defenses. In addition, forewarning also provides us with more time in which to recall relevant facts and information from memory—facts that may prove useful in refuting a persuasive message (Wood, 1982). Such effects are more likely to occur with respect to attitudes we consider to be important (Krosnick, 1989), but they occur to a smaller degree even for attitudes we view as fairly trivial. For these reasons, to be forewarned is to be forearmed where persuasion is concerned.

SELECTIVE AVOIDANCE

Still another way in which we resist attempts at persuasion is through **selective avoidance**, a tendency to direct our attention away from information that challenges our existing attitudes. In the context of social cognition (see chapter 2), selective avoidance is one of the ways in which attitudes (a type of schema) guide the processing of new information. For example, consider the act of television viewing. People do not simply sit in front of the tube and absorb whatever the media decide to dish out. Instead, they change channels, push the mute button, or cognitively tune out when confronted with information contrary to their existing views. The opposite effect occurs as well: When we encounter information that supports our views we tend to give it increased attention. We stop changing channels and listen carefully. Together, these tendencies to ignore or avoid information that contradicts our attitudes while actively seeking information consistent with them constitute the two sides of *selective exposure*—deliberate efforts to obtain information that supports our views. Through this mechanism, we often protect our current attitudes against persuasion and assure that they remain largely intact for long periods of time.

To conclude: because of the operation of reactance, forewarning, and selective avoidance, our ability to resist persuasion is considerable. Of course, attitude change *does* occur in some cases; to deny that it does would be to suggest that all forms of advertising, propaganda, and political campaigning are worthless (see Figure 3.8). But the opposite conclusion—that we are helpless pawns in the hands of all-powerful persuaders—is equally false. Resisting persuasion is an ancient human art, and recent political events around the globe (e.g., the demise of communism in Eastern Europe and the former Soviet Union) suggest that it is alive and well as we approach the twenty-first century.

Are attitudes easier to influence at some times of life than at others? Are we equally open to change throughout the lifespan? For information on this intriguing question, please see "Focus on Research: The Cutting Edge—Age and Attitude Change."

COGNITIVE DISSONANCE: HOW WE SOMETIMES CHANGE OUR OWN ATTITUDES

Imagine the following situation: You have always been in favor of affirmative action (special programs for hiring and promoting members of minority groups and women). Now, however, you learn that because of this policy one of your friends has been passed over for promotion, even though your friend has more experience and better qualifications than a minority candidate who *was* promoted. While you are in favor of affirmative action, you also believe that people should be promoted on the basis of merit. How do you feel? If you are like most people, you find this situation disturbing. After all, you have come face to face with the fact that two of your attitudes are inconsistent—they just don't seem to fit together.

■ **Resistance to persuasion: High, but not perfect**

FIGURE 3.8 The fact that political campaigning is so effective indicates that our resistance to persuasion is not perfect.

Age and Attitude Change: Are We Open to Change throughout Life?

"Set in their ways," "Rigid," "Closed-minded." We hate to admit it, but when we ask students in our classes to list the characteristics of middle-aged people (which some define as "anyone over thirty"!), these are some of the adjectives they offer. Such descriptions suggest that once people reach a specific age (or age range), their capacity for change diminishes—they become "locked in," so to speak. Applied to the realm of attitude change, this view suggests that during our youth our attitudes are flexible and can readily be changed. Afterwards, however, they become relatively fixed and are more difficult to alter.

Is this view—sometimes known as the *impressionable years hypothesis*—really true? Are our attitudes more open to change when we are young, and less so later in life? Or, as a competing view known as the *openness to experience hypothesis* suggests, do we remain equally open to such change throughout life? Evidence on this issue is somewhat mixed (e.g., Krosnick & Alwin, 1989). Sophisticated research conducted by Tyler and Schuller (1991), however, points to the optimistic conclusion that in fact we remain open to attitude change throughout life.

In order to gather evidence on this issue, Tyler and Schuller (1991) phoned almost sixteen hundred people living in the Chicago metropolitan area and asked them to answer several questions concerning their obligation to obey the decisions of judges or police officers and their support for these authorities. In addition, they asked these people to describe any experiences they had had with judges or police officers during the past year. One year later the researchers phoned again a randomly selected sample of the same persons (more than eight hundred of them) and asked the same questions. Participants were classified into four age groups: 18–25, 26–35, 36–50, and 51–95.

Results offered several kinds of support for continued openness to attitude change throughout life. First, it was found that in all four age groups, participants' attitudes toward judges and police officers were affected by recent experiences with these authorities. Moreover, if anything, the magnitude of such effects was somewhat *greater* for older than for younger persons. Second, it was found that while attitudes prior to recent experiences with judges or police officers predicted current attitudes, there were no differences among the various age groups in this respect. In other words, older persons were not locked into stable attitudes that were resistant to change in the face of experiences that might be expected to shift them. Finally, among persons who had had recent experiences with the police or judges, current attitudes were less strongly influenced by previous attitudes than was true for persons who did not have such experiences—and again, this was true regardless of age.

That these findings were not specific to attitudes regarding law enforcement authorities is suggested by an additional study conducted by Tyler and Schuller (1991). In that investigation, attitudes toward government agencies were measured. Again, it was found that these were strongly affected by recent experiences and that the impact of such experiences on attitudes was about equal for people of various ages (18–25, 26–35, 36–45, and 46–60).

Taken as a whole these findings, and related research on attitude change throughout the lifespan (Alwin, Cohen, & Newcomb, 1991), point to a fairly optimistic conclusion: Contrary to popular belief, attitude change in response to life experiences is possible over the entire lifespan. Thus, at least where this kind of change is concerned, age definitely does not seem to equal rigidity.

In the terminology of social psychology, you would be experiencing a state known as **cognitive dissonance** (Festinger, 1957). This is the feeling, usually unpleasant, that arises when we discover inconsistency between two of our attitudes or between our attitudes and our behavior. We have already illustrated inconsistency between two attitudes in the example above, in which favorable attitudes toward affirmative action ran smack up against attitudes toward promotion on the basis of merit (see Figure 3.9). And there are many other causes of dissonance as well. It occurs whenever individuals must choose between two attractive alternatives, for rejecting one job, school, or lover in favor of another is inconsistent with the positive features of the rejected option. Most relevant to our present discussion, though, is the fact that dissonance is generated whenever individuals say things they don't mean or behave in ways that are inconsistent with their underlying attitudes or values. In such cases, the dissonance produced can have a startling effect: It can lead the people involved to change their attitudes so that these more closely reflect their words and deeds. In other words, saying or doing things that are inconsistent with their own attitudes sometimes causes people to change the attitudes themselves. How can this be so? Read on.

DISSONANCE AND ATTITUDE CHANGE: THE EFFECTS OF FORCED COMPLIANCE

There are many occasions in everyday life when we must say or do things inconsistent with our real attitudes. For example, your friend buys a new car and proudly asks you how you like it. You have just read an article indicating that this model is such a lemon that the manufacturer puts a free ten-pound bag of sugar in the trunk. But what do you say? Probably something like "Nice, really nice." Similarly, imagine that

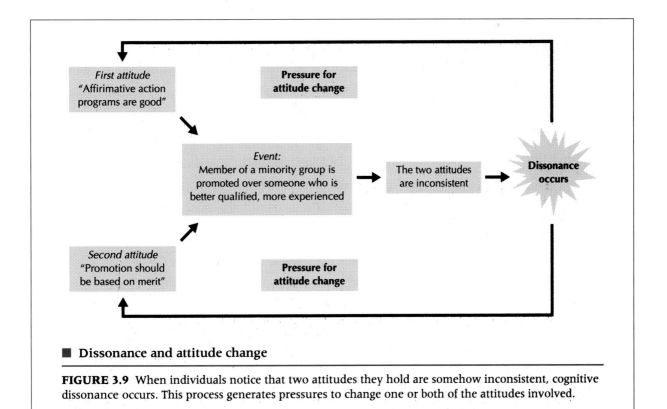

■ Dissonance and attitude change

FIGURE 3.9 When individuals notice that two attitudes they hold are somehow inconsistent, cognitive dissonance occurs. This process generates pressures to change one or both of the attitudes involved.

FOCUS ON RESEARCH:
CLASSIC CANADIAN CONTRIBUTIONS

Dissonance Reduction at the Race Track: Does Confidence Increase After Placing a Bet?

A classic study by Canadian researchers demonstrated that cognitive dissonance can play a part in decision-making processes in a real-life context. Knox and Inkster (1968) were interested in the effects of a phenomenon called "postdecisional dissonance." Festinger (1957, 1964) had suggested that whenever we have committed ourselves to one particular decision, there will be some dissonance created by the fact that we have had to reject alternative choices that also had attractive features. In order to reduce this postdecisional dissonance, we will change our cognitions so that the chosen alternative is seen as more desirable and the rejected alternatives as less desirable.

If you have ever had to commit yourself publicly to an important decision (e.g., to apply to or accept one university) and reject attractive alternatives, you know that a lot of doubt and uncertainty can be involved in that predecision period. But did your feelings and cognitions change once that commitment had been made, to more positive certainty (your chosen university was definitely the best)? This is the hypothesis that Knox and Inkster tested in the context of Vancouver's Exhibition Park Race Track and at a harness racing track nearby. Subjects were approached either just before they placed their bet at the $2 Win window (prebet group) or a few seconds after they had placed their $2 Win bet (postbet group). They were asked only one question: to rate the chances of their horse winning the race.

Their hypothesis predicted that in order to reduce the dissonance produced by having committed themselves to one horse, subjects in the postbet group would show greater confidence in their horse's chances than those in the prebet group. This is exactly what they found both in the horse-racing and in the harness-racing context (see Figure 3.10).

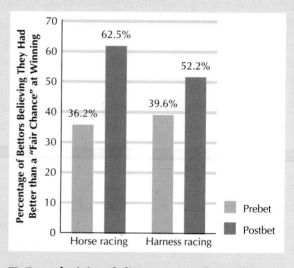

■ **Post-decisional dissonance reduction**

FIGURE 3.10 Knox and Inkster asked racegoers their chances of winning before they placed a bet or after they had bet. A higher percentage of subjects who had already bet (postbet) believed they had better than a "fair chance" of winning than those who were about to bet (prebet).

Source: Adapted from Knox and Inkster, 1968.

at an important meeting your boss turns to you and asks your opinion of her new plan. Since you value your relationship with her (and your job!) you praise the plan, even though you realize it has serious problems. In these and countless other situations, our actions and our attitudes are inconsistent. What happens in these situations, which social psychologists describe as involving *forced compliance*? (This term derives from the fact that in such incidents we are forced by circumstances to say or do things contrary to our real views.)

Since dissonance is an unpleasant state, people who experience it are motivated to reduce it. So something has to give (change). Several possibilities exist. First, individuals can change their attitudes so that these are now consistent with their behavior. For example, you may convince yourself that this is the right car for your friend or that your boss's plan is actually better than you thought. To the extent you do, you would experience the self-generated attitude change referred to in the title of this section.

Second—and this option is somewhat harder—individuals experiencing dissonance can change their cognitions about their own behavior. Thus, you might tell yourself that supporting your boss's views at meetings is an important part of your job. Thus, doing so is quite consistent with your attitudes.

Third, dissonance can be reduced by acquiring *new information*—information that is consistent with the attitudes or actions that, at first blush, seem inconsistent. For example, people who smoke cigarettes usually know that this is harmful to their health. They often try to reduce the dissonance produced by such counterattitudinal behavior by eagerly seeking evidence that smoking is truly not all *that* bad. They read reports of studies suggesting that smoking has few ill effects (ignoring the fact that these studies are sponsored by large tobacco companies). And they repeatedly remind themselves about Uncle Hal, who lived to be ninety-eight despite the fact that he smoked more than two packs a day.

Fourth, dissonance can be reduced by minimizing the importance of the inconsistency. For instance, in the incident involving affirmative action, you might convince yourself that this particular promotion is relatively unimportant since your friend plans to leave the company soon anyway.

In which of these ways do people actually seek to reduce dissonance? The answer is simple: in the way that is least effortful. In this, as in most other situations, we follow the path of least resistance and seek to reduce dissonance by changing whatever is easiest to change. Since it requires effort to change cognitions about our own actions, acquire new information, or minimize the importance of outcomes that really *are* important, the easiest route may well be to change our own attitudes. This, in essence, is why saying or doing things inconsistent with our attitudes sometimes leads us to change them.

DISSONANCE AND THE LESS-LEADS-TO-MORE EFFECT

Social psychologists generally agree that the forced compliance effect is a fact: When individuals say or do things they don't believe, they often experience a need to bring their attitudes into line with these actions. There is one complication in this process we have not yet considered, however: How strong are the reasons for engaging in counterattitudinal actions? If these reasons are quite strong, little or no dissonance will be generated. After all, if the last person to disagree with your boss publicly was fired on the spot, you would have strong grounds for praising the boss's plan even if you don't like it. Similarly, if you expect your friend to give you a lift to school in his new car every morning, you have strong reasons for praising, not belittling it. But what if good, convincing reasons for engaging in such actions are lacking? Under these conditions, dissonance will be stronger, for you must confront the fact that you said or did something you didn't believe *even though you had no strong or clear basis for doing so*. In short, dissonance theory points to the unexpected prediction that the weaker the reasons for engaging in counterattitudinal behavior, the stronger the dissonance generated, and hence the greater the pressure to change these views. Social psychologists often refer to this paradoxical prediction as the **less-leads-to-more effect**: The more inducements there are for engaging in attitude-discrepant behavior, the weaker the pressures toward attitude change (see Figure 3.11).

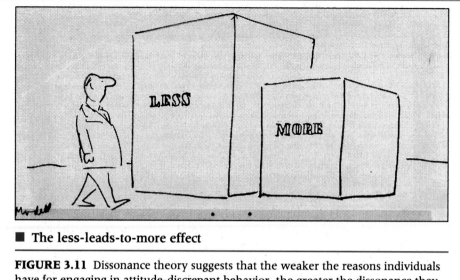

■ The less-leads-to-more effect

FIGURE 3.11 Dissonance theory suggests that the weaker the reasons individuals have for engaging in attitude-discrepant behavior, the greater the dissonance they will experience and the stronger the pressure to actually alter these views.
Source: The New Yorker.

Surprising as it may seem, this effect has been confirmed in many different studies (e.g., Riess & Schlenker, 1977). For example, in the first and most famous of these experiments (Festinger & Carlsmith, 1959), subjects were offered either a small reward (one dollar) or a large one (twenty dollars) for telling another person that some dull tasks they had just performed were very interesting. (One of the tasks consisted of placing spools on a tray, dumping them out, and repeating the process over and over again.) After engaging in this attitude-discrepant behavior (telling another subject the tasks were interesting when they knew full well that they were not), participants were asked to indicate their own liking for the tasks. As predicted by the less-leads-to-more effect, subjects actually reported greater liking for the dull tasks when they had received the small reward than when they had received the large one.

While this and several other studies lend support to predictions based on dissonance theory, we should note that the less-leads-to-more effect occurs only under certain conditions (Sogin & Pallak, 1976). First, it occurs only in situations in which people believe that they have a choice as to whether or not to perform the attitude-discrepant behavior. Second, small rewards lead to greater attitude change than large ones do only when people believe that they were personally responsible for both the chosen course of action and any negative effects produced (Goethals, Cooper, & Naficy, 1979). And third, the less-leads-to-more effect does not occur when people view the payment they receive as a bribe rather than well-deserved pay for services rendered. These and related findings suggest that there are significant limits on the impact of forced compliance. Still, we should note that often the conditions just outlined do exist—often people do have (or think they have) freedom of action. And they frequently accept responsibility for their own behavior, even when doing so produces negative consequences. As a result, the strategy of offering others just barely enough reward to induce them to say or do things contrary to their beliefs can often be effective in inducing attitude change—and self-generated change at that.

The less-leads-to-more effect revisited:
Inferred values and induced compliance

As we noted above, the less-leads-to-more effect was first predicted by dissonance theory and has often been studied within this context. More recent research on compliance, however, suggests it may also stem from a simpler and even more basic mechanism involving attributions. To see how this mechanism operates, consider the following events.

Imagine that someone offers to hire you to perform an unspecified job. This person says that she or he will pay you $100 to do the job and that the job will take only ten minutes of your time. Choose a number from one to seven to indicate how difficult, dangerous, or embarrassing you think the job is (1 = not very difficult or dangerous; 7 = very difficult or dangerous). Next, imagine that the same person offers you $5 to perform this job. Rate the job on the same scale once again. Did your ratings differ in the two instances? In all likelihood they did, for generally we assume that the more someone is willing to pay us for doing something, the more demanding or risky it must be. In short, we infer the nature or value of the task from the pay associated with it.

Turning this relationship between price and value around, assume that someone offers to sell you a painting for $10 000. How famous or talented is the artist? Now, imagine that you are offered the same painting for only $100; how famous or talented is the artist under these conditions? Once again, your ratings will probably differ, and this too will reflect the fact that you inferred value from price: The higher the price, the more famous or talented the artist.

What does all this have to do with forced compliance? According to Freedman, Cunningham, and Krismer (1992), quite a lot. These researchers argue that the less-leads-to-more effect may stem, at least in part, from the kind of attributions or inferences we have just described. In other words, they suggest that the reason people who engage in counterattitudinal behavior sometimes change their attitudes *more* when they have received a small reward than a large one is this: The large reward suggests that the counterattitudinal behavior is difficult or unpopular, while the small reward suggests that this behavior is easy or popular. Since people are more likely to change their attitudes toward popular views than unpopular ones, it is not surprising that greater attitude change occurs in the context of a small reward.

To test this explanation—which Freedman et al. describe as *inferred value theory*—the researchers performed a series of closely related studies. In one, college students were asked to rate the stressfulness and painfulness of a hypothetical experiment for which participants would be paid either $25 or $100 for serving as subjects. Results were clear: They rated the experiment as more stressful and painful in the $100 than in the $25 condition. Similar findings were also obtained when participants were asked to rate the extent to which a child would enjoy a new food under two different conditions: When her father offered her no incentive for eating it or when he offered her a large incentive (extra dessert). As expected, participants assumed that the girl would enjoy the food more in the low-incentive than in the high-incentive condition.

In a follow-up study Freedman et al. (1992) attempted to determine whether these effects will occur even when individuals have no choice about performing the action in question. Dissonance theory suggests that the less-leads-to-more effect will occur only when free choice about engaging in attitude-discrepant behavior exists. In contrast, inferred value theory suggests that having such choice is *not* necessary. To obtain evidence on this prediction, the researchers told students that a study in which they were participating involved either memory for rhythms or memory for words. They were then informed that they had been assigned to the rhythm task—they had no choice in this matter. Then they were reminded of the fact that because they were

FIGURE 3.12 Individuals who learned that other participants in a study received a large payment ($12) for performing a task rated this task as less enjoyable and were less willing to perform it again than participants who learned that others received a smaller payment ($5). These findings provide support for the role of inferred values in the less-leads-to-more effect.

Source: Based on data from Freedman et al., 1992.

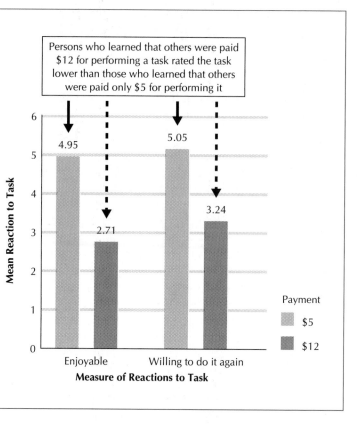

participating in the study as part of a course requirement, they would not be paid for their time. However, they were also told either that other participants, who were volunteers, received $12 for being in the study or that others received $5 for being in the study. Participants were then asked to rate the enjoyableness of the rhythm task and how willing they were to perform it again. As inferred value theory predicts, those in the high-incentive group (who had heard about the $12 fee) rated it as less enjoyable and were less willing to perform it again than those in the low-incentive group ($5) (see Figure 3.12).

In sum, it appears that when we are paid for engaging in some activity or when we must pay for some object or experience, we use the amounts involved as a basis for inferring the value of the objects or the difficulty of the tasks. And these inferences, in turn, can strongly affect our attitudes about the activities or objects in question. This may be one important reason why when we engage in actions discrepant with our attitudes, the smaller the inducement for doing so, the greater our tendency to change these attitudes.

DISSONANCE: DOES IT REALLY STEM FROM INCONSISTENCY?

Ever since the concept of cognitive dissonance was first developed in the 1950s, social psychologists have assumed *inconsistency* to be its most basic feature. It has been reasoned that people dislike inconsistency and strive to reduce it when it arises. More recently, however, Cooper and his colleagues (Cooper & Fazio, 1984; Cooper & Scher, 1992) have offered a contrasting interpretation of dissonance. This theory suggests that inconsistency is *not* the essential ingredient in dissonance. Rather, dissonance—and the motivation to reduce it—stems primarily from feelings of responsibility for negative events or outcomes. The reasoning behind this theory is as follows. Whenever people notice that they have brought about an aversive (harmful) event, they are motivated to determine whether they were responsible for this outcome or whether, perhaps, it stemmed from factors beyond their control. If they conclude that they were indeed personally responsible for the outcome, dissonance is generated, and all the effects described above (e.g., efforts to reduce it) then follow. Sometimes, of course, saying or doing things we don't believe can produce negative outcomes and so generate dissonance. But Cooper and his colleagues argue that attitude-discrepant behavior is not necessary for the occurrence of dissonance. What is essential, they maintain, is that people accept responsibility for producing aversive events.

In support of this view, Cooper and his coworkers point to evidence indicating that attitude change can follow from either attitude-consistent or attitude-discrepant behavior, provided the individuals involved learn that these actions produced negative outcomes (e.g., Scher & Cooper, 1989). When they believe that attitude-discrepant behaviors produced no harmful effects, in contrast, attitude change occurs to a much lesser degree.

While such evidence seems convincing, it is our view that the case for changing our basic conception of dissonance is far from complete. Recent research does call attention to several factors that may influence dissonance and the attitude change it often produces, but such research does not seem to account for all the intriguing findings generated in studies that have defined dissonance in the traditional, inconsistency-based manner (e.g., Baumeister, 1986). Further, it seems possible to interpret personal responsibility for aversive outcomes within the context of traditional dissonance theory. Most persons, after all, have a relatively positive self-image; discovering that they personally have been responsible for causing negative outcomes is in a sense inconsistent with that image. Accordingly, attitude change in such cases may stem, at least in part, from inconsistency.

Until such complexities are fully resolved, we believe it is reasonable to continue to view dissonance as deriving from and centering on the effects of inconsistency (e.g., Aronson, 1993). To repeat: When people discover that their various attitudes or their attitudes and behaviors don't fit neatly together, they may experience considerable pressure for change. And one of the important things that may give way in such contexts is their attitudes.

SUMMARY AND REVIEW

THE NATURE AND FORMATION OF ATTITUDES

Attitudes are enduring mental representations of features of the social or physical world. These representations include evaluations of "attitude objects" plus information pertaining to them. Attitudes are acquired through experience and exert a directive influence on subsequent behavior. Attitudes can be acquired indirectly, from other persons, through *social learning*. This process involves three basic forms of learning: classical conditioning, instrumental conditioning, and mod-

eling. Recent evidence indicates that *subliminal conditioning* of attitudes is also possible and may play a role in their development. Attitudes can also be acquired directly, through personal experience.

ATTITUDES AND BEHAVIOR

Attitudes are related to behavior, but this relationship is far from simple. Specific attitudes predict behavior better than general ones. Similarly, strong attitudes, or ones in which people have a *vested interest*, are better predictors of behavior than weak or irrelevant ones. The cognitive component of attitudes predicts certain types of behavior (e.g., career decisions) better than the affective component. The opposite is true for other forms of behavior (e.g., romantic involvements). Most, if not all, of these effects can be understood in terms of *attitude accessibility*—the ease with which various attitudes can be retrieved from memory.

PERSUASION

Persuasion is the process of changing attitudes through the presentation of various types of information. The *traditional view* of persuasion focused on identifying crucial characteristics of communicators, communications, and audiences. A newer *cognitive approach* focuses on the cognitive processes that underlie persuasion. An important cognitive model of persuasion is the *elaboration likelihood model (ELM)*. It suggests that persuasion can occur either (1) through careful processing of attitude-relevant information, or (2) in a relatively automatic manner in response to various persuasion cues (e.g., cues relating to the expertise or likableness of would-be persuaders). Personal characteristics such as *self-awareness* play a role in determining which of these two forms of persuasion actually occurs in a given situation.

RESISTANCE TO PERSUASION

Several factors play a role in our strong ability to resist persuasion. These include *reactance* (efforts to protect or restore personal freedom), *forewarning* (advance knowledge of persuasive intent on the part of others), and *selective avoidance* of information inconsistent with our attitudes. Contrary to popular belief, it appears that we remain open to changing our attitudes throughout life.

COGNITIVE DISSONANCE: CHANGING OUR OWN ATTITUDES

When individuals discover inconsistency between two attitudes they hold or between their attitudes and their behaviors, they experience *cognitive dissonance*. Dissonance motivates persons experiencing it to attempt to reduce it. When individuals say or do things inconsistent with their attitudes, they may seek to reduce the dissonance generated by changing these attitudes. The fewer good reasons they have for engaging in attitude-discrepant behavior, the greater the dissonance and the stronger the pressure for change—the *less-leads-to-more effect*. Interestingly, recent findings suggest that the less-leads-to-more effect may stem, at least in part, from attributions suggesting that actions for which individuals receive large rewards are more valuable or difficult than those for which they receive small rewards.

KEY TERMS

Attitude Accessibility The ease with which specific attitudes can be remembered and brought into consciousness.

Attitudes Mental representations of features of the social or physical world (including evaluations of those features) that are stored in memory.

Central Route (to persuasion) Attitude change resulting from systematic processing of information presented in persuasive messages.

Classical Conditioning A basic form of learning in which one stimulus, initially neutral, acquires the capacity to evoke reactions through repeated pairing with another stimulus. In a sense, one stimulus becomes a signal for the presentation or occurrence of the other.

Cognitive Dissonance An internal state that results when individuals notice inconsistency between two or more of their own attitudes or between their attitudes and their behavior.

Cognitive Perspective (on persuasion) An approach that attempts to understand persuasion by identifying the cognitive processes that play a role in its occurrence.

Demand Characteristics Cues that reveal the hypothesis or purpose of an experiment to participants. In the context of such information, participants may decide to "help" the researcher, by confirming the hypothesis, or may hinder the researcher by behaving in a manner opposite to the hypothesis.

Elaboration Likelihood Model (of persuasion) A theory suggesting that persuasion can occur in either of two distinct ways, differing in the amount of cognitive effort or elaboration they require.

Forewarning Advance knowledge that one is about to become the target of an attempt at persuasion. Forewarning often increases resistance to the persuasion that follows.

Instrumental Conditioning A basic form of learning in which responses that lead to positive outcomes or permit avoidance of negative outcomes are strengthened.

Less-Leads-to-More Effect The fact that offering individuals small rewards for engaging in counterattitudinal behavior often produces more dissonance, and so more attitude change, than offering them larger rewards.

Modeling A basic form of learning in which individuals acquire new forms of behavior through observing others.

Negative Attitude Change Attitude change in a direction opposite to that recommended in a persuasive communication.

Peripheral Route (to persuasion) Attitude change that occurs in response to persuasion cues—informa-tion concerning the expertise or status of would-be persuaders.

Persuasion The process through which one or more persons attempt to alter the attitudes of one or more others.

Reactance Negative reactions to perceived threats to one's personal freedom. Reactance often increases resistance to persuasion.

Selective Avoidance A tendency to direct one's attention away from information that challenges existing attitudes. Such avoidance increases resistance to persuasion.

Social Learning The process of acquiring new forms of behavior (including attitudes) by observing or interacting with others.

Subliminal Conditioning (of attitudes) Classical conditioning of attitudes by exposure to stimuli that are below the threshold of conscious awareness.

Vested Interest The extent to which an event or issue has a strong effect upon the life of a person holding an attitude about it.

Values Values are broad and abstract principles of life. They contain our moral beliefs and our standards of conduct.

FOR MORE INFORMATION

Eagly, A., & Chaiken, S. (1993). *The psychology of attitudes*. San Diego, CA: Harcourt Brace & Jovanovich.

   This book provides a comprehensive review of the vast existing literature on attitudes. Written by two expert researchers, it contains much valuable information about the nature of attitudes, how they can be changed, and their effects on behavior.

Pratkanis, A. K., Breckler, S. J., and Greenwald, A. G. (Eds.) (1989). *Attitude structure and function*. Hillsdale, NJ: Erlbaum.

   An examination of a wide range of information on attitudes. Each chapter has been prepared by expert researchers. A must for anyone interested in the nature and function of attitudes.

Rajecki, D. W. (1989). *Attitudes* (2nd ed.). Sunderland, MA: Sinauer Associates.

   A very broad introduction to current knowledge about attitudes. Covers a wide range of topics, from methods of attitude research through attitude change through group discussions. All in all, an interesting and valuable text.

Chapter FOUR

Identity and Culture: The Self in a Multicultural Context

··

The Self: Multiple Components of One's Personal Identity

Self-concept: The Central Schema/Self-esteem: Attitudes about Oneself/Self-monitoring Behavior: Emphasis on Internal versus External Factors/Self-focusing: The Relative Importance of Self

Social Identity: The Self in a Multicultural Context

Social Identity Theory: The Importance of a Group-based Sense of Self/Culture and the Self: Social Identity Across Cultures/The Independent and the Interdependent Self

Cross-cultural Psychology: Comparing Cultures

Concepts of Cross-cultural Psychology/Cross-cultural Research: Questioning Some Traditional Findings/Implications for a Multicultural Society

SPECIAL SECTIONS

FOCUS ON RESEARCH: CLASSIC CANADIAN CONTRIBUTIONS
    Acculturation: The Immigrant Experience

For each of us, the sense of *self* is extremely important in defining who we are, what we do, and how we evaluate both ourselves and others (Brewer, 1991; Deaux, 1993). Our sense of self combines both the private or internal person and the more public or social person who identifies with various groups—including cultural, racial, religious, political, gender, age, and occupational groups, to name just a few. The more private self provides us with a sense of *personal identity,* while the more public self provides us with a sense of *social identity* (Tajfel & Turner, 1979). In this chapter we will discuss these two major aspects of the self. First, we will describe some of the crucial elements of the *personal* self, including the self-concept, self-esteem, self-monitoring behavior, and self-focusing. Second, we will turn to the more *social* aspects of the self, concentrating on the sense of cultural or ethnic identity, which is so important to a Canadian context. Finally, we will look at the area of *cross-cultural psychology* that has begun to provide insights into the importance of culture to the way people define and think about the self and to social behavior in general. Indeed, the findings of cross-cultural psychology have led to questioning of some long-cherished assumptions about social behavior.

THE SELF: MULTIPLE COMPONENTS OF ONE'S PERSONAL IDENTITY

We acquire our personal identity, or **self-concept**, primarily through our social interactions, and the self and its acquisition are matters of long-standing interest in social psychology (Higgins, 1987; Markus & Wurf, 1987; Suls & Greenwald, 1986). The first part of this chapter will review current knowledge about the self from the point of view of social cognition (see chapter 2). In other words, we will focus on the self in terms of its cognitive framework—a special framework that influences how we process not only social information (Klein, Loftus, & Burton, 1989) but our own motivation, emotional states, and our feelings of well-being (Van Hook & Higgins, 1988). From this perspective, the self is the center of each person's cognitive and social universe.

SELF-CONCEPT: THE CENTRAL SCHEMA

If you wanted to describe your current concept of yourself, what information would be relevant? Most people describe their physical appearance (tall, short, blond, brunette, etc.), indicate their major traits (outgoing, shy, anxious, calm, etc.), and sometimes mention their major goals and motives (to get rich, to make the world a better place, etc.). Altogether, the self-concept is a complex collection of diverse information that somehow is held together as *you*. If each of us is not just a random collection of information (like the mixed-up pieces of dozens of jigsaw puzzles), what is the "glue" that holds all of the information together in a unified self-image? For most social psychologists interested in the self, the answer lies in the concept of the *schema*, which was described in chapter 2.

The self-schema and its cognitive effects

A schema is an organized collection of beliefs and feelings about some aspect of the world. Each of us has a **self-schema** in which our self-knowledge is organized (Markus & Nurius, 1986). That is, the self-schema is a cognitive framework that guides the way we process information about ourselves. Self-schemas reflect all of our past self-relevant experiences; all of our current knowledge and existing memories about ourselves; and our conception of what we were like in the past, what we are like now, and what we may be like in the future. A person's self-schema is the sum of everything that individual knows or can imagine about herself or himself.

If the self is the center of our social universe and if our self-schemas are well developed, it follows that we should do a better job of processing information that is relevant to ourselves than any other kind of information. Self-relevant information should be more likely to capture our attention, to be entered into memory, and to be recalled (Higgins & Bargh, 1987), as suggested in Figure 4.1. These hypotheses have been confirmed in studies of memory in which words deliberately made relevant to self ("Does this word describe you?") were later recalled more easily than words not made relevant ("Is

---

■ Self-schema: Organized knowledge relevant to oneself

FIGURE 4.1 The self-schema consists of the organized knowledge relevant to each individual's self. Attention is more likely to be focused on self-relevant information than on any other type of information, and self-relevant information is more readily entered into memory and more easily recalled, as suggested by the thought processes of this rhinoceros.

Source: The New Yorker, February 8, 1988, p. 36.

this word printed in big letters?"). This tendency for information related to the self to be most readily processed and remembered is known as the **self-reference effect**.

Though the self-reference effect has been firmly established experimentally, think for a minute about *why* it should occur. What is it about relating information to the self that enhances our ability to process it effectively? Experiments by Klein, Loftus, and their colleagues (e.g., Klein, Loftus, & Burton, 1989) offer valuable insights. For example, in an important study Klein and Loftus (1988) reasoned that recall of self-relevant information might be facilitated in one of two ways—each of which has been shown to enhance memory. First, self-relevance encourages what is termed *elaborative* processing—the tendency to think about the meaning of words or events. Second, self-relevance might facilitate *categorical processing*—the tendency to place stimuli in specific categories. To determine whether the self-relevance effect rests on either (or both) of these mechanisms, Klein and Loftus presented each of three different groups of subjects with a list of thirty words. The words on each list were either related to one another (Canada, Mexico, France, etc.; jazz, opera, rock, etc.) or unrelated to one another (aspirin, library, boat, etc.). The first group was told to think of a definition of each word (the *elaboration* task). The second group was told to place each word in one of five categories—things associated with a day by the sea, for example—(the *categorization* task). The third group was asked to indicate whether each word brought to mind an important personal experience (the *self-reference* task). After completing its task, each group was given a surprise recall task—"Write down as many of the words as you can remember."

Klein and Loftus predicted that for the unrelated words, the categorical processing task would be especially helpful for memory, because without such processing, relations among the words would not be readily apparent. In contrast, for the related words, the elaborative processing task would be helpful; because the relations were already obvious, but thinking about definitions would add something extra. Klein and Loftus reasoned that if the self-reference effect was based on elaborative processing, the self-reference task and the elaborative processing task would have the same effect on memory (each would enhance performance on the list of related words). If, however, the self-reference effect was based on categorical processing, the self-reference task and the categorical processing task would have the same effect on memory (each would enhance performance on the unrelated words). The results were clear in that the self-reference task had both effects. For the unrelated words, the recall performance of the self-reference group was equal to that of the categorization group; for the related words, performance was equal for the self-reference group and the elaboration group. In summary, the ability to process information related to the self more readily than other information seems to derive from two powerful mechanisms. We think about such information more deeply than we do about other information, and we categorize it more effectively. Both mechanisms underlie the self-reference effect, making it easier to recall self-relevant information (see Figure 4.2).

Some interesting recent Canadian research by Campbell and her colleagues (Campbell, Trapnell, Katz, and Lavallee, 1992; Campbell, Trapnell, Heine, Katz, Lavallee, & Lehman, 1994) has focused on the clarity of the self-concept—the extent to which a person's beliefs about the self are clearly defined, internally consistent, and stable over time. A scale to measure this characteristic has been developed that when scored in one direction tests for *self-concept clarity* and when scored in the opposite direction tests for *self-concept confusion*. Attesting to the importance of a clearly defined idea of the self, they find that those who are high in self-concept clarity tend also to have higher self-esteem than those who are lower in self-concept clarity or are more confused. This relation between self-concept clarity and esteem will be discussed further in the section below on culture and the self.

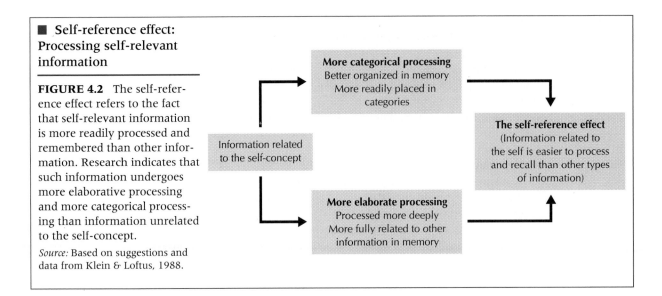

FIGURE 4.2 The self-reference effect refers to the fact that self-relevant information is more readily processed and remembered than other information. Research indicates that such information undergoes more elaborative processing and more categorical processing than information unrelated to the self-concept.

Source: Based on suggestions and data from Klein & Loftus, 1988.

For each person many selves are potentially possible

When people speak about themselves, they often assume stability and the absence of change. Despite this, most of us realize that we can and do change. You are not the same person you were ten years ago, and you can safely assume that ten years from now you will not be exactly the same person you are today. Your daydreaming fantasies are likely to involve how you might change once you get out of school, get married, enter a career, make more money, or move to a new location. So, along with a self-concept, we are each somewhat aware of other, **possible selves**, as well.

Markus and her colleagues (e.g., Markus & Nurius, 1986) contend that each person's self-concept at any given time is actually only a *working self-concept* that is open to change in response to new experiences, new feedback, and new self-relevant information. We also actively imagine and sometimes take steps to bring about alternate selves by getting in better shape physically, learning to play the piano, changing our hair styles, and so forth. We can also imagine alternate selves that are less desirable—ourselves gaining weight, losing our friends, developing lung disease, and so forth.

Alternative possible selves affect us in several ways (Markus & Nurius, 1986). First, they affect motivation, because an image of a future self acts as an incentive to work hard, study, exercise, stop smoking, save money, and so on, so that you can become a college graduate, an attorney, a businessperson, a homeowner, or whatever seems an ideal goal to you. Second, there is sometimes a discrepancy between self-perceptions and the way others perceive us. We see ourselves as we are *and* as we hope to become; other people are likely to see only the current self. Third, discrepancies between how we are and how we would like to be can be painful and emotionally upsetting (Van Hook & Higgins, 1988). Fourth, individual differences arise, in that some people (optimists) envision positive self-changes in the future while others (pessimists) view their future selves in negative terms.

The concept of possible selves has led to some interesting research. In one such study Porter, Markus, and Nurius (1984) asked thirty individuals who were the victims of a major crisis in their lives (death of someone close to them, a critical illness, etc.) to describe their current selves and possible future selves. Those who reported having recovered from the crisis and those who had not recovered were found to describe similar current selves—they were fearful, resentful, and depressed, and felt a loss of control. The two groups differed, however, in their imagined future selves. The recovered group described future selves that were happy, confident, secure, optimistic, and involved with many friends; while the poor-recovery group envisioned future selves that were unpopular, unimportant, weak, depressed, and prone to failure.

In considering possible selves ("What do you want to be when you grow up?"), one person may imagine many alternatives while another considers only a very limited number. This is termed *possible self-concept complexity* (number of aspects or categories of one's possible self). Recent research suggests that it may be emotionally beneficial to consider multiple alternatives for one's future and for one's present. People who had fewer possible selves were found to react more strongly to both failure and success (Niedenthal, Setterlund, and Wherry 1992). It seems that having your life wrapped up in only one possible future self makes the idea of failure more devastating (or success more intense) than if you have many options.

The realization that individuals have many possible selves in addition to their current working self-concepts presents a more complicated, but probably more accurate picture of how human beings conceive of themselves.

SELF-ESTEEM: ATTITUDES ABOUT ONESELF

We have just seen how people differ in describing their future selves in optimistic versus pessimistic terms. They also differ in describing their current selves in positive or negative terms. **Self-esteem** refers to the self-evaluations each individual makes. A person expressing *high self-esteem* believes himself or herself to be fundamentally good, capable, and worthy; *low self-esteem* is a view of oneself as useless, inept, and unworthy. The opinions expressed by others probably help shape these attitudes, and outsiders' opinions may sometimes bring about changes in one's self-esteem. Self-evaluations are also affected by the characteristics of others with whom we compare ourselves (Brown et al., 1992). With respect to people in general or those with whom we are not psychologically close, our self-views become more positive when we identify something *deficient* or *inadequate* about another person—a contrast effect. Thus, comparing oneself with someone who is worse off (downward comparison) results in a more positive mood and higher self-esteem (Reis, Gerrard, & Gibbons, 1993). When we feel psychologically close to another person, self-appraisals become more positive when we identify something *exceptionally good* about that person—an assimilation effect (Brown et al., 1992).

At any given time, of course, self-esteem refers to one's own evaluations of oneself rather than to the reactions or characteristics of others (see Figure 4.3). A large body of research has concentrated on this concept, because it is a central and pervasive aspect of the self, influencing behavior even when esteem does not seem to be especially relevant to what is going on at the time (Greenwald, Bellazza, & Banaji, 1988).

The discrepancy between self and ideal self

The difference between a person's perception of how he or she is and how that person believes he or she *should be* is known as **self-ideal discrepancy**. The less discrepancy between one's self and one's ideal self, the higher one's self-esteem.

Consider a situation in which you find a wallet containing $100 lying on the sidewalk. We all know the right thing to do, and ideally your behavior will match that standard; if you return the wallet, you will probably feel proud of yourself and evaluate yourself highly, experiencing high self-esteem. But the money may look very tempting, and you may decide to keep it. If so, any guilt about not doing the right thing and not living up to your ideals will result in a negative self-evaluation.

■ Low self-esteem affects feelings and behavior

FIGURE 4.3 A person's attitude about himself or herself is also known as self-esteem. As suggested here, low self-esteem is associated with unhappiness and interpersonal difficulties.

The consequences of negative self-evaluations

Research has consistently shown that having positive self-regard is generally beneficial, provided that it is not carried to extremes. For example, people with high self-esteem tend to be less lonely than those whose self-esteem is low, suggesting that a positive self-evaluation is associated with good social skills (Omstead et al., 1991). In addition, the lower an individual's self-esteem, the more depressed that person feels (Pillow, West, & Reich, 1991). These effects of low self-esteem are shown in Figure 4.4.

Other research indicates that depression is not just a matter of low self-esteem; it is also related to *variable self-esteem*. That is, those whose self-esteem frequently goes up or down in response to changes in the situation are the ones most likely to become depressed (Roberts & Monroe, 1992). The explanation is that anyone whose self-esteem is strongly affected by each minor occurrence has feelings of self-worth that are based on less stable sources than is true for those whose self-esteem remains at a fairly constant level.

Anyone who has felt lonely and depressed is likely to agree that these are unsatisfactory conditions. What can be done? Within the framework of self-discrepancy theories, self-esteem can be elevated either by changing behavior to match one's ideals

■ Some negative effects of low self-esteem

FIGURE 4.4 Research indicates several ways in which low self-esteem has negative consequences for the individual. As shown here, low self-esteem is associated with inadequate social skills. Poor social skills lead to loneliness, and loneliness results in feelings of depression. Depression is also intensified simply by the tendency to evaluate oneself in a negative way.

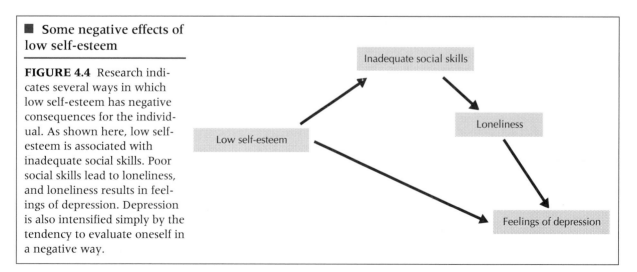

or by lowering ideal standards to match more closely one's actual behavior. This may sound strange, but consider the people who set impossibly high standards for themselves. If, for example, you wish to be perfect in all that you do, never making mistakes and being liked by everyone you meet, these are almost certainly unreasonable goals, and your self-evaluation will be unnecessarily low. The best way to raise self-esteem in this context is to lower your expectations about what you want to be.

Is it common to adjust ideal standards in order to protect self-esteem? Most people are, in fact, attuned to do just this. Students who receive a favorable outcome—such as a good test score—are likely to internalize the result and take credit for being intelligent or for working hard (Burke, Hunt, & Bickford, 1985). An unfavorable outcome is more likely to be attributed to external factors (such as "the room was too hot" or "the instructor was unfair"). If this point seems familiar, it is because in chapter 2 we discussed taking credit for favorable outcomes and looking elsewhere for the cause of unfavorable events as attributional biases. Many common attributional biases serve to protect self-esteem. However, there are some cultures where use of such *self-serving biases* in attribution is much less common than in the West, as we will see in the last part of this chapter.

If self-esteem represents the characteristic evaluation an individual makes, it would seem to be an internal trait or dispositional variable. If self-esteem can be raised or lowered in response to the evaluations of others, it would seem to be a temporary *state* that fluctuates with changes in the external situation. In fact, both trait and state concepts of self-esteem are accurate, and in the following section we will discuss research consistent with each.

Dispositional and situational influences on self-esteem

When self-esteem is conceptualized as a trait or part of a person's personality (i.e., it is *dispositional*), it is measured along a positive-negative dimension that indicates where the person falls in relation to others. Dispositional self-esteem does not indicate a totally unchanging characteristic set in concrete but rather a general tendency to evaluate oneself in a relatively consistent way at different times and in many different situations. If your dispositional self-esteem is higher than the person sitting next to you, you probably feel better about yourself than he or she does—both today and next month, both after doing well on an exam and after doing poorly.

Most studies of trait self-esteem concentrate on environmental factors that bring about individual differences. Childhood experiences can be especially important, because children's self-concepts are in the process of being formed. For example, Felson (1989) found that children tend to evaluate themselves in part on the basis of how they think their parents evaluate them. A classic example is that of a child whose parents divorce; self-blame follows when the child makes the false assumption that one parent is leaving because the child did something wrong (see Figure 4.5). Such childhood misperceptions may underlie the Kaplan and Pokorny (1971) finding that negative childhood events—having a parent enter a mental hospital, divorce, remarry, or die—are associated with low general self-esteem as an adult.

Data that require a more complicated explanation indicate that middle-born children have significantly lower self-esteem than first or last-born children (Kidwell, 1982). One suggestion is that the youngest child tends to receive the most parental affection and first-borns tend to be allowed the most freedom of action, leaving the middle-born offspring feeling unloved and mistrusted.

In contrast to the long-lasting effects of early experiences on dispositional self-esteem, situational effects in later life are likely to be temporary. Have you ever felt elated after something very positive happened to you, or really down in the dumps after an especially negative experience? If so, you know that your mood was affected, and

■ Negative childhood events can result in low self-esteem

FIGURE 4.5 Research indicates that a variety of negative childhood events ranging from parental divorce and re-marriage to the death of a parent can result in low self-esteem in adulthood. One reason seems to be the tendency for the child to assume that parents blame him or her for the problem and that they dislike the child as a consequence; the child then adopts this perceived negative evaluation as a self-evaluation.

very possibly your feelings about yourself as well. One explanation is that an immediate event (and the emotion that results) commands more of our attention than long-term factors, so self-esteem may shift up or down. As a result, a temporary change in mood leads to an equally temporary change in self-esteem (Esses, 1989). Those who are already low in self-esteem are especially vulnerable to the effects of negative moods (Brown & Mankowski, 1993). These situationally based effects wear off in time, and one's self-esteem returns to its more customary level.

Social identity and its consequences also influence self-esteem, as was shown in research by Hirt et al. (1992). Among sports fans, one aspect of social identity involves identification with a specific team or teams. Hirt and his colleagues reasoned that the success or failure of a fan's team would affect the self-esteem of the fan. In one experiment, one group of Indiana University basketball fans watched Bobby Knight's Hoosiers in a winning game while another group saw the team lose. (A control group watched a Division II basketball game between schools irrelevant to Indiana fans: South Dakota State versus Jacksonville State.) Self-esteem was found to become more positive after an I.U. victory and more negative after the team lost; no such effects were found in the control group. In addition, the changes in the fans' self-esteem influenced their mood, their estimates of the team's future success, and their estimates of their own future performance in tasks involving mental and social skills. Considering that this study involved identification with a basketball team rather than the individual's gender, race, religion, or any other central aspect of self, these findings provide clear indications of the importance of social identity in our lives.

SELF-MONITORING BEHAVIOR: EMPHASIS ON INTERNAL VERSUS EXTERNAL FACTORS

Snyder and his colleagues have identified self-monitoring behavior as still another important component of the self (Gangestad & Snyder, 1985; Snyder & Ickes, 1985). Self-monitoring refers to the degree to which individuals regulate their behavior on the basis of the external situation and the reactions of others (high self-monitors) or on the basis of internal factors such as their own beliefs, attitudes, and interests (low self-monitors).

In the original formulation of self-monitoring, it was assumed that high self-monitors engage in role-playing in an attempt to behave so as to receive positive evaluations from others. Thus, high self-monitoring was described as a useful characteristic for people such as politicians, salespeople, and performers, who wish to please those with whom they interact. More recently, Schwalbe (1991) proposed that the high self-monitoring behavior of some individuals is based not on skillfully tuned role-playing in response to the reactions of other people but on relatively permanent images or "scripts" assumed to be appropriate in a given situation. For example, a college student may always be outgoing and amusing with those his own age and always quiet and shy with older individuals—regardless of how others are actually responding to his behavior. This theory suggests two types of high self-monitors—those guided by the audience and those guided by assumptions about what to do in particular situations, irrespective of any specific audience reaction.

Measuring self-monitoring behavior

The first measuring device for this construct was the **Self-monitoring Scale** developed by Snyder (1974). This test requires the respondent to express agreement or disagreement with a series of statements that reflect either emphasis on internal reasons to act or a tendency to be guided by external cues. Examples of these items are shown in Table 4.1.

Though various criticisms and modifications of the Self-monitoring Scale have been offered (Beauvois & Le Poultier, 1986; Briggs & Cheek, 1988; Montag & Levin, 1990), there is considerable evidence supporting the validity of the original measure. For example, Lippa and Donaldson (1990) conducted a field study in which Snyder's test was used. Students first responded to a computer program asking them to list the primary people with whom they interacted, the situations in which the interactions took place, and their characteristic behavior in such situations. Then they completed the Self-monitoring Scale, and—over a ten-day period—they kept a detailed behavioral diary. Scores on the scale were found to predict the consistency of their behavior as indicated on the computer program and in the diaries. That is, high self-monitors were responsive to specific situations and audiences, and low self-monitors behaved in consistent ways regardless of the situation. Other research also indicates that low self-monitors vary less from situation to situation than high self-monitors (Koestner, Bernieri, & Zuckerman, 1992).

Correlates of self-monitoring behavior

The differential attention paid to situation versus self is even reflected in how individuals react to advertising. Some ads emphasize information about quality and intrinsic rewards, while others emphasize image and extrinsic rewards—as shown in Figure 4.6. Debono and Packer (1991) found that high self-monitors rated advertised products more

---

■ On Snyder's Self-monitoring Scale, respondents answer each item by indicating whether it is true or false with respect to themselves. On the sample items presented here, high self-monitors would tend to agree with the first two and to disagree with the second two.

TABLE 4.1 Measuring self-monitoring behavior

Items from the Self-monitoring Scale

When I am uncertain how to act in social situations, I look to the behavior of others for cues.

In different situations and with different people, I often act like very different persons.

My behavior is usually an expression of my true inner feelings, attitudes, and beliefs.

I would not change my opinions (or the way I do things) to please someone else or to win their favor.

Source: Based on information in Snyder, 1974.

■ Advertising: Quality versus image

FIGURE 4.6 Studies of self-monitoring behavior indicate that high self-monitors rate an advertised product more positively when the ad stresses image and what other people will think if the consumer purchases it. Low self-monitors rate a product more positively when the ad stresses quality and information about how the consumer will benefit from it.

positively and perceived them as more self-relevant after seeing an image-based ad ("Heineken—you're moving up"). Low self-monitors liked the products better and perceived them as more self-relevant after seeing a quality-based ad ("Heineken—you can taste the difference"). The distinction seems to be based on whether one is concerned about the product making a good impression on others or about liking the product oneself.

Because high self-monitors are especially concerned about public approval, Cutler and Wolfe (1989) proposed that these individuals would express more confidence in their decisions in order to be liked more. Examples of such behavior can be found in politics. Politicians who waver in their opinions or qualify their beliefs are perceived as having low confidence in their decisions and as being deficient as leaders (see chapter 10). In the 1992 United States presidential election, H. Ross Perot lost many of his supporters when he entered the primaries, then dropped out of the race, then changed his mind a second time by reentering the contest. In their research Cutler and Wolfe found that, indeed, high self-monitoring, as hypothesized, was linked to being confident about one's decisions. Interestingly enough, this confidence was unrelated to the accuracy of the decisions!

Self-monitoring as a factor in interpersonal behavior

High self-monitors would be expected to pay attention to others and low self-monitors to pay attention to themselves. These hypothesized differences do occur, even in speech patterns. Ickes, Reidhead, and Patterson (1986) discovered that low self-monitors were more likely than high self-monitors to speak in the first person (I, me, my, mine, etc.). High self-monitors were relatively more likely to speak in the third person (he, she, her, his, their, etc.). Such differences suggest that high self-monitors are more attentive to and concerned with the actions and reactions of others, while low self-monitors are more concerned with themselves.

These differences in attention are also reflected in the interpersonal choices people make. High self-monitors tend to select a companion (for example, a tennis partner) on the basis of how well the other person performs; low self-monitors are more likely to choose a companion on the basis of how much they like the other person (Snyder, Gangestad, & Simpson, 1983). Why? The explanation is based on an emphasis on the situation (I want to *play tennis* with you) versus an emphasis on personal feelings about the other person (I want to play tennis with *you*). The results of this and other investigations (Snyder & Simpson, 1984) provide evidence that low self-monitors are more committed to individuals while high self-monitors are more committed to situations.

Some of these findings may suggest that low self-monitors are better adjusted than those who score high on this dimension. For example, people in the West tend to believe that consistency across situations is preferable to inconsistency (Beauvois & Dubois, 1988). Research indicates, however, that individuals who score between the two extremes are less maladjusted than those on the two ends of the spectrum (Miller & Thayer, 1989). Compared to people whose scores fall in the middle of the dimension, neuroticism was greater among high self-monitors (whose behavior fluctuates with the situation) *and* low self-monitors (whose behavior is unvarying, regardless of the situation).

SELF-FOCUSING: THE RELATIVE IMPORTANCE OF SELF

So far we have examined several aspects of the self, including the way one's self-esteem is affected by situational factors and also the way these elements of the self (along with self-monitoring tendencies) influence behavior. We now examine the self in a slightly different way. **Self-focusing** refers to the centrality of an individual's sense of self. The extent to which you are self-focused is indicated by the degree to which your attention is directed inward towards yourself as opposed to outward toward the environment (Fiske & Taylor, 1991).

Self-focusing is tied to memory and cognition. You can focus on yourself only if you can recall relevant past events and process relevant current information. Klein, Loftus, and Burton (1989) have identified two areas of memory involving self-focusing. Self-focus affects the accuracy of biographical recall (how well you can retrieve factual information about yourself) and the complexity of self-descriptive judgments (Dixon & Baumeister, 1991). If you were asked "Are you happy with your social life?", would you answer the same way as if you were asked "Are you unhappy with your social life?" In other words, does the wording (framing) of the question lead you to focus on specific positive versus negative aspects of yourself? Kunda et al. (1993) find that one's memory and one's working self-conception *are* affected by such questions, but only if one's self-knowledge contains both positive and negative elements. For example, if your social life were totally positive, the wording of a question about it would be irrelevant.

In addition, a brief period of self-focusing improves self-insight, in that research participants who are instructed to think briefly about themselves are better able to make accurate assessments of social feedback than those not given such an opportunity (Hixon & Swann, 1993). We will now describe how these processes operate.

Self-focusing as a trait, or at least a tendency

Duval and Wicklund (1972) suggested that a person who is high in self-focusing (or self-awareness) either acts to reduce any discrepancies between his or her self-concept and actual behavior or avoids situations in which such discrepancies occur. In both instances, behavior is influenced by whether or not attention is focused on the self (Carver & Scheier, 1981). As with self-monitoring behavior, those whose self-focus is strong would be expected to show consistent behavior across situations, while a weak self-focus would be associated with behavior that changed as the situation changed.

Because one's self-concept contains multiple elements, it is possible to focus on only a portion of it at any one time. For example, Showers (1992a) has provided evidence that many people store positive and negative aspects of themselves separately in memory. Thus, if the individual focuses on the negative, his or her mood and subsequent behavior will be different than if the focus is on the positive. Some individuals, however, seem to store positive and negative self-knowledge together; the result is less negative affect and higher self-esteem (Showers, 1992b). The most general conclusion is that the organization of self-evaluations affects self-esteem and mood beyond what could be predicted on the basis of simply the *amount* of positive and negative content.

Though the self-content on which a person focuses influences mood (Sedikides, 1992), mood also affects self-focusing behavior, and environmental factors in turn affect one's mood (Salovey, 1992). If you are in a negative mood, for example, because you have a toothache and are scheduled to visit the dentist, you are more likely to recall (focus on) negative aspects of your self. The extent and the content of the self-focusing behavior as well as mood can affect expectations. Thus, a depressed individual who is self-focused on negative content is more pessimistic than either nondepressed individuals or other depressed individuals who are *not* self-focused on negative content. Figure 4.7 presents examples of how these factors are interrelated.

Though little research has been done to determine why some people are more self-focused than others, Ullman (1987) examined some of the developmental aspects of this behavior. He found that young children tend to define themselves to others in terms of external characteristics (age, sex, etc.). As adolescents grow older, they concentrate more on defining themselves to others in terms of their "true" selves (personal qualities, etc.). Thus, from childhood to adolescence, self-focusing increases.

Situational influences on self-focusing

Though the tendency to be relatively self-focused or not reflects the trait aspects of focusing, no one is *uniformly* self-focused or situation-focused. People can even be induced to focus on themselves through simple instructions (Johnson, 1987). That is, you can direct where your attention is focused—right now, think about your most unpleasant characteristics. You can do that, or you can think about (recall) the most pleasant ones. In addition, external cues, such as the presence of a mirror, act to increase self-focusing.

In everyday behavior self-awareness is not always a conscious process (Epstein, 1983), so we may not notice how much self-focusing is occurring in a given situation. In general, if you are in a familiar, comfortable situation, you pay less attention to the environment and more attention to yourself. If the situation is unfamiliar and threatening, environmental cues become all-important. Think of the difference between driving along a familiar road in daylight and navigating an unfamiliar road on a rainy night. Self-focusing in the first situation is common, but in the second situation it could be fatal.

In some circumstances, self-focusing and the situation can have reciprocal effects. Strentz and Auerbach (1988) studied FBI agents in training who took part in a realistic simulated abduction in which they were assigned the role of hostages for four days. The trainees were abducted from an FBI van by staff members dressed like Middle Eastern terrorists. The abductors fired their guns (using blanks), and the van's driver and his

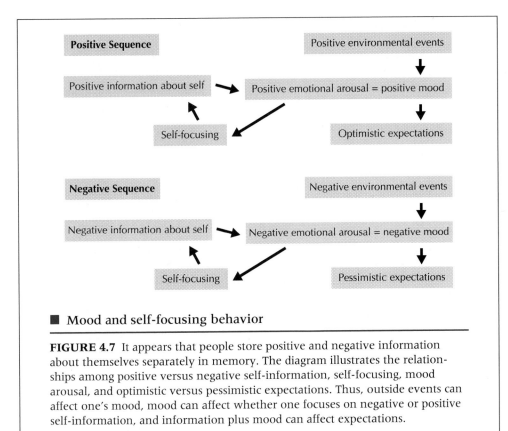

Positive Sequence

Positive information about self → Positive emotional arousal = positive mood

Positive environmental events

Self-focusing

Optimistic expectations

Negative Sequence

Negative information about self → Negative emotional arousal = negative mood

Negative environmental events

Self-focusing

Pessimistic expectations

■ Mood and self-focusing behavior

FIGURE 4.7 It appears that people store positive and negative information about themselves separately in memory. The diagram illustrates the relationships among positive versus negative self-information, self-focusing, mood arousal, and optimistic versus pessimistic expectations. Thus, outside events can affect one's mood, mood can affect whether one focuses on negative or positive self-information, and information plus mood can affect expectations.

assistant broke concealed blood bags as they dropped to the ground, apparently murdered. A few of the trainees thought that real terrorists had interrupted the exercise with an actual kidnapping. The trainees were handcuffed, a pillowcase was placed on each person's head, and they were driven to a secret location. Before the abduction began, some of the trainees were told to concentrate on their emotional state (self-focusing) during the experience; some were told to concentrate on the events (situation-focusing); and still others received no instructions. Those who focused on themselves reported the least anxiety and emotional distress, and observers rated their behaviors as showing less distress than the situation-focused or no-instruction groups. In addition, the self-focused individuals were found to seek more social support during the abduction than those in the other two conditions, as shown in Figure 4.8. Social support was measured on a Ways of Coping checklist, on which the participants indicated their behavior with respect to such items as "talked to someone to find out about the situation" and "talked to someone about how I was feeling" (Folkman & Lazarus, 1980; Vitaliano, 1985). Presumably, in an extremely unpleasant situation, self-focusing results in additional emotional awareness and hence the need for interpersonal contact and communication.

SOCIAL IDENTITY: THE SELF IN A MULTICULTURAL CONTEXT

Think about your own sense of self. How is it related to the social world? Is your self a private being, separate from others, within the bounds of your physical body? Or is your sense of self more integrated into your social world, extending out so that you

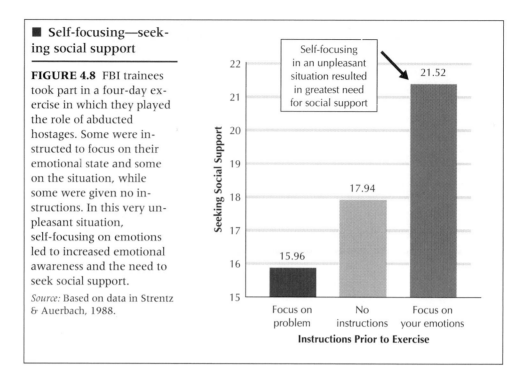

■ Self-focusing—seeking social support

FIGURE 4.8 FBI trainees took part in a four-day exercise in which they played the role of abducted hostages. Some were instructed to focus on their emotional state and some on the situation, while some were given no instructions. In this very unpleasant situation, self-focusing on emotions led to increased emotional awareness and the need to seek social support.

Source: Based on data in Strentz & Auerbach, 1988.

are part of your family, your community or even your society. The former, more separate sense of self, has been suggested to be typical of Western cultures and the latter, more socially integrated sense of self, more typical of Eastern cultures (e.g., Geertz, 1984). However, some of the earliest Western theorists of the self also put forward the idea that the self is essentially *social*. Other people, friends, family, and ancestors were seen by William James (1890), for example, as an important part of the self. Further, the development of a sense of self was seen as occurring only through interaction with others and with society (Cooley, 1902/1964; Mead, 1934). And today, those who take a sociocultural perspective, see the self as "property of the culture" (Sampson, 1991, p. 212). It is this social side of our identity on which we will focus in this second section of the chapter.

SOCIAL IDENTITY THEORY: THE IMPORTANCE OF A GROUP–BASED SENSE OF SELF

One of the most influential theories to emerge from European social psychology since the "crisis" of the 1970s is **Social Identity Theory** (Tajfel, 1978; 1982; Tajfel & Turner, 1979). Social identity theorists have stressed that group belonging is very important to the individual's self-concept. Your **social identity** is that part of your self-concept derived from membership in, and identification with, social groups. It is distinguished from **personal identity**, which is the unique and individual aspects of your self-concept. In other words, *social identity* is the part of your sense of self that comes from the knowledge that you are part of particular groups in society. Some of these groups are chosen by you, such as when you decide to become a student at one particular college or decide to join a club. But membership in other groups is involuntary: you are born into them or assigned them by your society. For example, we do not choose our gender group, our age group or our cultural background. By an accident of birth you may be a young, male, Italian-Canadian or a middle-aged, female, Anglo-Canadian. Notice that the group-title (e.g., Italian-Canadian) is one that is defined by the society in which you live (what is sometimes called being a "hyphenated-Canadian"). You may or may not identify yourself in that way. However, it is almost impossible not to be aware that such designations are of social significance in Canada. Whether you like it or not, others often identify *you* in that way (see Figure 4.9)

Often our sense of self-worth is tied to our group-membership or group-identification. For example, we saw above that sports-fans' self-esteem can rise and fall with the success or failure of their team (Hirt, et al., 1992). In line with this, a fundamental assumption of social identity theory is that individuals strive to maintain or achieve a *positive* and *distinctive* social identity. First, we are concerned that our group can be distinguished from other groups—this is what gives us an *identity*. So for example, when the North American Free Trade Agreement (NAFTA) was signed in 1993, there were fears expressed that Canada would suffer the loss of its distinctive identity through economic association with the United States. Second, as well as being distinctive, we are also concerned that our groups are positively evaluated, relative to other groups in society.

In order to establish whether our group has a positive or a negative social identity, we use *intergroup social comparison*. We compare the status and respect of our group with other groups in society. If you want a measure of how important group status can be to the individual, think how strongly you react when you hear someone in a public setting say something negative about a group to which you belong. For example, let's imagine that you happen to turn on the television when the Oprah Winfrey show is on, and the day's topic is "Our neighbours to the North." There is someone on the screen talking about how "these Canadians" are all very nice but they're not exactly exciting: if you visit Canada, it's like stepping back into the past; they're about ten years behind the times, and they don't have any "get-up-and-go." Now, if you are like many Canadians, your hackles would have begun to rise, or at the

■ Social identity: Your group and you

FIGURE 4.9 World Cup soccer excitement in Toronto and Chinese New Year celebrations

very least, you would have stopped and listened. When the expression "these Canadians" was used, they were referring to *you*—and you were just about to be saddled with a negative social identity.

The importance of social identity is evident here, and you can see some of its implications. In the example above, if you could magically transport yourself into the TV show, you might want to re-establish a more positive view of your group by describing the good things about Canada. Further, you might point out that America isn't so perfect.... This is just what social identity suggests: An individual who has a negative social identity is motivated to improve it. This often involves a clash of competing identities with other groups and can lead to prejudice and conflict. Social identity theorists would characterize the numerous nationalist movements and ethnic conflicts that have occurred around the world as examples of the struggle for a separate and positively evaluated social identiy (e.g., Taylor & Moghaddam, 1987). We will discuss the implications of social identity to the area of prejudice and discrimination in the next chapter (chapter 5).

Social identity theory has generated a great deal of research, particularly in Europe where it originated. In Canada, a number of researchers have worked with Tajfel and his colleagues (e.g., Taylor & Moghaddam, 1987; Bourhis, Giles, Leyens, & Tajfel, 1979). One recent example of such work from the United States is the **Collective Self-esteem Scale**. The goal of the scale is to measure feelings about the social groups to which the individual belongs (Luhtanen & Crocker, 1992): an individual's sense of *social identity*. This test assesses self-esteem with respect to membership in social groups. The items deal with how subjects feel about the social groups to which they belong, how they feel about their contributions to those groups, how others evaluate the groups, and how important the memberships are to their identity. Four different components (or factors) are measured by this new scale, as shown in Table 4.2.

Presumably, other more specific aspects of social identity could be measured in the same general way. For example, items such as "I often regret that I belong to some of the social groups I do" could be rewritten as "I often regret that I am a male (or, a Canadian, Catholic, homosexual, or Irish-Canadian).

■ The Collective Self-esteem Scale measures a specific aspect of self-esteem: the way an individual evaluates his or her membership in social groups. This scale consists of four components, and sample scale items are shown for each component.

TABLE 4.2
Components of collective self-esteem

The Collective Self-esteem Scale

Membership Component	*Private Component*	*Public Component*	*Identity Component*
I feel I don't have much to offer to the social groups I belong to.	I often regret that I belong to some of the social groups I do.	Overall, my social groups are considered good by others.	The social groups I belong to are an important reflection of who I am.
I am a worthy member of the social groups I belong to.	I feel good about the social groups I belong to.	Most people consider my social groups, on the average, to be more ineffective than other social groups.	Overall, my group memberships have very little to do with how I feel about myself.

Source: Based on information in Luhtanen & Crocker, 1992.

CULTURE AND THE SELF: SOCIAL IDENTITY ACROSS CULTURES

One of the most important aspects of a person's social identity is his or her **culture.** In chapter 1 we emphasized the importance of considering cultural context and recognizing multicultural diversity when studying human social behavior. But before we examine its relationship to the self, we should clarify the meaning of culture. Culture was defined as the organized system of shared meaning, perceptions, and beliefs held by persons belonging to a particular group. The shared understanding of a culture is often communicated among members by a shared language, or for some subcultural groups it is a particular *jargon*, a specialized way of speaking. For example, anyone who has become "computer-literate" knows the specialized language of "RAMs," "down-loading," and "hard-drives." Culture is also expressed in social customs, in cultural artifacts and products (from buildings to eating implements and food), and in artistic works. In Canada, for example, French-Canadian culture has its own system of communication, which has evolved with marked differences from the language spoken in France and has produced its own artistic traditions and cuisine. The shared understanding of a culture is passed from generation to generation and it both shapes, and is shaped by, each successive generation. As Moghaddam, Taylor, and Wright (1993) put it: "In essence, humans have an interactive relationship with culture: we create and shape culture, and are in turn influenced by our own cultural products" (1993, p. 3).

THE INDEPENDENT AND THE INTERDEPENDENT SELF

Two researchers who have written extensively about the importance of culture to the self are Markus and Kitayama (1991a, 1991b). Reviewing a considerable body of research conducted in Asian countries, they have concluded that there are fundamental differences in Eastern and Western conceptions of the self. The **independent conception of self** is of an individual who is separate and distinct from other individuals and from the social and physical environment. Those who have an independent sense of self will see themselves as autonomous and tend to strive to achieve individuality and uniqueness. Their behavior will tend to be influenced by reference to their own thoughts, feelings, and beliefs. This has been characterized as a construal of the self that is particularly Western (meaning, for example, the United States, Canada, and Western Europe):

> The Western conception of the person as a bounded, unique,… dynamic centre
> of awareness, emotion, judgement and action organised into a distinctive
> whole and set contrastively both against other such wholes and against its so-
> cial and natural background is, however incorrigible it may seem to us, a rather
> peculiar idea within the context of the worlds' cultures (Geertz, 1974, p.225).

Independence tends to be seen as the right, and even the healthy, way to be in Western culture. We tell someone to "stand on your own two feet," "think for yourself," "don't follow the crowd," "be true to yourself," but, as Geertz suggested in the quote above, this may not be how most cultures conceptualize the self.

In contrast, the **interdependent conception of self** views it as fundamentally connected to others and to the environment: the self is integrated into the social context. Those who have an interdependent sense of self will strive for acceptance, attempt to fit in with others and to maintain harmonious relations. Their behavior will be more likely to be influenced by the thoughts, feelings, and actions of significant others. Markus and Kitayama suggest that the interdependent construal of the self is more typical of non-Western cultures in Asia, Africa, South America and Southern Europe (see also, Smith & Bond, 1993; Triandis, 1989).

Research has begun to confirm these cultural distinctions in self-concept. Cousins (1989) found greater context-dependence in the self-concepts of students from Japan (an Eastern culture) compared to those from the United States (a Western culture). Half his subjects were asked to complete the Twenty Statements Test. This test is designed to elicit an individual's *spontaneous self-concept* and asks respondents to provide twenty answers to the question "Who am I?" However, a second version of this test was provided for the second group of subjects, asking them to describe themselves in various contexts (e.g., at home, at school, with close friends). As shown in Figure 4.10, when no context was provided, American students included more abstract and context-free personal trait statements such as "I am lazy" or "I am sociable" (an average of 57.8 percent of statements) compared to the Japanese (average 18.6 percent). In fact, when there was no context provided, Japanese students often spontaneously provided one for their behavior (e.g. "I am one who plays mah-jongg on Friday nights"). However, when a specific context was provided, the findings were reversed: Japanese students produced more personal trait statements (on average, 41.2 percent of statements) than American students (on average, 25.7 percent of statements). As might be expected from the conceptualizations of the interdependent and the independent self, the Japanese self-concept was more bound to particular contexts, whereas the American self-concept was more context-free. These results suggest that the *interdependent* self-concept might vary with the particular social context in which an individual found him or herself and, thus, be inconsistent from one situation to another. On the other hand, the *independent* self, being relatively context-free, might be expected to be more consistent and more clearly distinct from its environment.

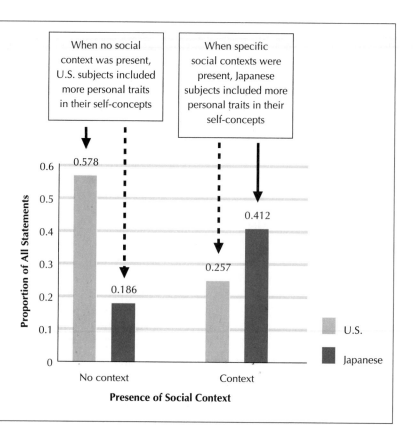

■ The independent and interdependent self in context and context-free

FIGURE 4.10 When asked "Who am I?" without any accompanying social context, students in the United States described themselves in terms of personal attributes to a greater extent than students in Japan. However, when the students were asked the same question with respect to specific social contexts (e.g., "Who am I at home … at school … with close friends…"), Japanese students were more likely to describe themselves in terms of personal attributes. These findings suggest the American self-concept tends to be more independent of social context, whereas the Japanese self-concept tends to be more dependent on the social context in which the self is considered.

Source: Based on data from Cousins, 1989.

Clarity and esteem in the independent and the interdependent self

How is self-esteem related to these cultural differences in the self-concept? A study comparing Canadian and Japanese students (Heine, Lehman, Okugawa, & Campbell, 1992) began to explore this issue. These researchers examined the clarity and consistency of the self-concept as it related to self-esteem. Japanese students who were on an eight-month exchange program at the University of British Columbia were compared to a sample of undergraduates from the same university. The student body at UBC is richly multicultural, as in most Canadian universities. However, in order to ensure that the cultural background of this second group was clearly Western, this study used only those students who were at least third generation Canadian, or second generation Canadian of European descent. The measure of self-concept clarity mentioned previously was used (Campbell, Trapnell, Katz, & Lavallee, 1992), testing the extent to which individuals feel that they have a clear (e.g., "In general I have a clear sense of who I am and what I am"), consistent (e.g., "I seldom experience conflict between the different aspects of my personality") and unchanging (e.g., "My beliefs about myself don't often change") understanding of their own self.

In line with Markus and Kitayama's cultural distinction between the independent and interdependent self (1991), they predicted that Canadian subjects would show greater self-concept clarity than Japanese. Further, because the consistency and clarity of the self-concept should be more important to an independent than an interdependent sense of self, they anticipated that self-concept clarity would be more related to self-esteem for Canadians than for Japanese. This is exactly what was found: Canadian subjects scored higher on the measure of self-concept clarity than Japanese subjects, and these scores showed a stronger relation to measures of self-esteem for the Canadian subjects (r=.69) than for the Japanese subjects (r=.37). Not only was the sense of self more distinct and consistent for Canadians in this study, but Canadians who had a very clear self-concept had higher self-esteem than those with an unclear self-concept. In contrast, for Japanese subjects self-concept clarity was much less strongly related to self-esteem. As Heine and his colleagues suggest: "the Japanese seem less likely to view their selves as unchanging and constant across different occasions and situations.... [Further,] reduced correlations between clarity and self-esteem for the Japanese suggest that relatively less importance is ascribed to maintaining a consistent and autonomous sense of self, compared with the Canadians."

In sum, research has begun to explore the nature of these differing cultural conceptions of the self. And indeed, findings seem to have far-reaching implications for the *personal* self, as discussed in the first section of this chapter. For example, the research above on self-concept clarity suggests that self-esteem may be differently determined for those from different cultures. In a second area of the personal self, Gudykunst and colleagues (e.g., Gudykunst, Gao, & Franklyn-Stokes, 1992) adapted the original Self-monitoring Scale for Eastern respondents. Using this revised scale, they found that American and British subjects scored high on items measuring monitoring of *own* behavior, whereas Japanese and Chinese subjects score high on items measuring monitoring of *others'* behavior. Such research underlines the importance of culture to the self and, in general, suggests greater cultural variation in the sense of self than had orginally been assumed by many Western researchers. If the sense of self is closely bound to one's culture, what happens when a person moves from one culture to live in another? Surely, the "culture-shock" (Oberg, 1960) must create tremendous stresses for the individual? The difficulties of adjusting to a new culture have been explored in John Berry's classic research described in the section, "Acculturation: the Immigrant Experience."

Acculturation: The Immigrant Experience

Many readers or their parents will have experienced the tremendous upheaval of immigration: traveling thousands of miles across the world to a strange land with stranger customs and perhaps a different language. The attempt to take in this new context is overwhelming at first. But that is the least of your problems. You may have to find and settle into a new home, a new job, a new community, while you are more than likely suffering from a severe case of homesickness and are sharply missing family or the friends you have left behind. John Berry has been studying the effects of this experience and the stress it involves since the 1960s. He has carried out extensive research and devised a complex model of what is termed *acculturative stress* (Berry, Kim, Minde, & Mok, 1987).

The process of **acculturation** involves changes in culture which result from continuous, first-hand contact between two distinct cultural groups (Redfield, Linton, & Herskovits, 1936). At the individual level, when applied to individual members of cultural groups, this process is termed *psychological acculturation*. Acculturation occurs most commonly when there is large-scale migration. Canada's multicultural population was formed in this way. Both immigrants and resident populations may suffer from acculturative stress if change in their own culture is involved. The obvious example here is Canada's First Nations, whose way of life was changed extensively, and in some cases completely destroyed, by contact with colonial immigrants. Also notice that for aboriginal people generally, contact with other cultures is not voluntary: that is, they do not choose to undergo acculturation—often it is forced upon them.

Individuals who undergo the period of adjustment that immigration entails, may suffer from **acculturative stress**: a reduction in the health status of individuals that is related to the process of psychological acculturation and includes physical, psychological, and social difficulties. For example, individuals suffering acculturative stress may experience an increase in psychosomatic symptoms such as headaches or stomach upsets, anxiety and depression due to the changes and losses involved in immigration, and they may feel confused in identity or alienated from society, at least for a while. Such problems are not an inevitable outcome of acculturation, and in some cases it can enhance a person's life in the long-run.

Berry et al.'s model of acculturative stress is complex, as is the experience it describes. It suggests that many factors can affect the level of acculturative stress, from the individual's personal characteristics, to the nature of the larger or host society, the form of acculturation that is desired, and the type of cultural group from which the individual comes. We will consider these latter two moderating factors: the mode or form of acculturation and the type of acculturating group.

MODES OF ACCULTURATION

Berry proposes that the consequences for an acculturating group or individual will partly depend upon their attitudes to contact with respect to two factors: (1) the maintenance of their own group's cultural identity; and (2) the value given to relations with the larger society. Whether groups or individuals are high or low on each of these dimensions will determine their choice of four different ideologies or modes of acculturation: (1) *Integration*—places a high value on maintenance of own group culture, but is also highly interested in relating to the larger society; (2) *Assimilation*—puts little value on maintenance of own cultural identity and seeks relations with the larger society; (3) *Separation*—places a high value on maintenance of own group's cultural identity and places little value on relations with the larger society; and (4) *Marginalization*—places little value on maintenance of own cultural group and little value on contact with the larger

►

society. Berry suggests that often the latter is not a chosen mode of acculturation but results from enforced cultural loss and exclusion through discrimination by the larger society.

This framework can be used to describe the ideology of an acculturating group, a nation, or an individual. For example, the multicultural policy of Canada is *integrationist*, encouraging groups to retain their own cultural heritage, while also participating in the larger society. In contrast, a Quebec *separatist* might place a high value on maintenance of Quebec's cultural heritage and deemphasize relations with the larger society, to the extent that the larger society is seen as a threat to cultural identity.

There is potential for tension and conflict in Canada between groups with differing ideologies, or between those groups and the national policy of multiculturalism. For example, Berry and colleagues (Berry, 1976) measured acculturation attitudes among members of ten aboriginal samples across Canada. In eight of these ten Native groups, they found a negative correlation between stress and two of the modes: integration and assimilation. This indicates that, in general, the greater subjects' belief in integration or assimilation, the less stress they were experiencing. Across all ten Native samples, there was a positive correlation between separatist beliefs and stress: those attempting to distance themselves from or reject the larger society were experiencing greater stress. For a person with separatist beliefs, contact with the larger society is undesirable by definition and most likely to involve stress, whereas for an integrationist or an assimilationist, contact is welcomed and, therefore, less likely to be as stressful.

NATURE OF THE ACCULTURATING GROUP

The type of acculturation that a group is undergoing can also affect the experience of its members. Berry et al. classify acculturating groups on two dimensions: (1) the *voluntariness* of their contact with the larger culture; and (2) the extent of *mobility* involved in contact. That is, the extent to which a group is permanent and settled (sedentary) or temporary and still in transition (migrant). Using this classification, as shown in Table 4.3, they identified five separate types of group: ethnic groups, Native people, refugees, immigrants, and sojourners. For groups such as settled *ethnic groups*, they or their ancestors chose to travel and stay in this society. Therefore, contact can be regarded as voluntary.

■ Types of acculturating group and their levels of acculturative stress

TABLE 4.3 Groups going through acculturation (the process of cultural change resulting from contact between cultures) vary in (1) the extent to which the contact is voluntary and (2) the extent to which they are mobile. Figures below each group show average levels of acculturative stress.

EXTENT OF MOBILITY	VOLUNTARINESS OF CONTACT	
	VOLUNTARY	*INVOLUNTARY*
SEDENTARY	Ethnic Groups (Anglocelts & European) 2.68	Native Peoples (Cree, Ojibway, Carrier & Tsimshiam) 5.45
MIGRANT	(i) Immigrants (Korean) 3.08 (ii) Sojourners (Foreign Students) 4.14	Refugees (Vietnamese) 5.62

Source: Adapted from Berry, Kim, Minde, & Mok (1987).

▶

In terms of mobility, they are sedentary: that is, long-term, permanent residents. *Native peoples* are also sedentary (extremely long-term and permanent residents), but, as mentioned above, their contact with the larger society was not voluntary and was often destructive. *Refugees* also have involuntary contact: that is, migration was not their choice, they were forced from their homes. Further, being relatively recent arrivals, they are still unsettled within the society (or migrant). Two types of voluntary and migrant groups are identified: *immigrants*, who are recent arrivals but who have chosen to come and stay in the society; and *sojourners*, recent and temporary visitors. Berry et al. reasoned that acculturation experiences would be less stressful for those who are involved in voluntary contact with the larger society and for those who are more sedentary. That is, voluntary migrants would have a more positive attitude towards contact, and those who were settled and permanently resident in Canada would have a greater sense of security and belonging compared to recent or temporary residents.

Data were gathered over more than ten years from 1197 subjects, who were part of 19 separate samples. There are multiple samples for some types of acculturating group (10 Native samples, 4 ethnic samples, and 3 sojourner samples), but only one sample for other types (refugees and immigrants), though individual samples are over 70 subjects each. Their measure of acculturative stress was adapted from the Cornell Medical Index by Cawte (1972) and contained items measuring psychosomatic symptoms, anxiety and irritability, and depression.

Average scores for each group are displayed immediately beneath them in Table 4.3. As you can see, voluntariness of contact was a major factor in acculturative stress, with the highest average scores shown by refugees and Native people (5.62 and 5.45 respectively). Where contact is voluntary, average stress is lower, the lowest being the ethnic groups (2.68) and immigrants and sojourners being somewhat higher (3.08 and 4.14, respectively). Mobility appears to have less relationship to acculturative stress. Although not as dramatic, it can be seen from Table 4.3 that the degree of permanence or mobility has some relation to level of stress. As Berry et al. predicted, the more temporary the stay, the greater the stress (for foreign students compared to Korean immigrants, and for both those groups compared to settled ethnic groups). Caution is necessary in interpretation of these data, however, as they were collected over a long period and for somewhat different purposes.

A number of other factors were found to be associated with lower stress, including higher education, knowledge of English, similarity of social structure between the culture of origin and the larger society, having a system of social support and Canadian friends if one is an immigrant, and even similarity of climate between one's homeland and Canada. Clearly the relationship between acculturative stress, characteristics of individuals, their group, and the larger society is not simple. Yet John Berry and his colleagues have undertaken the task of comparing Canada's many subcultures in terms of these factors and have contributed to our understanding of the experience of cultural adjustment.

CROSS-CULTURAL PSYCHOLOGY: COMPARING CULTURES

Since the 1970s, social psychologists have begun systematically to examine social behavior in different cultures. This is the task of **cross-cultural psychology,** which is defined as "the systematic study of behavior and experience as it occurs in different cultures, is influenced by culture, or results in changes in existing culture" (Triandis, 1980, p.1). Cross-cultural psychology, therefore, is concerned with *differences* between cultures in behavior and experience, the way in which culture *influences* behavior and experience, and with *changes* in culture. This task involves more than simple replication of studies first carried out in the United States, followed by examination of any differences found. The cross-cultural approach has required a fundamental re-thinking of theory and research in psychology. We will first examine some of the original theoretical concepts that have emerged from cross-cultural psychology. These concepts lay the groundwork for research in cross-cultural psychology. In the second part of this section, we will describe some research that has challenged a number of traditional and well-established "truths" in social psychology.

CONCEPTS OF CROSS-CULTURAL PSYCHOLOGY

Before discussing cross-cultural research, it is useful to define a number of terms or concepts that will be used later. In addition, exploring the implications of these concepts can help us to begin to think about the importance of culture in our own social behavior. Perhaps you have been *ethnocentric* and assumed the kind of behavior you and your group exhibit is universal (or *etic*).

Ethnocentrism: Seeing things from your culture's perspective

If you have travelled to a foreign country or spent time with people from another cultural group, you may have found yourself thinking that their customs were strange or, perhaps, that their food was odd and their accents funny. If so, you were displaying **ethnocentrism**. This term was first used in 1906 by William Sumner and was defined by him as: "the view of things in which one's own group is the centre of everything and all others are scaled and rated with reference to it" (in Brewer, 1986, p. 88). That is, the culture in which you were raised tends to be seen as the "centre of everything," the norm, and, by comparison, other cultural groups are seen as "abnormal" or "wrong"—they don't quite do things in the right way. Beyond this, ethnocentrism can often make us deride other groups' customs as ridiculous, or make us feel morally superior. In sum, ethnocentrism is the cultural equivalent of egocentrism. When we say that someone is egocentric, we mean that they only see things from their own point of view. Someone who is ethnocentric only sees things from the perspective of their own culture. Adorno and colleagues (1950) developed an Ethnocentrism Scale for use with European-Americans in the post-war years. The following items from this scale can give you an idea of ethnocentrism of that time:

> America may not be perfect, but the American way has brought us about as close as human beings can get to a perfect society;

> The people who raise all the talk about putting Negroes on the same level as whites are mostly radical agitators trying to stir up conflict;

> Certain religious sects who refuse to salute the flag should be forced to conform to such patriotic action, or else be abolished.

A highly ethnocentric person would strongly agree with such statements. It is obvious from these scale items that strong ethnocentrism is a part of prejudice, and this will be further discussed in the next chapter.

You may not be strongly ethnocentric, but there are few people who have not at times seen things from their culture's perspective, taken pride in their groups' superiorities, or ridiculed the ways of other groups. Many Canadians believe that they live in the best country in the world—by comparison, other countries just don't match up. Social psychology itself may have been guilty of ethnocentrism (or "eurocentrism") when it overgeneralized its theories and findings based on a largely European-American population to other non-Western subcultures within that society or to other nations.

Etic versus emic: A universal or a cultural perspective?

A distinction made by John Berry (1969) has proved very useful for examining ethnocentric biases in social psychology. He suggested that social psychological research and findings can be approached in two different ways. An **etic analysis** of social behavior focuses on universal factors—ones that apply across all cultures. For example, all cultures have family relations or a set of cultural norms. An **emic analysis** focuses upon factors that are culturally specific—that vary between cultures and have specific meaning within a particular culture. For example, the concepts of "masculinity" or "the self," as we saw above, have different meanings in different cultures.

The importance of this distinction is in its implications for social-psychological research. An etic analysis has often led researchers to assume that their measures, or the distinctions they made between variables, were of equal significance in another culture. If other cultures were of interest, studies originating largely in the United States would be replicated in those cultures without change (Smith & Bond, 1993). Berry terms this approach to research an *"imposed etic."* We have seen, in relation to the self, that we cannot make assumptions of universality of meaning between cultures. For example, when another of Adorno et al.'s scales (the "F" scale, 1950) was used in Turkey, items in the scale did not correlate with each other as they had in the U.S.A. testing. This suggests that the meaning of scale items was less closely related in a Turkish context (Kagitcibasi, 1970). The scale was also found not to predict anti-black prejudice among white South Africans, as it had in the U.S.A.(Pettigrew, 1958). Many concepts used in research have been assumed to be etic when in fact they are emic.

The increasing awareness of this danger has led to a call by Canadians and non-Western psychologists for indigenous psychologies (Berry, 1989; Moghaddam, 1990; Sinha, 1992). Psychologists would begin by examining psychological issues that arise within their own culture and would analyze them from that culture's perspective. This is an emic level of analysis. A comparison of such indigenous findings could then more clearly identify universal or etic factors: ones that arose across all cultural contexts. John Berry has termed this approach a *"derived etic."* This approach is not common, as yet, but researchers from the West are increasingly aware of the need to understand the meaning of psychological phenomena and terms within the culture studied.

An example of such research can be found in the area of cross-cultural values. In constructing a set of values for cross-cultural comparison, Schwartz (1992; Schwartz & Bilsky, 1987) included values from both Western and non-Western sources. In addition, he asked colleagues in countries where he collected data, to insert values from their own culture that did not seem to be represented in the final list. Analysis of his results suggested that the values important to people in the twenty countries studied, can be represented by eight to ten value-clusters, shown in Table 4.4. These represent the best attempt, as yet, to identify a universal set of values. Further research is needed, however, to verify their universality.

Individualism and collectivism

A value dimension that emerged from earlier cross-cultural research (Hofstede, 1980) and has received particular attention is the individualism-collectivism dimension. **Individualism** refers to a focus on individual rights and goals, individual self-determination, and the independence of the individual from others. **Collectivism**, in contrast, refers to the importance of group goals (those of the community, work, or family groups) rather than those of the individual; individuals are seen as interdependent with their groups, and importance is given to the need to maintain harmony and balance between people. The dimension of individualism-collectivism is reflected by the values of self-direction and conformity, for example, in Schwartz's work (1992, see Table 4.4).

> ■ A "derived etic" approach to cross-cultural values
>
> **TABLE 4.4** Schwartz (1992) used values derived from both Western and non-Western research in his value-set for cross-cultural research in twenty countries around the world. Analysis of subjects' ratings of each of these values as "a guiding principle in my life" revealed that between eight and ten value-clusters applied in all twenty countries.
>
> 1. **Self-direction**: independent thought and action, choosing, creating, exploring.
> 2. **Stimulation**: need for variety, excitement, challenge in life.
> 3. **Hedonism**: seeking pleasure, enjoying life.
> 4. **Achievement**: success through competence, gaining social approval.
> 5. **Power**: attaining social status and prestige, control, or dominance over others and over resources.
> 6. **Security**: safety, harmony, stability of society, relationships, and self.
> 7. **Conformity**: restraint of actions, inclination and impulses that would upset others or violate social expectations.
> 8. **Tradition**: respect, commitment, and acceptance of customs.
> 9. **Benevolence**: preservation and enhancement of the welfare of other people (e.g., forgiveness, helpfulness, honesty, loyalty).
> 10. **Universalism**: appreciation and tolerance for all people and for nature (e.g., equality, protecting environment, world at peace).
>
> *Source:* Schwartz (1992).

You have probably also realized the parallel between these terms and the distinction made between the independent and interdependent construal of the self in the preceding section. Indeed, as with the concept of the self, Western cultures (e.g., United States, Canada, Western Europe) tend to be more individualist, and Eastern and many other non-Western cultures (e.g., in Africa, South and Central America and Southern Europe) tend to be more collectivist. Although distinctions between cultures can be made on many dimensions, this particular one has proved useful in research because cultures that vary on this dimesion have been shown to vary in other psychological processes from the cognitive to the interpersonal and the intergroup (see Triandis, 1990). We will discuss some of this research in the next section.

CROSS-CULTURAL RESEARCH: QUESTIONING SOME TRADITIONAL FINDINGS

One measure of the impact of cross-cultural psychology is that most recent textbooks include sections on this topic and some texts are wholly devoted to it (e.g, Matsumoto, 1994; Moghaddam, Wright, & Taylor, 1993). Furthermore, the expansion of cross-cultural research in the past decade has been astonishing (see Smith & Bond, 1993), and its findings are fascinating. We will describe a small but important selection of this research in three major areas of social psychology: social cognition, social interaction, and group behavior.

Social cognition: Attributional biases

Two major biases in attribution that were discussed in chapter 2 have been challenged by cross-cultural research: the self-serving bias and the fundamental attribution error.

It is well established in a North American context that we have a tendency to be self-enhancing. That is, we tend to process information so as to enhance or maintain our own level of self-esteem. We even tend to be more optimistic about our own future, seeing it as much rosier than other people's (Taylor, 1989). An example of this tendency from the area of causal attribution is the *self-serving bias*, which is the tendency to take credit for our own positive outcomes (make internal attributions) and deny responsibility for our negative outcomes (make external attributions). Western research had shown this to be a general tendency, except among those with low self-esteem or depression (Miller & Ross, 1975; Taylor, 1989). However, recent cross-cultural research has often failed to find this bias among those from more collectivist cultural backgrounds.

For example, in a Canadian context, Moghaddam, Ditto, and Taylor (1990) found that women who were immigrants from India tended to attribute both success and failure to internal causes. A similar pattern, showing no difference in attribution for success and failure, was also found among junior and high school students in Hong Kong (Hau & Salili, 1991). One Canadian study put this attributional bias strongly to the test by ensuring that the failure and success situations were very important to subjects. Fry and Ghosh (1980) studied eight-to-ten-year old Canadians who were either of European-Canadian or (East) Indian-Canadian backgrounds but were similar in socioeconomic status. They were given bogus feedback indicating that they had done very well or very poorly at a task. Under conditions of high involvement, they were told that their performance on the task indicated their intelligence and, to add to the pressure, that the results would be shared with their peers, their parents, and their teachers. After they received the bogus feedback, subjects rated various internal and external causes of their task performance on five-point scales, ranging from 1 (not at all important) to 5 (very important).

Results (in Figure 4.11) indicate that only EuroCanadian children showed the self-serving bias, giving very high ratings to internal causes (ability and effort) when they were successful and low ratings to internal causes when they failed. IndoCanadian children, on the other hand, took less credit (made fewer internal attributions) when they succeeded and only slightly less credit when they failed.

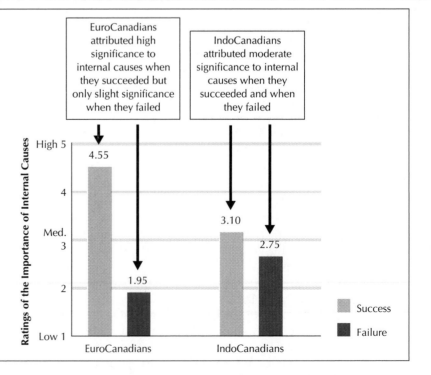

■ **Self-serving bias across cultures**

FIGURE 4.11 EuroCanadian and IndoCanadian children's average ratings of the importance of internal causes (ability and effort) when they succeeded and when they failed. While EuroCanadian children give high significance to their own ability and effort when they are successful and very little significance to effort and ability when they fail, IndoCanadian children's attributions vary little whether they succeed or fail. Results suggest that it is only EuroCanadian children who demonstrate a self-serving bias in attribution.

Source: Adapted from Fry and Ghosh (1980).

The tendency for those from more collectivist cultures to make fewer internal attributions when they succeed (and often more internal attributions for failure) has been termed a *self-effacement or modesty bias* and has been shown to occur among Chinese (Crittenden, 1991; Bond, Leung, & Wan, 1982) and Japanese (Kashima & Triandis, 1986). Further, Chinese students who used this style of attribution were liked more by their peers than those who did not (Bond et al., 1982), suggesting that such attributions are an important part of social relations.

There is also evidence from cross-cultural research that these cultural styles of attribution are learnt through socialization: they increase as we get older. This has been most strongly demonstrated in relation to the fundamental attribution error (Miller, 1984). The *fundamental attribution error,* a tendency to attribute others' behavior to internal causes, shows similar cross-cultural patterns to the self-serving bias. That is, it is much less common in collectivist cultures than in individualistic cultures and in some cases does not appear to occur at all (see Korten, 1984; Miller, 1984; Shweder & Bourne, 1982).

In sum, cross-cultural research has shown that those from more collectivist cultures either do not use the self–serving bias and the fundamental attribution error, or use them less than North Americans. Further, the evidence that these cultural differences in attribution increase with age suggests that social learning in line with cultural beliefs may be the source of these differing attributional styles. If internal cognitive processes such as self-concept formation and causal reasoning are shown to vary between cultures, it seems probable that social interaction will also vary. One area where research is beginning to accumulate evidence is that of justice or fairness in social exchange.

Social interaction: Fairness in social exchange

When do we perceive a social interaction, or the distribution of resources between people, as fair or just? This has been a question of philosophers going back to the time of Aristotle and continues to be important today (e.g., Rawls, 1970). Justice is usually regarded as central to the organization of society or governments. At the individual level, social psychologists have been examining the issue of individual perceptions of fairness since the 1960s (Adams, 1965; Greenberg & Cohen, 1982). The dominant model of fairness or justice perception has been equity theory (Walster, Walster, & Berscheid, 1978). Simply stated, this theory suggests that resource distributions will be perceived as fair when they are proportional to *individual inputs*. That is, people should receive what they deserve on the basis of their inputs or contributions. For example, in a work setting you would expect the appropriate pay (resource distribution) based on hours worked or experience on the job (your contribution). Walster et al. (1978) claim that it is not only economic relationships that use the equity principle. It will also determine the satisfaction and stability of intimate and loving relationships.

This *equity principle* of justice (suggesting that resources should be distributed on the basis of individual inputs) can be contrasted with others. The two major alternatives are the *equality principle,* which suggests that resources should be distributed equally to everyone in a group regardless of individual differences in contributions, and the *needs principle,* according to which resources should be distributed on the basis of individual needs. Equity theory has been characterized by one critic as reflecting a North American form of economic individualism (Sampson, 1978). Others have pointed out that even in North America, different principles of justice are used for the distribution of different kinds of resources (e.g., Lerner, 1981; Leventhal, 1976). So, for example, although in Canada the *equity* principle is usually applied in economic exchange, we distribute medical resources according to *needs* and believe that everyone should be *equal* before the law.

Cross-cultural differences in perceptions of fairness might be expected on the individualism-collectivism dimension. Individualist cultures stress individual entitlement and achievement. The *equity* principle, which bases resource distribution on individual inputs, should be seen as fair more frequently in such cultures. Indeed, hundreds of studies have demonstrated its widespread use in the United States (see, Greenberg & Cohen, 1982; Walster et al., 1978). However, in collectivist cultures, group goals are paramount and harmony in relationships is stressed. Research in a Western context has shown that if subjects are asked to share resources so as to maintain harmony, the distribution they tend to choose is equality (Lerner, 1974; Leventhal, Michaels, & Sanford, 1972) and when individuals are very closely linked (relationships of dependency or "identity") or resources are scarce, then there is a tendency to prefer distribution on the basis of the needs of participants (Greenberg, 1982; Lerner, 1982). We could, therefore, expect a greater endorsement of the *equality* or the *needs* principles in more collectivist cultures.

A study by Leung and Bond (1984) found that, compared to Americans, Chinese students showed a greater preference for *equal* distributions of money when friends worked together on a task. However, when strangers worked together, an *equity* distribution (on the basis of individuals' contributions to the group) was preferred by Chinese students to a greater extent than American students. The fact that Chinese students made a marked distinction in resource distributions between friends and between strangers was interpreted as showing their greater concern to maintain harmony among friends. American students, on the other hand emphasized the importance of individual entitlement by more closely adhering to equity in relationships with both friends *and* strangers.

Another study carried out in India and the United States examined the needs principle in addition to equity and equality (Murphy-Berman, Berman, Singh, Pachauri, & Kumar, 1984). Researchers asked subjects to distribute a hypothetical bonus or pay cut between two workers who were needy or meritorious. The needy person was described as an average worker who was in a poor financial situation and had an illness in the family. The meritorious person was described as an excellent worker who was in adequate financial shape. Subjects were given an opportunity to allocate the bonus or the pay cut in one of three ways: (1) favoring the needy person (following the *needs* principle); (2) favoring the meritorious person (following the *equity* principle); or (3) equally to both workers (following the *equality* principle). Figure 4.12 shows the results for distribution of the bonus. Indian subjects consistently favored allocation according to needs in both types of distribution and equity least, but this was particulary marked when there were cutbacks (a scarcity of resources). American subjects, on the other hand, resolved the dilemma between the meritorious (excellent) worker and the needy (average) worker by allocating according to equality or equity when a bonus was distributed, and allocating according to equality most often when there was a cut-back. Overall, Indian respondents showed greater use of the needs principle and less use of the equity and equality principles than American subjects.

A preference for equality over equity among more collectivist cultures has been shown for Koreans compared to Americans (Leung & Park, 1986), for Japanese compared to Australians (Kashima & Triandis, 1986; Mann, Radford, & Kanagawa, 1985) and for Chinese compared to Americans (Hui, Triandis, & Yee, 1991). In support of the idea that it is differences in values that determine these culture differences, some studies have shown that those individuals from any country who endorsed more interdependent or collective values, also showed greater preference for equality (Hui, Triandis, & Yee, 1991; Leung & Iwawaki, 1988). In reviewing the available evidence, Smith and Bond (1993) conclude that "studies of distributive justice... yield a rather clear picture. In more collectivist countries there is greater reliance on the criteria of equality and needs *within* the in-group, but greater use of the equity criterion *outside* the group." However, we can see from the results discussed above that the particular social and economic context needs to be taken into account as well as the cultural background of the individual when predicting usage of these principles of justice.

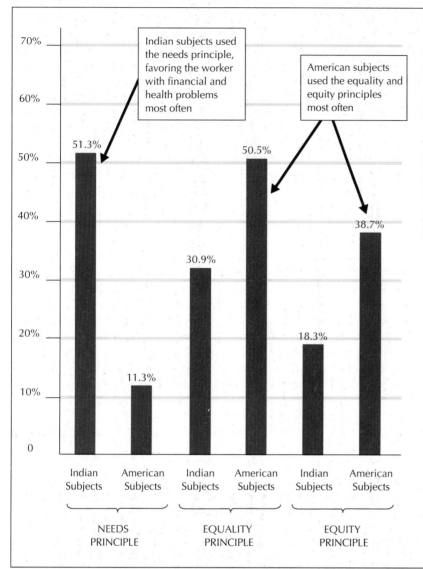

Justice in India and the United States: Needs, equality, or equity?

FIGURE 4.12 When Indians and Americans were asked to distribute a bonus between a needy person (needs principle of justice) and a meritorious person (equity principle of justice), Indians favored the needs principle of justice more and equality and equity principles less than Americans.

Source: Adapted from Murphy–Berman et al.(1984).

Within the chart:

- Indian subjects used the needs principle, favoring the worker with financial and health problems most often
- American subjects used the equality and equity principles most often

Bar values:
- NEEDS PRINCIPLE: Indian Subjects 51.3%, American Subjects 11.3%
- EQUALITY PRINCIPLE: Indian Subjects 30.9%, American Subjects 50.5%
- EQUITY PRINCIPLE: Indian Subjects 18.3%, American Subjects 38.7%

Group processes: Cultural differences in conflict-resolution

People all over the world spend much of their time working together in groups. At work, in school, and at play, groups constitute an important fact of daily life. Do these groups function in the same manner everywhere? Or are the processes that take place within them influenced by cultural factors? A growing body of evidence points to the following conclusion: The events that occur within groups, and the relationships that develop among their members, are strongly affected by cultural forces. In order to provide you with some insight into the nature of such effects, we'll examine cultural differences with respect to a key aspect of group functioning: conflict-resolution techniques.

Individualist cultures tend to value individual goals over group goals and individual rights and needs over collective responsibilities. Collectivist cultures, in contrast, tend to value group goals over individual ones and collective needs over individual rights. Differences along this dimension are related to many aspects of group functioning, from how groups handle *free-rider* effects (Yamagishi, 1988) through the extent to which leaders are held responsible for group failures (Takahashi, 1991), as we shall see in chapter 9. Perhaps the impact of such differences in cultural values is most visible, however, in group reactions to conflict. According to Ting-Toomey (1988), a researcher who has studied this issue in detail, people from collectivist cultures show greater concern than people from individualist cultures with saving *others' face*—with others' desire to maintain their self-respect and personal image. This implies that they would avoid humiliating their opponents in a conflict and would try to provide them with an out—a good excuse for a negative performance or a poor outcome. In contrast, people from individualist cultures show much more concern with protecting or enhancing their own image and self-respect—what might be termed *self-face*.

A second difference between people from collectivist and individualist cultures proposed by Ting-Toomey involves specific strategies for resolving ongoing conflicts. Presumably, persons from individualist cultures would tend to use more active strategies, such as direct competition or efforts to collaborate with opponents, while those from collectivist cultures would tend to use such tactics as accommodating their opponents or avoiding conflict altogether.

Research conducted by Ting-Toomey and her colleagues (e.g., Ting-Toomey et al., 1991) provides support for these predictions. In these studies, thousands of persons in various cultures (the United States, Japan, China, Korea, Taiwan) completed questionnaires designed to measure their concern with maintaining their own face and their opponent's face in conflict situations, and other questionnaires designed to measure their preferred techniques for resolving conflicts with others (competition, accommodation, compromise, avoidance, etc.).

Results indicated that, as predicted, persons from China, Korea, and Taiwan all reported more concern with maintaining others' face than participants from the United States. With respect to maintaining their own face, participants from Japan reported the highest concern and those from Korea the lowest concern. Participants from the United States, China, and Taiwan fell in between in this respect.

Cultural differences in preferred modes of handling conflict also emerged. As expected, participants from the United States reported stronger preference for dominating others than did participants from Japan and Korea. In contrast, participants from Taiwan and China showed the strongest preference for giving in to their opponents and for avoiding conflict (see Figure 4.13).

Finally, cultural factors do appear to play an important role where group processes are concerned. Concern with others' and one's own face, preferred means of resolving conflict—these and many other aspects of behavior in group settings are affected by culture. In order fully to understand groups, therefore, we must take account of the cultures in which they operate; failure to do so is like trying to understand the growth of a beautiful plant without considering the soil that nurtures its roots.

To summarize, the cross-cultural research above shows systematic variations on the basis of cultural background, in patterns of attributional bias, in perceptions of fairness or justice between people, and in strategies for resolving group conflict. One dimension for understanding such cultural differences is the collectivism-individualism dimension. Individuals and cultural groups whose values differ along this dimension also show measurable differences in a wide range of behaviors and responses. However, it should be noted that this research is just a beginning. There are other value dimensions upon which cultures differ, and research has not yet explored those (see Schwartz,1992, and the values listed in Table 4.4). Most of the cross-cultural research has been initiated in the West, and very little indigenous input has occurred as yet. Until that time, it is difficult to be sure that research has not imposed Western values and meaning in non-Western settings (Sinha, 1992; Moghaddam 1990). There are, therefore, still many avenues and implications to be explored before we can consider that we have a true grasp of the importance of culture to social behavior.

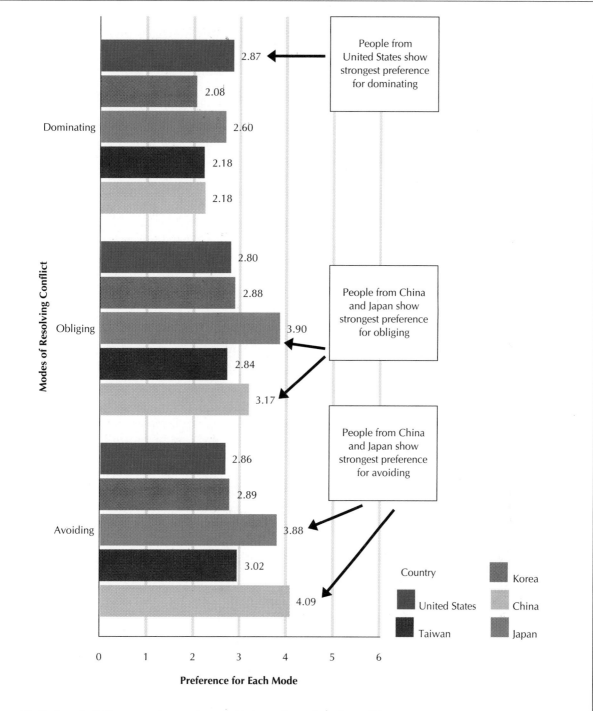

■ Cultural differences in preferred means of resolving conflicts

FIGURE 4.13 As shown here, people from individualist cultures such as the United States showed a stronger preference than people from collectivist cultures such as China and Taiwan for resolving conflicts through dominating. In contrast, people from collectivist cultures showed stronger preferences for resolving conflicts through giving in to opponents and avoiding the situation.

Source: Based on data from Ting-Toomey et al., 1991.

IMPLICATIONS FOR A MULTICULTURAL SOCIETY

The findings of this section have profound implications for social psychology. Social psychologists can no longer assume that findings in one culture apply in others. Indeed, we have seen that some social processes that are well established and widespread in the West, such as the self-serving bias and the fundamental attribution error, can no longer be regarded as universal. Beyond the assumption of universality of results, social psychologists will also have to question the universality of many scales and measurement instruments developed in the West using European-origin subjects.

While cross-cultural psychology has questioned some cherished and long-accepted assumptions of social psychology, it has also opened up new vistas. For example, this approach has already produced new dimensions for understanding social behavior and some methodological innovations. It may eventually provide a way of distinguishing the universal (etic) from the cultural (emic) and ultimately deepen our understanding of the scope of human nature (Matsumoto, 1994).

However, the lessons of cross-cultural theory and research go beyond the purely academic. They have implications for multicultural societies such as Canada and the United States. Like social psychologists, societies can be unwittingly ethnocentric—or, in the case of much of North America, "Eurocentric," assuming that the European forms of behavior and beliefs apply to everyone. If we take the policy of multiculturalism seriously and desire the full participation of Canada's cultural groups, then we must attempt to understand each other's ways of thinking and behaving. And social psychology has an important part to play in the extension of such understanding (Berry, 1984). Unless we continue to learn about each other's cultures, society's Eurocentrism can implicitly exclude groups from their full place in the cultural mosaic.

Social identity refers to an individual's group-based self-concept, where *personal identity* refers to the unique and individual aspects of a person's self-concept. It includes the many facets of one's self-concept and identification with various categories of people defined in terms of sex, race, religion, political affiliation, age, occupation, and so on.

ASPECTS OF THE SELF-CONCEPT AS PERSONAL IDENTITY

A person's self-concept is defined as a *schema*—an organized collection of beliefs and feelings about everything relating to that individual's self-knowledge. Such schemas guide the way we process self-relevant information. In addition to our current self, we can and do imagine a variety of possible selves we could be. *Self-esteem* refers to self-evaluation—the attitude a person has about himself or herself. Positive self-esteem occurs when there is minimal difference between an individual's ideal and his or her current behavior, and most evidence indicates that a positive self-evaluation is a beneficial attribute. *Self-efficacy* is the aspect of self that involves a person's perceived abilities and competencies to deal with specific tasks. Feelings of self-efficacy lead to better task performance on the job, in school, in interpersonal situations, and in dealing with fears. *Self-monitoring behavior* refers to whether a person regulates his or her behavior in response to the external situation and the reactions of others (high self-monitors) or on the basis of internal factors (low self-monitors). High self-monitoring is associated with a positive response to image-based advertising, low behavioral consistency across situations, and interpersonal preferences based on the activity at hand rather than on feelings about the other individual. *Self-focusing* refers to the extent to which one's attention is directed inward toward the self or outward toward the environment.

SOCIAL IDENTITY IN A MULTICULTURAL CONTEXT

Social Identity theory suggests that the groups to which we belong form an important part of our identity. We are motivated to achieve a positive and distinctive social identity. Cultural groups are an important source of social identity and can determine our understanding of the self. Cultures can vary in terms of whether they have an *independent* or *interdependent conception of the self*. When individuals come in contact with those from other cultures, such as through the process of immigration, *acculturative stress* can occur. This is the psychological stress resulting from *acculturation*, cultural change associated with prolonged cross-cultural contact. The complex process of acculturation and acculturative stress depends upon the nature of the acculturating group, beliefs about modes of acculturation, the nature of the host society and individual characteristics and experiences of the immigrant.

CROSS-CULTURAL PSYCHOLOGY

Cross-cultural psychology investigates the influence of culture, cultural differences and cultural change. If we are raised in one culture, we can suffer from *ethnocentrism* and evaluate other cultural groups from the perspective of our own. Social psychology has tended to have a somewhat ethnocentric perspective in understanding social behavior. It has tended to assume that it is studying *etic* factors—universal factors—when in fact it is studying factors which are specific to Western culture—that is, they are *emic* or culturally specific. An important dimension for comparison of cultures is the *individualism-collectivism* dimension. Western cultures tend to be individualist, focusing on individual goals and independence. Eastern and other non-Western cultures tend to be more collectivist, focusing on group goals and the interdependence of individuals. Research has shown that cultural variations on this dimension also predict differences in social cognition, perceptions of fairness, and preference for resolving group conflict.

Acculturation Culture change which results from continuous, first-hand contact between two distinct cultural groups

Acculturative Stress A reduction in health status related to the process of acculturation that can include physical, psychological, and social difficulties.

Collective Self-esteem Scale A measure of self-esteem linked to the person's membership in social groups.

Collectivism A cultural value emphasizing the importance of group goals. Individuals are seen as interdependent with their group.

Cross-cultural Psychology The branch of psychology concerned with the systematic study of cultural differences, cultural influences, and cultural changes in behavior.

Culture The organized system of shared meaning, perceptions, and beliefs held by persons belonging to a particular group. This often includes a particular language or system of communication, social customs and organization, as well as artifacts and artisitic products of the group.

Emic A finding or concept that differs between cultures: that is, it is culturally specific.

Ethnocentrism Evaluating other cultures from the perspective of your own. Your own group standards are used as the norm and other groups are then seen as "abnormal" or "wrong."

Etic A finding or concept that appears to be consistent across cultures: that is, it is universal.

Independent Conception of the Self The self is viewed as separate and distinct from other individuals and from the environment. Such individuals will tend to see themselves as autonomous and unique. This construal of the self is typical of Western cultures.

Individualism A cultural value emphasizing the importance of individual rights and goals. Individuals are seen as independent from others.

Interdependent Conception of the Self The self is viewed as fundamentally connected to others and to the environment: the self is integrated into the social context. Such individuals will strive for acceptance and to maintain harmonious relations with others. This construal of the self is more typical of non-Western cultures.

Personal Identity The unique aspects of the individual's internal and private self-definition.

Possible Selves Mental representations of what we might become, or should become, in the future.

Self Our unique individuality, as delineated by all of our knowledge, feelings, and ideas about ourselves.

Self-concept A system of affective and cognitive structures (schemas) about the self that lends coherence to each individual's self-relevant experiences.

Self-esteem The self-evaluations made by each individual; the general attitude a person holds about himself or herself.

Self-focusing Self-awareness; the directing of attention inward toward oneself as opposed to outward toward the environment.

Self-ideal Discrepancy The difference between a person's perception of how he or she is and how that person believes he or she should be.

Self-monitoring Behavior The degree to which an individual regulates his or her behavior on the basis of the external situation and the reactions of others (high self-monitors) or on the basis of internal factors such as beliefs, attitudes, and values (low self-monitors).

Self-monitoring Scale Snyder's test for measuring individual differences in self-monitoring behavior.

Self-reference Effect The tendency for information related to the self to be processed more efficiently (in several respects) than other forms of information.

Self-schema An organized collection of beliefs and feelings about the self.

Social Identity The group-based aspects of an individual's self-definition, derived from membership in and identification with social groups.

Social Identity Theory The theoretical approach that stresses the importance of a person's *social identity* to the self-concept. Individuals are motivated to achieve or maintain a positive and distinctive social identity.

Bednar, R. L., Wells, M. G., & Peterson, S. R. (1992). *Self-esteem: Paradoxes and innovations in clinical theory and practice*. Washington, DC: American Psychological Association.

A description of a therapeutic process that focuses on the client's self-esteem as a central concern. The therapist emphasizes the situations in which the individual constructs his or her self-evaluations, and the client learns to face problems rather than avoid them. The goal is improved self-esteem and the attendant reduction of various maladaptive symptoms.

FIVE

Prejudice and Discrimination: Understanding Their Nature, Countering Their Effects

Virtually everyone reading this chapter has experience of prejudice or discrimination. You may have been the victim of spiteful remarks about your race, gender, or physical attributes, or perhaps you were systematically excluded by a group on the same basis. If so, you know about prejudice and discrimination from the receiving end. And, if you are like many victims, this has left a lasting and painful memory.

On the other hand, you may have been the perpetrator of prejudice or discrimination. You may have made a negative assumption about someone based on their gender, ethnicity, age, or appearance, or acted negatively towards someone purely on that basis. Perhaps you have repeated a joke that contains racist or sexist stereotypes, or laughed at one. If so, then you know about prejudice and discrimination from the other side—as an actor. In contrast to the experiences of victims, being the perpetrator does not lead to emotional scars, at least for you—in fact, you have probably dismissed any suggestion that *you* could be a "bigot." It is almost certainly inconsistent with your self-concept. After all, you "didn't mean anything" by that joke you told; it's just that the listener "doesn't have any sense of humor!" Our point is that none of us is immune from the experience of prejudice and discrimination as either victim or perpetrator, or both. Even if you are the (very rare) person who has been neither victim nor perpetrator, you have certainly observed its destructive effects in society as a whole.

What, precisely, is *prejudice*, and how does it differ from another term with which we are also, unfortunately, too familiar—*discrimination*? What factors contribute to the existence of prejudice and discrimination? And perhaps even more important, how can these negative forces in human society be reduced? Given the great diversity of the human species, plus the fact that contact among people of different racial, ethnic, and national backgrounds is increasing, these are vital questions and ones with which we surely must grapple in the mid-1990s. In fact, it does not seem too extreme to suggest that overcoming prejudice and discrimination is one of the most crucial tasks confronting humanity today. The alternative—permitting them to exist unchecked—seems to condemn us to an ever-rising tide of hatred and violence. If nothing else, then, social psychology's commitment to understanding, and combating, prejudice and discrimination seems more timely than ever.

■ Realistic conflict theory

FIGURE 5.1 According to this theory, prejudice stems from competition over valued commodities or opportunities.

A quick review of human history indicates that prejudice and discrimination have always, alas, been part of human society. At first glance, therefore, it is tempting to assume that everything that could be learned about these topics was probably uncovered long ago. In fact, nothing could be farther from the truth. Despite the best efforts of philosophers, poets, historians, and others, the nature and causes of prejudice remained unclear until very recent times. This picture has changed—and changed radically—as social psychologists have applied the increasingly sophisticated methods and concepts of their field to this subject. The result, we believe, has been nothing short of a series of major breakthroughs in our understanding of the psychological foundations of prejudice—its cognitive, social, and interpersonal roots (Devine, 1989; Dovidio & Gaertner, 1993). To provide you with an overview of this valuable information, our discussion of prejudice will proceed as follows.

First, we'll examine the nature of both prejudice and discrimination, indicating what these concepts are and how they differ. Second, we will consider the causes of prejudice and discrimination—why they occur and what makes them so intense and so persistent. Third, we will look at reponses of the victims of prejudice and discrimination. Finally, we will explore various strategies for reducing prejudice and discrimination.

PREJUDICE AND DISCRIMINATION: WHAT THEY ARE AND HOW THEY DIFFER

In everyday speech, the terms *prejudice* and *discrimination* are used interchangeably. Are they really the same? Most social psychologists draw a clear distinction between them. **Prejudice** refers to a special type of *attitude*—generally, a negative one—toward the members of some social group. In contrast, **discrimination** refers to negative *actions* toward those individuals. Since this is an important difference, let's consider it more closely.

PREJUDICE: CHOOSING WHOM TO HATE

We'll begin with a more precise definition: *Prejudice is an attitude (usually negative) toward the members of some group, based solely on their membership in that group.* In other words, a person who is prejudiced toward some social group tends to evaluate its members in a specific manner (usually negatively) merely because they belong to that group. Their individual traits or behavior play little role; they are disliked (or, in a few cases, liked) simply because they belong to a specific social group (see Figure 5.2).

When prejudice is defined as a special type of attitude, two important implications follow. First, as we noted in chapter 3, attitudes often function as *schemas*—cognitive frameworks for organizing, interpreting, and recalling information (Fiske & Taylor, 1991). Thus, individuals who are prejudiced toward particular groups tend to process information about these groups differently from the way they process information about other groups. Information consistent with their prejudiced views often receives more attention, is rehearsed more frequently, and, as a result, tends to be remembered more accurately than information that is not consistent with these views (Bodenhausen, 1988; Judd, Ryan, & Park, 1991). To the extent that this happens, prejudice becomes a kind of closed cognitive loop, and, in the absence of truly dramatic experiences that refute its accuracy, it can only grow stronger over time.

Second, if prejudice is a special kind of attitude, then it may involve more than negative evaluations of the groups toward whom it is directed. In addition, it may involve negative feelings or emotions on the part of prejudiced persons when they are in the presence of, or merely thinking about, members of the groups they dislike (Stephan & Stephan, 1988). Prejudice may also involve beliefs and expectations about members of these groups—specifically, **stereotypes** suggesting that all members of

■ Prejudice as blanket condemnation or rejection

FIGURE 5.2 Prejudice leads those who hold it to reject the members of some group simply because they belong to that group.
Source: The New Yorker, 1980.

"Well, sir, then I take it you would vote for any cat in preference to a capable dog."

these groups demonstrate certain characteristics and behave in certain ways. Finally, it may involve tendencies to act in negative ways—or intentions of doing so—toward those who are the object of prejudice.

One additional point: When most people think about prejudice, they tend to focus on its emotional or evaluative aspects. They emphasize the strong negative feelings and irrational hatreds that so often characterize racial, ethnic, or religious prejudice. Such reactions are important and play a key role in many forms of prejudice. Yet it is crucial to note that prejudice also is related to, and involves, certain aspects of *social cognition*—the ways in which we notice, store, process, recall, and then use information about others. Because we have only limited capacity to perform these complex tasks (Gilbert & Hixon, 1991), we often adopt various cognitive shortcuts in our efforts to make sense out of the social world (Fiske, 1989). We described several of these shortcuts in chapter 2 and as you may recall, they *do* help to reduce cognitive effort. However, they can also lead us to draw false conclusions about others (Schaller, 1992): to place them in convenient, if inaccurate, categories and to rely on existing cognitive frameworks (schemas, memories) rather than attempting to adjust these to reflect social reality more accurately (Devine, 1989). For example, once we hold negative stereotypes about members of a specific social group, we tend to evaluate persons belonging to this group unfavorably on dimensions relating to these stereotypes *simply because they belong to this group* (e.g., Bodenhausen, 1990). Because of these and related tendencies, prejudice is often as much a reflection of the limits and operation of our cognitive processes as it is of deep-seated hatred, strong emotions, and rampant ill will. We will return to this point in more detail below, but please try to keep it in mind as you read the pages that follow.

DISCRIMINATION: PREJUDICE IN ACTION

Attitudes, we noted in chapter 3, are not always reflected in overt action—far from it. Prejudice is definitely no exception to this rule. In many cases, persons holding negative attitudes toward the members of various groups cannot express these views directly. Laws, social pressure, fear of retaliation—all serve to deter them from putting their prejudiced views into open practice. In other instances, however, such restraining forces are absent. Then the negative beliefs, feelings, and behavioral tendencies referred to above may find expression in overt actions. Such discrimination (or *discriminatory behaviors*) can take many forms. At relatively mild levels it involves simple avoidance—prejudiced persons simply avoid or minimize contact with the objects of their dislike. While such discrimination may seem relatively benign, it can sometimes have serious consequences for its victims. For example, recent studies indicate that sizable proportions of health-care professionals (physicians, nurses, hospital workers) report spending less time with AIDS patients than with people suffering from other illnesses (Gordin et al., 1987, Hunter & Ross, 1991). Clearly, such discrimination can add to the pain and the suffering of the victims.

At stronger levels, discrimination can produce exclusion from jobs, educational opportunities, or neighborhoods. Finally, in the most extreme cases, prejudice leads to overt forms of aggression against its targets. Anyone who has watched scenes of racial and ethnic violence on the evening news—whether they come from the former Yugoslavia or the streets of American cities—is familiar with these frightening expressions of prejudice.

Subtle forms of discrimination: Prejudice in disguise

Bigots, like other persons, prefer to have their cake and eat it, too. They prefer, if possible, to harm the targets of their prejudice without any cost to themselves. How can they accomplish this goal? One answer involves the use of *subtle forms of discrimination*—ones that permit their users to conceal the underlying negative views from which they stem. Several of these subtle forms exist, ranging from heaping excessive praise on even minimal accomplishments (the implication being that good performance by members of some group is surprising; Gaertner & Dovidio, 1986), to displaying unfriendly nonverbal behavior (e.g., standing slightly too far away, failing to make appropriate eye contact; Neuberg, 1989). In this discussion, however, we'll focus on two that seem to be most common: *tokenism* and *reverse discrimination*.

Tokenism: Small benefits, high costs.   Imagine that you are hired for a job you really wanted and at a higher starting salary than you expected. At first, you are happy about your good fortune. Now assume that one day you learn that you got the job mainly because you belong to a specific group—one whose members the company must hire in order to avoid legal actions by a government agency charged with the task of eliminating discrimination in the workplace. How will you react? In all probability, you will be upset. After all, few persons enjoy discovering that they are a victim of **tokenism**: that they have been hired solely as a token member of a racial, ethnic, or religious group rather than on the basis of their qualifications. Direct evidence of such negative reactions to tokenism in work settings has been reported in several studies. For example, in one study, Chacko (1982) found that among women holding management-level jobs, the greater the extent to which they felt they had been hired purely because of their gender, the lower their satisfaction with their jobs. Similarly, other findings indicate that persons who are hired or promoted because of their gender, race, or ethnic identity may actually receive lower performance ratings from others in their company (Heilman & Herlihy, 1984). This is not surprising, since others tend to attribute the achievements of these persons to the special hiring or promotion factors rather than to hard work or talent. Summers (1991) found that women whose promotions are attributed to the influence of affirmative action policies (policies that encourage the hiring and promotion of women and minorities) are often seen as less qualified by others than women whose promotions are attributed to their own hard work and talent.

We should hasten to note that tokenism occurs in many other contexts as well. More generally, it takes the form of trivial positive actions toward the targets of prejudice that are then used as an excuse or justification for later discrimination. "Don't bother me," prejudiced persons who have engaged in tokenism seem to say; "Haven't I done enough for those people already?" (e.g., Dutton & Lake, 1973; Rosenfield et al., 1982). Wherever it occurs, tokenism seems to have at least two negative effects. On the one hand, it lets prejudiced people off the hook; they can point to tokenistic actions as public proof that they are not really bigoted or that they have followed the letter if not the spirit of antidiscrimination laws. On the other hand, it can be damaging to the self-esteem and confidence of the targets of prejudice, including those few persons who are selected as tokens or who receive minimal aid. Clearly, then, tokenism is one subtle form of discrimination worth preventing.

Reverse discrimination: Giving with one hand, taking with the other.   A second type of subtle discrimination occurs in situations in which persons holding at least some degree of prejudice toward the members of a social group lean over backward to treat those group members favorably—more favorably than they would were the individuals not members of that particular group. Such **reverse discrimination** effects have been observed in several contexts. For example, Chidester (1986) had white students engage in a brief get-acquainted conversation with a stranger who was described as being either African-American or white. (The conversation took place through microphones and headphones.) When participants in the study later evaluated their partners in this conversation, they reported more favorable reactions when the unseen person was supposedly black than when she or he was supposedly white. (In fact, all participants were white; only subjects' beliefs about the race of their partner were varied.) Unless one assumes that the white participants actually held more favorable views of blacks than of members of their own race, these findings point to the occurrence of "lean over backward" reactions among participants.

At first glance such behavior may not seem to fit our definition of discrimination. After all, it yields positive rather than negative outcomes for its victims. On one level, this is certainly true; people exposed to reverse discrimination do receive raises, promotions, and other benefits. But on another level, such favorable treatment may prove harmful, especially over the long run. A clear illustration of the potential damage stemming from reverse discrimination is provided by a study conducted by Fajardo (1985).

In this investigation, several white teachers were asked to grade essays prepared in advance and deliberately written so as to be poor, moderate, or excellent in quality. Information attached to the essays indicated that they were written by either white or African-American students. If reverse discrimination existed, it would be expected that the teachers would rate the essays more favorably when they were supposedly prepared by black rather than by white students. Results indicated that this is precisely what happened. Moreover, the tendency of white teachers to favor black students was strongest under conditions where the essays were of moderate quality; in other words, when there was greatest uncertainty as to the rating students should receive.

In real life, as you can readily see, assigning favorable ratings to mediocre work by black students can indeed help them in the short run. But it can also set them up for later problems. It may lead some students, at least, to conclude that they are doing better in school than they actually are and to become over-confident about the likelihood of future success. The anguish that follows when these hopes are dashed can be devastating. Similarly, reverse discrimination may be a subtle (and perhaps largely unconscious) tactic on the part of teachers for minimizing close contact with minority students. Students who receive consistently high grades don't need special help, so by assigning inflated evaluations to minority students' work, teachers can avoid working closely with them. In these and other ways, reverse discrimination can be as harmful as the more obvious forms of discrimination it sometimes replaces.

How do individuals feel when they engage in discrimination—subtle or otherwise? And do such reactions differ for persons who are low or high in prejudice? These issues will be discussed below.

DISCRIMINATION WITH—AND WITHOUT—COMPUNCTION: WHEN ATTITUDES AND BEHAVIOR COLLIDE

Most people realize that there is sometimes a gap between their overt actions—how they actually behave in a given situation—and their views about how they *should* act in that situation. Indeed, as we noted in chapter 3, noticing such discrepancies is often a first step on the road toward attitude change. This is because generally, people find discrepancies between their overt actions and their internal standards disturbing, and therefore feel internal pressure (dissonance or related states) to close these gaps.

Such discrepancies raise important questions with respect to prejudice and discrimination. Many persons in Canada and elsewhere have struggled vigorously to overcome prejudices they acquired as children. As a result of doing so, they now accept egalitarian principles and would state, if asked, that they are no longer prejudiced toward various groups (e.g., African-Canadians, Jews, women). Yet they find that at some level, negative feelings about these groups persist. Consider the following example from the United States (Pettigrew, 1987, p. 20):

> Many Southerners have confessed to me... that even though in their minds they no longer feel prejudice toward Blacks they still feel squeamish when they shake hands with a Black. These feelings are left over from what they learned... as children.

How do individuals react to such ambivalence? And does the nature of such reactions differ with the intensity of their prejudice? These and related questions have been investigated by Devine and her colleagues (Devine et al., 1991) in a series of enlightening studies.

In these investigations Devine and her colleagues asked college students identified as low, moderate, or high in prejudice toward various groups (i.e., blacks, homosexuals) to indicate how they believed they *should* feel in various situations involving contact with these groups and how they actually *would* feel in these situations. For example, participants were asked to indicate how they should feel when a black person boarded a bus and sat next to them and how they actually would feel in that situation. Similarly, they were asked how they should feel and how they actually would feel about having dinner with a gay individual. In addition, participants were asked to indicate their current feelings about how well their actual responses (their *would* ratings) matched their personal standards (their *should* ratings). They did this by rating their feelings on a number of different dimensions. Some of these dimensions reflected *compunction* (angry at myself, guilty, embarrassed, disappointed with myself). Other dimensions reflected more global discomfort (negative, concerned, frustrated, tense, anxious).

Results indicated that, as expected, highly prejudiced persons held internal standards that permitted more open expression of such prejudice—greater discrimination toward blacks or homosexuals. Further, persons low in prejudice reported that their personal standards regarding behavior in situations where they came into contact with targets of discrimination were highly internalized—these standards were very important to them, and they felt strong obligations to behave consistently with them. In contrast, highly prejudiced persons did not report such well-defined or internalized personal standards and reported weaker felt obligations to behave in accordance with them.

Perhaps the most important—and revealing—findings of the study concerned the affective (emotional) reactions of persons high and low in prejudice to observed discrepancies between their own behavior and their internal standards. Devine and her colleagues (1991) expected that persons low in prejudice would react negatively to such discrepancies and, in particular, that they would respond to these gaps with feelings of *compunction*—guilt and shame over failing to meet their own standards. In contrast, persons high in prejudice would report weaker reactions of this type, although they might report equally strong feelings of general discomfort. As shown in Figure 5.3, these predictions were strongly confirmed. Persons low and moderate in prejudice did experience stronger feelings of guilt and shame when there was a sizable gap between their actual behavior and internal standards than when the discrepancy was smaller. Among highly prejudiced persons, in contrast, large discrepancies did not produce significantly more compunction than small discrepancies. In other words, highly prejudiced persons did not feel guilty about experiencing negative reactions toward blacks and gays; low prejudiced persons did.

These findings have important implications for understanding the nature of prejudice, and especially for understanding how individuals attempt to deal with—and eliminate—prejudices they acquired early in life. One view (Dovidio & Gaertner, 1993) suggests that when people embrace egalitarian beliefs but continue to experience negative feelings toward specific social groups, they cope with such ambivalence by excluding such feelings from consciousness. The results obtained by Devine et al. (1991)

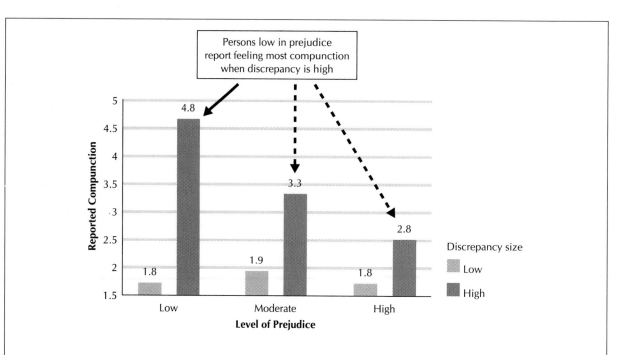

When attitudes and actions collide: Contrasting reactions of highly prejudiced and relatively unprejudiced persons

FIGURE 5.3 Individuals low or moderate in prejudice reported experiencing strong feelings of compunction—shame or guilt—when their attitudes concerning tolerant, unprejudiced behavior failed to find expression in their actions. In contrast, persons high in prejudice reported experiencing weaker reactions of this sort.

Source: Based on data from Devine et al., 1991.

indicate, in contrast, that such persons remain aware of these feelings, and—if they have truly adopted an unprejudiced perspective—are made uneasy by them. The feelings of compunction (guilt, shame, self-criticism) they experience may then serve as an important force for further change in the direction of reduced prejudice. In sum, the findings of this research provide evidence for the view that where prejudice is concerned, change is possible: People who wish to eliminate racist, sexist, and other prejudiced attitudes from their thinking can succeed in doing so. Indeed, recognition of the fact that they are still far from perfect in this respect and that gaps remain between their egalitarian attitudes and certain aspects of their behavior may be just the psychological nudge they need to keep them on the road toward unprejudiced beliefs and standards.

THE ORIGINS OF PREJUDICE: CONTRASTING PERSPECTIVES

That prejudice exists is all too obvious. The question of *why* it occurs, however, is more complex. Why do so many people hold negative views about the members of specific social groups? What factors or conditions foster such reactions and lead to their persistence? Many different answers to these questions have been proposed. Here, we will consider several views that have proved most influential.

INSTITUTIONAL ORIGINS OF PREJUDICE: CANADA'S RACIST HISTORY

Canada today has a reputation as a tolerant society, as we mentioned in chapter 1. However, even the most tolerant of Western countries has a history that is riddled with **racism**: prejudice and discrimination based upon race or ethnicity. This is one of the most destructive forms of prejudice in a multicultural society. Historians of racist groups in Canada agree that racism has been an integral part of Canadian society (Barrett, 1987; Sher, 1983). As Stanley Barrett concluded from his analysis of racism and racist groups in Canada:

> My argument…is that racism—quite apart from the formally organized [racist] groups—has been institutionalized into Canadian society since the country's beginning. The right wing, including the most extreme racists and anti-semites, simply represent a more crystallized and overt form of a broader phenomenon (Barrett, 1987, p.4).

Barrett believes that racism in Canada has an *institutional* origin—that, historically, it was a product of the "institutional framework" of this society, built into its system of stratification and legitimized by regulations and laws. Examples from Canadian history are numerous. A few are shown in Table 5.1. Today, there are laws banning such discrimination and the dissemination of hatred, but the subtle forms that prejudice and discrimination often take have prevented many successful prosecutions.

■ **Institutional racism in Canadian history**

TABLE 5.1 Some examples of institutional racism from Canada's history

■ At the end of the last century, Chinese men were encouraged to emigrate to Canada to help build the great railway that links this country. Once it was completed, a head tax of $50 was imposed on all Chinese immigrants. When this did not stem the tide of immigrants, it was increased to $500, effectively preventing many families from being united. Moreover, given that the Chinese who built the railway were not well paid, they often could not afford to return to China.

■ From 1920 to the 1950s and 60s, it was mandatory for Native children to be sent away from their often remote homes to special residential schools. There, they were discouraged from maintaining their own cultural heritage. If they spoke their own language or practiced their own customs they were punished. Laws had also been passed banning important Native ceremonies such as the potlach. The effect of this program was to severely disrupt the Native culture and way of life. Family relationships were destroyed by enforced separation for two or three generations, and today communities are still recovering.

■ Subsequent to the Japanese attack on Pearl Harbour in December, 1941, 23 000 people of Japanese descent were placed in internment camps. Their property was placed in the hands of the "Custodian of Enemy Alien Property" and later sold at well below market prices. Approximately 75 percent of these people were Canadian citizens. Again, this government action was clearly discriminatory. People of German descent did not receive this harsh treatment although Germany was also an enemy of Canada during World War Two.

■ Voting: Canadians of Chinese descent did not receive the vote until 1947. Canadians of Japanese descent did not receive the vote until 1949. Note that for both groups immigration had begun as early as the 1880s. The Inuit first received the federal vote in 1962 and Status Indians first received the vote in 1960. A person who could not vote could not hold public office, could not be in the public service and was prevented from entering many professions such as law and pharmacy.

■ Schooling and Housing: Until 1942, McGill University entrance requirements were a 65 percent average for Jews, but a 50 percent average for non-Jews. The law authorizing segregated schools was not repealed until 1965. As late as 1973, residential property deeds in Vancouver's affluent "British Properties" stipulated that no person of Asiatic or African ancestry could stay on the premises overnight unless he or she was a servant.

Source: Barrett (1987) and others.

DIRECT INTERGROUP CONFLICT: COMPETITION AS A SOURCE OF PREJUDICE

It is an axiom of life that the things people value most—good jobs, nice homes, high status—are always in short supply. There's never quite enough to go around. This fact serves as the foundation for what is perhaps the oldest explanation of prejudice—**realistic conflict theory** (e.g., Bobo, 1983). According to this view, prejudice stems from competition among social groups over valued commodities or opportunities. In short, prejudice develops out of the struggle over jobs, adequate housing, good schools, and other desirable outcomes. The theory further suggests that as such competition continues, the members of the groups involved come to view each other in increasingly negative terms (White, 1977). They label one another as "enemies," view their own group as morally superior, and draw the boundaries between themselves and their opponents ever more firmly. The result, of course, is that what starts out as simple competition relatively free from hatred gradually develops into full-scale emotion-laden prejudice (refer to Figure 5.4).

Evidence from several different studies seems to confirm the occurrence of this process: As competition persists, the individuals or groups involved come to perceive each other in increasingly negative ways. Even worse, such competition often leads to direct and open conflict. Perhaps the most dramatic evidence for this process is provided by a classic study in social psychology conducted by Hovland and Sears (1940). These researchers examined the relationship between the number of lynchings of blacks in fourteen states in the American South and two indexes of economic conditions: farm value of cotton and acre value of cotton. (Cotton was the most important crop in the South at that time.) Their data covered a forty-nine-year period, and results were clear: The more negative economic conditions were, the greater the incidence of this atrocious type of violence.

These findings have often been interpreted as suggesting that under adverse economic conditions, competition for increasingly scarce economic resources increases. Such competition in turn increases prejudice toward groups other than one's own (in this case, prejudice on the part of whites toward blacks) and so increases the incidence of prejudice-driven violence. Interestingly, a reanalysis of Hovland and Sears's data using the more sophisticated statistical techniques available today and a more accurate measure of economic conditions has confirmed these results (Hepworth & West, 1988). Thus, it appears that increased competition between groups during periods of economic decline may indeed be one of the factors contributing to prejudice and resulting violence.

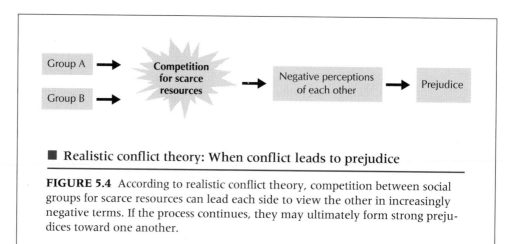

■ Realistic conflict theory: When conflict leads to prejudice

FIGURE 5.4 According to realistic conflict theory, competition between social groups for scarce resources can lead each side to view the other in increasingly negative terms. If the process continues, they may ultimately form strong prejudices toward one another.

While direct conflict between racial or ethnic groups may indeed sometimes contribute to the development of strong prejudice between them (e.g., Bobo, 1983), it is important to note that this process appears to occur primarily with respect to *group conflict*—perceived threats to one group's interest by another group. When, instead, threats to individual interests are considered, there is little support for the view that conflict leads inevitably to prejudice. For example, Sears and his colleagues (e.g., Sears & Allen, 1984; Sears & Kinder, 1985) found that whites whose self-interests are threatened by forced busing—those with children in public schools—are not more prejudiced against blacks or more opposed to such busing than whites whose self-interests are not threatened by busing (whites without school-age children, whites whose children attend private schools). These and related findings indicate that it is primarily perceived conflict between *groups*, not individuals, that leads to intergroup prejudice. Since there are many situations in which individuals perceive that their group's interests are being threatened by members of some other group, however, it seems likely that intergroup conflict plays a role in prejudice in some instances.

For additional evidence concerning the impact of intergroup conflict on prejudice, please see the "Classic Contributions" section below.

FOCUS ON RESEARCH

Conflict and Prejudice in a Summer Camp: The Robber's Cave Experiment

It was the mid-1950s, and in America Eisenhower was president, the economy was humming along, and—at least for the moment—domestic tranquility prevailed. Yet even then social psychologists were deeply concerned with the topic of prejudice. To acquire new insights into prejudice, Sherif and his colleagues (1961) decided to conduct an intriguing project.

Their study involved sending eleven-year-old boys to a special summer camp in a remote area where, free from external influences, the nature of conflict and its role in prejudice could be carefully observed.

When the boys arrived at the camp (named *The Robber's Cave*), they were divided in two separate groups and assigned to different cabins located quite far apart (see Figure 5.5). For one week, the campers in each

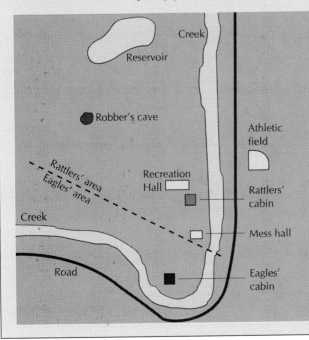

■ **Setting for the Robber's Cave experiment**

FIGURE 5.5 The summer camp represented here served as the site of the famous Robber's Cave experiment. Note the distance between the cabins of the two opposing groups (Rattlers and Eagles) and division of the camp into two separate territories.

Source: Based on information in Sherif et al., 1961.

group lived and played together, engaging in such enjoyable activities as hiking, swimming, and other sports. During this initial phase, the boys quickly developed strong attachments to their own groups. They chose names for their teams (the Rattlers and the Eagles), stenciled them onto their shorts, and made up separate flags with their groups' symbols on them.

At this point the second phase of the study began. The boys in both groups were told that they would now engage in a series of competitions. The winning team would receive a trophy, and its members would earn prizes (pocket knives and medals). Since these were prizes the boys strongly desired, the stage was set for intense competition. Would such conflict generate prejudice? The answer was quick in coming. As the boys competed, the tension between the groups rose. At first it was limited to verbal insults, teasing, and name-calling. Soon, though, it escalated into more direct acts—for example, the Eagles burned the Rattlers' flag. The next day the Rattlers struck back by attacking the rival group's cabin, overturning beds, tearing out mosquito netting, and seizing personal property. Such actions continued until the researchers intervened to prevent serious trouble. At the same time the two groups voiced increasingly negative views of each other. They labeled their opponents "bums" and "cowards," while heaping praise on their own group at every turn. In short, after only two weeks of conflict, the groups showed all the key components of strong prejudice toward each other.

Fortunately, the story (and the research project) had a happy ending. In the study's final phase, Sherif and his colleagues attempted to reduce the negative reactions described above. Merely increasing the amount of contact between the groups failed to accomplish this goal; indeed, it seemed to fan the flames of anger. But when conditions were altered so that the groups found it necessary to work together to reach *superordinate goals*—ones they both desired—dramatic changes occurred. After the boys worked together to restore their water supply (previously sabotaged by the researchers), pooled their funds to rent a movie, and jointly repaired a broken-down truck, tensions between the groups largely vanished. In fact, after six days of such experiences, the boundaries between the groups virtually dissolved, and many cross-group friendships were established.

It is important to note that there are major limitations to this research. The study took place over a relatively short period; the camp setting was a special one; all participants were boys; and, perhaps most important, the boys were quite homogeneous in background—they did not belong to distinctly different social groups. Despite these restrictions, however, the findings reported by Sherif and his colleagues are compelling. They offer a chilling picture of how what starts out as rational competition over scarce resources can quickly escalate into full-scale conflict, which then in turn fosters accompanying strong, negative attitudes.

SOCIAL IDENTITY AND SOCIAL CATEGORIZATION AS A BASIS FOR PREJUDICE: THE US-VERSUS-THEM EFFECT

A second perspective is based upon Tajfel' social identity theory (Tajfel & Turner, 1979; Tajfel, 1970). Tajfel's work suggested that the process of social categorization is at the basis of prejudice and discrimination. You will recall from chapter 4 that according to this theory, we are motivated to achieve or maintain a distinctive and positive social (or group-based) identity. One way that we can do this is through the *us–versus–them effect*.

People generally classify the social world into groups along socially important dimensions—this is the process of **social categorization**. But we go beyond mere categorization and identify—*us* and *them*. We identify the groups to which we belong (usually termed the **ingroup**) and the groups to which we do not belong (the **outgroup**). Such distinctions are based on many dimensions, including race, religion, sex, age, ethnicity, occupation, and income, to name just a few.

If the process of dividing the social world into "us" and "them" stopped there, it would have little bearing on prejudice. Unfortunately, however, it does not. Our desire for a positive social identity leads to sharply contrasting feelings and beliefs about members of one's ingroup and members of various outgroups. Persons in the former ("us") category are viewed in favorable terms, while those in the latter ("them") category are perceived more negatively. Outgroup members are assumed to possess more undesirable traits, are perceived as being more alike (i.e., more homogeneous) than members of the ingroup, and are often strongly disliked (Judd, Ryan, & Park, 1991; Linville, Fischer, & Salovey, 1989; Schaller & Maas, 1989). The ingroup-outgroup distinction also affects *attribution*, the way we explain the actions of our own group and other groups, as we saw in chapter 2 when discussing the *ultimate attribution error*.

That strong tendencies exist to divide the social world into these contrasting groups has been demonstrated in many studies (e.g., Stephan, 1985; Tajfel, 1982; Turner et al., 1987). In these investigations, participants generally expressed more negative attitudes toward members of outgroups and treated them less favorably than members of their own group. Further, these patterns held true even when these categories were purely arbitrary and had no existence beyond the experiment, and when the persons involved never met face to face. On the other side of the coin, growing evidence indicates that when individuals shift the boundaries of this *us-versus-them* distinction so that persons previously on the "wrong" side of the ingroup-outgroup boundary are now viewed as being inside, prejudice toward them tends to disappear as well (Gaertner et al., 1989). Together, these findings indicate that in some settings, prejudice may well stem from a basic aspect of the way in which we think about and respond to the social world: our tendency to identify ingroups and outgroups and, further, to show bias on the basis of this categorization.

But why, precisely, is this the case? Why does the definition of others as outgroup members leads us to view them in biased and mainly negative ways? Tajfel and his colleagues (e.g., Tajfel, 1982) suggest that social identity processes are the key. Individuals seek to enhance their self-esteem by becoming identified with specific social groups. This tactic can succeed, however, only to the extent that the persons involved perceive their groups as somehow superior to other, competing groups. Since all individuals are subject to the same forces, the final result is inevitable: Each group seeks to view itself as somehow better than its rivals, and prejudice arises out of this clash of social perceptions (see Figure 5.6).

Support for the accuracy of these suggestions has been obtained in several experiments (e.g., Meindl & Lerner, 1985). Thus, it appears that our tendency to divide the social world into two opposing camps often plays a role in the development of important forms of prejudice.

EARLY EXPERIENCE: THE ROLE OF SOCIAL LEARNING

A third explanation for prejudice is one you will not find surprising: it suggests that prejudice is *learned* and that it develops in much the same manner, and through the same basic processes, as other attitudes (refer to our discussion in chapter 3). According to this **social learning view**, children acquire negative attitudes toward various social groups because they hear such views expressed by parents, friends, teachers, and others and because they are directly rewarded (with love, praise, and approval) for adopting them. In addition to direct observation of others, social norms—rules within a given group suggesting what actions or attitudes are appropriate—are also important (Pettigrew, 1969). As we will see in chapter 7, most persons choose to conform to

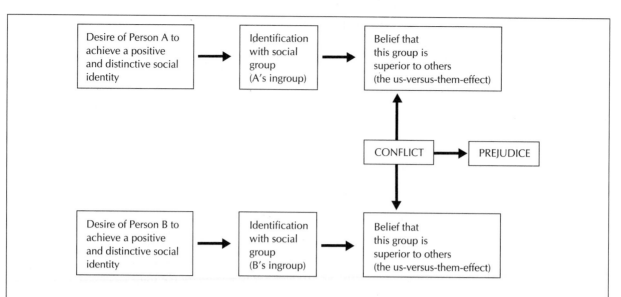

■ **Why social identity and social categorization processes sometimes lead to prejudice**

FIGURE 5.6 According to Tajfel's Social Identity theory (1982), prejudice sometimes arises out of social competition. This process reflects the desire of individuals to achieve a positive and distinctive social identity by identifying with groups they view as desirable or superior. Since the members of many groups have the same desire, conflict between them occurs. Prejudice then follows from this clash of social perceptions.

Source: Based on suggestions by Tajfel, 1982.

most *social norms* of groups to which they belong. The development and expression of prejudice toward others often stems from this tendency.

While persons with whom children have direct contact are central both in social learning and in pressures toward adhering to social norms, the mass media, too, are important. Until quite recently members of racial and ethnic minorities were shown infrequently in movies or on television. Further, when they did appear, they were usually cast in low-status or comic roles. Given repeated exposure to such materials for years or even decades, it is not at all surprising that many children came to believe that the members of these groups must be inferior. After all, why else would they always be shown in this manner?

The situation has changed greatly in recent years in Canada and elsewhere. Members of various racial and ethnic minorities now appear more frequently and are shown in a more favorable manner than was true in the past. Whether these shifts will contribute to reduced prejudice remains uncertain, but at least they constitute a few steps in the appropriate (counter-prejudicial) direction.

COGNITIVE SOURCES OF PREJUDICE: STEREOTYPES, ILLUSORY CORRELATIONS, AND OUTGROUP HOMOGENEITY

A fourth source of prejudice is in some ways the most unsettling of all. As we noted earlier, it involves the possibility that prejudice stems, at least in part, from basic aspects of *social cognition*—how we think about other persons. We will now consider several forms of evidence pointing to this conclusion.

Stereotypes: What they are and how they operate

Consider the following groups: Afro-Americans, Asian-Americans, homosexuals, Jews. Suppose you were asked to list the traits most characteristic of each. Would you experience much difficulty? Probably you would not. You would be able to construct quite easily a list of traits for each group. Moreover, you could do this *even for groups with which you have had limited personal contact*. Why? The reason involves the existence and operation of stereotypes. As we saw in chapter 2, these are cognitive frameworks consisting of knowledge and beliefs about specific social groups. As noted by Judd, Ryan, and Park (1991), stereotypes involve generalizations about the typical or "modal" characteristics of members of various social groups. That is, they suggest that all members of such groups possess certain traits, at least to a degree. Once a stereotype is activated, these traits come readily to mind; hence the ease with which you could construct the lists described above (Higgins & Bargh, 1987).

Like other cognitive frameworks or *schemas*, stereotypes exert strong effects on the ways in which we process social information. For example, information relevant to a particular stereotype is processed more quickly than information unrelated to it (Dovidio, Evans, & Tyler, 1986). Similarly, stereotypes lead the persons holding them to pay attention to specific types of information—usually, information consistent with the stereotypes. Alternatively, if information inconsistent with a stereotype does manage to enter consciousness, we may actively refute it, perhaps by recalling facts and information that are consistent with the stereotype (O'Sullivan & Durso, 1984). Stereotypes also determine what we remember—usually, again, information that is consistent with these frameworks.

Now consider the relevance of such effects to prejudice. Once an individual has acquired a stereotype about some social group, she or he tends to notice information that fits readily into this cognitive framework and to remember "facts" that are consistent with it more readily than "facts" that are inconsistent with it. As a result, the stereotype becomes, to a large degree, self-confirming. Even exceptions to it make it stronger, for they simply induce the person in question to bring more supporting information to mind (see Figure 5.7).

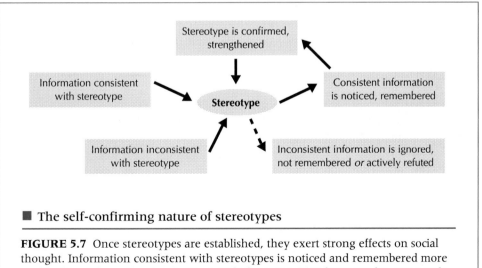

■ The self-confirming nature of stereotypes

FIGURE 5.7 Once stereotypes are established, they exert strong effects on social thought. Information consistent with stereotypes is noticed and remembered more readily than information inconsistent with these cognitive frameworks. As a result, stereotypes become largely self-confirming, and even exceptions to them serve to increase their strength.

Evidence for the ways in which stereotypes influence (we might actually say *bias*) social thought has been provided by many different studies (e.g., Brewer, 1989; Fiske & Neuberg, 1990). Research performed by Bodenhausen (1988) provides an especially clear illustration. Bodenhausen asked students to play the role of jurors in an imaginary court case. Some participants received information designed to activate a negative stereotype toward Hispanics—the defendant was named Carlos Ramirez, and he came from Albuquerque, New Mexico. Others received more neutral information, unrelated to existing stereotypes—the defendant was named Robert Johnson and came from Dayton, Ohio. Half the participants learned the defendant's name before receiving evidence about the case, while the others learned his name only after reading the evidence. Bodenhausen suggested that the impact of stereotypes on subsequent social judgments and behavior derives from the fact that stereotypes bias the processing of information received after their activation. Specifically, he suggested that stereotypes change recipients' interpretation of such information, cause them to devote more effort to processing stereotype-consistent than stereotype-inconsistent information, or both.

After learning the defendant's name and reading information about the case, participants in all conditions rated the likelihood that he was guilty. Bodenhausen predicted that the defendant would be rated as more guilty when he had an ethnic name, but only when participants learned the name *before* reviewing the evidence. Results offered clear support for this prediction. Additional evidence, gathered in a follow-up study, indicated that stereotypes seem to affect the processing of social information by increasing the amount of attention and rehearsal directed to stereotype-consistent input.

But are stereotypes always activated in such situations? Research by Gilbert and Hixon (1991) suggests that the activation of stereotypes, and their subsequent impact upon our social thought, are not inevitable. If we are busy with other tasks, they may fail to emerge, and our thinking may be relatively free of their biasing influence. Once they are activated, however, their impact on our social thought may be profound. What do these findings mean with respect to prejudice? One implication is quite encouraging: Social interaction is a complex and absorbing task. Thus, when individuals from different backgrounds who hold stereotypes about each other meet, the very fact that they must interact may help to prevent activation of stereotypes. This may be one reason why face-to-face contact helps to weaken stereotypes and associated prejudice. (We'll return to this topic in more detail in the section on direct intergroup contact.) But persistent, and largely negative stereotypes can have detrimental effects. For evidence that they do, please see the "Applied Side" section that follows.

SOCIAL PSYCHOLOGY: ON THE APPLIED SIDE

Negative Effects of Gender Stereotypes: Why, Often, Men Get the Jobs

Overt discriminatory practices have been banned by legislation in many nations, and there has been at least some weakening of **sexism**, or negative gender-based stereotypes, about women. Yet such progress has been spotty at best (Steinberg & Shapiro, 1982). Prejudice and open discrimination against females have decreased noticeably in some countries and regions, while in others there has been virtually no change in centuries-old patterns of restriction

▶

and bias (see Kanekar, Kolsawala, & Nazareth, 1988). Because prejudice based on gender affects more individuals than any other single kind (more than half the human race!) and because it produces negative outcomes for males as well as females, it is important to examine its impact.

The **gender stereotypes** of many cultures assume that males possess such desirable traits as *decisiveness, forcefulness, confidence, ambition*, and *rationality*. In contrast, the corresponding assumptions about females include less-desirable traits such as *passivity, submissiveness, indecisiveness, emotionality*, and *dependence* (Deaux & Lewis, 1984). Some positive characteristics, too, are included—such as warmth, nurturance, sensitivity, and understanding. Overall, however, the traits assigned to females are less desirable and less suited for many valued roles (e.g., leadership, authority) than the traits assigned to males (Heilman, Martell, & Simon, 1988).

Stereotypes do not exist in a social vacuum. On the contrary, they exert powerful effects on judgments and evaluations of the persons to whom they are applied. Gender stereotypes are no exception—they influence the perceptions and behavior of large numbers of persons. In the case of females, the impact of such stereotypes is largely negative. Such effects are visible in many areas of life, but perhaps they are most unsettling with respect to jobs and the world of work. A growing body of evidence suggests that when selecting applicants for various jobs—and especially for relatively high-level ones—organizations seek a good match: They want to hire the people whose characteristics resemble most closely those that they view as necessary for effective performance. This is a reasonable point of view, but, in the context of gender stereotypes, it turns out to be highly damaging to females.

What traits are assumed to be necessary for success in high-level jobs? In general, it appears, ones closer to the content of male gender stereotypes than to the content of female gender stereotypes. Leaders, most people believe, should be bold, assertive, tough, and decisive—all traits traditionally viewed as masculine in nature. In contrast, few persons want or expect leaders to be kind, sensitive, emotional, and nurturant. To the extent females are subject to

traditional gender stereotypes, then, they face a difficult uphill struggle in efforts to launch and advance their careers.

Evidence for the negative impact of gender stereotypes on females in work settings has been obtained in many studies (e.g., Heilman & Martell, 1986; Heilman, Martell, & Simon, 1988). These experiments have repeatedly found that females are perceived as less suited for high-level jobs than males, primarily because they are viewed as possessing the traits required for successful performance of these jobs to a lesser extent than males.

While such findings are unsettling, much of this research used *simulation* procedures in which college students or others played the role of job interviewers or other persons charged with the task of choosing among applicants. A study by Van Vianen and Willemsen (1992), however, examined the effects of gender stereotypes on the decisions of actual members of employment selection boards.

These individuals (some of whom were female and some male) had the responsibility of interviewing applicants for high-level scientific and technical jobs at a university in the Netherlands. They completed two questionnaires: one on which they rated the attributes of ideal candidates and another on which they rated the perceived qualities of each actual job applicant. Ratings on both questionnaires involved traits previously found to be part of masculine and feminine gender stereotypes. For example, positive traits that were part of the masculine gender stereotype included *daring, forceful, logical, confident*; negative traits included *aggressive, arrogant, dominant, reckless*. Positive traits on the feminine gender stereotype included *understanding, sociable, spontaneous, warm, gentle*; negative traits included *dependent, dreamy, changeable, affected*.

Results provided strong support for the view that these gender stereotypes play a role both in conceptions of ideal job candidates and in the actual selection of applicants. First, descriptions of the ideal candidate provided by the interviewers included mainly traits present in the masculine gender stereotype. This implies that in the eyes of these interviewers, the traits required for success in these high-level jobs were primarily

▶

ones typically attributed to males. Second, the candidates they recommended for the job were rated as possessing masculine attributes to a greater extent than candidates they rejected. Third, as shown in Figure 5.8, accepted and rejected female candidates differed significantly in terms of their perceived possession of masculine traits: Accepted females were much closer to the description of the "ideal candidate" than rejected ones, and of course the ideal candidate was described largely in masculine terms. In contrast, rejected and accepted males did not differ significantly in perceived possession of masculine traits.

Fortunately, it appears that the impact of gender stereotypes can be reduced when clear evidence of a woman's ability or competence is provided to interviewers (Heilman, Martell, & Simon, 1988). Nevertheless, the findings reported by Van Vianen and Willemsen (1992) and other researchers suggest that in many instances persistent gender stereotypes can—and do—exert negative effects on the prospects and outcomes of working females.

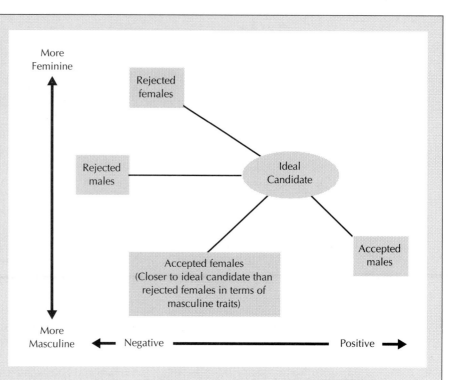

■ **The perceived characteristics of successful and unsuccessful job candidates**

FIGURE 5.8 Women applicants who were accepted for a high-level job were perceived as possessing more traits typically associated with males than female applicants who were rejected. Accepted candidates were also closer to interviewers' ideal candidate. Accepted and rejected male applicants did not differ in this respect.

Source: Based on data from Van Vianen & Willemsen, 1992.

Stereotyping in intergroup relations: Are the effects always negative?

Don Taylor at McGill University has suggested that, in the context of intergroup relations, stereotyping is not always destructive (1981; Taylor & Moghaddam, 1987). His model explores both negative and positive forms of stereotyping and suggests that when groups are not in conflict, intergroup stereotyping can have a constructive effect on intergroup relations. How can this occur? First, Taylor points out that the content of stereotypes is not necessarily negative. For example, groups with high status are often viewed positively by other groups in society (e.g., Berry, Kalin, & Taylor, 1977). Frequently, groups will also characterize themselves positively. Kirby and Gardner (1973), for instance, found that English Canadians stereotyped themselves as "clean, intelligent, good and modern." Second, he suggests that such positive stereotypes help to create a distinct identity for a group. Building on notions of social identity theory, Taylor's *intergroup stereotyping model* then suggests that if groups wish to maintain a distinctive and positive social identity, they will welcome stereotyping to the extext that it has two qualities: (1) it is perceived as accurate by the group itself; and (2) it is positively evaluated by others. Thus, in the context of intergroup relations we have to consider the positivity and accuracy of each group's stereotypes of other groups and of themselves. One means of representing this is shown in Figure 5.9. The two matrices in Figure 5.9 represent the negative effects (Matrix A) and the positive effects (Matrix B) of intergroup stereotyping.

Matrix A shows a negative form of intergroup stereoyping: *intergroup conflict*. In this situation, groups agree about each other's attributes (ABC or XYZ) but disagree about their evaluations (+ or −). As in the ultimate attribution error, each group sees itself positively and the other group negatively. In Matrix B both groups agree about each other's attributes (ABC or XYZ), and they agree in their positive evaluations (+) of each other. This is seen as a situation where intergroup stereotyping has *desirable consequences*: each group is distinctive from the other and each is positively evaluated. For example, in a survey of ethnic attitudes in Canada, French and English Canadians had largely positive views of each other, especially relative to other ethnic groups in Canada (Berry, Kalin, & Taylor, 1977). Further, common attributes are found between the self-stereotype and the outgroup stereotype of English and French Canadians (Taylor, 1981). For example, Aboud and Taylor (1971) found that English Canadians characterized themselves as ambitious, likable, competent, and proud, and that they were characterized by French Canadians as ambitious, educated, dominant, and authoritarian. The implications of this model for intergroup relations in Canada are that stereotyping need not be a destructive force. When groups are in conflict, then, this is reflected in their negative stereotyping of each other. However, if groups understand and respect each other, stereotyping can, at times, provide the positive and distinctive identity for which groups strive (Tajfel, 1982).

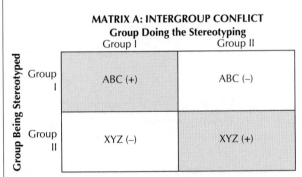

MATRIX A: INTERGROUP CONFLICT
Group Doing the Stereotyping

Group I sees itself as having stereotypical attributes ABC and evaluates those attributes positively (+). It sees Group II as having XYZ attributes and evaluates those negatively (−). Group II agrees about the nature of the attributes of each group (ABC or XYZ) but reverses the evaluations, seeing its own group's attributes as positive and those of Group I as negative.

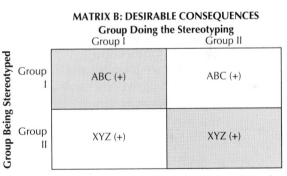

MATRIX B: DESIRABLE CONSEQUENCES
Group Doing the Stereotyping

Group I sees itself as having stereotypical attributes ABC and evaluates those attributes positively (+). It sees Group II as having XYZ attributes and evaluates those positively (+). Group II agrees both with the description of the stereotypical attributes and with their positive evaluation for both groups.

■ **Intergroup stereotyping**

FIGURE 5.9 In the context of intergroup relations, groups will welcome stereotyping of themselves if the stereotype is perceived as accurate and positive (Matrix B). On the other hand if groups stereotype each other negatively, this can contribute to intergroup conflict (Matrix A).

Illusory correlations: Perceiving relationships that aren't there

Consider the following set of information: (1) there are one thousand members of Group A but only one hundred members of Group B; (2) one hundred members of Group A were arrested by the police last year, and ten members of Group B were arrested. Suppose you were asked to evaluate the criminal tendencies of these two groups: would your ratings of them differ? Your first answer is probably "of course not—why should they?" After all, the rate of criminal behavior is equal in the two groups (10 percent in both cases). Yet a large body of evidence suggests that you might actually assign a less-favorable rating to Group B (Hamilton & Sherman, 1989; Mullen & Johnson, 1990). Why? The answer seems to involve what social psychologists term *distinctiveness-based illusory correlations*, or, more simply, **illusory correlations**: perceived relationships between two variables when in fact none exists. In this case, you might perceive a correlation between membership in one of these groups and the tendency to commit criminal acts. Illusory correlations seem to stem, at least in part, from the fact that infrequent events are highly distinctive; thus, when two relatively infrequent events occur together, we tend to perceive that they are linked (correlated). Being arrested and belonging to Group B are both relatively infrequent events, so we perceive a stronger correlation between them than we do between being arrested and belonging to Group A (which is ten times as large).

What do illusory correlations have to do with prejudice? A great deal. For example, in the United States, whites outnumber African-Americans by approximately nine to one. Even in the mid 1990s, violent crimes are still relatively rare occurrences (except for persons living in devastated areas of major cities). Thus, when whites read or hear about a violent crime committed by an African-American, two relatively infrequent stimuli co-occur. As a result, an illusory correlation suggesting a strong link between race and violent behavior may emerge. Please note: We are not suggesting that no such relationship exists. In the United States, members of some minority groups do commit a higher proportion of violent crimes than would be predicted solely on the basis of their numbers in the total population. Illusory correlations, however, lead many persons to assume that this relationship between racial or ethnic identity and violence is even *higher* than it actually is. Further, illusory correlations also lead people to ignore the many factors that may be responsible for such relationships and that have nothing whatsoever to do with race or ethnic background (e.g., poverty, growing up in a highly violent environment, and so on; please see Figure 5.10).

Are illusory correlations inevitable? In other words, do the workings of our own cognitive systems condemn us to perceive relationships between variables that don't really exist? Research findings offer a relatively optimistic answer (Schaller & Maas, 1989). First, it appears that illusory correlations can be reduced or prevented by conditions that promote thorough and extensive processing of social information (Sanbonmatsu, Shavitt, & Sherman, 1991). For example, if individuals are encouraged to take account of the relative size of various groups as well as the frequency with which their members perform various actions, the tendency to perceive group membership and such actions as correlated is reduced. Second, and perhaps somewhat paradoxically, illusory correlations can be reduced by factors or conditions that occupy individuals' cognitive resources and prevent the illusion from forming (Stroessner, Hamilton, and Mackie, 1992). It appears that illusory correlations are most likely to occur when individuals have a moderate amount of cognitive resources at their disposal for processing information about different social groups. When they are distracted or have relatively few cognitive resources available, the strength or likelihood of illusory correlations is reduced. And when they direct very careful attention to such information, the tendency to perceive illusory correlations also decreases. Unfortunately, individuals often appear to function at that critical moderate level:

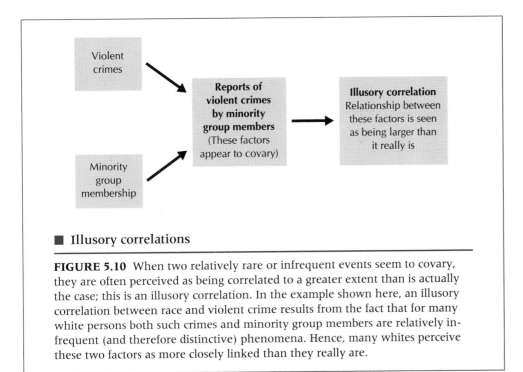

■ Illusory correlations

FIGURE 5.10 When two relatively rare or infrequent events seem to covary, they are often perceived as being correlated to a greater extent than is actually the case; this is an illusory correlation. In the example shown here, an illusory correlation between race and violent crime results from the fact that for many white persons both such crimes and minority group members are relatively infrequent (and therefore distinctive) phenomena. Hence, many whites perceive these two factors as more closely linked than they really are.

They pay just sufficient attention to information from the news media and other sources to form erroneous perceptions of the social world. Thus, illusory correlations appear to be quite common and may contribute to the persistence of negative stereotypes in many real-life contexts.

Ingroup differentiation, outgroup homogeneity: "They're all the same"—or are they?

One remark people with a strong prejudice toward some group often make goes something like this: "You know what *they're* like; they're all the same." What such comments imply, of course, is that the members of some outgroup are much more similar to one another (i.e., are more homogeneous) than the members of one's own ingroup. This tendency to perceive persons belonging to groups other than one's own as all alike is known as the **illusion of outgroup homogeneity** (Linville et al., 1989). The mirror image of this tendency is known as the **ingroup differentiation hypothesis**—the view that we tend to perceive members of our own groups as showing much larger differences from one another than those of other groups.

Existence of the illusion of outgroup homogeneity has been demonstrated in many different contexts. For example, individuals tend to perceive persons older or younger than themselves as more similar to one another in terms of personal traits than persons in their own age group—an intriguing type of "generation gap" (Linville et al., 1989). Perhaps the most chilling example of such outgroup homogeneity effects, however, appears in the context of *cross-racial facial identification*—the tendency for persons belonging to one racial group to be more accurate in recognizing the faces of strangers from their own group than strangers from another racial group (e.g., Bothwell, Brigham, & Malpass, 1989; see Figure 5.11). In the United States this tendency has been observed among both blacks and whites, although it appears to be somewhat stronger among whites (Anthony, Cooper, & Mullen, 1992).

■ Cross-racial facial identification: The illusion of outgroup homogeneity strikes again

FIGURE 5.11 Look at the photos shown here. If you are Asian, would you find it easier to recognize the strangers in the bottom row than those in the top row? If you are white, would the reverse be true? A large body of research evidence suggests that in fact most people find it easier to recognize strangers from their own racial or ethnic group.

Taking account of existing evidence, it seems clear that a strong tendency does exist to perceive members of outgroups as more homogeneous than members of our own ingroup. Since it is reasonable to assume that in reality, all groups of human beings are equally diverse in their traits and behaviors, this implies that we are probably more accurate in making judgments about members of our own group than about members of various outgroups. And in fact this prediction, too, has been confirmed (Judd, Ryan, & Park, 1991).

Unfortunately, the tendency to perceive persons belonging to groups other than our own as "all alike" is yet another force operating to maintain the existence of stereotypes. After all, if we are convinced that members of outgroups show little variability with respect to important traits, why should we take the trouble to deal with them as individuals? It is much easier to conclude that we already know what they are like—and, given the negative nature of most stereotypes, this picture is usually not a favorable one. Little wonder, then, that persons belonging to different racial, ethnic, and religious groups rarely seek increased contact with each other. On the contrary, as we have noted before, they often go out of their way to minimize such contact. And this, in turn, helps assure that each group remains secluded in its own social world, insulated from change by a comforting—if dangerous—blanket of prejudice.

THE AUTHORITARIAN PERSONALITY REVISITED

One of the earliest approaches to prejudice was Adorno and colleagues' (1950) work on the authoritarian personality. This approach focused upon a type of highly conventional individual who was submissive to strong leaders and threatened by those in society who were different or unconventional. High authoritarians were found particularly likely to be racially prejudiced and homophobic.

Current research in this area is dominated by the work of Bob Altemeyer in Manitoba (1981; 1988). He has carried out a thorough revision and validation of the original scales, which are now much more reliable and measure what is termed **right-wing authoritarianism**. The right-wing authoritarianism scale (RWA) measures three basic attitudinal clusters. Those who are high in right-wing authoritarianism will show (1) *authoritarian submission*, a high degree of submissiveness to figures of authority who are perceived as legitimate and established; (2) *authoritarian aggression*, a general aggressiveness towards various people (often minorities, the unconventional and socially deviant) when it appears that such aggression is sanctioned by established authority; and (3) *conventionalism*, a high degree of adherence to social values and customs that are perceived as endorsed by society and established authorities.

The term "right-wing" as it is used here does not imply a necessarily conservative political perspective. In general, Altemeyer does not find a very strong relationship between political allegiance and the RWA score. An interesting exception, however, was among provincial members of legislative assemblies (MLAs). Responses of one hundred MLAs from Manitoba, Ontario, British Columbia, and New Brunswick showed that Progressive Conservative Party (PC) and Social Credit Party (Socred) MLAs had higher RWA scores than New Democratic Party (NDP) MLAs. The scores of Liberal Party MLAs tended to overlap those of the two more right- and left-wing political groups. Moreover, in none of the provinces was there overlap between the scores of MLAs from right-wing parties and those from left-wing parties. That is, the lowest score of a PC or Socred MLA was higher than the highest score of an NDP politician. Thus, for professional politicians the right-wing authoritarianism scale was very much a predictor of political allegiances, although scores over all did not tend to be at the extremely high end of the scale (indicating very few extremely authoritarian politicians). One limitation in these data that may account for the non-overlap in scores is that this was a self-selected sample: many more MLAs were sent this questionnaire than actually returned it. It is possible that those who returned the questionnaire were, for example, those who felt particularly strongly about the issues within it and, therefore, their responses may not reflect the average responses of such politicians.

Extensive studies have found that high scores in right-wing authoritarianism correlate with ethnic and racial prejudice, acceptance of government high-handedness or illegality (e.g., illegal wire-taps and intimidation of opponents), endorsement of severe punishment for law-breakers, and religious orthodoxy and fundamentalism.

RESPONSES OF THE VICTIMS OF PREJUDICE

It was suggested in chapter 4 that social psychology may have been ethnocentric or specifically *Eurocentric*, perceiving the world through a lens of European history and European values. The term *Eurocentric* also seems to apply, at least to a degree, to the study of prejudice and discrimination. Most theorizing and research on these topics has focused, at least in the United States, on prejudice *by* the European-descended majority *toward* other groups in North American society. Certainly, it has been the prejudice of European-Canadians and Americans that has been most responsible for the pain, suffering, and deprivation of other groups in North America. But in recent years it has become apparent that it is equally important to investigate the reactions of these other groups to prejudice. How have the targets of majority prejudice coped with such treatment? What has it done to their self-concept, their self-esteem, and their identification with their own group? These are the kinds of questions that have been raised with increasing frequency in systematic research.

During the past few decades a growing literature has considered prejudice from the perspective of the persons who are its targets. We will first describe two theoretical approaches that have described the range of possible responses of the victims of prejudice and discrimination. Second, we will look at individual responses related to a sense of self: self-presentation, self-esteem, and negative emotion. Third, we will examine some recent research that indicates differences in the way we evaluate discrimination against our group and against ourselves as individuals. Finally, we will describe a recent model and some related research that explores the effects of prejudice and discrimination on racial and cultural identification.

TYPES OF POSSIBLE RESPONSE TO PREJUDICE AND DISCRIMINATION

An early and influential theoretical approach to prejudice was presented in Gordon Allport's book, *The Nature of Prejudice* (1954). Among the topics considered was the responses of victims of prejudice. Allport described a broad range of possible responses from passivity to aggression against the source of prejudice. However, these responses were classified into two fundamental types based on whether the victim attributed blame for prejudice and discrimination internally or externally. An **intropunitive response** turns the blame for victimization inward, on the self or on the victim's group. Thus, intropunitive defenses against others' prejudice include self-hatred, aggression against or denial of one's own group, sympathy for other victims, clowning (a form of self-ridicule), or neuroticism and passive withdrawal. In contrast, an **extrapunitive response** turns the blame for victimization outward, upon other individuals or groups. Specific extrapunitive defenses are prejudice, aggression, and obsessive suspicion of outgroups, fighting back and militancy, strengthening of ingroup ties, and increased striving for self-improvement.

A more recent perspective, which is related to Allport's, comes from social identity theory (Tajfel, 1982; Tajfel & Turner, 1979). Social identity theory suggests that those who have a negative social identity (i.e., their group is perceived and evaluated negatively by other groups in society) can respond in one of three ways: (1) acceptance and passivity; (2) personal improvement strategies; and (3) group improvement strategies. Individuals may accept the negative view of their group and not attempt personal or group change, though it is suggested that they will feel resentment towards more advantaged groups in society. Those who are motivated to improve their social identity can use *personal* strategies or *group-based* strategies. Examples of personal strategies are attempting personal upward mobility (termed a *social mobility* strategy) or perhaps leaving one's own group. In addition, individuals may simply change the direction of social comparison. By ceasing to compare oneself with members of more positively viewed groups and comparing oneself to other members of the ingroup, one can come to view oneself more positively. Group-based strategies for improvement of social identity will be used when individuals can see the possibility of change in the structural relations between groups in society (termed *social change* strategies). Use of such strategies improves an individual's social identity through improvement of the whole group's position in society. For example, groups may attempt to change the negative social definition of their own characteristics, or they may directly challenge and compete with more advantaged groups in society. This is something that African-American groups did in the 1960s and '70s when they challenged the current negative view and position of their group in the United States. One slogan that emerged from this movement was "black is beautiful," which clearly aimed to redefine the negative view of their characteristics.

These broad categories provide a useful way of organizing and understanding the varied responses of victims of prejudice. While Allport (1954) classified these responses on the basis of attribution of blame (internal or external), Tajfel (1982; Tajfel & Turner, 1979) distinguished between personal and social (or group-based) strategies for improvement. Only a few of the specific responses mentioned have been studied and the following sections examine some of these more specific emotional, cognitive, and strategic responses.

SELF-PRESENTATION, EMOTIONS, AND SELF-ESTEEM

In Canada, Ken Dion and his colleagues (Dion, 1975; Dion & Earn, 1975; Dion, Earn, & Yee, 1986) carried out a series of laboratory experiments investigating the different responses of minority group members to the perception that they had been the victims of prejudice from majority group members. Typically, minority subjects in these studies were asked to carry out a task whose completion depended on the actions of majority individuals. Although subjects did not meet these majority group subjects (who were, in fact, fictitious), they believed that their own minority status was known to them. When the experimenter engineered the minority subjects' failure, apparently through the actions of majority group members, subjects were able to, and often did, attribute blame to the prejudice of these fictitious others. In this way, Dion et al. (1986) were able to examine the responses of Jewish males, Chinese males, and women to perceived prejudice and discrimination by members of the majority (respectively, Christians, non-Chinese, and men). Specifically, they measured differences in stereotypic self-presentations, self-esteem, and emotional responses compared to those who did not perceive themselves as the victim of prejudice.

They found that Chinese males who perceived themselves as the victims of prejudice responded on measures of self-stereotyping by denying the negative side of their social stereotype. On the other hand, Jewish men (Dion & Earn, 1975) and women (Dion, 1975) enhanced identification with the positive aspects of their stereotype. For example, Jewish men might have emphasized how hardworking they were (a positive aspect of the social stereotype of Jews) or women might have focused on their nonviolent or nurturing characteristics (again positive aspects of the female stereotype).

Based on their own work and that of Miller and associates with African-Americans (Boye & Miller, 1968; Miller, Boye, & Gerard, 1968), Dion et al. (1986) suggest that members of minority ethnic groups that are clearly identifiable as outgroups (e.g., Chinese or African-Americans) respond with denial of the negative aspects of their social stereotype. In contrast, those whose minority status is less identifiable (e.g., Jews) or is not always salient (e.g., women) will respond by increased identification with positive aspects of their social stereotype. Dion et al. (1986) suggest that the reason for these contrasting responses may be that different groups socialize their members differently in the ways to cope and respond to prejudice. It may also be due to the fact that clearly identifiable ethnic groups are the target of a more extreme and constant form of prejudice and discrimination. Often the stereotypes of such groups are more negative in content (see Karlins, Coffman, & Walters, 1969; Katz & Braly, 1933). If negative characterization of your group is extreme or constant, it may be difficult not to respond by rejecting that very unflattering description. However, if the negative characterization of your group is mild or infrequent, it may be easier to dismiss it and to focus on positive aspects of your group. Also, the stereotype of less identifiable groups may have more positive content on which to focus (e.g., the English-Canadian stereotype described earlier).

Among *extrapunitive* responses that have been suggested are negative feelings about others. Results for measures of emotion did demonstrate such negative effects of perceiving oneself the target of prejudice. As shown in Figure 5.12, the emotional responses of Jewish men, while including greater sadness and anxiety, also showed greater egotism, aggression, and less social affection toward majority-group members when they perceived themselves as the object of antisemitic prejudice and discrimination.

One type of *intropunitive* response which has been suggested to result from such victimization is a lowering of self-esteem. These studies, counter to expectation, did not find negative effects on self-esteem. Indeed, women who perceived themselves as failing because they were the target of prejudice from a male opponent showed higher self-esteem than those who did not perceive themselves as victims of prejudice (Dion, 1975). This may reflect the fact that subjects in the prejudice condition were able to make an external attribution for their failure to another's prejudice and, thus, maintain self-esteem. Responses of the women and Jewish men in these studies tend towards the extrapunitive rather than intropunitive. However, these laboratory-created situations were short-term and do not tell us about the impact of such experiences in a person's real life. Long-term and relentless experiences of prejudice and discrimination may have the effect of gradually eroding self-esteem.

FOCUSING ON ONE'S GROUP, NOT ONESELF, AS THE TARGET OF PREJUDICE AND DISCRIMINATION

An intriguing finding from recent research in the area of victim responses is that members of minority groups often perceive higher levels of discrimination as directed at their group as a whole than at themselves personally (Crosby, 1982, 1984; Guimond & Dubé-Simard, 1983; Taylor, Wright, Moghaddam, & Lalonde, 1990). It is as if individuals are saying, "My group as a whole has been treated badly, but personally

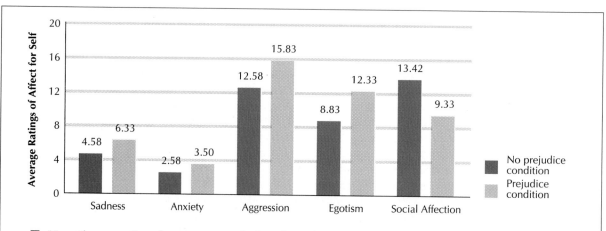

■ Negative emotional responses to being the victim of prejudice

FIGURE 5.12 When Jewish men perceived that their failure at a task was due to prejudice and discrimination by non-Jews, their emotional responses of aggression, sadness, anxiety, and egotism were higher and their social affection for others was lower compared to those who did not perceive prejudice as the cause of their failure.

Source: Adapted from Dion, Earn & Yee, 1978.

I've been lucky enough to avoid such treatment." While it is possible that an occasional individual from a group that is the target of widespread discrimination may be lucky enough to avoid this treatment, it is not possible that this is the *typical* experience of its members. The question then arises—why do group members typically perceive themselves (or present themselves) in this way?

Crosby (1982), for example, found that when asked about their working life, women expressed some resentment and bitterness about "women's employment situation." However, they did not generally feel discriminated against personally at work. This *personal/group discrimination discrepancy* (Taylor et al., 1990) has been shown among Canadian cultural groups such as Francophone Québecois (Guimond & Dubé-Simard, 1983), Anglophone Québecois (Taylor, Wong-Rieger, McKirnan, & Bercusson, 1982), and more recently among Haitian and Indian women immigrants to Quebec (Taylor et al., 1990). In the latter study, despite the fact that fairly high levels of personal discrimination were reported, particularly by the Haitian subjects, both groups of subjects saw greater racial and cultural discrimination directed at their group in general than at themselves personally.

A number of explanations have been put forward for this discrepancy (Crosby, 1982; Taylor et al., 1990). One is that individuals may be motivated to deny the discrimination that they have experienced, presumably because this protects them from perceived threat, shame in front of others, or lowered self-esteem (Taylor et al., 1990). Or, similarly, they may see it as less appropriate to complain about their own personal situation than about that of the group as a whole (Crosby, 1982).

A second explanation has pointed to differences in the cognitive processes of social comparison or group-identification that may occur when someone is asked about discrimination towards the self or towards the group as a whole. When a person is asked about discriminative treatment of his or her group, this directs attention towards the individual's group-based identity and may lead to comparisons of the whole group with other groups in society (a process of *intergroup* social comparison). For example, when asked about women's situation in general (as in Crosby's study, 1982), the obvious source of comparison is men in general. However, when asked about discrimination against the self, attention may be more focused upon personal identity, and evaluation may involve comparison of the self with other individuals within one's group (a process of *intragroup* social comparison). Such differences in identification and social comparison will lead to different sources of information being accessed and, therefore, to differing estimates of levels of discrimination for the self and the group as a whole. This kind of pattern was shown in Crosby's study (1982). Seventy percent of the employed women in her study believed that they personally were better off than most working women, and, when asked to name specific individuals they used as a point of comparison, 71 percent named others of their own gender (intragroup comparisons). Yet these same women (relative to male subjects or housewives) gave the highest ratings of dissatisfaction, and of bitterness and resentment when asked about "women's employment situation" in general.

Finally, the personal/group discrimination discrepancy may occur because of greater certainty about discrimination against groups than against particular individuals. When someone evaluates personal experiences of discrimination, it is often difficult to be certain whether it really did occur, particularly when prejudice and discrimination take the subtle forms discussed earlier. For example, if you have been the victim of *tokenism* in the work place, it may not be clear to you personally that this is the case. Certainly, your employer is unlikely to openly admit that you have been employed on this basis. However, when we can actually measure differences in overall treatment of groups in society (for example, in the workplace or the legal system), then the fact of discrimination at the group level becomes obvious.

RACIAL AND CULTURAL IDENTIFICATION

Racial identification of African-Americans: A theoretical model

One crucial effect of exposure to racial prejudice is heightened **racial identification**. When others exclude you from their schools, offices, and neighborhoods, assume that you possess stereotyped traits, and describe your physical characteristics in negative terms, one obvious effect is to make you, as an individual, conscious of your own membership in a specific racial group. That this is part of the experience of many African-Americans is apparent (e.g., Asante, 1980; Williams, 1976). But what, precisely, does racial identification involve? Is it an all-or-nothing process in which individuals conclude that they belong to a particular racial group and to no other? Modern conceptions of racial identification, based on careful research with African-Americans, suggest that this is not so (Hilliard, 1985). In what is perhaps the most influential current model of this process, Sanders Thompson (1988, 1991) suggests that racial identification of African-Americans involves three key aspects: *physical, psychological,* and *sociocultural* components.

The physical component refers to a sense of acceptance and comfort with the physical attributes of blacks (skin color, hair texture, etc.). The psychological component refers to the individual's sense of concern for and commitment to the racial group. Group pride and feelings of group membership and responsibility are central to this aspect of racial identity. Finally, the sociocultural aspect refers to the individual's attitudes toward cultural, social, and economic issues. These include expressions of cultural heritage, as well as attitudes concerning the economic and political advancement of African-Americans. According to Sanders Thompson (1990, 1991), all three are essential components of an individual's racial identification (see Figure 5.13).

If racial identification is not an all-or-nothing state, a reasonable question to ask about it is this: What factors influence the development of such identification? In other words, what factors determine the extent to which individuals develop the physical, psychological, and/or sociocultural reactions described above? Clearly, it might be possible for a given individual to develop some aspects of racial identification but not others. For example, she or he might be comfortable with the physical features

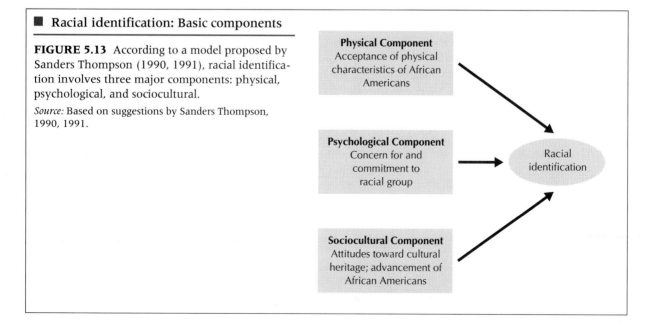

■ Racial identification: Basic components

FIGURE 5.13 According to a model proposed by Sanders Thompson (1990, 1991), racial identification involves three major components: physical, psychological, and sociocultural.

Source: Based on suggestions by Sanders Thompson, 1990, 1991.

Physical Component
Acceptance of physical characteristics of African Americans

Psychological Component
Concern for and commitment to racial group

Sociocultural Component
Attitudes toward cultural heritage; advancement of African Americans

Racial identification

of African-Americans (in fact, recent evidence suggests that such satisfaction exists for many African-Americans; Bond & Cash, 1992). Concurrently, though, the same person might feel little attachment to black culture and little concern over the economic or political opportunities of other blacks. If individuals can vary in the extent to which they demonstrate these different components of racial identification, then perhaps each component is affected by somewhat different factors. A well-conducted study by Sanders Thompson (1991) provides revealing evidence on this issue.

Through interviews and a questionnaire, Sanders Thompson obtained information from almost two hundred African-Americans concerning numerous variables she felt might influence racial identification. She included demographic variables (age, income, level of education, etc.) and variables relating to a wide range of social factors, such as when and to what extent respondents had personally experienced racism, whether there had been conflict within respondents' families relating to skin color or social class, and the extent to which respondents interacted with white Americans (the proportion of whites in their neighborhood and school, their experience with interracial dating, etc.). Additional items were designed to assess the physical, psychological, and sociocultural components of racial identification.

Results indicated that by far the most important predictor of all three aspects of racial identification was the extent to which respondents had personal experience with racial prejudice. The greater such experience, the stronger their racial identification. In general, demographic factors such as age, income, and education were less important (although they did seem to play a role in the psychological aspect of racial identification). Not surprisingly, conflicts within one's own family related to skin color or social class significantly predicted physical racial identification.

What do these findings mean? For one thing, that exposure to white prejudice is a key factor in the development of a strong sense of racial identification among African-Americans. Such experiences seem to drive home the fact that blacks are viewed as different—as a definite outgroup—by the majority. And this in turn leads many African-Americans to identify strongly with their own group. Such identification can then serve as a crucial source of personal strength and support for the individuals involved (White & Parham, 1990). So, in one crucial respect, majority prejudice may have somewhat paradoxical—and largely unintended—effects: It can actually serve to strengthen the sense of group cohesion and the personal convictions of many African-Americans, thus enhancing their ability to resist.

Cultural identification of Canadian ethnic groups

Research has indicated that most Canadian ethnic groups strongly favor maintenance of their own cultural identity (Berry, Kalin, & Taylor, 1977; Lambert, Mermigis, & Taylor, 1986; Moghaddam & Taylor, 1987). In addition, they mostly favor *integration* (maintenance of own group's identity whilst taking part in the larger society) over *assimilation* (loss of own group's separate identity and merging into the larger society, Berry, 1984). Such findings raise questions about the role of a society's policy towards its cultural groups. Can national cultural policies have an impact upon the responses and experiences of minority individuals?

In chapter 1 we saw that the policies of Canada and United States towards their cultural groups differ. The United States has been characterized as having an assimilationist approach (or a *melting pot*), whereas Canada has an integrationist approach (a *cultural mosaic*). The Canadian policy of multiculturalism encourages ethnic groups to maintain their own cultural heritage while participating fully in the larger society. When introduced in 1971, the prime minister at that time, Pierre Trudeau, stated that the policy's intention was to "help to break down discriminatory attitudes and cultural jealousies...[and to provide] confidence in one's own individual identity; out of this can grow respect for that of others and a willingness to share..." (Government of Canada, 1971). It has been pointed out that this statement is expressed in social psychological terms, assuming that the promotion of multiculturalism would increase the confidence of individuals in their own cultural identity, which in turn would lead to increased respect for the identity of other cultural groups and increased interaction (Kalin, 1981; Berry, 1984). This assumption, now termed the **multiculturalism hypothesis,** has been examined by a number of Canadians researchers.

A national survey of ethnic attitudes carried out by Berry, Kalin, and Taylor (1977) found some support for the multiculturalism hypothesis among the two Canadian "charter" groups (French and English Canadians). Greater cultural and economic security in Canada's multicultural context was associated with greater tolerance for other ethnic groups and generally supportive attitudes towards the policy of multiculturalism. In contrast, the response pattern of those with an insecure cultural identity suggested ethnocentrism (Adorno, et al., 1950; Kalin, 1981; Le Vine & Campbell, 1972). That is, those who were most insecure culturally and economically, tended to give the most extreme positive rating for their own group while rating other ethnic groups most negatively.

The 1977 national survey's supportive findings were restricted to French and English Canadians, two large and well-established ethnic groups in Canada. However, when a sample of Greek Canadians was used to test the multiculturalism hypothesis, findings were more mixed (Lambert, et al., 1986). Once again results showed that the more culturally and economically secure Greek subjects felt about the standing of the Greek community, the more favorable were their social perceptions of other ethnic groups in Canada. But this favorability did not extend to a greater desire for social contact. A sense of cultural security was not related to willingness to enter into close social contact with someone from another ethnic group (e.g., as a personal friend or a son-in-law). In addition, a greater belief in the status of Greek Canadians was associated with greater ethnocentrism. Findings, for this group, which is smaller and less long-established compared to French and English Canadians, are less clearly supportive of the multiculturalism hypothesis: A greater sense of cultural identity was not necessarily associated with greater tolerance and desire for increased interaction with other ethnic groups. Finally, as John Berry's review of this literature makes clear (1984), more research is necessary to clarify the conditions under which an integrationist policy can best be carried out.

What are the implications of such research for multicultural societies? While the experience of being the victim of prejudice and discrimination can lead to stronger racial or cultural identification with one's group, this may be a mixed blessing for community relations. On the one hand, it may provide a much needed sense of pride and self-esteem for the individual group member. In addition, theorists have suggested that increased group consciousness may be a necessary stage on the path towards *social change*—the use of a group-based strategy for improvement of one's negative social identity (Tajfel, 1982; Tajfel & Turner, 1979; Taylor & McKirnan, 1984). For example, a sense of group awareness and pride was a part of the movements of the 1960s that advocated a change of social status for African-Americans. On the other hand, increased pride in one's own group is sometimes associated with greater ethnocentrism, or negative attitudes towards other ethnic groups, in addition to a reluctance for close social contact. This would seem to be particularly true when groups are not culturally or economically secure. If the ultimate goal in a multicultural society is a high degree of tolerance and cooperation, *not* a series of groups fortified inside their own cultures, then this research suggests that a sense of *security* in their group's position and future may be needed before individuals feel a "respect for others and a willingness to share" (Government of Canada, 1971).

CHALLENGING PREJUDICE: POTENTIALLY BENEFICIAL STEPS

Whatever the specific origins of prejudice, there can be no doubt about the following point: Prejudice is a brutal, negative force in human society. Wherever and whenever it occurs, it is a drain on precious human resources. So reducing prejudice and countering its effects are important tasks—and especially crucial at a time when world population exceeds 5.5 billion and the potential harm stemming from irrational hatred is greater than ever before. Do any effective strategies for accomplishing these goals—for lessening the impact of prejudice—exist? Fortunately, they do; and while they cannot totally eliminate prejudice or discrimination, these strategies *can* make a substantial dent in the problem. Several of these tactics will now be reviewed.

BREAKING THE CYCLE OF PREJUDICE: ON LEARNING *NOT* TO HATE

Are children born with prejudices firmly in place? Or do they acquire these through experiences at home, in school, and elsewhere? At present, it would be difficult to find someone willing to support the first view, for a vast body of knowledge on human development indicates that bigots are definitely made, not born. Children acquire prejudice and related reactions from their parents, other adults, and their peers. Given this fact, one useful technique for reducing prejudice follows logically: Somehow we must discourage parents and other adults who serve as models for children from providing training in bigotry, and we must encourage them instead to help children develop more positive views about others.

Having stated this principle, we must now admit that putting it into practice is anything but simple. How can we induce parents who may be themselves highly prejudiced to encourage unbiased, prodiversity views among their children? One possibility involves calling parents' attention to their own prejudiced views. As we noted at the start of this chapter, few persons are willing to describe themselves as prejudiced; instead, they view their own negative attitudes toward various groups as entirely justified. A key initial step, therefore, is somehow convincing parents that the problem exists. Once they come face to face with their own prejudices, many do seem willing to modify their words and their behavior. True, some extreme fanatics actually want to turn their children into hate-filled copies of themselves. Most people, however, recognize that we live in a world of increasing ethnic and racial diversity and realize that this environment requires a higher degree of tolerance than ever before.

Adding to the weight of these arguments is a growing body of evidence indicating that prejudice harms those who hold prejudiced views as well as its victims (Dovidio & Gaertner, 1993; Jussim, 1991). Persons who are prejudiced, it appears, live in a world filled with fear, worry, and anger—much of it of their own creation. They fear attack from presumably dangerous social groups, they worry about the economic and health risks stemming from contact with such groups, and they experience anger and other emotional turmoil over what they view as unjustified incursions by these groups into *their* neighborhoods, schools, or offices. Even at less intense levels, however, prejudice can exert negative effects on those who hold it. For example, consider a study conducted by Harris et al. (1992).

These researchers were interested in studying the impact of negative expectancies about others—expectancies closely related to certain types of prejudice—on children's social interactions. To investigate this topic, they arranged for pairs of boys in third through sixth grade, who were previously unacquainted, to play together on two different tasks. Half of the boys in the study had previously been diagnosed as being *hyperactive*, and half were normal. Before the interaction began, half of the boys were told—independently of their partner's actual behavior—that their partner had a special problem: He disrupted the class, talked when he shouldn't, and got into trouble a lot. The remainder were not provided with this information.

One of the tasks on which the boys worked involved building a design with Legos (plastic blocks); the other was more competitive in nature and involved coloring two pictures of a dinosaur with only one set of crayons. The boys' behavior during these interactions was videotaped and later rated by two trained observers on several different dimensions, such as friendliness, giving commands, and offering plans or suggestions. In addition, the boys also reported on their own feelings and reactions to the tasks.

Results indicated that, as expected, boys whose partners had been led to believe that they had a behavioral problem enjoyed the task less, rated their own performance as poorer, and took less credit for success than boys whose partners had not been led to believe they had such a problem. Thus, as has been found in many previous studies (e.g., Snyder & Swann, 1978), negative expectations, which are often part of prejudiced reactions, did adversely affect the targets of such expectations. This is sometimes known as the *self-fulfilling prophecy*; when others hold—and communicate—negative expectations about us, this may undermine our confidence or self-esteem and so lead us to act in ways that tend to confirm these expectancies. Needless to say, self-fulfilling prophecies can exert damaging effects on the targets of prejudice.

Another, and perhaps even more interesting, aspect of the findings obtained by Harris et al. (1991) involved the effects of such expectancies on the boys who had held them—those who had been told that their partners were hyperactive. As shown in Figure 5.14, they enjoyed the tasks less, worked less hard on them, talked less, liked their partners less, and were less friendly toward their partners than boys not given these expectations. In sum, the persons who held negative expectancies, too, were adversely affected by them. These and other findings strongly suggest that in many situations prejudice is definitely a two-edged sword: It harms its intended victims, but it exacts significant costs from the holders of prejudice, too. Educating parents about these effects may indeed cause them to think twice before indoctrinating their children with their own prejudiced views.

Please note: We don't wish to imply that holding prejudiced views, or derogating the members of outgroups, produces mainly negative effects on prejudiced persons. If that were so, prejudice would probably not constitute a major social problem. In fact, as suggested by Tajfel (1982), derogating outgroup members may help the persons who engage in such actions to establish a positive social identity. A growing body of empirical findings (e.g., Branscombe & Wann, 1993) indicates that when prejudiced persons derogate outgroup members, they sometimes experience a boost in self-esteem. So there are indeed some rewards for engaging in such behavior. The trick, it would seem, is to convince parents that the potential harm more than offsets any temporary benefits resulting from prejudiced views or actions.

DIRECT INTERGROUP CONTACT: THE POTENTIAL BENEFITS OF ACQUAINTANCE

We often have little contact with other cultural groups or minorities, particularly if we hold strong prejudices against them. For example, a study carried out in Toronto found that only 18 percent of those who described themselves as "very prejudiced" had had close contact with minority groups. Whereas, over 56 percent of those who were "very tolerant" had had such close contact (Henry, 1978, in Alcock, Carment, & Sadava, 1988). This state of affairs raises an intriguing question: Can prejudice be reduced by

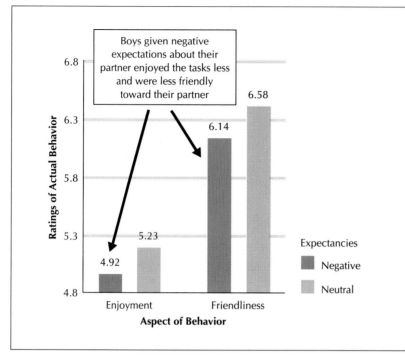

Negative effects of prejudice on those who hold such views

FIGURE 5.14 Boys who were told that a stranger with whom they interacted was hyperactive enjoyed the tasks on which they worked less and were less friendly toward their partner than boys who were not given such information. In this case, their negative expectations (one aspect of prejudice) seemed to interfere with their own performance and enjoyment.

Source: Based on data from Harris et al., 1992.

somehow increasing the degree of contact between different groups? The idea that it can is known as the contact hypothesis, and there are several good reasons for predicting that such a strategy might prove effective (Pettigrew, 1981). First, increased contact between persons from different groups can lead to growing recognition of similarities between them. As we will see in chapter 6, perceived similarity can generate enhanced mutual attraction. Second, while stereotypes are resistant to change, they can be altered when sufficient information inconsistent with them is encountered. Increased contact between persons from different social groups may provide such information. Third, increased contact may help counter the illusion of outgroup homogeneity described earlier. For these reasons it seems possible that direct intergroup contact may be one effective means of combating prejudice. Is it? One large-scale correlational study in Canada suggested that it is (Kalin & Berry, 1982).

Rudolf Kalin and John Berry used responses of over 1800 subjects in order to test the contact hypothesis. They measured three variables: the attitudes of outgroup members towards seven Canadian ethnic groups: English, French, Native, German, Jewish, Italian, and Ukranian; familiarity of subjects with those ethnic groups; and the percentage presence of an ethnic group in the subject's geographical area of residence. If findings were supportive of the contact hypothesis, then as the percentage presence of an ethnic group in a neighborhood increased, subjects should report greater familiarity with that group (which suggests greater contact with its members) and increased positive attitudes. This is exactly what they found, with two exceptions. For all ethnic groups, outgroup members reported greater familiarity with that group as their presence in a neighbourhood actually increased (a positive correlation between familiarity and percentage presence). Further, as the presence of an ethnic group in an area increased, outgroup members reported more positive attitudes towards them. This positive correlation between percentage presence and evaluation of an ethnic group was true for all but two of the group evaluations: The increased presence of French Canadians and Native people was not always associated with increased positive attitudes by outgroup members. There was a significant positive relationship between percentage presence of French Canadians and the evaluation of them by Angloceltic subjects, as the contact hypothesis would predict. However, this relationship was not significant for non-Angloceltic subjects. Similarly, as the presence of Native Canadians in a neighborhood increased, this was not associated with increased positive attitudes by outgroup subjects. These two exceptions perhaps reflect problem areas in intergroup relations in Canada. Certainly, the data mentioned earlier, which showed high levels of acculturative stress for Native people (Berry et al, 1987, in chapter 4), suggest that contact with other cultures has often had negative results for these groups. On the whole, however, Kalin and Berry's correlational test of the contact hypothesis is supportive: for the majority of the Canadian ethnic groups studied, greater contact was associated with more positive attitudes.

A large number of studies, both in the laboratory and in the field, have investigated the contact hypothesis (Cook, 1985; Stephan, 1985). This accumulated evidence has confirmed that intergroup contact can reduce prejudice, but only under certain conditions.

First, the groups interacting must be roughly equal in social, economic, or task-related status. If they differ sharply in such respects, communication may be difficult and prejudice can actually be increased by contact. Second, the contact situation must involve cooperation and interdependence so that the groups work toward shared goals (as in the Robber's Cave experiment described earlier). Third, contact between the groups must be informal so that they can get to know one another as individuals. Fourth, contact must occur in a setting in which existing norms favor group equality. Fifth, the groups must interact in ways that permit disconfirmation of negative stereotyped beliefs about one another. And sixth, the persons involved must view one another as typical of their respective groups; only then will they generalize their pleasant contacts to other persons or situations (Wilder, 1984).

When contact between initially hostile groups occurs under these conditions, prejudice between them does seem to decrease (Cook, 1985; Riordan, 1978). Such effects have been observed in the United States, where increased contact between African-Americans and whites has been found to reduce prejudice between them (Aronson, Bridgeman, & Geffner, 1978), and in many other nations as well. For example, increased school contact between Jews of Middle Eastern origin and Jews of European or American origin tends to reduce ingroup bias among Israeli soldiers (Schwarzwald, Amir, & Crain, 1992).

On the basis of these findings, it seems reasonable to suggest that, when used with care, direct group contact can be an effective tool for combating cross-group hostility and prejudice. When people get to know one another, it seems, many of the anxieties, stereotypes, and false perceptions that have previously kept them apart seem to melt in the warmth of new friendships. Or, to put it another way, when stereotypes and other preconceived notions about others collide with social reality, it is sometimes reality that carries the day. As Schwarzwald et al. (1992, p. 366) put it:

> ... despite the strong social and psychological forces working to maintain the vicious circle of prejudice, change can be induced and preserved over time. Interethnic contact can alter the character of later interethnic relations.

RECATEGORIZATION: REDRAWING THE BOUNDARY BETWEEN "US" AND "THEM"

In the town of Siena, Italy, different neighborhoods (wards) form tight-knit groups. Residents identify strongly with these groups, which date back to the Middle Ages, and proudly display the symbol of their ward (e.g., a turtle, a seashell, a falcon; see Figure 5.15). Once a year, the various neighborhoods engage in a citywide horse race, and the struggle for victory in this event is fierce. For many days prior to the event, crowds of young people from the various neighborhoods gather in the streets to taunt one another. These sessions often become so intense that violent fights erupt, sometimes with tragic consequences. During the race itself almost any action that might bring victory is acceptable, so jockeys frequently use tactics that would be banned on most racetracks throughout the world.

To an outsider these events seem puzzling. Siena is a small city, and the persons involved all speak the same language, share the same culture, and practice the same religion. Yet because they choose to divide their social world into competing groups, hostility and conflict between them run high. But now consider what happens when sports teams from Siena play against teams from other Italian cities. During such events, neighborhood distinctions disappear and all Sienese join together in rooting for *their* teams, which represent the entire city of Siena. What has happened? In terms of the principles discussed in this chapter, the citizens of Siena have shifted the location of the boundary between "us" and "them." At the time of the citywide horse race, this boundary falls between neighborhoods. When their city competes with other towns, however, the boundary is moved outward and falls between Siena and these rivals.

Such shifts in the boundary between "us" and "them" are a common part of social life. Many of us have had the experience of rooting for our school's team when it plays against teams from other schools but of forgetting such distinctions and rooting for our city's or our state's team when it competes in a wider arena. Can this kind of boundary shift or **recategorization** be used to reduce prejudice in other contexts? Research by Gaertner and his colleagues (1989) indicates that it can. In these

■ The us-versus-them effect

FIGURE 5.15 When neighborhoods within Siena (a small Italian city) compete against one another in a yearly horse race, each neighborhood perceives itself as us and the other neighborhood as them. Sometimes the competition becomes so intense that it leads to violent outbursts in which many persons are injured.

studies, groups of six participants first worked on a task in separate three-person teams. This was done to establish a firm *us-them* boundary between the teams. Then, in a second phase of the research, the same individuals worked on the same tasks again, but under one of several contrasting conditions. Some groups of participants continued to work as two separate teams, others worked as separate individuals (i.e., each worked alone), and still others worked together as a single six-person group. Finally, the groups rated one another on various dimensions. Gaertner and his colleagues (1989) reasoned that the experience of working either as individuals or as part of a single group would shift the us-them boundary so as to include persons who were originally members of the competing three-person team; thus, prejudice toward these persons would decrease in these conditions relative to that expressed in the condition where the boundary between these teams was maintained. Results offered strong support for this prediction.

Can this principle of recategorization (or, in the case of people working as individuals, *de*categorization) be put to practical use? Gaertner and his colleagues believe that it can, and have formulated a theoretical model—the **common ingroup identity model**—to explain how this might be so. According to this model, which is derived from social identity theory and research (Tajfel, 1982), when various factors (e.g., perceptions of a shared fate, cultural norms stressing egalitarian values) lead individuals belonging to different groups to view themselves as members of a single social entity, attitudes toward former outgroup members become more positive. These favorable attitudes then promote increased positive contacts between members of the two previously separate groups. Such contact, in turn, reduces intergroup bias still further. In short, weakening or eliminating initial us-them boundaries starts a process that carries the persons involved toward major reductions in prejudice and hostility.

How can this process be launched? The results of a study by Gaertner et al. (1990) suggest that one factor that can get it started is "cooperative interaction" among members of the two initially distinct groups. In this investigation, two separate three-person groups were created and then brought into contact with each other under two different conditions. In the *cooperative interaction* condition, they worked together toward common goals and expected to share the same outcomes. In the *no cooperative interaction* condition, in contrast, they merely listened to the other group's discussion and did not work together in a cooperative manner. As expected, cooperative interaction increased the tendency of the two groups to perceive themselves as one entity. Moreover, cooperative interaction also reduced feelings of bias toward the former outgroup (that is, the other group). These findings and those of other research (e.g., Brewer et al., 1987; Vanbeselaere, 1987) suggest that strategies based on shifting individuals' perceived boundaries so as to include a wider range of persons inside the us-them boundary offers a very promising approach to the reduction of prejudice.

Prejudice in a Multicultural High School: Testing the Common Ingroup Identity Model in a Field Setting

While the research conducted by Gaertner and his colleagues provides strong support for the common ingroup identity model, this research does suffer from one obvious drawback: It used short-lived, artificially created groups. How does the model fare when tested under more natural conditions? To find out, Gaertner et al. (1993) have recently conducted follow-up research in a multicultural high school in the United States. Students in the school came from many different ethnic backgrounds—African-American, Chinese, Hispanic, Japanese, Korean, Vietnamese, and Caucasian. More than thirteen hundred students in the school completed a survey designed to measure their perceptions of conditions shown in previous research to influence the effects of increased contact with persons from other groups (e.g., equal status, cooperative interdependence, norms supportive of friendly intergroup contact). Other items on the survey measured students' perceptions of the extent to which the student body at the school was a single group, consisted of distinct groups, or was composed of separate individuals. Finally, students also completed items designed to measure their feelings toward both their ingroup and various outgroups.

Results offered strong support for the model. First, as predicted, perceptions of cooperative interdependence between students from different groups were positively related to the students' belief that the student body was a single group. Similarly, the extent to which the students felt as though they belonged to one group was significantly related to positive feelings toward outgroup members. Finally, the stronger the students' feelings of interdependence, the smaller the difference between their feelings toward ingroup and outgroup members. In sum, as the model predicts, the greater the extent to which students at the school felt that they belonged to a single cooperative group, the lower their feelings of intergroup bias. When combined with the results of systematic laboratory studies, these findings suggest that efforts to induce persons belonging to different groups to engage in *recategorization*—to shift the boundary between "us" and "them" so as to include persons previously excluded—can be an important first step toward the reduction of many forms of prejudice.

THE NATURE OF PREJUDICE AND DISCRIMINATION

Prejudice is a negative attitude toward the members of some social group that is based solely on their membership in that group. *Discrimination* refers to harmful actions directed toward the persons or groups who are the targets of prejudice. Discrimination can be overt, ranging from relatively mild forms such as avoidance or exclusion to physical violence. However, it often occurs in more subtle forms such as *tokenism* or *reverse discrimination*. Highly prejudiced persons experience relatively little guilt or shame when they engage in discriminatory behavior toward the targets of their prejudice.

ORIGINS OF PREJUDICE

Several contrasting views have been offered concerning the origins of prejudice. The *realistic conflict* view suggests that prejudice stems from competition for scarce resources between social groups. A second theory, *social categorization*, suggests that prejudice stems from our strong tendencies to divide the social world into two camps, "us" and "them." A third perspective calls attention to the role of early experience, in which children acquire prejudiced attitudes from parents, teachers, friends, and others.

Much recent evidence supports the view that prejudice stems from certain aspects of *social cognition*—the way in which we think about others and the social world. *Stereotypes*, cognitive frameworks involving generalizations about the typical characteristics of members of social groups, play an especially important role in this regard. Once stereotypes are activated, they exert profound effects on social thought. Other aspects of social cognition that play a role in prejudice include *illusory correlations*—perceptions of stronger relationships between unusual or distinctive events than actually exist—and the illusion of *outgroup homogeneity*, which involves the tendency to perceive lower variability in the behavior of outgroup members than in the behavior of persons belonging to our own social group.

RESPONSE OF THE VICTIMS OF PREJUDICE

Since the mid-1970s, a growing number of studies have examined the effects of prejudice from the perspective of those who are its targets. Theorists have distinguished between *intropunitive* responses of victims, which involve self-blame, and *extrapunitive* responses, which involve other-blame. Further, responses can be classified as strategies aimed at personal improvement or at group improvement. Research has demonstrated changes in self-presentations and affect as a response to perceived prejudice. Reported levels of discrimination also vary as

a function of whether victims are focusing on their group as a whole or themselves personally, with group levels reported to be higher. Modern theories of *racial identification* propose that such identification consists of several distinct components, including *physical, psychological,* and *sociocultural identification*. While these are influenced by demographic variables (age, income, education), racial identification appears to be most strongly affected by personal experiences with racial prejudice. The *multiculturalism hypothesis,* which assumes that confidence in cultural identification will lead to improved relations with other ethnic groups, has received some, but mixed, support in a Canadian context. Increased tolerance for other ethnic groups is most strongly related to a sense of security in the standing of one's own cultural group.

STRATEGIES FOR REDUCING PREJUDICE

One way to reduce prejudice is to encourage parents and others to transmit tolerant rather than prejudiced attitudes to children. Direct intergroup contact also seems to be helpful in this respect, provided that the contact occurs under appropriate conditions. Another useful technique involves somehow inducing individuals to shift the boundary between "us" and "them" so that former outgroup members are included in the ingroup. Cognitive interventions, such as inducing individuals to think about others in terms of their individual attributes rather than in terms of stereotypes, and inducing them to form counterstereotypic inferences, can also be effective in reducing prejudice.

KEY TERMS

Common Ingroup Identity Model A theory suggesting that to the extent individuals in different groups view themselves as members of a single social entity, positive contacts between groups will increase and intergroup bias will be reduced.

Contact Hypothesis The view that increased contact between members of various social groups can be effective in reducing prejudice between them. Such efforts seem to succeed only when contact takes place under specific, favorable conditions.

Discrimination Negative behaviors directed toward members of social groups who are the object of prejudice.

Extrapunitive Response A response of the victim of prejudice and discrimination that turns the blame outward, towards other individuals or groups.

Gender Stereotypes Stereotypes concerning the traits supposedly possessed by females and males, traits that distinguish the two genders from each other.

Illusion of Outgroup Homogeneity The tendency to perceive members of outgroups as more similar to one another (less variable) than the members of one's own ingroup.

Illusory Correlations Perceptions of stronger associations between variables than actually exist. Illusory correlations come about because each variable is a distinctive event and the co-occurrence of such events is readily entered into and retrieved from memory.

Ingroup The social group to which an individual perceives herself or himself as belonging ("us").

Ingroup Differentiation Hypothesis The view that individuals perceive greater variability among members of their ingroup than they do among members of various outgroups.

Intropunitive Response A response of the victim of prejudice and discrimination that turns the blame inward towards the self or the victim's group.

Multiculturalism Hypothesis The assumption that the promotion of multiculturalism will increase the confidence of individuals in their own cultural identity, which in turn will lead to increased respect for the identity of other cultural groups and increased interaction with them.

Outgroup Any group other than the one to which individuals perceive themselves as belonging ("them").

Prejudice Negative attitudes toward the members of specific social groups.

Racism Prejudice and discrimination based upon a person's race or ethnicity.

Racial Identification The process through which individuals (especially those belonging to minority groups) acquire identification with their own racial group. Current models of racial identification suggest that it involves physical, psychological, and sociocultural components.

Realistic Conflict Theory The view that prejudice sometimes stems from direct competition among social groups over scarce and valued resources.

Recategorization Shift in the boundary between an individual's ingroup ("us") and some outgroup ("them"). As a result of such recategorization, persons formerly viewed as outgroup members may now be viewed as belonging to the ingroup.

Reverse Discrimination The tendency to evaluate or treat persons belonging to other groups (especially ones that are the object of strong ethnic or racial prejudice) more favorably than members of one's own group.

Right-wing Authoritarians Those who are particularly vulnerable to prejudice and show submissiveness to figures of authority, agression towards nonconformists or those who are different and who hold conventional values.

Sexism Prejudice based on gender.

Social Categorization Our tendency to divide the social world into two separate categories: our ingroup ("us") and various outgroups ("them").

Social Learning View (of prejudice) The view that prejudice is learned—acquired through direct and vicarious experience—in much the same manner as other attitudes.

Stereotypes Beliefs to the effect that all members of specific social groups share certain traits or characteristics. Stereotypes are cognitive frameworks that strongly influence the processing of incoming social information.

Tokenism Instances in which individuals, businesses, educational institutions, and so on perform trivial positive actions for members of outgroups toward whom they feel strong prejudice. Such tokenistic behaviors are then used as an excuse for refusing more substantive beneficial actions for these groups.

FOR MORE INFORMATION

J. F. Dovido & S. L. Gaertner (Eds.). (1986). *Prejudice, discrimination, and racism.* Orlando, FL: Academic Press.

Contains chapters prepared by various experts on the topics of prejudice and discrimination. Several call attention to the fact that racial prejudice has not actually decreased or disappeared in recent years—it has simply shifted into more subtle forms.

Knopke, H., Norrell, & Rogers, R. (Eds.). (1993). *Opening doors: An appraisal of race relations in contemporary America.* Tuscaloosa: University of Alabama Press.

A valuable overview of the current state of race relations in the United States. Chapters by social psychologists who have studied racial prejudice in their research provide valuable insights on this important and timely topic.

Stephan, W. G. (1985). Intergroup relations. In G. Lindzey and E. Aronson (Eds.), *Handbook of social psychology* (Vol. 2, 599–658). New York: Random House.

A very thorough review of current knowledge about intergroup relations. Carefully examines many processes that play a role in the development of prejudice as well as several techniques for combating prejudice and discrimination.

Chapter SIX

Relationships: From Attraction to Loneliness

SPECIAL SECTIONS

For most people, relationships constitute a crucial aspect of their lives. Despite changes in our society and widespread changes in various attitudes and values, most of us believe that an ideal life includes interacting with cherished relatives, having close friends, falling in love, getting married, and becoming parents. However, this is not always easy to achieve. Sometimes choosing friendships or dating relationships can be difficult enough and even established family life is not without its difficulties. We are all aware, after exposure to films and novels as well as to real-life experiences, that relatives often don't get along, friendships fade, and love can turn to hate. Sometimes close relationships cause more pain than joy. Still, despite negative examples all around us, we tend to maintain our hopes about what relationships can and should be.

Levinger (1980) has described relationships as passing through five possible stages: *initial attraction, building a relationship, continuation,* and—for some—*deterioration* and *ending*. This chapter will follow this outline, beginning with the initial attraction and building stages of the relationship. The majority of the research on relationships, until recent years, has concentrated on these first two stages, under the heading of **interpersonal attraction**. This area is concerned with the initial steps involved in establishing relationships. We will first show how most interpersonal contacts are controlled by factors that are only indirectly related to the characteristics of the people involved. Most of the individuals we meet happen to come into close *physical proximity* with us because of such impersonal environmental determinants as the location of seats in a classroom, rooms in a dormitory, or desks in an office. The likelihood that proximity will lead to a positive versus a negative relationship is based in part on each person's *emotional state*. We tend to like others when our emotions are positive and to dislike others when our emotions are negative, regardless of the reason for feeling good or feeling bad. Even though the physical setting fosters contact and positive feelings facilitate positive evaluations, two people will progress toward getting to know one another only if they are sufficiently motivated to *affiliate*—that is, only if they feel the need to establish a relationship. Each individual is also influenced in positive and negative ways by attitudes and beliefs about the *external characteristics* of the other person (physical attractiveness, accent, skin color, height, clothing style, and so forth). Once interaction begins, interpersonal attraction is strongly determined by the extent to which the two people discover that they are *similar* in various attitudes, beliefs, values, and interests.

Such relationships become even more positive if each person is able to communicate his or her *positive evaluations* of the other, either in words or in actions.

Beyond these initial stages, we will turn to the *continuation* of relationships on the long term. Social psychologists, as well as other behavioral scientists, are focusing more and more attention on the study of long-term close relationships (Duck & Barnes, 1992; Hatfield & Rapson, 1992a, 1993; Morgan & White, 1993; Werner, Altman, & Brown, 1992)—mostly among heterosexuals, but increasingly among gays and lesbians as well (Schullo & Alperson, 1984). Given the importance of family, friendship, love, and marriage to most people, what makes close relationships thrive, and how can such relationships lead to problems?

At the basis of most ongoing relationships is *love* and we will consider the different forms it can take. Next we will turn our attention to the nature and maintenance of *long-term intimate relationships*. The final two stages of relationship in the Levinger model (1980) are *deterioration* and *ending*. This is not to suggest that relationships inevitably reach this point. However, few relationships are entirely trouble-free, and it is often our response to problems that occur that determines whether the relationship continues or ends. Therefore, we'll also consider *troubled relationships*, how *problems* arise and the effects of *dissolution*. Finally, the phenomenon of *loneliness*, which can result when relationships fail, or are not formed at all, will be examined.

INTERPERSONAL ATTRACTION: WHEN STRANGERS MEET

There are five and a half billion people living on our planet. Each one of us interacts with only a very small percentage of the total group; nevertheless, it would be possible to know thousands of people. In fact, however, we tend to form close relationships with a quite limited number of individuals. During the last half of this century, social psychologists have been actively attempting to identify the basis we each use to narrow our social world to a manageable number of acquaintances—and to determine what factors lead us to like some of these individuals and dislike others. At the earliest stage, two people are likely to become acquainted if they are brought into contact through simple physical proximity, or **propinquity**, and if each is experiencing positive rather than negative affect at the time.

PHYSICAL PROXIMITY

Friendships often begin because of a series of unplanned encounters that are controlled by the physical details of the immediate environment. On the basis of these casual, accidental contacts, each person begins to recognize the other. At this point it is common for people to exchange greetings when they see one another and to exchange remarks about the weather or whatever. This positive response to a familiar face can be observed even among infants. They are, for example, more likely to smile when exposed to a photograph of someone they have seen before than in response to a stranger's picture (Brooks-Gunn & Lewis, 1981).

The first empirical data suggesting a propinquity effect were provided by sociological studies in the 1930s, which demonstrated that prior to marriage most couples had lived within the same neighbourhood (Bossard, 1932; Davie & Reeves, 1939). Later studies in student residences, where individuals or couples had been randomly assigned to units, showed similar effects of propinquity. Most friendships occurred among those who were on the same or adjacent floors in dormitories, or within 22 feet of each other in apartments (e.g., Evans & Wilson, 1949; Festinger, Schachter, & Back, 1950).

The power of propinquity

The generality of the propinquity effect is shown by its extension to friendship patterns in such diverse populations as urban residents in a housing project for the elderly (Nahemow & Lawton, 1975) and young suburban families in a housing development (Whyte, 1956). It seems to be a general truth that the closer two people live, the better their chance of becoming close friends (Ebbesen, Kjos, & Konecni, 1976). When residential propinquity brings blacks and whites together in a nonconfrontational atmosphere, prejudice decreases (Deutsch & Collins, 1951).

Classroom investigations permit more precise study of such effects, because seats can be assigned and the amount of contact in this setting is limited to specific days and times. Once again, classroom friendships are clearly determined by where each person is seated. Those sitting side by side are most likely to become acquainted. When students are seated alphabetically, friendships form between those whose last names begin with the same or a nearby letter (Segal, 1974). This may not seem important until you consider the fact that you may meet some of your friends (and perhaps even your future spouse) simply because of an instructor's seating chart. For example, a couple who donated a large sum of money to a New York university in 1990 told a reporter that they met in an economics class at that institution during the 1930s because they were seated in alphabetical order—Edward George met and married Frances Gildea.

Among other implications, those given a corner seat or a seat on the end of a row make fewer friends (Maisonneuve, Palmade, & Fourment, 1952). So, the total number of friends you make in a class depends in part on where you sit. If you have someone sitting on your right and someone on your left, you are likely to make two friends, whereas a seat on the end of a row yields the likelihood of only one new friend (Byrne & Buehler, 1955). Further, if the instructor changes seat assignments once or twice during the semester, each student becomes acquainted with additional classmates (Byrne, 1961).

Why does propinquity lead to attraction?

To some extent, we are affected by propinquity because we tend to avoid strangers unless we are forced to come in contact because of where we live, where we are seated in a classroom, and so forth. But there is another, more basic, reason. As Zajonc (1968) and his colleagues have reported, **repeated exposure** to a new stimulus (frequent contact with that stimulus) leads to a more and more positive evaluation of the stimulus—as long as the initial reaction is not an extremely negative one. Whether the stimulus is a drawing, a word in an unknown foreign language, a new product being advertised, a political candidate, or a stranger, the greater the exposure, the more positive the response (Moreland & Zajonc, 1982). Perhaps in part because of the repeated exposure effect, even a letter of the alphabet that occurs in one's own name is perceived to be more attractive than a letter not in one's name (Nuttin, 1987). The general idea is that we respond with at least mild discomfort to anything or anyone new. With repeated exposure we become desensitized, anxiety decreases, and that which was *new* becomes *familiar*.

In a test of how repeated exposure operates in a college classroom, Moreland and Beach (1992) found that as the number of exposures to a fellow student increases, the greater the attraction toward that person. At the end of a semester, these researchers asked students in a large college course to evaluate four different female classmates (actually, experimental assistants). One of these women never attended the class, one attended four times, one ten times, and one fifteen times. To control for other variables that might influence attraction, the experimenters selected assistants who were similar in appearance, and they instructed the assistants not to interact with any of the actual students, in or out of class. As shown in Figure 6.1, attraction toward these strangers increased as the number of classroom exposures increased; thus, the effect of repeated exposure was clearly evident.

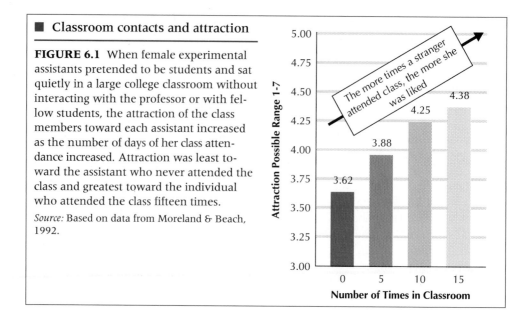

■ Classroom contacts and attraction

FIGURE 6.1 When female experimental assistants pretended to be students and sat quietly in a large college classroom without interacting with the professor or with fellow students, the attraction of the class members toward each assistant increased as the number of days of her class attendance increased. Attraction was least toward the assistant who never attended the class and greatest toward the individual who attended the class fifteen times.

Source: Based on data from Moreland & Beach, 1992.

Note that propinquity is not 100 percent effective in fostering attraction. Repeated exposure to a stranger who behaves in an unpleasant fashion leads to more and more dislike (Swap, 1977). Even a stranger who is not unpleasant can be evaluated negatively if propinquity involves interference with your need for **privacy**: your need to limit others' knowledge of your personal life (Larson & Bell, 1988). Sometimes you prefer to be by yourself rather than with another person—no matter who that person is. At such times, too much propinquity can be aversive. This is one reason that those who live in close physical proximity (sailors on submarine duty, siblings sharing a bedroom, and even some married couples) may come to feel less and less attraction over time rather than more and more.

AFFECT: EMOTIONS AND ATTRACTION

Humans experience and express emotions throughout their daily lives, and these emotions strongly affect perception, cognition, learning, motivation, decision making—and attraction (Erber, 1991; Forgas, 1993a, 1993b; Zajonc & McIntosh, 1992). As you'll recall from chapter 2, psychologists often use the term **affect** in referring to emotions or feelings. A person's emotional state can most concisely be described as falling along a positive-negative (or pleasant-unpleasant) dimension (McIntyre et al., 1991; Russell, Weiss, & Mendelsohn, 1989). Within these broad categories, more specific emotions can also be distinguished; the basic elements of negative affect, for example, seem to consist of fear, hostility, guilt, and sadness (Watson & Clark, 1992).

Affect as the basis of attraction

A great many experiments have established that positive feelings lead to liking, while negative feelings lead to dislike. So anything that arouses positive versus negative affect influences attraction. Music is an example. We know that music has a powerful effect on emotions and on behavior. For example, slow-tempo music played in a grocery store results in increased sales, presumably because shoppers relax, walk slowly, and consider a greater number of products (Milliman, 1982). In contrast, fast-tempo music speeds up behavior; if it is played while people eat, they respond with more bites per minute (Roballey et al., 1985; see figure 6.2). Besides tempo, music also can arouse positive versus negative feelings. In an attraction experiment, female college students were asked to rate male strangers depicted in photographs. While they engaged in this task, the experimenter played pleasant music (rock), unpleasant music (avant-garde classical), or no music (May & Hamilton, 1980). Compared to the no-music condition, students listening to rock music liked the strangers better and even thought they were more physically attractive; the opposite was true for those listening to avant-garde tapes.

Sometimes the affect is created by the affective state of the other person; that is, happy or sad moods can prove to be contagious (Goleman, 1991; Hsee, Hatfield, & Chemtob, 1992; Sullins, 1991). This may explain in part why depressed people are rated negatively by others (Holowaty, Pliner, & Flett, 1990). Also, people tend to laugh and smile when they hear laughter, even if they don't know what is funny (Provine, 1992). When emotional contagion was studied in public settings such as shopping centers and grocery stores, it was found that when an experimental assistant smiled at a stranger, that person was very likely to smile back. When the assistant frowned, however, this did not elicit a frown (Hinsz & Tomhave, 1991). In other words, "Smile and the world smiles with you; frown and you frown alone." The investigators also noted sex differences in that women were more likely to smile back than were men, and strangers of both sexes were more likely to return the smile of a female than of a male.

Whatever the source of an individual's emotional state, happy feelings lead to liking, but if that person feels unhappy, he or she likes other people less well (Swallow & Kuiper, 1987) and evaluates them in negative terms (Shapiro, 1988). And emotions influence interpersonal behavior as well as attraction responses (Clark & Watson, 1988). Cunningham (1988) induced happy or sad feelings in male subjects (some saw movies and others received false evaluations), then sent the subjects to a waiting room in which a female confederate was seated. The males in a positive mood communicated with the female stranger more and disclosed more about themselves than did those in a negative mood.

■ **Music influences our emotions and our overt behavior**

FIGURE 6.2 Music affects how we feel and what we do in many situations. For example, when grocery stores play background music with a slow tempo, shoppers go down the aisles more slowly and purchase more items. Also, music that has an effect on emotions influences attraction responses. People like strangers more when listening to music they like, while they like strangers less when disliked music is playing.

Why does affect influence attraction?

Many investigators have concluded that a simple process underlies the relationship between emotions and liking. According to the **reinforcement-affect model** (Clore & Byrne, 1974), we like anyone or anything that makes us feel good and dislike whoever or whatever makes us feel bad. The role of affect in this process is all-important. The role of reinforcement is less obvious, however. As shown in figure 6.3, we react not only to the person or event *responsible* for arousing our emotions but also to anyone or anything simply *associated* with those feelings. For example, you view a funny movie, feel happy, and like the movie; if someone is with you at the time, you associate that person with your positive emotions and like him or her. This conditioning process is often the basis on which we form our likes and dislikes (Byrne & Clore, 1970).

As we discussed in chapter 3, there is ample evidence that attitudes can be acquired through classical conditioning when the attitude object is paired with a stimulus that evokes negative affect or with one that evokes positive affect. In the Krosnick et al. (1992) experiment on subliminal conditioning that was described, researchers conditioned attitudes toward a female stranger by pairing her pictures with either pleasant

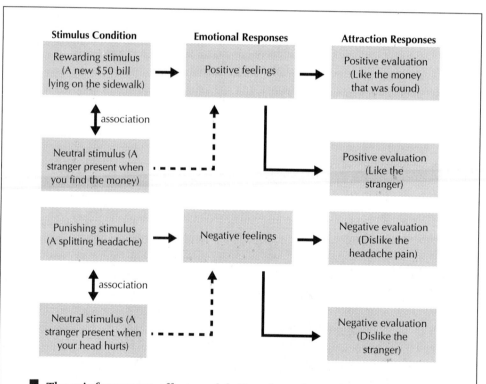

■ The reinforcement-affect model: Emotions determine attraction

FIGURE 6.3 According to the reinforcement-affect model, likes and dislikes are based on the arousal of positive versus negative feelings. We like any rewarding person, thing, or event because they create positive emotions. We dislike any punishing person, thing, or event because they create negative emotions. When someone else happens to be present at the time (even though not responsible for the emotions), he or she becomes associated with the positive or negative feelings. Thus, on the basis of simple classical conditioning, we like anyone who is associated with positive emotions and dislike anyone associated with negative emotions.

or unpleasant pictures that were presented at speeds so rapid that the participants were unaware of them. In addition to providing new evidence consistent with the reinforcement-affect model, these investigators were able to show that it is possible to like or dislike someone—and to hold positive or negative beliefs about them—without having any realization of the basis for these reactions. It seems probable that in our everyday lives we develop some of our interpersonal likes and dislikes on the basis of just such associations; we're not always sure just why we "like Jill and dislike Jack."

Conditioning of affective responses has been studied in a somewhat different context by Rozin, Millman, and Nemeroff (1986). These investigators point out that even brief contact between a neutral object and something that arouses positive or negative feelings leads to a transfer of the emotional response to the neutral object. For example, a laundered shirt that had been worn by a disliked person was rated as less desirable than a laundered shirt that had been worn by a liked person. Even though the shirts did not actually differ, one elicited a positive evaluative response and the other a negative response on the basis of learned associations.

If two people are brought into repeated contact by propinquity and if both experience relatively positive affect, they are at a transition point. They may simply remain superficial acquaintances who nod and perhaps say hello when they happen to see one another. Another possibility is that they may begin to converse from time to time, learn each other's names, and begin to exchange information about themselves, thus becoming close acquaintances. Which alternative is chosen depends on two factors—*affiliative needs* and reactions to *observable characteristics*.

THE AFFILIATION NEED: INDIVIDUAL DIFFERENCES AND EXTERNAL EVENTS

People spend a great deal of their time interacting with friends and acquaintances (see Figure 6.4), perhaps because our species has found it beneficial to behave in this way (Wright, 1984). Studies of chimpanzees and monkeys provide interesting evidence that the need to affiliate may be based on biological factors (de Waal, 1989).

■ **Affiliation is a major aspect of human behavior**

FIGURE 6.4 Most of us spend a large portion of our free time interacting with people we know and like. Affiliation is one of the basic human needs. Individuals differ in the strength of their need to affiliate, and this motive is also affected by various external events.

Beyond such proposed evolutionary underpinnings, people differ a great deal in the strength of their **need for affiliation** or need for interpersonal relationships. Those whose need is weak prefer to spend much of their time alone, while those with a strong need prefer to interact with others whenever possible. The stronger a person's need for affiliation, the more likely he or she is to take advantage of propinquity and positive affect by attempting to move toward a close acquaintanceship.

Dispositional differences in affiliation need

Beginning with the pioneering work of Murray (1938/1961), psychologists have constructed various tests to measure individual differences in the need to affiliate and have conducted research to determine how such differences influence behavior. The tests used most are in the form of questionnaires. A typical finding is that males high in affiliation need are more self-confident and spend more time talking to attractive females than is true for males whose need to affiliate is low (Crouse & Mehrabian, 1977). Affiliation motivation is also positively related to the frequency of letter writing and the desire to be with other people rather than alone (McAdams & Constantian, 1983).

Much of the current research on affiliation has emphasized the existence of different varieties of motivation. McAdams and Losoff (1984), for example, focus on **friendship motivation**, the need to establish warm interpersonal relationships. Children whose friendship motivation is strong are found to know a great deal about their friends, to form stable relationships, and to be perceived by their teachers as friendly, affectionate, cooperative, happy, and popular.

There are, however, other reasons to affiliate, and Hill (1987) suggests that four basic motives may be involved. He proposes that affiliation is based on *social comparison* (the need to reduce uncertainty), *positive stimulation* (the need for interesting, lively contact with others), *emotional support* (the need for companionship when problems arise), and *attention* (the need for praise and admiration). Table 6.1 provides examples of items that measure each of these motives. A person's score on each dimension indicates the type of situation in which he or she is most likely to engage in affiliative behavior.

■ The Interpersonal Orientation Scale measures the types of motivation that underlie the need for affiliation. Shown are sample items based on four quite different reasons for seeking the company of others, together with college situations in which they might be likely to occur.

TABLE 6.1 Different aspects of the need for affiliation

Type of Need	Sample Test Items That Measure the Need	Typical Situation
Social Comparison	When I am not certain about how well I am doing at something, I usually like to be around others so I can compare myself to them.	When class papers are returned to students.
Positive Stimulation	Just being around others and finding out about them is one of the most interesting things I can think of doing.	After several hours of studying in the library.
Emotional Support	One of my greatest sources of comfort when things get rough is being with other people.	After receiving a very low grade on an exam.
Attention	I like to be around people when I can be the center of attention.	When the opportunity arises to make the class laugh.

Source: Based on information in Hill, 1987.

Social skills can help or hinder affiliation

Beyond motivational differences, people also vary in how well they deal with interpersonal situations. Socially skilled individuals are friendly, possess high self-esteem, seldom react angrily, and find it easy to make conversation (Reisman, 1984). Those who are least skilled tend to be unfriendly, have low self-esteem, frequently become angry, and consider casual conversation to be a difficult task.

Langston and Cantor (1989) studied the interpersonal successes and failures of students over a period of time to find out why some do well socially while others do not. These investigators proposed the model shown in Figure 6.5 to describe the crucial variables. Students who succeeded interpersonally differed from those who failed interpersonally in how they perceived the task of meeting new people and in the strategy they used when interacting with others. Specifically, unskilled individuals appraised the situation negatively and experienced anxiety. This *social anxiety* leads to cognitive distortions (for example, assuming that you are disliked by others) and feelings of depression (Johnson, Johnson, & Petzel, 1992). In response to their negative perceptions of the situation, unskilled individuals developed social strategies that were restrained and conservative—striving to reveal very little about themselves. For most people social anxiety and awkwardness are reduced by attempts to find out about another person (Leary, Kowalski, & Bergen, 1988). When socially unskilled students ask questions about another person's experiences and attitudes, however, they are too fearful to communicate anything meaningful about themselves (Thorne, 1987). This tendency to hold back and play it safe makes a negative impression on others. Other students, who were successful interpersonally, felt it was an interesting challenge to make new friends, and they felt comfortable in letting the other person know as much as possible about themselves. This friendly, open, outgoing strategy is a useful one in establishing friendships.

External events can arouse affiliation needs

Though people differ in their need to interact with others, external events can also arouse this motive. You have probably been in certain situations in which total strangers began to talk to one another: the stress of a flood, the excitement of a special event such as Mardi Gras, or some other out-of-the-ordinary occurrence. Humphriss

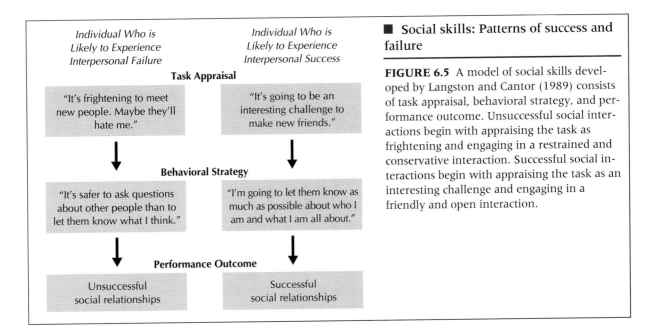

■ Social skills: Patterns of success and failure

FIGURE 6.5 A model of social skills developed by Langston and Cantor (1989) consists of task appraisal, behavioral strategy, and performance outcome. Unsuccessful social interactions begin with appraising the task as frightening and engaging in a restrained and conservative interaction. Successful social interactions begin with appraising the task as an interesting challenge and engaging in a friendly and open interaction.

(1989) described the aftereffects of a California earthquake—the dreadful destruction of property served to unite neighbors and create friendly feelings. As suggested in the cartoon in figure 6.6, "An emergency makes things different."

The psychological basis of these affiliative reactions was first identified by Schachter (1959) in his investigations of the effect of fear on affiliation. In an experimental setting, many of the subjects who had been told that they would soon receive painful electric shocks preferred waiting with other subjects rather than remaining alone. When they expected a nonfrightening experience, subjects preferred to wait alone or expressed no preference. Why should fear or anxiety increase the motivation to affiliate?

The explanation is that we seek out others—even strangers—in order to talk about what is going on, to compare perceptions, and to decide what to do (Morris et al., 1976). This behavior is an example of the **social comparison process**, the general tendency to evaluate what we think and do by comparing our reactions with those of others, thus reducing uncertainty and anxiety. A positive emotional atmosphere can occur even in very upsetting situations, because there is an opportunity to share the experience with others and to engage in novel activity (Byrne, 1991).

A related phenomenon does not rest on social comparison or sharing a novel experience: Sometimes there is the possibility of obtaining information about a frightening upcoming event by interacting with someone who has already gone through it and therefore knows the score. For example, in a medical setting those facing surgery prefer having a roommate who has already undergone the same operation (Kulik & Mahler, 1989).

RESPONDING TO OBSERVABLE CHARACTERISTICS

Even though we realize that "beauty is only skin deep" and that most stereotypes are incorrect, most of us nevertheless react to those we meet on the basis of *positive* stereotypes about physical attractiveness (Albright, Kenny, & Malloy, 1988) and *negative* stereotypes about physical defects (Fichten & Amsel, 1986), as well as with a multitude of specific prejudices. For example, we are apt to evaluate people on the basis of whether they appear old (Perdue & Gurtman, 1990), whether they wear eyeglasses (Terry & Macy, 1991), what kind of clothing they wear (Bushman, 1988; Cahoon &

■ Emergencies can bring people together

FIGURE 6.6 It is frequently observed that emergency situations such as power failures and natural disasters can motivate people to affiliate, to help one another, and to experience camaraderie. As the cartoon character notes, "Just for a while today ... everyone cared about everyone else."

Source: Universal Press Syndicate, February 6, 1988.

Edmonds, 1989), and how well groomed they are (Mack & Rainey, 1990). These judgments—along with those based on such variables as skin color, sex, height, and accent—are likely to be worthless in making accurate behavioral predictions, as we indicated in the discussion of prejudice in chapter 5. Much of the research on the effects of observable characteristics has concentrated on **physical attractiveness**, but we will first describe how several other physical attributes influence attraction.

The effects of superficial characteristics

It is surprisingly commonplace for people to express like or dislike toward a stranger simply because of some irrelevant aspect of that person's outward appearance. Attention to overt characteristics is part of a general screening process known as **cognitive disregard**. According to Rodin (1987), we deal with strangers by first excluding all who strike us at first glance as "unsuitable" as acquaintances. Anyone placed in that category becomes "invisible" and is no longer an object of attention; subsequently, he or she is not even remembered. Undergraduates, for example, are found to disregard anyone who is elderly or middle-aged; middle-aged individuals disregard those who are young; and males disregard unattractive females. After we decide who doesn't count, we find out more about those who remain in order to decide whom we like. Engaging in cognitive disregard is an efficient way of eliminating anyone whom we feel would not be acceptable as an acquaintance or a friend. The problem with such behavior is that evaluations based on observable characteristics are unfair, and they prevent us from ever getting to know some people who might have become our good friends.

Other physical attributes also evoke stereotypes. Research shows that people perceive adults who look or sound very young as being weak, naive, incompetent, warm, and honest (Berry & Brownlow, 1989; Berry & Zebrowitz-McArthur, 1988; Montepare & Zebrowitz-McArthur, 1987). Though these perceptions tend to be almost totally inaccurate, they continue to influence first impressions and interpersonal attraction.

In addition to physical appearance, *behavioral cues* also influence judgments in equally unfair ways. People react more positively to those whose walking style seems youthful, for example, than to those whose gaits are perceived as elderly, regardless of the person's actual age or sex (Montepare & Zebrowitz-McArthur, 1988). Emotional expressiveness and extroverted behavior create a positive first impression in the United States (Friedman, Riggio, & Casella, 1988). It is commonly found in that culture that males who behave in a dominant way are liked better than those who behave submissively (Sadalla, Kenrick, & Vershure, 1987). Thus, there is a preference for a male who gestures a lot, has a strong tennis serve, and is competitive and authoritative as opposed to one who looks down, nods his head in agreement, and plays tennis for fun rather than to win. Female dominance, in contrast, does not affect attraction one way or the other.

Sometimes overt behavior is easily altered, and most people try to act so as to create a good impression. For example, Patricia Pliner of the University of Toronto and her colleague Shelly Chaiken found that both men and women tend to eat less in the presence of someone of the opposite sex than when they are alone or with a same-sex companion (Pliner & Chaiken, 1990). The reason is that overeating is perceived as unattractive in general and specifically as unfeminine for women (Mori, Chaiken, & Pliner, 1987).

Is behavior ever related to observable characteristics?

Is it possible that behavior *is* sometimes predictable on the basis of the kind of overt cues we have been discussing? In a few instances, there is a relationship.

We have already pointed out that people respond to various aspects of clothing. Is it also possible that clothing affects the behavior of the wearer? Sometimes that seems to be the case. In one experiment with college women, those who were given nurses' uniforms to wear were less aggressive toward a stranger than those who were dressed in Ku Klux Klan uniforms (Johnson & Downing, 1979). Response to clothing color is another example. Probably because black is associated with negative characteristics in our culture (*blacklist, blackball, blackmail,* etc.), Frank and Gilovich (1988) found that professional football and hockey players wearing black uniforms (e.g., the Vancouver Canucks) are rated as bad, mean, and aggressive. More surprisingly, they also found that those team members who wear black uniforms play more aggressively and receive more penalties than those wearing light-colored uniforms (see Figure 6.7). It seems that when a player wears black, his behavior becomes more aggressive.

The effect of clothing on behavior was shown even more convincingly in an experiment in which the researchers told male subjects they would be competing against one another in several tasks (Frank & Gilovich, 1988). The tasks differed in aggressiveness (for example, stacking blocks versus engaging in a dart-gun duel). Each subject picked five of these activities in which to compete. Then the subjects were divided into teams of three and given either a black or a white uniform to wear over their clothing. At this point each team considered the tasks again, and the members were asked to agree on which five they preferred. As shown in Figure 6.8, those given white uniforms made the same choices in terms of task aggressiveness as they did before the uniforms were issued. Those given black uniforms, however, shifted toward more aggressive choices. It appears that clothing not only affects how one is perceived, but also how one behaves.

Attracted by attractiveness

Both sexes respond strongly to the physical attractiveness of those they meet (Cash & Killcullen, 1985; Hatfield & Sprecher, 1986), though males are more responsive to female attractiveness than females are to male attractiveness (Feingold, 1990, 1992b; Pierce, 1992). Also, individuals differ in the importance they attach to physical appearance (Cash

■ **You are what you wear? Black uniforms and aggressiveness**

FIGURE 6.7 People respond to one another in part on the basis of the clothes they wear. We tend to perceive hockey players who wear dark uniforms as being more aggressive than those who wear light-colored uniforms. Such stereotypes also affect the behavior of those wearing the uniforms. Teams that wore black uniforms (such as the Vancouver Canucks) in the National Hockey League between 1970 and 1985 received more penalties than teams wearing non-black uniforms.

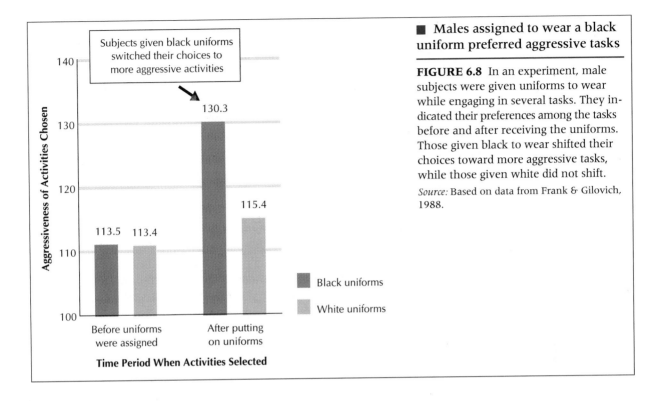

■ Males assigned to wear a black uniform preferred aggressive tasks

FIGURE 6.8 In an experiment, male subjects were given uniforms to wear while engaging in several tasks. They indicated their preferences among the tasks before and after receiving the uniforms. Those given black to wear shifted their choices toward more aggressive tasks, while those given white did not shift.

Source: Based on data from Frank & Gilovich, 1988.

& Jacobi, 1992). The attractiveness effect has been demonstrated in settings ranging from college dances to commercial dating services (Green, Buchanan, & Heuer, 1984).

A person who is very attractive is assumed to have other positive qualities as well (Calvert, 1988). People generally believe that attractive men and women are more poised, interesting, sociable, independent, dominant, exciting, sexy, well adjusted, socially skilled, and successful than the unattractive (Dion & Dion, 1987; Moore, Graziano, & Miller, 1987). Also, handsome men are perceived as more masculine and beautiful women as more feminine than are less attractive individuals (Gillen, 1981). Analogous stereotypes apply to vocal attractiveness; the more attractive a person's voice, the more positive the ratings of that individual's personality traits (Zuckerman & Driver, 1989). For male undergraduates, the more attractive a female stranger, the more sexually desirable she is judged to be and the better she is rated as a potential date and potential spouse (G. Smeaton, personal communication, 1990).

At the opposite age extreme, research results indicate that people assume attractiveness among adults aged sixty to ninety-three to be indicative of desirable personality traits (Johnson & Pittenger, 1984). Relative attractiveness remains stable over the years (Pittenger, Mark, & Johnson, 1989), and the bias favoring those with a pleasing appearance operates from birth to old age.

Given the pervasive effects of attractiveness, it follows that many people may worry about their appearance. Canadian researchers, Dion, Dion, and Keelan (1990) developed a scale to measure **appearance anxiety**, defined as apprehension concerning one's physical appearance and the evaluations made by others. Subjects indicate their agreement or disagreement with a series of statements such as "I enjoy looking at myself in the mirror" and "I feel that most of my friends are more physically attractive than myself." Among college students, women indicate more appearance anxiety than men, and high scores on this test are associated with experiencing social anxiety, feeling unattractive in childhood, and having had fewer dates in high school.

In recent research, described in the following "Work in Progress" section, appearance anxiety has been found to predict behavioral differences in specific social situations and to be relevant to some of the issues discussed in chapter 4.

A few negative attributes are associated with being attractive. Many people believe that beautiful women are more vain and materialistic than unattractive ones (Cash & Duncan, 1984). Attractiveness is a plus for males running for political office, but not for female candidates (Sigelman et al., 1986), possibly because elected officials are not "supposed" to be feminine. Though attractiveness is believed to lead to success, people often assume that the resulting good fortune is undeserved and simply based on looks (Kalick, 1988).

Beyond the assumptions people make about those who are physically attractive, is there any evidence that attractiveness is actually related to specific characteristics? Most of the characteristics attributed to attractive people represent inaccurate stereotypes (Feingold, 1992a). For example, there is a general stereotype that "what is beautiful is good," and one supposed correlate of physical attractiveness is intelligence (Dion, Berscheid, & Walster, 1972). Even though experimental subjects rate essays written by attractive students more positively than those written by unattractive ones (Cash & Trimer, 1984), there is in fact no relationship between attractiveness and college grade point average (Baugh & Parry, 1991).

Some of the other stereotypes seem to be true, however. Probably because people respond favorably to anyone who is good looking, attractive men and women learn to interact well with those of the opposite sex, and they have more dates than

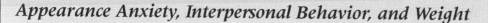

WORK IN PROGRESS

Appearance Anxiety, Interpersonal Behavior, and Weight

Currently, Professors Dion and Dion are actively exploring additional aspects of appearance anxiety (Dion, 1993). They proposed, for example, that anxiety about one's appearance would cause one to feel uncomfortable in interacting face to face with an attractive member of the opposite sex. On the basis of scores on the Appearance Anxiety Scale, the researchers selected high- and low-anxiety students to take part in a study supposedly dealing with "interpersonal communication." An attractive opposite-sex research assistant interviewed each participant and asked such innocuous questions as "What is your major?" The interview was videotaped, and judges (who did not know the appearance anxiety scores of the participants) rated the apparent comfort/discomfort of these individuals during the interaction. Women—but not men—high in appearance anxiety were rated by the judges as behaving in ways suggesting they were uncomfortable while being interviewed.

In research that is consistent with findings reported in chapter 4, the Dions found that overweight women scored higher in appearance anxiety than women whose weight was normal or below average—and also higher than men, including overweight men. Thus, women who depart from the expected standards of physical appearance with respect to weight are most anxious about how they look.

Additional work, now in progress, is designed to test the hypothesis that, among women, appearance anxiety is associated with depression. The general theoretical assumption is that concern about appearance is more closely tied to self-esteem for women than for men. As a result, when women perceive themselves (accurately or inaccurately) to be unattractive, their self-esteem drops and their depression rises.

their less-attractive peers (Reis, Nezlek, & Wheeler, 1980). Similarly, a study of fifth-graders found attractive students to be more popular and less aggressive than unattractive kids (Johnstone, Frame, & Bouman, 1992). Altogether, good interpersonal skills appear to be associated with ratings of attractiveness (O'Grady, 1989).

You might assume that being attractive would increase an individual's self-esteem, but the two characteristics are unrelated (Kenealy et al., 1991). A possible reason that good-looking people don't necessarily evaluate themselves highly, is that when you are very attractive, you tend to believe that others value you only for your appearance (Major, Carrington, & Carnevale, 1984).

The matching hypothesis: Seeking an equally attractive partner

Despite the fact that most of us like those who are most attractive, men and women who are seeking actual relationships often fear being rejected by someone more attractive than themselves (Bernstein et al., 1983). Also, they themselves are likely to reject anyone less attractive than they are. As a result—the **matching hypothesis** states—romantic partners tend to pair off on the basis of being *similar* in physical attractiveness (Berscheid et al., 1971; Kalick & Hamilton, 1986). See figure 6.9. This tendency affects not only who dates whom, but also the choice of a marriage partner (Price & Vandenberg, 1979; Zajonc et al., 1987).

■ The matching hypothesis: Selecting a similar partner

FIGURE 6.9 Research indicates that the matching hypothesis is correct. People tend to choose friends, lovers, and spouses who are similar to themselves in physical attractiveness.

Matching does not occur 100 percent of the time, of course, and mismatches sometimes are observed. When people perceive an extreme appearance discrepancy between partners, it apparently makes them uncomfortable. When Forgas (1993) asked research participants to evaluate couples on the basis of their pictures, pairs similar in attractiveness (matched) were rated more positively—with respect to ability, likability, and quality of the relationship—than the couples dissimilar in attractiveness (mismatched). These differences in evaluation were intensified by the observer's mood. Participants who were first shown a comedy film rated the matched couples even more positively, and those who were first shown a film about death from cancer rated the mismatched couples even more negatively.

Matching for attractiveness also occurs in same-sex friendships (Cash & Derlega, 1978), and this tendency is actually stronger for men than for women (McKillip & Reidel, 1983). In addition, a person's perceived attractiveness is affected by the appearance of his or her friends. If, for example, you become friends with someone less attractive than yourself, you are perceived as less good looking than if your friend is as attractive or more attractive than yourself (Wedell, Parducci, & Geiselman, 1987).

BUILDING A RELATIONSHIP: SIMILARITY AND RECIPROCITY

As we have seen, once two people are brought together by physical proximity, the probability that they will like each other and establish some kind of relationship is increased if each is (1) in a positive emotional state, (2) motivated by affiliative needs, and (3) favorably impressed by the appearance and other observable characteristics of the other. Further steps toward a closer relationship depend on the two individuals' beginning to communicate and on the content of that communication (Byrne, 1992). The development of a friendship rests on the discovery of various kinds of *similarity* and on the indication of *reciprocal positive evaluations*.

SIMILARITY: WE LIKE THOSE MOST LIKE OURSELVES

Over twenty centuries ago, Aristotle described the nature of friendship and hypothesized that people who agree with one another become friends, while those with dissimilar attitudes do not. As the gentleman in Figure 6.10 indicates, **attitude similarity** is acceptable in conversation—but not a different point of view. In books and movies opposites may attract, but in real life birds of a feather flock together. As tennis pro Bjorn Borg said of his new wife, "She's a great woman. She's just like me" (Milestones, 1989).

Similar attitudes, dissimilar attitudes, and attraction

The association between attitude similarity and attraction was first documented in correlational studies such as Schiller's (1932) investigation of married couples; eventually laboratory experiments (beginning with Schachter, 1951) established a cause-and-effect relationship. That is, the expression of a similar attitude, belief, or value results in liking, while dissimilar statements result in dislike. These effects hold true across age groups ranging from elementary school children to the elderly, across socioeconomic levels, and across cultures as different as those of India, Japan, Korea, Mexico, Singapore, and the United States.

When people interact, their conversation often involves the expression of their attitudes about whatever topics come up—school, music, television shows, politics, religion, and so on. As people talk, each person indicates his or her likes and dislikes (Hatfield & Rapson, 1992; Kent, Davis, & Shapiro, 1981). Research has shown that each

"No, I would not welcome a contrasting point of view."

FIGURE 6.10 As centuries of observation and decades of research have shown, attitude similarity is an important component of interpersonal attraction. As the man in the cartoon indicates, most people don't even want to hear about views different from their own.

Source: The New Yorker, March 18, 1985, p. 46.

individual in the interaction reponds to the other on the basis of the **proportion of similar attitudes** that are expressed. For example, we are equally attracted to someone who has views like our own on two of the four topics we discuss or on fifty of the one hundred topics we discuss; the proportion is .50 in each instance. The higher the proportion of similar attitudes, the greater the liking. This relationship is sufficiently strong that it is possible to express it in mathematical terms as a linear function, as shown in Figure 6.11 (Byrne & Nelson, 1965).

Attempts to identify dispositional differences in response to attitude similarity/dissimilarity have most often been unsuccessful. In some instances, however, individual diversity does occur. For example, Grover and Brockner (1989) hypothesized that people high in empathy would be more sensitive to the views of others and thus more responsive to similarity or dissimilarity than would people low in empathy. When subjects who differed in level of empathy responded to an attitudinally similar or dissimilar stranger, the high-empathy individuals responded more strongly than the low-empathy individuals, especially when the stranger was similar (see Figure 6.12).

Despite the fact that several critics have questioned one or more aspects of the concept of similarity-attraction (Bochner, 1991; Rosenbaum 1986; Sunnafrank, 1992),

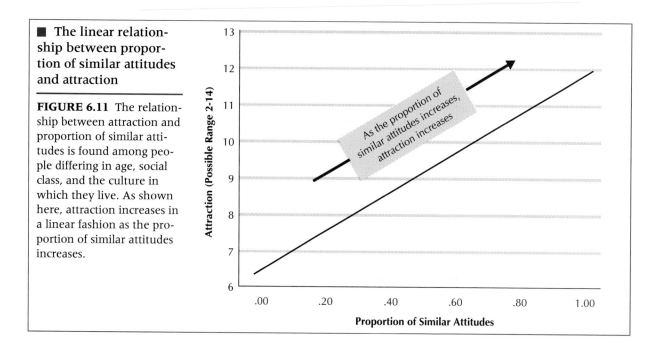

■ The linear relationship between proportion of similar attitudes and attraction

FIGURE 6.11 The relationship between attraction and proportion of similar attitudes is found among people differing in age, social class, and the culture in which they live. As shown here, attraction increases in a linear fashion as the proportion of similar attitudes increases.

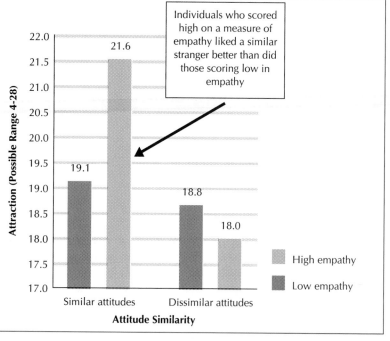

■ The effect of empathy on response to similarity/dissimilarity

FIGURE 6.12 Though almost everyone likes attitudinally similar others in preference to those with dissimilar attitudes, individuals vary in how strongly they are affected by the views of others. When subjects are divided into those scoring high and low on the dispositional characteristic of empathy, those high in empathy respond more positively to a similar stranger than do those low in empathy.

Source: Based on data from Grover & Brockner, 1989.

most social psychologists and sociologists conclude that the effect is an extremely solid and reliable one. Extensive research has suggested that attraction is a function of the *proportion* of similar attitudes another person holds. In addition, *expectations* about similarity can modify how people respond. It is basically a matter of how much a stranger's attitudes deviate from what is expected. The greater the deviation (either more dissimilarity or more similarity than one's expectations), the greater the effect on attraction (either negatively or positively). With such minor modifications, Cappella and Palmer (1990, p. 161) have represented the general view when they say that, "perhaps the most well known and well established finding in the study of interpersonal relations is that attitude similarity creates attraction."

Why do we care about the attitudes of others?

Three possible explanations have been offered as to why people respond emotionally to the similar and dissimilar attitudes expressed by others.

The oldest formulation, **balance theory** (Heider, 1958), rests on the concept that humans organize their likes and dislikes in a symmetrical way. **Balance** exists when two people like each other and agree about some topic (Newcomb, 1961). When they like each other and disagree, however, an unpleasant state of **imbalance** is created (Orive, 1988). Each person attempts to restore balance through such means as changing attitudes, convincing the other person to change attitudes, or reducing liking. When two people dislike each other, they are in a state of **nonbalance** and don't care whether they agree or disagree.

While balance theory leads to a number of interesting predictions about how people will respond to agreement and disagreement, it really doesn't explain *why* such information is important. As a result, many theorists have taken the question a step farther; they have suggested that attitudes are important because we turn to other people to obtain **consensual validation** of our views about the world through a social comparison process (Festinger, 1954; Goethals, 1986). According to this theory, when someone agrees with you, the agreement validates your views—provides "evidence" that you are correct. You are pleased to discover that you have sound judgment, are intelligent, have good taste, and so forth. Not surprisingly, you like the person who makes you feel good about yourself. Disagreement has just the opposite effect; perhaps you have faulty judgment, are not too bright, and have poor taste. Such information makes you feel bad about yourself, and you dislike the other person. If this conceptualization is correct, it means that when we sound out others on their views, we are not really seeking evidence; we simply want to identify others who agree with us. One example of this process occurs when people complain about something or about someone to their acquaintances; they are not usually attempting to solve a problem but simply to find someone who will express sympathy and agree that their complaint is a just one (Alicke et al., 1992).

More recently, a third possible explanation has been offered by Canadian researcher Phillipe Rushton (1989). He hypothesizes that people use attitude similarity, among other cues, to detect those who are genetically similar to themselves. Friends, for example, exceed chance in their similarity on such genetically determined characteristics as blood type and Rh factor. If you like someone who is similar to you, become friends, and provide that person assistance when it is needed, you are unconsciously helping to ensure that genes like your own will be protected and eventually transmitted to the next generation. For this reason, we are each biologically programmed to attend to and respond positively to similarity of all kinds. Choosing a similar mate is even more crucial as a way to protect your portion of the gene pool.

Other kinds of similarity influence attraction, too

For most characteristics that have been investigated, similarity results in liking and friendship (Griffin & Sparks, 1990). Though **complementarity** is often proposed as a contrast to similarity (dominant people should like submissive ones, etc.), research seeking this kind of attraction effect has generally been unsuccessful (Nowicki & Manheim, 1991). Complementary pairs of workers *are* found to perform tasks better than noncomplementary pairs (Estroff & Nowicki, 1992), however. Despite the overall research support for similarity, we can each come up with examples of pairs of friends or even spouses who are dissimilar in a variety of ways. Then we nod and say, "opposites attract." Though research has not confirmed this common observation, perhaps it is partially true. That is, if two people are *very* similar with respect to 95 percent of their attitudes, values, beliefs, and interests, it is *possible* that differences on a few other characteristics are perceived as interesting or intriguing—if nothing else, it gives them something to talk about. Such examples of minor dissimilarities in the context of major similarities may account for the persistence and popularity of the complementarity hypothesis in our culture.

Examples of similarity factors associated with liking include age (Ellis, Rogoff, & Cramer, 1981); religion and race (Kandel, 1978); skills (Tesser, Campbell, & Smith, 1984); smoking, drinking, and engaging in premarital sex (Rodgers, Billy, & Udry, 1984); using marijuana (Eisenman, 1985); experiencing the same emotions (Alliger & Williams, 1991); being a morning versus an evening person (Watts, 1982); and many different personality dispositions (Morell, Twillman, & Sullaway, 1989; Rosenblatt & Greenberg, 1988; Smith, 1989). Also, the more two people interact, the more similar they become in personality (Blankenship et al., 1984; Funder & Colvin, 1988), including self-concept (Deutsch et al., 1991) and ideal-self concept (LaPrelle et al., 1990).

One advantage of having friends who are similar to ourselves is that we are able to communicate better with them than with strangers (Fussell & Krauss, 1989).

RECIPROCITY: MUTUAL LIKING

Once two people discover areas of similarity, a friendship is likely to develop. One additional step is crucial, however. Each individual must indicate that the other person is liked and evaluated positively (Condon & Crano, 1988). Almost everyone is pleased to receive such feedback and very upset to receive negative evaluations (Coleman, Jussim, & Abraham, 1987). Often, even an inaccurate positive evaluation (Swann et al., 1987) or an obvious attempt at flattery (Drachman, DeCarufel, & Insko, 1978) is well received. Individuals also differ in the kind of evaluations they want from others. People with positive self-concepts (see chapter 4) are most inclined to want positive evaluations from others; in contrast, those with negative self-concepts sometimes respond well to accurate negative appraisals (Swann, Stein-Seroussi, & Giesler, 1992). It appears that some people primarily want to be praised, while others feel a stronger need to be correct about their negative self-evaluations.

Though mutual liking can easily be expressed in words, the first signs are often nonverbal (see the discussion of nonverbal cues in chapter 2). For example, when a woman converses with a man while maintaining eye contact and leaning toward him, he often interprets her behavior (sometimes incorrectly) as an indication that she likes him, and so he may be attracted to her (Gold, Ryckman, & Mosley, 1984).

When the evaluation is verbalized, there is much less ambiguity about its meaning, and there is an immediate effect on interpersonal behavior. In one experiment, some subjects were led to believe that they were liked by a stranger and others to believe that they were disliked (Curtis & Miller, 1986). When each subject then engaged in a ten-minute discussion with someone supposed to be that stranger (actually, just another subject), behavior was strongly influenced by whether a positive or a negative evaluation had been given. As shown in Figure 6.13, those who had received positive feedback and thus expected to be liked made more eye contact, spoke in a warmer tone, and were more self-disclosing than those who expected to be disliked. One result in the positive condition was greater reciprocal liking afterward.

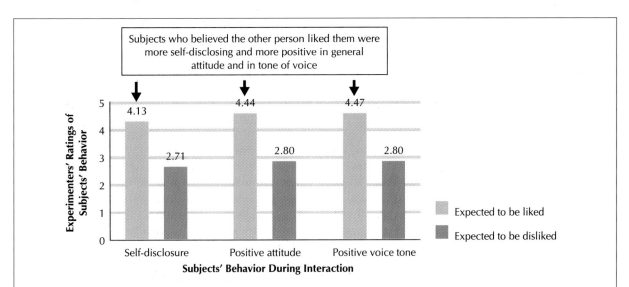

FIGURE 6.13 Reciprocal liking is a vital element in the formation of a relationship. In an experiment, subjects who had been led to believe that another subject liked them engaged in more self-disclosure, expressed more positive attitudes, spoke in more positive tones, and were liked more than subjects who had been led to believe that another subject disliked them.

Source: Based on data from Curtis & Miller, 1986.

WHAT IS THIS THING CALLED LOVE? MOVING BEYOND CASUAL FRIENDSHIPS

Love has long been a familiar theme in our songs, stories, and everyday lives, and a poll of 1000 North American adults reveals that 75 percent of the men and 70 percent of the women say that they are now "in love" (Vox pop, 1993). What does this mean? One suggestion is that a friendship between a man and a woman is transformed into *love* when the two individuals begin to perceive themselves as potential sexual partners. As we shall see, over two decades of social psychological research indicates that love is sometimes less sensible and less straightforward than that.

PASSIONATE LOVE

Aron et al. (1989) point out that many people fall in love, but that there is no analogous experience of "falling in friendship." As we saw, propinquity and similarity are major determinants of friendship. Love, in contrast, is much more likely to be precipitated by desirable aspects of the other person, such as an attractive appearance, pleasing personality, and reciprocal liking. It is even possible to experience love toward someone who doesn't love you—*unrequited love*. The most common instances involve loving someone in your immediate environment who fails to respond and longing for a past partner who is no longer interested. Bringle and Winnick (1992), with a sample of over 400 respondents, found that most (60 percent) had experienced unrequited love at least once during the previous two years. In such situations, both individuals experience emotional distress (Baumeister, Wotman, & Stillwell,

1993). Those who are rejected as lovers respond with a decrease in self-esteem, and they believe that they were misled. Those who reject a would-be lover perceive that person as intrusive and annoying, but they still feel guilty about hurting him or her.

In any event, romance often begins as a sudden, intense, all-consuming response to another person. Phrases such as *falling head over heels in love* imply that love is an accident—something like slipping on a banana peel (Solomon, 1981). This kind of interpersonal response is labeled **passionate love** (Hatfield, 1988), one of several varieties of love that have been identified. A person experiencing passionate love tends to be preoccupied with his or her partner—and to perceive the love object as being perfect. Responses include sexual attraction, physiological arousal, the desire to be in constant contact, despair at the thought of the relationship ending, and the intense need to be loved in return. This emotional response can be measured by a test called the Passionate Love Scale (Hatfield & Sprecher, 1986). Some of the test items are shown in Table 6.2, and you may notice that passionate love (like attitudes) combines cognitive, emotional, and behavioral elements.

Under the "right" conditions, passionate love can arise suddenly and without warning, possibly accompanied by the secretion of neurochemicals that produce feelings of excitement and happiness (Toufexis, 1993). Even a brief contact with a stranger can sometimes lead to love at first sight (Averill & Boothroyd, 1977). When

---

■ Hatfield and Sprecher (1986) developed the Passionate Love Scale to measure the intense emotional reactions that are characteristic of this kind of love. Those taking the test are also informed that other terms for this feeling are infatuation, lovesickness, and obsessive love. The sample items shown here constitute only a portion of the total scale.

TABLE 6.2 The Passionate Love Scale

Please think of the person whom you love most passionately right now. If you are not in love right now, please think of the last person you loved passionately. If you have never been in love, think of the person whom you came closest to caring for in that way.

1. I would feel deep despair if _____ left me.
2. Sometimes I feel I can't control my thoughts; they are obsessively on _____ .
3. I feel happy when I am doing something to make _____ happy.
4. I would rather be with _____ than anyone else.
5. I'd get jealous if I thought _____ were falling in love with someone else.
6. I yearn to know all about _____ .
7. I want _____—physically, emotionally, mentally.
8. I have an endless appetite for affection from _____ .
9. For me, _____ is the perfect romantic partner.
10. I sense my body responding when _____ touches me.
11. _____ always seems to be on my mind.
12. I want _____ to know me—my thoughts, my fears, and my hopes.
13. I eagerly look for signs indicating _____'s desire for me.
14. I get extremely depressed when things don't go right in my relationship with _____ .

Responses to each item are made along the following scale:

Not at all true			Moderately true			Definitely true		
1	2	3	4	5	6	7	8	9

two opposite-sex strangers in a laboratory experiment are simply asked to gaze into each other's eyes for two minutes, they are likely to report feelings of passionate love for each other (Kellerman, Lewis, & Laird, 1989). What is the explanation for this seemingly irrational response?

Three conditions are required for passionate love to occur (Hatfield & Walster, 1981), as summarized in Figure 6.14. First, you must learn what love is and develop the expectation that it will happen to you (Dion & Dion, 1988). Beginning in early childhood, most of us are exposed to the idea that people fall in love and get married. Think of *Snow White* and *Cinderella*. Though it has long been assumed that romantic love was invented in medieval Europe, some psychologists, historians, and anthropologists have recently become convinced that it is a universal phenomenon (Gray, 1993; Hatfield & Rapson, 1992b). One explanation of the origin of love is based on evolutionary theorizing (Fisher, 1992). It is assumed that about four or five million years ago, when people began to stand on two legs and forage for food to be carried back to a safe place, adequate child care and survival were most likely if there was male-female bonding. That is, males could venture forth to seek food, and females could remain safe and take care of their offspring; but—the couple had to like and trust one another. Reproductive success was enhanced by the development of brain chemistry that led to love and hence to bonding. In relatively modern times, this natural response has often been repressed and hidden by the customs and practices of a given culture. For example, while most Americans (87 percent) believe today that love is crucial to a good marriage, such beliefs are much less widely held elsewhere—in Russia and in India, for example. Fisher's prediction is that cultural changes will lead to more and more expressions of love because it is a natural, biological aspect of the relationship between men and women.

The second condition required for the occurrence of passionate love is the presence of an appropriate target person with whom one can fall in love. Social learning theorists propose that we have been taught by parents, movies, books, songs, and

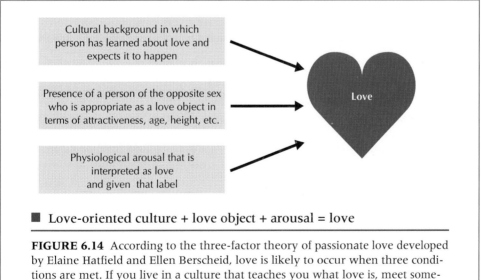

■ Love-oriented culture + love object + arousal = love

FIGURE 6.14 According to the three-factor theory of passionate love developed by Elaine Hatfield and Ellen Berscheid, love is likely to occur when three conditions are met. If you live in a culture that teaches you what love is, meet someone who is an appropriate love object, and are physiologically aroused, you may very well interpret your aroused state as indicating love. This process underlies the behavior that has led to such familiar phrases as "love at first sight," "love is blind," and "head over heels in love." Sadly enough, passionate love is not likely to last, and enduring love requires a more realistic foundation.

peers to seek an attractive partner of the opposite sex—someone similar to ourselves in most respects. Thus, we base our romantic choices on culturally prescribed criteria.

In contrast, evolutionary theory hypothesizes that love objects are chosen on the basis of maximizing reproductive success. From this perspective, an appropriate love object is one who will be able to reproduce and to care and/or provide for the offspring (Buss, 1988), and similarity is desirable because it improves the odds for the continued existence of one's personal corner of the gene pool (Rushton, 1989, 1990; Rushton & Nicholson, 1988).

The third requirement for passionate love is that a state of emotional arousal occur while the love object is present. As described in chapter 2, Schachter's theory of emotion suggests that we use external cues to tell us which emotional labels to apply when we are physiologically aroused. If arousal occurs in the presence of an attractive person of the opposite sex, attraction, romantic feelings, and sexual desire often result. The Capilano Bridge experiment (Dutton & Aron, 1974) described in chapter 1 demonstrated that this arousal can involve such states as fear, and in other research it has been frustration and anger (Driscoll, Davis, & Lipetz, 1972). In such cases the term "passionate love" is simply a misattribution. When the arousal involves sexual excitement (Istvan, Griffitt, & Weidner, 1983), love may be a more accurate label for one's aroused state. As Hatfield and Rapson (1987) point out, *passionate love* may not be very different from *sexual desire*. Perhaps we say "I love you" because that is more socially acceptable than saying "I want to have sex with you."

OTHER VARIETIES OF LOVE

Despite—or because of—its intensity, passionate love is not long-lasting, As Momma suggests in figure 6.15. Fortunately, there are other kinds of love that *can* be sustained over time.

Companionate love involves not the dazzling and dizzying emotional state of passionate love but "the affection we feel for those with whom our lives are deeply entwined" (Hatfield, 1988, p. 205). Companionate love represents a very close friendship in which two people are attracted, have much in common, care about each other's well-being, and express reciprocal liking and respect (Caspi & Herbener, 1990). Clearly, this kind of love can be expected to lead to a satisfactory long-term relationship more often than does passionate love; but companionate love does not lead to romantic songs and stories.

Some theorists (Borrello & Thompson, 1990; Hendrick & Hendrick, 1986; Lasswell & Lobsenz, 1980) propose that in addition to passionate and companionate love, there are four additional varieties or "love styles." Table 6.3 presents the elements of this six-part model of love along with examples of test items that have been designed to measure each type. Research based on this model has found that men score higher than women in both passionate (Eros) and game-playing (Ludus) love. *Storge* is the ancient Greek word for loving affection, and females score higher than males in these friendly relationships as well as in logical (Pragma) and possessive (Mania) love (Hendrick et al., 1984). As you might guess on the basis of the earlier discussion, romantic partners tend to be similar to one another in the kind of love they express (Hendrick, Hendrick, & Adler, 1988). Game-playing love seems to be the least satisfactory type, in that it leads to relationship dissatisfaction and failure. Those who favor a game-playing approach to love tend to be concerned primarily with themselves and their own autonomy and self-fulfillment (Dion & Dion, 1991).

Another conceptualization of love describes it as consisting of three basic components: Sternberg's (1986, 1988) **triangular model of love**. The first component is **intimacy**—the closeness two people feel and the strength of the bond holding them together. Partners high in intimacy are concerned with each other's welfare and happiness, and they value,

Cultural Variation in Love, Intimacy and Mate Selection: International Commonalities and Differences

CULTURAL VARIATIONS IN LOVE

A study of college students in Germany, Japan, and the United States found differences with respect to the students' attitudes about romantic love (Simmons, vom Kolke, & Shimizu, 1986). Among both men and women, researchers found that Japanese students placed much less value on romantic love than did students in the two Western nations. Unlike their Western counterparts, Japanese believe in male chivalry and in a dependent female role for women. Further, in Japan being in love seems to have primarily negative connotations—being in a dazed state and feeling jealous. Also, Japanese students expect marriage to bring disillusionment. American and German students were alike in most respects, but German students held the most passionate view of romance.

Other research compared the love styles of French and American college students (Murstein, Merighi, & Vyse, 1991), using the measure described earlier in Table 6.3. Americans were much more likely to endorse friendship love than were the French, possibly because of the prevalence of coeducational school experiences and repeated interactions between the sexes. American men were higher on passionate love than those in France; this may reflect cultural differences, in that privacy and self-control are important in France, while Americans tend to be more open, "letting it all hang out." French women were higher on selfless love than were American women, and the authors suggested that the high proportion of Catholics in the French sample might explain this. That is, unlike the other types, selfless love better expresses a religious view involving self-sacrifice and giving.

EXPRESSING INTIMACY

Ting-Toomey (1991) points out that all interpersonal relationships are culture-bound to some extent, and she has proposed that we each learn how to express intimacy to a romantic partner in ways that are acceptable in a given society. Her research concentrated on love commitment (perceived interdependence in a relationship), disclosure maintenance (communication about the relationship), ambivalence (expressed uncertainties about the relationship), and conflict (overt arguments and disagreements).

According to Ting-Toomey's hypothesis, behavior in intimate relationships was expected to differ as a function of cultural *individualism/collectivism*. In an individualist society the focus is on the nuclear family, while a collectivist society has a communal orientation with extended kinship, neighborhood, and work groups. The investigator chose the United States, France, and Japan for comparison because research has shown them to represent high, medium, and low individualism, respectively. It was hypothesized that the higher a society's individualism, the greater would be all four types of intimacy expression.

University students in the three nations responded to a scale measuring the expression of intimacy in relationships. As shown in Table 6.4, the hypothesis was supported with respect to love commitment, disclosure maintenance, and relational ambivalence. But the expression of conflict did not follow the expected pattern, being high in both the United States and Japan and low in France (possibly because of the high level of selfless love found among French women). Apparently, conflict is equally likely in individualistic and collectivist societies.

MATE SELECTION

Buss and 49 colleagues around the world carried out a massive cross-cultural study of preferences in mate selection (1990). The total

►

■ In a cross-cultural study of college students, it was predicted that various kinds of expressive behavior in intimate relationships would occur more strongly as cultural individualism increased. The United States (high individualism), France (intermediate individualism), and Japan (low individualism) were compared. The expected relationships were found for expressions of love commitment, disclosure (communication), and ambivalence about the relationship. But the expression of conflict in relationships was equally high in the United States and Japan, and lowest in France.

TABLE 6.4 Cultural individualism/collectivism and behavior in intimate relationships

Behavior in Intimate Relationships	Culture Type		
	Individualist *(U.S.)*	*Intermediate* *(France)*	*Collectivist* *(Japan)*
Love commitment	High	Medium	Low
Disclosure	High	Medium	Low
Ambivalence	High	Medium	Low
Conflict	High	Low	High

Source: Based on data in Ting-Toomey, 1991.

subject sample was over 9000 people from 37 cultures on 6 continents. Their interest was in cultural and gender differences in the kinds of characteristics we look for in a mate. Subjects were asked to rank order eighteen characteristics of a potential mate from 1, the most desirable, to 18, the least desirable.

Perhaps their most surprising finding was the extent of agreement among those from different cultures (the average correlation between cultures was r = .78): Overall, cultures had more in common than they differed. Interestingly, their English-speaking Canadian sample had an order of preference that was almost identical to the average rankings for the entire international sample, differing only in giving a somewhat lower ranking than average to similar education and religious background. Table 6.5 shows the average rankings of mate characteristics for the North American section of the sample. Because of its average profile, the English-Canadian sample can be taken as demonstrating the typical response of the entire sample. As you can see in Table 6.5, the most highly valued attributes in a mate were "mutual attraction—love," followed by three personality dispositions: "dependable character,"

"emotional stability and maturity," and having a "pleasing disposition." It is interesting to note that while the English-Canadian sample reflected the international average and was extremely similar to the United States sample (the correlation between these two was r = .98), the French-Canadian sample differed somewhat, particularly in giving a higher ranking to "refinement, neatness" and a slightly lower ranking to "emotional stability and maturity." The distinctiveness of French-Canadian values in the North American context was also shown when we discussed a range of more abstract values in chapter 3 (Lipset, 1989).

Despite the commonalities between cultures, there were also some important differences. In particular, cultural variation had a strong effect in relation to more traditional values of "chastity (no previous experience in sexual intercourse)", "good housekeeper" and "desire for home and children," as well as the value of having an "exciting personality." Cultures placing a high or low value on these characteristics are shown in Table 6.6. Further analysis, using a statistical technique called multidimensional scaling, revealed two value dimensions that distinguished between groups ▶

■ A cross-cultural study of preferences in mate characteristics found a remarkably high level of agreement between cultures. The ranking of preferences shown by the English-Canadian sample of the study was very close to the overall international average rankings. For both males and females, mutual attraction or love, a dependable character, and emotional stability were ranked among the most important characteristics in a mate.

TABLE 6.5 The average ranking of potential mate characteristics in Canada and the United States. (The lower the number the more important that characteristic is in a mate)

Mate Characteristics	Canada English		Canada French		U. S. A.	
	Male	Female	Male	Female	Male	Female
Mutual Attraction—Love	1	1	2	2	1	1
Dependable Character	3	3	1	1	3	3
Emotional Stability	2	2	6	4	2	2
Pleasing Disposition	4	4	3	5	4	4
Education and Intelligence	6	8	7	7	5	5
Good Health	5	5	8	9	6	9
Sociability	7	6	5	6	8	8
Desire for Home and Children	8	9	9	11	9	7
Refinement, Neatness	11	12	4	3	10	12
Ambition and Industriousness	10	7	10	8	11	6
Good Looks	9	13	1	15	7	13
Similar Education	13	11	14	14	12	10
Good Financial Prospects	15	10	13	10	16	11
Good Cook and Housekeeper	12	15	12	12	13	16
Favorable Social Status	14	14	15	13	14	14
Similar Religious Background	16	16	16	16	15	15
Chastity (no experience of sexual intercourse)	17	18	17	18	17	18
Similar Political Background	18	17	18	17	18	17

Source: Adapted from Buss and 49 others (1990).

of cultures. One dimension ranged from modern industrial values to more traditional values. China, India, Iran, and Nigeria placed on the traditional end of this dimension, while Netherlands, Great Britain, Finland, and Sweden placed on the modern end. The second dimension ranged from valuing education, intelligence, and refinement at one pole of the dimension, to valuing a pleasant personality at the other pole. Spain, Colombia, and Greece placed at the pole where education and intelligence was highly valued, while Indonesia, Estonia, Ireland, and Japan placed at the opposite pole. Canadians, especially English-speaking Canadians, placed centrally on each of these dimensions, reflecting their generally average profile of values.

All together, these studies suggest the important role cultural influences play in determining the meaning and form of loving relationships.

▶

■ In a cross-cultural study of preferences in mate characteristics, three characteristics in particular distinguished between cultures: chastity, good housekeeper, and an exciting personality.

TABLE 6.6 Three mate characteristics which showed a strong effect for culture. Shown are those cultures which placed a high value on these characteristics (saw them as important or indispensable) and those which placed a low value (saw them as irrelevant or less important).

Mate Characteristic	High Value	Low Value
Chastity	China, India, Indonesia, Iran, Ireland, Palestinian Arab, Taiwan	Britain, Finland, Netherlands, Norway, Sweden, West Germany
Good Housekeeper	South African Zulu, Estonia, Colombia	Canada (both French & English), United States, all Western European samples (except Spain)
Exciting Personality	Brazil, France, Ireland, Japan, Spain, United States	China, India, Iran, South African Zulu

Source: Based on data in Buss and 49 others (1990).

LONG-TERM CLOSE RELATIONSHIPS

The common element found in each type of close relationship is **interdependence**. This means that two people influence one another's lives and regularly engage in joint activities.

When college students are asked to identify the *one person* in the world to whom they feel most close, they describe one of three types of relationship (Berscheid, Snyder, & Omoto, 1989). Some (14 percent) specify a family member, 36 percent identify a friend, and almost half (47 percent) name a romantic partner. The remaining 3 percent mention someone else, such as a fellow worker.

CLOSE RELATIVES

Though family relationships are important during a large portion of our lives, surprisingly little research has focused on this kind of interpersonal closeness.

There are some exceptions, such as several recent studies of sibling relationships. The great majority of children (about 80 percent) grow up with siblings, and interactions with siblings clearly provide a way to learn and practice interpersonal skills (Dunn, 1992). Brothers and sisters often experience a mixture of love and hate, closeness and rivalry; and these mixed feelings recur throughout one's life, because friendships, love affairs, and marriages tend to evoke the reactions originally associated with siblings (Klagsbrun, 1992).

Siblings interact differently at different ages; most siblings are close in childhood but then grow apart in adolescence and young adulthood. By middle age about 80 percent again establish positive relationships, while 10 percent express hostility and another 10 percent feel only indifference. Closeness in adulthood is more likely if siblings are no more than five years apart in age; both sister-sister and brother-sister pairs tend to be closer than brother-brother pairs (Rosenthal, 1992).

Another important, and often neglected, relationship is that between parents and their offspring, especially in adolescence and afterward. No matter how close parents feel toward a baby or a young child, they are often apprehensive when these same young people approach puberty. Parents fear being rejected and hated by rebellious teenagers; but most adolescents report very positive feelings about their parents, though they are naturally less close and dependent than they were in childhood (Galambos, 1992).

Jeffries (1987, 1990, 1993) has also pursued the question of the love adolescents feel for their parents. Based on the writings of St. Thomas Aquinas, Jeffries's model suggests that love for one's parents consists of two basic components: *attraction* and *virtue*. Each component in turn consists of five factors, as shown in Figure 6.17. To the extent that feelings of attraction and virtuous behaviors occur, adolescents also feel loved by their parents, experience happiness and satisfaction with this relationship, indicate high self-esteem, trust other people, and behave in an altruistic way (see chapter 8). This and other studies provide evidence that positive parent-child relationships are of vital importance to the success of subsequent interpersonal relationships. We will return to this topic later in the chapter.

Another aspect of family relationships was studied by Kennedy (1991), who asked young adults to describe their interactions with and feelings about their grandparents. These subjects reported feeling close to at least one of their grandparents (most often the grandmother)—a person they enjoyed being with, who loved them and expressed special interest in them, and made them feel relaxed, comfortable, and proud. When parents divorce and remarry, the children are more likely to spend a great deal of time with their grandparents. In some cultural groups, grandparents may assume the role of substitute or surrogate parents.

CLOSE FRIENDS

Close friends, compared with casual friends, spend more time together, interact in more varied situations, are more likely to exclude others from the relationship, and provide more emotional support to each other (Hays, 1989). One result is that friends are more accurate than nonfriends in inferring what the other person is thinking and feeling (Stinson & Ickes, 1992). Canadian researchers Paulhus and Bruce (1992) found that the continued interaction of two close friends results in increasingly accurate descriptions of each other's personality. A casual friend is often someone who is "fun to be with," while close friends are valued for such qualities as generosity, sensitivity, and honesty (Urbanski, 1992).

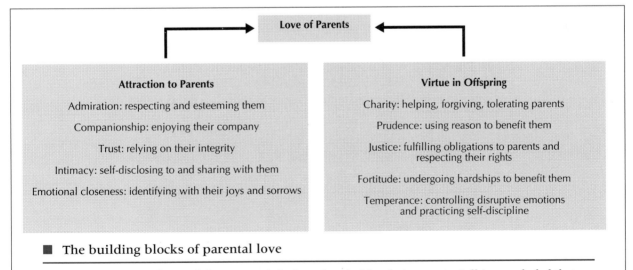

■ The building blocks of parental love

FIGURE 6.17 In studying adolescents and the love they feel for their parents, Jeffries concluded that this kind of love is built on two basic components—attraction toward one's parents and personal virtue. Those who like their parents and are themselves virtuous are able to experience parental love and to treat their mothers and fathers lovingly.

Source: Based on concepts presented by Jeffries, 1987, 1990, 1993.

When close same-sex friendships are compared with opposite-sex romantic relationships, other specific characteristics emerge (Winn, Crawford, & Fischer, 1991). Surprisingly, pairs of friends report more contentment and commitment than do dating partners. Both friends and dates respond to inequity with anger, but friendships are less likely to include feelings of guilt.

In adolescence, friendships tend to be more intimate than in childhood, and such friendships generally have positive effects on the individuals involved (Berndt, 1992). Among friends of the same or of the opposite sex, an "intimate relationship" means that the two individuals feel free to engage in self-disclosing behavior, express their emotions, provide and receive support, experience trust, engage in physical contact, and feel relaxed with one another (Monsour, 1992; Planalp & Benson, 1992).

MARITAL AND FAMILY RELATIONSHIPS

Although patterns of marital and family relationships are changing in Canada, marriage and family are still strong institutions. Changes are indicated by census figures which show that between 1971 and 1991 the marriage rate fell from 8.9 to 6.4 per 1000 population and divorce rates doubled from 1.3 to 2.8 per 1000 population (Che-Alford, Allen, & Butlin, 1994). In addition, the number of couples living in common-law relationships doubled between 1981 and 1991. However, before we worry about the "breakdown of the family," it should be noted that marriage and family are still by far the most preferred form of living arrangement. In 1991, 84 percent of all Canadians lived in families (defined by Statistics Canada in this case as married couples or common-law couples, with or without children, or single parents and children). Table 6.7 shows the changes in family structure in the decade prior to 1991. The proportion of families in which the husband-and-wife couples are common-law spouses increased from 5.6 percent to 9.9 percent between 1981 and 1991(Che-Alford et al., 1994). And in that same time period, the proportion of families with lone parents increased from 11.3 percent in 1981 to 13 percent in 1991. However, in total we can say that the "traditional" family is still the preferred form of relationship: Today in Canada almost 89 percent of

---

■ The structure of family life in Canada has been changing gradually. In the decade from 1981 to 1991, the proportion of all families in which the couple were married decreased by 6 percent, while the proportion of unmarried couples and single parents increased by the same amount. However, marriage remains the preferred form of family life in Canada.

TABLE 6.7 Changing family structure in Canada 1981, 1986 and 1991

		1981	1986	1991
Now-married Couples (with or without children)		83.1 %	80.1 %	77.2 %
Common-law Couples (with or without children)		5.6 %	7.2 %	9.9 %
Lone-parents: (with children)	Female	9.3 %	10.4 %	10.7 %
	Male	2.0 %	2.3 %	2.3 %

Source: Based on Che-Alford, Allan & Butlin, Statistics Canada (1994).

the husband-wife couples are married and 80 percent of families with children still contain both a father and a mother (Che-Alford et al., 1994).

In sum, there are gradual changes in family life and marriage in Canada, but tradition still dominates. Rather than talk of the "breakdown of the family," we should perhaps recognize that family life tends to *evolve* or *adapt* to social and economic changes. For example, at the beginning of this century the *extended* family (consisting of children, parents, grandparents and possibly aunts or uncles) was much more likely to live together than today, although this is still a common form of arrangement in some non-Western cultural groups. Somewhere around the middle of the century the *nuclear* family (consisting of parents and their young children) became the more common form and now seems "traditional" to many North Americans. As our society changes economically and socially, family and marital living arrangements will probably continue to evolve.

Most of the research in this area in social psychology has focused on marriage, although increasingly it is investigating common-law and same sex couples. One of life's greatest challenges continues to be finding happiness in such relationships and discovering how to avoid dispute or break up. However, in general we don't expect our own relationships to be anything like those expressed by Hagar's wife in Figure 6.18.

Similarity and marriage

As we indicated earlier, similarity plays a key role in attraction and in the development of relationships. It has also been established in studies dating back to the beginning of this century that married couples are similar in their attitudes, values, interests, and other attributes (e.g., Pearson & Lee, 1903; Schuster & Elderton, 1906).

While we know that similarity leads to attraction, it has also been proposed that the shared experiences within a long-term relationship would result in even greater similarity over time. The question of whether spouses become more similar over the years was answered by Caspi, Herbener, and Ozer (1992). Data were available on more than 150 couples whose values and attitudes were measured before their weddings and then again after twenty years of marriage. The measure of values dealt with their basic interests in theoretical, economic, aesthetic, political, and religious issues. The attitude items concentrated on marital issues such as premarital sex, infidelity, engaging in the same recreational activities, and how best to structure daily interactions with one

■ The effect of marriage on romantic love

FIGURE 6.18 Most of us expect to fall in love and get married, and most of us do exactly that. Though examples of fading love and unhappy marriages are common, few of us ever expect to feel the way Hagar's wife does here.

Source: King Features Syndicate, Inc., March 8, 1983.

another and with offspring. As expected, husbands and wives showed greater than chance similarity at the time they were engaged and also after two decades as a married couple. There was, however, *no* change in the degree of similarity over time. Similarity was maintained, but it neither increased nor decreased.

There is one type of similarity that leads to a rather odd outcome. As we indicated in chapter 4, people are motivated to confirm their self-concepts in responding to self-relevant information. In interpersonal relationships, confirmation is also important, so a person seeks a marital partner who shares his or her perception of self (Swann, Hixon, & De La Ronde, 1992). For example, if you evaluate many aspects of yourself positively, you want a spouse who also thinks highly of you. What happens, however, when your self-concept is negative? Swann and his colleagues reasoned that anyone with a negative self-concept would want a partner who viewed him or her negatively. To test this proposition, they recruited married couples (ranging in age from seventeen to seventy-eight) at a horse ranch and at a shopping mall. These husbands and wives were given self-concept tests and a questionnaire about their marriage. As you might expect, those with a positive self-concept were more committed to partners who evaluated them positively than to partners expressing negative views. As predicted, however, those with negative self-concepts were most committed to partners who thought badly of them. The investigators point out that even people who evaluate themselves negatively like *positive* feedback, especially from relative strangers. Nevertheless, these same individuals are disturbed to receive positive feedback from a spouse, because that person is supposed "to know better."

Relationship patterns among young married couples

We realize that not all marriages are alike, but exactly how do relationships differ? A study of the everyday lives of husbands and wives who had been married about two years revealed four distinct types of relationship (Johnson et al., 1992). The researchers interviewed spouses separately and asked them about the details of just how they engaged in household tasks, leisure pursuits, interactions, conflicts, and conversations. Four marital patterns emerged, as described in figure 6.19: symmetrical, parallel, differentiated, and reversed.

Symmetrical marriages were found to be the most common type (about two out of five couples), with both working outside the home, spouses holding egalitarian beliefs about sex roles and dividing household labor in ways not based on traditional sex typing, and husbands and wives spending very little leisure time together. About one marriage in four is *parallel*, consisting of what was once the most typical relationship, in which the husband is the primary wage earner, housework is divided along sex-typed lines, and men and women go their separate ways to engage in leisure activities—he to his friends and she to her relatives. *Differentiated* couples (about one out of five) both work (though the husband is more involved in his job), divide the household work along traditional lines, and spend their leisure time together equally involved with friends and relatives. The smallest group (one out of ten) consists of relationships that are *reversed*—primarily because of the husband's unemployment. The wife is involved in her job, the household duties show little or no sex typing, the couple is highly companionate, and the husband is more involved than the wife with friends and relatives.

These groups differ considerably in parenthood. Both the parallel and differentiated couples are very likely to have children (77.8 and 71.4 percent); in contrast, 50 percent of those in reversed relationships and only 35.7 percent of those in symmetrical marriages are parents. However, despite obvious differences in employment patterns, division of household labor, and how they spend their leisure time, those in each group are equally satisfied with their marriages.

Type of Marriage	Characteristics of Marriage
Symmetrical 42%	Husband and wife both have jobs Household tasks are not sex-typed Sex role ideology is egalitarian Spouses spend little leisure time together 35.7% have children
Parallel 27%	Husband is primary wage earner Housework is divided in sex-typed way Spouses spend little time together Husband spends time with friends Wife spends time with relatives 77.8% have children
Differentiated 21%	Both work; husband's job emphasized Housework is divided in sex-typed way Spouses spend most leisure time together and are equally involved with friends and relatives 71.4% have children
Reversed 10%	Wife is involved with outside job Household jobs are not sex-typed Relationship is highly companionate Husband spends time with friends and relatives 50% have children

■ **Four types of marriages**

FIGURE 6.19 A study of the daily lives of couples who had been married about two years revealed four quite different types of relationship. These couples differed with respect to outside jobs, handling of household tasks, leisure time activities, and probability of having offspring. These very different patterns of married life were not, however, related to marital satisfaction.

Source: Based on data in Johnson et al., 1992.

TROUBLED RELATIONSHIPS: PROBLEMS, SOLUTIONS, FAILURES

What happens to turn a loving, romantic relationship into one filled with unhappiness and even hate? Some problems are universal. For example, by their very nature, intimate relationships create conflicts in each partner—between the desire for independence and the desire for closeness, between the need to be open and honest and the need for privacy, between the comfort of predictability and the excitement of the unexpected (Baxter, 1990).

Some problems are brought on by what one of the partners does or what the other partner believes that he or she has done; an example is jealousy (Johnson & Rusbult, 1989). Whatever the problem, solutions may be possible, but couples differ in how well they deal with them. In this section, we will explore some major sources of conflict, possible ways to prevent or resolve problems, and some of the consequences of a broken relationship.

PROBLEMS IN RELATIONSHIPS, AND POSSIBLE SOLUTIONS

At some point in most relationships, passionate love begins to fade, and each individual must face the reality of spending his or her life with someone who is less than perfect. People who believe they are ideally suited for one another can discover that there are negative as well as positive elements in the relationship. Studies of married couples indicate that most report having disagreements regularly (from more than once a week to monthly), while only 1.2 percent say they *never* have disagreements (McGonagle, Kessler, & Schilling, 1992).

Relationship awareness occurs when at least one member of the pair begins to think about how the two of them interact and to compare and contrast their respective roles. Such awareness is more characteristic of women than of men, but marital satisfaction is greater when husbands *do* talk about the relationship (Acitelli, 1992; Harrell, 1990). We will now examine some of the specifics that lead to conflict and dissatisfaction.

Sources of conflict in male-female interactions

Some behaviors are equally upsetting to both sexes (for example, unfaithfulness), while others are more annoying to one sex than to the other. Buss (1989a) asked several hundred men and women to describe the source of their conflicts with a romantic partner. Generally, women become upset if their partners are not loving and gently protective, while men become upset if their partners reject them sexually or ignore them.

It should be noted that some people are more likely than others to behave in ways that cause a partner to be angry and upset. For example, individuals who are characteristically disagreeable, emotionally unstable, and/or unperceptive are most likely to evoke conflict (Buss, 1991). Also, those who characteristically fear being exploited in interpersonal relationships have greater difficulty in establishing and maintaining them (Cotterell, Eisenberger, & Speicher, 1992).

Discovering dissimilarities

When partners belatedly realize that they are dissimilar in some of their attitudes, values, and preferences, negative feelings often arise. One of the problems with passionate love is that the overpowering emotional state in which "love is blind" makes it difficult or impossible to pay attention to such seemingly irrelevant details as the other person's similarities and dissimilarities to oneself. One obvious solution is for two individuals to know as much as possible about one another early in the relationship (Byrne & Murnen, 1988).

Some dissimilarities do not occur until after the couple is married, and thus are difficult to anticipate or avoid. For example, one of the partners may change his or her religious views, political beliefs, drinking behavior, or sexual preferences while the other does not. If so, initial similarity changes into dissimilarity (Levinger, 1988). Consider a situation in which a man marries a woman who plans to be a homemaker but who later decides to pursue a career. Her newfound interest in a life outside of the home can be a source of annoyance to her husband (Nicola & Hawkes, 1986).

Still other dissimilarities are hard to avoid because they are not relevant to a dating couple or even to the early stages of marriage. Two people may easily fail to discover (until too late) that they differ in long-range plans about saving money versus spending it, in beliefs about how best to raise children, or in concerns about health and hygiene. When their differences become apparent, marital dissatisfaction can increase.

Boredom

For some, a long-term relationship becomes a source of distress because it is boring. Many dating couples report breaking up simply because they became bored with one another (Hill, Rubin, & Peplau, 1976).

As Skinner (1986) pointed out, boredom is a major problem in our lives, but it has seldom been investigated. Married couples especially are likely to develop unchanging routines in their daily interactions, sexual and otherwise, and only gradually realize that they are in a rut. For some, this regularity and predictability is a positive feature. For others, it can be unpleasant; and then each attributes the problem to the other person, which causes marital dissatisfaction (Fincham & Bradbury, 1992, 1993).

When boredom arises, it can sometimes be overcome if the couple seeks new stimulation in the form of vacations, joint educational efforts, unfamilar dining experiences, new hobbies they can share, new sexual practices, and so on. The alternative—continuing to do the same things in the same way—can easily lead to dissatisfaction.

Though much of the research on marriage focuses on problems, it is helpful to remember that more marriages succeed than fail. Some of the secrets of success were identified by Lauer and Lauer (1985) through a study of 351 couples who had been married fifteen years or longer. When the investigators asked these couples to explain why their marriages lasted, the most common responses (shown in Figure 6.20) stressed friendship, commitment, similarity, and positive affect.

Positive versus negative communications

One of the oddest and most self-defeating aspects of a long-term relationship occurs when partners shift from providing one another with positive evaluations to words and deeds that indicate negative evaluations. As suggested in Figure 6.21, this kind of shift is characteristic of unsuccessful relationships.

Dating couples and newlyweds frequently express their positive feelings about one another. They make an effort to be together, they hold hands, they repeatedly demonstrate their love, they say kind things, they help each other, and they make it obvious that each finds the other socially and sexually desirable. Over time, however, quite different expressions of feeling occur. It is easy enough to think (or say), "I don't have to tell you I love you; I married you, didn't I?" Other indications of love can also fade away, as in "You don't bring me flowers anymore."

As dissatisfaction increases, negative interactions become more frequent (Margolin, John, & O'Brien, 1989). For one thing, some individuals make maladaptive attributions ("it's all his fault" or "it's all her fault") about the cause of any disagreement or difficulty. In an unhappy couple, instead of trying to solve problems, each person expresses negative evaluations and blames the other (Bradbury & Fincham,

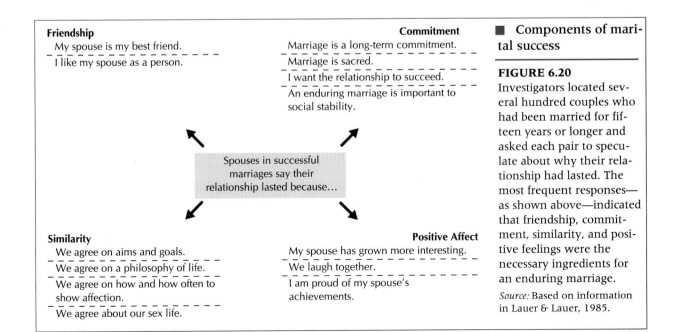

Friendship
My spouse is my best friend.
I like my spouse as a person.

Commitment
Marriage is a long-term commitment.
Marriage is sacred.
I want the relationship to succeed.
An enduring marriage is important to social stability.

Spouses in successful marriages say their relationship lasted because...

Similarity
We agree on aims and goals.
We agree on a philosophy of life.
We agree on how and how often to show affection.
We agree about our sex life.

Positive Affect
My spouse has grown more interesting.
We laugh together.
I am proud of my spouse's achievements.

■ **Components of marital success**

FIGURE 6.20
Investigators located several hundred couples who had been married for fifteen years or longer and asked each pair to speculate about why their relationship had lasted. The most frequent responses—as shown above—indicated that friendship, commitment, similarity, and positive feelings were the necessary ingredients for an enduring marriage.

Source: Based on information in Lauer & Lauer, 1985.

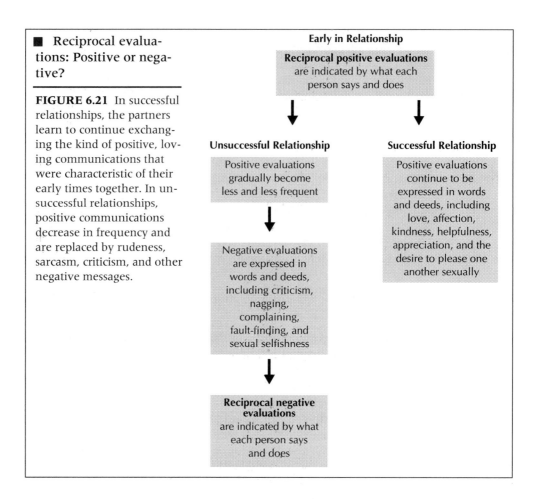

■ Reciprocal evaluations: Positive or negative?

FIGURE 6.21 In successful relationships, the partners learn to continue exchanging the kind of positive, loving communications that were characteristic of their early times together. In unsuccessful relationships, positive communications decrease in frequency and are replaced by rudeness, sarcasm, criticism, and other negative messages.

1992). Videotapes of the interchanges of satisfied and dissatisfied couples indicate much higher rates of negative verbal and nonverbal behavior among those whose marriages are in trouble (Halford & Sanders, 1990).

Miller (1991) notes how puzzling this new pattern of behavior really is:

> …why is it that some of our most hateful, caustic, and abusive interactions take place with those we say we love? Why is it that intimacy seems to give us a license to treat people in sarcastic, critical, and cruel ways that we reluctantly use with total strangers?

> Even in happy marriages, spouses are characteristically meaner to each other than to mere acquaintances or friends….(p.63)

Miller (1991) suggests that we become rude and impolite to intimate partners for three reasons. (1) In an intimate relationship there is more *opportunity* to discover a mate's many trivial imperfections than in other relationships, in part because each person feels confident of being accepted by the partner, feels less need for impression management, and so relaxes and becomes "himself" or "herself." (2) When the other person's flaws become apparent, *misplaced expectations* lead each spouse naively to assume that the other will change for the better; it is frustrating and annoying when change doesn't occur—and it usually doesn't. (3) It is easy enough to stop complimenting and rewarding a partner because of *lack of motivation*. It requires less effort and less thought to be selfish and impolite than to be socially skillful and thoughtful. We save that for others.

The solution is seemingly simple—people need to be aware of this deadly danger in intimate relationships, to be realistic, and to be as nice and as polite to an intimate partner as to strangers, acquaintances, and friends. Though behaving in this way appears to require special effort, it would seem to be well worth it.

Jealousy: A special threat

The possibility of attraction toward someone new is a common problem in relationships, and jealousy is the usual response of one's partner (White & Mullen, 1990). Among the negative emotions aroused by jealousy are suspicion, rejection, hostility, and anger (Smith, Kim, & Parrott, 1988).

Jealousy endangers a relationship. An individual who is low in self-esteem is most likely to become jealous (Salovey & Rodin, 1991), and jealousy also precipitates a decrease in self-esteem (Mathes, Adams, & Davies, 1985). Much like passionate love in reverse, jealousy elicits a flood of all-consuming negative thoughts, feelings, and behaviors (Pines & Aronson, 1983). Cultures differ greatly, however, in evaluating what it is that gives rise to jealousy. For example, if one's partner hugs someone of the opposite sex, this causes much more sexual jealousy in Hungary than in the United States (Buunk & Hupka, 1987).

Men and women also differ; men become more jealous in response to sexual infidelity, while women's jealousy is stronger in response to indications of a partner's emotional commitment to someone else (Buss et al., 1992). One explanation is an evolutionary one. If a man's mate is intimate with other men, any offspring she has may not be his—thus, a woman's infidelity is a genetic threat to a man. If, however, a woman's mate is intimate with other women, this is no genetic threat to the woman, because her children are still hers. But her well-being is threatened if her mate becomes emotionally involved with another woman, because his commitment may shift to a new relationship. Oddly consistent with this sex difference is the way in which men and women justify engaging in an extramarital relationship. For women involved in extramarital affairs, sex outside of marriage is justified only by love, while men feel that sexual pleasure and variety constitute sufficient justification (Glass & Wright, 1992).

Some people deliberately try to make their partners jealous as a way to gain attention and to strengthen the relationship. They may flirt with others or talk about former lovers (White, 1980). Among college students, these tactics are used by one in three women and one in five men, but the result is more likely to damage the relationship than to help it.

WHEN RELATIONSHIPS BREAK UP: FROM DISSATISFACTION TO DISSOLUTION

Social psychologists have become increasingly interested in understanding the last two stages in the relationship process: deterioration and ending.

Differences between friendships and intimate relationships

Friendships often fade away quietly when friends move to new locations or develop new interests (Rose, 1984). When love is involved, however, it is very difficult to drift apart peacefully. Instead, painful emotions are aroused, feelings are hurt, and anger can become intense.

Romantic relationships don't end easily because they involve the investment of one's time, the exchange of powerful rewards, and commitment (Simpson, 1987). If an acceptable substitute is readily available, the loss of a partner is less traumatic than when one is simply cast adrift (Jemmott, Ashby, & Lindenfeld, 1989).

Responding to relationship problems

Rusbult and Zembrodt (1983) point out that individuals respond to an unhappy partnership either actively or passively. An active response involves either ending the relationship ("exit") or working to improve it ("voice"). Passively, a person can simply wait for improvement to occur ("loyalty") or wait for further deterioration ("neglect"). These alternate choices are shown in figure 6.22.

Among diverse couples (college students, older couples, and gays and lesbians), a consistent finding is that men and women whose self-esteem is high respond to relationship failure by exiting, while those with low self-esteem engage in passive neglect (Rusbult, Morrow, & Johnson, 1990).

Once deterioration begins, a breakup becomes very likely. Sometimes the only reasonable solution is for each member of the pair to start over again with someone else. Actively solving the problems and maintaining the relationship is likely only if three factors are present: a high level of *satisfaction of various needs* on the part of each person, *commitment* to the relationship based on past investment of time and effort in building the relationship, and the *absence of alternative lovers* (Rusbult, 1983; Simpson, 1987). More generally, the **dependence model of breakups** proposes that the decision whether to break up or to continue a relationship is related to an individual's degree of dependence on that relationship (Drigotas & Rusbult, 1992). Even a bad relationship may satisfy important needs that can't be met with alternate partners.

Breakup and divorce

Although about 84 percent of Canadians have been married by the age of 34 years (Kerr & Ram,1994), in 1991 for every 100 marriages there were 44 divorces and the average duration of marriage was 10.9 years (Che-Alford et al., 1994). We have already

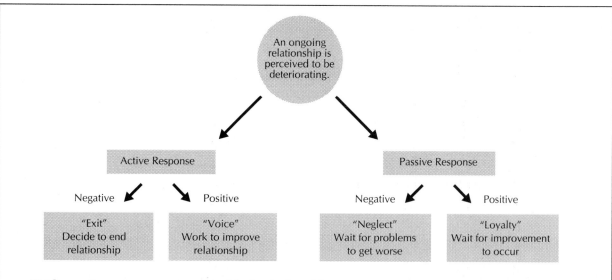

■ Alternative responses to a troubled relationship

FIGURE 6.22 When a relationship is beginning to fail, the partners can respond in either an active or a passive way. Either way, a partner can take a positive or a negative approach. Assuming the best, a partner can work actively to improve the situation or wait passively in the hope that improvement will simply occur. Assuming the worst, a partner can actively end the relationship or passively wait for it to fall apart. If the relationship is not hopeless, the most adaptive response is an active, positive one.

Source: Based on suggestions by Rusbult & Zembrodt, 1983.

discussed some of the factors that make relationships more or less likely to fail. Some additional predictors of divorce will be described here.

Observations of different infant-mother attachment styles led Hazan and Shaver (1990) to propose that adults follow similar attachment patterns in forming relationships with their peers in romantic or friendship relationships. A recent model developed by Kim Bartholomew of Simon Fraser University is the *four-category model of adult attachment* (Bartholomew, 1990, 1993; Bartholomew & Horowitz, 1991). Basing her model on the original writings of John Bowlby on attachment in children (1973), Bartholomew proposes that adult attachment patterns can be conceptualized as derived from two related dimensions: (1) The positivity of the individual's model of the self (the extent to which the individual's self-concept is characterized by *anxiety* related to the self); and (2) the positivity of the individual's model of others in general (the extent to which the orientation to others is *avoidant*). Table 6.8 shows the four categories of adult attachment which result from these two dimensions: *secure, preoccupied, dismissing,* and *fearful.* Beneath each one is the description used in research to define that particular type of attachment to others in general (Griffin & Bartholomew, 1994). For example, both the *secure* and the *preoccupied* patterns are shown by those who have a positive (non-avoidant) orientation towards other people, but they differ in that those who have a secure pattern feel positive towards themselves, whereas preoccupied individuals have a negative model of the self. The *dismissing* and *fearful* patterns are shown by those who have a negative (avoidant) response to others. However, the dismissing individual has a positive model of the self and the fearful individual has a negative view of the self. Most people, rather than showing a single type of response pattern, display elements of two or more (Bartholomew & Horowitz, 1991). Of these attachment styles, only the secure style is likely to enable individuals to form long-lasting, committed, satisfying relationships (Shaver & Brennan, 1992). Research indicates that self-reports of cold or inconsistent relationships with one's parents are associated with later avoidant and/or anxious-ambivalent romantic attachments, whereas parental relationships described as warm are associated with secure romantic attachments (Bringle & Bagby, 1992).

■ The pattern of attachment that adults demonstrate depends on the positivity of their model of the self and the positivity of their model of others.

TABLE 6.8 The four-category theory of adult attachment

	MODEL OF SELF	
	Positive (Low Anxiety)	**Negative (High Anxiety)**
Positive (Low Avoidance)	SECURE PATTERN "It's easy for me to become emotionally close to others. I am comfortable depending on them and having them depend on me. I don't worry about being alone or having others not accept me."	PREOCCUPIED PATTERN "I want to be completely emotionally intimate with others, but I often find that others are reluctant to get as close as I would like. I am uncomfortable being without close relationships, but I sometimes worry that others don't value me as much as I value them."
Negative (High Avoidance)	DISMISSING PATTERN "I am comfortable without close emotional relationships. It is very important to me to feel independent and self-sufficient, and I prefer not to depend on others or have others depend on me."	FEARFUL PATTERN "I am uncomfortable getting close to others. I want emotionally close relationships, but I find it difficult to trust others completely, or to depend on them. I worry that I will be hurt if I allow myself to become too close to others."

(Row group label: **MODEL OF OTHERS**)

What else is related to marital success and failure? Kurdek (1993) obtained data from 222 newlywed couples each year for five years. Over that period, 64 of the couples dissolved their marriages. Several demographic and psychological factors were found to predict marital outcome. For example, marital dissolution was associated with low income, low educational level of the wife, a previous divorce for either partner, neuroticism, unrealistic expectations about the relationship, and a brief courtship. Also associated with marital failure were dissimilarities in spouses' need for independence, in the value they placed on attachment, and in their motives for marriage. These and other factors (each present at the time of the marriage) permitted a fairly accurate prediction of which couples would and would not remain married. Such findings suggest the possibility that couples planning marriage might find it valuable to be interviewed, tested, and informed of the likelihood that their marriage would last.

Note also that poverty exerts a major influence on marital success and failure. According to census figures families below the poverty level were twice as likely to break up as couples above the poverty level (Pear, 1993). Other background characteristics making divorce more likely include failure to complete college, unstable employment, getting married before age twenty, and experiencing an out-of-wedlock pregnancy (McGue & Lykken, 1992).

The aftereffects of relationship failure

Both men and women suffer emotionally when a marriage fails, and those who do not remarry are likely to experience loneliness, depression, and lasting feelings of anger (Fischman, 1986). Most divorced individuals do remarry, especially males. In 1991, about 20 percent of marriages involved divorced persons and this number had risen from only 10 percent in 1960 (Che-Alford, et al., 1994).

Fourteen percent of Canadian children under 17 years of age are living with a single parent, 80 percent of whom are women. Poverty often results from separation or divorce for the single mother. The average family income of a female lone-parent in 1990 was just over half (57 percent) that of a male lone-parent, and only 38 percent of the average income of a two-parent family (Che-Alford et al., 1994). Psychologically, children of a broken marriage suffer more than their parents, and they frequently respond with very negative feelings, lowered self-esteem, anxiety, and feelings of powerlessness; social and academic problems also tend to develop (Guidubaldi, Perry, & Nastasi, 1987; Slater & Calhoun, 1988).

Research on relationships can help people make better decisions about entering romantic partnerships and provide needed information about how to maintain such relationships.

LONELINESS:
THE ABSENCE OF CLOSE RELATIONSHIPS

Though most of us place a high value on establishing relationships, some people have difficulty in doing so. In addition, it is not unusual to find oneself without a relationship as the result of the departure or death of a partner. In either instance, the result can be **loneliness**: the unfulfilled desire to engage in close interpersonal relationships (Peplau & Perlman, 1982). One of the major theorists in this area is Dan Perlman of the University of British Columbia. He and Anne Peplau (1981) describe loneliness as having three essential characteristics: (1) it results from perceived deficiences in a person's social relationships; (2) it is unpleasant and distressing; and (3) it is a subjective phenomenon. That is loneliness is determined by individuals' subjective perceptions and feelings about the lack of sufficient relationships in their lives, *not* by their objective social isolation. Loneliness is not, therefore, the same as being alone—sometimes we can be lonely in a crowd, or we can feel quite content being by ourselves. Research on this topic has concentrated on the consequences of loneliness, the reasons for being lonely, and ways to overcome loneliness (Marangoni & Ickes, 1989).

UNDERSTANDING AND MEASURING LONELINESS

Because of the subjective nature of loneliness, theorists have focused on attempting to understand and explain the feelings and perceptions of the lonely person. Perlman and Peplau's **discrepancy-attributional model of loneliness** (Peplau & Perlman, 1982; Perlman & Peplau, 1986) emphasizes the way in which the perceptions and interpretations of the lonely individual can mediate their emotional response. Two principles underly their model. First, loneliness is conceived as the "response to a discrepancy between one's desired and achieved levels of social relationship" (Perlman & Peplau, 1986, p.137). Both the desired level of social contact (the number and quality of the relationships a person wants) and the achieved level of social contact are subjectively evaluated by each individual. The second principle is that cognitive processes, especially causal attributions for loneliness, have a moderating effect on the experience of loneliness. When you feel lonely, your attributions about the cause of that state are important. For example if you blame your circumstances (e.g., you have just moved away from home for the first time) rather than yourself (I'm just an unlikeable person), your emotional response to the loneliness and your expectations of future social contacts probably will be radically different. In the first situation, you might feel more hopeful that the loneliness is merely temporary, perhaps only lasting until you have found your feet and begun to make friends in this new context. In the second situation where you blame yourself, a much greater sense of depression and hopelessness could be anticipated. Among the implications of this model is that relieving loneliness can also take a subjective approach. As we will see below, the focus could be on the specific type of relationship that a person desires or upon altering his or her subjective perceptions of the causes of loneliness.

The **UCLA Loneliness Scale** is a personality test constructed to assess individual differences in the experience of loneliness (Russell, Peplau, & Cutrona, 1980). Subjects are asked to respond along a scale ranging from "never" to "often" on items such as "I feel left out" and "I have a lot in common with the people around me." A person who feels lonely is likely to indicate *often* in response to the first item, *never* in response to the second.

In samples of American, Puerto Rican, and Portuguese adolescents, high scores on the UCLA Loneliness Scale are found to be associated with feelings of depression, anxiety, dissatisfaction, unhappiness, and shyness (Jones, Carpenter, & Quintana, 1985; Neto, 1992). Lonely individuals are also disliked by others and evaluated negatively on characteristics such as adjustment, achievement, strength, attractiveness, and sincerity (Lau & Gruen, 1992; Rotenberg & Kmill, 1992). As you might expect, someone who feels lonely reports spending leisure time alone, seldom engages in social activities such as dating, and has only casual friends or acquaintances (Berg & McQuinn, 1989; Williams & Solano, 1983). Lonely individuals don't have a network of friends (R. A. Bell, 1991).

LONELINESS IN CHILDHOOD

Young people commonly go through periods of loneliness. For example, one's parents or a close friend's parents may move to a new location, making it necessary to start over again in establishing close relationships. The situation is usually temporary, and such experiences do not cause adult loneliness.

In contrast to these short-term situational experiences of loneliness, a more serious, long-lasting problem develops when children fail to learn appropriate social skills (Rubin, 1982). It is rare for any of us to be taught the best way to make and keep friends, to make others feel comfortable, to manage disagreements, and to be sensitive to the feelings of others. A child's parents or older siblings may serve as good role models; in other instances, children develop good skills by accident. But if a child fails to learn appropriate ways to interact, he or she is likely to react inappropriately. For example, interpersonal failures can lead to aggressive behavior or to withdrawal and loneliness.

Studies of preschool children have revealed four patterns of interpersonal relationships. Some children are very popular; some are average in the number and warmth of their relationships; other youngsters are ignored; and a few are actively rejected. Those in the latter two categories are the ones most likely to be lonely and to require help in changing their style of interacting with peers (Johnson, Poteat, & Ironsmith, 1991). Without such intervention, interpersonal inadequacies tend to remain as consistent problems from the preschool years through adulthood (Asendorpf, 1992).

INTERPERSONAL SKILLS AND LONELINESS

Adolescence is a peak time for loneliness (Brennan, 1982). Young people are involved in the process of separating themselves from their parents and forming outside relationships. If this interpersonal effort fails, loneliness results. The person feels alienated from parents, teachers, and peers. Among the worst possible consequences is **hopelessness**, a feeling of despair that is potentially associated with suicide (Page, 1991). Again, good interpersonal skills are crucial.

Socially unskilled teenagers or adults are unaware of how best to deal with other people, and as a consequence they fail to do the right things. The interactions of a socially unskilled person with a stranger are characterized by few references to the other person, failure to follow up on topics introduced by that individual, and an absence of questions that indicate interest (Jones, Hobbs, & Hockenbury, 1982). Those who are lonely also tend to disclose very little about themselves, or to make inappropriate disclosures (Solano, Barren, & Parish, 1982).

Such interpersonal behaviors drive potential friends away, and these experiences result in expectations of interpersonal failure, along with cynicism, pessimism, and the belief that one's life is uncontrollable (Davis et al., 1992). Romantic relationships are especially troublesome, and loneliness is associated with the belief that friendship, love, and marriage are relatively unimportant and doomed to fail (B.Bell, 1991).

DOING SOMETHING TO RELIEVE LONELINESS

Unless a major effort is made to improve interpersonal interactions, loneliness will not magically go away. Lonely individuals tend to retreat into wish-fulfilling fantasies, become absorbed in their occupations, or turn to alcohol and drugs (Revenson, 1981). Some rely on music as a substitute for interpersonal relationships, but songs of separation, heartache, and sadness actually increase feelings of loneliness (Davis & Kraus, 1989). Because these coping strategies only make things worse, what is the solution? Two successful techniques, often used together, are **cognitive therapy** and **social skills training**.

The cognitions of lonely and nonlonely people are found to differ. The *self-schema* of a lonely individual brings about selective attention to negative information involving himself or herself, thus confirming and strengthening an already negative self-concept (Frankel & Prentice-Dunn, 1990). Cognitive therapy is designed to alter such cognitions, especially with respect to social situations. If, for example, a man perceives himself as dull and boring, a therapist may be able to convince him that this self-perception is incorrect or to help him give up his false belief that only witty and exciting people can make friends. If a woman reacts to social situations as stressful because she feels others are always evaluating her (Asendorpf, 1989), she can learn that she really isn't the center of everyone else's attention.

Such changes in cognitions need to be accompanied by behavioral changes. Those who are lonely not only lack appropriate social skills, they also are anxious about not possessing these skills (Solano & Koester, 1989). One form of social skills training is to expose a lonely individual to interpersonally successful role models on videotape. The person can also practice social skills in a nonthreatening situation and view the results on tape. Specific interactions (such as initiating a conversation) can be prescribed and rehearsed. Sometimes the needed skills are very specific—how to speak easily on the telephone, give compliments, or improve one's physical appearance.

The effects of these efforts can be remarkable, even in a short period of time (Young, 1982). Once a lonely person thinks about social situations in a new way, learns how best to interact with others, and changes his or her interpersonal style, the resulting interpersonal successes can eliminate loneliness.

SUMMARY AND REVIEW

Our attitudes about other people range from strong liking to strong dislike, and research on interpersonal attraction focuses on the factors that determine these attitudes.

INTERPERSONAL ATTRACTION

Friendships often begin on the basis of unplanned encounters that are controlled by the physical details of the environment. When neighborhoods, dormitory assignments, or classroom seating arrangements bring people into regular contact, they are likely to become acquainted. Thus, proximity (or *propinquity*) leads to repeated exposure, which results in familiarity and the increased likelihood of friendly interaction.

A basic determinant of attraction is *affect*, or one's emotional state during an interpersonal interaction. Positive affect results in liking while negative affect causes dislike, whether the other person is responsible for the emotion or not. We learn to associate our emotional state with anyone who is present at the time, and attraction is sometimes a function of emotional conditioning.

A relationship is most likely to form if two people are each motivated to affiliate. People differ in the dispositional variable known as *need for affiliation*, and the strength of this motive determines attraction-related behaviors. In addition, several specific underlying motives—such as the need for emotional support and the need for attention—provide different reasons for seeking relationships. Not only dispositions but external events involving stress or excitement can act as powerful motivators of affiliation, in that people seek out others with whom to engage in social comparison and information-gathering interactions.

Initial attraction or avoidance is often based on responses to stereotypes associated with the *observable characteristics* of others—race, sex, age, height, physique, accent, clothing, and so forth. Among the most pervasive of these characteristics is *physical attractiveness*. There is a generally positive response to both males and females who are attractive, and people tend to select others approximately as attractive as themselves (according to the *matching hypothesis*) as friends, dates, and marriage partners.

BUILDING A RELATIONSHIP: SIMILARITY AND RECIPROCITY

Observers of human behavior since before the time of Christ have noted that *attitude similarity* is associated with liking and attitude dissimilarity with negative responses. Research in the latter half of this century established a precise linear relationship between attraction and proportion of similar attitudes. Because we tend to assume that others agree with us (the false consensus effect), initial attraction to a stranger tends to be high, and subsequent attraction is a function of how far the person's actual attitudes deviate from our expectations. Also, similarity in many aspects of behavior and appearance is found to be positively related to attraction. Explanations of the similarity effect include balance theory, the need for consensual validation, and the sociobiological importance of genetic similarity.

A crucial variable in friendship formation is the expression of mutual liking (reciprocity) either in words or in nonverbal behavior.

WHAT IS THIS THING CALLED LOVE ?

A crucial aspect of our lives is the establishment of close, loving *relationships*. Most people report that they feel closest to a romantic partner. The basis for romantic relationships is often *passionate love*, an intense, overpowering emotional experience. A close, caring friendship with a romantic partner is labeled *companionate love*—a less intense and more lasting state than passionate love. Additional elements and types of love have been described by Hendrick and Hendrick and by Sternberg.

Cross-cultural research has shown how the perception and expression of love, and preference for particular characteristics in a mate can differ in different countries.

LONG–TERM CLOSE RELATIONSHIPS

Interdependence occurs when two people influence one another's lives and engage in many joint activities over an extended time period. This kind of relationship often involves *relatives* such as parents and siblings and also *close friends*.

Despite a high divorce rate, most people marry. Couples develop a variety of relationship patterns in dealing with jobs, household duties, leisure activities, and parenthood.

TROUBLED RELATIONSHIPS

Problems and conflicts arise in long-term relationships. Among the common difficulties are dissimilarities between the partners, boredom, increasingly negative interactions, and *jealousy*. When the problems become sufficiently intense, the relationship sometimes can be restored, but breakups often occur. Whether the relationship is maintained or dissolved depends on such factors as personality, patterns of attachment, the meaning of the relationship to each partner, and the availability of alternate partners.

LONELINESS

Those who want a close relationship but fail to establish one express feelings of *loneliness*. The *discrepancy-attributional model* of loneliness stresses that loneliness results from a response to a discrepancy between desired and achieved levels of social contact. Secondly, response is influenced by attributions about the causes of loneliness. Chronic loneliness often has roots in a person's childhood. With more effective social skills and cognitive restructuring, loneliness can be overcome.

Affect Emotions or feelings.

Appearance Anxiety Apprehension or worry about the adequacy of one's physical appearance and about how others evaluate it.

Attitude Similarity The extent to which two individuals share the same attitudes about a series of topics.

Balance In Newcomb's theory, the pleasant emotional state that results when two people like each other and agree about a topic of discussion.

Balance Theory A cognitively oriented theory of the relationships among an individual's liking for another person, his or her attitude about a given topic, and the other person's perceived attitude about that same topic.

Close Friends Friends who spend a great deal of time together, interact in varied situations, exclude others from the relationship, and provide one another with emotional support.

Cognitive Disregard Part of the screening process whereby some of the people we meet are excluded from further consideration as possible acquaintances or friends on the basis of our reaction to one or more of their observable characteristics. We pay little attention to those we exclude from consideration, and we tend to forget them.

Cognitive Therapy An interpersonal therapy stressing the importance of altering the client's maladaptive beliefs and thought processes.

Companionate Love Feelings of love that are based on friendship, mutual attraction, common interests, mutual respect, and concern for each other's happiness and welfare.

Complementarity Possession of different but complementary traits. The complementarity hypothesis suggests that people with complementary traits should like one another; for example, a dominant person should be attracted to a submissive one. There is, however, very little empirical support for this appealing idea.

Consensual Validation The "validation" of one's views about any aspect of the world that one perceives on finding that someone else holds the same views.

Decision/Commitment In Sternberg's triangular model of love, the cognitive elements involved in deciding to form a relationship and in being committed to it.

Dependence Model of Breakups A formulation proposing that an individual's decision to end a relationship is more likely the less the individual is dependent on that relationship.

Discrepancy-Attributional Model of Loneliness The experience of loneliness depends upon a person's response to a discrepancy between desired and achieved levels of social contact and attributions about the causes of loneliness.

Friendship Motivation The motive to establish warm and friendly interpersonal relationships.

Hopelessness A feeling of despair in which an individual gives up on life. Sometimes hopelessness leads to suicide.

Imbalance In Newcomb's theory, the unpleasant emotional state that results when two people like each other but disagree about a topic of discussion. Each is motivated to change some element in the interaction (the actual or perceived attitude of one of the individuals or the feeling of attraction) in order to achieve balance or nonbalance.

Interdependence The characteristic common to all close relationships; means that two people influence one another's lives and engage in many joint activities over an extended period of time.

Interpersonal Attraction The degree to which we like other individuals. Interpersonal attraction varies along a dimension ranging from strong liking on one extreme to strong dislike on the other.

Intimacy In Sternberg's triangular model of love, the closeness or bondedness of two partners.

Jealousy The thoughts, feelings, and actions that arise when a relationship is threatened by a real or imagined rival for a partner's affection.

Loneliness The emotional state of a person who wants to be in a relationship but is not. Can also be a personality disposition. The lonely person feels unhappy and isolated but lacks the necessary social skills and cognitive awareness to overcome the problem.

Matching Hypothesis The proposal that individuals with approximately equal social assets (such as physical attractiveness) select one another as friends, lovers, and/or spouses.

Need for Affiliation The motive to seek interpersonal relationships.

Nonbalance In Newcomb's theory, the indifferent emotional state that results when two people dislike each other and don't care whether they agree or disagree about a topic of discussion.

Passion In Sternberg's triangular model of love, the sexual drives and sexual arousal associated with an interpersonal relationship.

Passionate Love An intense and often unrealistic emotional response to another person. When two individuals respond to one another in this way, they interpret their feelings as "true love," while observers often label their response as "infatuation."

Physical Attractiveness The combination of facial features, physique, and grooming that is perceived as aesthetically appealing by members of a given culture at a given time period.

Privacy The need to limit how much other people know about one's past, present, or future activities.

Propinquity Physical proximity. As propinquity between two individuals increases, the probability of their coming in contact increases. Repeated interpersonal exposure leads to increased familiarity, and familiarity generally leads to a positive evaluative response.

Proportion of Similar Attitudes The number of topics on which two individuals hold the same views in relation to the total number of topics on which they compare their views. Expressed as a percentage or proportion: the number of topics on which there is agreement divided by the total number of total topics discussed.

Reinforcement-Affect Model A theory proposing that positive versus negative evaluations are based on positive versus negative emotions. The evaluations are directed at the person who is *responsible* for the emotions or (through classical conditioning) *simply associated* with the arousal.

Relationship Awareness Consciousness of the pros and cons of an existing relationship; occurs when at least one member of a romantic couple begins to think about how the two of them interact and to compare and contrast their respective roles.

Repeated Exposure Frequent contact with a stimulus. According to Zajonc's theory of repeated exposure, as the number of contacts with any neutral or mildly positive stimulus increases, the evaluation of that stimulus becomes increasingly positive.

Social Comparison Process The tendency to evaluate one's abilities, accomplishments, views, actions, appearance, beliefs, and other attributes by comparing them with those of other relevant people.

Social Skills Training A therapeutic process that teaches individuals what to do and say in interpersonal interactions.

Triangular Model of Love Sternberg's formulation that conceptualizes love relationships in terms of the relative emphasis placed on intimacy, passion, and decision/commitment.

UCLA Loneliness Scale A personality test that assesses the extent to which an individual feels lonely and isolated from others.

Derlega, V. J., & Winstead, B. A. (Eds.). (1986). *Friendship and social interaction*. New York: Springer-Verlag.

> Authors from various fields discuss friendship. Included are such topics as friendship formation, the importance of friendship in our lives, and the effects of sex and social situations on friendship functioning.

Hatfield, E., & Sprecher, S. (1986). *Mirror, mirror ... The importance of looks in everyday life*. Albany, NY: SUNY Press.

> A well-written and extremely interesting summary of research dealing with the effects of physical attractiveness on interpersonal relationships. The scientific literature is well covered, and the findings are illustrated throughout with anecdotes, photographs, and drawings that consistently enliven the presentation.

Nardi, P. M. (Ed.) (1992). *Men's friendships*. Newbury Park, CA: Sage.

> A series of contributors provide chapters that cover many aspects of male friendship patterns. Included are discussions of men's power, networking, self-disclosure, friendships with women, gay relationships, and cross-cultural comparisons focused on Native American, Asian-American, and African-American men.

Brehm, S. S. (1992). *Intimate relationships*. New York: McGraw-Hill.

> In this second edition of a book aimed at undergraduate readers, Professor Brehm covers the primary topics relevant to relationships including attraction, love and romance, sexual interactions, equity, jealousy, loneliness, and the dissolution of relationships.

Duck, S. (1991). *Human relationships*. Newbury Park, CA: Sage.

> A very readable summary of social psychological work on interpersonal relationships. Among the many topics covered are love, long-term relationships, family interactions, and the effects of divorce on children.

Hatfield, E., & Rapson, R. L. (1993). *Love, sex, and intimacy: Their psychology, biology, and history*. New York: Harper Collins.

> This unique book was coauthored by a social psychologist and her historian husband, and it covers a wide range of material relevant to love, sex, intimacy, and relationships in an interesting, readable fashion. In discussing these topics, the authors draw on psychology, biology, history, literature, arts, and their personal observations.

Hendrick, S. S., & Hendrick, C. (1992). *Romantic love*. Newbury Park, CA: Sage.

> Two psychologists who are at the forefront in investigating the phenomenon of love bring together what is known on the subject. They combine material from psychologists, sociologists, historians, and philosophers in dealing with the history of love, love in close relationships, love styles, and the way love affects our everyday lives.

SEVEN

Social Influence: Changing Others' Behavior

Recently, as part of a social psychology class project on social influence, a student at the University of British Columbia went out onto the university campus to attempt to influence people to behave in a way that they wouldn't normally—namely to do three push-ups there and then on the ground. She would exert this influence simply by asking them politely. The idea was that differences in her apparent role (either she dressed in her own casual student clothes or like a researcher in white lab coat, carrying a clipboard) would result in differing levels of compliance with her request. She first tried out the casual dress condition and much to her surprise received almost total compliance—even when she did not have the authority of the researcher's lab coat, people would drop to the ground instantly and bob up and down three times. Now, this describes a fairly common student project which has probably been replicated many times since Garfinkel introduced such ideas in his "breaching studies" (1967). What makes this one unusual was that, unknown to her, she encountered a psychology professor who was himself unaware of this class project. She approached him with her standard request: "Excuse me, I'm conducting some research. I wonder if you would do three push-ups for me?" No other information was provided. Yet despite his advancing years and his broad psychological knowledge, there was the professor dropping to the ground and complying. As he later said, he didn't understand why he had done it, particularly as he had recently hurt his shoulder and had a permanently troublesome back. This serves to show you that even psychology professors are human and, like everyone, are vulnerable to the forces of social influence.

You may well have encountered situations in which you found yourself doing or saying things you would not normally have said or done in the absence of pressure from others. And turning the situation around, you have probably also engaged in such efforts yourself on many occasions. In a practical sense, therefore, you already know quite a lot about the topic on which we'll focus in this chapter—**social influence**: efforts on the part of one person to alter the behavior or attitudes of one or more others.

As suggested by Figure 7.1, social influence takes many different forms, some blatant and obvious, others more subtle or disguised. There can be little doubt, however, that this is an important process. Every day we are subjected to many attempts by others to influence us in some manner; and we in turn often engage in efforts to influence *them*. Thus, from the standpoint of sheer frequency, social influence is an important form of social behavior—one worthy of careful attention. In addition, as we'll note in later chapters, success in changing others' behavior also plays a key role in many other aspects of social interaction, ranging from *helping behavior* on the one hand to *leadership* and *bargaining* on the other (see chapters 8 and 9). Social influence is an important topic for this reason, too.

In a sense, we began the discussion of social influence in chapter 3, where we examined the nature of *persuasion* and other forms of *attitude change* (Judd et al., 1991). Here, we'll expand the scope of this earlier discussion by examining several additional forms of social influence. We'll start by focusing on *conformity*: Pressures to go along with the crowd, to behave in the same manner as other persons in one's group or society. Such pressures toward conformity play an important role in our decisions to go along with friends' plans even when risky or senseless acts are involved. After all, as part of the group, how can we resist, especially when doing so would lead to our expulsion from the group! Little wonder that pressures toward conformity can often exert compelling and seemingly irresistible effects.

Next, we'll consider a second major form of social influence known as *compliance*. A person seeking compliance attempts to alter the behavior of one or more others through direct requests or similar tactics. This is an extremely common form of influence, but one that takes a wide variety of specific forms. The guiding principle in all these techniques can be described as follows: Do anything that will tip the balance in your favor—anything that will increase the likelihood that others will say yes to your requests.

Finally, we'll examine a third form of social influence—*obedience*. Here, one person simply orders one or more others to change their behavior in specific ways. Usually the persons who issue such orders have some means of enforcing submission to them: They have *power* over those on the receiving end (Yukl & Falbe, 1991). Research findings indicate, however, that direct orders can often be effective in inducing

■ **The many faces of social influence**

FIGURE 7.1 Efforts to exert social influence take many different forms. Some of these are blatant and obvious, while others, like the one shown here, are much more subtle.
Source: The New Yorker.

"I like it"

obedience even in situations where the persons who issue these commands have little or no means for backing them up.

As we consider each of these major forms of social influence, we'll address two crucial questions: (1) Why do they succeed—why are they effective in changing others' behavior? and (2) What factors or conditions determine their degree of success in this regard?

CONFORMITY: GROUP INFLUENCE IN ACTION

Have you ever found yourself in a situation in which you felt that you stuck out like the proverbial sore thumb? If so, you have already had direct experience with pressures toward **conformity**. In such situations, you probably experienced a strong desire to "get back into line"—to fit in with the other people around you. Such pressures toward conformity stem from the fact that in many contexts, there are spoken or unspoken rules indicating how we *should* or *ought to* behave. These rules are known as **social norms**. In some instances, norms can be both detailed and precise. For example, governments generally function through constitutions and written laws; athletic contests are usually regulated by written rules; and signs in many public places (e.g., along highways, in parks, and at airports) frequently describe expected behavior in considerable detail.

In contrast, other norms are unspoken or implicit. Most of us obey such unwritten rules as "Don't stand too close to strangers on elevators if you can help it" and "Don't arrive at parties or other social gatherings exactly on time." Similarly, we are often strongly influenced by current and rapidly changing standards of dress, speech, and personal grooming. Regardless of whether social norms are explicit or implicit, one fact is clear: *Most people obey them most of the time*. For example, few persons visit restaurants without leaving a tip for their server. And virtually everyone, regardless of personal political beliefs, stands when the national anthem of their country is played at sports events or other public gatherings.

At first glance, this strong tendency toward conformity—toward going along with society's expectations about how we should behave in various situations—may strike you as objectionable. After all, it does prevent people from "doing their own thing." Actually, though, there is a strong basis for the existence of so much conformity: Without conformity we would quickly find ourselves facing social chaos. Imagine what would happen outside movie theaters or voting booths or at supermarket checkout counters if people did not follow the simple rule, "Form a line and wait your turn." And consider the danger to both drivers and pedestrians if there were not clear and widely followed traffic regulations. In many situations, then, conformity serves a useful function. But this in no way implies that it is always helpful. Some norms governing individual behavior appear to have no obvious purpose; they simply exist. For example, even today many companies require that their male employees wear neckties and that their female employees wear skirts or dresses, despite the facts that (1) such clothing is not directly related to performance of their jobs, and (2) it may cause them considerable personal discomfort when temperatures are very high (neckties) or very low (short skirts; see Figure 7.2). In cases such as these, the existence of strong pressures toward conformity can seem quite unacceptable.

Given that strong pressures toward conformity do exist in many settings, it is surprising to learn that conformity, as a social process, was not the subject of systematic investigation by social psychologists until the 1950s. At that time Solomon Asch (1951) carried out a series of experiments that added much to our knowledge of this important form of social influence. For a description of his research, please see the "Classic Contributions" section that follows.

■ **Pressures to conform: Sometimes they are objectionable**

FIGURE 7.2 When pressures to conform force individuals to behave in ways that cause discomfort, these pressures can be viewed as objectionable.

FOCUS ON RESEARCH: CLASSIC CONTRIBUTIONS

Group Pressure: The Irresistible Social Force?

Suppose that just before an important exam, you discover that your answer to a homework problem is different from that obtained by another member of the class. How do you react? Probably with mild concern. Now imagine that you learn that a second person's answer, too, is different from yours. Moreover, to make matters worse, it agrees with the answer reported by the first person. How do you feel now? The chances are good that your anxiety will rise to high levels. Next you discover that a third person agrees with the other two. At this point you know that you are in big trouble. Which answer should you accept? Yours or the one obtained by your three friends? There's no time to find out, for at this moment the exam starts. Sure enough, the first question on the exam relates

to this specific problem. Which answer should you choose? Can all three of your friends be wrong while you are right?

Life is filled with such dilemmas—instances in which we discover that our own judgments, actions, or conclusions are different from those reached by other persons. What do we, and others, do in such cases?

The answer is provided by a series of studies conducted by Asch (1951) that are considered to be true classics in social psychology. In his research Asch asked participants to respond to a series of simple perceptual problems such as the one in Figure 7.3. On each problem they indicated which of three comparison lines matched a standard line in length. Several other persons (usually six to eight) were also present

➤

during the session; but, unknown to the real participant, all were accomplices of the experimenter. On certain occasions (twelve out of eighteen problems) the accomplices offered answers that were clearly wrong (e.g., they unanimously stated that line A matched the standard line in Figure 7.3). Moreover, they gave their answers before the participant responded. Thus, on such trials, the participants faced the type of dilemma described above. Should they go along with the other persons present or stick to their own judgments? A large majority of the participants in Asch's research opted for conformity. Indeed, fully 76 percent of those tested in several different studies went along with the group's false answers at least once. In contrast, only 5 percent of the subjects in a control group, who responded to the same problems in the absence of any accomplices, made such errors.

While most persons conformed at least once, however, it is important to note that they also *resisted* such influence on many other occasions. As shown in Figure 7.4, almost 24 percent never conformed, and many others yielded on only a few of the trials on which the accomplices gave wrong answers. Yet a large majority did conform to the accomplices' false answers, and the implicit norm these generated, at least part of the time. These results, and those obtained in many later studies (Tanford & Penrod, 1984) point to an unsettling conclusion: Many persons find it easier publicly to contradict the evidence of their own senses than to disagree openly with the unanimous judgments of other persons—even those of total strangers.

In later research, Asch (1957) repeated the above procedures with one important change: Instead of stating their answers out loud, participants wrote them down on a piece of paper. As you might guess, conformity dropped sharply. This finding points to the importance of distinguishing between *public compliance*—doing or saying what others around us say or do—and *private acceptance*—actually coming to feel or think as they do. Often, it appears, we overtly adhere to social norms or yield to group pressure without changing our private views or interpretations of the social world (Maas & Clark, 1984). Thus, in Asch's research, and in many real-life situations too, individuals may modify their overt actions so as to get into line with others while at the same time maintaining their attitudes and personal views largely intact. We will return to this distinction between public compliance and private acceptance at several points in this chapter.

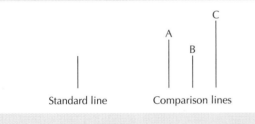

■ **Asch's line judgment task: An example**

FIGURE 7.3 Participants in Asch's research were asked to report their judgments on problems such as this one. On each problem, they indicated which of the comparison lines (A, B, or C) best matched the standard line in terms of length.

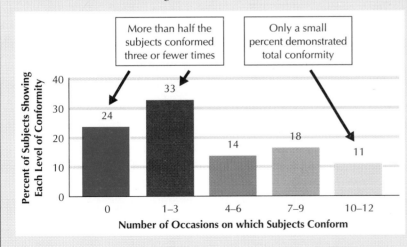

Number of Occasions on which Subjects Conform

■ **Asch's key results: Most people conform, but only part of the time**

FIGURE 7.4 While most participants in Asch's research yielded to the false group judgments at least once, most resisted group pressure on most occasions. For example, fully 58 percent conformed three times or less during the twelve critical trials (occasions when the accomplices gave false answers).
Source: Based on data from Asch, 1957.

FACTORS AFFECTING CONFORMITY:
COHESIVENESS, GROUP SIZE, AND SOCIAL SUPPORT

Asch's research demonstrated the existence of powerful pressures toward conformity. Even a moment's reflection, however, indicates that conformity does not occur to the same degree in all settings or among all persons. This fact raises an intriguing question: What factors determine the extent to which individuals yield to conformity pressure? Many variables play a role, but among them three have received most attention: (1) *cohesiveness*—degree of attraction to the group or persons exerting influence; (2) *group size*—how many persons are exerting influence; and (3) the presence or absence of *social support*.

Cohesiveness and conformity:
Accepting influence from those we like

Consider the following situation. After graduation from college, you go to work for a large corporation. You like your job very much and feel that you have a bright future with the company. There's only one minor problem. In the past, you have considered yourself to be a political moderate with a slight preference for New Democratic candidates. Now, however, you discover that most of the people with whom you work are relatively conservative. They repeatedly voice their opposition to various government programs and criticize judges who, in their opinion, are too lenient toward criminals. Will your own views change as a result of exposure to these statements? Perhaps. You may find yourself agreeing with your new friends more and more as time passes. And even if you do not, you may demonstrate the kind of public compliance noted above: Sometimes you may voice agreement with your coworkers even if you don't really share their views.

Now, in contrast, imagine that you have signed up for an evening course in personal self-defense. During the sessions you hear other members of the class express extremely conservative views about law and order, the right to own guns, and punishing criminals. Will you be influenced by these statements? Probably not. In fact, the chances are good that you will pay little if any attention to them. Why do you react so differently in these two contexts? Partly because of contrasting levels of attraction to these different groups of persons. You are fairly neutral toward the persons in your self-defense class, but you like your coworkers very much and want to gain their acceptance. Thus, while you have little motivation for adopting the views of persons in your evening class, you have strong motivation for agreeing with people where you work.

In social psychology, this kind of attraction toward a particular group or its individual members is usually described by the term **cohesiveness**, and there is little doubt about its impact on conformity. When cohesiveness is high (i.e., when we are strongly attracted to a group and want badly to be accepted by it), pressures toward conformity are generally much greater than when cohesiveness is low (Forsyth, 1992). This is one basic reason why most persons are much more willing to accept social influence from friends or persons they admire than from others.

A compelling illustration of the impact of cohesiveness on conformity is provided by a study by Crandall (1988). In this investigation, members of two different sororities completed two questionnaires: one designed to measure patterns of friendship within these social organizations (i.e., who was friends with whom), the other to measure tendencies toward the potentially serious health problem of *binge eating*, in which individuals report uncontrollable urges to eat and actually consume tremendous amounts of food (see Figure 7.5). Both questionnaires were completed by members of the two sororities on two occasions: at the start of the academic year and again when it was nearly over. The purpose was to allow Crandall to determine whether shifts in friendship patterns over time would be related to changes in tendencies toward binge

FIGURE 7.5 In binge eating individuals report uncontrollable urges to eat and consume incredibly large amounts of food. Growing evidence suggests that this potentially harmful disorder is sometimes influenced by pressures to conform to the norms of specific social groups.

eating. Specifically, Crandall hypothesized that the young women who participated in the study would report becoming more like their friends with respect to binge eating as time passed and bonds of friendship (cohesiveness) deepened. Results offered strong support for this prediction. Groups of friends become increasingly like one another over time in terms of binge eating. Initially, friends were no more similar to one another in this respect than they were to other members of the sorority. After approximately seven months had passed, however, their patterns of binge eating grew increasingly similar. Additional findings indicated that relatively clear social norms concerning binge eating had emerged and were operating in both sororities. The nature of these norms, however, differed in the two organizations. In one sorority, the more individuals binged, the more popular they were. In the other, women were most popular when they engaged in binge eating with moderate frequency; binging too often or not often enough reduced their popularity.

These findings provide a clear illustration of the fact that the more we like others and wish to gain their approval, the more we tend to be influenced by them. Moreover, they also underscore the fact that pressures toward conformity can affect virtually any aspect of behavior—even something as basic as eating habits.

Conformity and group size: Why "more" isn't always "better" with respect to social influence

A second factor that exerts important effects upon the tendency to conform is the size of the influencing group. Studies designed to investigate this relationship indicate that up to a point—about three or four members—rising group size does increase conformity. Beyond this level, however, further increments in group size produce less and less additional effect (e.g., Gerard, Wilhelmy, & Conolley, 1968). It's important to note, by the way, that these findings were obtained in short-term laboratory studies; informal observation suggests that under natural conditions conformity may increase with increments in group size up to a somewhat larger number than three or four. But it still seems likely that at some point further increments in group size exert little or no effect on conformity.

Why is this the case? One reason seems to involve the fact that as group size rises beyond three or four members, individuals exposed to social pressure begin to suspect *collusion*. They conclude that group members are not expressing individual views or behaving in accordance with individual preferences but working together to exert influence (Wilder, 1977). This makes a great deal of sense; after all, it is rare to find all the people around us agreeing unanimously with one another. Usually people hold varying opinions and engage in a wide range of behaviors reflecting different preferences. When too many people agree, therefore, this may be a signal that it is time to be on guard.

Regardless of the reason for this leveling off in conformity pressure as group size mounts, there is another complication in the picture. Groups do not always seek to exert influence upon a single, holdout member. On the contrary, conformity pressure may be directed to several persons rather than to only one. How does this factor affect the picture? One answer is provided by a theory known as the **social influence model** (or **SIM** for short; Tanford & Penrod, 1984). This model suggests that the function relating group size to conformity or social influence is as follows. At first, each person added to the group (each additional source of influence) produces a larger increment in conformity pressure than the one before. Soon however, this function levels off so that each additional person adds *less* to the total amount of influence than did the preceding ones. The SIM model also suggests that as the number of targets of social influence increases, the impact of group size on conformity decreases. This is because the impact of the influencing group is now spread over several target persons rather than a single holdout.

Is the SIM model accurate? Some evidence suggests that it is. When Tanford and Penrod (1984) applied their model to the findings of many previous studies dealing with the impact of group size on conformity, they found that this model predicted the obtained results quite accurately. Thus, the SIM model appears to provide a useful description of how pressures toward conformity vary both with group size and with the number of persons who are the target of such influence.

Beyond transitory factors such as group size and cohesiveness, another more enduring feature of group influence is the importance of *culture*. That is, some cultures may encourage greater conformity in their members than others and such socialization differences could be expected to have lasting influence upon individuals. This was the subject of a Canadian study on conformity by John Berry, which is described in the following "Classic Canadian Contributions" section.

FOCUS ON RESEARCH: CLASSIC CANADIAN CONTRIBUTIONS

Conformity and Culture in Subsistence-level Societies

John Berry (1967) carried out an early cross-cultural study of conformity in two non-industrialized cultures: the Temne of Sierra Leone, who were farmers, and the Inuit of Baffin Island, who were hunters. A group of Scots from near Edinburgh were also used as a Western comparison-group. Berry was interested in exploring cultural differences as they related to the way of life of each group.

He reasoned that the extent of conformity would be related to cultural norms and socialization practices. In turn, these cultural norms would be related to the society's means of subsistence. Specifically, agricultural communities tend to be very interdependent because the cooperation of all members is usually needed in

▶

order to achieve successful planting, harvesting, and storage of food. Therefore, these cultures would emphasize conformity to group needs. In contrast, societies based upon hunting do not usually require such extensive accumulation of food and are not, therefore, as interdependent. Where hunting is a viable way of life, hunters are usually able to acquire food throughout the year. Rather than depending upon others to achieve the one harvest for the year, as in an agricultural society, the hunter can achieve greater independence from others.

This description of high versus low *food-accumulating* societies derived from anthropological research (Barry, Child, & Bacon, 1959) and was applied to the Temne (farmers) and the Inuit (hunters) respectively. Anthropological evidence had also suggested that the socialization of children differed markedly in the high and low food-accumulating societies. The Temne farmers imposed severe disciplinary measures on children past the age of about two-and-a-half years, and expressions of individuality were strongly discouraged (Dawson, 1963). Among the Inuit hunters, independence and self-reliance was emphasized, and there was a great deal of leniency in the disciplining of children (Chance, 1960; Honigmann & Honigmann, 1965; Kardiner, 1939). In sum, while the Temne encouraged conformity to the group and dependence, the Inuit encouraged independence and individualism. Berry, therefore, hypothesized that greater conformity would be shown by Temne subjects than by Inuit subjects.

To test this hypothesis, he used an adaptation of Asch's (1950) line judgment task. Subjects were asked to choose the one line (from a series of eight lines of varying length) which matched a standard line. Social influence occurred when the experimenter pointed to one line among the eight, which was marked with an *X*, and said, "I am going to give you a hint. Most [Temne, Inuit, or Scots, depending upon the subject's culture] say this line is equal to the one at the top [the standard line]." This "hint" actually indicated the wrong line; therefore, subjects were being influenced to conform to an erroneous judgment by their group. The marked line was five lines (and five increments in length) away from the correct line. Thus, subjects' degree of conformity could be measured by how many lines away from the correct one (and towards the marked wrong one) their choice was.

Results confirmed the hypothesis, as shown in Figure 7.6. Temne subjects showed the greatest conformity to their group's erroneous choice (as indicated by their higher score),

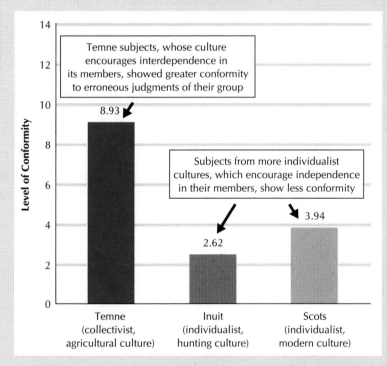

■ Culture and conformity in subsistence-level societies

FIGURE 7.6 When John Berry compared the conformity of subsistence-level and modern industrial cultures, he found that conformity was greater for the (collectivist) culture—the Temne of Sierra Leone—which encouraged dependence and discouraged individualism in children. In more individualist cultures such as the Inuit of Baffin Island and the Scots, where independence was encouraged in children, less conformity was shown.
Source: Based on data from Berry, 1967.

and Inuit subjects showed the least conformity. Scots subjects were in between these two but were closer to the Inuit scores, as might be expected from a fairly individualist culture. Later studies confirmed the high level of independence in perceptual judgments among hunting cultures, for example among Canadian Native groups (Berry & Annis, 1974).

Berry's study was one of the earliest in social psychology to compare individualist and collectivist cultures (though these terms were not widely used at that time) and to suggest that social influence and conformity vary along this cultural dimension. But his work goes further in suggesting the origins of such cultural differences in a society's means of survival: If subsistence requires a high level of cooperation, then greater conformity may be required of individuals in that culture. As one Temne spontaneously remarked during the study, "When Temne people choose a thing, we must all agree with the decision—this is what we call cooperation."

The effects of support from others: When having an ally helps

In Asch's research, and in many later studies of conformity, subjects were exposed to social pressure from a unanimous group: All the other persons present seemed to hold views different from their own. Under those conditions it is hardly surprising that most persons yielded to social pressure. What would happen if persons facing pressure to conform discovered that they had an ally—someone who shared their views or at least failed to accept the position of the majority? Under such conditions, perhaps, conformity might be reduced. That this is actually so is indicated by the results of several experiments (e.g., Allen & Levine, 1971; Morris & Miller, 1975). In these studies subjects provided with an ally or partner showed much less conformity than ones who did not receive such social support.

Perhaps the importance of such support in reducing conformity is best illustrated by two additional facts. First, conformity is reduced even when the partner or ally is someone not competent in the present situation. For example, in one study involving visual judgments, conformity was reduced even by a partner who wore thick glasses and could not see the relevant stimuli (Allen & Levine, 1971). Second, it is not crucial that the ally even share the subject's views. Conformity is reduced even if this person merely differs from the other group members—breaks their united front in some manner.

These and other findings suggest that almost any form of social support can help a person resist social pressure. As you might guess, though, certain types of support are more effective than others. For example, it appears that support received early—before pressures toward conformity are in place—is more effective than support received later (Morris, Miller, & Spangenberg, 1977). Apparently, learning that someone else shares their views can help strengthen individuals' ability to resist group pressure as it grows. This fact has important implications for many real-life settings. If you ever find yourself in a situation in which pressures toward conformity are rising and you feel that they should be resisted, try to speak out as quickly as possible. The sooner you do, the greater your chances of rallying others to your side and resisting the majority.

THE BASES OF CONFORMITY: WHY WE OFTEN CHOOSE TO "GO ALONG"

As we have just seen, several factors determine whether and to what extent conformity occurs. Yet this does not alter the essential point: Conformity is a basic fact of social life. Most people conform to the norms of their groups or societies most of the time.

Why is this the case? Why do people so often choose to go along with these social rules or expectations instead of combating them? The answer seems to center primarily on two powerful needs possessed by all human beings: the desire to be liked or accepted by others and the desire to be right (Insko, 1985).

The desire to be liked: Normative social influence

How can we get others to like us? This is one of the eternal puzzles of social life. As we noted in chapter 6, many tactics can prove effective in this regard. One of the most successful, though, is to appear to be as similar to others as possible. From our earliest days, we learn that agreeing with the persons around us and behaving much as they do causes them to like us. Parents, teachers, friends, and others often heap praise and approval on us for demonstrating such similarity (refer to our discussion of attitude formation in chapter 4). One important reason we conform, therefore, is simple: we have learned that doing so can yield the approval and acceptance we strongly crave. This source of social influence—and especially of conformity—is known as **normative social influence**, since it involves altering our behavior to meet others' expectations. Clearly, it is a common aspect of daily life.

The desire to be right: Informational social influence

If you want to know your weight, you can step onto a scale. Similarly, if you want to know the dimensions of a room, you can measure them directly. But how can you establish the "accuracy" of your own political or social views or decide which hairstyle suits you best? There are no simple physical tests or measuring devices for answering these questions. Yet most of us have just as strong a desire to be correct about such matters as about questions relating to the physical world. The solution is obvious: to answer these questions, or at least to obtain information about them, we must turn to other people. We use *their* opinions and *their* actions as guides for our own. Obviously, such reliance on others can be another source of conformity, for in an important sense, other people's actions and opinions define social reality for us. This source of social influence is known as **informational social influence**, since it is based on our tendency to depend upon others as a source of information about many aspects of the social world.

Direct evidence for the operation of such informational social influence is provided by a field study conducted by Weenig and Midden (1991) in the Netherlands. These investigators reasoned that individuals obtain much of their information about new government programs from other persons in their neighborhoods. Thus, the greater the number of communication ties people have with friends, neighbors, and relatives, the greater their awareness of such programs should be and the greater the amount of attention they will direct to them. In short, the researchers predicted that *information diffusion*—the spread of information about new programs or initiatives—would be greater in neighborhoods where many communication links existed among residents than in neighborhoods where relatively few links existed.

To test this hypothesis, they studied the spread of information about a new energy conservation program in two neighborhoods that were similar in all major respects except one: In one neighborhood residents had many informal friendly contacts (cohesiveness was high), while in the other residents had relatively few social contacts (cohesiveness was low). The program was designed to induce residents to adopt such practices as putting insulation into the walls of their homes and adding storm windows (double glazing). The investigators measured awareness of the new program by asking neighborhood residents whether they had heard of the program and then asking them to mention as many program activities (newsletters, information meetings, booklets, and so on) as they could remember. The researchers also measured attention to the program by asking residents to rate the extent to which they had taken notice of the information provided in each aspect of the program. As predicted, persons in the cohesiveness neighborhood did discuss the program with others more frequently than those in the less cohesive neighborhood. In addition, they reported receiving more advice on the various options than persons in the less-cohesive neighborhood (see Figure 7.7). Further, and of even greater importance, both awareness of the program and attention to it increased with the number of communication ties between residents. So, in sum, persons in these neighborhoods did seem to rely on one another for information about new and potentially important programs: Neighbors served as sources of *informational social influence* about energy conservation.

Together, normative and informational social influence provide a strong basis for our tendency to conform—to act in accordance with existing social norms. In short, there is nothing mysterious about the compelling and pervasive occurrence of conformity; it stems directly from basic needs and motives that can be fulfilled only when we do indeed decide to "go along" with others.

THE NEED FOR INDIVIDUATION AND THE NEED FOR CONTROL: WHY, SOMETIMES, WE CHOOSE *NOT* TO GO ALONG

Having read this discussion of normative and informational social influence, you may now have the distinct impression that pressures toward conformity are all but impossible to resist. If that's so, take heart. While such pressures are indeed powerful, they are definitely *not* irresistible. In many cases, individuals—or groups of individuals—decide to dig in their heels and say *no*. This was certainly true in Asch's research, where, as you may recall, most of the subjects yielded to social pressure, but only part of the time. On many occasions they stuck to their own judgments, even in the face of a disagreeing, unanimous majority. What accounts for this ability to resist even powerful pressures toward conformity? Research findings point to two key factors.

First, as you probably already realize, most of us have a strong desire to maintain our uniqueness or individuality. We want to be like others, but not to the extent that

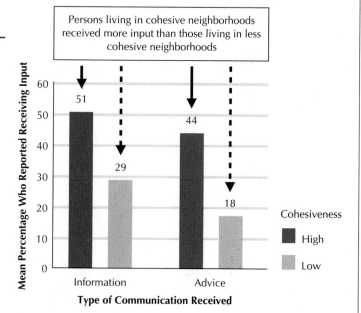

■ Informational social influence in operation

FIGURE 7.7 Individuals who lived in a cohesive neighborhood reported receiving more information and advice on a new government-sponsored program for energy conservation than individuals who lived in a less-cohesive neighborhood.

Source: Based on data from Weenig & Midden, 1991.

we lose our personal identity. In other words, along with the needs to be right and to be liked, most of us possess a desire for **individuation**—for being distinguished in some respects from others (e.g., Maslach, Santee, & Wade, 1987; Snyder & Fromkin, 1980). The result is that most people want to be similar to others *generally*, but don't want to be *exactly* like the people around them. In short, they want to hold on to at least a modicum of individuality (e.g., Snyder & Endelman, 1979). It is partly because of this motive that individuals sometimes choose to disagree with others or to act in unusual or even bizarre ways (see Figure 7.8). They realize that such behavior may be costly in terms of gaining the approval or acceptance of others, but their desire to maintain a unique identity is simply stronger than various inducements to conformity.

A second reason why individuals often choose to resist group pressure involves the desire to maintain control over the events in their lives (e.g., Burger, 1992; Burger & Cooper, 1979). Most persons want to believe that they can determine what happens to them, and yielding to social pressure sometimes runs counter to this desire. After all, going along with a group implies behaving in ways one might not ordinarily choose, and this can be interpreted as a restriction of personal freedom and control.

Direct evidence for the powerful impact of this factor has been reported by Burger (1987) in several related studies. In one of these experiments, male and female students

■ The need to be unique

FIGURE 7.8 Most people seem to have a need for individuation—a need to establish their unique identity. This is one factor that sometimes operates against yielding to conformity pressures.

were asked to rate each of ten cartoons in terms of how funny they found them to be. Half of the participants rated these cartoons while alone; the others rated them after hearing the ratings provided by several other persons. As in Asch's research, these other persons were all accomplices of the researcher. The accomplices rated the cartoons as being quite funny (an average rating of almost seventy on a one-hundred-point scale), despite the fact that other evaluators had previously rated them as quite dull. Before rating the cartoons, all participants had completed a questionnaire designed to measure the strength of their desire for personal control (the *Desirability of Control Scale*; Burger & Cooper, 1979). It was predicted that those high in the desire for personal control would show less yielding to the accomplices' influence than those low in desire for personal control, and this prediction was confirmed. In the absence of the accomplices, subjects high and low in desire for personal control did not differ in their ratings of the cartoons; both groups rated them as not very funny. In the presence of social influence from the accomplices, however, subjects low in desire for personal control rated the cartoons as funnier than those high in desire for personal control. They yielded to pressures toward conformity to a greater extent.

In sum, while pressures toward conformity often win out and induce individuals to behave in ways they would not otherwise choose, this is not always the case. On some occasions, at least, our desires to maintain our uniqueness and to exert control over our lives help us to resist even strong social influence.

MINORITY INFLUENCE: ONE MORE REASON WHY THE MAJORITY DOESN'T ALWAYS RULE

As we have just noted, individuals can—and often do—resist group pressure (Wolfe, 1985). Lone dissenters or small minorities can dig in their heels and refuse to go along. Yet even this is not the total story; in addition, there are cases in which such persons or groups can turn the tables on the majority and *exert* rather than merely receive social influence. History provides numerous examples of such events. Such giants of the scientific world as Galileo, Pasteur, and Freud faced virtually unanimous majorities who rejected their views in harsh terms. Yet over time they won growing numbers of colleagues to their side until, ultimately, their opinions prevailed. More recent examples of minorities influencing majorities are provided by the success of environmentalists. Initially such persons were viewed as wild-eyed radicals operating at the fringes of society. Over time, however, they have succeeded in changing strongly held attitudes and laws, with the result that society itself has been altered through their efforts.

When do minorities succeed in exerting social influence on majorities? Research findings suggest that they are most likely to be successful under certain conditions (Moscovici, 1985).

First, the members of such groups must be *consistent* in their opposition to majority opinions. If they waffle or show signs of yielding to the majority view, their impact is reduced. Second, in order for a minority to affect a larger majority, its members must avoid appearing rigid and dogmatic (Mugny, 1975). A minority that merely repeats the same position over and over again is less persuasive than one that demonstrates a degree of flexibility in its stance. Third, the general social context in which a minority operates is important. If a minority argues for a position that is consistent with current social trends (e.g., conservative views at a time of growing conservatism), its chances of influencing a majority are greater than if it argues for a position that is out of step with such trends. Finally, *single minorities*, minorities that differ from the majority only with respect to beliefs or attitudes, are more effective in exerting influence than *double minorities*—ones that differ both in attitudes and in their group membership. For example, a female M.P. who belonged to either the New Democratic or Conservative parties would be in a double minority position (women are a minority gender group in parliament and the N.D.P. or Conservatives are minority political parties). However, a male M.P. belonging to either of these parties would be in a single minority position due to his political affiliation.

Even when minorities are consistent and flexible and promote views consonant with current social trends, however, they may fail to exert much influence. The power of majorities to evoke conformity is great, so most people may continue to comply with established norms even in the presence of eloquent vocal minorities. While minorities may fail to change overt behavior in many cases, they can still produce important effects. For example, they may induce large numbers of persons to think more deeply or carefully about the issues in question (Nemeth, 1986). "How can they [the vocal minority] be wrong and yet be so sure of themselves?" "Why are they willing to go to so much trouble for such a ridiculous cause?" These are the kind of questions observers may ask themselves when confronted with an unpopular but highly committed minority. And the minority may lead some persons to consider ideas and alternatives they would otherwise have ignored. As we noted in chapter 3, such cognitive effort can often serve as an initial step to attitude change, placing individuals on the *central route* to persuasion. In sum, even when minorities fail to sway majorities initially, they may launch processes that lead eventually to social change. In this respect, at least, there is much truth to the phrase "Long live the loyal opposition!"

COMPLIANCE: TO ASK—SOMETIMES—IS TO RECEIVE

How many times each day do you receive requests from others? If you kept a record, you'd probably be surprised by the total; for friends, coworkers, acquaintances, family members, lovers, and roommates frequently ask us to change various aspects of our behavior. Advertisers, politicians, and many others also get into the act, so that finally, the list of people attempting to exert such influence upon us is large indeed.

Social psychologists term efforts to influence us through direct requests **compliance**, and in its most basic form, it is quite straightforward: Persons seeking compliance state their wishes and hope these will be granted. In many instances, however, the workings of this type of influence are somewhat more complex. Rather than presenting their requests cold, persons seeking compliance begin with preliminary steps designed to tip the balance in their favor—tactics they hope will increase the likelihood of the targets' saying yes. Persons seeking compliance use many different procedures for this purpose, but here we'll concentrate on the ones that appear to be most successful.

INGRATIATION: LIKING AS A BASIS FOR INFLUENCE

Earlier we noted that most people have a strong desire to be liked by others. While this motive probably stems from several different sources, one of the most important of these is this: We realize that if others like us, they are more willing to do things for us. They are more likely to help us with various tasks, to evaluate us favorably, and to say yes to our requests. Recognition of this basic fact lies behind a common technique for gaining compliance: **ingratiation** (Jones, 1964). What this involves, in essence, is efforts by individuals to enhance their attractiveness to a target so that this person will then be more susceptible to their requests (Liden & Mitchell, 1988; Wortman & Linsenmeier, 1977).

What ingratiation techniques are effective? As noted in our discussion of *impression management* (see chapter 2), several can be useful. First, individuals seeking to ingratiate themselves to others can employ *target-directed* tactics (Liden & Mitchell, 1988). These concentrate on inducing positive feelings in the target person. Presumably, such feelings will transfer to the ingratiator and will increase liking for him or her (refer to our discussion of attraction in chapter 6). Included among target-directed tactics are *flattery*, expressing *agreement* with the target person's views, showing *interest* in the target (e.g., appearing to hang on their every word), and directing many positive nonverbal cues toward them (e.g., smiling, leaning in their direction; Wortman & Linsenmeier, 1977). As suggested by Figure 7.9, such tactics often work—they increase the likelihood that target persons will say yes to various requests (e.g., Godfrey, Jones, & Lord, 1986; Kacmar, Delery, & Ferris, 1993). As you probably know from your own experience, however, such techniques can be overdone; and when they are, they can sometimes backfire. For example, recent evidence suggests that *excessive flattery*—flattery that is recognized as undeserved praise by the recipient—can increase rather than reduce interpersonal conflict (Baron et al., 1990).

Other tactics include efforts by would-be ingratiators to enhance their personal appeal to target persons—techniques sometimes described as involving *self-enhancement*. As we noted in chapter 2, the goal is to make a favorable impression on the target person (Schlenker, 1980). This can involve trying to improve one's personal appearance through dress or grooming; presenting information that suggests that one possesses desirable characteristics (e.g., sincerity, competence, intelligence, friendliness); or merely associating oneself with positive events or people the target already likes. In this latter category, ingratiators can name-drop, thus linking themselves to important or respected persons, and can casually introduce evidence of their past accomplishments into the conversation. Additional tactics include *self-deprecation*—providing negative information about oneself as a means of promoting the image of modesty—and *self-disclosure*, or offering personal information about oneself even if it is not requested. This latter tactic fosters the impression that the ingratiator is honest and likes the target person (Tedeschi & Melburg, 1984).

Do such tactics work? A growing body of evidence suggests that, if used with skill and care, they do. For example, in one laboratory study on this topic, Godfrey, Jones, and Lord (1986) asked pairs of unacquainted subjects to carry on two brief conversations with one another. After the first conversation, one individual in each pair was asked to try to make the other person like him or her as much as possible. The others were not given such instructions. After the conversations, subjects rated one another on a number of dimensions. In addition, videotapes of their conversations were carefully coded and analyzed by two trained raters. Results indicated that subjects told to ingratiate themselves with their partners succeeded in this task: They were indeed rated as more likable after the second conversation than after the first. In contrast,

■ Flattery: Often, it succeeds

FIGURE 7.9 Flattery is sometimes a highly effective technique for obtaining compliance.
Source: King Features Syndicate, Inc., 1986.

subjects in the control group did not show such gains. Further, some of the factors behind this success were apparent in the tapes. The ingratiating subjects reduced the amount of time they spoke and showed more agreement with their partners in the second conversation. Again, control subjects failed to show such changes.

Other studies point to the success of ingratiation in applied contexts. It is now well established that job applicants who dress and groom appropriately and who emit positive nonverbal cues (e.g., smile frequently, maintain eye contact with the interviewer) receive higher ratings than applicants who do not engage in such actions (e.g., Arvey & Campion, 1982). However, additional evidence suggests that as is true in other contexts involving ingratiation, these tactics can be overdone. And if overdone they result in lower rather than higher ratings. For example, Rasmussen (1984) found that when applicants with poor credentials emit many nonverbal cues, they are down-rated relative to applicants who do not engage in such behavior. This may happen because interviewers think such applicants are trying to distract them and shift their attention away from their poor credentials. In short, the use of too many ingratiatory tactics seems to backfire and worsen rather than enhance reactions to the applicants.

MULTIPLE REQUESTS: TWO STEPS TO COMPLIANCE

Suppose you wanted a fairly large favor from one of your friends. Would you simply approach this person and make your request? Perhaps, but it is more likely that you would try to prepare the ground before seeking compliance. One way in which you might do this would be to begin with an initial request—asking for something different from what you really wanted. Then you would somehow use this as an entering wedge for gaining the compliance you really seek, and you would follow up with your actual request. Several variations on this *multiple request* strategy exist, and under appropriate circumstances, all can be effective.

The foot in the door: Small request first, large request second

Experts in gaining compliance—skilled salespersons, confidence artists—often start their campaigns for gaining compliance with a trivial request. They ask potential customers to accept a free sample, or potential victims to do something that seems totally without risk (e.g., hold a receipt or the key to a safe deposit box). Only after these small requests are granted do they move on to the requests they really want—ones that can prove quite costly to the target persons. In all such instances, the basic strategy is much the same: somehow induce another person to comply with a small initial request and thereby increase the chances that he or she will agree to a much larger one. Is this technique—often known as the foot-in-the-door technique—really successful? Evidence from many different studies suggests that it is (Beaman et al., 1983).

In what is perhaps the most famous study concerned with this topic (Freedman & Fraser, 1966), a male experimenter phoned homemakers and identified himself as a member of a consumers' group. During this initial contact, he asked subjects to answer a few simple questions about the kinds of soap they used at home. Several days later, the same person called again and made a much larger request: Could he send a crew of five or six persons to the subject's home to conduct a thorough inventory of all the products he or she had on hand? It was explained that this survey would take about two hours, and that the crew would require freedom to search in all closets, cabinets, and drawers. As you can see, this was a truly huge request! In contrast, subjects in a one-contact control group were called only once and were presented with the large, second request "cold." Results were impressive: While only 22.2 percent of those in the one-contact condition agreed, fully 52.8 percent of those in the two-contact "foot-in-the-door" group complied. While results have not been as strong in several later studies (Beaman et al., 1983), existing evidence suggests that the foot-in-the-door tactic is effective in producing enhanced compliance in many settings, and in response to a wide range of requests—everything from signing a petition (Baron, 1973) through contributing to charity (Pliner et al., 1974). But how, precisely, does it operate? Why does agreeing to an initial small request increase one's likelihood of saying yes to a later and much larger one? Two possibilities exist.

First, it may be that after consenting to a small request, individuals come to hold a more positive view of helping situations generally. They now perceive such situations as less threatening or costly than would otherwise be the case. As a result, they are more willing to comply with later—and larger—requests (Rittle, 1981).

Second, once individuals agree to a small initial request, they may experience subtle shifts in their own self-perceptions. Once they have agreed to an initial request, they may come to view themselves as the kind of person who does that sort of thing—one who offers help to people who need it. Thus, when contacted again and presented with a much larger request, they agree in order to be consistent with their enhanced self-image.

Both of these explanations have received some support from research findings (DeJong & Musilli, 1982; Rittle, 1981). A study conducted by Eisenberg, Cialdini, and their colleagues (1987), however, offers impressive and convincing evidence for the accuracy of the second (the self-perception view). This study was based on the fact that before age seven, children do not possess sufficient cognitive capacity to use their past behavior, and inferences about it, as predictors of their future behavior. That is, they are not capable of reasoning, "I was helpful before; therefore, I will probably be helpful again." Since they lack the capacity for such reasoning, they experience few, if any, pressures to be consistent in their behavior.

On the basis of these facts, Eisenberg and her colleagues reasoned that children younger than age seven would not demonstrate susceptibility to the foot-in-the-door effect. Children seven and above, however, would indeed be affected by it. To test this prediction, the investigators exposed children in three age groups (five to six, seven to eight, and ten to eleven) to an initial small request, or to no initial request. This request involved donating coupons that could be used to win prizes to poor children described as having no toys. Subjects received six coupons apiece, and virtually all complied with the experimenter's request that they donate one of these to the poor youngsters.

In a second session one or two days later, children were given a choice of either playing with an array of attractive toys or helping "sick children in the hospital" by sorting colored paper into four color-coded piles. Doing this rather than playing with the toys constituted the second, larger request. (It involved considerable effort and giving up the opportunity to play with the attractive toys.)

Results offered support for the hypothesis that the foot-in-the-door effect would not occur among the youngest children. For the five- to six-year-olds, there was no difference between the foot-in-the-door group and the control condition (children who were not exposed to the initial request) in terms of willingness to expend effort for the "sick children." Among the older children, in contrast, those in the foot-in-the-door group sorted more papers than those in the control condition. This difference was significant for the ten- to eleven-year-olds, and approached significance for the seven- to eight-year-olds (see Figure 7.10).

The findings reported by Eisenberg and her colleagues support the self-perception interpretation of the foot-in-the-door effect. Apparently, exposing individuals to small initial requests they are unlikely to refuse leads them to view themselves as *helpful* persons. This, coupled with strong internal pressures to be consistent (to live up to their enhanced self-image), then produces greater compliance with subsequent, larger requests. In a sense, therefore, the foot-in-the-door technique works because target persons help it to work: Their desire to be consistent is stronger than their desire to avoid the costs associated with saying yes.

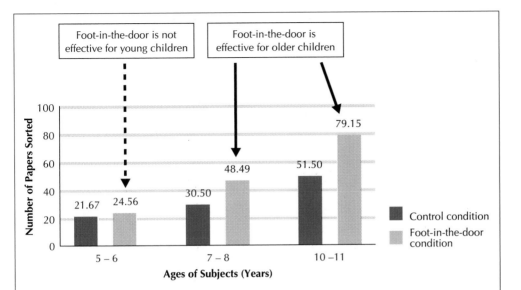

■ Evidence for the self-perception explanation of the foot-in-the-door effect

FIGURE 7.10 Young children (ages five to six) were not affected by the foot-in-the-door tactic. However, older children (ages seven to eight and ten to eleven) were affected by this tactic. These results stem from the fact that children below the age of seven are not yet able to draw inferences about themselves from their own behavior or to use their past actions as a basis for predicting their own future actions.

Source: Based on data from Eisenberg et al., 1987.

The door in the face: Large request first, small request second

Another strategy for gaining compliance that is also based on multiple requests is, in a sense, opposite to that behind the foot in the door. Here, persons seeking compliance start by asking for a very large favor—one the target is almost certain to refuse. Then, when refusal occurs, they shift to a smaller request, the favor they really wanted all along. This approach is known as the **door-in-the-face technique** or the *rejection-then-retreat tactic* and also appears to be quite effective.

In one well-known study designed to investigate this strategy, Cialdini and his colleagues (1975) stopped college students on the street and presented a huge request: Would they serve as unpaid counselors for juvenile delinquents two hours a week for the next *two years*! As you can guess, none agreed to this proposition. When the experimenters then scaled down their request to a much smaller one—would the same students take a group of delinquents on a two-hour trip to the zoo—fully 50 percent agreed. In contrast, less than 17 percent of those in a control group agreed to this smaller request when it was presented alone rather than after an initial giant request.

The use of this technique can be observed in many real-life situations. Negotiators often begin with a position that is extremely favorable to themselves but very unfavorable to their opponents. When this initial proposal is rejected, they back down to a position much closer to the one they really hope to obtain. Similarly, television writers who wish to get certain lines or scenes past the network censors often sprinkle throughout their scripts words or situations they know will be cut. Then they agree to the elimination of many of these while still retaining the key lines they wanted all along (Cialdini, 1988).

Why does this tactic sometimes succeed? Two explanations have been proposed. The first relates to the notion of *reciprocal concessions*. When individuals who start with a very large request back down to a smaller one, target persons may view this as a concession. Such persons then feel obligated to make a matching concession themselves. As a result, they become more willing to comply with the requester's second, scaled-down proposal.

Another possibility involves our concern over *self-presentation*—our wish to present ourselves in a favorable light to others. If we refuse a large and unreasonable request, this appears justifiable and our image doesn't suffer. If we then also refuse a much smaller request from the same source, however, we may appear unreasonable. Thus, we may often yield to the rejection-then-retreat tactic because of our concern that failing to do so will cause us to look rigid or intransigent (Pendleton & Batson, 1979).

Comparing the foot-in-the-door and door-in-the-face tactics: The role of source legitimacy

Research findings, as well as informal observations of daily life, indicate that both the foot-in-the-door and the door-in-the-face techniques sometimes succeed. Is one of these tactics preferable to the other? In general, the answer seems to be no. Neither has a clear overall advantage over the other. Several factors do suggest, however, that the foot-in-the-door tactic may operate successfully in a somewhat wider range of situations.

First, consider the issue of time between the first and second requests. Since shifts in self-perception tend to persist, the foot-in-the-door technique should succeed even when the first and second requests are separated by substantial periods of time (several hours or more). In contrast, the door-in-the-face procedure may fail under such conditions, because the tendency to make a reciprocal concession to the requester after he or she backs down may quickly dissipate. Existing evidence suggests that this is indeed the case (e.g., Cann, Sherman, & Elkes, 1975).

Second, it appears that the foot-in-the-door tactic can succeed even when the first and second requests are made by two different persons. Again, this is due to the fact that shifts in self-perception, once induced, tend to persist. Thus, internal pressure toward being consistent (i.e., toward helping others) may enhance compliance even when the second request is made by a different person. In contrast, target persons should feel little or no obligation to make concessions to a person different from the one who proposed the initial large request. This technique, therefore, may succeed only when the two requests are made by the same individual.

Third, the foot-in-the-door technique may succeed regardless of the legitimacy of the requester, while the door-in-the-face tactic may work only when the requester is judged to be high on this dimension. This would be the case because pressures to be consistent by agreeing to a second, larger request should operate regardless of source legitimacy. In contrast, individuals might feel little obligation to reciprocate for concessions by a source of influence that is low in legitimacy. This prediction has been confirmed by several studies (e.g., Patch, 1986).

In sum, while both techniques are useful in gaining compliance, existing evidence suggests that the foot-in-the-door tactic is applicable in a somewhat broader range of contexts than the door-in-the-face tactic. For this reason, it may often—though certainly not always—prove more effective as a means of exerting social influence.

SWEETENING THE DEAL: THE "THAT'S NOT ALL!" TECHNIQUE

One television program popular during the 1950s ("The Milton Berle Show"), contained a segment that many people found highly amusing. A man would come out onto the stage and set up a small platform. He would then roll up his sleeves and begin to offer members of the audience what he described as "incredible deals" (see Figure 7.11). During this comedy routine he would mention a deal and then immediately indicate how he would sweeten it by throwing in something extra. "Tell you what I'm gonna do," he'd comment. "You say that's not enough? You say you want more for your money? Tell you what I'm gonna do…"

The deals offered in this comic routine were preposterous, but the technique itself is an intriguing one. Have you ever been in a situation where someone tried to sell you something and then, before you could answer yes or no, offered to add some bonus to the deal? Auto dealers sometimes do this, offering to add an option to the car in question as a "closer." Similar techniques are used in many other settings, too. Does this approach, sometimes termed the **that's not all (TNA) technique**, really work? Evidence gathered by Burger (1986) suggests that it does.

In an initial study on this tactic, Burger conducted a bake sale on a college campus. Cupcakes were displayed on a table, but no price was indicated. In one condition of the study (the *that's not all* condition), when potential buyers asked the price for the cupcakes, they were given this information and then, before they could respond, were also shown a bag containing two cookies. The seller noted that the price included the cookies. In a second (control) condition, in contrast, subjects were shown the cookies and told that these were included in the deal before being given the price. Results indicated that the TNA technique worked: 73 percent of subjects in the TNA group bought the cupcakes, while only 40 percent of those in the control condition did so.

In a follow-up study, the seller told subjects in the TNA condition that the cupcakes were priced at $1.25. Then, before they could respond, the seller indicated that he would lower the price to $1.00 since he was planning to close his booth very soon. In a control condition, in contrast, subjects were simply told that the cupcakes were priced at $1.00. Finally, in a third (*bargain*) condition, the experimenter indicated that the cupcakes were now $1.00, although formerly they had been $1.25. This group was included to determine if any increased tendency to buy the cupcakes in the TNA condition was due merely to the fact that these items were now a bargain (their price had been reduced).

■ The "that's not all!" technique in operation

FIGURE 7.11 In order to close a deal, persons like the one shown here often throw something extra in before the potential customer has made her or his decision. This is the essence of the that's not all technique for gaining compliance.

Results indicated that the TNA technique was effective once again. More than 50 percent of subjects in this condition bought the cupcakes; the corresponding percentages were much lower in both the control and bargain conditions. This latter finding suggests that the TNA technique is not effective merely because it offers items at a bargain price; rather, there is something about sweetening the deal in midstream that generates increased compliance.

Why does the TNA technique work? One possibility involves the *norm of reciprocity*. As we noted in our discussion of the door-in-the-face technique, we often feel obligated to reciprocate when another person makes a concession. In view of the norm of reciprocity, persons who are the target of the that's not all technique may feel an increased obligation to say yes when the requester lowers the price, throws in a bonus, or takes some similar action. Support for this view is provided by the fact that the TNA technique succeeds only when subjects perceive the requester's addition of a bonus as a personal gesture; if it is viewed as something the requester had to do, this tactic fails.

Whatever its precise basis, the that's not all technique can be quite effective. Moreover, as we noted previously, it appears to be in widespread current use. For this reason you should definitely be on guard whenever someone attempts to induce you to say yes by offering more than they did initially. The chances are good that in such situations, the new, "improved" deal is the one the requester had in mind all along.

In your everyday interactions you seldom use this kind of "hard sell" technique when attempting to influence someone. But what tactics of influence do people actually use most frequently, and which of these are most successful? For information on this important issue, please see the "Focus on Research" section below.

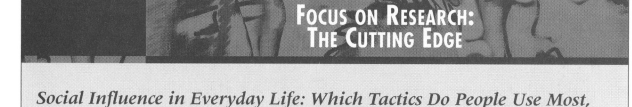

FOCUS ON RESEARCH: THE CUTTING EDGE

Social Influence in Everyday Life: Which Tactics Do People Use Most, When Do They Use Them, and with What Effect?

By this point it should be clear that persons seeking compliance from others have a wide range of tactics at their disposal. They can seek to influence target persons through ingratiation, impression management, multiple requests, somehow sweetening the deal, offering them various incentives, or complaining, to name just a few techniques. Informal evidence, as well as a wealth of research findings (e.g., Cialdini, 1988), indicates that all of these tactics are used—and used frequently—in the course of social interaction. But which ones are the most common? And which are the most effective? Further, are some tactics preferred over others in specific kinds of situations?

These are intriguing questions relating to what might be described as *the use of social influence in everyday life*, and a growing body of research is providing at least partial answers to all of them (Kipnis & Schmidt, 1988; Kipnis, Schmidt, & Wilkinson, 1980). In these studies researchers have asked individuals to indicate how they go about the task of influencing others, how successful these attempts at influence are, and why, precisely, they perform them. The answers paint a very rich portrait of the use of social influence in everyday life.

Perhaps the most revealing research in this respect is a series of studies conducted by Yukl and his colleagues (e.g., Yukl & Falbe, ▶

1990; Yukl & Falbe, 1991; Yukl & Tracey, 1992). In one of these investigations, Yukl and Falbe (1990) asked almost two hundred persons to describe their own use of influence tactics in their jobs. Specifically, they asked the participants to rate the extent to which they used the various influence techniques described in Table 7.1. In addition, participants indicated the extent to which they used these techniques on their peers, subordinates, or bosses. It was predicted that the use of various tactics would vary with the nature of the target. For example, Yukl and Falbe predicted that *pressure tactics* (demands, threats, intimidation), *inspirational appeals* (emotional requests), *consultation* (involving the target in a decision), and *exchange tactics* (promising reciprocation in the future) would be used more often on subordinates than on bosses; while *coalition tactics* (seeking the aid of others to persuade the target) would be used more often with peers or bosses (refer to Table 7.1). All these predictions were confirmed; not surprisingly, participants in the study did report that they used somewhat different tactics of influence on subordinates than on bosses. Similarly, they reported somewhat different objectives for influence attempts directed toward subordinates or toward bosses.

Participants indicated that they used influence on subordinates to get them to perform new tasks or work harder but that they used influence on bosses to acquire resources from them.

In additional research, Yukl and Falbe (1990) asked another sample of employed persons to indicate how often others (bosses, peers, or subordinates) used the various techniques of influence shown in Table 7.1 on *them*. Results tended to confirm the findings of the initial study. Participants reported that bosses were more likely than subordinates to use pressure tactics and inspirational appeals on them. However, in contrast to the findings of the first study, they did not report that bosses were more likely to use exchange tactics, coalition tactics, or consultation.

Perhaps the most important findings of these studies, however, involve the relative frequency with which various tactics of influence are employed. Both users and targets of social influence agreed very closely in this respect, indicating that consultation, rational persuasion, inspirational appeals, and ingratiating tactics were the most commonly used tactics. In contrast, pressure tactics, upward appeals, and exchange tactics were the least common (refer to Figure 7.12).

■ The techniques described here are ones that individuals report using quite frequently in their interactions with others.

TABLE 7.1 Techniques of social influence in everyday life

Tactic of Social Influence	Description
Pressure Tactics	Demands, threats, intimidation
Upward Appeals	Statements to the effect that persons with authority support the request
Exchange Tactics	Promises of reciprocal benefits for current compliance
Coalition Tactics	Statements indicating that others support the request
Ingratiating Tactics	Efforts to put target in a good mood or enhance the appeal of the requester
Rational Persuasion	Logical arguments and factual evidence
Inspirational Appeals	Emotional appeal based on values or ideals
Consultation Tactics	Involvement (by requester) of target person in decision or plan related to request

Source: Based on information in Yukl & Falbe, 1990.

▶

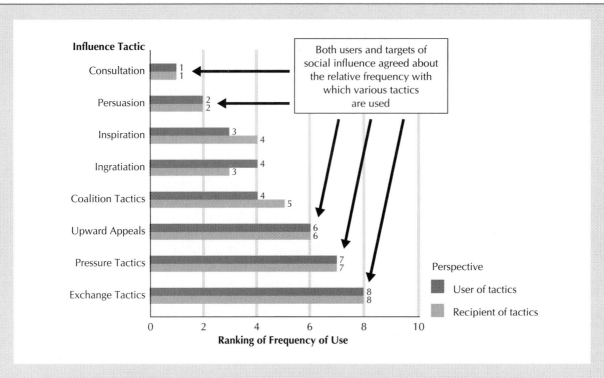

Influence Tactic

Perspective
■ User of tactics
■ Recipient of tactics

Ranking of Frequency of Use

Both users and targets of social influence agreed about the relative frequency with which various tactics are used

■ **Tactics of social influence: Which ones are used most?**

FIGURE 7.12 As shown here, individuals report using, and being the target of, such tactics as rational persuasion, inspirational appeals, and ingratiating tactics much more often than pressure tactics, upward appeals, and exchange tactics. (Higher ranks = more frequent use.)

Source: Based on data in Yukl & Falbe, 1990.

Yukl and Tracey (1992) have also investigated a related issue: Which influence tactics are most successful in gaining enthusiastic commitment, as opposed to mere compliance, from target persons? The results of this research indicated that consultation, inspirational appeals, and rational persuasion were moderately effective in gaining commitment on the part of a wide range of target persons—peers, subordinates, and superiors in organizations. Two other tactics—ingratiation and exchange (promises of later reciprocation)—were moderately successful with subordinates and peers but were not effective in gaining commitment from superiors.

Together, these findings paint a rich and informative picture of social influence in everyday life. Consistent with the research findings on resistance to persuasion described in chapter 3, most persons seem to react negatively to pressure tactics and other blatant attempts at social influence. They much prefer the "velvet glove" approach based on eloquence, consultation, rational argument, and inspirational appeals. Indeed, even various forms of *ingratiation* are preferred to demands or threats to go over the target's head. The message in these results for persons seeking compliance from others is clear: Proceed, but choose your strategies with care; and never forget that where social influence is concerned, less really is often more!

OBEDIENCE: SOCIAL INFLUENCE BY DEMAND

What is the most direct technique one person can use to change the behavior of another? In one sense the answer is as follows: He or she can order the target to do something. This approach is less common than either conformity pressure or tactics for gaining compliance, but it is far from rare. Business executives issue orders to their subordinates; military officers bark commands that they expect to be followed at once; and parents, police officers, and sports coaches, to name just a few, seek to influence others in the same manner. **Obedience** to the commands of sources of authority is far from surprising; such sources usually possess some means of enforcing their directives (e.g., they can reward obedience and punish resistance). More surprising, though, is the fact that even persons lacking in such power can sometimes induce high levels of submission from others. The clearest and most dramatic evidence for the occurrence of such effects has been reported by Stanley Milgram in a series of famous—and controversial—investigations (Milgram, 1963, 1974).

DESTRUCTIVE OBEDIENCE: SOME BASIC FINDINGS

In his research Milgram wished to learn whether individuals would obey commands from a relatively powerless stranger requiring them to inflict what appeared to be considerable pain on another person—a totally innocent stranger. Milgram's interest in this topic derived from the occurrence of tragic real-life events in which seemingly normal, law-abiding persons actually obeyed such directives. For example, during World War II, troops in the German army obeyed commands to torture and murder unarmed civilians—millions of them—in infamous death camps set up specifically for this grisly purpose. Similar appalling events have occurred in many other cases and at many other points in history (e.g., the My Lai massacre during the Vietnam war; the massacre of thousands of Kurds and members of other ethnic minorities in Iraq by supporters of Saddam Hussein; see Figure 7.13).

■ Obedience to authority: Sometimes the results are tragic

FIGURE 7.13 Soldiers, members of secret police forces, and others often obey orders directing them to inflict serious harm on innocent victims. Such tragic instances of destructive obedience are all-too-common events in recent history. Shown here is a refugee camp for Kurds—victims of ruthless oppression by the troops of Saddam Hussein.

To try to gain insights into the nature of such events, Milgram designed an ingenious, if disturbing, laboratory simulation. The experimenter informed participants in his studies (all males) that they were participating in an investigation of the effects of punishment on learning. Their task was to deliver electric shocks to another person (actually an accomplice) each time he made an error in a simple learning task. These shocks were to be delivered by means of thirty switches on the equipment shown in Figure 7.14. Participants were told to move to the next higher switch each time the learner made an error. Since the first switch supposedly delivered a shock of 15 volts, it was clear that if the learner made many errors, he would soon be receiving powerful jolts. Indeed, according to the labels on the equipment, the final shock would be 450 volts! In reality, of course, the accomplice (the learner) *never received any shocks* during the experiment. The only real shock ever used was a mild demonstration pulse from one button (number three) to convince subjects that the equipment was real.

During the session the "learner" (following prearranged instructions) made many errors. Thus, subjects soon found themselves facing a dilemma: Should they continue punishing this person with what seemed to be increasingly painful shocks? Or should they refuse to go on? The experimenter pressured them to continue, for whenever they hesitated or protested, he made one of a series of graded remarks. These began with "Please go on," escalated to "It is absolutely essential that you continue," and finally shifted to "You have no other choice; you *must* go on."

Since subjects were all volunteers and were paid in advance, you might predict that they would quickly refuse the experimenter's orders. Yet, in reality, fully *65 percent showed total obedience* to the experimenter's commands, proceeding through the entire series to the final 450-volt level (see Figure 7.15). In contrast, subjects in a control group who were not given such commands generally used only very mild shocks

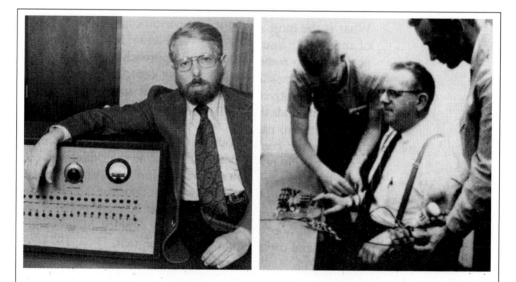

■ **Studying obedience in the laboratory**

FIGURE 7.14 Left: Stanley Milgram with the apparatus he used in his famous experiments on obedience. (It has recently been displayed in a special exhibit at the Smithsonian Institution in Washington, D.C.) Right: The experimenter (right front) and a participant (rear) attaching electrodes to the learner's (accomplice's) wrists.

Source: From the film *Obedience,* distributed by the New York University Film Library, Copyright 1965 by Stanley Milgram. Reprinted by permission of the copyright holder.

during the session. Many persons, of course, protested and asked that the session be ended. When ordered to proceed, however, a majority yielded to the experimenter's social influence and continued to obey. Indeed, they continued to do so even when the victim pounded on the wall as if in protest against the painful treatment he was receiving (refer to Figure 7.15).

In further experiments, Milgram (1965a, 1974) found that similar results could be obtained even under conditions that might be expected to reduce such obedience. When the study was moved from its original location on the campus of Yale University to a run-down office building in a nearby city, subjects' level of obedience remained virtually unchanged. Similarly, a large proportion continued to obey even when the accomplice complained about the painfulness of the shocks and begged to be released. Most surprising of all, many (about 30 percent) continued to obey even when they were required to grasp the victim's hand and force it down upon the "shock" plate! That these chilling results were not due to special conditions present in Milgram's laboratory is indicated by the fact that similar findings were soon reported in studies conducted in several different nations (e.g., Jordan, West Germany, Australia) and with children as well as adults (e.g., Kilham & Mann, 1974; Shanab & Yahya, 1977). Thus, these findings seemed to be alarmingly general in scope.

DESTRUCTIVE OBEDIENCE: WHY DOES IT OCCUR?

The results obtained by Milgram and others are disturbing. The parallels between the behavior of subjects in these studies and atrocities against civilians during time of war or civil uprising seem clear. (For example, consider the willingness of Chinese

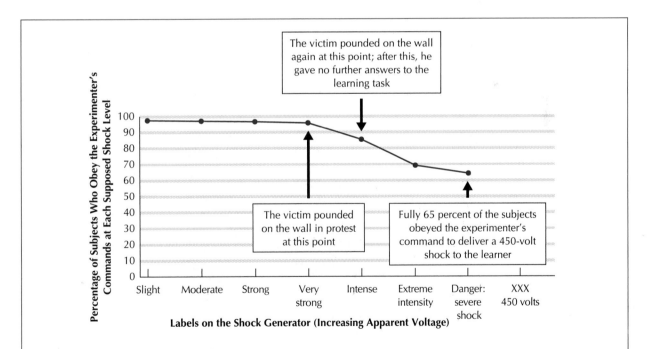

■ Obedience to the commands of a powerless authority

FIGURE 7.15 A surprisingly large proportion of the male participants in Milgram's research obeyed the experimenter's orders to deliver electric shocks of increasing strength to an innocent victim. Fully 65 percent demonstrated total obedience to these commands.

Source: Based on data from Milgram, 1963.

troops to fire upon civilians during the Tiananmen Square demonstrations of spring 1989.) But why, precisely, do such effects occur? Why were subjects in these experiments—and many persons in tragic situations outside the laboratory—so willing to yield to the commands of authority figures? Several factors appear to play a role.

First, in many situations, the persons in authority relieve those who obey of the responsibility for their own actions. "I was only carrying out orders," is the defense many offer after obeying harsh or cruel directives. In life situations this transfer of responsibility may be implicit. In Milgram's experiments, in contrast, it was quite explicit. Subjects were told at the start that the experimenter (the authority figure), not they, would be responsible for the victim's well-being. Given this fact, it is not surprising that many tended to obey.

Second, persons in authority often possess visible badges or signs of their status and power. These consist of special uniforms, insignia, titles, and similar factors. Faced with such obvious reminders of who's in charge, most people find it difficult to resist. The powerful impact of such cues has been demonstrated by Bushman (1984, 1988) in several similar experiments. For example, in one of these investigations, a female accomplice of the researcher ordered pedestrians to give a nickel to a young man who needed it for a parking meter. In one condition the accomplice was dressed in a uniform (although its precise nature was ambiguous). In a second condition she was dressed as a business executive, and in a third she was dressed as a panhandler. Not surprisingly, a higher percentage of subjects obeyed in the first condition (72 percent) than in the others (48 and 52 percent respectively). Other data, which the researcher collected by asking subjects who obeyed why they did so, indicated that the uniform had the expected effect: Subjects in this condition reported that they obeyed simply because they had been ordered to do so by someone with authority. These findings, and those in related studies, suggest that the possession of outward signs of authority, even if they are largely irrelevant to the present situation, play an important role in the ability of authority figures to induce high levels of obedience to their commands.

A third reason for obedience in many situations where the targets of such influence might resist involves its gradual nature. Initial commands are often relatively small and innocuous. Only later do they increase in scope and come to require behavior that is dangerous or objectionable. For example, police or military personnel may at first be ordered to question, arrest, or threaten potential victims. Gradually, demands are increased to the point where they are commanded to beat, torture, or even kill unarmed civilians. In a similar manner, subjects in the laboratory research on obedience were first required to deliver only mild and harmless shocks to the victim. Only as this person continued to make errors on the learning task did the intensity of these "punishments" rise to harmful levels.

In sum, several factors contribute to the high levels of obedience witnessed in laboratory studies and in a wide range of real-life contexts. Together these merge into a powerful force—one that most persons find difficult to resist. Unfortunately, the consequences of this compelling form of social influence can be disastrous for many innocent and largely defenseless victims.

DESTRUCTIVE OBEDIENCE: RESISTING ITS EFFECTS

Now that we have considered some of the factors responsible for the strong tendency to obey sources of authority, we will turn to a related question: How can this type of social influence be resisted? Several strategies seem to be effective in helping reduce the tendency to obey.

First, individuals exposed to commands from authority figures can be reminded that they—not the authorities—are responsible for any harm produced. Under these conditions sharp reductions in the tendency to obey have been observed (e.g., Hamilton, 1978; Kilham & Mann, 1974).

Second, individuals can be provided with an indication that beyond some point, unquestioning submission to destructive commands is inappropriate. For example, they can be exposed to the actions of *disobedient models*—persons who refuse to obey an authority figure's commands. Research findings suggest that this strategy, too, is quite effective in reducing obedience (Milgram, 1965b; Powers & Geen, 1972).

Third, individuals may find it easier to resist influence from authority figures if they question the expertise and motives of the authority figures. Are such persons really in a better position to judge what is appropriate and what is inappropriate? What motives lie behind their commands—socially beneficial goals or selfish gain? By asking such questions, persons who might otherwise obey may find support for independence rather than submission.

Finally, simply knowing about the power of authority figures to command blind obedience may be helpful in itself. Growing evidence (e.g., Sherman, 1980) suggests that when individuals learn about the findings of social psychological research, they may change their behavior to take account of this knowledge. With respect to destructive obedience, there is some hope that knowing about this process can enhance individuals' ability to resist. To the extent this is the case, then even exposure to findings as disturbing as those reported by Milgram can have positive social value. As they become widely known, they may produce desirable shifts within society.

To conclude: The power of authority figures to command obedience is certainly great, but it is definitely *not* irresistible. Under appropriate conditions it can be countered and reduced (see Figure 7.16). As in many other spheres of life, there is a choice. Deciding to resist the dictates of authority can, of course, be dangerous. Those holding power wield tremendous advantages in terms of weapons and technology. Yet, as recent events in Eastern Europe, the former Soviet Union, and elsewhere demonstrate, the outcome is by no means certain when committed groups of citizens choose to resist. Ultimately, victory may go to those on the side of freedom and decency rather than to those who possess the guns, tanks, and planes. The human spirit, in short, is not so easily controlled or extinguished as many dictators would like to believe.

■ **Resisting sources of authority: The potential benefits are great**

FIGURE 7.16 Pressure to obey from sources of authority is *not* irresistible. When large numbers of persons decide to disobey, the results can be dramatic. (Shown here are German students dismantling the Berlin Wall in 1989.)

CONFORMITY

Conformity occurs when individuals change their attitudes or behavior to comply with *social norms*—rules or expectations about how they should behave in various situations. Conformity increases with *cohesiveness*—liking for the sources of such influence—and with the number of persons exerting conformity pressure; but only up to a point. Some cultures place greater emphasis on the need for conformity among members and this appears to derive from the need for cooperation in order to survive. Conformity is reduced by the presence of *social support*—one or more individuals who share the target persons's views, or who at least depart from the majority's position in some manner. One reason individuals sometimes resist conformity pressure is that they wish to maintain their unique identity as individuals. Minorities can sometimes influence larger majorities, especially when they appear to be deeply committed to the views they support.

COMPLIANCE

Compliance involves direct efforts by individuals to change the behavior of others. Many techniques can be used to increase the likelihood that target persons will say yes. *Ingratiation* involves efforts by requesters to increase their attractiveness to target persons, and may include flattery, expressing agreement with the target persons, and self-deprecation. Other techniques are based on the use of *multiple requests*. Here the *foot-in-the-door* and the *door-in-the-face* techniques are most prevalent. Another tactic for gaining compliance is the *that's not all* technique. Here, target persons are offered something extra before they decide to accept or reject a request.

Among the most common tactics used for gaining compliance are *rational persuasion, ingratiation,* and *inspirational appeals.*

OBEDIENCE

The most direct form of social influence is *obedience*—direct orders from one person to another. Research findings indicate that many persons obey commands from an authority figure even when such persons have little power to enforce their orders. These tendencies toward obedience stem from several causes (e.g., authority figures gradually escalate the scope of their orders; they have visible signs of power). Obedience can be reduced or resisted through several procedures, such as reminding individuals that they, not the authority figures, will be responsible for any harmful outcomes and exposing the targets of obedience to disobedience models.

KEY TERMS

Cohesiveness In the context of social influence, the degree to which individuals like or are attracted to other members of a group or to persons who attempt to influence them.

Compliance A form of social influence in which one or more persons attempts to influence one or more others through direct requests.

Conformity A type of social influence in which individuals change their attitudes or behavior in order to adhere to existing social norms.

Door-in-the-Face Technique A procedure for gaining compliance in which requesters begin with a large request and then, when this is refused, retreat to a smaller one (the one they actually desired all along).

Foot-in-the-Door A procedure for gaining compliance in which requesters begin with a small request and then, when this is granted, escalate to a larger one (the one they actually desired all along).

Individuation Differentiation of oneself from others by emphasis on one's uniqueness or individuality.

Informational Social Influence Social influence based on the desire to be correct (i.e., to possess accurate perceptions of the social world).

Ingratiation A technique for gaining compliance in which requesters first induce target persons to like them, then attempt to change their behavior in some desired manner.

Normative Social Influence Social influence based on the individual's desire to be liked or accepted by other persons.

Obedience A form of social influence in which one person simply orders one or more others to perform some action(s).

Social Influence Efforts on the part of one person to alter the behavior or attitudes of one or more others.

Social Influence Model (SIM) A general model of social influence designed to account for the impact of group size, number of targets, and several other factors upon the acceptance of influence in a wide range of settings.

Social Norms Rules indicating how individuals are expected to behave in specific situations.

That's Not All (TNA) Technique A technique for gaining compliance in which requesters offer additional benefits to target persons before the target persons have decided whether to comply with or reject specific requests.

FOR MORE INFORMATION

Cialdini, R. B. (1988). *Influence: Science and practice* (2nd ed.). Glenview Ill.: Scott-Foresman.

    An insightful account of the major techniques people use to influence others. The book draws both on the findings of systematic research and on informal observations made by the author in a wide range of practical settings (e.g., sales, public relations, fund-raising agencies, organizations). This is the most readable and informative account of knowledge about influence currently available.

Hendrick, C. (Ed.). (1987). *Group processes*. Newbury Park, CA: Sage.

    Contains chapters dealing with several of the topics covered in this chapter (e.g., majority and minority influence, how groups affect the behavior of their members). Each chapter is written by experts on the lines of research and concepts covered.

This is a useful source to consult if you'd like to know more about key aspects of social influence.

Milgram, S. (1974). *Obedience to authority*. New York: Harper & Row.

    This book remains the definitive work on obedience as a social psychological process. The untimely death of its author only added to its value as a lasting contribution to our field.

Milgram, S., Sabini, J., & Silver, M. (1992). *The individual in a social world*. New York: McGraw-Hill.

    Presents a collection of essays written by Stanley Milgram, whose research on obedience is a classic in social psychology. Several of the chapters included deal with obedience, conformity, and other aspects of social influence. The style is very readable, and the content is thought-provoking, to say the least.

Chapter
EIGHT

Helping and Harming: Prosocial Behavior and Aggression

··

SPECIAL SECTIONS

E ven brief inspection of any newspaper or magazine reveals the fact that human social behavior is extraordinarily varied. One page may feature a story of domestic violence and another page may report atrocities inflicted by one national group on another. Yet an adjacent column may give details of heroism—an incident where someone took considerable risks to help rescue a stranger (see Figure 8.1). Social psychologists have focused a great deal of attention on both topics—the factors that influence whether we *help* or *harm* others.

In this chapter we will examine some of what is known about the variables that predict who does and does not engage in *prosocial behavior* when emergency situations arise. By **prosocial behavior**, we mean actions that provide benefit to others rather than the person who carries them out. A related term, **altruistic behavior**, refers to acts that suggest an unselfish concern for the welfare of others, in which there are costs for the actor. In this chapter we begin with the story of how an important research program began with efforts to explain why *response to an emergency* sometimes consists of tremendous effort, risk-taking, and sacrifice—and sometimes consists of doing little or nothing. We then examine some of the specific variables that increase or decrease the likelihood that *helping behavior* will occur, as well as its effect on the recipient.

The second part of this chapter examines **aggression**, the intentional infliction of some form of harm on others. In view of its destructive impact on society and its prevalence (Geen, 1990), it is hardly surprising that aggression has been an important topic of research in social psychology for several decades (Baron & Richardson, 1994). First, we'll describe several different theoretical perspectives on aggression—contrasting views about the nature and origins of such behavior. Next, we'll review important social causes of aggression—aspects of others' behavior (or our interpretations of their actions) and of the situation that play a role in the initiation of aggressive outbursts. Finally, we'll end on an optimistic note by examining various techniques for the prevention and control of human aggression. As will soon become apparent, a degree of optimism really is justified in this respect, for several effective techniques for reducing overt aggression do indeed exist.

■ Hurting and Helping

FIGURE 8.1 Aggression and prosocial behavior: Two very important social phenomena

RESPONDING TO AN EMERGENCY: WHAT DO BYSTANDERS DO?

The daily news provides many examples of people helping one another, even risking their lives to provide aid to strangers in distress. The following story is not an uncommon one. Two men who happened to live in the same building heard a woman (a stranger to them) screaming in the parking lot. Independently, they rushed out to provide help:

> The two "good Samaritans"… said screams awakened them. Both said they could see what appeared to be an attack from their windows. As one ran out the door, his wife said she'd call the police, but he said there wasn't time. When he reached the parking lot, the man was sitting on the woman's back, hitting her on the head, and telling her he was going to rape her. The attacker pretended he was her boyfriend, but the rescuer said, "I don't care, get off of her." He pulled the woman to her feet, and the second rescuer ran up, saying the police were on their way. The assailant ran off, but was later caught and arrested. (De Mare, 1992)

Despite these dramatic incidents, we seem to pay more attention to the opposite extreme: **bystander apathy**, when witnesses seem to ignore the problem and fail to provide help. An extreme example of such seeming indifference occurred in New York. On March 13, 1964, at 3:20 A.M., Kitty Genovese was returning from her job as manager of a bar. She had parked her car and was about to enter her apartment building. Suddenly a man ran up to her brandishing a knife. She ran, but he chased after her, caught up, and stabbed her. Ms. Genovese screamed for help, and lights came on in many of the apartment windows that overlooked the scene. The attacker started to leave but then came back to resume his assault on the screaming victim. Almost forty-five minutes after the initial attack, Kitty Genovese lay dead as the result of multiple stab wounds. Afterward, thirty-eight people reported that they had heard her screams, but not one had offered assistance or even placed a call to the police (Rosenthal, 1964).

Why not? Many columnists, editorial writers, and TV commentators suggested that the bystanders were unresponsive because our society had become apathetic, selfish, and indifferent to the plight of others. Similar themes still appear in newspapers and on TV: Americans have been described as turning away from the outstretched hands of those who are homeless with feelings of apathy, numbness, and confusion (Steinfels, 1992). Though such characterizations are plausible, social psychologists John Darley and Bibb Latané, discussing the Genovese story over lunch, proposed a different explanation of why people fail to help (Krupat, 1975). We will turn now to the research that grew out of that noontime conversation. Though very little was known about prosocial behavior at the beginning of the 1960s, we are now able to identify the situations in which it occurs (and those in which it does not) as well as the personality dispositions and motivational states associated with it (Darley, 1991).

BYSTANDER "APATHY" VERSUS DIFFUSION OF RESPONSIBILITY

The initial hypothesis (Darley & Latané, 1968) was that the inaction of the bystanders in the Genovese murder resulted from the fact that many people were present at the scene and that no one person felt responsible for taking action. Thus, there was **diffusion of responsibility**. Darley and Latané tested the hypothesis that as the number of bystanders increases, the diffused responsibility results in a decrease in prosocial behavior. Each subject in their initial experiment was exposed to a bogus medical emergency and believed himself or herself to be either the only one who knew about the problem, one of two bystanders, or one of five bystanders. The basic question was whether helpfulness would decrease as the number of bystanders increased.

When undergraduate subjects arrived at the laboratory to take part in a psychological experiment, the instructions indicated that they would discuss with fellow students some of the problems involved in attending college in a high-pressure urban setting. The participants were told that each of them would be assigned to a separate room and could communicate only by an intercom system; they could hear each other, but the experimenter would not be listening. This arrangement was supposedly designed to avoid any embarrassment about discussing personal matters.

Some subjects were told that they were one of two discussants, others that they were part of a group of three, and still others that six students were participating. Each participant was supposed to talk for two minutes, after which the listener or listeners would comment on what the others had said. In reality, only one subject took part in each session, and the other participant or participants were simply tape recordings. Thus, the stage was set for a controlled emergency apparently overheard by varying numbers of bystanders.

In each session the first person to speak was the tape-recorded individual who was to be the "victim." He said, sounding embarrassed, that he sometimes had seizures, especially when facing a stressful situation such as exams. After the participant (and, in two of the conditions, other "participants") had given a two-minute talk about college problems, the victim spoke again.

I er I think I need er if if could er er somebody er er help because I er I'm er h-h-having a a a real problem er right now and I er if somebody could help me out it would er er s-s-sure be good ... because er there er er a thing's coming on and and I could really er use some help so if somebody here er help er uh uh uh (choking sounds)... I'm gonna die er er I'm gonna die er help er er seizure (chokes, then is quiet). (Darley & Latané, 1968, p. 379.)

Two aspects of bystander responsiveness were measured, and the results are shown in Figure 8.2. A helpful response consisted of leaving the experimental room to look for the imaginary victim. As the number of apparent bystanders increased, the percentage of subjects attempting to help decreased. Further, among those who did respond, an increase in the number of bystanders led to increased delay in taking action. Such findings are consistent with Darley and Latané's hypothesis that the presence of others leads to diffused responsibility and makes helpfulness less probable.

Beyond demonstrating the **bystander effect**, this experiment also called into question the idea of the "apathetic bystander." For example, among those who thought they were the only witness, 85 percent tried to help, and did so within the first minute. Such responsiveness decreased and slowed down as more bystanders were present. But the subjects who failed to respond were not indifferent. Instead, they seemed emotionally upset, confused, and uncomfortable.

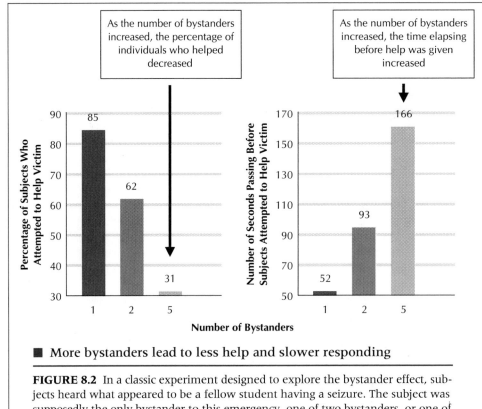

■ More bystanders lead to less help and slower responding

FIGURE 8.2 In a classic experiment designed to explore the bystander effect, subjects heard what appeared to be a fellow student having a seizure. The subject was supposedly the only bystander to this emergency, one of two bystanders, or one of five. As the number of bystanders increased, the percentage of subjects who tried to help the victim decreased. In addition, among those who did help, more time passed before help was offered as the number of bystanders increased. This bystander effect was initially explained on the basis of diffusion of responsibility.

Source: Based on data in Darley & Latané, 1968.

PROVIDING OR NOT PROVIDING HELP: FIVE NECESSARY COGNITIVE STEPS

Following the initial experiment on diffusion of responsibility, Latané and Darley (1970)—as well as others—carried out numerous interrelated experiments, and they eventually formulated a theoretical model to explain why bystanders sometimes do and sometimes do not help a victim. They described a helping response as the end point of a series of cognitive decisions, as outlined in Figure 8.3. Help is provided only if the appropriate decision is made at each step. What are these crucial choice-points?

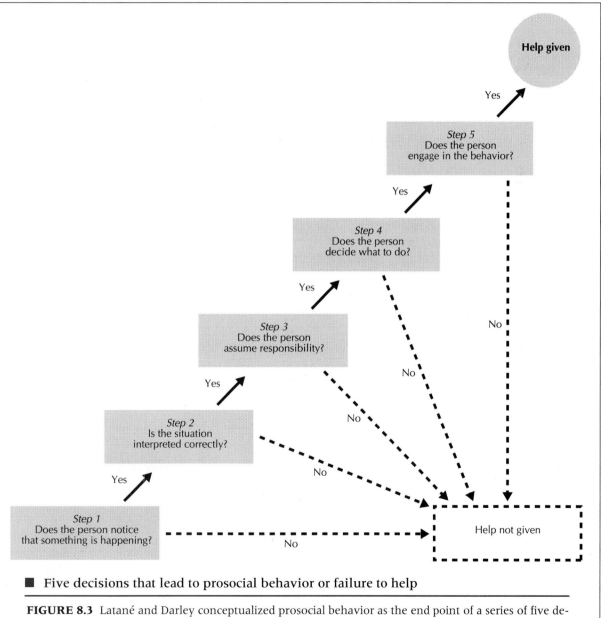

■ Five decisions that lead to prosocial behavior or failure to help

FIGURE 8.3 Latané and Darley conceptualized prosocial behavior as the end point of a series of five decisions. At each step in the process, one decision results in no help being given, while the other decision leads the individual one step closer to a prosocial act.

Source: Adapted from Byrne & Kelley, 1981.

Attending to the emergency

The first decision is whether to shift one's attention from whatever one is doing to the unexpected emergency—to *notice* that something is wrong. Many factors can prevent this. You may not be facing the emergency situation, so seeing or hearing it may be impaired. Other people or sounds in your immediate vicinity may distract you. Or you may be so involved in your present activity that you notice very little else.

The role of such preoccupation was studied by Darley and Batson (1973). Seminary students served as experimental subjects, and their task was to go to a nearby building to present a talk. In an attempt to prime a helping response, the researchers specified that the talk was to be either about providing help to a stranger in need (Luke's parable of the Good Samaritan) or about jobs. To manipulate preoccupation, the investigators told the subjects that they were (1) ahead of schedule, with plenty of time; (2) right on schedule; or (3) late for the speaking engagement. It was assumed that the third group would be the least attentive to an emergency situation.

On their way to give the talk, the subjects each encountered an experimental assistant who was slumped in a doorway, coughing and groaning. Would they notice this individual and offer help? The topic of the upcoming speech had no effect on their response, but the time pressure did. As shown in Figure 8.4, help was offered by 63 percent of those who believed they had time to spare, 45 percent of those who were on schedule, and only 10 percent of those who were told they were late. The preoccupied subjects were in such a hurry that even when they were going to talk about the Good Samaritan, some simply stepped over the victim and rushed along to keep the speaking appointment.

Perceiving that an emergency exists

Once the situation gets a bystander's attention, the second step is to interpret the situation correctly. What is going on? In general, it is easier to imagine a routine, everyday explanation of events than a highly unusual and unlikely one (Macrae & Milne,

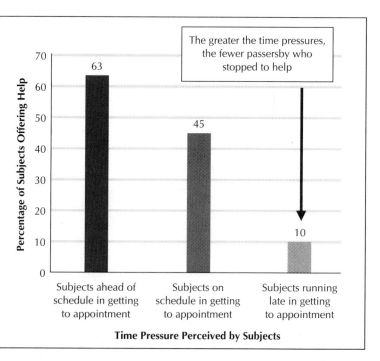

■ Too preoccupied to attend to an emergency

FIGURE 8.4 When potential helpers are preoccupied by other concerns, they are much less likely to help a person in need—in part because they are too busy to pay attention to the victim. Subjects who believed they had plenty of time to get to an appointment were most likely to stop and help a stranger who was slumped in a doorway, coughing and groaning. Those who believed they were late for the appointment were least likely to help.

Source: Based on data in Darley & Batson, 1973.

The greater the time pressures, the fewer passersby who stopped to help

1992). And a problem with interpreting an everyday situation as an emergency is that you can end up looking foolish (see Figure 8.5).

To avoid being embarrassed about being incorrect and behaving in an inappropriate way, most people fail to engage in any drastic action until the evidence is clear and convincing that an emergency is actually occurring. Often there is some degree of ambiguity in emergency situations, so potential helpers hold back and wait for additional information in order to be sure about what is going on. The more ambiguous the situation, the less likely people are to offer help (Bickman, 1972). Because it is easier *not* to help than to take an active helping role, and because we tend to give more weight to negative than to positive information (see chapter 2), people are especially attentive to any information that suggests there is no reason to be concerned (Wilson & Petruska, 1984).

When more than one bystander witnesses an emergency, each interprets the event in part on the basis of what the others do or say—each relies on *social comparison* (see chapter 6). If fellow witnesses fail to react, helping behavior is strongly inhibited. A special problem is that in our culture we are taught to remain calm in an emergency; it isn't socially acceptable to begin screaming when we see a stranger slip on an icy path, for example. As a result, most bystanders pretend to be calm, and this cool response is perceived by other bystanders as evidence that nothing serious is occurring. In an actual emergency, therefore, multiple bystanders can inadvertently and incorrectly inform one another that everything is all right.

This phenomenon is known as **pluralistic ignorance**, and an experiment by Latané and Darley (1968) demonstrates how it operates. The investigators asked subjects to fill out questionnaires in a room either alone or in groups of three. Shortly after they began, smoke was pumped into the room through a vent. The experimenters waited for the subjects to respond (but terminated the experimental session after six minutes if the subjects remained in their seats and failed to act). When subjects were in the room alone, 75 percent went out to report the smoke, and half of those who responded

■ Fear of looking foolish

FIGURE 8.5 Most people are very concerned about the reactions of others and feel that it is best not to stand out from the crowd by doing something that may elicit ridicule. Engaging in an overt act when you are alone is safe, because there is no one to evaluate your actions as foolish. For this reason, a bystander who is the sole witness to what appears to be a stranger in distress is more likely to help than a bystander who is one of several witnesses.

Source: Universal Press Syndicate, May 31, 1978.

did so within two minutes. When three people were in the room, only one person reacted in the first four minutes—the majority (62 percent) did nothing for the entire six minutes even though the smoke became thick enough to make it difficult to see.

Ambiguity and social acceptability also inhibit the tendency to help when a man is hurting a woman. Suppose you heard the sounds of a fight in a neighboring apartment, and the woman yelled, "I hate you! I don't ever want to see you again!" Would you do anything? Most people would decide that it was simply a lovers' quarrel and none of their business. Bystanders would probably be likely to respond, however, if the woman shouted, "Whoever you are, just get out of my apartment!" In an experimental version of such interactions, Shotland and Strau (1976) found that three times as many interventions took place when a fight was between a man and woman who were strangers than when it involved a married couple.

Ambiguity sometimes includes indecision as to whether a victim does or does not *want* to be helped. That is one reason why people are hesitant to respond to a domestic quarrel; sometimes the victim of domestic aggression resents an outsider's interference as much as the aggressor does.

Is it my responsibility to help?

At the third decision point in the model, the bystander either does or does not assume responsibility to act. Even though you notice that an emergency exists and correctly interpret what is going on, you are not likely to do anything about it unless you decide that it's your responsibility to help. For example, you see an elderly person lying on the sidewalk—moaning in pain—and an ambulance has just pulled up (see Figure 8.6). Will you dash over to help or will you assume that in this situation

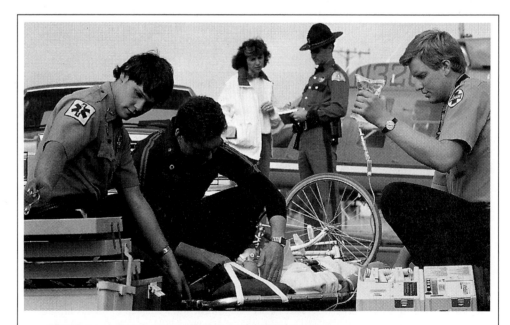

■ Whose responsibility? Leave it to the experts

FIGURE 8.6 If one of the bystanders witnessing an emergency has special skills and training that are relevant to providing help, other bystanders are much less likely to offer assistance to a victim. For example, a medical emergency is best handled by medical personnel.

responsibility for providing aid belongs to the trained medical personnel? When the responsibility is reasonably clear, you will probably do nothing.

Many situations are not that clear, of course. If you are in a classroom and a fellow student falls to the floor and lies there with his eyes closed, you will probably expect your instructor to take some appropriate action. That is, the leader of a given group is perceived to be responsible for taking charge and deciding what to do (Baumeister et al., 1988). In that same classroom, if the instructor collapses on the floor, what will you do? Because none of the students has any clear responsibility, this is the kind of situation in which everyone may very well stand back and fail to do anything.

The direct link between the number of bystanders and perceived responsibility was tested by Schwartz and Gottlieb (1980). These investigators arranged for participants to witness an "emergency" either alone or with a second person. As in many other studies, helping behavior was less likely to occur when there were two bystanders than when there was one. The investigators determined perceived responsibility by asking participants afterward why they helped or failed to help. Of those who were alone, 80 percent said that they felt personally responsible for offering help; only 17 percent of those who had a fellow bystander mentioned any feelings of responsibility.

How to help? Knowing what to do

Once a bystander assumes responsibility, there is a fourth decision point. How can the victim be helped? As suggested in Figure 8.7, in an emergency situation, it seldom makes sense to take time to consult with others about what to do. In some emergencies, almost anyone is able to provide the necessary aid—by telephoning the police, helping a victim stand up on a slippery sidewalk, and so forth. Other emergencies call for special skills, and useful help can be provided only by those who have the required training. For example, a bystander who could not swim would be unable to rescue someone who was having difficulty in the water.

■ **Deciding what to do in an emergency situation**

FIGURE 8.7 A necessary step in the prosocial sequence is deciding how to provide help. If the bystander doesn't know what to do, there obviously isn't time to turn the matter over to a committee.

Source: The New Yorker, July 16, 1990, p. 37.

"Under new business: Peterson, at Hammond Point Beach, reports that a person in the water is flailing about and calling for help. Peterson wants to know what action, if any, he should take."

When a bystander is able to help, he or she is likely to act even though other bystanders are present and unresponsive. Cramer et al. (1988) found that when another bystander was present, registered nurses were more likely than college students to offer assistance to an accident victim. When no other bystanders were present, however, a college student was as likely to offer assistance as was a nurse.

Deciding to help

The final decision in the model is whether or not to act. Among the factors influencing this behavior are the possible costs involved—being rejected by the victim or getting one's clothes dirty, for example. When others are present, additional costs arise, such as making a mistake and appearing foolish. Social blunders can be avoided if the bystanders are able to communicate about what is going on and what to do about it. For this reason, prosocial behavior is less inhibited by the bystander effect if the bystanders are acquainted than if they are strangers (Rutkowski, Gruder, & Romer, 1983).

Another factor that reduces the fear of making a blunder and also increases the tendency to communicate with strangers is the consumption of alcohol. Even a modest amount of alcohol increases the tendency to help, and additional drinking leads to still more prosocial actions (Steele, Critchlow, & Liu, 1985). Steele and his colleagues hypothesized that intoxication causes "cognitive myopia." The inebriated person perceives the victim's need and is unaware of the ambiguities of the situation or of possible negative consequences of providing aid. Steele notes, "Now you may not want the help of a drunk...I don't know about the quality of the help you'd get, but they're more likely to do it" (quoted in Kent, 1990, p. 13).

INTERNAL AND EXTERNAL FACTORS THAT INFLUENCE ALTRUISTIC BEHAVIOR

We have discussed several variables that affect altruism, including the number of bystanders who witness an emergency, cognitive appraisal and decision making, and dispositional differences in help-related characteristics. Additional factors also affect whether or not altruistic responses will occur: the presence of *role models*, the *emotional state* of potential helpers, and various *victim characteristics*.

ROLE MODELS: PROVIDING HELPFUL CUES

If you are out shopping and pass someone collecting money to help the homeless, provide warm coats for needy children, buy food for those in poverty, or whatever, do you reach in your pocket or purse to make a contribution? One determinant of your behavior is whether you see someone else contribute. People are much more likely to give money if they observe others do so (Macauley, 1970). Even the presence of paper money and coins in the collection box acts as an encouragement to a charitable response.

The presence of fellow bystanders who fail to respond to an emergency inhibits helpfulness, as we have seen. In an analogous way, the presence of a helpful bystander provides a role model and encourages helpfulness. This modeling effect was shown in a field experiment in which a female confederate was parked by the side of a road with a flat tire. Male motorists were much more likely to stop and help if (several minutes earlier) they had observed another woman with car trouble receiving help (Bryan & Test, 1967).

The positive effect of models is not limited to real-life encounters. Television is found to influence viewers in a variety of ways, and altruism is one of them (see Figure 8.8). In a study of the effects of TV, investigators showed six-year-olds an episode of "Lassie" that contained a rescue scene, an episode of the same program unrelated to prosocial behavior, or a humorous segment of "The Brady Bunch"

(Sprafkin, Liebert, & Poulous, 1975). Afterward, while the subjects were playing a game in which the winner would receive a prize, they came in contact with some puppies who were whining unhappily. Despite the fact that helping the puppies would decrease their chance of winning, the children who had watched the "Lassie" rescue scene spent much more time trying to comfort the animals than did those in the other two TV conditions.

Other investigators have found that when preschool children are exposed to prosocial programs such as "Mister Rogers' Neighborhood" or "Sesame Street," they are more likely to behave in an altruistic way than children who have not watched such shows (Forge & Phemister, 1987). These studies consistently indicate that television can exert a very positive influence on the development of prosocial responses.

EMOTIONS:
EFFECTS OF POSITIVE VERSUS NEGATIVE MOODS

It might seem obvious that being in a good mood would make an individual more likely to provide help to someone in need and that a bad mood would interfere with altruistic behavior. Research indicates, however, that the effects of mood on helping are somewhat more complicated than that. Other variables must be taken into account before we can predict how mood operates in specific situations (Salovey, Mayer, & Rosenhan, 1991).

Positive emotions

Children sometimes wait for their parents to be in an especially good mood before asking for something. They assume that a happy parent is more likely to do something for them than an unhappy one. Research has identified many instances supporting this underlying assumption. When a pleasant mood is created by experiences such as listening to Steve Martin on a comedy album (Wilson, 1981), finding money or being given cookies (Isen & Levin, 1972), or going out on a day when the sun is shining (Cunningham, 1979), the result is an increase in the tendency to assist others in need. Even the presence of a pleasing fragrance in the room increases helping behavior (Baron & Thomley, 1992).

■ **TV can provide prosocial models**

FIGURE 8.8 Though television often provides models for undesirable behavior such as aggression, some programs depict prosocial models and are found to increase the likelihood of helpful behavior.

Despite these findings, other investigations have reported less prosocial behavior among individuals in a positive mood (Shaffer & Graziano, 1983)—especially when helping is potentially too embarrassing or risky (Rosenhan, Salovey, & Hargis, 1981). An individual experiencing positive emotions is more likely than a less happy person to engage in helpful acts only if these acts are rewarding rather than costly (Cunningham, Steinberg, & Grev, 1980) or if others are present to encourage helpfulness (Cunningham et al., 1990).

The explanation for the inhibition of costly prosocial behavior is that happy people are reluctant to do anything that might spoil their present mood (Isen, 1984). Another factor is that a good mood leads the person to feel powerful (*I can do anything*), and this includes the power to say no to a person requesting help. Figure 8.9 summarizes the findings on the effects of positive emotions on helping behavior.

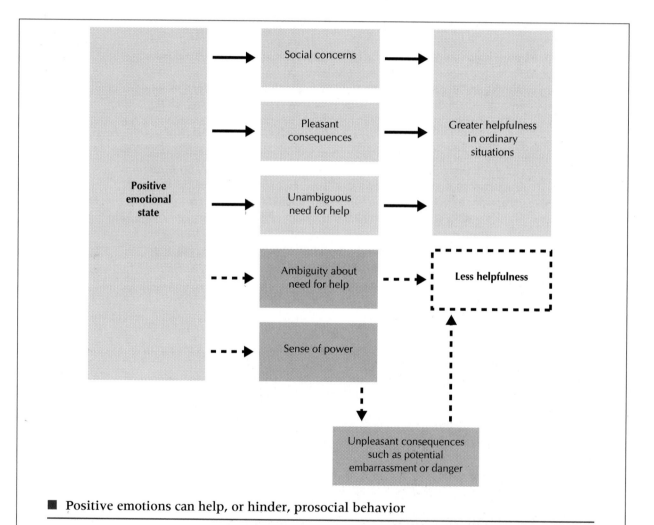

■ Positive emotions can help, or hinder, prosocial behavior

FIGURE 8.9 A positive emotional state sometimes increases and sometimes decreases the likelihood of engaging in prosocial actions. Positive feelings lead to greater helpfulness if social concerns are involved, the consequences of helping are pleasant rather than unpleasant, and the need for help is not ambiguous. Positive emotions result in less helpfulness if the need is ambiguous or if the consequences of helping are unpleasant; under such circumstances, the happy bystander feels sufficiently powerful that he or she can refuse to help.

Negative emotions

The effects of negative moods on prosocial behavior are slightly more complex than the effects of positive emotions. Sometimes negative moods increase helping, sometimes they inhibit it, and sometimes they are found to have no effect. When negative emotions increase prosocial responding, it can be explained by the *negative state relief model*—helping makes people feel good, and those in a negative mood are motivated to do anything to make themselves feel better (Cialdini, Kenrick, & Bauman, 1982). Depressed individuals, for example, are especially likely to help if what they have to do to help is interesting or pleasant (Cunningham et al., 1990) and if they feel *personally responsible* for their bad mood (Rogers et al., 1982).

As you might guess, helping others is not always a remedy for a negative mood. If you are sufficiently angry or depressed, no amount of helping will make you feel better. Helping as a way to relieve negative feelings is most likely to occur if (1) the required behavior is perceived as relatively easy and effective, (2) it seems clear that the helpful act will lead to more positive feelings, and (3) the negative feelings are not too intense (Berkowitz, 1987).

The effects of negative emotions also have to do with the focus of those emotions. When the potential helper is concentrating on his or her own unhappy circumstances, helping is less likely to occur; helping increases when the focus is on the other person's problems (Thompson, Cowan, & Rosenhan, 1980). These investigators suggested that when attention is directed toward the misfortunes of others, empathy is aroused, and this motivates a prosocial response. This hypothesis was supported by an Australian study of the extent to which help was provided in a real-life emergency. When a destructive bushfire occurred near the city of Melbourne, a sample of the residents described their emotional reactions when they first heard about the fire and about their subsequent helping behavior (Amato, 1986). Those who were upset by the news reports of the plight of the victims (shocked, horrified, sick, etc.) and who felt sympathy for them donated significantly more money to the relief efforts than did those whose reactions were more self-centered (angry at authorities, indifferent, etc.).

The various factors that determine the effect of negative emotions on helping behavior are summarized in Figure 8.10.

CHARACTERISTICS OF THE HELPER: THE ALTRUISTIC PERSONALITY

Over the years, despite the demonstrated importance of situational variables, numerous investigations have suggested that some individuals are more altruistic than others. In some instances, altruistic behavior seems to be motivated by other concerns. Certain individuals, for example, have a strong *need for approval*, and they are more likely to provide help *if* they have previously received positive interpersonal feedback for this kind of behavior (Deutsch & Lamberti, 1986). Other research indicates that altruistic motives are important predictors of who will help (Clary & Orenstein, 1991) and that an individual's altruism is probably based on his or her socialization experiences (Grusec, 1991). What exactly are the components of the **altruistic personality**?

Bierhoff, Klein, and Kramp (1991) reviewed the literature and identified a number of possible variables that had been found to be relevant in previous research. The investigators selected several of these personality variables and administered measures to assess their levels in two groups of German citizens. The first group consisted of men and women who had been at the scene of an accident and administered first aid before an ambulance arrived. To obtain such a sample, the investigators asked members of an ambulance team for names and addresses of individuals who had been administering first

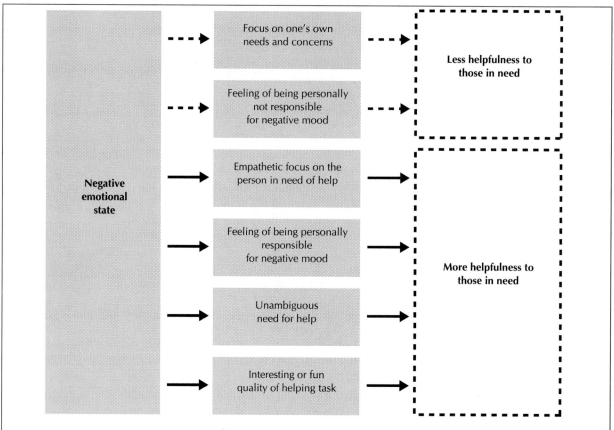

■ Negative emotions can lead to more, or less, prosocial behavior

FIGURE 8.10 As with positive emotions, negative feelings can foster or inhibit prosocial behavior, depending on specific circumstances. Helpfulness increases if there is an empathic focus on the person needing help, if the potential helper feels responsible for his or her own negative mood, if the need for help is not ambiguous, and if the helping task is interesting or fun. Negative emotions lead to less helpfulness if the person focuses on his or her own concerns and if the potential helper does not feel responsible for the negative mood.

aid at the scene of an accident when the ambulance arrived. These "first aiders" were sent a questionnaire. They ranged in age from 13 to 65, with a mean of 37.8. The second group consisted of control subjects who reported witnessing an automobile accident but providing no help to the victims. The researchers matched these nonhelpers to the helpers with respect to sex, age, and social status. Five of the measures administered to the subjects significantly differentiated these two groups, as summarized in Table 8.1. Social psychologists see the characteristics identified in this study as major components of the altruistic personality. Each characteristic is described below.

First, the altruistic sample scored higher than the control group on a measure of **self-concept encompassing empathy**. A high score on this measure indicates that an individual has rated himself or herself as being responsible and socialized, having self-control, wanting to make a good impression, achieving goals by means of conformity, and being tolerant.

Those who had given first aid to accident victims also scored higher than control subjects in the tendency called **belief in a just world**. Those who hold this belief

■ In an attempt to identify the factors that make up the altruistic personality, investigators compared citizens who witnessed a traffic accident and provided first aid to the victim with citizens who witnessed such an accident and did not provide first aid. As indicated here, five personality characteristics were found to differentiate the two groups. Together these characteristics identify altruistic individuals.

TABLE 8.1 Components of the altruistic personality

Individuals Who Administered First Aid after a Traffic Accident	Individuals Who Failed to Administer First Aid
Were higher in internal locus of control	Were lower in internal locus of control
Believed more strongly in a just world	Believed less strongly in a just world
Felt more socially responsible (were interested in public matters and involved in the community; felt a sense of duty)	Felt less socially responsible
Had higher empathy component in self-concept	Had lower empathy component in self-concept
Were less egocentric	Were more egocentric

Source: Based on data in Bierhoff, Klein, & Kramp, 1991.

perceive the world as a fair and predictable place in which good behavior is rewarded and bad behavior punished. In other words, everybody gets what they deserve. The person giving first aid is doing the right thing and will benefit from doing so.

A third variable differentiating the two groups was **social responsibility**. Those who accept the norm of social responsibility—the idea that we should all do our best to help others—are more helpful than those who deny responsibility, believing that it doesn't apply to them.

The fourth characteristic of those who provided first aid was **internal locus of control**—the assumption that you can behave in such a way as to maximize good outcomes and minimize bad ones; in other words, that you are not a helpless pawn at the mercy of luck, fate, and other uncontrollable forces.

The altruistic group was *lower* than the control group on a measure of **egocentrism**, or self-absorption. People who are primarily concerned with themselves are often found to be high in competitiveness and less willing to help others. Other research is consistent in finding that people whose social values place an emphasis on cooperation are more helpful than those who stress individualistic or competitive values (McClintock & Allison, 1989).

These five characteristics of the altruistic personality were confirmed in another study of people who helped a quite different kind of victim. Oliner and Oliner (1988) obtained personality data on people throughout Europe who were actively involved in rescuing Jews from the Nazis during World War II (see Figure 8.11). Those who bravely defied the authorities and protected Jews were found to be remarkably similar to those who provided first aid to accident victims.

Altogether, people with an altruistic personality have a strong sense of internal control, a high belief in a just world, a sense of duty, a self-concept involving empathy, and a concern for others rather than an egocentric concern for self. How would you rate yourself on these five dimensions?

■ Altruistic individuals: Saving Jews from Nazi persecution

FIGURE 8.11 Current studies of those who provide first aid to accident victims and studies of those who helped protect Jews from Nazi persecution during World War II reveal very similar personality characteristics. Those who are altruistic have an internal locus of control, believe in a just world, feel socially responsible, feel empathic, and are not egocentric.

WHO NEEDS HELP?
CHARACTERISTICS OF THE VICTIM

If you were walking down the sidewalk in a large city and noticed a man passed out next to the curb, would you be more likely to stop and help if he wore filthy clothes and clutched a wine bottle next to his stained shirt or if he were neatly dressed and had a dark, swollen bruise on his forehead? The odds are you would be more strongly motivated to help the victim in the second case. Why?

Victim responsibility

A generally accepted social norm is that when anyone runs into difficulties because of his or her own irresponsibility or carelessness, it's up to that person to solve the problem (Schmidt & Weiner, 1988). "you've made your bed, now lie in it." That is one reason why most people would help an unconscious stranger who apparently has been injured but not one who drank enough alcohol to pass out.

As shown in Figure 8.12, a model formulated by Weiner (1980) proposes that we respond with disgust to a victim who is responsible for the problem, and that this reaction does not motivate helping. When the victim is not responsible for the problem, we respond with empathy, which does motivate a helpful response.

Attraction

On the basis of the material presented in chapter 6, you might assume that the more we like a person, the stronger our tendency to provide assistance, and you would be correct (Clark et al., 1987; Schoenrade et al., 1986). The variables that increase attraction also increase prosocial responses. For example, help is provided more often for an attractive victim than for an unattractive one (Benson, Karabenick, & Lerner, 1976), and more often for a victim who is similar to the helper than for a dissimilar one (Dovidio, 1984).

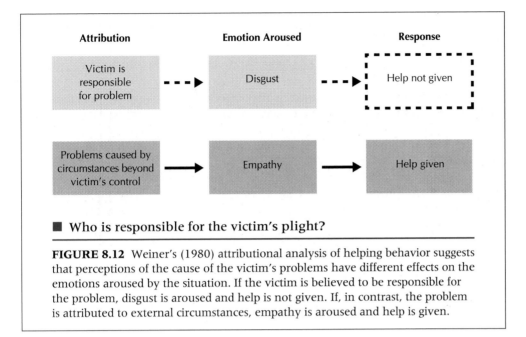

Attribution	Emotion Aroused	Response

Victim is responsible for problem → Disgust → Help not given

Problems caused by circumstances beyond victim's control → Empathy → Help given

■ Who is responsible for the victim's plight?

FIGURE 8.12 Weiner's (1980) attributional analysis of helping behavior suggests that perceptions of the cause of the victim's problems have different effects on the emotions aroused by the situation. If the victim is believed to be responsible for the problem, disgust is aroused and help is not given. If, in contrast, the problem is attributed to external circumstances, empathy is aroused and help is given.

Asking for and responding to help

Research on prosocial behavior has focused primarily on the person who provides or fails to provide help, but the victims can also play a central role in an emergency situation when they ask for or respond to help from others.

Earlier in this chapter we saw how ambiguity can inhibit a prosocial response. One way to resolve ambiguity is for the victim to ask for help; this makes the need quite clear. But some people find it difficult to ask and thus are less likely to be helped. For example, shy individuals are very reluctant to seek help from a member of the opposite sex (DePaulo et al., 1989). Whether or not a person who needs help actually seeks it also depends on demographic factors—women seek help more than men, the elderly seek help less than young adults, and those high in socioeconomic status make more requests for help than those low in socioeconomic status (Nadler, 1991).

One reason that some people are reluctant to ask for help is the belief that they will be viewed as less competent if they do so (DePaulo & Fisher, 1980). Interestingly enough, the more the potential helper resembles the person needing help, the greater the reluctance to seek help (Nadler, 1987; Nadler & Fisher, 1986), in part because the similarity emphasizes the incompetence of the one who needs help.

In somewhat more general terms, Nadler (1993) finds that help-seeking can be stigmatizing. He suggests that the act of asking for help touches on a basic human dilemma—the conflict between dependence and independence. Western culture values independence and self-reliance as indicators of personal strength and adequacy. To seek help is to violate those values. An experiment examined people's perceptions of the person who asks for help. Compared to those of high socioeconomic status, an individual from a low socioeconomic background "loses" more by seeking help, because this request seems to confirm the stereotype that such a person is dependent, incompetent, and unsuccessful. That effect is moderated by requests that imply independence ("help me because I want to understand what to do") rather than dependence ("help me because I can't do it by myself").

A related reason not to request aid is the realistic assumption that potential helpers may view the victim's emotional response as inappropriate. For example, if a natural disaster occurs but the victim suffers only minor property damage, indications of distress and the need for help are viewed as inappropriate behavior caused by character faults (Yates, 1992).

Because needing help and receiving it implies a lack of competence, the victim's self-esteem decreases when help is provided, especially if the help comes from a friend or a similar person and suggests that the victim is lacking in important skills and abilities (DePaulo et al., 1981; Nadler, Fisher, & Itzhak, 1983). And when the victim's self-esteem is threatened, the victim responds with negative feelings and dislikes the helper. The only positive result is that the victim is motivated to provide self-help in the future (Fisher, Nadler, & Whitcher-Alagna, 1982). Help by someone who is a dissimilar or disliked other does not threaten self-esteem or evoke negative feelings (Cook & Pelfrey, 1985), but the victim is also not motivated to help him- or herself in the future. These various reactions are outlined in Figure 8.13.

CULTURAL VALUES AND HELP–SEEKING

We have discussed several aspects of help-seeking, but it should be added that cultural values also influence whether or not an individual seeks help from others. In the following section, we examine societal differences in such behavior.

Cross-cultural comparisons often focus on societies that differ in their emphasis on individual versus communal behavior. At the individualistic extreme on the spectrum, each person strives to be a self-contained unit and seeks success and recognition on the basis of individual achievement. It's every man for himself, every woman for herself. In contrast, communal societies stress interlocking familylike connections in which individuals depend on one another, sharing both hardship and success. It's one for all and all for one. These differences in individualism versus collectivism were also discussed in chapter 4. Given such differences in outlook, differences in help-seeking behavior might well be expected.

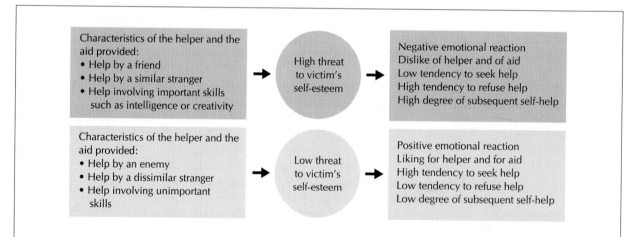

■ How do victims respond to being helped? It depends on who helps

FIGURE 8.13 When a victim is helped, he or she sometimes responds negatively and sometimes positively. According to Fisher, Nadler, and Whitcher-Alagna (1982), being helped by a friend on important tasks is threatening, lowers one's self-esteem, and evokes negative emotions, but leads to more self-help afterward. Being helped by a nonfriend on an unimportant task is not threatening, does not lower self-esteem, and evokes positive emotions, but leads to less self-help afterward.

City dwellers and kibbutz dwellers in Israel

Comparisons of behavior in different parts of the world often focus on cultures that differ in a specific way; behavioral differences may be attributed to that particular difference (although the cultures may differ in other ways that may also affect behavior). Nadler (1986) was able to concentrate on citizens of a single nation, Israel, and yet examine the effect of individualistic versus communal living on help-seeking behavior. He points out that his country provides a unique opportunity for such comparisons because there are both urban dwellers whose environment stresses typical Western attitudes such as self-reliance and individual achievement and kibbutz dwellers whose environment stresses egalitarian-communal ideology (see figure 8.14).

Based on these cultural differences, Nadler predicted that those living in a kibbutz would expect to be dependent on one another and thus should be willing to seek help when it is needed. This should be an expected and normative way to cope with problems. Those living in a city, however, should view self-reliance as all-important and thus should be reluctant to turn to others for help; as in the studies described earlier in the chapter, these individuals should feel uncomfortable about seeking help.

■ Individualistic versus communal cultures affect helping behavior

FIGURE 8.14 In Israel both communal and individualistic cultures are represented (kibbutz dwellers versus city dwellers). Nadler (1986) found that those raised communally in a kibbutz are more likely to seek help than those raised individualistically in a city, especially when the help benefits the group rather than the individual.

Nadler asked study participants from kibbutzim and urban settings to imagine a series of everyday situations in which they faced a problem and a potential helper was available; for each situation the participants were to indicate the likelihood that they would actually seek help from the other person. As predicted, kibbutz dwellers indicated more help-seeking than did city dwellers.

Nadler further hypothesized that the type of situation requiring help would also influence help-seeking by the two cultural subgroups. Some high school students were placed in a situation that involved a group, while others were supposed to be working only for themselves. In other words, they were given a communal task or an individual task. Specifically, subjects worked on anagrams that were supposedly a measure of success at the university; a score would be assigned either to the person's group or to the individual. They were allowed to ask for hints on those anagrams for which they needed help. Again, kibbutz and city dwellers differed. Those raised on a kibbutz were more likely to seek help when the task involved the success of the group, while city dwellers sought help primarily when individual success was at stake. Thus, it appeared that socialization in different subcultures within Israel resulted in differences in help-seeking behavior.

RURAL VERSUS URBAN HELPING:
THE IMPORTANCE OF CONTEXT

Even if you have always lived in a city, you are probably aware of the cliché that people from small towns are friendlier and more helpful than people in the big city. But is this just a stereotype or does it have some basis in fact? A wide range of studies in places as far apart as the United States (Korte & Kerr, 1975; Latané & Darley, 1970) and Australia (Amato, 1983) have suggested this is fact rather than mere cliché.

One study carried out in Toronto (Rushton, 1978), had students from an undergraduate psychology class make requests of passersby in three locations of increasingly less population density in and around the city: downtown Toronto, a northern suburb of Toronto, and a small town north of the city. All these requests were made on one street (Yonge Street), which stretches from the city center to rural areas. Requests were made by one student, while others unobtrusively observed the subject's response. The approach always began with, "Excuse me, I wonder if you could...," followed by one of four specific requests: (1) "...tell me what time it is?" (2) "...tell me how you get to the nearest post office?" (3) "...give me change for a quarter?" (4) "...tell me what your name is?" Helpfulness was counted both as those who complied with the request and those who stopped and indicated regretfully that they were unable to comply (e.g., didn't know the location of the post office). Figure 8.15 shows the very consistent results of this study. People in the small town north of Toronto were more helpful than those in the suburb, who were in turn more helpful than passersby in downtown. This is true whether it was a common and simple request (e.g., for the time) or an unusual one (e.g., for the person's name). Incidentally, the level of helpfulness shown in downtown Toronto was not significantly different from data Latané and Darley gathered in New York City (1970). The robustness of this rural-urban dicrepancy has been confirmed for a wide range of prosocial behaviors from donations to charity to emergency intervention (Amato, 1983).

A number of explanations have been put forward for this effect. For example, Milgram's (1970) *stimulus overload* explanation suggests (in a concept similar to the notion of *information overload*—see chapter 2) that the more crowded and urbanized the setting, the more a person is bombarded with stimuli (the sight, sound, and smell of the city). This state of stimulus overload makes us put on what might be termed "psychological blinkers": In order to cope, we cut out all extraneous stimulation that we can. Because of this self-protective response, we may not either notice or want to help a stranger. A second type of explanation refers to the *aversive* nature of such overstimulation. If the

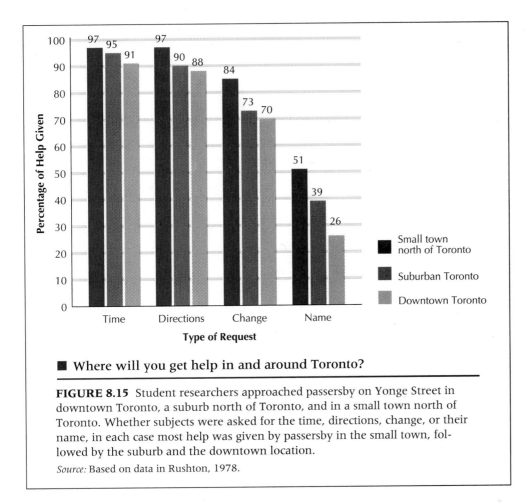

■ **Where will you get help in and around Toronto?**

FIGURE 8.15 Student researchers approached passersby on Yonge Street in downtown Toronto, a suburb north of Toronto, and in a small town north of Toronto. Whether subjects were asked for the time, directions, change, or their name, in each case most help was given by passersby in the small town, followed by the suburb and the downtown location.

Source: Based on data in Rushton, 1978.

downtown areas of cities are more unpleasant than the suburbs or rural areas, then this may affect our mood (Amato & McInnes, 1983), which we have seen can influence helpfulness. A third explanation has referred to the *difference in numbers* of people in the helping context. With the greater density of bystanders in a downtown area diffusion of responsibility, which can prevent or delay helping, is more likely to occur. Finally, *socialization* practices with reference to helpfulness may differ in the city and in the small town. Certainly, research has shown that those who are raised in a small town (even when they are in the city) tend to be more helpful than those raised in a large city (Latané & Darley, 1970). These day, when urban children are brought up to be "street smart" and avoid all contact with strangers on the streets, the gap between helpfulness on city streets and rural streets may widen.

AGGRESSION, ITS NATURE AND CAUSES: THEORETICAL PERSPECTIVES

Why do human beings aggress against others? What makes them turn, with brutality unmatched by even the fiercest of predators, against their fellow human beings? Scholars and scientists have pondered such questions for centuries, with the result that many contrasting explanations for the paradox of human violence have been proposed. Here, we'll examine several that have been especially influential.

AGGRESSION AS AN INNATE TENDENCY

The oldest and probably best known explanation for human aggression centers on the view that human beings are somehow "programmed" for violence by their biological nature. According to this **instinct theory** of aggression, people aggress because, quite simply, it is part of their essential human nature to do so. The most famous early supporter of this perspective was Sigmund Freud, who held that aggression stems mainly from a powerful *death wish* or instinct (thanatos) possessed by all persons. According to Freud, this instinct is initially aimed at self-destruction but is soon redirected outward, toward others. Freud believed that the hostile impulses it generates increase over time and, if not released periodically, soon reach high levels capable of generating dangerous acts of violence. It is interesting to note that a death instinct was not originally part of Freud's theories. Rather, he added it after witnessing the atrocities and wholesale slaughter of World War I. Freud also suggested that directly opposed to this death wish is another instinct, *eros*, which is focused on pleasure, love, and procreation. The complex relationship between these two powerful forces fascinated Freud, and is reflected in modern research on the potential links between sex and aggression discussed later in this chapter.

A related view was proposed by Konrad Lorenz, a Nobel Prize-winning scientist. Lorenz (1966, 1974) proposed that aggression springs mainly from an inherited *fighting instinct* that human beings share with many other species. Presumably, this instinct developed during the course of evolution because it yielded important benefits. For example, fighting serves to disperse populations over a wide area, thus ensuring maximum use of available natural resources. Further, because it is often closely related to mating, fighting helps assure that only the strongest and most vigorous individuals will pass their genes on to the next generation. Very similar views have been proposed by Ardrey (1976), who contends that because early in the development of our species "we either attacked or starved" (1976, p. 337), our ancestors quickly evolved into a species of hunters. It is our anatomical, physiological, and psychological adaptations to a life as hunters, Ardrey suggests, that underlie our strong and innate aggressive tendencies.

A third perspective suggesting that aggression is at least partly innate is provided by the field of *sociobiology* (Barash, 1977; Buss, 1991; Rushton, 1989). According to sociobiologists all aspects of social behavior, including aggression, can be understood in terms of evolution. Briefly, behaviors that help individuals get their genes into the next generation will become increasingly prevalent in the species' population. Since aggression aids the males of many species in obtaining mates, principles of natural selection will, over time, favor increasing levels of aggression, at least among males. Sociobiologists further contend that since human beings, too, evolved in the context of natural selection, our strong tendencies toward aggression behavior can be understood in this context. Thus, they are now part of our inherited biological nature.

Is there any basis for the views just described? Do biologically inherited tendencies toward aggression actually exist among human beings? Most social psychologists doubt that they do, primarily for two important reasons. First, they note that proponents of instinct views such as those of Freud and Lorenz use somewhat circular thinking. These theorists begin by observing that aggression is a common form of behavior. On the basis of this fact, they then reason that such behavior must stem from universal, built-in urges or tendencies. Finally, they use the high incidence of aggression as support for the presence of such instances and impulses! As you can see, this is questionable logic.

Second, and perhaps more important, several findings argue against the existence of universal, innate human tendencies toward aggression. Comparisons among various societies indicate that the level of at least some forms of aggression varies tremendously. For example, in Norway murder is a very rare event: Fewer than one person per 100 000 is a victim of homicide each year. In Canada this figure is triple the

Norwegian rate and in the United States it is more than eight times higher; but in part of New Guinea, it is almost *eight hundred* times higher! (Please see Figure 8.16.) Such huge differences in the incidence of aggression suggest that aggression is strongly influenced by social and cultural factors, and that even if it is based on innate tendencies, these are literally overwhelmed by other determinants of such behavior.

For these and other reasons, an overwhelming majority of social psychologists reject instinct theories of aggression. This does not imply, however, that they also reject any role of biological factors in such behavior. On the contrary, there is increasing awareness among social psychologists of the importance of biological factors in a wide range of social behavior (Nisbett, 1990). Further, evidence points to the conclusion that some biological factors do indeed predispose specific individuals toward aggression (Gladue, 1991; Mednick, Brennan, & Kandel, 1988). For example, several studies suggest that individuals arrested for violent crimes are considerably more likely than persons not arrested for such crimes to have suffered mild neurological damage during the prenatal period (Denno, 1982; Baker & Mendick, 1984). These and related findings indicate that biological factors do indeed play a significant role in at least some instances of aggression. However, this is still a far cry from the suggestion that human beings possess a universal, inherited instinct toward aggression. Theories such as those offered by Freud, Lorenz, and others, therefore, should be viewed as intriguing but largely unverified proposals concerning the origins of human violence.

AGGRESSION AS AN ELICITED DRIVE: THE MOTIVE TO HARM OR INJURE OTHERS

An alternative view concerning the nature of aggression, and one that continues to enjoy more support among psychologists, suggests that such behavior stems mainly from an externally elicited drive to harm or injure others. This approach is reflected in several different **drive theories** of aggression (e.g., Berkowitz, 1988, 1989; Feshbach, 1984). Such theories propose that external conditions (e.g., frustration, loss of face) arouse a strong motive to engage in harm-producing behaviors. This aggressive drive, in turn, leads to the performance of overt assaults against others. By far the most famous of these theories is the well-known *frustration-aggression hypothesis*. According to this view frustration leads to the arousal of a drive whose primary goal is that of

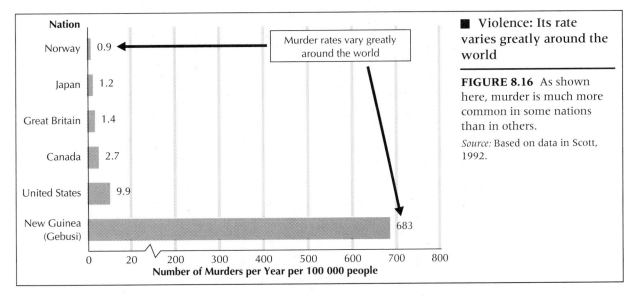

■ Violence: Its rate varies greatly around the world

FIGURE 8.16 As shown here, murder is much more common in some nations than in others.

Source: Based on data in Scott, 1992.

harming some person or object. This drive, in turn, leads to attacks against various targets—especially the source of frustration. Berkowitz (1989) has recently offered a sophisticated revision of this hypothesis; we'll consider it in detail in a later section.

Because they suggest that external conditions rather than innate tendencies are crucial in the occurrence of aggression, drive theories seem somewhat more optimistic about the possibility of preventing such behavior than instinct theories. Since being frustrated or thwarted in various ways is a common aspect of everyday life, however, drive theories, too, seem to leave us facing continuous—and often unavoidable—sources of aggressive impulses.

AGGRESSION AS A REACTION TO AVERSIVE EVENTS: THE ROLE OF NEGATIVE AFFECT

Think back over occasions when you have behaved in an aggressive manner. Now, try to remember how you felt at those times. The chances are good that you will recall feeling upset or annoyed. In short, you probably were experiencing some type of *negative affect* in situations where you aggressed against others. This relationship between negative, unpleasant feelings and overt aggression serves as the basis for a third theoretical perspective on aggression, sometimes known as the **cognitive neoassociationist** view (Berkowitz, 1984, 1988). According to this theory, exposure to aversive events (ones we prefer to avoid) generates negative affect (unpleasant feelings). These feelings, in turn, automatically activate tendencies toward both aggression and flight (efforts to escape from the unpleasant situation), as well as physiological reactions and thoughts or memories related to such experiences. Whether overt aggression then follows depends on several factors, such as higher levels of thought and cognition. For example, consider a woman shopping in a supermarket who is bumped by another shopper's cart. This experience is painful, and the shopper reacts with tendencies toward aggression, plus thoughts and memories related to similar unpleasant events. Then the other shopper apologizes profusely, explaining that she lost her footing on a wet spot on the floor. At this point the angry shopper reappraises the situation and decides that the incident was truly an accident. As a result her anger subsides, and aggression is unlikely.

Considerable evidence offers support for the accuracy of this theory. Individuals exposed to a wide range of unpleasant, aversive events do tend to behave more aggressively than persons not exposed to such conditions, even when their aggression cannot possibly eliminate the causes of such negative affect (Berkowitz, 1989). Further, negative affect, induced in several different ways, encourages aggressive thoughts and memories, as Canadian Brendan Rule and her colleagues showed (Rule, Taylor, & Dobbs, 1987). Thus, the cognitive neoassociationist theory seems to offer important insights into the origins and nature of aggressive behavior. Unfortunately, unpleasant events, and the negative affect they generate, are an all-too-common part of daily life. Thus, this modern approach is similar to earlier ones in at least one respect: It too suggests that instigations to aggression, if not aggression itself, are an ever-present fact of life.

AGGRESSION AS LEARNED SOCIAL BEHAVIOR

Yet another important perspective on aggression, the **social learning view**, is more of a general framework than a fully developed theory. This approach (Bandura, 1973; Baron & Richardson, 1994) emphasizes the fact that aggression, like other complex forms of social behavior, is largely *learned*. Human beings, this perspective contends, are *not* born with a large array of aggressive responses at their disposal. Rather, they must acquire these in much the same way that they acquire other complex forms of social behavior: through direct experience or by observing the behavior of others (i.e., social models; Bandura, 1973). Thus, depending on their past experience, people in different cultures learn to attack others in contrasting ways—by means of kung fu, blowguns, machetes, or revolvers. But this is not all that is learned where aggression is concerned. Through direct and vicarious experience, individuals also learn (1) which persons or groups are appropriate targets for aggression, (2) what actions by others either justify or actually require aggressive retaliation, and (3) what situations or contexts are ones in which aggression is either appropriate or inappropriate.

In short, the social learning perspective suggests that whether a specific person will aggress in a given situation depends on a vast array of factors, including that person's past experience, the current reinforcements associated with aggression, and many variables that shape the person's thoughts and perceptions concerning the appropriateness and potential effects of such behavior (refer to Figure 8.17). Since most if not all of these factors are open to change, the social learning approach is quite positive with respect to the possibility of preventing or controlling overt aggression. Indeed, it is more encouraging in this respect than any of the other views we have considered.

SOCIAL DETERMINANTS OF AGGRESSION: HOW OTHERS' ACTIONS, OR OUR UNDERSTANDING OF THEM, INFLUENCE AGGRESSION

Think back to the last time you lost your temper. What made you "lose your cool?" The chances are quite good that your anger, and any subsequent aggression, stemmed from the actions of another person. In fact, when asked to describe situations that made them angry, most persons refer to something another person said or did—

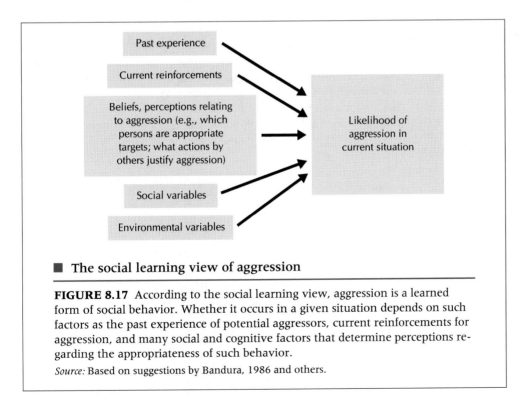

■ The social learning view of aggression

FIGURE 8.17 According to the social learning view, aggression is a learned form of social behavior. Whether it occurs in a given situation depends on such factors as the past experience of potential aggressors, current reinforcements for aggression, and many social and cognitive factors that determine perceptions regarding the appropriateness of such behavior.

Source: Based on suggestions by Bandura, 1986 and others.

something that caused them to become upset and to view aggression against this person as justified (Torestad, 1990). They are much less likely to mention purely physical events, such as a flat tire, bad weather, or the like. In short, aggression often stems from various social conditions that either initiate its occurrence or increase its intensity. As you can probably guess, many factors play a role in this regard. We'll examine several of these below.

FRUSTRATION: WHY NOT GETTING WHAT YOU WANT (AND WHAT YOU EXPECT) CAN SOMETIMES LEAD TO AGGRESSION

Suppose that you asked twenty people you know to name the single most important cause of aggression. How would they reply? The chances are good that a majority would answer, *frustration*. And if asked to define frustration, many would state, "The way I feel when something prevents me from getting what I want to get and expect to get in some situation." In short, many persons would indicate that in their experience, aggression often stems from interference with their efforts to reach various goals.

The widespread acceptance of such views stems, at least in part, from the famous **frustration-aggression hypothesis**, first proposed by Dollard and his colleagues more than fifty years ago (Dollard et al., 1939). In its original form, this hypothesis made the following sweeping assertions: (1) Frustration *always* leads to some form of aggression, and (2) aggression *always* stems from frustration (Dollard et al., 1939). In short, the theory held that frustrated persons always engage in some type of aggression and that all acts of aggression, in turn, result from frustration. Bold statements like these are always appealing—they are intellectually stimulating if nothing else. But growing evidence suggests that both portions are also far too sweeping in scope to be accurate.

First, it is now clear that frustrated individuals do not always respond with aggressive thoughts, words, or deeds. On the contrary, they show a wide variety of reactions to frustration, ranging from resignation and despair on the one hand to attempts to overcome the source of their frustration on the other.

Second, it is also apparent that *not* all aggression results from frustration. People aggress for many different reasons and in response to many different factors. For example, professional boxers hit and sometimes seriously injure others because it is their role to do so and because they wish to win valued prizes—not because of frustration. Similarly, during times of war, many pilots report that flying their planes is a source of intense pleasure, and that they bomb and strafe enemy targets while feeling elated, not frustrated. In these and many other cases, aggression definitely stems from factors other than frustration.

In view of these considerations, few social psychologists now accept the idea that frustration is the only, or even the most important, cause of aggression. Instead, most believe that it is simply one of a host of different factors that can potentially lead to aggression. Along these lines, Berkowitz (1989) has recently proposed a revised version of the frustration-aggression hypothesis that seems consistent with a large amount of existing evidence. According to this view, frustration is an aversive, unpleasant experience, and frustration leads to aggression because of this fact. In short, frustration sometimes produces aggression because of the basic relationship between negative feelings and aggressive behavior we described earlier in this chapter.

These suggestions seem to be quite straightforward, and they contribute much to our understanding of the role of frustration in aggression. In particular, they help explain why *unexpected* frustration and frustration that is viewed as *illegitimate* (e.g., the result of someone's whims or hostile motives) produce stronger aggression than frustration that is expected or viewed as legitimate. Presumably this is so because unexpected and illegitimate frustration generates stronger negative feelings than that which is expected or legitimate.

Going farther, Berkowitz (1989) also explains why frustration, even when strong, unexpected, and illegitimate, does not always lead to aggression. He notes that the negative feelings generated by frustration do initially produce tendencies toward aggression; but these tendencies are soon modified by higher-level cognitive processes. Individuals who have been frustrated may examine the nature of their feelings, attempt to understand *why* they have experienced frustration, consider the relative appropriateness of aggression and other possible reactions, and engage in efforts to control their anger or annoyance. Given the unpredictable outcome of these processes, it is hardly surprising that frustration does not always lead to aggression.

In sum, frustration is indeed one potential cause of overt aggression (Gustafson, 1989). It is certainly not the only cause behind such behavior, however, and is not necessarily the strongest or most important cause. Thus, it does not play the very central role in human aggression that many people seem to assume.

DIRECT PROVOCATION: WHEN AGGRESSION BREEDS AGGRESSION

Imagine the following scene: One morning you hand in an important report that your boss had asked you to write. That afternoon she storms into your office, throws the report onto your desk, and says, "Where did you ever learn to write? I've seen better from my eight-year-old son!" After this she continues, disparaging your report in every conceivable way. How do you react? If you are like most people, you probably make excuses or just stand there sullenly; after all, she's the boss, and there's not much else you can do. But all the while she is attacking your work, you are thinking such thoughts as "Who does she think she is?" "How dare she speak to me like that?" and "Just wait—I'll get even for this!"

This incident illustrates an important point about aggression: Often, it is the result of verbal or physical **provocation** from others. That is, when we are the victims of some form of aggression from others, we rarely "turn the other cheek"—at least not if we can help it. Instead, we tend to reciprocate, returning as much aggression as we have received, or perhaps slightly more. Many studies have provided evidence for such effects (Dengerink, Schnedler, & Covey, 1978; Ohbuchi and Ogura, 1984). In all these investigations, individuals provoked either verbally or physically by others tended to retaliate in kind. In fact, as we just noted, their reactions to such provocation were often stronger than the provocations themselves. This finding helps explain why aggression often spirals upward from mild taunts to stronger insults, and from pushing or shoving to kicks, blows—or worse (see Figure 8.18).

But what actions by others, precisely, serve as direct provocation? A study by Torestad (1990) provides some intriguing answers. Torestad asked teenagers to describe situations in which they became angry, then analyzed the more than 900 situations described to determine whether basic patterns could be uncovered. In fact, these were readily apparent. As shown in Table 8.2, participants in the study indicated that they were frequently angered by certain kinds of actions by others. At the top of the list was what might be described as *unreasonable* or *opinionated* behavior by others: instances in which other persons disagreed with participants' views and would not listen to reason in this respect. A close second was actions by others in which they unfairly *blamed* or *slandered* the participant. Among other types of behaviors that participants found to be anger- and aggression-provoking were direct insults, thoughtless or inconsiderate actions by others, teasing, nagging, and physical assault or harassment. Examples of these potential causes of anger and aggression are presented in Table 8.2.

■ Aggression: The dangerous spiral upward

FIGURE 8.18 Aggression often begins with the trading of verbal provocations—taunts, insults. But it may quickly escalate into physical violence.

Source: King Features Syndicate, 1990.

■ When asked to describe events that make them angry, individuals generally list ones that fall into the major categories shown here.

TABLE 8.2 Causes of anger

Category of Anger-Provoking Events	Example
Unreasonable Behavior	I say something I know is true but nobody believes me.
Unfair Blame, Slander	I am blamed for doing something I haven't done.
Direct Insults	Someone insults me and it is unjustified.
Thoughtless Behavior	People in high positions abuse their power.
Teasing	I am teased about my appearance.
Thwarted Plans	My parents don't allow me to go out in the evening.
Nagging, Yelling	Somebody takes his bad mood out on me.
Physical Harassment	My brother hits me without cause.
Frustration (Environmental)	I go to see a film listed in the paper, but when I get there it isn't playing.
Assaults on Belongings	Something I own is stolen or damaged.

Source: Based on data from Torestad, 1990.

INTERPRETING OTHERS' PROVOCATION: INTENTIONALITY AND ATTRIBUTION

While reactions to direct provocation from others generally follow the rule of *reciprocity*, it is important to note that this is not always the case. Several factors seem to determine whether, and to what extent, individuals choose to overlook provocation or to respond to it in kind. Perhaps the most important of these factors is the *perceived intentionality* of such provocation. When individuals conclude that provocation from another person was *intended*—purposely performed—they generally become quite angry and engage in strenuous efforts to reciprocate. If, instead, they conclude that provocation was *unintended*—the result of accident or factors beyond others' control—they are much less likely to lose their temper and behave aggressively. In short, *attributions* concerning the causes behind provocative actions by others play a key role in determining our reactions to them.

In another study carried out by Thomas Johnson and Brendan Rule of the University of Alberta (1986), when individuals perceived annoying actions by others as stemming from malicious intentions they were much more likely to retaliate than when they perceived the same actions as stemming from problems in the others' lives (i.e., receiving a low mark on an important exam). Additional evidence for the importance of attributions in determining response to provocation is provided by several experiments (e.g., Kremer and Stephens, 1983). The results of these studies suggest that when provoked or angered by another person, we do not always automatically dish out what we have received: Sometimes this is the case, but often our reactions reflect our interpretations of the causes behind provocative actions. As is true in many other contexts, therefore, our behavior toward others is strongly determined by our thoughts about them.

A related personal characteristic may potentially play an important role in the occurrence of aggression: the tendency to perceive hostile intent in others even when it is totally lacking. Presumably, the stronger this tendency—known as **hostile attributional bias**—the greater individuals' likelihood of engaging in reactive aggression in response to provocation from others.

Evidence that this is actually the case has been provided by several studies (Dodge, Murphy, & Buchsbaum, 1984). For example, in one revealing investigation, Dodge and Coie (1987) measured boys' tendency falsely to attribute hostile intentions to others and then observed these boys' behavior while playing with other children. Results supported the major prediction: The greater the boys' tendency to demonstrate hostile attributional bias, the greater their tendency to engage in aggression.

While much of the research concerned with the hostile attributional bias has focused on children, several recent investigations have extended these findings to adolescents and adults. For example, in one of these studies, Dodge et al. (1990) examined the relationship between hostile attributional bias and aggression among a group of male adolescents confined to a maximum security prison for juvenile offenders. These young men had been convicted of a wide range of violent crimes, including murder, sexual assault, kidnapping, and armed robbery. The researchers hypothesized that hostile attributional bias among these men would be related to the number of interpersonally violent crimes they had committed and to trained observers' ratings of the prisoners' tendencies to engage in reactive aggression in response to provocation. However, the researchers also predicted that the hostile attributional bias would *not* be related to observers' ratings of the young men's *proactive* aggression—aggressive acts performed in the absence of provocation for purposes of gaining dominance over others. In order to measure individual differences in hostile attributional bias, the researchers asked the prisoners to watch videotapes of incidents in which one person's actions toward another appeared to stem from hostile intent, appeared to stem from prosocial intent, or were ambiguous. After viewing each incident, participants indicated whether the actor's intent was hostile, helpful, ambiguous, or accidental in nature. Hostile attributional bias was measured in terms of the tendency to attribute hostile intent to others in situations where most observers would agree that it was *not* present. Results offered support for the major predictions: Hostile attributional bias was related to reactive but not to proactive aggression.

Taken as a whole, the findings reported by Dodge and other investigators indicate that hostile attributional bias is an important personal characteristic with respect to aggression. In short, the tendency to perceive malevolence or malice in the actions of others, even when it doesn't really exist, is an important trait—one that can involve individuals in a higher-than-average incidence of aggressive encounters with others.

HEIGHTENED AROUSAL:
EMOTION, COGNITION, AND AGGRESSION

Have you ever found yourself "over-reacting" to mild frustration or someone else's careless remark? If you have, you may later have realized that the recipient of your anger did not really deserve it; that you were "taking it out on" this person. How do we explain such incidents? Could it be that the emotional arousal from some earlier negative incident or mood had somehow transferred to your current situation? Growing evidence suggests that it could (Zillmann, 1983, 1988). Under some circumstances, heightened arousal—whatever its original source—can enhance aggression in response to annoyance, frustration, or provocation. In different experiments, arousal stemming from participation in competitive games (Christy, Gelfand, & Hartmann, 1971), vigorous exercise (Zillmann, 1979), and even some types of music (Rogers & Ketcher, 1979) has been found to facilitate subsequent aggression. Why is this the case? A compelling explanation is offered by **excitation transfer theory** (Zillmann, 1983, 1988).

This framework begins by noting that physiological arousal, however produced, dissipates slowly over time. As a result, some portion of such arousal may persist as a person moves from one situation to another. In the example above, some portion of the arousal you experienced as a result of a near miss in traffic may still be present as you approach the security gate in the airport terminal. Now, when you encounter minor annoyance, such arousal intensifies your emotional reactions to it. The result: You become enraged rather than just mildly irritated. When are such effects most likely to occur? Excitation transfer theory offers two related answers. First, they are most likely to take place when the persons involved are relatively unaware of their residual arousal—a common occurrence, since small elevations in arousal are difficult to detect (Zillmann, 1988). Second, such effects are also most likely to occur when the persons involved recognize the presence of such arousal but attribute it to events occurring in the present situation (Taylor et al., 1991). Thus, in the incident we have been describing, if you attributed your residual feelings of arousal to the delay you were now experiencing, your anger would be intensified. (Please see Figure 8.19 for a summary of excitation transfer theory as it applies to this situation.)

Interestingly, recent findings suggest that excitation transfer effects are most likely to occur when individuals experience a state known as **deindividuation**—one in which they experience reduced self-awareness and reduced awareness of social norms in a given situation (e.g., Prentiss-Dunn & Rogers, 1982). Deindividuation often occurs when individuals feel that they are an anonymous part of a large crowd. In fact, a combination of heightened arousal and deindividuation has been used to explain rioting (McPhail, 1991) such as the sports riots in Vancouver or Montreal in recent years, or the Los Angeles riots related to the beating of Rodney King. When they experience deindividuation, individuals may be less aware of any residual arousal and more likely to attribute it to external causes (Taylor et al., 1991). The result is that the likelihood of excitation transfer—and increased aggression—is enhanced. Thus, a sports fan who still feels some residual excitement after a playoff or championship game, leaves the stadium to mill with the crowd in the street. The reduced self-awareness or *deindividuation* induced by the crowd, together with this continuing excitement, increase the likelihood that the fan will get involved in any aggressive and antisocial behavior that occurs. Multiply this effect by the number of people in the crowd and you have the stage set for a riot. And often it only needs one incident to trigger it.

In sum, it appears that aggression, like many other forms of social behavior, is influenced by a complex interplay between emotion and cognition. As we noted in

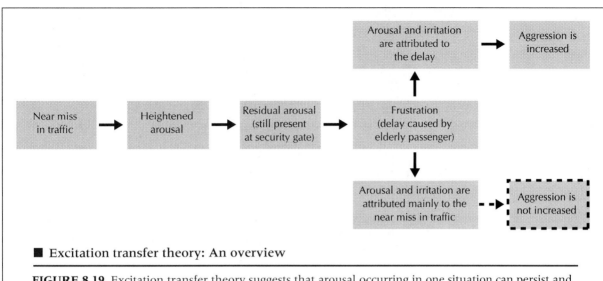

■ **Excitation transfer theory: An overview**

FIGURE 8.19 Excitation transfer theory suggests that arousal occurring in one situation can persist and can intensify emotional reactions in later, unrelated situations. Thus, the arousal generated by a near miss in traffic can intensify feelings of annoyance or frustration produced by later delays occurring at an airport security gate. Such effects are most likely to occur if the person involved is unaware of the residual arousal or attributes such arousal to events in the present (airport) situation.

Source: Based on suggestions by Zillmann, 1988.

chapter 2, cognition frequently influences emotional reactions, and these in turn often shape cognition. In other words, what we think influences what and how we feel, and what we feel influences what and how we think. And together, the complex pattern of thoughts and emotions we experience determines whether and to what degree we aggress against others.

EXPOSURE TO MEDIA VIOLENCE: THE EFFECTS OF WITNESSING AGGRESSION

List five films you have seen in recent months. Once you have formulated this list, answer the following question: How much aggression or violence did each of these films contain? How often did characters in these movies hit, shoot at, or otherwise attempt to harm others? Unless your moviegoing habits are somewhat unusual, you probably recognize that many popular films contain a great deal of violence—much more, we hope, than you will ever see in your real life. The fact that many films, television shows, and even televised sports events have a great deal of aggressive content has led social psychologists and others to pose the following question: Does exposure to a steady diet of such materials have any effect upon the behavior of viewers? This is an important question, so it is not surprising that it has been the subject of literally hundreds of research projects. The findings of these studies have not been entirely consistent; indeed, given the complexity of the issues addressed, this is only to be expected. However, taken together, they point to the following conclusion: *Exposure to media violence may in fact be one factor contributing to levels of violence in Canada and elsewhere.*

Evidence for the effects on aggression of media violence

Several different lines of research, conducted in very different ways, are consistent with the interpretation stated above. First, this interpretation is supported by many short-term laboratory studies. In the earliest of these investigations, Bandura, Ross, and Ross (1963) exposed young children to one of two short films. In one film, an adult model aggressed in various ways against an inflated toy clown known as a Bobo doll (e.g., she sat on the toy and punched it repeatedly in the nose). In the other, the same model behaved in a quiet and nonaggressive manner. Later the children in both groups were allowed to play freely in a room containing many toys, including a Bobo doll and other toys used by the model. Observations of the children's behavior revealed that those who had seen the model behave aggressively were much more likely to attack the Bobo doll than those who had not witnessed such behavior. These findings suggest that even very young children can acquire new ways of aggressing against others through exposure to filmed or televised violence.

In subsequent laboratory studies, subjects viewed actual television programs or films and were then given an opportunity to attack (supposedly) a real victim rather than an inflated toy (e.g., Liebert & Baron, 1972). Once again, results were the same: Participants in such studies (both children and adults) who witnessed media violence later demonstrated higher levels of aggression than participants who were not exposed to such materials (Josephson, 1987; Liebert, Sprafkin, & Davidson, 1989).

Additional and in some ways even more convincing evidence for the aggression-enhancing impact of media violence has emerged from a wide range of *field studies* conducted under more realistic conditions. Some of these investigations have used experimentation to examine the effects of prolonged exposure to media violence (e.g., Leyens et al, 1975; Parke et al., 1977). In these studies investigators exposed groups of children to contrasting amounts of media violence, and then observed the children's overt levels of aggression in natural situations (e.g., Leyens et al., 1975; Parke et al., 1977). Again, results indicated that youngsters exposed to violent movies or programs demonstrate higher levels of aggression than those exposed to nonviolent materials.

One of the most interesting field studies was a natural experiment carried out in Canada by Tannis Williams and her colleagues at the University of British Columbia (Williams, 1986). These researchers were able to take advantage of the fact that a small logging town in B.C. was about to have television (one channel of the CBC) introduced into its community for the first time. This enabled the research team to observe the impact of television in a natural setting. However, because any changes in observed levels of aggression before and after the introduction of television might be due to other societal or environmental changes, a control or comparison group was needed. Two other small logging towns in B.C. were found that were remarkably similar in terms of socioeconomic levels, population size, major sources of occupation, and geographical remoteness. The only major difference was that the first town, which they called "Notel," had no television at the beginning of the study, the second town, which they called "Unitel," had one channel (CBC), and the third town, "Multitel," had four channels (CBC and three American channels: ABC, CBS and NBC).

Children's level of physical and verbal aggression in the school playground was measured before the introduction of television to Notel (Time 1) and nearly two years after the introduction (Time 2). Ratings of aggressivness by peers and teacher were also obtained. Figure 8.20 shows that at Time 1 (before Notel had any television), the three towns showed virtually no difference in levels of aggression and a nonsignificant difference in levels of verbal aggression (Joy, Kimball, & Zabrack, 1986). However, almost two years after the introduction of one CBC channel, the children of Notel were significantly more aggressive both physically and verbally than in the other logging towns that already

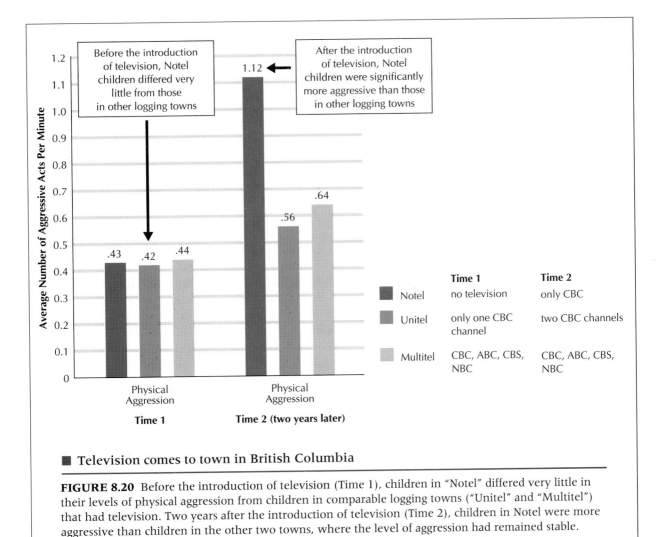

Television comes to town in British Columbia

FIGURE 8.20 Before the introduction of television (Time 1), children in "Notel" differed very little in their levels of physical aggression from children in comparable logging towns ("Unitel" and "Multitel") that had television. Two years after the introduction of television (Time 2), children in Notel were more aggressive than children in the other two towns, where the level of aggression had remained stable.

had some television. It should be noted that in this study children initially classified (at Time 1) as low and high in aggressiveness were similarly affected and showed the same levels of increase.

In chapter 1 we discussed the problems of interpretation that occur in natural experiments where, because random assignment of subjects is not possible, there may be confounding variables. This carefully conducted study attempted to rule out major confounds that might explain the increase in aggression in Notel at Time 2 (Williams, 1986). The use of two comparable towns where no significant changes in aggression were shown helps to rule out the possibility that greater aggressiveness at Time 2 in Notel occurred merely because the children were older. Another possibility might be significant changes in the population or economic conditions in Notel, but no such changes were reported during the two-year interval of the study. The researchers point out that the children in Unitel and Multitel had grown up with television (Joy, et al., 1986). It is possible that they may have been habituated to its level of violence by the time their behavior was measured initially in grades 1 and 2 (at Time 1). Children in Notel, in contrast, had reached grades 1 and 2 without television in their lives, and its impact may not have had sufficient time to wear off by Time 2 (two years after its introduction). Such an interpretation, while compelling, is speculative. What we can say is that the changes in levels of aggression in Notel children do appear to be due to the introduction of television, and are not of short-term duration in this real-life setting.

Other field studies, in contrast, have employed *systematic observation* (the correlational method) to study this issue. For example, consider a study conducted by Black and Bevan (1992). These researchers approached persons waiting in line to see either violent movies or ones lacking in violent content and asked them to complete a brief questionnaire designed to measure the tendency to engage in aggressive behavior. Other moviegoers were asked to complete the same questionnaire as they left the theater. Results were both revealing and unsettling. First, they indicated that, as the researchers predicted, scores on the aggression scale were higher among those who had just seen a violent movie than they were among persons waiting to see such films. In contrast, a similar increase in reported aggression did *not* occur among persons who watched nonaggressive movies. Second, individuals waiting to see the violent films scored higher on the aggression scale than those waiting to see the nonviolent films. As noted by Black and Bevan (1992, pp. 42–43), these findings, taken together, suggest "not only that films featuring violence attract an audience with a propensity for aggression, but that viewing the film further heightens this tendency."

At this point we should note that similar effects have also been observed among people who view aggressive sports events (Russell, 1981). Many sports involve actions by players that can be described as aggressive in nature—sports such as football, hockey, and boxing, to name just a few. And exposure to such sports does seem to increase aggression among viewers and fans (e.g., Russell, 1981).

Finally, other investigators have conducted long-term studies in which the amount of media violence watched by individuals as children is related statistically to their rated levels of aggression several years—or even decades—later (e.g., Eron, 1982; Huesmann, 1982). Once again, results indicate that these two variables are indeed related: The more media violence individuals watch as children, the higher their rated levels of aggression as adults.

At this point we should insert an additional note of caution: Not all findings obtained to date have been consistent with the view that exposure to media violence (or participation in aggressive video games) increases actual aggression (Freedman, 1984). Further, the evidence for relatively short-term effects of viewing violence are more firmly established by research evidence than the potential long-term effects of such experience. Still, taken as a whole, existing evidence does seem to offer at least moderately strong support for the conclusion that exposure to media violence can contribute, along with many other factors, to the occurrence of aggressive behavior (Wood, Wong, & Chachere, 1991). The importance of factors other than media in contributing to levels of violence in society is underlined when you consider that Canada and the U.S. have virtually the same media but very different levels of violence.

The fact that exposure to media violence can facilitate similar behavior among viewers is, by itself, somewhat unsettling. Perhaps even more disturbing, however, is evidence pointing to the conclusion that even inanimate objects can sometimes encourage dangerous instances of aggression. For a discussion of such possibilities, please see the "Classic Contributions" section on the following page.

The Role of Aggressive Cues:
Does the Trigger Sometimes Pull the Finger?

Suppose that someone you knew owned a large collection of guns, and that one evening you got into an argument with this person while sitting in the room containing the personal arsenal. Would you be more likely to lose your temper and behave aggressively in this setting than elsewhere? In other words, would the presence of racks of weapons on the walls actually facilitate the likelihood of aggression? (Assume, by the way, that all the guns are unloaded!)

According to one noted authority on aggression, Leonard Berkowitz (1969, 1974), this might well be the case. He has proposed that one important determinant of aggression is the presence of what he terms **aggressive cues**. These are stimuli that have been associated or linked with aggression in the past. Berkowitz suggests that such aggressive cues serve to elicit aggressive responses from persons who have been angered or otherwise made ready to aggress. Thus, the greater the presence of such cues on the scene, the higher the level of aggression that is likely to occur.

What does this have to do with the gun collection example presented above? According to Berkowitz, the objects in this collection (guns) have been intimately associated with aggression on numerous occasions. As a result, they become aggressive cues, and their mere presence on the scene may facilitate aggressive behavior *even if they are not themselves used in such actions*. Support for this reasoning comes from a famous experiment by Berkowitz and LePage (1967). In this study, male participants were first angered or not angered by an accomplice and were then provided with an opportunity to aggress against this person by means of electric shock. (Participants were given an opportunity to evaluate the accomplice's work by giving him from one to nine "shocks." The lower their evaluation, the higher the number of shocks.)

In the control condition (*no-objects condition*), only the equipment used by subjects ostensibly to deliver shocks to the accomplice was present. In two other conditions, in contrast, a .38 caliber revolver and a 12-gauge shotgun were lying on the table near the shock button. In one of these groups, it was explained that the weapons were being used in another study and had no connection with the present experiment (*unassociated-weapons* condition). In the other, participants were told that the weapons were being used by the accomplice in another study that he was conducting (*associated-weapons* condition). Berkowitz and LePage (1967) predicted that the mere physical presence of the weapons would facilitate aggression by the angry subjects, but would fail to enhance aggression by those who had not been angered. As you can see from Figure 8.21, this is precisely what occurred. Individuals who had previously been angered by the victim delivered more shocks to the accomplice in the presence of weapons than in their absence. There was little difference between the associated- and unassociated-weapons conditions, however.

These findings seem to suggest that the presence of weapons can indeed facilitate aggression, even if the weapons themselves are not used in the subsequent assaults. As Berkowitz himself has put it (1968, p. 22):

> Guns not only permit violence, they can stimulate it as well. The finger pulls the trigger, but the trigger may also be pulling the finger.

Unfortunately, the relatively neat picture provided by this initial study has been somewhat complicated by subsequent research (Buss, Booker, & Buss, 1972; Turner and Simon, 1974). These later studies suggest that the **weapons effect** reported by Berkowitz

▶

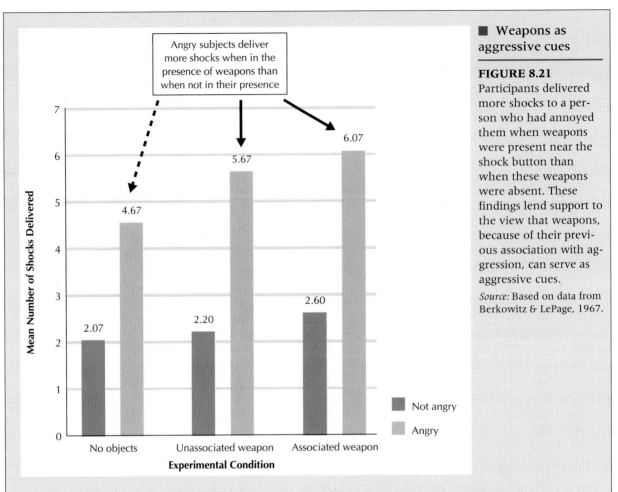

Weapons as aggressive cues

FIGURE 8.21
Participants delivered more shocks to a person who had annoyed them when weapons were present near the shock button than when these weapons were absent. These findings lend support to the view that weapons, because of their previous association with aggression, can serve as aggressive cues.

Source: Based on data from Berkowitz & LePage, 1967.

Angry subjects deliver more shocks when in the presence of weapons than when not in their presence

2.07
4.67
2.20
5.67
2.60
6.07

Mean Number of Shocks Delivered

Not angry
Angry

No objects   Unassociated weapon   Associated weapon
Experimental Condition

and LePage (1967) may occur only under relatively restricted conditions (e.g., when participants have no suspicions concerning the presence of these unusual items in a research laboratory; Carlson, Marcus-Newhall, & Miller, 1990). Regardless of the ultimate validity of the weapons effect, however, there can be little doubt that Berkowitz's more general suggestion that aggression is *pulled* from without rather than merely *pushed* from within has gained widespread acceptance among social psychologists. In this respect, certainly, his research on the impact of aggressive cues has been highly influential.

The impact of media violence: Why does it occur?

The finding that exposure to violence on television or in the movies can encourage similar behavior among viewers has important implications. It suggests that steps designed to limit such exposure, or to reduce the violent content in TV and Hollywood offerings, might help to lessen one potential cause of aggression. But assuming that such effects occur, another question arises: *How*, precisely, does exposure to media violence stimulate increased aggression among viewers? Several processes seem to play a role.

First, exposure to media violence weakens the *inhibitions* of viewers against engaging in such behavior. After watching many characters—including heroes and heroines—handle many situations through aggression, some viewers feel less restrained about engaging in similar actions themselves. "If *they* can do it," such persons seem to reason, "then so can I."

Second, exposure to media violence provides viewers with new techniques for attacking and harming others not previously at their disposal. And such behaviors, once acquired, tend to be used when individuals are angered or annoyed by others.

Third, watching others engage in aggressive actions can influence viewers' cognitions in several different ways (e.g., Berkowitz, 1984, 1988). Violent materials can serve to *prime* aggressive thoughts and memories, making these more readily available in viewers' cognitive systems. (See our discussion of priming in chapter 2.) Such thoughts and memories may then serve to pave the way for overt aggressive actions. Interestingly, priming can influence the impact of media violence in another way. When individuals have been exposed to aggressive words—words such as *insult, stab, anger*—the aggressive schema activated can increase their interest in watching violent films or television programs (Langley, O'Neal, Craig, & Yost,1992).

Finally, repeated exposure to media violence may reduce emotional sensitivity to violence and its harmful consequences. That is, after watching countless murders, fights, and assaults, viewers may become *desensitized* to such materials and show lessened emotional reaction to them (Geen, 1981). Then they may find real-life aggression, too, less disturbing; and they may demonstrate reduced empathy toward its victims, even when the victims evidence signs of considerable pain and suffering (Baron, 1971, 1979).

In sum, media violence seems to enhance the occurrence of overt aggression for several different reasons, and through several different mechanisms. Given this fact, it is not at all surprising that such materials influence the behavior of children and adults alike.

CULTURE AND AGGRESSION: THE SOCIAL CONTEXT OF VIOLENCE

Early in this chapter, we called attention to the existence of huge variations in the rate of violence around the world. For example, murder rates in the United States are ten to twenty times higher than in other industrialized nations; but in several tribal societies they are fifty to eighty times higher (Scott, 1992). Perhaps a more concrete example—one that places such numbers in a specific context—will prove helpful.

Aggression: The role of microculture

In the Mexican state of Oaxaca, there are two Zapotec villages located less than four miles apart. The two villages have existed in their present locations for at least 450 years, and in terms of language, religion, economics, and virtually every other aspect, they are identical. Yet the murder rate in one is more than six times higher than in the other. Thus, while residents of the nonviolent village might expect to witness one murder every fourteen years, those in the violent village could expect to see one every eighteen months to two years (Fry, 1990). What accounts for this difference? Careful comparison of the villages suggests that the key difference lies in what sociologists term *microculture*—cultural differences between groups within a larger culture. In this case, it appears that the nonviolent villagers view themselves as peaceful people who have a high amount of respect for others. In contrast, those in the violent village perceive themselves as tough and aggressive; they have a much higher rate of fist fights, spouse abuse, and, of course, homicides. What underlies these differences? In attempting to explain them, Scott (1992) calls attention to what might be termed *social inertia*—the tendency of a social system or culture to remain unchanged and stable in certain dimensions once it is established. Researchers theorize that when these two villages were founded, they were organized along different lines, perhaps by persons with different perspectives on aggression. The norms established in those long-gone days have persisted, and find expression in the sharply contrasting rates of violence we now observe.

In short, *culture* does seem to play an important role in aggression. Growing evidence suggests that it determines not only the rate of violence but the forms it generally takes and the targets selected. Various cultures hold contrasting beliefs about the appropriateness and reasons for aggression and consequently have different child-rearing practices. For example, a study by Osterwell and Nagano-Nakamura (1992) indicates that Japanese mothers view aggression as a natural part of their children's behavior but believe that it should be expressed *within* the family, where it can be regulated and so do little serious harm. In contrast, Israeli mothers believe that aggression is mainly a response to external provocations, and they believe that aggression should be expressed outside the family rather than within it. Such contrasting beliefs about aggression influence child-rearing practices in various cultures, and these, in turn, help explain why cultural differences in the rate and intensity of many forms of aggression tend to persist over time (Fraczek & Kirwil, 1992).

THE PREVENTION AND CONTROL OF AGGRESSION: SOME USEFUL TECHNIQUES

An underlying theme in this discussion of aggression—perhaps the most important theme—has been this: Aggression stems from the complex interplay between a variety of external events (e.g., provocation, frustration), cognitions concerning these events (e.g., attributions, memories), and individual differences (e.g., a tendency to be hostile). As such, aggression is definitely *not* a "programmed," automatic response. To the extent you accept this point of view, you will also find our next proposal to be a reasonable one: Aggression can be prevented or at least reduced. It is *not* an inevitable pattern, either for individuals or for our entire species. On the contrary, several techniques for controlling its occurrence or intensity exist and can be put to practical use (Baron & Richardson, 1994). In this final section, we'll consider several of these procedures.

PUNISHMENT: AN EFFECTIVE DETERRENT TO VIOLENCE?

Throughout history, most societies have used **punishment** as a means of deterring human violence. Nations have established harsh punishment for such crimes as murder, rape, and assault. Are such tactics actually effective? In one sense, of course, they are. Persons who are imprisoned or executed for performing violent acts cannot repeat these offenses. But what about deterrence: Will the threat of severe punishment prevent individuals from engaging in aggressive acts in the first place? The pendulum of scientific opinion on this issue has swung back and forth for decades. At present, however, the weight of existing evidence seems to suggest that if used in an appropriate manner, punishment *can* be an effective deterrent to violence. In order for it to succeed, however, several conditions must be met (Bower & Hilgard, 1981).

First, punishment must be prompt—it must follow aggression as soon as possible. Second, it must be strong—it must be of sufficient magnitude to be highly aversive to potential recipients. Third, it must be very likely—the likelihood that it will follow aggressive actions must be quite high. Unfortunately, of course, these conditions are precisely the ones lacking from the criminal justice systems of many nations. In many societies, the delivery of punishment for aggressive actions is delayed for months or even years; the magnitude of punishment itself is variable from one locale to another; and it is well known that many violent crimes go unpunished—no one is ever apprehended, tried, or convicted of them. In view of these facts, it is hardly surprising that punishment has often seemed to fail as a deterrent to violent crime. The dice, so to speak, are heavily loaded against the possibility of its succeeding.

In sum, the fact that punishment does not currently seem to be successful in deterring the rising tide of violence in many nations does not necessarily mean that punishment itself is useless. Rather, it may simply stem from the fact that this procedure is being used in ways that virtually guarantee its failure. If these conditions were changed, we believe, the potential impact of punishment might well be enhanced. And then the safety and well-being of countless innocent victims might also be better protected.

CATHARSIS: DOES GETTING IT OUT OF YOUR SYSTEM REALLY HELP?

Are devices such as the one shown in Figure 8.22 of any use? In other words, does somehow blowing off steam really help individuals get rid of—or at least control—their aggressive impulses? The belief that such activities are effective in this respect is very widespread. Many persons accept some version of what psychologists describe as the **catharsis hypothesis** (Dollard et al., 1939)—the idea that participation in activities that allow individuals to vent their anger and hostility in some relatively safe way will actually reduce later aggression. Presumably, such activities yield two important benefits: (1) They help to reduce emotional tension; and (2) since they help eliminate anger, they reduce the likelihood of more dangerous forms of aggression.

However, research provides little confirmation of such suggestions. First, any relief of emotional tension appears to be only temporary (Zillman, 1988), particularly if the person is reminded of or relives the original frustration. Second, research indicates that overt aggression is *not* reduced by (1) watching scenes of filmed or televised violence (Geen, 1978), (2) attacking inanimate objects (Mallick & McCandless, 1966), or (3) aggressing verbally against others. Indeed, there is some evidence that aggression may actually be increased by each of these conditions.

■ Catharsis: Is it really effective?

FIGURE 8.22 Can the tendency to aggress against others actually be reduced by devices designed to let people release their aggressive impulses? Existing evidence casts doubt on the widespread belief that such catharsis is effective for this purpose.

Contrary to popular belief, then, catharsis does not appear to be as effective a means for reducing aggression as is widely assumed. Because of the strong impact of cognition upon arousal, feelings of anger and irritation may quickly reappear when individuals encounter or merely think about the persons who previously annoyed them. For this reason, catharsis may be less effective in producing long-term reductions in aggression than has often been assumed.

COGNITIVE INTERVENTIONS: THE ROLE OF APOLOGIES AND ACCOUNTS

Imagine the following scene: You are waiting for another person with whom you have an appointment. She is late, and as time passes, you become more and more upset. Finally, fully thirty minutes after the agreed-upon time, she shows up. Before you can say a word, she apologizes profusely: "I'm so sorry. My car wouldn't start. Then, I got stuck in a traffic jam on the highway. I'm really upset; please forgive me." Would you be angry and criticize this person severely? Probably you would not. Her apology—an admission of wrongdoing plus a request for your forgiveness—would go a long way toward defusing your annoyance. Of course, your reactions would depend strongly on the nature of her excuses. Research findings suggest that ones that make reference to causes beyond the excuse-giver's control are much more effective than ones that refer to events within this person's control (e.g., "Sorry... I just forgot"; Weiner et al., 1987).

In addition, excuses or explanations for provocative actions (sometimes termed *causal accounts*) that appear to be *sincere* and are *specific* in nature—provide a clear and detailed explanation of the factors involved—are much more effective in defusing anger and subsequent aggression than excuses that appear to be insincere or are lacking in detail (e.g., Shapiro, Buttner, & Barry, 1993).

In sum, systematic research on the effects of cognitive interventions such as apologies and reasonable explanations confirm informal observations about the effectiveness of such procedures: In many cases, they do go a long way toward reducing anger aroused by provocative actions and so also toward preventing overt aggression (e.g., Baron, 1988; Ohbuchi, Kameda, & Agarie, 1989). In short, while it is often difficult to admit wrongdoing and to say "I'm sorry," the value of doing so may well make this effort worthwhile. However, cognitive processes and interpretation of aggression can have both positive and negative results in the area of spousal abuse (see "On the Applied Side–Cognitive Processes in Spousal Abuse").

SOCIAL PSYCHOLOGY: ON THE APPLIED SIDE

Cognitive Processes in Spousal Abuse: A Double-edged Sword

One area of aggression where cognitive processes, especially attribution, can be a double-edged sword is in the prevention and treatment of spousal abuse. On the one hand, abusers often use cognitive distortions about the abuse in order to direct blame away from themselves or to minimize their assaultive behavior. For example, they have been found to make external attributions for their abuse (Henderson & Hewstone, 1984; Shields & Hanneke, 1983), or

►

they may recall an assault in such a way that it minimizes the violence, its frequency, and its consequences (Ganley, 1981; Sonkin, Martin, & Walker, 1986). On the other hand, treatments for spousal abuse make use of these same cognitive processes by challenging the often unrealistic or self-excusing cognitions of spousal abusers.

Don Dutton of the University of British Columbia has been involved in research and treatment of male abusers (or wife assaulters) over a number of years. His own research (Dutton, 1987; Kennedy & Dutton, 1989) and that of others (Straus, Gelles, & Steinmetz, 1980) has shown that spousal abuse is often under-reported and is surprisingly prevalent. For example, a survey of spousal abuse levels in Alberta found that 11.2 percent of men reported they had used violence against their partners in the previous year (Kennedy & Dutton, 1989). This is very similar to the 11.3 percent found in a 1985 United States national survey (Straus & Gelles, 1985). While milder forms of physical and verbal abuse by both sexes are not uncommon in intimate relationships (Sigelman, Berry, & Wiles, 1984), when physical injury requiring treatment occurs, in 94 percent of the cases the victim is female and in only 14 percent of the cases is the victim male. (Berk, Berk, Loseke, & Rauma, 1981).

Dutton's own research has examined both wife-assaulters and their treatment. In one study of wife assaulters (Dutton, 1986a), the explanations of those who had voluntarily come for treatment and those who had been referred by the courts was compared. Subjects were asked to describe their most recent assaultive action in detail. Their explanations for the cause of the violence were classified in terms of *locus of attribution* (whether the assaulter assigned responsibility to the self, the victim, or the situation) and the extent to which they *minimized* the severity, the frequency, or the effect of the assault. As Figure 8.23 shows, self-referred men were more likely to take responsibility for assault (52 percent) than court-referred men (14 percent). Court-referred men were more likely to attribute assault to the situation or circumstances (e.g., acute stress or intoxication) or to the behavior or characteristics of the victim (e.g.,

she showed disrespect). Despite their tendency to accept blame for the assault, many self-referred men minimized their assaultive behavior, that is, their descriptions underestimated the frequency of the assaults, the severity of their own actions, and the consequences (in term of physical injury) for the victim. Fifty-two percent of the self-referred men showed this highly minimizing pattern, whereas only 18 percent of the court-referred men did. This minimization is explained by Dutton as a way that the self-referred men could "compensate for acknowledging personal responsibility" (1986a, p. 388). Such research can aid professionals in understanding how abusive behavior is sustained and can help the therapist in devising treatments.

Most treatments of wife assaulters use cognitive and behavioral techniques stemming from Bandura's social learning theory of aggression (1979; Dutton, 1992). A major component of treatment is to confront the self-excusing and minimizing cognitions of assaulters. The reality of the abuse, its consequences, and the assaulter's responsibility is repeatedly pointed out. In parallel, treatment attempts to alter the assaulters unrealistic expectations about his wife and to build empathy for her. Often, the latter is accomplished by comparing her experience to the assaulter's own experience as a child. It is not uncommon for abusers to have been abused themselves or to have observed abuse during childhood (Kalmus, 1984; Straus et al., 1980). Such empathy can increase the probability that the abuser's own guilt will act as a deterrent to future assaults. A further part of treatment, is to improve assertive communication skills as part of teaching nonviolent conflict resolution. Assaulters are often found to have poor communication skills and to resort to physical aggression as a learned response to conflict situations in the family. Finally, assaulters are taught to recognize and manage their anger. As part of this process, the individual might keep an "anger diary" in which he detailed the situations and stimuli that initiate anger and his own physical and cognitive responses to it.

Do such treatment techniques work? This is an important question because of the devastating effects of continued spousal abuse for all members of a family. While arrest has been shown to have some deterrent effect, in many cases this appears to be short-lived (Dutton, 1992). Can treatment reduce the tendency to re-offend? Studies seem to indicate that it can, even for involuntary recipients (those who have been referred for treatment by the courts). Dutton (1986b) compared men arrested and convicted of wife assault who received no treatment, with a similar group of convicted men who received four months of treatment (as described above) by the order of the courts. Three years after their conviction, 40 percent of the untreated group had repeated assaults according to police records. However, only 4 percent of treated men had re-offended. Further, where couples had remained together, 84 percent of wives reported no acts of severe violence since termination of treatment. Results of this and similar programs (Edleson & Grusznski, 1988; Edleson, Syers, & Brygger, 1987; Shepard, 1987) suggest that mandatory treatment for those convicted of wife assault can have a significant impact in improving their control and in diminishing recidivism.

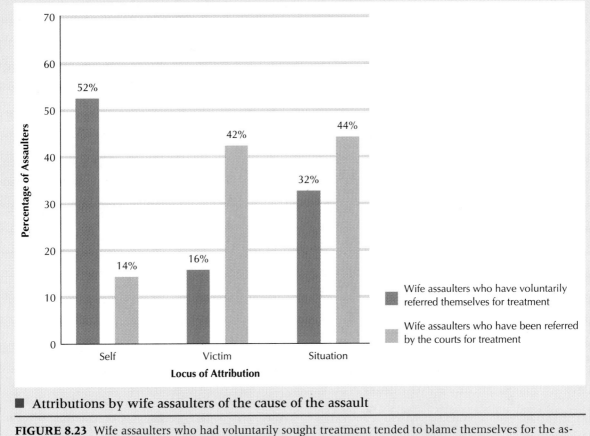

■ Attributions by wife assaulters of the cause of the assault

FIGURE 8.23 Wife assaulters who had voluntarily sought treatment tended to blame themselves for the assault. However, wife assaulters who had been referred to treatment through the court system tended to blame the victim (their wife) or the situation (stress, being drunk).

Source: Based on data in Dutton , 1986.

Prosocial behavior refers to acts of helping that have no obvious benefit to the person who helps.

RESPONDING AND NOT RESPONDING TO EMERGENCIES

Latané and Darley proposed a decision-making model to predict helping responses in emergency situations. Individuals must make the appropriate decision at each of five steps in order to engage in a prosocial act: attending to the emergency, perceiving that it is an emergency, assuming responsibility, determining what needs to be done, and deciding to provide help. Other research indicates that dispositional factors are also involved, and a combination of characteristics constitutes the *altruistic personality*.

FACTORS INFLUENCING ALTRUISTIC BEHAVIOR

Helping behavior is influenced by the presence of helpful models, the potential helper's emotional state, feelings of attraction toward the recipient, and the degree to which the victim is perceived to be responsible for the problem. Some people are more likely to seek help than others. Though receiving help may seem to be a positive experience, it is often uncomfortable and threatening to one's self-esteem.

Studies in Israel indicate that help-seeking is more likely among individuals familiar with a communal experience (living in a kibbutz) than among those with an individualistic background (living in a city). Also, those raised on a kibbutz were most likely to seek help when the group needed it, while city dwellers were most likely to seek help when they needed it as individuals.

THEORETICAL PERSPECTIVES ON AGGRESSION

Aggression—the intentional infliction of harm on others—has been attributed to many different causes. *Instinct theories*, such as the ones proposed by Freud and Lorenz, suggest that aggression stems from innate urges toward destructive actions. *Drive theories* suggest that aggression stems from externally generated motives to harm or injure others. In contrast, modern perspectives (the *neoassociationist* and *social learning views*) suggest that aggression stems from negative reactions to aversive experiences, memories, cognitions, learning, and present reinforcement or punishments for aggressive actions.

SOCIAL DETERMINANTS OF AGGRESSION

Many acts of aggression are triggered by the words or deeds of persons with whom the aggressor interacts, or by social conditions generally. *Frustration*, interference with goal-directed behavior, can facilitate aggression, perhaps because of the negative feelings it generates. *Direct provocations* from others are an important cause of aggression. Attribution and interpretation of others' provocation will often determine retaliation. We are especially likely to retaliate when such actions appear to stem from malevolent intent. There are some individuals who perceive hostile intent behind others' actions even when this is lacking and are, therefore, more aggressive than those without such *hostile attributional bias*. *Heightened arousal* can increase aggression, depending upon the complex interplay between emotions and cognitions. Cognitions sometimes shape emotions and hence aggression. Considerable evidence suggests that exposure to *media violence* (in films or television shows) can increase aggression on the part of viewers.

THE REDUCTION OF AGGRESSION

Several techniques are effective in reducing aggression. *Punishment* can serve as an effective deterrent to aggression if it is delivered swiftly, it is intense, and its likelihood of occurrence is high. Participation in *cathartic activities* (e.g., vigorous nonaggressive behaviors) can sometimes lower arousal and anger. But such reductions appear to be temporary, and anger can readily reemerge when individuals bring thoughts and memories associated with aggression (or past sources of provocation) to mind.

Direct *apologies* and *reasonable explanations* for provocative actions are often highly effective in reducing anger and subsequent aggression. Explanations for spousal abuse given by the abusers can relieve themselves of blame. However, therapeutic intervention can also utilize knowledge about the kinds of excuses and justifications used by abusers in its attempt to alter cognitions and aid in control of aggressive behavior.

Aggression Behavior directed toward the goal of harming or injuring another living being who is motivated to avoid such treatment.

Aggressive Cues Stimuli that, because of previous association with aggression, acquire the capacity to elicit such behavior.

Altruistic Behavior Acts that suggest an unselfish concern for the welfare of others, are costly for the individual who behaves altruistically, and sometimes involve risk.

Altruistic Personality The combination of dispositional variables that make an individual more likely to engage in altruistic behavior. Included are an empathic self-concept, belief in a just world, feelings of social responsibility, internal locus of control, and low egocentrism.

Belief in a Just World The tendency to believe that the world is a predictable and fair place in which good behavior is rewarded and bad behavior punished.

Bystander Apathy Indifference on the part of witnesses to an emergency; formerly assumed to explain bystanders' failure to help a stranger in distress. Research indicates, however, that bystanders are often quite concerned by the distress of a stranger; their failure to help is based on quite different factors.

Bystander Effect The finding that as the number of bystanders witnessing an emergency increases, the likelihood of each bystander's responding, and the speed of responding, decrease.

Catharsis Hypothesis The view that providing angry persons with an opportunity to engage in vigorous but noninjurious activities will reduce their level of emotional arousal and lower their tendencies to aggress against others.

Cognitive Neoassociationist View A theory suggesting that aversive experiences generate negative affect, which in turn activates tendencies toward both aggression and flight. Which of these actions follows depends in part on higher-level cognitive processes.

Deindividuation A psychological state characterized by reduced self-awareness and major shifts in perception; encourages wild, impulsive forms of behavior, including aggression. Deindividuation is encouraged by external conditions such as anonymity.

Diffusion of Responsibility The presence of multiple bystanders at the scene of an emergency, resulting in the responsibility for taking action being shared among all members of the group. As a result of diffusion of responsibility, each individual feels less responsible and is less likely to act than if he or she were alone.

Drive Theories Theories suggesting that aggression stems from external conditions that arouse the motive to harm or injure others. The most famous of these theories is the frustration-aggression hypothesis.

Egocentrism The tendency to be primarily concerned with oneself and to hold individualistic and competitive values.

Empathy The tendency to respond to another person's emotional state with a vicarious emotional reaction that resembles what the other person is experiencing. For example, a person who observes someone in distress may also feel distressed.

Excitation Transfer Theory A theory suggesting that arousal produced in one situation can persist and intensify emotional reactions occurring in subsequent situations.

Frustration-Aggression Hypothesis The suggestion that frustration is a very powerful determinant of aggression.

Hostile Attributional Bias The tendency to perceive others' actions as stemming from hostile intent even when this is not clearly the case.

Instinct Theory A view suggesting that specific forms of behavior (e.g., aggression) stem from innate tendencies that are universal among members of a given species.

Internal Locus of Control The belief that you are not at the mercy of outside forces but can behave in such a way as to make a difference—to maximize good outcomes and minimize bad ones.

Pluralistic Ignorance A phenomenon that can occur when multiple bystanders witness an emergency: Each interprets the event in part on the basis of what the others do or say, but when none of them is sure about what is happening, all hold back and pretend that everything is all right. Each then uses this "information" to justify not responding.

Prosocial Behavior Acts that benefit others rather than the person who carries them out.

Provocation Actions by others that are perceived as acts of aggression deriving from hostile intentions.

Punishment Procedures in which aversive consequences are delivered to individuals each time they engage in specific actions. Under appropriate conditions, punishment can serve as an effective deterrent to human aggression.

Self-concept Encompassing Empathy An individual's perception of himself or herself as responsible, socialized, self-controlled, interested in making a good impression, conforming in order to achieve, and tolerant.

Social Learning View A perspective suggesting that aggression is a complex form of learned behavior.

Social Responsibility A social norm to the effect that each of us has a responsibility to do our best to help others, taking care of those in need.

Weapons Effect The facilitation of aggression by the presence of weapons even when the weapons are not used in the aggressive actions performed.

FOR MORE INFORMATION

Clark, M. S. (Ed.). (1991). *Prosocial behavior*. Newbury Park, CA: Sage.

A review of the current status of research on prosocial behavior, with individual chapters written by those most active in this field of inquiry. Included are such topics as empathy, volunteerism, mood, and help-seeking.

Eisenberg, N. (1985). *Altruistic emotion, cognition, and behavior*. Hillsdale, NJ: Erlbaum.

Two of the crucial factors determining altruism—emotions and cognitions—are the central focus of this book. Specific topics include sympathy, conceptions of altruism, and moral decision making.

Baenninger, R. (Ed.). (1991). *Targets of violence and aggression*. Amsterdam: Elsevier/North-Holland.

This book deals with aggression toward targets that are either helpless or unable to retaliate. Separate chapters (each written by a different expert) examine such important and timely topics as human aggression toward other species, child abuse, athletes as targets of aggression, aggression toward homosexuals, and aggression along roadways. A comprehensive overview of what we currently know about several especially distressing forms of violence.

Baron, R. A., & Richardson, D. R. (1994). *Human aggression* (2nd ed.). New York: Plenum.

A broad introduction to current knowledge about human aggression. Separate chapters examine the biological, social, environmental, and personal determinants of aggression. Additional chapters examine the development of aggression and the occurrence of aggression in many natural settings.

Geen, R. G. (1991). *Human aggression*. Pacific Grove, CA: Brooks/Cole.

A well-written and relatively brief overview of research findings concerning aggressive behavior. One unique chapter integrates laboratory research on aggression with findings in behavioral medicine concerning potential links between hostility and heart disease.

Chapter NINE

Groups and Individuals:
The Consequences of Belonging

···

Groups: Their Nature and Function

Group Formation: Why Do People Join?/How Groups Function: Roles, Status, Norms, and Cohesiveness

Groups and Task Performance: The Benefits—and Costs—of Working with Others

Social Facilitation: Performance in the Presence of Others/Groups versus Individuals: Which Has the Edge in Task Performance?/Social Loafing: Letting Others Do the Work in Group Tasks

Decision Making by Groups: How It Occurs, the Outcomes It Yields, and the Pitfalls It Faces

The Decision-making Process: How Groups Move toward Consensus/The Nature of Group Decisions: Moderation or Polarization?/Decision Making by Groups: Some Potential Pitfalls

Leadership: Its Nature and Impact in Groups

The Trait Approach: Are Leaders Born or Made?/Gender Differences in Leadership: Do Male and Female Leaders Differ?/Leader Effectiveness: Two Influential Views/Transformational Leadership: Leadership through Vision and Charisma/Cultural Differences in Leadership in American and Asian Corporations

SPECIAL SECTIONS

SOCIAL PSYCHOLOGY: ON THE APPLIED SIDE
    Signing the Meech Lake Accord: An Example of Groupthink?

Throughout this book, we have emphasized the importance of group belonging. One major theme has been the impact of a person's cultural group on his or her social behavior. Membership in cultural, gender, or family groups is seldom voluntary: We are born into such groups and raised within them. However, later in life we can choose to join various other groups: clubs, political parties, groups of friends or work groups. It is on this latter, more voluntary, type of group belonging that this chapter will focus. Once persons belong to a number of groups, whether involuntarily or by choice, they are subject to a wide variety of forces and processes—ones that can affect their behavior, attitudes, and values in many ways. These processes of *group influence*—the effects of group membership on individual behavior—will be the major topic examined here. First, to set the stage for further discussion, we'll examine the basic nature of groups—what they are and how they function. Second, we'll consider the impact of groups on *task performance*. Here we'll examine the ways in which performance in various tasks can be affected by the presence of others or their potential evaluations—a process known as *social facilitation*. In addition, we'll address the complex question of whether groups or individuals are better at performing various tasks. Third, we'll turn to *decision making* in groups, examining both the process through which groups move toward consensus and various factors that can distort or bias the decisions they reach. Finally, we'll return to the topic of our opening story, *leadership*, considering the question of whether leaders are born or made, their style of exerting influence, and several factors that seem to determine their effectiveness.

One final point before proceeding: While the emphasis in this chapter will be on the many ways in which groups influence their individual members, it is important to note that groups, in turn, are shaped by their members. Indeed, *group composition*—the background, gender, characteristics, and attitudes of group members—can strongly influence the nature and operation of groups (Moreland & Levine, 1992a). So, in a key sense, the relationship between individuals and groups is very much a two-way street.

GROUPS: THEIR NATURE AND FUNCTION

Look at the photos in Figure 9.1. Which show social groups? In order to answer, we must first define the term **group** in concrete terms. According to most social psychologists, a group consists of *two or more interacting persons who share common goals, have a stable relationship, are somehow interdependent, and perceive that they are in fact part of a group* (Paulus, 1989). In other words, the term group does not apply to mere collections of individuals who happen to be in the same place at the same time but who have no lasting relationship to one another. Rather, this term is restricted to collections of persons that meet certain criteria.

First, such persons must *interact* with each other, either directly or indirectly. Second, they must be *interdependent* in some manner—what happens to one must affect what happens to the others. Third, their relationship must be relatively *stable*; it must persist over appreciable periods of time (e.g., weeks, months, or even years). Fourth, the individuals involved must share at least some goals that they all seek to attain. Fifth, their interactions must be *structured* in some manner, so that, for example, each performs the same or similar functions each time they meet. Finally, the persons involved must perceive themselves as members of a group—they must recognize the existence of a lasting relationship among them.

■ Groups: More than just collections of individuals

FIGURE 9.1 Which of these photos show true social groups? According to the definition offered in the text, only the bottom one.

This is quite a lengthy list: Are all these conditions really necessary before it makes sense to describe several persons as belonging to a group? Opinion is split on this issue (e.g., Turner, 1985), but many feel that awareness of group membership may be the most important. In other words, people belong to a group when they perceive that they belong to it. In any case, it is also clear that groups do not spring into existence as fully formed entities. Rather, they emerge out of a continuous process of social *integration* in which bonds between potential members strengthen gradually, as people develop shared feelings, beliefs, and behaviors (Moreland, 1987).

Applying this definition to the photos in Figure 9.1, it is easy to see that the people in the bottom picture are members of a group. In contrast, those in the top two photos are not; they are simply persons who happen to be in the same place at the same time but who have no real relationship to one another.

GROUP FORMATION: WHY DO PEOPLE JOIN?

At present you probably belong to several different groups. Why did you join them in the first place? Existing evidence on this question suggests that individuals generally enter groups for several major reasons (Greenberg & Baron, 1993). First, groups help us to satisfy important psychological or social needs such as those for belonging and receiving attention and affection. Second, groups help us achieve goals that we could not attain as individuals. By working within groups we can perform tasks we could not perform alone. Third, group membership often provides us with knowledge and information that would otherwise not be available to us. For example, individuals are often denied access to sensitive or restricted information held by a group until they are admitted to full membership. Fourth, groups help meet our need for security; in many cases there is a degree of safety in numbers, and belonging to various groups can provide protection against common, external enemies.

Finally, group membership also contributes to establishment of a positive *social identity*—it becomes part of the self-concept (refer to chapter 4). Simply put, the greater the number of prestigious, restrictive groups to which an individual is admitted, the more her or his self-concept is bolstered. In sum, there are many important reasons for joining groups, so it is not at all surprising that most persons seek entry to many over the course of their lives.

HOW GROUPS FUNCTION: ROLES, STATUS, NORMS, AND COHESIVENESS

That groups often exert powerful effects upon the behavior and cognitions of their members is obvious. Indeed, we will devote much of this chapter to the task of describing such effects. Before turning to specific types of *group influence*, however, we should address a more basic issue: How, precisely, do groups affect their members? A complete answer to this question involves many processes, including several we have examined in previous chapters (e.g., conformity, persuasion, attraction). However, there is general agreement that four aspects of groups play a crucial role in this regard. These are known, respectively, as *roles*, *status*, *norms*, and *cohesiveness* (Forsyth, 1983; Paulus, 1989).

Roles: Differentiation of function within groups

Think of a group to which you have belonged—anything from the scouts to a professional association relating to your occupation. Now consider the following question: did everyone in the group act in the same way or perform the same functions? Your answer is probably no. On the contrary, a considerable degree of differentiation may well have existed. Specific persons worked at different tasks and were expected to accomplish different things for the group. In short, they fulfilled different **roles**. Sometimes roles are assigned in a formal and specific manner. For example, an individual may be chosen by a group to serve as its leader, secretary, or treasurer. In other cases individuals gradually acquire certain roles without being formally assigned to them. Leaders often emerge in this manner (Ellis, 1989). And within a given group, different persons gradually come to fulfill either *task-oriented roles* (focusing on getting the group's major jobs done), or *relations-oriented roles* (focusing on reducing interpersonal friction and maintaining good relations between members). However roles emerge, people often *internalize* them; they link their roles to key aspects of their self-concept or self-perceptions (see chapters 2 and 4). When this happens, roles may exert truly profound and general effects on behavior, even at times when individuals interact with other persons not in their group. For example, a high-powered attorney may find herself behaving toward her children in the same aggressive, confrontational ways she uses to good advantage in the courtroom; or a police officer may approach friends and neighbors with the swagger that says, "look out—here comes authority!"

Roles help to clarify the responsibilities and obligations of the persons belonging to a group. In addition, roles constitute one key way in which groups shape the behavior and thoughts of their members. They do have a downside, however. First, group members sometimes experience *role conflict*—pressures stemming from the fact that they must play two or more roles concurrently, or from the fact that a single role requires competing forms of behavior. A very common example of role conflict is shown in Figure 9.2. Second, because they prescribe specific forms of behavior, roles tend to restrict individual freedom, and this in turn can lead to negative reactions on the part of group members.

■ Role conflict: The downside of group membership

FIGURE 9.2 When you carry out two conflicting roles—such as being a parent and an employee—the pressures of group membership can get you down.

Status: The prestige of various roles

Suppose you visited the office of the president of your university; would it be different in any respect from the office of a new assistant professor? Absolutely! Unless your school is a very unusual one, the president's office would be much larger and much more luxurious. Such differences are hardly surprising—we view them as a normal part of social life. They reflect the fact that within any group (and organizations like colleges can be viewed as being large and complex groups), different roles (positions) are associated with different degrees of **status**—social standing or rank. And status, in turn, is related to a wide variety of outcomes, including the size and plushness of one's office, use of a reserved parking spot, and having or not having an expense account. So status is as important aspect of groups and the way they function.

Norms: The rules of the game

A third factor responsible for the powerful impact of groups upon their members is one we have already considered—norms. As you may recall from chapter 7, **norms** are rules—implicit or explicit—established by groups to regulate the behavior of their members. They tell group members how to behave (*prescriptive norms*) or how not to behave (*proscriptive norms*) in various situations. Most groups insist upon adherence to their norms as a basic requirement for membership. Thus, it is not surprising that individuals wishing to join or remain in specific groups generally follow these rules of the game quite closely. If they do not, they may soon find themselves on the outside looking in!

Norms develop in several different ways (Feldman, 1984). First, they can be established by leaders, who state them as explicit principles. Second, they may derive from critical events in the group's history. For example, a costly leak of information from a decision-making group may lead its members to adopt strict rules about secrecy. Third, norms are often carried over from past situations. Individul members know how they have behaved in other groups, and they may import such patterns—and the expectations that these are the correct or preferred ways of behaving—into a newly formed group. However they are formed, once group norms take shape, they often exert strong effects upon members and upon all activities that occur within the group.

Cohesiveness: The effects of wanting to belong

Consider two groups. In the first, members like one another very much, strongly desire the goals their group is seeking, and feel that they could not possibly find another group that would better satisfy their needs. In the second, the opposite is true: members don't like one another, they do not share common goals, and they are actively seeking other groups that might offer them a better deal. Which group would exert stronger effects upon its members? The answer is obvious: the first. The reason for this difference lies in the fact that **cohesiveness**—all pressures or forces causing members to remain part of a group—is much higher in the first group than in the second. In other words, individuals in the first group want to retain their membership much more strongly than those in the second.

While cohesiveness has sometimes been viewed as a unitary dimension ranging from low to high, growing evidence suggests that it actually involves at least two distinct aspects (Zaccaro & McCoy, 1988). The first involves the degree to which members like each other—*interpersonal cohesiveness*. The second involves the extent to which group membership provides for the attainment of important personal goals—*task-based cohesiveness*. Interestingly, it appears that under some conditions, only groups that are high in both will be successful. Specifically, on tasks that require members to work together to generate and choose correct solutions, both high interpersonal cohesiveness and high task-based cohesiveness are necessary for good performance (Zaccaro & McCoy, 1988). This is because on such tasks members must be committed to the task *and* willing to expend effort for the group. When members can work alone and close coordination between them isn't needed, in contrast, only task-based cohesiveness is required. In fact, high levels of interpersonal cohesiveness may actually be detrimental by generating social interactions that interfere with performance.

Additional factors that influence cohesiveness include (1) the amount of effort required to gain entry into the group (the greater the costs of joining the group in the first place, the higher members' attraction to it; as dissonance theory suggests—see chapter 3—the harder we must work to attain a goal, such as group membership, the higher our evaluation of it); (2) external threats or severe competition (Sherif et al., 1961); and (3) size—small groups tend to be more cohesive than large ones.

In sum, several aspects of groups determine the extent to which they can, and do, influence their members. Since these play an important role in group influence, keeping them in mind is well worthwhile as we consider some of the specific ways in which groups shape the behavior and thought of individuals.

GROUPS AND TASK PERFORMANCE: THE BENEFITS—AND COSTS—OF WORKING WITH OTHERS

Some activities, such as studying, balancing one's chequebook, or writing love letters, are best carried out alone. Most tasks we perform, however, are done either with others or in their presence. This raises an intriguing question: What impact, if any, do groups exert upon task performance? In order to answer this question, it is necessary to consider two separate but related issues: (1) What are the effects of the mere presence of others on individual performance; and (2) are groups more, or less, efficient than individuals in carrying out various tasks?

SOCIAL FACILITATION: PERFORMANCE IN THE PRESENCE OF OTHERS

Imagine that you must make a speech in front of a large audience. You have several weeks to prepare, so you write the speech and then practice it alone over and over again. Now, finally, the big day has arrived. You are introduced and begin to speak. How will you do? Better or worse than was true when you delivered it to the four walls of your own room? In short, will the presence of an audience facilitate or interfere with your performance? Early research concerned with this question (Triplett, 1898) yielded a confusing pattern of results. Sometimes performance was improved by the presence of an audience, and sometimes the opposite was true. How could this puzzle be resolved? An insightful answer was offered by Zajonc (1965).

The drive theory of social facilitation: Other persons as a source of arousal

Before describing Zajonc's theory, we should clarify a basic point. The term **social facilitation** is used by social psychologists to refer to any effects on performance stemming from the presence of others. Thus, it includes decrements as well as improvements in task performance.

Now, back to Zajonc's theory. The basic idea behind his theory, now known as the **drive theory of social facilitation**, is that the presence of others produces increments in level of arousal. As you can readily see, this suggestion agrees closely with our informal experience. The presence of other persons—especially when they serve as an audience—does seem to generate signs of increased arousal (e.g., feelings of tension or excitement). But how do such increments in arousal then affect our performance? Zajonc suggests that the answer involves two facts.

First, it is a basic principle of psychology that increments in arousal enhance the occurrence of *dominant responses*—the responses an individual is most likely to make in a given situation. Thus, when arousal increases, the tendency to make dominant responses increases, too (Davis & Harvey, 1992). Second, such dominant responses can be either correct or incorrect for any task currently being performed.

When these two facts are combined with the suggestion that the presence of others is arousing, two predictions follow: (1) The presence of others will facilitate performance when an individual's dominant responses are the correct ones for the particular situation; (2) the presence of others will impair performance when a person's dominant responses are incorrect for the situation. (Please see Figure 9.3 for a summary of these suggestions.) Another implication of these predictions is that the presence of others will facilitate the performance of strong, well-learned responses, but may interfere with the performance of new and as yet unmastered ones.

Initial studies designed to test these predictions generally yielded positive results (e.g., Matlin & Zajonc, 1968; Zajonc & Sales, 1966). Individuals were in fact more likely to emit dominant responses when in the presence of others than when alone, and performance on various tasks was either enhanced or impaired depending on whether these responses were correct or incorrect in each situation (Geen, 1989; Geen & Gange, 1977). For example, in one ingenious investigation, Davis and Harvey (1992) found that the batting performance of major league baseball players declines in high-pressure situations (such as when there are runners on base during late innings or when there are already two outs). Since audience-induced arousal would be expected to be very high in such situations, and since batting is a difficult task (even most professionals fail to get a hit more than 70 percent of the time), these findings are consistent with the predictions based on Zajonc's theory.

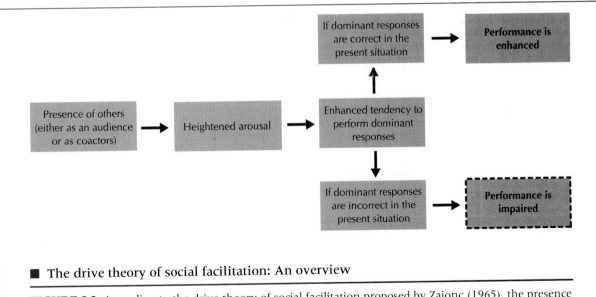

■ The drive theory of social facilitation: An overview

FIGURE 9.3 According to the drive theory of social facilitation proposed by Zajonc (1965), the presence of others increases arousal. This in turn enhances the performance of dominant responses. If these responses are correct in a given situation, performance is also enhanced. If they are incorrect, performance is reduced.

Source: Based on suggestions by Zajonc, 1965.

Additional research, however, soon raised an important question: Does social facilitation stem from the mere physical presence of others (and, perhaps, the increased tendencies to monitor carefully what's happening); or do other factors (e.g., concern over others' possible evaluations) also play a role? Support for the latter possibility was provided by the results of several interesting studies suggesting that social facilitation occurred only when individuals believed that their performance could be observed and evaluated by others (e.g., Bond, 1982; Bray & Sugarman, 1980; Cottrell et al., 1968). Such findings led some researchers to propose that social facilitation actually stems either from **evaluation apprehension**—concern over being judged by others—or related concerns over *self-presentation*—looking good in front of others (Carver & Scheier, 1981). Thus, it may be these factors, not the mere physical presence of others, that are crucial in determining the impact of an audience or coactors upon task performance.

At first glance, such suggestions seem quite reasonable. Most of us are concerned with the impressions we make on others and care about others' evaluations of us. Further, such concerns might be motivating or arousing in many situations. Other evidence, however, points to the conclusion that social facilitation effects can sometimes occur even in situations where these factors do not seem to play a role (e.g., Markus, 1978; Schmitt et al., 1986). For example, it has been found that animals—even insects!—perform simple tasks better in the presence of an audience than when alone. Since it is difficult to assume that insects are concerned about the impression they are making on other insects (common roaches were actually used in one of these studies; Zajonc, Heingartner, & Herman, 1969), these findings raise serious questions about an interpretation of social facilitation based solely on evaluation apprehension.

Research conducted with humans raises similar questions. For example, in one carefully conducted study on this issue, Schmitt and his colleagues (Schmitt et al., 1986) had participants perform both a simple task and a more complex one under one of three conditions: alone in the room, in the presence of another person who wore a blindfold and earphones (the *mere presence* condition), or in the presence of another person who could directly observe their performance (*evaluation apprehension* condition). The simple task was that of typing their own names. The complex one involved typing their names backward and inserting ascending numbers between every two letters. If the mere presence of others is arousing, then social facilitation effects should occur in this condition. This was indeed the case. Participants in the mere presence condition performed the simple task faster, but the complex task more slowly, than those in the control (alone) condition. Moreover, those in the evaluation apprehension condition performed the simple task the most quickly of all. These findings suggest that the mere presence of others is arousing, and that the possibility of being evaluated increases such arousal still further—at least for the purposes of performing simple tasks.

One potential resolution: Distraction-conflict theory

How can the diverse and seemingly contradictory findings we have described so far be explained? One answer is provided by **distraction-conflict theory**, developed by R. S. Baron, Sanders, and Moore (e.g., R. S. Baron, 1986; Sanders, 1983).

Like other explanations of social facilitation, this theory assumes that audiences and coactors (others performing the same task as subjects) heighten arousal. In contrast to earlier views, however, distraction-conflict theory suggests that such arousal stems from conflict between two tendencies: (1) the tendency to pay attention to the task being performed, and (2) the tendency to direct attention to an audience or coactors. The conflict produced by these competing tendencies is arousing, and such arousal in turn enhances the tendency to perform dominant responses. If these are correct, performance is enhanced; if they are incorrect, performance is reduced (refer to Figure 9.4).

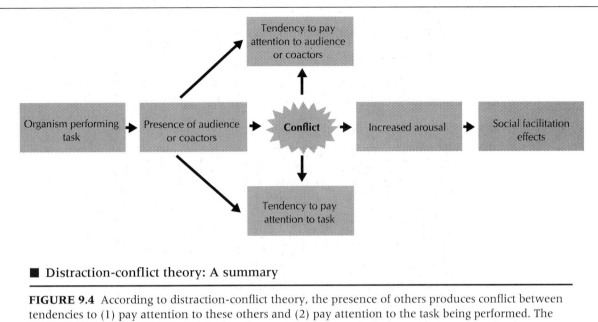

■ **Distraction-conflict theory: A summary**

FIGURE 9.4 According to distraction-conflict theory, the presence of others produces conflict between tendencies to (1) pay attention to these others and (2) pay attention to the task being performed. The conflict generated by these competing tendencies increases arousal. This in turn accounts for the occurrence of social facilitation effects.

Source: Based on suggestions by R. S. Baron, 1986.

Several different findings support this theory. For example, audiences produce social facilitation effects only when directing attention to them conflicts in some way with task demands (Groff, R. S. Baron, & Moore, 1983). When paying attention to an audience does not conflict with task performance, social facilitation fails to occur. Similarly, individuals experience greater distraction when they perform various tasks in front of an audience than when they perform them alone (R. S. Baron, Moore, & Sanders, 1978). Finally, when individuals have little reason to pay attention to others present on the scene (e.g., these persons are performing a different task), social facilitation fails to occur; when they have strong reasons for paying close attention to others, social facilitation occurs (Sanders, 1983).

Distraction-conflict theory offers two additional advantages worth considering. First, since animals as well as people can experience the type of conflict shown in Figure 9.4, this theory may account for the occurrence of social facilitation among animals. Second, with certain modifications (R. S. Baron, 1986), the theory can explain the occurrence of social facilitation without reference to the notion of arousal. The reasoning is as follows. The presence of an audience (or coactors) threatens the persons involved with *information overload*—they have more things demanding their attention than they can readily handle. As a result, they focus their attention primarily on those cues most central to the task at hand. Such focused attention can enhance performance on simple tasks, but may reduce it on complex ones that require attention to a wide range of stimuli. In short, a modified form of distraction-conflict theory can explain social facilitation effects in terms of our limited information-processing capacity.

To conclude: While distraction-conflict theory may not provide a final answer to the persistent puzzle of social facilitation, it is quite promising in this respect. In any case, it has added substantially to our understanding of what many social psychologists consider to be the simplest type of group effect.

GROUPS VERSUS INDIVIDUALS: WHICH HAS THE EDGE IN TASK PERFORMANCE?

At the start of this discussion, we called attention to the fact that many tasks people perform involve working with others. One reason why this is so involves the nature of the tasks themselves: Many simply cannot be performed by one person alone (refer to Figure 9.5). Another basis for this reliance on groups where tasks are concerned is as follows: There is a general, widespread belief that people can accomplish more by working with others than by working alone. In one sense, this suggestion must be true; several people working together do generally accomplish more than any one of them in isolation. But more to the point, are groups really more *efficient* than individuals—do they accomplish more *per member*—than persons working alone?

Pros and cons of working in groups

The answer, it turns out, is fairly complex (Stroebe, Diehl, & Abakoumkin, 1992). Working in groups does indeed offer certain advantages. It allows individuals to pool

■ Group effort: Required for many tasks

FIGURE 9.5 Many tasks, such as the ones shown here, can be successfully completed only by groups of individuals working together in a coordinated manner.

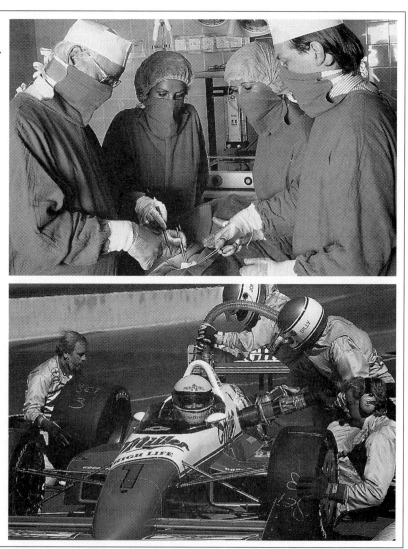

knowledge, skills, and equipment. Similarly, it allows for an efficient division of labor.

On the other hand, working in groups has important costs as well. When cohesiveness is high, members may spend a lot of time engaging in pleasant but nonproductive interactions. Further, strong pressures to adhere to existing norms may interfere with the development of new and better procedures for completing essential tasks. The likelihood of conflict between group members, too, can interfere with effective performance (e.g., Thomas, 1992). Finally, as group size increases, it may become increasingly difficult for members to coordinate their activities, with the result that output suffers. In sum, group settings offer a mixed bag of potential pluses and minuses where task performance is concerned. What determines the final balance between these factors? Research findings suggest that the most important single factor in this regard is the type of task being performed.

Type of task and group performance

One useful framework for understanding the different types of tasks performed by groups has been proposed by Steiner (1972, 1976). According to this perspective, most tasks fall into one of four different categories.

First, there are **additive tasks**. These are ones in which the contributions of each member are combined into a single group product. For example, when several persons combine their efforts to lay the foundation for a house, move a heavy object, or pick up litter, the tasks being performed are additive ones. The group's output is based upon the sum of its members' individual efforts, and the extent to which these are coordinated in a useful way.

A second category is that of **compensatory tasks**. These are ones on which the contributions of the various members are averaged together to form a single group outcome. For example, consider a group of economic forecasters trying to predict next year's rate of inflation. The group outcome is the average of all their predictions. Presumably, since the rosy predictions of optimists in the group will be offset by the dire predictions of pessimists, the final prediction will tend to be more accurate than the judgments of any individual member.

Third, there are **disjunctive tasks**. Here, the group's product is determined by the performance of its best or most competent person. Many complex problem-solving tasks faced by groups are disjunctive in nature: The correct solution will be obtained only if one member discovers it and can then convince the others of its accuracy. For example, if a group of mathematicians is trying to solve a difficult equation, a solution will be obtained only if at least one member of the group can generate it and then gain the acceptance of the others.

Finally, there are **conjunctive tasks**. Here, the group's final product is determined by its weakest link—the poorest-performing member. A clear example of this type of task is a team of mountain climbers. The entire team can advance only as fast as its slowest member.

Now, to return to our basic question: How do groups and individuals compare with respect to each of these types of tasks? Many factors play a role in the performance of both individuals and groups, so a complete answer would require many pages. A useful rule-of-thumb reply, however, is as follows. On both additive and compensatory tasks, groups usually outperform individuals. (Please see Figure 9.6 for a summary of these conclusions.) In fact, they often do better than the best individual member. In such cases, then, the whole is indeed greater than the sum of its individual parts. (But see the next section for a discussion of one important exception to this conclusion, at least where additive tasks are concerned.) On disjunctive tasks, groups tend to do better than the average individual, because the final outcome is determined

Groups, individuals, and task performance: Who has the edge?

FIGURE 9.6 Groups often outperform individuals on additive tasks, on which individual members' contributions are combined into a single group product, and on compensatory tasks, on which group performance is determined by the average performance of group members. Groups are about equal to individuals on disjunctive tasks, on which performance is determined by the best member. They are less productive than individuals on conjunctive tasks, where performance is determined by the weakest group member.

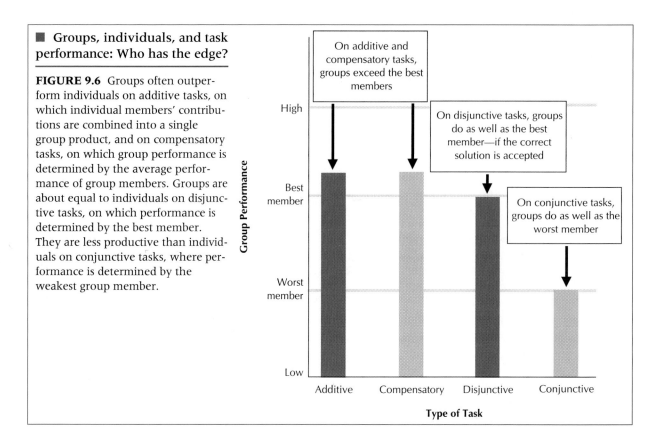

On additive and compensatory tasks, groups exceed the best members

On disjunctive tasks, groups do as well as the best member—if the correct solution is accepted

On conjunctive tasks, groups do as well as the worst member

largely by the talents and contributions of the best (most effective) member. Finally on conjunctive tasks, groups generally perform more poorly than individuals, since overall performance is determined by the weakest member.

One final point: As we suggested earlier, group output is also often strongly affected by group size (Kerr & Bruun, 1983). As group size increases, potential productivity increases, especially on additive tasks. But the possible occurrence of what Steiner terms *process losses*—reductions in productivity due to lack of coordination or reduced motivation—also rises. Recent findings indicate that as Steiner's model predicts, performance on additive tasks generally increases with group size; this is so because productivity gains exceed process losses. In contrast, performance on disjunctive tasks at first increases, but then declines, with increasing group size (Littlepage, 1991). This is because at some point, gains in potential productivity are more than offset by incoordination and other process losses. So, in sum, in answer to the question "Are groups or individuals more productive?" the most reasonable answer seems to be: It depends on several factors, including the nature of the task and the size of the group.

SOCIAL LOAFING: LETTING OTHERS DO THE WORK IN GROUP TASKS

Suppose that you and several other people are helping a friend to move. In order to lift the heaviest pieces of furniture, you join forces, with each person lending a hand. Will all of the people helping exert equal effort? Probably not. Some will take as much of the load as possible, while others will simply hang on, appearing to help without really doing much.

This pattern is quite common in situations where groups perform *additive tasks*. Some persons work hard while others engage in **social loafing**, doing as little as they can get away with. Why do such effects occur? Because it is difficult, in many additive tasks, to identify the contributions of each participant. The group outcome depends on the combined efforts of all members, and the efforts exerted by each cannot be separated or identified.

Direct evidence for the occurrence of social loafing has been obtained in many experiments. For example, in one of the first of these studies, Latane, Williams, and Harkins (1979) asked groups of male students to clap or cheer as loudly as possible at specific times, supposedly so that the experimenter could determine how much noise people make in social settings. Subjects engaged in clapping and cheering either alone or in groups of two, four, or six persons. Results were clear: The magnitude of the sounds made by each person decreased sharply as group size rose. In other words, each participant put out less and less effort as the number of other group members increased. And the experimenters were able to confirm that this was not due to an increasing lack of coordination between group members. Additional research suggests that such social loafing is quite general in Western cultures; it occurs in both sexes and under a wide range of work conditions (e.g., Brickner, Harkins, & Ostrom, 1986; Harkins, 1987; Harkins & Petty, 1982). Moreover, it occurs with respect to cognitive tasks as well as ones involving physical effort (Weldon & Mustari, 1988).

How do individuals react to evidence that other members of their group are engaging in social loafing or that these persons may soon be tempted to do so? You might guess that other group members would react negatively or perhaps become less interested in participating themselves. And research supports this suggestion. Typical reactions are resentment, annoyance and even withdrawal from the group (Messick & Brewer, 1986). However, research findings suggest that in some instances a very different reaction known as **social compensation** may occur (Williams & Karau, 1991). Social compensation involves increased effort on the part of some group members in order to make up for a lack of effort on the part of others. Considered as a whole, the findings reported by Williams and Karau suggest that social loafing by others is not always contagious. When confronted with *free-riders* in their groups, individuals do not necessarily engage in such behavior themselves. On the contrary, under some conditions, they may actually attempt to compensate for such behavior and increase their own effort. Such effects will not occur in all cases, however. Rather, they are most likely to occur when individuals care about the evaluation their group will receive and when they expect to remain in the group. In addition, social compensation is probably not a permanent state of affairs: If individuals find that others continue to loaf despite their own best efforts, feelings of anger or resentment may become so strong that they give up and loaf themselves or actually leave the group. At least for a while, however, some persons do appear willing to "carry" other members of their groups toward shared group goals.

Cultural differences in social loafing: North America and Asia

One result of the greater interdependence shown in more *collective* cultures (e.g., Japan, China and India—see chapter 4) may be that individuals within those cultures are more likely to feel responsible and committed to their groups than similar individuals in Canada or the United States. On that basis, we might expect cultural differences in attitude and response to social loafing. For example, social loafing could be expected to be more frowned-upon in collective cultures and "free-riders" responded to more negatively. Recent research suggests that this may be the case, particularly when group tasks in experiments are more realistic and important to the group (Smith & Bond, 1993).

When tasks are trivial, such as in the group cheering or clapping methodology mentioned above, there is evidence for some social loafing in many non-Western cultures: India, Thailand, Taiwan, Japan, and Malaysia (Gabrenya, Wong, & Latané, 1985). However, when the tasks are more meaningful, cultural differences appear. For example, Chinese and American schoolchildren were given an auditory tracking task (counting tones) that they carried out individually or in pairs (Gabrenya et al., 1985). While American school children showed the expected tendency to socially loaf when in pairs, the Chinese school children showed an opposite pattern termed "social striving"; that is, individuals performed better in pairs than when alone. Similar findings were also reported for managers from China compared to those from the U.S.A. when carrying out an "in-basket" simulation task (Earley, 1990), and for Japanese students carrying out a numerical task (Matsui, Kakuyama, & Onglatco, 1987).

Further, there is evidence of a stronger reaction to the possibility of social loafing by Japanese students than American (Yamagishi, 1988). In this investigation, male and female subjects in the United States and in Japan worked on a simple letter-matching task in groups of three. The conditions of the game were such that subjects could *not* observe and monitor one another's behavior. Thus, there was no procedure designed to guard against free riders. However, the experimenter explained that rewards would be divided equally among team members. On each trial, subjects were given the choice of either remaining in the group or withdrawing from it. If they chose the latter course, their earnings on that trial would depend only on their own performance. The cost of exiting was also varied so that in one condition it was low (points earned by subjects were worth the same amount of money whether they remained in the group or not) and in another it was high (points had less value when subjects chose to withdraw from the group). Results are shown in Figure 9.7 and indicate that when there was a possibility of social loafing by others in the group, Japanese students were more likely to choose to leave their group than American students. These findings suggest that Japanese subjects disliked the possibility of social loafing so strongly that they chose to withdraw on many trials, even if the cost was high. In contrast, American subjects were deterred from withdrawing from their group when this action was costly.

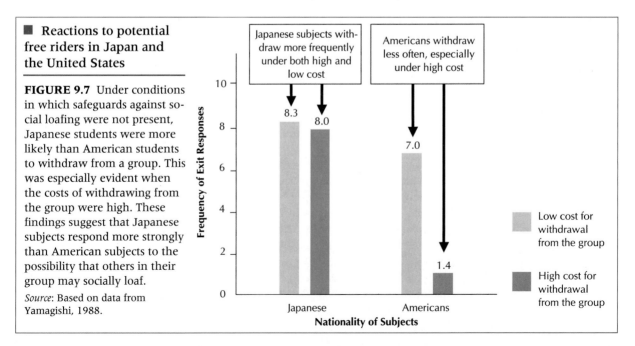

■ Reactions to potential free riders in Japan and the United States

FIGURE 9.7 Under conditions in which safeguards against social loafing were not present, Japanese students were more likely than American students to withdraw from a group. This was especially evident when the costs of withdrawing from the group were high. These findings suggest that Japanese subjects respond more strongly than American subjects to the possibility that others in their group may socially loaf.

Source: Based on data from Yamagishi, 1988.

To summarize, it appears that there are important cultural differences in social loafing, a phenomenon that had been assumed to be similar across cultures. Differences between American and Asian subjects were shown both in the frequency of social loafing and in the strength of response to others' social loafing. Research has still to discover how widespread is the "social striving" shown by Asian subjects in these studies, and to clarify the conditions under which this response will occur. Nevertheless, it is not difficult to imagine, in our multicultural society, that such cultural differences in response to working in a group could pose difficulties. Since so many important tasks are performed under group conditions, the implications for society are quite unsettling. It is, therefore, important to consider techniques for the reduction of social loafing in groups.

Reducing social loafing: Some useful techniques

Fortunately, research evidence points to several techniques that may be useful in countering social loafing tendencies. The most obvious of these involves making the output or effort of each participant readily identifiable (e.g., Williams, Harkins, & Latané, 1981). Under these conditions, individuals cannot conceal minimal effort within the group, and the tendency to sit back and let others do the work is greatly reduced.

Second, groups can reduce social loafing by increasing group members' commitment to successful task performance (Brickner et al., 1986; Zaccaro, 1984). Pressures toward working hard will then serve to offset temptations to engage in social loafing. Moreover, the larger the group, the stronger such pressures will be. Thus, output per group member may actually *increase* rather than decrease as group size rises.

Third, several recent studies suggest that social loafing can be reduced by conditions that provide individuals with an opportunity to evaluate their own contributions or those of the entire group relative to other groups (Harkins & Szymanski, 1988; Szymanski & Harkins, 1987). In other words, social loafing seems to occur not simply because individuals believe that their contributions cannot be identified, but also, at least in part, because they feel these cannot be evaluated, either by themselves or others. Conditions that afford the opportunity for such evaluation greatly reduce tendencies toward social loafing (Harkins & Szymanski, 1989).

Finally, social loafing can be reduced by strengthening of group cohesiveness. This increases the extent to which members care about the group's outcomes, and so too their level of individual effort.

Together, these findings suggest that tendencies toward social loafing are not an unavoidable part of task performance by groups. On the contrary, they *can* be reduced under appropriate circumstances. Further, in order to reduce social loafing it is not necessary to convince individuals that their outputs will be readily identifiable. Providing them with a standard against which to evaluate their contributions, or even those of the entire group, may be sufficient.

DECISION MAKING BY GROUPS: HOW IT OCCURS, THE OUTCOMES IT YIELDS, AND THE PITFALLS IT FACES

Groups are called upon to perform a wide range of tasks—everything from conducting delicate surgical operations through harvesting the world's crops. One of the most important activities they perform, however, is **decision making**. Governments, large corporations, military units, and virtually all other social entities entrust key decisions to groups. As a result, most of the laws, policies, and business practices that affect our daily lives are determined by committees, boards of directors, and similar groups—not by single individuals. There are several reasons for this fact, but perhaps the most important is this: Most people believe that groups, by pooling the expertise of their members and by avoiding extreme courses of action, can usually reach better decisions than individuals.

Are such assumptions accurate? Do groups actually make better (i.e., more accurate) decisions than individuals? In their efforts to deal with this practical question, social psychologists have focused on three major, and closely related, topics: (1) How do groups actually go about moving toward consensus and reaching decisions? (2) Do decisions reached by groups differ in any way from those reached by individuals? And (3) what accounts for the fact that groups sometimes make truly disastrous decisions—ones that are so bad they seem hard to explain?

THE DECISION-MAKING PROCESS: HOW GROUPS MOVE TOWARD CONSENSUS

When a group first begins to discuss an issue, its members rarely voice unanimous agreement. Rather, they support a wide range of views and favor competing courses of action. After some period of discussion, however, they usually reach a decision. This is not always the case—for example, juries become hung, and other decision-making groups, too, may deadlock. In most cases, though, *some* decision is reached. Is there any way of predicting this final outcome? In short, can we predict the decision a group is likely to reach from information about the views initially held by its members? Growing evidence suggests that we can (e.g., Kerr & MacCoun, 1985; Kaplan & Miller, 1987).

Social decision schemes

To summarize some very complex findings in simple terms, it appears that the final decisions reached by groups can often be predicted quite accurately by relatively simple rules known as **social decision schemes**. These rules relate the initial distribution of member views or preferences to the group's final decisions. For example, one scheme—the *majority-wins rule*—suggests that in many cases the group will opt for whatever position is initially supported by a majority of its members. According to this rule, discussion serves mainly to confirm or strengthen the most popular view. In contrast, a second decision scheme—the *truth-wins rule*—indicates that the correct solution or decision will ultimately come to the fore as its correctness is recognized by a growing number of members. A third decision scheme, adopted by many juries, is the *two-thirds majority rule*. Here, juries tend to convict defendants if two-thirds of the jurors initially favor this decision (Davis et al., 1984). Finally, some groups seem to follow a *first-shift rule*. They tend, ultimately, to adopt a decision consistent with the direction of the first shift in opinion shown by any member.

Surprising as it may seem, the results of many studies indicate that these straightforward rules are quite successful in predicting even complex group decisions. Indeed, they have been found to be accurate in this regard up to 80 percent of the time (e.g., Stasser, Taylor, & Hanna, 1989). Of course, different rules seem to be more successful under some conditions than others. Thus, the majority-wins scheme predicts decisions best in *judgmental tasks*—ones that are largely a matter of opinion. In contrast, the truth-supported rule seems best in predicting group decisions on *intellective tasks*—ones for which there is a correct answer (Kirchler & Davis, 1986).

Procedural processes: When decisions are influenced by the procedures used to reach them

While the decisions reached by groups can often be predicted from knowledge of members' initial positions, it is clear that many other factors play a role in this complex process. Among the most important of these are several aspects of the group's *procedures*—the rules it follows in addressing its agenda, managing the flow of interaction among members, and handling related issues (Stasser, Kerr, & Davis, 1989). One procedure adopted by many decision-making groups is the **straw poll,** in which members indicate their present positions or preferences in a nonbinding vote. While straw polls are non-binding and leave members free to change their views, it seems possible that simply learning about the current distribution of opinions within a group may have strong effects upon the individual members. That this is actually the case is confirmed by research findings (e.g., Davis et al., 1988; MacCoun & Kerr, 1988). Specifically, it appears that when a straw poll is held early in a group discussion, and especially when it involves each member reporting her or his views sequentially, the straw poll can lead to important shifts in the positions held by each member and so, ultimately, in the decision reached by the group.

A second procedural factor that can exert powerful effects on group decisions is what has been described as *deliberation style* (Hastie et al., 1983). This refers to the manner in which group members exchange information about their individual views. In one approach, known as *verdict-driven* (or *compound*) *deliberation*, members of a group first reach their personal decisions and then discuss these with other members. In another, known as *evidence-driven* (or *elemental*) *deliberation*, each piece of relevant information is examined by the group first, before individual decisions are made. In sum, in compound deliberation group members discuss their personal decisions, while in elemental deliberation they discuss the evidence or information before them. What effect does this procedure have on group decisions? A study by Kameda (1991) provides revealing information on this issue.

Kameda (1991) asked groups of six male and female students to act as mock juries and reach a decision concerning a case of fraud: A businessman was charged with serving as an accessory to a crime in which the businessman's friend cheated an old farmer. Groups were instructed to make their individual judgments first and then discuss them (compound deliberation), or to discuss the evidence first (elemental deliberation). Because Kameda reasoned that the effects of deliberation procedures would vary for two types of decisions, half of the participants in each condition were told that they could reach a guilty decision only if two criteria were met: The defendant knew of the intention of his friend to swindle the farmer, *and* he played an active role in perpetrating the fraud. This is called a *conjunctive decision*. The other half were told that they could reach a verdict of guilty if either of these two criteria were met; this is a *disjunctive decision*.

Results indicated that in the conjunctive situation, jurors were more likely to report a guilty verdict when using the elemental (evidence-driven) deliberation style than the compound (verdict-driven) style. However, in the disjunctive situation, the opposite was true: Jurors judged the defendant to be guilty more frequently in the compound condition (see Figure 9.8). These findings indicate that the procedures used by a decision-making group can play an important role in its final decision. The precise effects of various procedures may interact in complex ways, however, with the kind of decisions being reached. To repeat a comment we made in chapter 1: Who ever said that understanding people—and especially their relations with others—would be simple?!

THE NATURE OF GROUP DECISIONS: MODERATION OR POLARIZATION?

Truly important decisions are rarely entrusted to individuals. Instead, they are generally the responsibility of groups whose members' training, expertise, and background seem to qualify them for this crucial task. Indeed, even kings, queens, and dictators usually consult with groups of advisers before taking major action. As we noted earlier, the

■ Deliberation style and group decisions

FIGURE 9.8 When the presence of both of two different criteria was required for a guilty verdict (a conjunctive decision), jurors were more likely to report a guilty verdict when using an evidence-driven deliberation style than when using a verdict-driven style. When either criterion was sufficient for a guilty verdict (a disjunctive decision), however, the opposite was true: A verdict-driven deliberation style yielded more guilty verdicts.

Source: Based on data from Kameda, 1991.

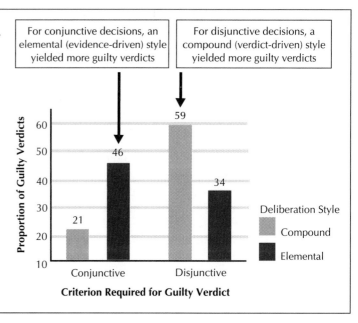

For conjunctive decisions, an elemental (evidence-driven) style yielded more guilty verdicts

For disjunctive decisions, a compound (verdict-driven) style yielded more guilty verdicts

major reason behind this strategy is the belief that groups are far less likely than individuals to make serious errors—to rush blindly over the edge. Is this really true? Are groups actually better at making wise decisions than individuals? Research conducted by social psychologists offers some surprising answers.

Groups versus individual decisions: A shift toward risk or a shift toward polarization?

Around 1960 a graduate student named James Stoner decided to examine this question in his master's thesis. In order to do so, he asked college students to play the role of advisers to imaginary persons supposedly facing decisions between two alternatives: one choice that was attractive but relatively high in risk, and another that was less appealing but quite conservative (Stoner, 1961). For example, in one of these situations, a character had to choose between a low-paying but secure job and a higher-paying but uncertain one.

During the first part of Stoner's study, each subject made individual recommendations about these situations. Then the subjects met in small groups and discussed each problem until a unanimous agreement was attained. Stoner expected that the decisions recommended by the groups would be more conservative than those offered by their individual members. Surprisingly, however, just the opposite was true: Groups actually recommended riskier decisions than individuals. The size of this difference was small, but it had important implications. After all, if groups make riskier decisions than individuals, the strategy of entrusting important decisions to committees, juries, and so on may be a poor one. In fact, it may be downright dangerous.

Impressed by these possibilities, many researchers conducted additional studies on this so-called **risky shift** (e.g., Burnstein, 1983; Lamm & Myers, 1978). At first these experiments seemed to confirm Stoner's initial findings. Gradually, however, a more mixed pattern of results emerged. In some cases group discussion actually seemed to produce shifts toward *caution* rather than risk (e.g., Knox & Safford, 1976). How could this be? How could group discussion produce both shifts toward caution and shifts toward risk? Eventually, a clear answer emerged. What had at first seemed to be a shift toward risk was actually a more general phenomenon—a *shift toward polarization*. Group discussion, it appeared, led individual members to become more extreme, not simply more risky or more cautious. In short, it enhanced or strengthened initial views. Thus, if an individual group member was mildly in favor of a course of action before the group discussion, he or she might come to favor it more strongly after the group deliberations. Similarly, if an individual was mildly opposed to some action before the discussion, he or she might come to oppose it even more strongly after the exchange of views. Since such shifts occur in the direction of greater extremity, this effect is known as **group polarization** (please see Figure 9.9.)

As we noted earlier, the tendency for groups to become increasingly extreme in their views has important—and unsettling—implications. Thus, it is not surprising that group polarization has been the subject of a considerable amount of research (Burnstein, 1983). Much of this research has focused on the following question: Why, precisely, does this polarization occur? What is it about group discussions that tends to intensify the initial beliefs of individual members?

Group polarization: Why it occurs

Several different explanations for group polarization have been proposed, but two have received most support. These are known as the *social comparison* and *persuasive arguments* views.

The social comparison approach suggests that before group discussion, most persons assume that they hold "better" views than the other members. They assume that their views are more extreme in the right (valued) directions. Since it is impossible for everyone to be above average in this respect, many individuals experience a rude awakening during group discussion: They discover that their own views are not nearly as far above average as they assumed. The result: They shift to more extreme positions (Goethals & Zanna, 1979).

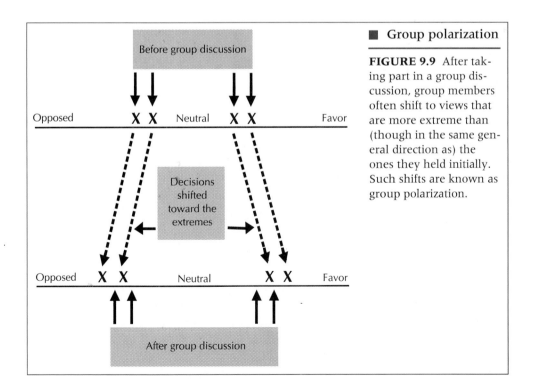

■ Group polarization

FIGURE 9.9 After taking part in a group discussion, group members often shift to views that are more extreme than (though in the same general direction as) the ones they held initially. Such shifts are known as group polarization.

The persuasive arguments view offers a contrasting explanation for the occurrence of polarization. In essence, it suggests that group members gradually convince themselves of the correctness of their initial views, and so come to adopt these even more strongly. The result, of course, is a shift toward extremity. More specifically, this view suggests that during group discussion, most of the information presented by group members supports their own views. Thus, if even a slight majority of the members lean in a particular direction, most of the arguments tend to favor this view. Gradually, then, the view that predominated initially gains greater and greater support (Vinokur & Burnstein, 1974).

Both explanations are supported by research findings, but some recent evidence (Zuber, Crott, & Werner, 1992) seems to cast doubt upon the ability of the role of persuasive arguments in group polarization. Specifically, when all group members are provided with an extensive list of arguments concerning an issue, polarization effects still occur. According to the persuasive arguments hypothesis, this should not be true, since all members would already have full information about the various arguments. In view of these and related findings, several researchers have recently concluded that group polarization can be better understood in terms of social decision schemes, such as the ones discussed under "The Decision-making Process," above (Zuber, Crott, & Werner, 1992). Specifically, it appears that the view that the median group member supports is the best predictor of the final group decision. To the extent this position leans toward one of the existing alternatives, then, this is the one most likely to be chosen, and the group will shift in this direction.

Regardless of the precise basis for group polarization, it definitely has important implications. The occurrence of polarization may lead many decision-making groups to adopt positions that are increasingly extreme—and therefore increasingly dangerous. In this context, it is interesting to speculate about the potential role of such shifts in disastrous decisions by political, military, or business groups who should, by all accounts, have known better—for example, the decision by President Johnson and his advisers to escalate U.S. involvement in Vietnam, and the decision by hard-liners in the Soviet government to arrest Mikhail Gorbachev—an action that soon led to dissolution of the Soviet Union. Did group polarization influence these events? It is difficult to say for sure. But the findings of many careful experiments suggest that this is a possibility well worth considering.

DECISION MAKING BY GROUPS: SOME POTENTIAL PITFALLS

The tendency of many decision-making groups to drift toward polarization is a serious factor that can interfere with their ability to make accurate decisions. Unfortunately, this is not the only process that can exert such negative effects. Several others, too, seem to emerge out of group discussions and can lead groups into disastrous courses of action. Among the most important of these are (1) *groupthink* and (2) the apparent inability of groups to pool expertise by discussing information not shared by all members.

Groupthink: When too much cohesiveness is a dangerous thing

Common sense suggests that a high level of cohesiveness among group members is beneficial. After all, if members are strongly attracted to a group, their motivation—and hence the group's performance—should be enhanced. Up to a point, this seems to be true. But, as shown in Figure 9.10, when very *high levels of cohesiveness* are coupled with *high stress, insulation* of the group from external input, a *lack of impartial leadership,* and a *lack of methodological procedures,* an unsettling process known as **groupthink** may emerge (Janis, 1982). Groupthink is a mode of thinking by group members in which concern with maintaining group consensus—*concurrence seeking*, in Janis's terms—overrides the motivation to evaluate all potential courses of action as accurately and realistically as possible. In short, groupthink involves a shift from primary concern with making the best decision to primary concern with reaching and maintaining consensus.

Once groupthink develops, several trends—all potentially catastrophic from the point of view of effective decision making—soon follow. (These "symptoms of groupthink" are shown in Figure 9.10). Members come to view their group as *invulnerable*—one that can't possibly make mistakes. Similarly, they engage in *collective rationalization*, discrediting or ignoring any information counter to the group's current views. Third, they conclude that their group is not only right, it is also *inherently morally superior*, and that all others (especially those who do not share its views) are confused, evil, or worse. Once groupthink develops, *pressures on members* to go along with the group's stated views become intense. Members who have lingering doubts engage in

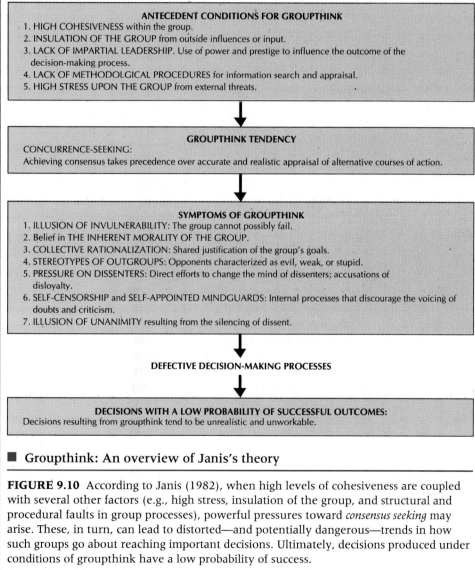

ANTECEDENT CONDITIONS FOR GROUPTHINK
1. HIGH COHESIVENESS within the group.
2. INSULATION OF THE GROUP from outside influences or input.
3. LACK OF IMPARTIAL LEADERSHIP. Use of power and prestige to influence the outcome of the decision-making process.
4. LACK OF METHODOLGICAL PROCEDURES for information search and appraisal.
5. HIGH STRESS UPON THE GROUP from external threats.

GROUPTHINK TENDENCY
CONCURRENCE-SEEKING:
Achieving consensus takes precedence over accurate and realistic appraisal of alternative courses of action.

SYMPTOMS OF GROUPTHINK
1. ILLUSION OF INVULNERABILITY: The group cannot possibly fail.
2. Belief in THE INHERENT MORALITY OF THE GROUP.
3. COLLECTIVE RATIONALIZATION: Shared justification of the group's goals.
4. STEREOTYPES OF OUTGROUPS: Opponents characterized as evil, weak, or stupid.
5. PRESSURE ON DISSENTERS: Direct efforts to change the mind of dissenters; accusations of disloyalty.
6. SELF-CENSORSHIP and SELF-APPOINTED MINDGUARDS: Internal processes that discourage the voicing of doubts and criticism.
7. ILLUSION OF UNANIMITY resulting from the silencing of dissent.

DEFECTIVE DECISION-MAKING PROCESSES

DECISIONS WITH A LOW PROBABILITY OF SUCCESSFUL OUTCOMES:
Decisions resulting from groupthink tend to be unrealistic and unworkable.

■ Groupthink: An overview of Janis's theory

FIGURE 9.10 According to Janis (1982), when high levels of cohesiveness are coupled with several other factors (e.g., high stress, insulation of the group, and structural and procedural faults in group processes), powerful pressures toward *consensus seeking* may arise. These, in turn, can lead to distorted—and potentially dangerous—trends in how such groups go about reaching important decisions. Ultimately, decisions produced under conditions of groupthink have a low probability of success.
Source: Adapted from Janis, 1982.

self-censorship; and if they do not, they are quickly silenced by other group members. Finally, *self-appointed "mind guards"* shield the group from external sources of information that are inconsistent with the group's position. The final result: A powerful illusion takes hold that the group is correct and infallible and has no dissent—or need for it. Janis (1982) analyzed a number of political decision-making "fiascoes" of this kind in the United States, such as the escalation of the Vietnam war, the Bay of Pigs, and the Watergate cover-up. However, closer to home, Canadians may have witnessed such defective decision-making in relation to recent constitutional discussions between the Prime Minister and provincial premiers. This possibility can be examined through a graphic and detailed account of the processes leading to the signing of the Meech Lake Accord provided by Andrew Cohen in his book, *A Deal Undone* (1990). As you will see in the following Applied Side section, "The signing of the Meech Lake Accord: An example of groupthink?" many of Janis's conditions and symptoms of groupthink were present at that time.

Is groupthink a real effect? And does it develop under the conditions proposed by Janis? Despite many efforts to answer these questions (e.g., Flowers, 1977; Moorhead & Montanari, 1986), the issue remains somewhat in doubt. Perhaps the most revealing evidence to date concerning its nature and occurrence has been provided by Tetlock and his colleagues (Tetlock et al., 1992) through subjects' analyses of factual accounts of several historic U.S. decisions that potentially involved groupthink. The results they obtained provided mixed support for the theory. On the one hand, it was found that historic events involving disastrous decisions were indeed described by participants as showing more characteristics of groupthink than events that led to successful decisions. This finding offered support for the model. Further, participants also associated structural and procedural faults in the groups with increased tendencies toward concurrence seeking; this too was consistent with the groupthink model. However, Tetlock and his colleagues did not find that group cohesiveness or high stress were necessarily associated with concurrence seeking on the part of the groups.

Together, these findings, and those of several other studies (e.g., McCauley, 1989) seem to point to two conclusions. First, something like groupthink does exist, and it affects the decisions of important decision-making groups. However, the precise nature and form of groupthink may be somewhat different from what Janis (1982) initially proposed. In other words, Janis has called attention to an important aspect of group decision making, but the precise nature of this process remains to be determined.

Assuming that groupthink exists, an important question arises: What steps can be taken to counter its effects—which, as we have already noted, can be disastrous? Several procedures may prove helpful. First, groups wishing to avoid the development of groupthink should promote open inquiry and skepticism among their members. Group leaders should encourage careful questioning of each alternative or policy and should, if necessary, play the role of devil's advocate, intentionally finding fault with various options as they are discussed. Second, the use of *subgroups* can be helpful. Such groups consider different aspects of the problem, and any final decision is then based on discussion of their recommendations. Since the subgroups work independently, spirited disagreements among them are far from rare; and this, of course, can halt any drift toward premature consensus and groupthink. Third, once a decision is reached, *second-chance* meetings, in which group members are asked to express any lingering doubts, can be extremely helpful. Such meetings provide a setting in which pressures toward conformity and consensus are reduced; this gives new ideas and criticism a chance to emerge and may effectively counter tendencies toward groupthink.

In sum, groupthink is a real danger faced by decision-making groups, especially under certain conditions. However, through steps such as those outlined above, the drift toward such premature closure can be halted, or even reversed.

Signing the Meech Lake Accord: An Example of Groupthink?

With the benefit of hindsight, many have seen Canada's recent attempts at constitutional reform—the Meech Lake Accord and its successor, the Charlottetown Accord—as faulty and unworkable. But that is not how it appeared in June 1990. After seven days sequestered together in the Government Conference Centre in Ottawa, the ten provincial premiers and the Prime Minister emerged triumphant (as Figure 9.11 shows) with an agreement to save the Meech Lake Accord (originally signed in 1987). The premiers were generous in their praise for each other and the prime minister: the adoption of the accord by the separate provincial legislatures seemed a *fait accompli* (Cohen, 1990).

We now know that this failed to occur, but why? How could the prolonged and joint efforts of so many talented and intelligent people produce an agreement which was unworkable? One contributory reason may have been that the Meech Lake Accord and its creators were the victims of groupthink (Janis, 1982). If this was the case, then, whatever the merits of its content, the conditions of its creation may have doomed the Accord to failure. Particularly in those final seven days of negotiation in Ottawa (and perhaps at the original signing of the Accord), many of the conditions and symptoms of groupthink were exhibited (refer to the overview of Janis's theory: Figure 9.10).

The *antecedent conditions* for groupthink were clearly present. First, the premiers, when they met in Ottawa, were under particularly *high stress*. The end of the three-year period for adoption of the original 1987 accord was less than a month away, and a number of provinces (Newfoundland, Manitoba, and New Brunswick) had not yet ratified it. The Prime Minister, Brian Mulroney, and his financial and political advisors were emphasizing that there could be serious economic and political consequences if Meech failed. From Andrew Cohen's account, their meeting had an "apocalyptic tone ... suggesting the country would live or die by the accord" (1990, p. 235).

Second, as had been the case when the premiers originally met at Meech Lake, their negotiations were in secret: they were *insulated* from the outside world and any external input. Many of the premiers were separated from their advisors during the lengthy negotiation sessions, and there was little communication with the public

■ **Signing the Meech Lake Accord: A triumph or a case of groupthink?**

FIGURE 9.11 When Brian Mulroney and the ten provincial premiers emerged from the Government Conference Centre on June 9, 1990 with an agreement to save the Meech Lake Accord, it appeared as if constitutional reform was assured. Subsequent events belied this impression. Could these highly experienced and intelligent politicians have been the victims of groupthink?

▶

or press for that seven-day period. They even held their meetings in a windowless boardroom.

Third, because this final meeting was not an official first ministers' conference, there were *few official procedures* for appraisal and consultation with outside experts. In retrospect, these faulty procedures were seen as a major cause of problems by Clyde Wells, the Newfoundland premier, who was most opposed to the Accord. He objected, specifically, to the secrecy of the proceedings: "That's no way to build a constitution … That's what's wrong with that god-awful process …" (Cohen, 1990, p. 241).

Fourth, Brian Mulroney does *not* appear to have played the role of an *impartial leader*. His belief in and support for the Accord was clear. He had engineered this last-minute effort, deliberately leaving the meeting until it was almost too late, so that he would have more control or, in his own words, could "roll all the dice." Andrew Cohen describes him at that time as

> charming, shrewd, mellifluous, he isolated the dissidents and, one by one, brought them to heel. There was, in Mulroney … the student of human weakness, the merchant of persuasion, the purveyor of favour. That week, he was all of those (1990, p. 252).

The final antecedent condition, *high cohesiveness*, was not initially a characteristic of the premiers' group in Ottawa. Three new premiers had been elected since the 1987 Accord had been signed, and they were, to differing degrees, opposed to the original agreement. However, over the week in Ottawa the premiers appear to have become more unified, turning into what was termed the "Premier's Club." Describing the ten premiers as they signed their agreement on the final day, Andrew Cohen suggests a highly cohesive group: "It was here that the most prominent features of the Premiers' Club—the male bonding, the union of the jocks, the fidelity and fraternity—were on display" (1990, p. 255).

Strong tendencies towards groupthink, or *concurrence-seeking*, were shown in the group. Even Clyde Wells describes himself as strongly influenced (Cohen, 1990, p.246):

> A kind of collegiality develops …. No one wants to do things to make life dif-

ficult. So you keep going, you make the concession, you agree. A little bit more, a little bit more … and finally you are on that thing and there's no way off it.

Many of the *symptoms of groupthink* were also manifested. *Pressure on dissenters* was particularly evident in the case of Clyde Wells, though other premiers also felt the pressure to suppress their doubts. An *illusion of unanimity* developed in which holdouts felt that they were the only ones being difficult. The group's belief in its *own inherent morality* was also apparent when they characterized themselves as great Canadians or saviours of the nation and condemned dissenters as uncaring or even traitorous. An *illusion of invulnerability* appeared to arise once the agreement was signed on June 9: Its ratification by the provincial legislatures was assumed to be a certainty. This final decision was *collectively rationalized*, even by those with serious doubts, as "a way for Quebeckers to feel truly a part of a united Canada" (Brian Mulroney quoted by Cohen, 1990, p. 255).

In the end, as the groupthink model would predict, these processes produced an unworkable decision. The premiers' apparent unanimity fractured as soon as they returned to their provinces. In Manitoba, the ratification of the Accord was blocked by a Native MLA, Elijah Harper. Clyde Wells rediscovered his original opposition to the Accord, and it was not submitted for a vote in the Newfoundland legislature. By the end of June 1990, the Meech Lake Accord had died.

Whatever the merits of its content, the Meech Lake Accord (and its successor the Charlottetown Accord) may have been doomed to failure, at least in part, because of the conditions and procedures through which it was devised: ones producing a state of groupthink. Given the intial lack of cohesiveness and the strong opposition among the new premiers, the fact that seven days of meetings in a hot-house atmosphere had managed to produce a "conversion of dissenters" was, as Cohen describes it, "ultimately… the triumph of the Group, the power of the Premiers' Club. In Ottawa, not even a Wells seemed able to resist its persuasion" (1990, p.242).

To share or not to share information: Or, why group members often tell each other what they already know

As we noted earlier, one reason why many key decisions are entrusted to groups is the belief that members will pool their resources—share ideas and knowledge unique to each individual. In this way, the decisions they reach will be better informed, and presumably more accurate, than those that would be reached by individuals working in isolation. Is this actually the case? Do groups really share the knowledge and expertise brought to them by individual members? A series of sophisticated studies conducted by Stasser and his colleagues (Stasser, 1992; Stasser & Titus, 1985, 1987; Stasser, Taylor, & Hanna, 1989) suggests that in fact such pooling of resources may be the exception rather than the rule.

These studies were undertaken to test the validity of a model of group discussion known as the **information sampling model** (Stasser & Titus, 1985). This model suggests that because information shared by many members is more likely to be mentioned during group discussion than information held by only a single member, decision-making groups are more likely to discuss—and discuss again—information shared by most members than information known to only a single member. More specifically, the model predicts that the larger the group, the greater the advantage of shared over unshared information. Further, and even more discouraging, the model also indicates that efforts to increase the pooling of resources by structuring group discussions will usually fail. This will happen because such efforts will enhance each member's recall of available information, and this in turn will actually increase the discussion of shared information.

In general, the results of studies undertaken to test this model have offered support for it (Stasser, 1992). Groups tend to discuss information shared by all members, and this tendency may actually be increased rather than reduced if groups are urged to review all information carefully before reaching a decision (Stasser, Taylor, & Hanna, 1989). There is some room for optimism, however: Some research findings indicate that group members can be encouraged to discuss *unshared* information, and so to discover "hidden profiles" in the available information, if they are convinced that there is a correct answer or decision. Under these conditions more extensive discussion may ensue, because if members perceive their task as uncovering the correct solution rather than simply reaching consensus, they may recognize the importance of unshared information to a greater extent and focus more attention on uncovering it (Stasser and Stewart, 1992).

These findings have important implications for many decision-making groups. They suggest that in general such groups are much better at rehashing and repeating information already shared by most members than at bringing new, unshared information into focus. But such problems can be overcome—at least to a degree—if group members believe that there is a correct decision. This implies that the group may have enough information at its disposal to make the right choice. And this, in turn, increases the likelihood that group members will uncover, and discuss, unshared information.

LEADERSHIP:
ITS NATURE AND IMPACT IN GROUPS

Suppose you surveyed persons belonging to a wide range of groups (businesses, sports teams, charities, social clubs) and asked them to name the single most important factor in determining the success of their group. What would you find? The chances are good that many—perhaps most—would reply "Effective leadership." This answer reflects the widespread belief that leadership is a key ingredient in group activities.

Indeed, many people believe that a group without an effective leader is worse than no group at all—the members would do better, in terms of reaching key goals, on their own. But what, precisely, is leadership? Like love, it is something we all feel we can recognize but can't precisely define. For social psychologists, however, leadership does have a clear focus: *influence*. Thus, many experts on this topic agree that **leadership** is *the process through which one member of a group (its leader) influences other group members toward the attainment of specific group goals* (Yukl, 1989).

In the remainder of this section, we will consider several issues related to the leadership process. First, we'll consider the question of who, precisely, becomes a leader— why some persons but not others rise to positions of authority. Second, we'll examine evidence concerning the possibility of *gender differences* in leadership. Finally, we'll examine current views concerning the basis of leaders' *effectiveness*, and a new perspective that deals with the inspirational (*transformational*) aspect of leadership.

THE TRAIT APPROACH: ARE LEADERS BORN OR MADE?

Are some people born to lead? Common sense suggests that this is so. Eminent leaders of the past such as Alexander the Great, Queen Elizabeth I, and Abraham Lincoln do seem to differ from ordinary human beings in several respects. Such observations led early researchers to formulate the **great person theory** of leadership. According to this approach, great leaders possess key traits that set them apart from most human beings. Further, the theory contends that these traits remain stable over time and across different groups. Thus, it suggests that all great leaders share these characteristics regardless of when and where they live or the precise roles they fulfill.

Certainly, these are intriguing suggestions, and they seem to fit quite well with our own informal experience. You will probably be surprised to learn, therefore, that they have *not* been confirmed. Decades of research (most conducted before 1950) failed to yield a short, agreed-upon list of key traits shared by all leaders (Geier, 1969; Yukl, 1981). Although a few consistent findings did emerge (e.g., leaders are slightly taller and more intelligent than their followers), these were hardly dramatic in nature or in scope. Indeed, the overall results of this persistent search for traits associated with leadership were so disappointing that most investigators gave up in despair and reached the following conclusion: Leaders simply do not differ from followers in clear and consistent ways.

Until quite recently this conclusion was widely accepted as true. Now, however, it has been called into question by a growing body of evidence indicating that leaders do actually differ from other persons in several important—and measurable—respects. After reviewing a large number of studies concerned with this issue, Kirkpatrick and Locke (1991) have recently contended that in business settings, at least, traits do matter—that certain traits, together with other factors, contribute to leaders' success. What are these traits? Table 9.1 presents a summary of the ones identified as most important by Kirkpatrick and Locke, plus descriptions of their basic nature. Most of these characteristics are ones you will readily recognize (drive, honesty and integrity, self-confidence). Others, however, seem to require further clarification.

Consider first what Kirkpatrick and Locke term *leadership motivation*. This refers to leaders' desire to influence others—in essence, to lead. Such motivation, however, can take two distinct forms. On the one hand, it may cause leaders to seek power as an end in itself. Leaders who demonstrate such *personalized power motivation* wish to dominate others, and their desire to do so is often reflected in an excessive concern with status. In contrast, leadership motivation can cause leaders to seek power as a means to achieve desired shared goals. Leaders who evidence such *socialized power motivation*

> ■ **Research findings indicate that successful business leaders demonstrate the traits listed here.**

TABLE 9.1 Characteristics of successful leaders

Trait	Description
Drive	Desire for achievement; ambition; high energy; tenacity; initiative
Honesty and Integrity	Trustworthiness; reliability; openness
Leadership Motivation	Desire to exercise influence over others to reach shared goals
Self-confidence	Trust in own abilities
Cognitive Ability	Intelligence; ability to integrate and interpret large amounts of information
Expertise	Knowledge of the group's activities; knowledge of relevant technical matters
Creativity	Originality
Flexibility	Ability to adapt to needs of followers and to changing requirements of the situation

Source: Based on suggestions by Kirkpatrick & Locke, 1991.

cooperate with others, develop networks and coalitions, and generally work with subordinates rather than trying to dominate or control them. Needless to add, this type of leadership motivation is usually far more adaptive for organizations than personalized power motivation.

With respect to *cognitive ability*, it appears that to be effective, leaders must be intelligent and capable of integrating and interpreting large amounts of information. Mental genius, however, does not seem to be necessary and may, in some cases, prove detrimental (Lord, DeVader, & Alliger, 1986).

While the list of traits presented in Table 9.1 is quite comprehensive and provides a good overall summary of recent evidence concerning this issue, we should note that one particular characteristic seems to play an especially crucial role in effective leadership. This trait, *flexibility*, refers to the capacity of leaders to recognize what actions are required in a given situation and then to act accordingly. For example, Zaccaro, Foti, and Kenny (1991) found that the greater a person's degree of flexibility, the higher the leadership ratings he or she received from other group members. In short, it appears that flexibility—the ability to match one's style and behavior to the needs of followers and the demands of the situation—may be an important trait where effective leadership is concerned.

In additional, follow-up research, Zaccaro and his colleagues (Mumford et al., in press) examined the relationship between a large number of personal characteristics and leadership activities among high school students and college freshmen. They found that several of these characteristics, including *achievement motivation, persuasiveness, good social skills, creativity, and good social adjustment* (i.e., popularity), were all significant predictors of students' serving as leaders. Moreover, these characteristics were predictive of leadership behavior by both females and males.

In sum, recent evidence seems to require some revision in the widely accepted view that leaders do not differ from other persons with respect to specific traits. As noted by Kirkpatrick and Locke (1991, p. 58):

> Regardless of whether leaders are born or made … it is unequivocally clear
> that *leaders are not like other people*. Leaders do not have to be great men or
> women by being intellectual geniuses or omniscient prophets to succeed,
> but they do need to have the "right stuff" and this stuff is not equally present in all people….

GENDER DIFFERENCES IN LEADERSHIP: DO MALE AND FEMALE LEADERS DIFFER?

Do male leaders and female leaders differ in their style or approach to leadership? The authors of many popular books suggest that they do (e.g., Grant, 1988). Is there any validity to these claims? Do male and female leaders really differ? Systematic research on this issue suggests that, in general, *they do not* (Powell, 1990). While female and male leaders do appear to differ in a few respects, these differences are smaller in magnitude, and fewer in number, than widely held gender role stereotypes suggest. Perhaps the most comprehensive evidence on this issue is that reported by Eagly and Johnson (1990).

These researchers examined the results of more than 150 separate studies of leadership in which comparisons between females and males were possible. They performed this task by means of the highly sophisticated technique known as *meta-analysis*, a statistical procedure for evaluating the effects of one or more variables across many different studies. Eagly and Johnson included three types of investigations in the analysis: *laboratory studies* (in which participants interacted with a stranger), *assessment studies* (in which measures of subjects' leadership style were obtained), and *organizational studies* (in which leadership behavior in actual organizations was assessed). The researchers reasoned that any differences between males and females would be more apparent in the first two types of studies than in the third type. This would be the case because in actual organizations, leadership roles would require similar behavior from males and females. As a result, any gender differences would tend to disappear. In laboratory and assessment studies, in contrast, differences between males and females would not be reduced by such role requirements.

The investigators examined potential differences between male and female leaders with respect to two key dimensions generally viewed as playing a crucial role in leader behavior or style: (1) concern with maintenance of good interpersonal relations (often known as *showing consideration*) versus concern with task performance (known as *initiating structure*) and (2) participative versus autocratic decision-making style. Gender role stereotypes suggest that female leaders might show more concern with interpersonal relations and tend to make decisions in a more participative manner than male leaders. Results, however, offered only weak support for such beliefs. With respect to showing consideration and initiating structure, there were few significant findings. In laboratory studies, females were slightly higher than males on *both* dimensions. In organizational studies, no differences on these dimensions were observed.

Turning to decision-making style, females did appear to adopt a more democratic or participative style than males; moreover, this was true across all three groups of studies (laboratory, assessment, and organizational studies). What accounts for this difference? One possibility is that female leaders are more concerned than males with interpersonal relations and realize that permitting subordinates to offer input to decisions is one way of maintaining good relations with them. Another possibility, suggested by Eagly and Johnson, involves the fact that women are higher than men in interpersonal skills. Such superiority, in turn, may make it easier for them to adopt a decision-making approach utilizing considerable give-and-take with subordinates. Whatever the precise basis for this difference, the overall findings of the meta-analysis conducted by Eagly and Johnson suggest that female and male leaders may indeed differ in some respects, but that these differences are smaller in magnitude and less consistent than gender role stereotypes suggest.

LEADER EFFECTIVENESS: TWO INFLUENTIAL VIEWS

All leaders are definitely not equal. Some are effective and contribute to high levels of performance and satisfaction on the part of their followers. Others are much less successful in these respects. Why is this the case? What factors determine leaders' success in directing their groups? This has been a central issue in much research concerned with leadership (Kiesler, Reber, & Wunderer, 1987; Vecchio, 1987). As yet, no definitive answers have emerged. But the two theories described below—Fiedler's *contingency theory* (Fiedler, 1978; Fiedler & Garcia, 1987) and Vroom and Yetton's *normative theory* (Vroom & Yetton, 1973)—have added considerably to our understanding of this issue.

Contingency theory: Matching leaders and tasks

Fiedler labels his approach the **contingency theory**, and this term is quite appropriate, for the theory's central assumption is this: A leader's contribution to successful performance by his or her group is determined both by the leader's traits and by various features of the situation. For a full understanding of leader effectiveness, both types of factors must be considered.

With respect to characteristics possessed by leaders, Fiedler identifies *esteem* (liking) for *least-preferred coworker* (LPC for short) as most important. LPC refers to a leader's tendency to evaluate in a favorable or in an unfavorable manner the person with whom she or he has found it most difficult to work. Leaders who perceive this person in negative terms (low-LPC leaders) seem primarily concerned with successful task performance. In contrast, those who perceive their least-preferred coworker in a positive light (high-LPC leaders) seem mainly concerned with good relations with subordinates. Which of these types of leaders is more effective? Contingency theory's answer is: It depends. And what it depends on is several situational factors. Fiedler suggests that whether low-LPC or high-LPC leaders are more effective depends on the degree to which the situation is favorable to the leader—provides this person with control over subordinates. This, in turn, is determined largely by three factors: (1) the nature of the leader's relations with group members (the extent to which he or she enjoys their support); (2) the degree of structure in the task being performed (the extent to which task goals and subordinates' roles are clearly defined); and (3) the leader's position power (his or her ability to enforce compliance by subordinates). Combining these three factors, the leader's situational control can range from very high (positive relations with members, a highly structured task, high position power) to very low (negative relations, an unstructured task, low position power).

To return to the central question: When are different types of leaders most effective? Fiedler suggests that low-LPC leaders (ones who are task-oriented) are superior to high-LPC leaders (ones who are people-oriented) when situational control is either very low or very high. In contrast, high-LPC leaders have an edge when situational control falls within the moderate range (see Figure 9.12). The reasoning behind these predictions is as follows: Under conditions of low situational control, groups need considerable guidance to operate effectively. Since low-LPC leaders are more likely to provide firm guidance, they will usually be superior in such cases. Similarly, low-LPC leaders have an edge under conditions that offer leaders high situational control. Here such leaders realize that conditions are very favorable and that task performance is assured. As a result, they often adopt a relaxed hands-off style, which is appreciated by subordinates. In contrast, high-LPC leaders, feeling that they already enjoy good relations with subordinates, may shift their attention to task performance. Their attempts to provide guidance in this respect may then be perceived as needless meddling, with the result that performance suffers.

To repeat: Fiedler's theory predicts that low-LPC (task-oriented) leaders will be more effective than high-LPC (relations-oriented) leaders under conditions of either low or high situational control. In contrast, high-LPC leaders will have an edge under conditions in which situational control is moderate.

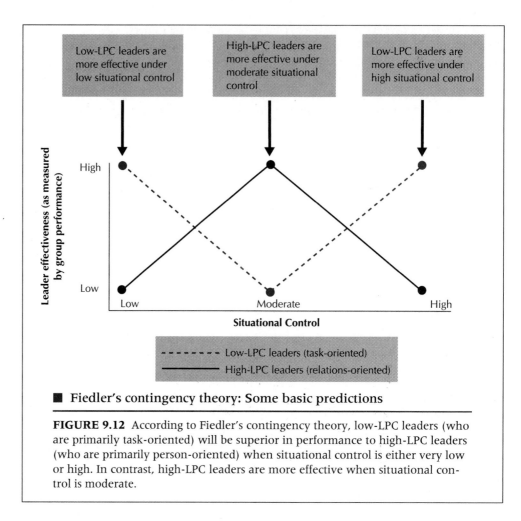

Low-LPC leaders are more effective under low situational control

High-LPC leaders are more effective under moderate situational control

Low-LPC leaders are more effective under high situational control

Leader effectiveness (as measured by group performance)

High

Low

Low   Moderate   High

Situational Control

- - - - - - - Low-LPC leaders (task-oriented)

——————— High-LPC leaders (relations-oriented)

■ Fiedler's contingency theory: Some basic predictions

FIGURE 9.12 According to Fiedler's contingency theory, low-LPC leaders (who are primarily task-oriented) will be superior in performance to high-LPC leaders (who are primarily person-oriented) when situational control is either very low or high. In contrast, high-LPC leaders are more effective when situational control is moderate.

Contingency theory: Its current status

Have these predictions been supported by research findings? Existing evidence presents something of a mixed picture. On the one hand, most laboratory studies performed to test various aspects of contingency theory have yielded positive results (Strube & Garcia, 1981). On the other, the results of studies conducted with naturally existing groups have not been as favorable (Peters, Hartke, & Pohlman, 1985). Such investigations have sometimes yielded results contrary to what contingency theory predicts. In addition, the theory has been criticized on several important grounds. A degree of ambiguity exists with respect to the placement of specific situations along the dimension of situational control (Ashour, 1973). Unless situations can be accurately classified as low, moderate, or high in situational control, predictions concerning leader effectiveness are difficult to make. Similarly, some critics have questioned the adequacy of the procedures used to measure leaders' standing along the LPC dimension, and even the validity of this dimension itself (e.g., Peters, Hartke, & Pohlman, 1985).

Taking such criticism plus existing evidence into account, the following tentative conclusions seem justified. Contingency theory has indeed added to our understanding of key aspects of leadership and leader effectiveness. Several questions about its accuracy remain, however, and require further careful attention. Therefore, this theory should be viewed as one still undergoing refinement rather than as one that offers a fully developed framework for understanding all aspects of leader effectiveness.

Normative theory: Decision making and leader effectiveness

One of the key tasks performed by leaders is making decisions. Indeed, a defining characteristic of leadership positions is that they are places where "the buck stops" and concrete actions must be taken. Yet leaders do not operate in a social vacuum; even when they possess considerable power and authority, there is no guarantee that their decisions will be accepted or implemented by followers. Thus, leadership is always something of a two-way street, in which leaders influence followers and followers, in turn, exert some degree of influence over leaders.

Given this fact, an intriguing question arises: In making decisions, how much participation by followers should leaders permit? According to one theory of leadership, **normative theory**, this question is an important determinant of leader effectiveness (Vroom & Yetton, 1973). Leaders who permit an appropriate amount of participation by followers will generally be more effective, over the long haul, than leaders who permit either too much or too little. But how much participation is enough? Vroom and Yetton's theory suggests that this depends on several issues relating, primarily, to the importance of the decision's being high in quality and the importance of its being accepted by subordinates. For example, consider a situation in which a high-quality decision is crucial (the stakes are high), the leader has enough information or expertise to make the decision alone, and acceptance by subordinates is not crucial (the decision will work even without their support). Here, a relatively *autocratic* style of decision is best. It is efficient, and getting the decision implemented will cost very little. In contrast, consider a situation in which a high-quality decision is necessary, the leader has enough information to make the decision alone, but acceptance by subordinates is crucial—the decision won't work without their active support. Here, a more participative style would be preferable.

Vroom and Yetton's theory suggests that by answering a series of such questions, leaders can arrive at the appropriate decision style—one that affords subordinates just the right amount of participation to maintain their morale while retaining the highest degree of efficiency possible. In general, these guidelines and suggestions seem to work: Leaders who adapt their style of decision making to existing conditions are generally more successful than ones who are either uniformly autocratic or participative in style (Vroom & Jago, 1978). Additional evidence, however, suggests the need for certain adjustments in the theory.

First, it appears that most persons prefer a participative approach by their leader even under conditions where normative theory recommends an autocratic style (Heilman et al., 1984). Second, leaders and subordinates seem to differ in their reactions to various methods for reaching decisions. Leaders tend to prefer those methods suggested by the normative model in any given situation, while subordinates tend to prefer participative strategies in all cases (Heilman et al., 1984). Third, it appears that certain personal characteristics of a leader may play a key role in determining the relative effectiveness of various decision strategies (Crouch & Yetton, 1987). For example, in situations involving conflicting opinions, only managers who are relatively high in conflict-handling skills should use the kind of participative decision-making strategy recommended by the Vroom and Yetton model. Managers low in conflict-handling skills, in contrast, obtain better results with a relatively autocratic style, despite the fact that this is not predicted by the model.

To conclude: Existing evidence suggests that the normative theory offers useful guidelines to leaders for choosing the most effective approach to decision making. However, adjustments in the model seem necessary, to take account of strong general preferences for participative procedures, differences in the perspectives of leaders and subordinates, and the personal skills or traits of leaders. With the addition of such modifications, the Vroom and Yetton model may prove very helpful in our efforts to understand this key aspect of leader effectiveness.

TRANSFORMATIONAL LEADERSHIP: LEADERSHIP THROUGH VISION AND CHARISMA

In the darkest days of the Depression, the United States seemed poised on the brink of social chaos. With millions out of work and the economy in a seemingly endless decline, despair was rampant. Through his inspiring speeches ("The only thing we have to fear is fear itself ...") and vigorous actions, President Franklin Roosevelt pulled the nation back from the edge of violence and saved the grand American experiment in political democracy....

World history is filled with similar examples. Down through the ages, some leaders have demonstrated extraordinary success in generating profound changes in the beliefs, perceptions, values, and actions of their followers (see Figure 9.13). Indeed, it is not extreme to suggest that such persons have often served as key agents of social change, transforming entire societies through their words and actions (Bass, 1985). Individuals who accomplish such feats are often described as being **transformational** or **charismatic leaders**, and the terms seem fitting. Such persons do indeed transform social, political, or economic reality; and they do seem to possess unusual and special skills that equip them for this task. (The word charisma means *gift* in Greek.) What personal characteristics make certain leaders charismatic? How do such leaders exert their profound effects upon many other persons? Systematic research on this issue has begun to yield some intriguing answers to these and related questions.

The basic nature of charisma: Traits or relationships?

At first glance, it is tempting to assume that transformational or charismatic leaders are special by virtue of the possession of certain traits; in other words, such leadership might be understood as an extension of the *great person theory* described earlier in this chapter. While traits may well play a role in transformational leadership, there is growing consensus that it makes more sense to understand such leadership as involving a special type of *relationship* between leaders and their followers (House, 1977). Within this framework, charismatic leadership rests more on specific types of reactions by

■ Transformational (charismatic) leaders

FIGURE 9.13 Throughout recorded history, some leaders have exerted a profound impact on their followers and on entire societies. Research findings have begun to shed much light on how such persons achieve these dramatic effects.

followers than on traits possessed by leaders. Such reactions include: (1) levels of performance beyond those that would normally be expected; (2) high levels of devotion, loyalty, and reverence toward the leader; (3) enthusiasm for and excitement with the leader and the leader's ideas; and (4) a willingness on the part of subordinates to sacrifice their own personal interests for the sake of a larger collective goal. In short, transformational or charismatic leadership involves a special kind of leader-follower relationship, one in which the leader can, in the words of one author, "make ordinary people do extraordinary things in the face of adversity."

The behavior of transformational leaders

But what, precisely, do transformational or charismatic leaders do to generate this kind of relationship with their subordinates? Studies designed to answer this question point to the following general conclusion: such leaders gain the capacity to exert profound influence over others through many different tactics.

First, and perhaps most important, transformational leaders propose a vision (Howell & Frost, 1989). They describe, usually in vivid, emotion-provoking terms, an image of what their nation, group, or organization could—and should—become. A dramatic example of such leadership is provided by the words of Martin Luther King, in his famous "I Have a Dream" speech:

> "So I say to you, my friends, that even though we must face the difficulties of today and tomorrow, I still have a dream. It is a dream deeply rooted in the American dream that one day this nation will rise up and live out the true meaning of its creed—we hold these truths to be self-evident, that all men are created equal. This will be the day when all of God's children will be able to sing with new meaning "My country, 'tis of thee, sweet land of liberty… ."

But transformational leaders do not simply describe a dream or vision; in addition, they offer a clear road map for attaining it; they tell their followers, in straightforward terms, how to get from here to there. This too seems to be crucial, for a vision that seems perpetually out of reach is unlikely to motivate people to try to attain it.

Third, transformational leaders engage in what Conger (1991) terms *framing*: they define the purpose of their movement or organization in a way that gives meaning and purpose to whatever actions they are requesting from followers. Perhaps the nature of framing is best illustrated by the well-known anecdote of two stonecutters working on a cathedral in the Middle Ages. When asked what they are doing, one replies, "Why, cutting this stone, of course." The other replies, "Building the world's most beautiful temple to the glory of God." Which person would be more likely to expend greater effort? The answer is obvious.

In addition, transformational leaders often show greater-than-average willingness to take risks and engage in unconventional actions in order to reach their stated goals. In order to help thwart the coup that threatened the budding democracy of his nation, Boris Yeltsin rushed to the Russian parliament building, where he stood on top of a tank and pleaded with troops sent there by the hard-liners to withdraw. In this manner he demonstrated his deep commitment to the forces of reform.

Other tactics shown by transformational leaders include high levels of self-confidence and confidence in their followers; a high degree of concern for their followers' needs; excellent communication skills, such as the ability to "read" others' reactions quickly and accurately; and a stirring personal style (House, Spangler, & Woycke, 1991). Finally, transformational leaders are often masters of *impression management*, engaging in many actions designed to enhance their attractiveness and appeal to others. When these forms of behavior are added to the captivating and exciting visions they propound, the tremendous impact of transformational or charismatic leaders begins to come sharply into focus. Their influence, it appears, does not stem from the possession of semimagical traits; rather, it is a logical result of a complex cluster of behaviors and techniques. In the final analysis, however, the essence of transformational leadership does appear to rest on the ability of such persons to inspire others, through their words, their vision, and their actions. As Conger puts it (1991, p. 44): "If you as a leader can make an appealing dream seem like tomorrow's reality, your subordinates will freely choose to follow you."

CULTURAL DIFFERENCES IN LEADERSHIP IN AMERICAN AND ASIAN CORPORATIONS

Are the kind of leadership processes we have described above universal—present in all cultures? Or does leadership operate differently in different cultures? Once again, research has begun to reveal differences based on cultural values.

While the term leadership generally conjures up images of political or military leaders, it is clear that in these times of increasing economic competition a nation's fortunes rest to an important extent with its business leaders. And important differences have been noted in the style of such leaders in different countries (Kotter, 1982). Some of the most revealing information on this issue to date has been reported by Doktor (1990) in comparative studies of the heads of major companies in the United States, Japan, Korea, and Hong Kong. Doktor contends that cultural values strongly determine how people perceive the nature of their jobs, and this includes the chief executive officers (CEOs for short) of major companies. In Japan, he notes, business leaders perceive that what affects one part of society may well affect other parts as well. Thus, they view their corporate decisions in a broad context that takes account of the decisions' consequences for other segments of society outside the business community. According to Doktor (1990), Korean culture is similar, but also places stronger emphasis on authority and a top-down decision-making process. Hong Kong presents a mixed picture, since in that culture traditional Chinese values emphasizing mutual influences between various aspects of society are combined with Western beliefs that place a high value on individuality and independence. In the United States, in contrast, decisions are viewed in a somewhat narrower context, focused on a company and its goals.

How do these contrasting cultural values influence the leadership style of Asian and American CEOs? To find out, Doktor compared the workdays of CEOs in Japan, Korea, Hong Kong, and the United States. These comparisons yielded some revealing findings. First, he found that CEOs in each country spent about the same proportions of their days working alone (25 percent) and working in groups (75 percent). However, the duration of each task they performed varied greatly. In the United States, almost 50 percent of all tasks were completed in only nine minutes or less. In contrast, the comparable percentages of short tasks in Japan and Korea were much lower—10 percent and 14 percent, respectively; as expected, Hong Kong was in between. The reverse pattern appeared for tasks requiring more than one hour. American business leaders spent only 10 percent of their time on such activities; Japanese and Korean managers spent 42 and 44 percent of their time on such tasks. In short, a clear pattern of differences emerged: American leaders spent their days performing a large number of tasks of brief duration; Japanese and Korean managers divided their days into a smaller number of longer segments.

Doktor contends that these differences are consistent with cultural differences among these countries. Because Japanese and Korean managers consider the broader context of their actions and decisions, they feel strongly that these should not be rushed. Thus, they spend more time on each task they perform. In contrast, American managers adopt a more restricted view of the impact of their decisions, so they are more willing to make them quickly. These differences are magnified by the contrasting status of business leaders in U.S. and Asian cultures. Asian cultures generally confer very high status on top business leaders. Thus, it is inappropriate to rush these people through an overcrowded schedule. CEOs in the United States also enjoy high status and respect, but not, according to Doktor, quite as high as that in Japan and Korea. As a result, their subordinates are less reluctant to rush them through many brief meetings.

These findings suggest that even today, when modern technology dictates the form of many business practices, cultural differences can and do play a key role in shaping the actions and perceptions of business leaders. As T. Fujisawa, the cofounder of Honda Corporation, once put it, "Japanese and American management are 95 percent the same—and differ in all important respects." We might add: "And those differences can be traced, to an important degree, to specific cultural factors."

SUMMARY AND REVIEW

THE NATURE AND FUNCTION OF GROUPS

A *group* consists of two of more individuals who share common goals, whose fates are interdependent, who have a stable relationship, and who recognize the group's existence. Groups exert influence upon their members through *roles* (members' assigned functions within the group), *status* (their relative standing or influence), *norms* (rules concerning appropriate behavior), and *cohesiveness* (forces acting to keep members within the group, e.g., their attraction to it).

GROUPS AND TASK PERFORMANCE

Individuals' performance of various tasks is often affected by the presence of others or by the potential evaluation of their work. Such effects are known as *social facilitation*, although they can involve reduced as well as enhanced task performance. Social facilitation appears to stem from arousal induced by the presence of others. *Distraction-conflict theory* suggests that such arousal stems from conflict between paying attention to others and paying attention to the task at hand.

Groups are more efficient in performing certain types of tasks than are individuals (e.g., additive and compensatory tasks). However, they are worse than individuals in performing other types of tasks (e.g., conjunctive ones). In some cases where groups might prove relatively efficient, their output is hindered by *social loafing*—the tendency of some members to take it easy and let others do most of the work. There is cultural variation in the extent to which individuals indulge in social loafing and in their responses to its presence in their groups. Several techniques (e.g., making individuals' work identifiable, providing standards for self-evaluation) are effective in countering tendencies toward social loafing. When a task is important or meaningful to individuals, they may react to social loafing by others not solely with anger or withdrawal but with *social compensation*—an increase in their own effort.

DECISION MAKING IN GROUPS

Groups make many key decisions. These can sometimes be predicted by *social decision schemes*—simple rules relating the initial views of members to the group's final decision. Procedures such as *straw polls* can influence the views of individual members and hence the decisions reached by groups. In addition, group decision making is influenced by *deliberation style*—whether groups focus on information and evidence or on members' judgments.

As a result of their deliberations, groups often demonstrate *group polarization*, a tendency to shift toward more extreme views. Two other potential difficulties faced by decision-making groups are *groupthink*, a tendency to become concerned more with maintaining consensus than with choosing the best alternative, and an inability to pool unshared information. Groupthink may have played a part in the decision making processes leading to the signing of the Meech Lake Accord.

LEADERSHIP

Leaders are group members who exert influence on other group members in the direction of specific goals. The *great person theory* of leadership suggests that specific persons become leaders because they possess crucial traits. Recent evidence suggests that there may be a grain of truth in this theory: Successful leaders do appear to differ from other persons in several respects. In particular, they demonstrate great *flexibility* in responding to the needs of group members and to changing external conditions.

Male and female leaders do not differ in their relative concern with task performance and interpersonal relations. However, female leaders tend to adopt a more democratic leadership style than do males.

According to Fiedler's *contingency theory*, leader effectiveness stems from a complex interplay between leaders' characteristics and the situations they confront. Vroom and Yetton's *normative theory* proposes that one important determinant of such effectiveness is decision-making style—the extent to which leaders permit participation by followers in key decisions. Leaders who permit the most appropriate level of participation by followers in a given situation are more effective than leaders who permit too little or too much participation.

Transformational or *charismatic leaders* exert profound effects on their followers. They do this by establishing a special kind of relationship with their followers, and by proposing an inspiring vision of where the group could be or ought to be. Important cultural differences exist with respect to leadership processes. American business leaders and Asian business leaders show several differences in style.

KEY TERMS

Additive Tasks Tasks in which the group product is the sum or combination of the efforts of individual members.

Charismatic Leaders Leaders who induce high levels of loyalty, respect, and admiration for themselves among their followers. (See also *Transformational Leaders*.)

Cohesiveness All forces acting on group members to cause them to remain part of a group; including mutual attraction, interdependence, shared goals, and so on.

Compensatory Tasks Tasks in which the group product is the average of all members' contributions.

Conjunctive Tasks Tasks in which the performance of the poorest member determines the group product.

Contingency Theory A theory suggesting the leader effectiveness is determined by a complex interplay between the leader's characteristics and the favorability of the situation (situational control) for the leader.

Decision Making The processes through which groups move toward consensus and reach decisions.

Disjunctive Tasks Tasks in which the contribution of the best member determines the final group product.

Distraction-conflict Theory A theory suggesting that social facilitation stems from the conflict produced when individuals attempt simultaneously to pay attention to other persons and to the task being performed.

Drive Theory of Social Facilitation A theory suggesting that the mere presence of others is arousing and increases the tendency to perform dominant responses.

Evaluation Apprehension Concern over being evaluated by others. Such concern can increase arousal and so contribute to social facilitation.

Great Person Theory A theory of leadership suggesting that all great leaders share key traits that suit them for positions of authority.

Group Polarization The tendency of group members to shift toward more extreme positions than those they initially held as a result of group discussion.

Group Two or more persons who interact with one another, share common goals, are somehow interdependent, and recognize that they belong to a group.

Groupthink The tendency of members of highly cohesive groups to seek consensus so strongly that they ignore information inconsistent with their views and often make disastrous decisions.

Information Sampling Model A theory of group decision making suggesting that group members are more likely to discuss shared information than information not shared by all group members. This tendency increases with group size.

Leadership The process through which leaders influence other group members toward attainment of specific group goals.

Normative Theory A theory suggesting that leaders are most effective when they adopt the style of decision making (from autocratic to participative) most appropriate in a given situation.

Norms Rules within a group indicating how its members should (or should not) behave.

Risky Shift The tendency for groups to recommend riskier courses of action following group discussion than before its occurrence.

Roles The set of behaviors that individuals occupying specific positions within a group are expected to perform.

Social Compensation Increased effort on the part of one or more group members to compensate for social loafing on the part of one or more others.

Social Decision Schemes Rules relating the initial distribution of member views to final group decisions.

Social Facilitation Effects upon performance resulting from the presence of others.

Social Loafing The tendency of some group members to exert less effort on a task than they would if working on it alone.

Status Social standing or rank.

Straw Poll A procedure in which group members indicate their current preferences regarding a decision. These statements are not binding upon them, so they are free to shift to other positions.

Transformational Leaders Leaders who exert profound influence over followers by proposing an inspiring vision, among other techniques. (See also *Charismatic Leaders*.)

FOR MORE INFORMATION

Hendrick, C. (Ed.). (1987). *Group processes*. Newbury Park, CA: Sage.

    A collection of chapters dealing with various aspects of group processes (e.g., group decision making, leadership, minority influence). Each chapter is quite up to date and was prepared by established experts in the field.

Paulus, P. B. (Ed.). (1989). *Psychology of group influence* (2nd ed.). Hillsdale, NJ: Erlbaum.

    This book deals with many of the topics considered in this chapter (e.g., social facilitation, social loafing, leadership). If you'd like to know more about these aspects of behavior in group meetings, this is an excellent source to consult.

Chapter TEN

Applied Social Psychology: Health, Environmental, and Legal Applications

Health Psychology: Maintaining Good Health, Responding to Illness
Stress and Illness/Responding to Health Problems/Medical Care as a Source of Problems

Environmental Psychology: Effects of Environmental Factors on Behavior and Effects of Human Behavior on the Environment
How the Environment Affects Human Behavior/How Human Behavior Affects the Environment

Social Psychology and the Legal System
Before the Case Goes to Court: Police Interrogation and Media Publicity/The Testimony of Eyewitnesses/In the Courtroom: Lawyers' and Judges' Influence on the Verdict/Characteristics of Defendants and Jurors

SPECIAL SECTIONS

FOCUS ON RESEARCH: CLASSIC CANADIAN CONTRIBUTIONS
Second Language Learning and Bilingualism: The Contribution of Wallace Lambert

S ome of the many applications of social psychology will be described in this chapter. By **applied social psychology** we mean the utilization of social psychological principles and research methods in real-world settings in efforts to solve a variety of individual and societal problems (Weyant, 1986). Applications of social psychology have expanded tremendously in recent years. You will recall that this was one of the trends mentioned in chapter 1. The fact that social psychology can be utilized in this way in so many diverse areas, is a mark of the strength and relevance of its accumulated theory and research.

Social psychology is now being applied in settings as diverse as the courtroom (in *forensic psychology*), the work setting (in *industrial-organizational psychology*), medicine (in *health psychology*), the playing field (in *sports psychology*), and even in the arena of politics (in *political psychology*), to name just a few. In the present chapter, we will focus on only three of these areas: the ways in which the principles of social psychology can be applied to our health, the physical environment that surrounds us, and the legal system.

This chapter provides a fitting end for a book on social psychology. We have come full circle to where we, and social psychology itself, began: advocating the importance of applying social psychological knowledge to real-world problems. You may recall that in chapter 1 we stressed the need for examination of social behavior in many applied areas. In addition, one of the founders of modern social psychology, Kurt Lewin, was an advocate for applied social psychology and was himself the architect of an extensive program of applied research, which he called *action research* (1948). We also mentioned in chapter 1 that the origins of psychology in Canada were very much based in applied research responding to societal needs between and during the two world wars. This tradition of applied research in Canada has continued to the present. Many of the Canadian social psychologists mentioned in this book are involved in applying their ideas and research to Canadian social problems. Perhaps the most famous of these applied contributions comes from the work of Wallace Lambert at McGill University. The following section, "Focus on Research—Classic Canadian Contributions," describes his examination of second language learning.

Second Language Learning and Bilingualism: The Contribution of Wallace Lambert

Second language learning and bilingualism has been a particularly important issue in Canada's bilingual society. It is not surprising, therefore, that Canadian researchers were pioneers in this area and remain on the forefront of research today. The most notable of these researchers is Wallace Lambert of McGill University, whose work has extended over thirty years.

Canada became an officially bilingual country in 1969 when the Official Languages Act was endorsed by parliament, giving equal status to the English and French languages. The 1991 census shows that 60 percent of Canadians have English as their mother tongue and 24 percent have French (Harrison & Marmen, 1994). Currently, 83 percent of the population can speak English, 32 percent can speak French, and 16 percent are English-French bilingual. This latter figure represents a 33 percent increase since the 1950s in the proportion of the population who are bilingual.

One reason for this increase may be the growth of French immersion programs for non-Francophone children. These programs were initiated in Quebec in 1965, when the Protestant School Board of Montreal launched the "St. Lambert Project" for children of Anglophone and immigrant parents. Wallace Lambert and his colleagues investigated the children's progress, and the results of their research have guided the introduction of French immersion programs since that time (Genesee, 1984; Lambert & Tucker, 1972). Children in the project were taught entirely in French from kindergarten to grade two. English language was introduced for half-hour periods during grade two and the proportion of the curriculum taught in English was gradually increased until by grade seven this included about half of the classes. The progress of these mostly Anglophone children was compared with that of Anglophone children taught in English and Francophone children taught in French.

Parents at that time, as now, had many questions about the effects of French immersion. For example, does being initially taught exclusively in French create deficits in English language proficiency? Would problems arise if children were taught a particular subject (e.g., history or mathematics) in French originally and then had to switch to English? Results of Lambert's research were encouraging. Children in the St. Lambert project achieved a level of spoken French far superior to that of Anglophone children in conventional French-as-a-second-language programs, though they did not quite achieve the proficiency of native French speakers. Further, their written and oral skills in English were as good as those of the children taught in English (1974). There was also no deficit shown if children were tested in English on a subject that they had studied in French. In fact, the overall results of the St. Lambert project, and subsequent research into similar programs, tend to confirm that early French immersion produces no detrimental effects on English language development or progress of other academic subjects, while French language progress is much enhanced (Genesee, 1984).

Beyond the academic effects of acquiring a second language, Lambert has been interested in the *social* implications of such bilingualism for the individual and for group relations. For example, the St. Lambert project found that the children involved had a more positive attitude to Francophones than conventionally educated Anglophone children. However, later research suggested that this more positive attitude may not last into adulthood (Genesee, 1984).

Lambert has also suggested (1978; Lambert & Taylor, 1984) that acquiring a second

▶

language may have different implications for a majority individual and a minority individual. The acquisition of a second language may be entirely beneficial for persons who belong to the majority group in a particular society, enhancing their academic, employment, and social opportunities. Lambert termed this *additive bilingualism*. However, there may be some personal and social loss involved in second language acquisition (usually the language of the majority) for the minority individual. Because of their dominant position, the culture and language of a majority person are seldom threatened by learning another culture's language, whereas, for minority individuals there may be a danger of loss of one's own identity and of the strength of one's native language in the community (termed *subtractive bilingualism*). The bilingual minority individual may find him- or herself drawn increasingly to participate in the majority culture and communicate in that language, with consequent losses of own culture and sense of social identity. For example,

Bourhis's (1990) research examined communication in the bilingual New Brunswick civil service. Anglophones are a majority in that context and tend to be of higher status. He found that Francophones were more likely to switch to English (even if not fluent) when addressed in that language by an Anglophone colleague than a fully bilingual Anglophone was to switch to French when addressed in that language.

Lambert's body of work has combined theoretical and applied research in addressing social problems: a true example of Lewin's *action research*. As Lewin suggested (1948), social psychologists can also be agents of social change. Building on the pioneering research described above, many researchers in Quebec continue to investigate the social psychology of language, studying, for example, its importance to intergroup relations and cross-cultural communication (Bourhis, 1979, 1984; Genesee & Bourhis, 1988) or to individual social identity and acculturation (Clément, 1987; Young & Gardner, 1990).

In the remainder of this chapter, we will first turn to *health psychology* and research that ranges from preventive medicine to the ways people cope with illness. The second major focus is on *environmental psychology*, research that deals with the interaction between the physical world and human behavior (Sanchez & Wiesenfeld, 1987). Finally, we will examine one of the more recent areas of expansion: *forensic social psychology*, which is concerned with social psychological factors in the legal system.

HEALTH PSYCHOLOGY: MAINTAINING GOOD HEALTH, RESPONDING TO ILLNESS

Though you may think of health and illness in terms of physical processes and the field of medicine, we now know that psychological factors affect all aspects of our physical well-being (Rodin & Salovey, 1989). **Health psychology** is the specialty that studies the psychological processes affecting the development, prevention, and treatment of physical illness (Glass, 1989). Let's consider three examples of ways in which social psychological research has been applied to health.

STRESS AND ILLNESS

At least since World War II, psychologists have been interested in **stress** and its effects on human behavior (Lazarus, 1993). For purposes of this discussion, *stress* refers to the responses elicited by physical or psychological events that an individual perceives to be harmful or emotionally upsetting. The original focus on the physical causes of stress (Selye, 1956) was soon broadened to include *psychological stress* (Lazarus, 1966).

In response to either physical or psychological danger, the individual feels threatened and tries to **cope** with the situation; coping behavior is considered successful if it reduces or eliminates the threat (Taylor, Buunk, & Aspinwall, 1990). What is the connection between stress and illness?

The effects of stress

The most common sources of stress are occupational threats (such as pressure from a supervisor to work harder) and family threats (such as complaints from a spouse) (Hendrix, Steel, & Schultz, 1987). As stress increases, illness becomes more common. Among steel pipe mill workers, for example, increases in the work load are found to result in an increase in physical symptoms (Perrewe & Anthony, 1990). For college students, common sources of stress include low grades, the divorce of parents, or an unwanted pregnancy (Brody, 1989). For all of us, even such minor everyday hassles as driving in heavy traffic or having to interact with an annoying coworker can increase our likelihood of catching a cold or developing the flu (Weinberger, Hiner, & Tierney, 1987). With a more serious problem such as the death of a loved one, there is an even greater probability that illness will occur (Schleifer et al., 1983).

When several negative events occur in the same general time period, they have a cumulative effect (Seta, Seta, & Wang, 1991); and as the total number of stressful experiences increases, the probability of illness increases. Scales have been developed to quantify stress. (For example, death of a spouse = 100, losing your job = 47, going on a vacation = 13, etc.) These values are sometimes simply added (Crandall, 1992) and sometimes combined according to a complex formula (Birnbaum & Sotoodeh, 1991). Either way, as the number of negative events increases, both perceived stress and susceptibility to the common cold increase (Cohen, Tyrrell, & Smith, 1993).

One reason that physical illness is likely to occur during times of stress is that the resulting anxiety and worry may interfere with such health-related behaviors as eating a balanced diet or exercising (Wiebe & McCallum, 1986). In addition to this indirect effect, the body's immune system functions less well when stress is high (Stone et al., 1987). This finding of a direct link between psychological responses and the body's defense against disease has led to the development of the field of **psychoneuroimmunology**. This interdisciplinary approach studies stress, emotional and behavioral reactions, and the immune system simultaneously (Ader & Cohen, 1993).

As an example of such work, consider the fact that college students are found to develop upper-respiratory infections at exam time (Dorian et al., 1982). How could that happen? Jemmott and Magloire (1988) did a study of college students in which they obtained samples of the students' saliva, which contains secretory immunoglobulin A, the body's primary defense against such infections. The level of this substance was found to drop during final exams and then to rise again when exams were over. Thus, the psychological stress of finals resulted in a change in body chemistry that facilitated the development of disease.

Reducing the harmful effects of stress

Stress is unavoidable in our lives, so what can we do to reduce its harmful effects? A common recommendation is to stay as healthy as possible through a sensible pattern of diet, sleep, and regular exercise. The result is an increase in *fitness*—the maintenance of good physical condition as evidenced by endurance and strength. Fitness is associated with *hardiness*, or positive psychological characteristics such as self-confidence and self-discipline (Hogan, 1989; see below). Is there also evidence that simply being fit has any effect on whether a person gets sick?

The answer is yes, according to convincing data provided by Brown (1991). He studied over one hundred undergraduate students, obtaining self-reports about their physical exercise. In addition, the investigator obtained an objective indicator of fitness by measuring each student's heart rate before, during, and after he or she rode an exercise bike under standard conditions. Similarly, the investigator assessed illness episodes through students' self-reports and through the records of their visits to the college health center during two semesters. Stress was defined by the number and severity of negative events in the students' lives over the previous twelve months. The role of stress was quite clear. Students with little stress in their lives had very few illnesses, regardless of their physical fitness. When stress was high, however, fitness was of great importance. Among those who experienced high stress, the low-fitness students had significantly more health center visits to treat illnesses than did those high in fitness. As hypothesized, the health of those who are physically fit is found much less vulnerable to the negative effects of life stress.

Beyond one's physical condition, there is the psychological factor of **hardiness**. This involves a sense of commitment, a perception that difficulties represent a challenge that can be overcome, and a belief that you have control over your life (Kobasa, 1979). We'll look at further evidence about the importance of perceived control in the following section. Hardiness is found to be associated with a positive self-concept (Allred & Smith, 1989). Studies of adolescents indicate that individuals high in *either* commitment or control had fewer health problems than those low in both (Shepperd & Kashani, 1991). Zimmerman (1990) suggests that the term "learned hopefulness" (as contrasted with "learned helplessness") be applied to individuals who know how to solve problems and who feel a sense of control.

Together, exercise, fitness, and hardiness combine to protect against illness, as shown in a study of undergraduates by Roth et al. (1989). Kessler et al. (1992) present evidence indicating that genetic factors also play a role in determining how well an individual adjusts to stress.

How personality dispositions affect health

Several personality variables (in addition to hardiness) also predict who is likely to develop or not develop illness (Smith & Williams, 1992). For example, *neurotic* individuals react more negatively to stress than those who are not neurotic (Bolger & Schilling, 1991), and they are also more likely to become ill as a result (Larsen & Kasimatis, 1991).

An important reason for the negative effect of stressful events is the sense that we are powerless to prevent accidents, bad grades, failed love affairs, and so forth. When events appear to be beyond our control, we are more likely to become depressed (Brown & Siegel, 1988) and physically ill (McFarlane et al., 1983). Compas et al. (1991) propose a two-level process in our response to threat. As outlined in Figure 10.1, the first reponse is emotional distress and an attempt to cope with one's emotions. A second step is to examine the various contingencies and to assess one's competence in being able to deal with them; if the result is the perception of being in control, problem-focused coping takes place. There is a sex difference in coping styles, in that women more frequently use emotion-focused coping, while men tend to use problem-focused coping (Ptacek, Smith, & Zanas, 1992).

In some instances the only possibility is emotion-focused coping. A child about to undergo surgery can't do anything to avoid the threat or remove the need for an operation, but he or she can benefit from relaxation training and learning the techniques of cognitive distraction ("thinking about something else"). When the situation permits, a more satisfactory approach is to teach a child competence skills, provide a sense of control, and encourage problem-focused coping; for example, a child distressed about a math exam can be taught how to study and how to master the subject matter.

A widely studied aspect of personality, **locus of control**, refers to our tendency to hold generalized beliefs that either external or internal factors control our lives.

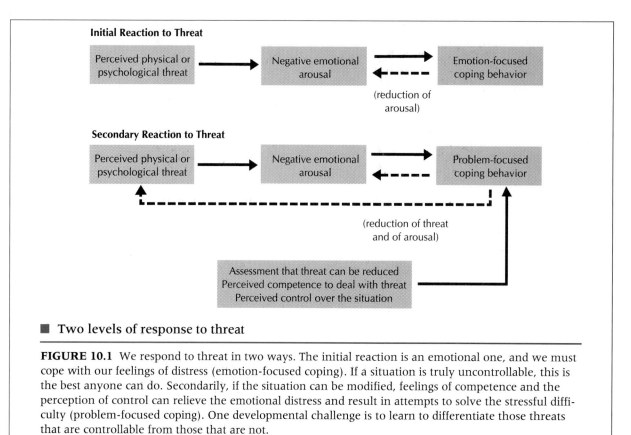

Initial Reaction to Threat

Perceived physical or psychological threat → Negative emotional arousal → Emotion-focused coping behavior

(reduction of arousal)

Secondary Reaction to Threat

Perceived physical or psychological threat → Negative emotional arousal → Problem-focused coping behavior

(reduction of threat and of arousal)

Assessment that threat can be reduced
Perceived competence to deal with threat
Perceived control over the situation

■ Two levels of response to threat

FIGURE 10.1 We respond to threat in two ways. The initial reaction is an emotional one, and we must cope with our feelings of distress (emotion-focused coping). If a situation is truly uncontrollable, this is the best anyone can do. Secondarily, if the situation can be modified, feelings of competence and the perception of control can relieve the emotional distress and result in attempts to solve the stressful difficulty (problem-focused coping). One developmental challenge is to learn to differentiate those threats that are controllable from those that are not.

Source: Based on proposals in Compas et al., 1991.

Those who express an *internal locus of control* seek more health-related information, remember the information better, and obtain medical examinations more readily than those with an external locus of control (Quadrel & Lau, 1989). Among patients who had recovered from a heart attack, "externals" were found to have higher serum cholesterol levels, to eat more fat, and to perceive themselves as less healthy than "internals" (Birkimer, Lucas, & Birkimer, 1991).

Related research indicates that health is also affected by the kind of goals for which we strive. Emmons (1992) identified undergraduates and older married couples in terms of their expressing high- or low-level strivings. Table 10.1 gives examples. Subjects who reported high-level strivings were found to experience more psychological distress but less physical illness. Low strivings were associated with less negative affect and more physical illness. The investigator suggested that in their everyday lives people have a trade-off between feeling depressed and getting sick. One explanation is that high, difficult goals require commitment and effort (thus increasing hardiness) but that in reality such goals are seldom met (thus increasing negative affect). Easy goals require little effort and commitment, but they are easy to reach.

People also differ in their characteristic feelings of **pessimism/optimism**. Those with a *pessimistic* outlook view events not only as uncontrollable but as likely to get worse; one result of this dark perception of life is that a given amount of stress causes more symptoms of illness than is true for optimistic individuals (Scheier & Carver,

■ Personal strivings are the characteristic recurring goals that a person is trying to accomplish in his or her life. People differ in whether they strive for relatively difficult, abstract goals or relatively easy, concrete ones. Those who emphasize high-level strivings experience more psychological stress (because they can't meet their goals) but less physical illness (because their commitment increases hardiness). Those who emphasize low-level strivings experience less emotional discomfort (because they can reach their goals) but more illness (because of a lack of commitment).

TABLE 10.1 High-level versus low-level goals in life

High-level, Abstract Strivings	Low-level, Concrete Strivings
I want to deepen my relationship with God.	I want to look well-groomed and clean-cut.
I want to be totally honest.	I want to be funny and make others laugh.
I want to be a fun person to be around.	I want to look attentive and not bored in class.
I want to compete against myself rather than against others.	I want to be organized and neat—clean my room and make my bed.
I want to increase my knowledge of the world.	I want to work hard or at least look like I'm working hard.

Source: Based on data in Emmons, 1992.

1987). When asked about their experiences with episodes of flu, pessimists perceive that the illness lasted longer and caused more stress than was true for optimists; pessimists also expected to catch the flu in the future (Hamid, 1990). Some research, such as that by Smith et al. (1989), suggests that pessimism is not distinguishable from the combination of anxiety and depression that is labeled *neuroticism*. Similarly, researchers at the University of British Columbia found that low self-esteem is associated with perceiving daily events in a more negative way (Campbell, Chew, & Scratchley, 1991).

The tangible benefits of *optimism* were demonstrated in a study of middle-aged men who had undergone heart bypass surgery. The more optimistic the patient, the faster his recovery and his return to a normal and active life (Scheier et al., 1989). Even more dramatic is the finding that pessimistic people die at an earlier age than optimistic ones (Peterson, Seligman, & Vaillant, 1988).

A more aggressive and hostile personality type has also been related to health problems. The **Type A** personality and behavior pattern has been associated with an increased risk of cardiovascular disease (Glass, 1977). This behavior pattern includes a continual sense of urgency about time, a workaholic lifestyle, extreme competitiveness, and a tendency to be particularly prone to anger and aggressiveness. The opposite, more relaxed pattern of behavior is termed *Type B*. Research indicates that people classified as Type A, compared to Type B, have higher blood pressure (Contrada, 1989); produce smaller amounts of HDL—"good cholesterol" (Type A's lack ..., 1992); and are twice as likely to suffer from heart disease (Weidner, Istvan, & McKnight, 1989). It appears that the anger component is a critical factor that leads to coronary problems (Smith & Pope, 1990). Thus, working hard to achieve does not cause heart disease, but failure to achieve elicits a hostile self-schema for the Type A person; this hostility in turn is detrimental to good health (Fekken & Jakubowski, 1990; Moser & Dyck, 1989).

What exactly is the effect of anger on the heart? One study of patients with coronary disease monitored heart functioning while people talked about events in their lives that still make them mad (Goleman, 1992). As these patients talked about being a prisoner of war, having someone back into their car, and so on, the pumping efficiency of their hearts dropped by 5 percent. Revealing the importance of anger was the fact that in response to other stressors (riding a stationary bicycle, doing difficult arithmetic problems, giving a speech), pumping efficiency showed no change or even improved. Anger thus seems to be the key element.

Studies of Type A children suggest the importance of attempting to alter this pattern of behavior *before* coronary heart disease develops (Hunter et al., 1991). Even something as simple as an aerobic exercise program results in a decrease in Type A behavior (Jasnoski et al., 1987).

HEALTH EFFECTS OF COMMUNICATING WITH OTHERS: SOCIAL SUPPORT AND SELF-CONCEALMENT

A familiar concept in health psychology is the importance of **social support**—physical and psychological comfort from friends and family. The general finding is that people who interact closely with friends and relatives are better able to avoid illness than those who remain isolated from others; if illness does occur, those who receive social support recover more quickly. What appears to be important is the degree of intimacy and communication between the individual and his or her social network. As Benjamin Gottlieb at the University of Guelph put it in his reveiw of this literature,

> …the quality of social support is a stronger predictor of health outcomes than the quantity…Health protection is not predicated on the sheer availability of social relationships, or on the structure of the social orbit in which the respondent participates, but instead on the character and strength of the respondent's most profound social ties.

One of the reasons that natural disasters (such as a severe flood) are distressing is that they disrupt networks of social support (Kaniasty & Norris, 1993). It is even found that adolescents who experience stress but lack social support are more likely to receive sports injuries than those who do have the support of an interpersonal network (Smith, Smoll, & Ptacek, 1990). As aging progresses, social support has important positive effects on cardiovascular responses and thus decreases the risk of heart disease (Uchino, Kiecolt-Glaser, & Cacioppo, 1992). An interesting tie-in between Type A hostility and social support is the finding that not only do mistrusting and antagonistic individuals have more cardiovascular problems, but their interpersonal style also makes social support less available (Smith & Christensen, 1992).

A crucial question is *why* social support should be beneficial. One answer is simple: Friends and relatives can help you get through a bad experience by providing housing, meals, affection, and encouragement (Pilisuk, Boylan, & Acredolo, 1987). One proposition, known as the *fever model,* suggests that talking about fears and problems is like having a high temperature (Stiles, Shuster, & Harrigan, 1992). That is, with an infection, fever is an indication that something is wrong, and it is also useful in helping to fight the bacteria. With psychological distress, talking about what is wrong may have these same two functions. Some research has stressed the cognitive processes involved, in that people whose schemas (see chapter 2) include social support perceive such support as more helpful (Lakey, Moineau, & Drew, 1992).

Part of the explanation for the benefits of social support seems to be biological, as indicated by studies of animals. When researchers placed male monkeys under stressful, unstable social conditions for more than two years, their affiliative behavior increased (Cohen et al., 1992). Further, stress led to suppressed immune system responsiveness, but those animals who were most affiliative showed an enhanced immune response. Similarly, when a person talks to someone else about unpleasant and threatening life events, physiological stress decreases, and this is beneficial to health. Pennebaker, Hughes, and O'Heron (1987) found that people who never confide their traumatic experiences to others have more major and minor health problems than those who *do* talk about such stressful events. The greatest benefit occurs, however, when people talk about solving problems rather than simply venting their negative emotions (Costanza, Derlega, & Winstead, 1988).

Such findings led Larson and Chastain (1990) to examine individual differences in **self-concealment.** They point out that most people have secret feelings, embarrassing thoughts, and distressing information about themselves; this is the kind of information that most of us may share with only one or two others or with no one else. One example is the experience of being sexually abused as a child. Some individuals, however, are consistently more concerned than others with maintaining secrecy about themselves and their experiences, even about relatively minor difficulties. It follows that individual differences in self-concealment may predict who seeks social support and thus benefits from it.

The investigators developed a **Self-concealment Scale** to measure the active tendency to maintain secrecy about information considered negative or distressing, as presented in Table 10.2. Research indicates that persons who score high on the scale report higher levels of anxiety and depression and indicate more bodily symptoms than those with low scores, even when such variables as the number of traumas experienced and the ease of access to a social network are held constant.

Experiments have shown that even in a laboratory setting, it is beneficial to let others know about one's negative experiences. Pennebaker and Beall (1986) asked subjects to write about a personal traumatic event for twenty minutes a day for four days. Compared with subjects who did not engage in this task, those who wrote about stressful events reported having fewer health problems in the months that followed. Similarly, in a study of the benefits of writing about secret traumas, Greenberg and Stone (1992) asked different groups of undergraduate men and women to spend some time each day for four days writing about trivial events (the day's activities, their shoes, a social function); about a traumatic and upsetting experience that had been discussed with others; or about the "most traumatic and upsetting experience of your

---

■ The Self-concealment Scale measures the active tendency to conceal from others any personal information thought to be negative or embarrassing. Individuals high in self-concealment experience more anxiety, depression, and physical symptoms. Other research supports this suggestion that failure to communicate about stressful events results in health problems.

TABLE 10.2 The Self-concealment Scale

Sample Items of the Self-concealment Scale

Subjects respond to each of the following statements on a five-point scale ranging from "strongly disagree" to "strongly agree."

I have an important secret that I haven't shared with anyone.

If I shared all my secrets with my friends, they'd like me less.

When something bad happens to me, I tend to keep it to myself.

Telling a secret often backfires and I wish I hadn't told it.

I have negative thoughts about myself that I never share with anyone.

Source: Based on information in Larson & Chastain, 1990.

entire life" that had not been talked about with anyone else in detail. Compared with other subjects, students who wrote about the most severe traumas reported fewer physical symptoms in the two months following the study. Both these studies indicate that there seem to be health benefits from disclosing traumatic events.

Further research has examined individual *ambivalence over emotional expression* (Katz & Campbell, 1994; King & Emmons, 1990, 1991). It has been suggested that whether expression of emotion is related to positive health effects depends upon the individual's degree of ambivalence about disclosing their feelings. Not everyone is equally at ease with such expression and this may determine its beneficial effects. When measured by the Ambivalence Over Emotional Expression Questionnaire (the AEQ), such ambivalence includes a desire to express emotions that are held back, expressing emotions but doing so reluctantly, and later regret about having expressed emotions (King & Emmons, 1990). Results of recent research in Canada (Katz & Campbell, 1994) suggests that *ambivalence* is a more important predictor of poor psychological well-being than actually being inexpressive.

With the proviso that one is not ambivalent, this line of research generally supports the conclusion that confession is good not only for the soul but also for the body.

RESPONDING TO HEALTH PROBLEMS

It might seem reasonable to assume that even though psychological factors affect the probability of becoming ill, only physiological factors are of importance once illness strikes. In fact, when illness strikes, physical symptoms must be noticed and interpreted, and then a series of critical decisions and choices must be made—whether to rely on self-diagnosis, seek informal or formal treatment, or do nothing, and how to cope with the symptoms or with the treatment. As a result, psychological processes affect each step of an illness episode.

Attending to symptoms:
You have to notice that something is wrong

A sudden and dramatic symptom such as fainting or vomiting is unlikely to go unnoticed by anyone, but what about less-obvious changes in your physical state? Considerable time may pass before you notice a slight pain in your lower back, a rash on your chest, or a gradual change in the workings of your gastrointestinal system. Also, some people pay less attention to internal sensations than others, and they are less likely to notice changes or to interpret them as indicating a possible illness (Mechanic, 1983). At the opposite extreme are *hypochondriacs*, sometimes characterized as the "worried well"—who constantly overestimate the seriousness of every minor symptom that occurs and seek unneeded medical help (Wagner & Curran, 1984).

The number of symptoms an individual reports is affected by *priming* (see chapter 2). That is, when subjects take part in a task requiring them to respond to health-related words such as "pain" and "pill," they report having more symptoms than if they are asked about symptoms *before* being given the task (Skelton & Strohmetz, 1990). Such findings suggest the possibility that exposure to health-relevant material in newspapers or on television may also prime people to attend to and report their physical symptoms.

One's mood also affects how much attention one pays to symptoms. College students who watched a movie that made them feel sad or depressed reported more physical symptoms than those in a more positive emotional state (Croyle & Uretsky, 1987).

Deciding what is wrong

Once you notice a pain, a lump, a stiffness, or whatever, you must decide what, if anything, is wrong. If you conclude that nothing is wrong, you do nothing. This is a self-attribution process in which people tend to use a commonsense attributional model when engaging in self-diagnosis (Leventhal, Nerenz, & Steele, 1984). Let's say that you have a pain in your stomach, and you begin throwing up; it's easy to decide that you picked up an intestinal virus that will go away in a few hours. Though your virus assumption is quite likely true, should you be incorrect in your self-diagnosis, the mislabeling could be dangerous (Routh & Ernst, 1984). For example, if you actually have appendicitis, you have made a mistake that discourages you from seeing a doctor. One possible result is a ruptured appendix, a serious and sometimes fatal complication.

Other common examples of mislabeling include the attributions made by elderly people who assume that every ache and pain is simply due to "old age." This assumption may convince them not to visit a physician (Prohaska et al., 1987). A related problem occurs when patients are taking drugs to control high blood pressure. Because this disorder has no symptoms, the patient may assume that the problem has been cured and thus stop taking the needed medication (Meyer, Leventhal, & Gutman, 1985).

Taking action

If a given symptom has been noticed and self-diagnosed, what is the next step? The person either ignores the problem, tries to treat it himself or herself, or seeks professional help.

According to Bishop (1987), four factors enter into most people's decision-making behavior: whether the person attributes the cause to a virus, whether the symptoms affect the upper or lower body, whether the problem is psychological or physiological, and whether it disrupts daily activities. The most common response to a supposed viral infection or a disruptive illness is self-care with over-the-counter remedies. A person is most likely to seek professional help if the symptom is interpreted as a nonviral physiological problem in the lower half of the body.

A personality disposition that affects decision making at this step is known as *monitoring* (being on the lookout for problems). High monitors are constantly on the alert for threatening information, and they are more likely to make a doctor's appointment in response to a mild problem than are low monitors (Miller, Brody, & Summerton, 1988).

MEDICAL CARE AS A SOURCE OF PROBLEMS

The process doesn't end when the individual decides to seek medical help. What is involved in interacting with a physician, undergoing necessary tests, and receiving treatment?

Patient-doctor interactions

After taking the major step of making an appointment, waiting to see the doctor, and then interacting with him or her, the patient is often sufficiently anxious and fearful that crucial symptoms go unreported or important questions are not asked. It helps to rehearse or even to write down what you want to say and what you need to find out (Roter, 1984). With this kind of preparation, patients say more and obtain more information than when they simply "play it by ear." A related problem arises when the physician is abrupt or disinterested or maintains control of the interaction by talking too much and interrupting; such behavior can discourage or prevent patients from describing and discussing their concerns (Goleman, 1991; Street & Buller, 1987). Again, coaching patients to focus on what they want to bring up is helpful, as is encouraging them to be assertive with medical personnel.

As you may have experienced, doctors differ in their ability to communicate. A patient is most satisfied and most likely to carry out the treatment plan if the physician is good at both sending and interpreting nonverbal messages (DiMatteo, Hays, & Prince, 1986).

When a medical practitioner cannot control his or her nonverbal communications (for example, feelings of anxiety or uncertainty), the patient is likely to assume the worst: *My condition is so bad that the doctor won't tell me the truth!* When physicians are taught good communication skills, these problems can be averted (Hays & DiMatteo, 1984).

Physicians also need to learn how to present medical information. Consider the possible effects of **framing**—that is, influencing decisions by the way relevant information is presented. For example, an individual can be told that a pregnancy has a 50 percent chance of producing a normal offspring or that there is a 50 percent chance of producing an abnormal child. The information is the same, but the negative framing of the second wording leads to more decisions to seek an abortion than when the more positive wording is used (Wilson, Kaplan, & Schneiderman, 1987). In a similar way, information can be provided that the chances of dying are 10 percent or that the chances of surviving are 90 percent; intensive care is more likely to appear necessary in response to the former than to the latter information.

Coping with diagnosis and treatment

Unlike the simple medical procedures on "Star Trek," the interventions we have to undergo in the twentieth century are often intrusive, painful, and even dangerous. Diagnostic tests and medical treatment are thus stressful, and patients must somehow cope with them. Is there any way to reduce these medical threats?

Though avoidance and denial may be dangerous at the self-diagnosis stage of an illness episode, they can be very useful techniques when treatment is actually under way (Suls & Fletcher, 1985). Sometime when you are in a dentist's office having your teeth cleaned or a cavity drilled, try concentrating on something else—past events, future plans, a movie you liked, seeking the solution of a difficult problem. To a surprising extent, these incompatible thoughts actually prevent or reduce pain or discomfort.

Distraction (e.g., thinking about one's room at home) is a helpful strategy in dealing with a painful experimental task such as cold-pressor, in which the volunteer's hand is placed in ice-cold water and left there "as long as possible" (Cioffi & Holloway, 1993). These investigators found, however, that paying close attention to the painful sensations (*monitoring*) results in a more rapid recovery from the experience. The worst strategy is to suppress awareness ("empty your mind") of the painful experience. To test the aftereffects of these different strategies, the experimenters later exposed the participants to an innocuous vibration—and it was perceived as more unpleasant by those who had used suppression than by those using either distraction or monitoring.

Related research also indicates that when one's mood is incompatible with pain, self-reported pain decreases. Thus, when Stalling (1992) induced a positive mood in subjects, their self-reports of pain decreased.

Attributions also affect how people respond to a serious illness. Male heart attack patients in intensive care were asked their opinions as to why the coronary problem had occurred (Bar-On, 1987). Those who emphasized external, uncontrollable factors—such as bad luck—had more problems with recovery than those who stressed internal, controllable causes—such as being an angry person. During a six-month follow-up, those making external attributions took more time before returning to work and before resuming their sex life than did those making internal attributions.

As emphasized earlier in our discussion, perceived control is important in relation to stress, and this is equally true with respect to physical symptoms and pain (Affleck et al., 1987). For example, it hurts much less if you remove a painful splinter from your own finger than if another person does it for you. Even when a person does not have control, *belief* in personal control can be adaptive. Studies of patients with heart disease, cancer, and AIDS found that those who felt that they personally were in control of their symptoms, care, and treatment adjusted much better to their condition than those who did not feel in control (Taylor et al., 1991; Thompson et al., 1993).

There are, however, realistic boundaries to perceived control. In studying heart patients, Helgeson (1992) told them that some people believe that they can exert control over the course of their disease by adopting a positive attitude, changing their diets, or engaging in more exercise. Then the researcher asked the patients to rate their belief in their ability to control their health. High perceived control was found to be adaptive, but this was most true when the threat was high and the perception of control was based on reality. Even patients' belief that doctors and others could control their condition (**vicarious control**) resulted in better adjustment, but only if the physicans had actually *done* something such as angioplasty or bypass surgery.

A different kind of control has been introduced in some medical settings, where patients may make use of an interactive laser-disk player, a touch-screen terminal, and a keyboard (Freudenheim, 1992). For example, a doctor may tell a man that he has an enlarged prostate gland and that surgery is one option. Rather than simply following the physician's advice, the patient enters his own health data (age, weight, symptoms, etc.) on the system and then can ask for and receive information about the pros and cons of having the surgery, trying drug treatment, or simply waiting to find out if his condition gets worse. The program explains the pluses and minuses of each option, and the final decision is up to the patient.

As suggested in the cartoon in Figure 10.2, we also gain a sense of control through accurate information about what is happening and what is going to happen (Jay et al., 1983). Such knowledge is far less stressful than ignorance and fear of the unknown (Suls & Wan, 1989). Information provides a cognitive "road map" that permits a patient to interpret the experience without frightening surprises.

In chapter 6 we reported that patients facing surgery prefer a roommate who has already successfully undergone the same kind of surgery rather than someone who has not yet had the operation. The effect of actually assigning roommates on this basis is startling. Kulik and Mahler (1987) compared patients who were assigned (randomly) to a room with someone who was about to have the same surgery or with someone who had already completed it. As shown in Figure 10.3, patients with a postoperative roommate walked farther each day after surgery than did those with a preoperative roommate; they also were less unhappy and anxious, needed less medication for their pain, and were able to go home more quickly.

"Relax, I'm just here to water your flowers."

■ **Fear of medical procedures**

FIGURE 10.2 Medical procedures are often frightening and mysterious. The patient benefits both emotionally and physically from being given details about what is happening and what is going to happen. What a patient does not need is fear based on a lack of knowledge.

Source: North America Syndicate, Inc., September 30, 1990.

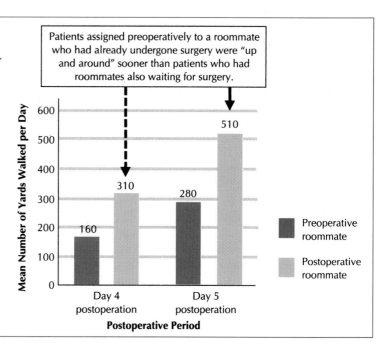

■ A postoperative roommate is better than a preoperative roommate

FIGURE 10.3 When surgery patients are assigned roommates who have already undergone the same operation, recovery proceeds faster. One example is shown here: Those assigned a postoperative roommate were found to walk farther each day than those with a preoperative roommate. Other benefits of such a roommate included less anxiety, the need for less pain medication, and an earlier discharge from the hospital.

Source: Based on data in Kulik & Mahler, 1987.

ENVIRONMENTAL PSYCHOLOGY: EFFECTS OF ENVIRONMENTAL FACTORS ON BEHAVIOR AND EFFECTS OF HUMAN BEHAVIOR ON THE ENVIRONMENT

In chapter 1 we identified five factors that influence social behavior and thought, and one of these was *ecological variables*—the direct and indirect influence of the physical environment. The study of such effects led to the growth of **environmental psychology**. In this section we will focus not only on how the environment affects our behavior but also on how human behavior affects the environment. Much of the initial research in this field dealt with how the presence of people influences each of us—studies of crowding, for example. During the 1960s and 1970s, however, interest broadened to include various environmental effects—such as air pollution, noise, and high temperature—on behavior. In the 1980s and 1990s, there has been increasing interest in pinpointing the negative effects of human activity on the environment and in promoting positive changes in this behavior.

HOW THE ENVIRONMENT AFFECTS HUMAN BEHAVIOR

To what extent are we adversely affected by environmental factors? **Environmental stress** refers to our reaction to perceived threats in the world around us. Throughout our existence, humans have faced such threats as floods, earthquakes, and tornadoes, but technological advances have brought us new dangers. For example, newspapers and television bring us stories of the possible increased risk of cancer associated with living or working near power lines (Brodeur, 1992; Gorman, 1992), using electrical appliances such as toasters and computer terminals (Toufexis, 1989), talking on cellular telephones (Angier, 1993), or being exposed to pesticides (Grieshop & Stiles, 1989). In some people such information has given rise to **technophobia**, the fear of living in a technological society (Pilisuk & Acredolo, 1988). Some of the most common specific concerns are shown in Table 10.3, along with the opinions of experts with respect to various hazardous risks. As you can see, public concern and expert concern often diverge.

Because environmental threats are a source of stress, people must find ways to cope, as discussed earlier. Perhaps the least effective coping strategy is "wishful thinking," in which people simply hope that the problem will go away (Hallman & Wandersman, 1992). Another way of coping is to assign responsibility for environmental problems. Though little research has concentrated on this tendency, it seems likely that coordinated efforts to blame the actions of a specific industry or to blame the government for failing to provide protection may result in beneficial changes.

Noise: Loud and unpredictable

One of the notable aspects of life in our increasingly crowded cities is the presence of noise both day and night—moving traffic, horns, sirens, police whistles, construction work, squealing brakes (Cooke, 1992). Some years ago, Glass, Singer, and Friedman (1969) proposed that it is harder to adapt to unpredictable than to predictable noise, because unpredictability involves a loss of perceived control. Subjects were given a proofreading task to carry out while they were exposed to one or the other type of noise. The proofreading was completed in both conditions, but with unpredictable noise there were more errors and a decrease in the subjects' tolerance for frustration. In general, exposure to unpredictable, uncontrollable noise leads to changes in behavior after the noise is terminated (Cohen, 1980). There is some evidence of a physiological basis for such effects, in that *endogenous opioids* (bodily secretions that reduce pain) are produced in response to stress as a bodily coping mechanism, and the effects of these opioids may include performance deficits (Davidson, Hagmann, & Baum, 1990).

The negative effects of noise are reduced, researchers find, when subjects gain *perceived control* upon learning that they can press a switch and turn off the noise. Performance improves and subjects feel less upset, even though most individuals do

■ Surveys indicate that people are concerned about the dangerous effects of technology on our health and safety. Scientific experts at the Environmental Protection Agency agree that hazards exist, but their assessments tend not to match those of the general public. People in general seem to worry most about immediate, short-term problems, while the scientists are more concerned about future, long-term problems.

TABLE 10.3 Concerns about technological hazards: The public versus the experts

	Perceptions of the General Public	Perceptions of Experts
Highest Concerns	Contaminated drinking water Storage of toxic chemicals Cancer-causing chemicals	Global climate change Species extinction and loss of biological diversity Soil erosion and deforestation
Moderate Concerns	Pesticide residue in food Air pollution Nuclear power plant accidents	Herbicides and pesticides Pollution of surface water Acid rain
Low Concerns	Car accidents Transport of explosives Food preservatives	Oil spills Groundwater pollution Escape of radioactive materials

Source: Based on data in Pilisuk & Acredolo, 1988, and Stevens, 1991a.

not actually press the switch (Glass et al., 1969). Personality also determines how people react to noise. For example, on a comprehension task, noise impairs the performance of introverts but not that of extroverts (Standing, Lynn, & Moxness, 1990).

Noise diminishes behavioral effectiveness not only in the laboratory but in daily life as well. Compared to children living in relatively quiet environments, children who are regularly exposed to the noise of highway traffic or of airplanes taking off and landing are found to have lower reading ability (Cohen, Glass, & Singer, 1973) and perform more poorly on math achievement tests and problem-solving tasks (Cohen et al., 1986). Noise disrupts adult behavior, too (Smith & Stansfeld, 1986). For example, as a result of daily exposure to loud aircraft, people suffer effects such as confusion about left versus right when giving directions, difficulty in finding items in a supermarket, problems with memory, and the tendency to drop things.

Exposure to loud, unpredictable noise in everyday life is also found to be associated with health risks, presumably because such stimulation is arousing and stressful (Topf, 1989). For example, children living on the lower floors of an apartment building in New York City that was built over a busy highway showed evidence of lowered auditory discrimination (Cohen, Glass, & Singer, 1973). Other research shows that regular exposure to noise in a busy industrial plant or in housing near an airport is associated with numerous health problems—hypertension (Cohen et al., 1986), hospitalization in mental institutions (Meecham & Smith, 1977), and fatal strokes (Dellinger, 1979).

Temperature and behavior

You often hear people say that climate and other meteorological factors affect behavior—that everyone seems more cheerful when there is a lot of sunshine or that they behave strangely when there is a full moon. Is behavior really affected by these aspects of the environment?

There is a large body of evidence that negative interpersonal responses increase and positive responses decrease when the temperature rises. When it is very hot, both interpersonal attraction and prosocial behavior are negatively affected (Bell et al., 1990). In a study of drivers in Phoenix, Arizona, the higher the temperature, the more they honked their horns at a car that failed to move when the light turned green (Kenrick & McFarlane, 1986).

Consistent with such findings is evidence linking temperature and serious interpersonal aggression (Anderson & DeNeve, 1992). For example, Anderson and Anderson (1984) examined the association between the number of aggressive crimes (murder and rape) and the daily temperature over a two-year period in two large American cities. The data indicate that criminal violence occurred more frequently as the temperature rose. Research in other cities shows similar effects; as the average monthly temperature rises, rapes and aggravated assaults become more frequent (Cohn, 1990; Simpson & Perry, 1990). It is also interesting to note that the relationship between temperature and nonviolent crimes such as burglary and car theft is much weaker (Anderson, 1987).

Beyond crime statistics, the effects of temperature on aggression are also evident in more "acceptable" kinds of human interaction. In major league baseball, it is not uncommon for a batter to be hit by the ball. Are such pitches accidents or evidence of aggression on the part of the pitchers? If aggression is the explanation, Reifman, Larrick, and Fein (1991) reasoned that more such hits would occur as the temperature rose. They analyzed data from 826 major league baseball games played during the 1986–1988 seasons. As shown in Figure 10.4, the hypothesis was strongly confirmed. The higher the temperature, the greater the mean number of players hit by a pitch.

Despite general agreement that the frequency of many types of aggressive behavior increases as the temperature rises, there is some disagreement about the effect

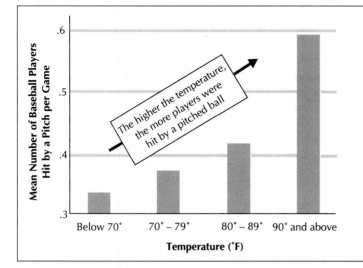

FIGURE 10.4 The relationship between temperature and aggressive behavior has been extended to baseball. Data based on hundreds of major league baseball games revealed that as the temperature rose, the average number of times the man at bat was hit by the ball increased.

Source: Based on data in Reifman, Larrick, & Fein, 1991.

of extremely high temperatures. Some argue that the data indicate a steadily rising curve in which aggression goes up as the temperature goes up (Anderson, 1989). In contrast, the *negative affect escape model* (Baron & Bell, 1976; Bell, 1992) proposes that when the discomfort caused by heat is sufficiently great, aggression actually begins to decline. The result is an inverted U-shaped curve. The explanation for this model is that the discomfort aroused by very high temperatures becomes so great that the individual is motivated to escape and seek relief by drinking a cold liquid, sitting under an air conditioner, going for a swim, or whatever. Proponents of both models agree that further research is needed to resolve the controversy.

Air pollution

Because of numerous human activities (driving cars, burning coal, smoking tobacco, etc.), our air is increasingly full of particles and gases that can have negative effects on our health and our interpersonal interactions. Despite the physical and emotional dangers of pollution, people quickly accept its presence. For example, newcomers to a heavily polluted area such as southern California almost always complain about the smog, but those who live there seldom notice it and do not even judge it to be an important issue for the community (Evans, Jacobs, & Frager, 1982). Nevertheless, pollution arouses negative emotions; one effect is an increase in the frequency of family disturbances reported to the police (Rotton & Frey, 1985).

In general, air that smells bad elicits negative feelings and less friendly interpersonal behavior (Rotton et al., 1979). Air that has a pleasant smell has the opposite effect—positive emotions and friendly behavior. Baron (1990) found that subjects who worked on a clerical task set higher goals, used more efficient strategies, and engaged in more friendly interpersonal behavior when surrounded by a pleasant artificial scent than when no air freshener was present. Presumably, the addition of pleasant smells to a work setting could enhance both morale and performance.

A troublesome form of atmospheric pollution is cigarette smoke. Not only does smoke smell foul, but smokers face serious health risks—and nonsmokers who breathe smoke-filled air also are more likely to develop health problems. "Passive smokers," such as a nonsmoking woman married to a heavy-smoking man, are more likely to develop lung cancer than similar women whose husbands do not smoke; also, children exposed to secondhand smoke have an increased likelihood of developing respiratory illnesses (Kenworthy, 1993).

Electrical ions in the atmosphere

Some environmental effects are based on natural phenomena, including some that you may never have noticed. Because of the presence of lightning, strong winds, and other meteorological disturbances, air molecules frequently split into positively and negatively charged particles called *ions*. The result is **atmospheric electricity**, which affects social behavior in several ways. For example, it has long been known that as the ion level in the atmosphere rises, there is an increase in the frequency of suicides, industrial accidents, and several categories of crime (Muecher & Ungeheuer, 1961; Sulman et al., 1974). Why?

One promising explanation is that negative ions activate people. As a result, they become more likely to do something they were already inclined to do. In laboratory studies, experimenters use special equipment to generate high levels of atmospheric electricity. As negative ions increase, participants' general activation level rises, adding to the strength of whatever responses are dominant for a particular person in a given situation. For example, negative ions increase the aggressiveness of Type A individuals, presumably because they already possess a strong tendency to aggress (Baron, Russell, & Arms, 1985).

A similar activation can be shown in studies of similarity and attraction of the kind described in chapter 6. When negative ions are present, attraction increases toward a similar stranger and decreases toward a dissimilar one (Baron, 1987). As shown in Figure 10.5, the usual reactions are intensified.

HOW HUMAN BEHAVIOR AFFECTS THE ENVIRONMENT

Almost everything that humans do has a measurable effect on the environment. Whenever someone becomes a parent, drives a car, uses hair spray, buys a product made of plastic, sends garbage to a landfill, uses salt on icy sidewalks or streets, or engages in thousands of other seemingly small acts, the environmental problems grow. As with population growth, the effects are neither obvious nor immediate.

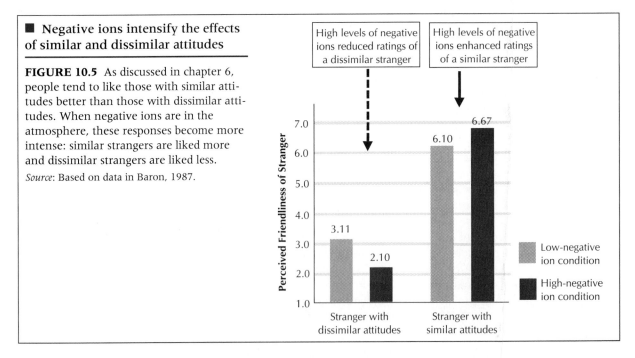

■ Negative ions intensify the effects of similar and dissimilar attitudes

FIGURE 10.5 As discussed in chapter 6, people tend to like those with similar attitudes better than those with dissimilar attitudes. When negative ions are in the atmosphere, these responses become more intense: similar strangers are liked more and dissimilar strangers are liked less.

Source: Based on data in Baron, 1987.

Though anything that you personally may do probably has only a very small effect, what you plus a few billion other people do can and does bring about changes in the environment (Stern, 1992). What are the most dangerous of these changes?

The greenhouse effect: A warmer, wetter world

Though experts are far from unanimous in their conclusions (Stevens, 1991b), there is a great deal of evidence that the earth is growing warmer at a rate that is being accelerated by human activities (Elmer-Dewitt, 1992). If **global warming** is occurring, scientists say that it will hasten the melting of the ice caps; this will cause the seas to rise, and many low-lying areas of land will be submerged (Schneider, 1989). The most agreed-upon forecast is that the sea level will rise two to three feet during the next century. The only force available to stop this disaster would be a complementary disaster in which the onset of the next ice age acted to reverse this trend (Olivenstein, 1992). Such predictions may seem like science fiction or, at most, a reason for minor adjustments in one's life (see Figure 10.6); however, the problem is sufficiently real that the nations meeting at the 1992 Earth Summit in Rio de Janeiro began to set goals and propose steps to try to keep our planet from slowly getting hotter without at the same time bringing economic development to a halt (Havel, 1992; Nasar, 1992).

Global warming will mean that many North American plants and animals, such as the sugar maple and the deer mouse, will survive only by migrating northward. Many other animal species, such as polar bears, monarch butterflies, tigers, and walruses may disappear entirely (Schneider, 1991; Stevens, 1992).

The cause of this climatic change is known as the **greenhouse effect**: the trapping of heat by rising levels of three gases in the earth's atmosphere, a rise that began around 1850. About half of the problem is attributable to *carbon dioxide*. Until the

"Don't worry, when the greenhouse effect really sets in we'll start growing orchids!"

■ **Adapting to global warming**

FIGURE 10.6 Though scientists are not in total agreement about the timing and the intensity, most agree that the atmospheric changes brought about by human activity will lead to gradual global warming through the *greenhouse effect*. Most people, however, do not take such threats seriously enough to change their present activities.

Source: North America Syndicate, Inc., January 7, 1990.

middle of the nineteenth century, this gas was produced almost entirely by the breath we and other animals exhaled and the natural decay of dead plants and animals. But when we began burning coal and oil to supply our need for energy, carbon dioxide production increased sharply, and there is now more of it in the atmosphere than at any time in the earth's existence (Fischer, 1989). Trees and other plants absorb carbon dioxide; but, paradoxically, excessive amounts of carbon dioxide also interfere with the health of plants and hence with crop growth (Browne, 1992b).

The other two gases that act to trap heat in the atmosphere are *methane* and the *chlorofluorocarbons*, each being responsible for about 25 percent of global warming. Most of the methane is generated in rice paddies, forest fires, landfills, and the digestive tracts of the 3.3 billion domesticated cattle and other mammals that humans raise for milk, food, and hides. Each time one of these animals releases gas in a belch or in flatulence, methane is expelled into the atmosphere (Chesek, 1992). Methane from all these sources has doubled the atmospheric methane level in the past three hundred years, and the total amount is growing at the rate of 1 percent each year. (Remember the effects of exponential growth?) The remaining cause of the warming trend, chlorofluorocarbons (or CFCs), are the gases used in refrigerators, air conditioners, and many spray cans. CFCs have two negative effects; they help trap heat in the atmosphere like the other two gases, but they also act to create holes in the ozone layer. As a result, the earth's plants and animals are less and less protected from the most intense and dangerous of the sun's rays (Lemonick, 1992).

Can anything be done to reverse these trends? The answer is yes, but change is not easy. To reduce carbon dioxide emissions, we need to develop an energy technology that is not based on burning organic matter (solar power and wind power are examples), and we need to alter our behavior (using public rather than private transportation; buying reusable artificial Christmas trees). You can even help by planting new trees; each tree absorbs up to forty-eight pounds of carbon dioxide annually (Grondahl, 1989). You need not be a Scrooge to note that North Americans cut down more than thirty-five million evergreen trees each December and discard them in January; these trees are thus prevented from absorbing carbon dioxide, while their decomposition over the next thirty years produces significant amounts of this gas (Cool, 1991).

The reduction of methane should be easy. One promising approach is to feed our cud-chewing animals (the *ruminants*—cattle, sheep, goats, buffalo, and camels) something other than the high-fiber diets they now eat. Chlorofluorocarbons must be banned completely and replaced with alternatives; fifty nations have agreed to do this. You may already have noted such changes as liquid deodorants that are sprayed out by a pump rather than by gas pressure. Such small changes can have major effects. More dramatically, new technology (such as refrigerators whose cooling is based on sound waves) is being developed to permit CFCs to be gradually phased out (Browne, 1992a).

Garbage, litter, and other waste products

It is possible to view our world as being buried in masses of trash and sewage, even though many individuals highly value a clean environment (Simmons et al., 1992). As the human population grows, we produce more and more waste. Where are we going to put it? Many landfills are reaching capacity and few new ones are being approved.

Rather than focusing on a problem of that magnitude, let's consider a simpler problem—litter. There is no reason for our sidewalks, parks, and other public places to be the final resting place for paper cups, candy wrappers, bottles, and so forth. How can you motivate people to avoid littering and also to pick up the litter of others? In university cafeterias, prominent reminders encouraging students to do what they know is right, or **prompts**, have been somewhat effective. An important element, however, is the tone of the prompt. Durdan, Reeder, and Hecht (1985) compared the effects of positive versus negative messages on cafeteria littering. Probably because they create a pleasant affective state, positive prompts ("Please be helpful!") resulted in less littering than mildly negative prompts ("Please don't litter!"). Before the prompts were used, over half of the students littered; when positive prompts were present, fewer than a third littered.

Several studies have focused on movie theaters and their attempts to change people's habit of throwing waste material under the seats. More than 80 percent of snack bar trash is simply dropped on the floor. Theaters have tried several prompting methods—making trash cans available, showing an antilittering cartoon on the screen, and passing out litter bags. Such techniques have an effect, but the reduction in littering is small. When Clark, Hendee, and Burgess (1972) provided rewards, however, a much greater effect was apparent. The investigators gave movie patrons litter bags; when these were filled and turned in, the customer received either a dime or a free movie ticket. This simple reward system reduced the percentage of litter discarded on the floor to 10 percent.

Even if there is only the *possibility* of a reward, people litter less. Hayes, Johnson, and Cone (1975) used the *marked item technique*. With this technique, only a few rewards are given, so each can be reasonably valuable (as in a lottery). The researchers scattered marked items among the litter on the grounds of a penal institution. They told inmates that some of the litter was marked in such a way that it could be seen only under a special light; anyone who picked up litter should bring it to a collection station and hold it under the light. If a marked item was in the litter, the person would win an attractive prize. The result was an immediate increase in the amount of litter collected.

These and other studies suggest that reminders can help change behavior, that positive wording is preferable to negative demands, and that small rewards can strongly affect environmental behavior.

Encouraging people to recycle

A major solution to the garbage problem is to recycle paper, glass, plastic, cans, and other products rather than to throw them away. Most of us indicate that we are in favor of recycling, but most of us don't actually recycle much without some form of extra encouragement, such as a series of persuasive communications (Burn & Oskamp, 1986). Even those who fail to recycle express concern for the environment, but they tend to be less knowledgeable about the process and more concerned about rewards for recycling than is true for more committed recyclers (Vining & Ebreo, 1990).

A surprisingly effective legislative approach to motivating people to recycle uses a combination of mild coercion and a small monetary reward. In many provinces in Canada and states in the U.S., customers who purchase beer, soft drinks, and other liquids in bottles or cans must pay a small deposit, included in the price of each item. The "reward" is a refund of the deposit when the customer returns the bottle or can to the store. Most people return their containers rather than lose the deposit money. Even when containers are thrown away, people who need the money often collect them from roadsides, parks, and other public places and turn them in.

Though such measures reduce the amount of waste and conserve resources, many consumers are at least mildly negative at first because of the trouble involved. Over time, though, attitudes become very positive. Kahle and Beatty (1987) conducted a longitudinal study of public reaction in Oregon and discovered an interesting sequence of events (shown in Figure 10.7). When a bottle bill is enacted into law, recycling behavior changes despite feelings of reluctance. This new behavior becomes habitual, and then attitudes change to correspond with the altered behavior (see the discussion of cognitive dissonance in chapter 3). There are also changes in subjective norms about what is the "right" thing to do. Once these behaviors and attitudes change, there is also an interesting generalization to other environmental concerns and to other proenvironment actions.

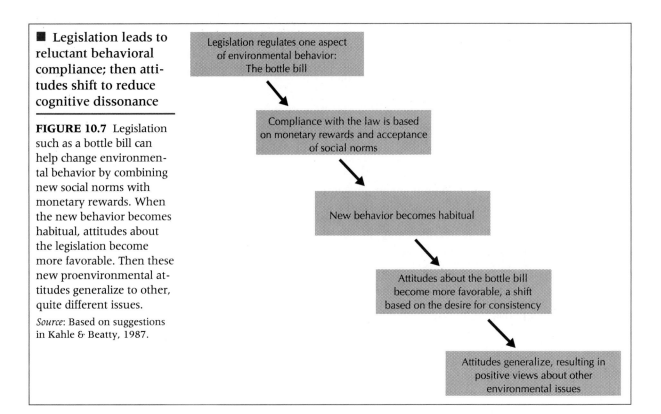

■ Legislation leads to reluctant behavioral compliance; then attitudes shift to reduce cognitive dissonance

FIGURE 10.7 Legislation such as a bottle bill can help change environmental behavior by combining new social norms with monetary rewards. When the new behavior becomes habitual, attitudes about the legislation become more favorable. Then these new proenvironmental attitudes generalize to other, quite different issues.

Source: Based on suggestions in Kahle & Beatty, 1987.

Legislation regulates one aspect of environmental behavior: The bottle bill

Compliance with the law is based on monetary rewards and acceptance of social norms

New behavior becomes habitual

Attitudes about the bottle bill become more favorable, a shift based on the desire for consistency

Attitudes generalize, resulting in positive views about other environmental issues

SOCIAL PSYCHOLOGY AND THE LEGAL SYSTEM

Ideally, the judicial process should provide the fairest set of procedures ever devised to reach objective, unbiased decisions about violations of society's criminal and civil laws. Our legal and judicial professions ordinarily strive to live up to that ideal. Yet research in **forensic psychology** (psychology specifically concerned with legal issues) repeatedly indicates that the human participants in the process do not always function according to rational guidelines (Davis, 1989). Social psychologists have provided a considerable body of evidence indicating that when people interact, their behavior and their judgments are affected by attitudes, cognitions, and emotions that may be biased, irrational, and unfair. And those same factors are equally relevant when people interact in a courtroom.

BEFORE THE CASE GOES TO COURT: POLICE INTERROGATION AND MEDIA PUBLICITY

Before a case reaches the courtroom, two major factors operate to influence both the testimony that is presented and the decisions that are made: police interrogation and publicity in the media.

Interrogation and suggestibility

In many instances the first interpersonal influence on the legal process takes place when police ask questions (see Figure 10.8). In both formal and informal questioning, police and others often ask **leading questions**—questions worded in such a way

■ Interrogation: Leading questions suggest what to answer

FIGURE 10.8 When the police interrogate eyewitnesses or suspected criminals, the setting is controlled by someone with authority and special knowledge, which increases the suggestibility of the person being questioned. *Leading questions* tend subtly to persuade people to respond with what they think the officer wants to hear. Once individuals give such an answer, however inaccurate it may be, they tend to believe what they have just said.

that they suggest what the answer should be. When the interrogator asks such questions, the person being questioned often accepts the assumptions underlying the inquiry. For example, an unbiased question would be, "what did you see on the afternoon of the accident?" A leading question, in contrast, would be "did you see the car strike the pedestrian and toss her body onto the curb?" Whether or not a witness is influenced by such questions depends on specific personality characteristics and on the setting in which the questioning takes place (Schooler & Loftus, 1986).

Gudjonsson and Clark (1986) point out that the way the usual interrogation is structured tends to reinforce the citizen's assumption that the official asking the questions possesses special knowledge. This increases the suggestibility of the witness or suspect, who then is more likely to respond as directed. For example, in police interrogations the officer is usually in charge, interruptions are not permitted, and the person being questioned is discouraged from answering back. This situation involves three components that encourage suggestible responses. When a leading question is asked, the witness usually feels some *uncertainty* about the "right" answer, some degree of *trust* in the officer asking the question, and an *expectation* that one is supposed to know the answer and should be able to provide it. As a result, rather than saying "I don't know" or "I'm not sure," the person is subtly persuaded to give a positive answer. Having given that answer, the individual is inclined to believe whatever he or she has just said, especially if the interrogator indicates approval.

As you might guess, witnesses are more accurate when asked only unbiased questions (Sanders & Chiu, 1988). In a study of police interrogation, subjects saw a videotape of a bank robbery and afterward were questioned about the crime (Smith & Ellsworth, 1987). The questioner was a confederate who had been described either as being very *knowledgeable* about the robbery or as being naive. Half the subjects were asked unbiased questions such as "Was there a getaway car?" Half were asked leading questions such as "Where was the getaway car parked?" As shown in Figure 10.9, the unbiased questions resulted in the most accurate answers, no matter who asked them. With the leading questions, accuracy decreased, especially when the questioner was supposed to be knowledgeable.

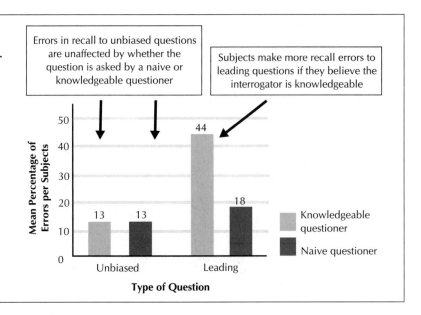

■ Mistakes are made when experts ask leading questions

FIGURE 10.9 Research indicates that witnesses make more errors in responding to *leading questions* than to *unbiased questions* and that the most inaccurate answers are given when the questioner is identified as knowledgeable.

Source: Based on data from Smith & Ellsworth, 1987.

Media publicity

On a regular basis, daily newspapers, radio and television news programs, and sometimes magazines and books devote a lot of space to information about crimes, accidents, and lawsuits, especially if they are dramatic or unusual or involve famous people (Barnes, 1989; Henry, 1991). One of the potentially negative aspects of a free press in this instance is that public opinion (including the opinion of individuals who might later be jurors) can be affected by how such news is presented. In Canada, the details of cases or evidence are sometimes suppressed by the courts if their publication might detract from a fair trial. An example is the ban on reporting of evidence related to the Paul Bernardo case. This produced an outcry from some Canadians against what was seen as censorship. At the other extreme, in the U.S., the mass of publicity and evidence disclosed in the O.J. Simpson case caused many people to question the possibility of an unbiased hearing. When should the rights of the accused to a fair trial supersede the rights of the press or of the public to see that justice is being done? The answer to this question obviously differs somewhat in Canada and the United States.

In research on two highly publicized cases involving defendants accused of distributing marijuana and a defendant charged with murdering a police officer, Moran and Cutler (1991) surveyed potential jurors. They found in each instance that the more knowledge people had about the details of the case, the more blame they placed on those arrested for the crimes. The investigators also found that knowledge of the crimes was unrelated to whether or not the respondents *believed* they could make impartial judgments. Given people's mistaken faith in their own lack of bias, Judge O'Connell (1988) suggests that asking potential jurors whether they can be fair and impartial is as useless as asking a man who is a practicing alcoholic if he has his drinking under control.

Not only does media publicity affect people's judgment about a specific case, but media information also has more general effects. For example, when people are exposed to descriptions of very serious crimes, they then view other crimes and other offenders more harshly than if they have not had such exposure—even to the extent of recommending more severe prison sentences (Roberts & Edwards, 1989). Presumably, they overgeneralize on the basis of the selective information in the crime stories.

Media reportage of crime also appears to influence the public's perception of the prevalence of crime. Anthony Doob of the University of Toronto's Centre of Criminology has been investigating such issues for many years (e.g., Doob & Macdonald, 1979; Roberts & Doob, 1990). A recently published survey of criminal victimization, part of Statistics Canada's 1993 General Social Survey (Gartner & Doob, 1994), shows that 46 percent of Canadians believe the level of crime has increased in the past five years, and 27 percent of the population (42 percent of women and 10 percent of men) do not feel safe walking alone in their own neighborhood. But what is the reality?

Despite the common perception that crime has increased, the crime victimization survey for 1993, compared to 1988, indicates overall rates have remained very stable: When asked both in 1988 and 1993, 24 percent of Canadians reported that they were the victims of at least one crime in the previous year (Gartner & Doob, 1994). Figure 10.10 shows that the "personal victimization" rates (which include violent crimes against the person) of Canadians between 1988 and 1993 have either remained the same or decreased.

Why should our perceptions be so at odds with reality? Doob's research indicates that the news media may be at fault insofar as they tend to overrepresent violent crime, as well as report it inadequately (Doob, 1985; Roberts & Doob, 1990). For example, Doob found that over 50 percent of newspaper crime reporting in Canada concerned violent crime (1985), though it is in fact a small percentage of all crime.

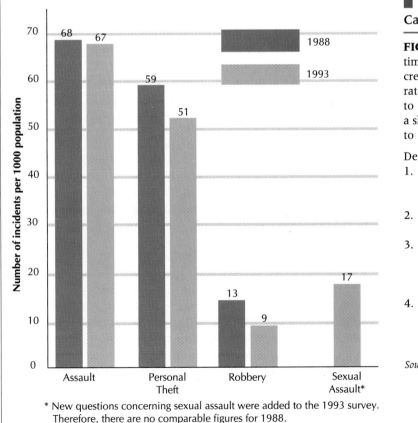

* New questions concerning sexual assault were added to the 1993 survey. Therefore, there are no comparable figures for 1988.

■ Has crime increased in Canada?

FIGURE 10.10 The 1993 crime victimization survey showed no increase in "personal victimization" rates per 1000 population compared to 1988. Most indices in fact showed a slight decrease for 1993 compared to 1988.

Definitions of Personal Victimization:
1. Assault: A weapon was present or there was an attack or threat of an attack.
2. Personal Theft: Cash or other personal property was taken.
3. Robbery: Something taken and the person who commited the act had a weapon or there was an attack or threat of violence.
4. Sexual Assault: Perpetrator sexually assaulted, molested, or attempted to sexually assault or molest victim.

Source: Gartner & Doob, 1994.

Furthermore, the news media appear to be the source of much of our information about sentencing. National surveys have shown that the Canadian public perceives sentencing as too lenient, particularly for violent crime (Doob & Roberts, 1983) and, further, that 95 percent of the public cite the news media as the source of "most of their information about sentencing offenders" (Roberts & Doob, 1990, p. 452). In a series of studies, Roberts and Doob investigated the influence of newspaper reporting on public perceptions of sentencing. One study compared subject responses to a lengthy newspaper account or to a detailed summary of the court documents relating to the sentencing proceedings of a real case of assault causing bodily harm. The sentence of 21 months given to the offender was relatively severe for a crime of this type. Subjects were adult visitors to the Ontario Science Centre who were randomly assigned to read either the newspaper account or the court documents. Results found that subjects who read the newpaper account were more likely to consider the sentence too lenient (63 percent) than those who read the court documents summary (19 percent). Further, they were more likely to consider that the judge did not weigh all factors in reaching his decision (newpaper group 46 percent; court documents group 24 percent). A second study comparing reportage in all three Toronto newspapers, demonstrated that dissatisfaction with sentencing was greatest when subjects had read a tabloid paper account rather than a broadsheet account (Roberts & Doob, 1990). This suggests that the kind of sensational reporting often found in tabloids may be particularly likely to produce negative views of the sentencing.

Doob's research clearly demonstrates that news media reporting can have an impact on public perception of crime in general and sentencing in particular. Roberts and Doob describe the newspaper accounts used in their research as "generally short and provid[ing] little information about the offense, the offender, or the judicial reasoning underlying the sentence" (1990, p. 464). The same could probably be said for much reporting on television and radio.

THE TESTIMONY OF EYEWITNESSES

When anyone witnesses a crime, an accident, or any other event relevant to a legal matter, he or she may later be called upon to testify about what was seen or heard, as shown in Figure 10.11. Each year in North American courtrooms, witnesses present crucial evidence concerning many suspects (Goldstein, Chance, & Schneller, 1989). This testimony has a major impact on jurors—even though eyewitnesses are frequently wrong (Wolf & Bugaj, 1990). Jurors are most convinced by such testimony when a witness presents many details (Bell & Loftus, 1988) or speaks with confidence and without hesitation (Whitley & Greenberg, 1986).

Eyewitness inaccuracy

Because the events that are witnessed are almost always totally unexpected, of brief duration, and stressful (Hosch & Bothwell, 1990), even the most honest, intelligent, and well-meaning citizen may be inaccurate when asked to recall the details of a past event or to identify a suspect. A study by Yuille and Cutshall of a crime in Burnaby, British Columbia, in which a gunstore owner and the man who had just robbed his store had a "shoot-out" on the street, throws further light on such inaccuracies. From police interviews around the time of the crime and from their own research interviews of eyewitnesses four or five months later, they were able to show that witnesses tend to have greater accuracy for recall of objects (e.g., the guns and the car) and events (i.e., the sequence of actions) than for identifying details of people (i.e., age, height, weight, hair color, and clothing), as shown in Figure 10.12. The level of accuracy

■ What happened?

FIGURE 10.11 Please look at the photograph for just ten seconds, then turn to the last page of this chapter and answer a few questions about what you remember.

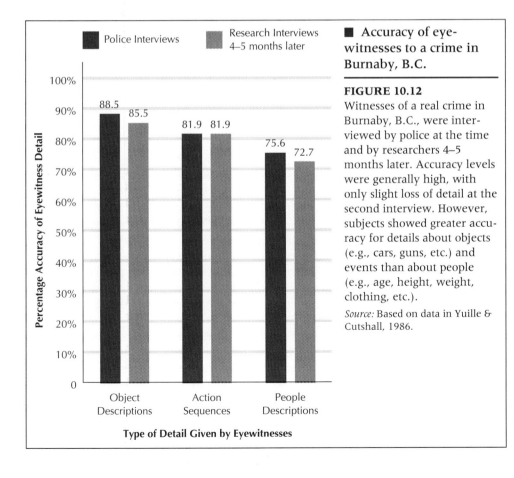

■ Accuracy of eye-witnesses to a crime in Burnaby, B.C.

FIGURE 10.12
Witnesses of a real crime in Burnaby, B.C., were interviewed by police at the time and by researchers 4–5 months later. Accuracy levels were generally high, with only slight loss of detail at the second interview. However, subjects showed greater accuracy for details about objects (e.g., cars, guns, etc.) and events than about people (e.g., age, height, weight, clothing, etc.).

Source: Based on data in Yuille & Cutshall, 1986.

found in this study of a real-life crime is greater than is generally found in laboratory research. The researchers suggest that this may be due to the greater level of involvement and the more severe consequences that result from being an eyewitness to an actual crime (Yuille, 1993; Yuille & Cutshall, 1986).

Many factors affect the accuracy of a witness (Wells & Luus, 1990). For example, accuracy decreases if there is a weapon in the suspect's hand (Tooley et al., 1987), if the suspect and the witness belong to different racial or ethnic groups (Platz & Hosch, 1988), and/or if misleading suggestions are made to the witness (Ryan & Geiselman, 1991). Yuille & Tollestrup of the University of British Columbia found that eyewitnesses who had been drinking alcohol were less accurate than sober eyewitnesses in recalling the details of a staged theft, but they were equally able to recognize the thief's picture (1990). A witness's certainty is found to be unrelated to his or her accuracy (Bothwell, Deffenbacher, & Brigham, 1987).

Before appearing in a lineup, guilty suspects may try to alter their appearance in an attempt to confuse witnesses, and this technique works. Also, if an innocent person is unlucky enough to wear the kind of clothing the criminal wore when committing the crime, witnesses are likely to identify him or her as the guilty party (Sanders, 1984).

Increasing the accuracy of witnesses

Correct identification of a criminal is improved when witnesses are first allowed to practice with a lineup containing only innocent volunteers. Any choice they make is wrong; they then receive information about the serious consequences of making such mistakes (Wells, 1984). As a result of this experience, their ability to recall crucial details about the suspect improves.

Another technique that bolsters memory and increases the accuracy of witnesses is to "reinstate the context" just before the identification is made; that is, first to show witnesses pictures of the crime scene and of the victim (Cutler, Penrod, & Martens, 1987). Witness reliability is also improved by exposure to just one suspect at a time, rather than to the usual lineup of several at once (Leary, 1988) and by instructions designed to improve witnesses' memory of an event (Yuille & McEwan, 1985).

Believability of eyewitnesses

Regardless of the accuracy of a witness, he or she must be believed if the testimony is to have any effect. What characteristics increase or decrease eyewitness believability?

To answer this question, Leippe, Manion, and Romanczyk (1992) conducted a laboratory experiment in which the "witnesses" were college students and children aged five to six and nine to ten. The experimenters told these individuals that the study dealt with skin sensitivity. Midway through the procedure, a female intruder entered the room, made an inquiry, and left. Afterward, each participant was asked to describe what had happened, the physical appearance of the experimenter and of the intruder, and what these two people had said and done. Participants were also asked to identify these two individuals from a group of photographs. The most and least accurate witnesses in each age group were thus identified.

A video camera recorded the participants' "testimony" from behind a one-way mirror. The researchers later asked other college students to view the tapes of accurate and inaccurate witnesses and to rate each one on several dimensions related to believability. The students perceived the most accurate witnesses as more accurate than the least accurate ones, but the difference was surprisingly small. One interesting finding was that the students rated the children as less believable and less accurate than the adults, even when they were equally accurate.

The student participants were most likely to believe a witness (regardless of age) if that person seemed confident. Ratings of witness confidence seemed to be based on the person's speaking without hesitation in long, elaborate sentences and not contradicting himself or herself. Altogether, believability was found to depend more on such characteristics as speaking style and age than on the accuracy of the testimony. Similarly, the more nervous the witness appears, the less accurate he or she is perceived to be (Bothwell & Jalil, 1992).

IN THE COURTROOM: LAWYERS' AND JUDGES' INFLUENCE ON THE VERDICT

Trials can be shaped in part by what is said and done by the opposing attorneys and by the judge. Lawyers make judgments as to which jurors are acceptable, which witnesses will be asked to testify, what evidence to present and when and how best to summarize the case to the jury. The judge presides over the interactions, rules on the admissibility of testimony and of exhibits presented as evidence, and explains the case and the legal ramifications to the jury. Each of these acts can influence what the jurors decide.

Lawyers: Advocates for one side, foes of the other

Lawyers obviously play a major role in a courtroom. Before the trial begins, jury selection takes place. Who does and does not serve on the jury can be critical, and some legal experts propose that the case has already been decided once the jury has been chosen (Hans & Vidmar, 1982).

Olczak, Kaplan, and Penrod (1991) conducted a series of investigations to determine how well the jury selection process operates. First, the researchers asked courtroom lawyers to react to a number of juror characteristics, in order to find out what information they typically use. Most lawyers were found to utilize just one or two characteristics while ignoring the remainder; Table 10.4 gives the characteristics thought most important and the questions most frequently asked in the *voir dire* process. Second, the researchers gave lawyers and introductory psychology students information about prospective jurors and asked the two groups to rate the jurors' desirability; these two groups responded to the characteristics in almost identical ways. Third, the lawyers and students were given information about individuals who really had served as jurors; the subjects were asked to decide how desirable each juror would be from the point of view of the defense. Both groups were wrong more often than right in their selections. The researchers concluded that even experienced courtroom lawyers use stereotypes in selecting jurors and that their choices are no better than those of college students.

The timing of opening statements turns out to be another important variable. Experimental evidence clearly shows that the defense is helped by presenting its opening statement early in the trial rather than after the prosecution presents evidence. Experimenters gave subjects the details of an actual trial, with variations in the timing of the defense opening statement. Early rather than delayed presentation affected the mock jurors' perceptions of the eyewitness testimony, the prosecutor's opening and closing statements, and the defense closing statement, as well as the perceived effectiveness of the lawyers—all in ways favoring the defense (Wells, Wrightsman, & Miene, 1985).

As in police interrogations, lawyers can ask leading questions of the person in the witness stand and thus bias the person's responses and the reactions of the jury. When questioning their own witnesses, lawyers tend to seek information by means of unbiased questions such as, "Can you tell me exactly what happened on the afternoon of the murder?" When cross-examining witnesses for the opposing side, however, they are more likely to ask leading questions such as, "You opened the door to the victim's apartment with your own key, didn't you?" Jurors perceive the witness as more competent and more credible when he or she is responding to unbiased questions (McGaughey & Stiles, 1983).

■ Before a trial begins, lawyers take part in a jury selection process in which they look for certain positive and negative characteristics and ask various questions in an effort to decide which prospective jurors should be retained and which should be excused. When lawyers were asked to indicate the most important characteristics and the *voir dire* questions they most often ask, these were the results.

TABLE 10.4 What do courtroom lawyers seek in selecting a jury?

Characteristics Lawyers Say Are Important in Jury Selection	*Voir Dire* Questions Lawyers Say They Ask Most Often
Intelligence	What is your attitude about this kind of crime?
Age	What is your general reaction to police officers?
Appearance	How much have you heard about this case in the media?
Occupation	
Open-mindedness	Were you ever the victim of this kind of crime?
Gender	How do you feel about someone who has been arrested?
Attentiveness	
Impressibility	Do you have any racial bias?
Race	Have any of your acquaintances ever been arrested or convicted?
	Do you have any relationship with any of the individuals connected with this case?

Source: Based on data from Olczak, Kaplan, & Penrod, 1991.

The effect of the judge

A judge's biases can affect the trial outcome. For example, when jurors are exposed to inadmissible evidence (Cox & Tanford, 1989) or to the judge's attack on the credibility of a witness (Cavoukian & Doob, 1980), the final verdict is swayed. Many of the cognitive processes described in chapter 2 (such as priming) obviously apply to how jurors respond to what the judge says and does.

People frequently express the view that some judges coddle criminals while others ("hanging judges") favor giving the maximum penalties. Carroll et al. (1987) found that judges actually do fall into one of two categories. Either they emphasize the social or economic causes of crime and the benefits of rehabilitation, or they blame the criminal for the crime and stress the importance of punishment and retribution. Whether you support "hard" or "soft" judges seems to depend on your views about what causes crime. As we saw in chapter 2, Canadian research found that college students who major in social sciences usually blame society, while business and engineering majors blame the individual who committed the crime (Guimond and Palmer, 1990).

Judges have a great deal of leeway in making various decisions about defendants, including the amount of bail that is set and the monetary level of fines—within maximum limits set by law. Because of the pervasive importance of physical attractiveness in interpersonal evaluations (see chapter 6), Downs and Lyons (1991) hypothesized that defendant attractiveness would affect the amounts of bail and fines. These researchers collected data on bail and fines assigned by forty actual judges in more than 1500 court cases involving misdemeanors. The appearance of the defendant in each case was rated by police officers who were not involved in the arrest and who did not know what the study was about. The findings, presented in Figure 10.13, strongly indicate that the more attractive the defendant, the lower the amount of bail or fine set by the judge. A similar analysis of felony cases revealed no attractiveness effect, however, so these biased judgments appear to be limited to relatively minor offenses.

CHARACTERISTICS OF DEFENDANTS AND JURORS

In earlier chapters we have described research on prejudice, attraction, attributions, and other phenomena—research that indicates how people respond to one another on the basis of race, sex, attractiveness, and other characteristics. These factors should, of course, be irrelevant in the courtroom. But, having read about the effect of physical attractiveness on the monetary decisions of judges, you may not be startled to learn that just such variables affect the outcome of both real and simulated trials (Dane, 1992).

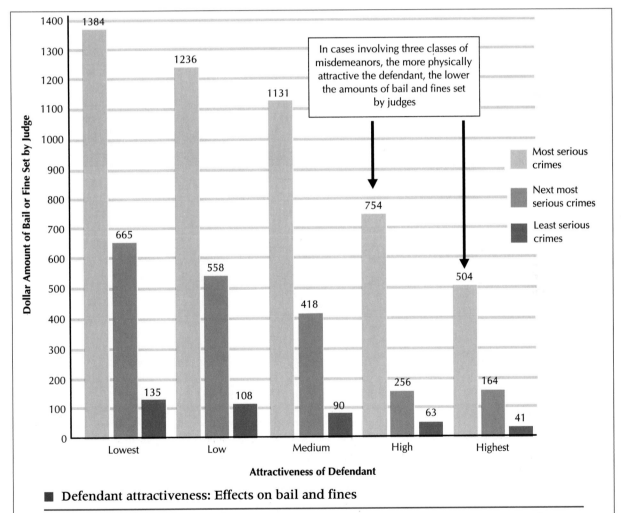

In cases involving three classes of misdemeanors, the more physically attractive the defendant, the lower the amounts of bail and fines set by judges

■ Defendant attractiveness: Effects on bail and fines

FIGURE 10.13 In a study of actual courtroom misdemeanor cases, policemen rated the physical attractiveness of defendants. Judges decided on bail amounts for those held in jail and on the amount of fines for those found guilty. For three classes of misdemeanors, the more attractive the defendant, the less the monetary amount set for bail and for fines.

Source: Based on data in Downs & Lyons, 1991.

Defendants: Equal under the law?

Research consistently indicates that attractive defendants are treated better than unattractive ones in gaining acquittals, receiving light sentencing, eliciting the sympathy of the jury, being considered dangerous, and so on (Esses & Webster, 1988; Wuensch, Castellow, & Moore, 1991). Because lawyers are aware of this attractiveness bias, they advise their clients to do everything possible to improve their appearance before entering the courtroom.

In a case involving sexual harassment, the attractiveness of both the plaintiff and the defendant can play a role (Castellow, Wuensch, & Moore, 1990). Study participants read the trial summary of a case in which a twenty-three-year-old secretary-receptionist accused her employer of repeatedly making suggestive remarks, attempting to kiss and fondle her, and providing detailed descriptions of the sexual activities he would enjoy sharing with her. Different groups of subjects also saw photographs purported to be of the two individuals; the photos showed (1) two attractive individuals, (2) two unattractive ones, or (3) and (4) the two possible attractive-unattractive combinations. As shown in Figure 10.14, attractiveness made a difference. Guilty judgments were most likely with an attractive plaintiff and an unattractive defendant (83 percent) and least likely with an unattractive plaintiff and an attractive defendant (41 percent).

The defendant's sex sometimes affects judicial decisions. In a mock trial, Cruse and Leigh (1987) presented jurors with testimony in an assault case. A couple was engaged in an argument about ending their relationship, and the defendant was alleged to have cut the victim with a kitchen knife. For half of the jurors, the defendant, "Jack Bailey," was accused of knifing "Lucy Hill," and 43 percent of the jurors found him guilty. The remaining jurors read the same evidence, except that Lucy was accused of knifing Jack; under these conditions, 69 percent found her guilty. The investigators suggested that the woman was more likely to be judged as guilty because stabbing someone with a knife was a masculine behavior—a woman "shouldn't act that way." In other words, she violated expectancies based on gender roles.

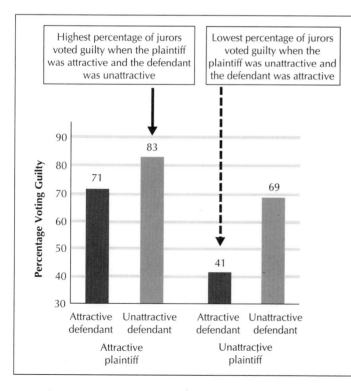

■ Sexual harassment: Attractiveness of plaintiff and defendant

FIGURE 10.14 Mock jurors were asked to decide on guilt and innocence with respect to charges of sexual harassment. They read a trial summary based on actual court cases and were shown photographs of the plaintiff and the defendant. The photographs were actually pictures of either an attractive or an unattractive man (identified as the defendant) and either an attractive or an unattractive woman (identified as the plaintiff). Judgments of guilt were clearly affected by the appearance of the two individuals. Both male and female jurors were most likely to give a guilty verdict when an attractive woman charged an unattractive man with harassment and least likely to vote guilty when an unattractive woman made that same charge against an attractive man.

Source: Based on data from Castellow, Wuensch, & Moore, 1990.

The defendant's ethnicity and race also influence the outcome. Defendants whose testimony is in another language that must be translated are judged more guilty than when the same testimony is originally given in English (Stephan & Stephan, 1986). In Canada, the Royal Commission of Inquiry into the wrongful conviction for murder of Donald Marshall, a Micmac Indian, identified racist attitudes of the police and other officials as one of the causes of this injustice. In the United States, African-American defendants are more likely to be convicted than white defendants, and are more likely to receive a prison sentence (Stewart, 1980) or the death penalty (Sniffen, 1991). A study of American trials also indicated that 11.1 percent of criminals (regardless of race) who kill a white victim receive a death sentence, while only 4.5 percent of those who kill a black victim are sentenced to die (Henderson & Taylor, 1985).

An unbiased jury of your peers?

Criminal verdicts are found to be determined in part by such seemingly irrelevant factors as the proportion of jurors with previous jury experience—the more such jurors, the more likely is conviction (Werner et al., 1985).

Some general attitudes are common among jurors, including a bias in favor of the defendant, known as a **leniency bias** (MacCoun & Kerr, 1988). On the opposite side are juror attitudes that are associated with a tendency to vote for conviction. One example is *legal authoritarianism*—a tendency to ignore the defendant's civil liberties and rights, including the presumption that the accused is innocent unless proven guilty. Narby, Cutler, and Moran (1993) reported a clear tendency across a series of studies for legal authoritarians to favor conviction. Other specific attitudes (such as how one evaluates psychiatrists) can affect the verdict in specific cases that require psychiatric testimony (such as those involving an insanity plea) (Cutler, Moran, & Narby, 1992).

Research on the legal system provides ample evidence that additional effort is needed to increase judicial fairness and objectivity. The elimination of all biases and inaccuracies is a difficult but important goal.

SUMMARY AND REVIEW

Applied social psychology utilizes social psychological principles and research methods in real-world settings in efforts to solve a variety of individual and societal problems. The findings and principles of social psychology have been applied to many of our social institutions and have provided a better understanding of how these institutions function and how they can be improved. One applied area where Canadians have been pioneers is second language learning and the social impact of bilingualism.

PSYCHOLOGY AND HEALTH

Health psychology is the specialty that studies how psychological processes affect the development, prevention, and treatment of physical illness. Considerable research has been directed at *stress* and the factors that make some individuals better

able to *cope* with environmental and psychological threat. Factors such as *fitness*, *hardiness*, and numerous personality dispositions are associated with how well individuals deal with stress. *Social support* is important in preventing and helping a person cope with illness, in part because of the importance of having someone with whom to talk about unpleasant life events rather than engaging in *self-concealment*. When an illness does strike, the person has to make a series of critical choices and decisions—noticing and interpreting symptoms, deciding to take action, and coping with medical procedures.

THE ENVIRONMENT

Environmental psychology is the field that deals with the interaction between the physical world and human behavior. Among the environmental factors that affect behavior are *environmental stress, noise, temperature, air pollution, atmospheric electricity*. The negative effects of human actions on the environment include *global warming* and the ever-mounting problem of *waste*. Studies designed to control littering suggest that proenvironmental behavior can be increased by the use of *prompts*, *rewards*, and legislation such as that requiring a deposit on cans and bottles.

THE LEGAL SYSTEM

Forensic psychology has produced ample evidence that the reality of our legal system often does not live up to its ideals. Witnesses and defendants are influenced by interrogation procedures and pre-trial media publicity. Eyewitness testimony is often inaccurate, and the behavior of lawyers and judges can influence verdicts. Jurors respond in part on the basis of cognitive reinterpretations of the evidence and on emotional biases for and against specific defendants.

KEY TERMS

Applied Social Psychology Social psychological research and practice in real-world settings, directed toward the understanding of human social behavior and the attempted solution of social problems.

Atmospheric Electricity The presence of positive and negative ions in the atmosphere. Higher numbers of ions create higher levels of atmospheric electricity.

Cope Respond to stress. Coping includes what a person does, feels, or thinks in order to master, tolerate, or decrease the negative effects of a stressful situation.

Environmental Psychology The field that deals with the interaction between the physical world and human behavior.

Environmental Stress A negative emotional reaction to perceived threats in the physical world.

Forensic Psychology Psychology as it relates to aspects of legal proceedings and the law, including eyewitness reliability and issues involving the police, the media, attorneys, judges, defendants, victims, plaintiffs, and jurors.

Framing Affecting judgments or decisions by the way in which relevant information is presented.

Global Warming The gradual increase in the earth's atmospheric temperature brought about by various human activities.

Greenhouse Effect The basis of global warming—gases released into the atmosphere (carbon dioxide, methane, and chlorofluorocarbons) trap the sun's heat, turning the earth into a "greenhouse."

Hardiness A cluster of characteristics that includes a sense of commitment, a perception of difficulties as representing challenges and opportunities, and a belief in one's ability to control one's own life.

Health Psychology The study and practice of the role of the psychological factors that affect the origin, prevention, and treatment of physical illness.

Leading Questions Questions (asked of witnesses by the police or by attorneys) that are worded so as to suggest answers. These questions can provide information that is inconsistent with what the witness actually observed.

Leniency Bias A general bias among jurors that leads them to tend to sympathize with and favor the defendant.

Locus of Control One's generalized belief that the control of one's life in terms of positive and negative outcomes rests either on controllable internal factors or on uncontrollable external factors.

Pessimism/Optimism Alternate outlooks on events of life in general—either a negative view that one's life is bad and getting worse or a positive view that it is good and getting better.

Prompts Reminders that encourage a person to engage in behavior about which he or she already holds favorable attitudes.

Psychoneuroimmunology The study of the way one's responses to external events affect internal physiological states that are crucial to the immune system in defending the body against disease.

Social Support The help provided by friends and relatives who give physical and psychological comfort to an individual facing stress. Those receiving social support tend to be in better physical health and to be better able to resist stress than those lacking such support.

Stress In social psychology, the responses elicited by physical or psychological events perceived by the individual to be harmful or emotionally upsetting.

Technophobia The fear that various aspects of a technological society are a source of danger.

Type A A personality type and behavior pattern characterized by high levels of competitiveness, time urgency, and hostility that has been associated with
an increased risk of cardiovascular disease.

Vicarious Control The generally beneficial belief that
medical personnel are able to control one's physical condition.

FOR MORE INFORMATION

Gore, A. (1992). *Earth in the balance.* Boston: Houghton
Mifflin.

 U.S. Vice President Al Gore wrote this book
while serving in the U.S. Senate, because he had
become convinced of the global environmental
crisis and wanted to try to convince others of the
reality and the seriousness of the problem. He
proposes a Global Marshall Plan with specific
steps to begin bringing about the necessary alter-
ations in behavior and in technology.

Shorter, E. (1992). *From paralysis to fatigue: A history of
psychosomatic illness in the modern era.* New York:
Free Press.

 Interest in the relationship between psychological factors and physical health began with the
identification of psychosomatic illnesses. This is a
fascinating history of nineteenth-century cases
such as "imaginary paralysis" and fainting fits and
their modern counterparts such as chronic fatigue
syndrome and environmental hypersensitivity.
The most general point is that some genuinely ex-
cruciating physical ailments do not have a physical cause and that psychosomatic conditions tend
to come suddenly into fashion and then eventually fade away.

Wrightsman, L. S. (1991). *Psychology and the legal system.*
Pacific Grove, CA: Brooks/Cole.

 This volume uses psychological concepts to
examine the legal system and is useful for students of law and psychology. It is meant to serve
as a bridge between social science issues and
methods on the one hand and the law and criminal justice system on the other. Topics include
moral judgment, children's rights, and psychologists' role in the legal system.

**How well do you recall what you have
seen?**
In the photograph in Figure 10.11:
What do you think happened?
How many vehicles were at the scene?
Were there people present? Male or female?
What were the road conditions?
What type of rescue apparatus was available?
What directions were the vehicles facing?

Aboud, F.E., & Taylor, D.M. (1971). Ethnic and role stereotypes: Their relative importance in person perception. *Journal of Social Psychology, 85,* 17–27.

Acitelli, L. HI (1992). Gender differences in relationship awareness and marital satisfaction among young married couples. *Personality and Social Psychology Bulletin, 18,* 102–110.

Adams, J. S. (1965). Inequity in social exchange. In L. Berkowitz (Ed.), *Advances in experimental social psychology* (Vol. 2, pp. 267–299). New York: Academic Press.

Ader, R., & Cohen, N. (1993). Psychoneuroimmunology: Conditioning and stress. In L. W. Porter & M. R. Rosenzweig (Eds.), *Annual review of psychology* (Vol. 44, pp. 53–85). Palo Alto, CA: Annual Reviews, Inc.

Adorno, T. W., Frenkel–Brunswick, E., Levinson, D. J., & Sanford, R. H. (1950). *The authoritarian personality.* New York: Harper & Row.

Affleck, G., Tennen, H., Pfeiffer, C., & Fifield, J. (1987). Appraisals of control and predictability in adapting to a chronic disease. *Journal of Personality and Social Psychology, 53,* 273–279.

Alagna, F. J., Whitcher, S. J., & Fisher, J. D. (1979). Evaluative reactions to interpersonal touch in a counseling interview. *Journal of Counseling Psychology, 26,* 465–472.

Albright, L., Kenny, D. A., & Malloy, T. E. (1988). Consensus in personality judgments at zero acquaintance. *Journal of Personality and Social Psychology, 55,* 387–395.

Alcock, J.E., Carment, D.W., & Sadava, S.W. (1994). *A textbook of social psychology.* (3rd ed.). Scarborough, Ont.: Prentice–Hall.

Alcock, J.E., Carment, D.W., & Sadava, S.W. (1988) *A textbook of social psychology.* Scarborough, Ont.: Prentice–Hall.

Alden, L. (1986). Self–efficacy and causal attributions for social feedback. *Journal of Research in Personality, 20,* 460–473.

Alicke, M. D., Braun, J. C., Glor, J. E., Klotz, N. L., Nagee, J., Sederhold, H., & Siegel, R. (1992). Complaining behavior in social interaction. *Personality and Social Psychology Bulletin, 18,* 286–29S.

Allen, V. L., & Levine, J. M. (1971). Social support and conformity: The role of independent assessment of reality. *Journal of Experimental Social Psychology, 4,* 48–58.

Alliger, G. M., & Williams, K. J. (1991). Affective congruence and the employment interview. *Advances in Information Processing in Organizations, 4,* 31–43.

Allport, G. W. (1985). Attitudes. In C. Murchison (Ed.), *Handbook of social psychology.* Worcester, MA: Clark University Press.

Allport, G.W. (1954). *The nature of prejudice.* Reading, MA: Addison–Wesley.

Allport, T. N. (1924). *Social psychology.* Boston: Houghton Mifflin.

Allred, K. D., & Smith, T. W. (1989). The hardy personality: Cognitive and physiological responses to evaluative threat. *Journal of Personality and Social Psychology, 56,* 257–266.

Altemeyer, B. (1981). *Right–wing authoritarianism.* Winnipeg: University of Manitoba Press.

Altemeyer, B. (1988). *Enemies of freedom.* San Fancisco: Jossey–Bass.

Alwin, D. F., Cohen, R. L., & Newcom¹ T. N. (1991). *Personality and social change: Attitude persistence and changes over the lifespan.* Madison: University of Wisconsin Press.

Amato, P.R. (1983). Helping behavior in urban and rural settings: Field studies based on a taxonomic organization of helping episodes. *Journal of Personality and Social Psychology, 45,* 571–586.

Amato, P.R., & McInnes, J.R. (1983). Affiliative behavior in diverse environments: a consideration of pleasantness, information rate, and the arousal–eliciting quality of settings. *Basic and Applied Social Psychology,4,* 109–122.

Anderson, C. A. (1987). Temperature and aggression: Effects on quarterly, yearly, and city rates of violent and non-violent crime. *Journal of Personality and Social Psychology, 46,* 91–97.

Anderson, C. A. (1989). Temperature and aggression: The ubiquitous effects of heat on the occurrence of human violence. *Psychological Bulletin, 106,* 74–96.

Anderson, C. A., & Anderson, D. C. (1984). Ambient temperature and violent crime: Tests of the linear and curvilinear hypotheses. *Journal of Personality and Social Psychology, 46,* 91–97.

Anderson, C. A., & DeNeve, K. M. (1992). Temperature, aggression, and the negative affect escape model. *Psychological Bulletin, 111,* 347–351.

Anderson, J. L. (1989). A methodological critique of the evidence for genetic similarity detection. *Behavioral and Brain Sciences, 12,* 518–519.

Anderson, N. H. (1981). *Foundations of information interaction theory.* New York: Academic Press.

Angier, N. (1993, February 2). Cellular phone scare discounted. *New York Times,* pp. C1, C3.

Anthony, T., Cooper, C., & Mullen, B. (1992). Cross–racial identification: A social cognitive integration. *Personality and Social Psychology Bulletin, 18,* 296–301.

Ardrey, R. (1976). *The hunting hypothesis.* New York: Atheneum.

Argyle, M. (1969). *Social Interaction.* London: Methuen.

Aron, A., Dutton, D. G., Aron, E. N., & Iverson, A. (1989). Experiences of falling in love. *Journal of Social and Personal Relationships, 6,* 243–257.

Aronoff, J., Woike, B. A., & Hyman, L. M. (1992). Which are the stimuli in facial displays of anger and happiness? Configurational bases of emotion recognition. *Journal of Personality and Social Psychology, 62,* 1050–1066.

Aronson, E. (1984). *The social animal.* (4th ed.). New York: W.H. Freeman.

Aronson, E., Bridgeman, D. L., & Oeffner, R. (1978). Interdependent interactions and prosocial behavior. *Journal of Research and Development in Education, 12,* 16–27.

Arvey, R. D., & Campion, J. E. (1982). The employment interview: A summary and review of recent research. *Personnel Psychology, 35,* 281–322.

Arvey, R. D., Bouchard, T. J., Jr., Segal, N. L., & Abraham, L. M. (1989). Job satisfaction: Genetic and environmental components. *Journal of Applied Psychology, 74,* 187–192.

Asante, M. K. (1980). *Afrocentricity: The theory of social change.* Buffalo, NY: Amulefi Publishing Company.

Asch, S. E. (1946). Forming impressions of personality. *Journal of Abnormal and Social Psychology, 41,* 258–290.

Asch, S. E. (1951). Effects of group pressure upon the modification and distortion of judgment. In H. Guetzkow (Ed.), *Groups, leadership, and men.* Pittsburgh, PA: Carnegie.

Asch, S. E. (1957). An experimental investigation of group influence. In *Symposium on preventive and social psychiatry,* 15–17. Walter Reed Army Institute of Research, Washington, DC: U. S. Government Printing Office.

Asendorpf, J. B. (1989). Shyness as a final common pathway for two different kinds of inhibition. *Journal of Personality and Social Psychology, 57,* 481–492.

Asendorpf, J. B. (1992). A Brunswickean approach to trait continuity: Application to shyness. *Journal of Personality, 60,* 55–77.

Atwood, M. (1984). *Second words: Selected critical prose.* Boston: Beacon Press.

Averill, J. R., & Boothroyd, P. (1977). On falling in love: Conformance with romantic ideal. *Motivation and Emotion, 1,* 235–247.

Baer, D.E., & Curtis, J.E. (1984). French–Canadian/English–Canadian differences in values: National survey findings. *Canadian Journal of Sociology, 9,* 405–427.

Baker, R. L., & Mednick, B. R. (1984). *Influences on human development: A longitudinal perspective.* Boston: Kluwer–Hijhoff Publishing

Bandura, A. (1973). *Aggression: A social learning analysis.* Englewood Cliffs, NJ: Prentice–Hall.

Bandura, A. (1979). The social learning perspective: Mechanisms of aggression. In H. Toch (Ed.), *Psychology of crime and criminal justice.* New York: Holt, Rinehart & Winston.

Bandura, A., Ross, D., & Ross, S. (1963). Imitation of film–mediated aggressive models. *Journal of Abnormal and Social Psychology, 66,* 3–11.

Bargh, J. A., Chaiken, S., Covender, R., & Pratto, F. (1992). The generality of the automatic attitude activation effect. *Journal of Personality and Social Psychology, 62,* 893–912.

Barnes, F. (1989). Fearless leader. *New Republic, 201*(22), 11–13.

Baron, R. A. (1971). Magnitude of victim's pain cues and level of prior anger arousal as determinants of adult aggressive behavior. *Journal of Personality and Social Psychology, 17,* 236–243.

Baron, R. A. (1973). The "foot–in–the–door" phenomenon: Mediating effects of size of first request and sex of requester. *Bulletin of the Psychonomic Society, 2,* 113–114.

Baron, R. A. (1979). Aggression, empathy, and race: Effects of victim's pain cues, victim's race, and level of instigation on physical aggression. *Journal of Applied Social Psychology, 9,* 103–114.

Baron, R. A. (1981). The "costs of deception" revisited: An openly optimistic rejoinder. *IRB: A Review of Human Subjects Research, 3,* 8–10.

Baron, R. A. (1987). Interviewer's moods and reactions to job applicants: The influence of affective states on applied social judgments. *Journal of Applied Social Psychology, 16,* 16–28.

Baron, R. A. (1987a). Effects of negative air ions on interpersonal attraction: Evidence for intensification. *Journal of Personality and Social Psychology, 52,* 547–553.

Baron, R. A. (1988a). Attributions and organizational conflict: The mediating role of apparent sincerity. *Organizational Behavior and Human Decision Processes, 41,* 111–127.

Baron, R. A. (1988b). Negative effects of destructive criticism: Impact on conflict, self–efficacy, and task performance. *Journal of Applied Psychology, 73,* 199–207.

Baron, R. A. (1989). Applicant strategies during job interviews. In G. R. Ferris & R. W. Eder (Eds.), *The employment interview: Theory, research, and practice* (pp. 204–216). Newbury Park, CA: Sage.

Baron, R. A. (1990). Attributions and organizational conflict. In S. Graham & V. Folkes (Eds.), *Attribution theory: Applications to achievement, mental health, and interpersonal conflict* (pp. 185–204). Hillsdale, NJ: Erlbaum.

Baron, R. A. (1993). Effects of interviewers' moods and applicant qualifications on ratings of job applicants. Manuscript submitted for publication.

Baron, R. A., & Bell, P. A. (1976). Aggression and heat: The influence of ambient temperature, negative affect, and a cooling drink in physical aggression. *Journal of Personality and Social Psychology, 33,* 245–255.

Baron, R. A., & Richardson, D. R. (1994). *Human aggression* (2nd ed.). New York: Plenum.

Baron, R. A., Fortin, S. P., Frei, R. L., Haver, L. A., & Shack, M. L. (1990). Reducing organiztional conflict: The potential role of socially–induced positive affect. *International Journal of Conflict Management, 1,* 133–152.

Baron, R. A., Rea, M. S., & Daniels, S. G. (1992). Effects of indoor lighting (illuminance and spectral distribution) on the performance of cognitive tasks and interpersonal behaviors: The potential mediating role of positive affect. *Motivation and Emotion, 16,* 1–33.

Baron, R. A., Russell, G. W., & Arms, R. I. (1985). Negative ions and behavior: Impact on mood, memory, and aggression among Type A and Type B persons. *Journal of Personality and Social Psychology, 48,* 746–754.

Baron, R. S. (1986). Distraction–conflict theory: Progress and problems. In L. Berkowitz (Ed.), Advances in experimental social psychology, Vol. 20. New York: Academic Press.

Baron, R. S., Moore, D., & Sanders, G. S. (1978). Distraction as a source of drive in social facilitation research. Journal of Personality and Social Psychology, 36, 816–824.

Barrett, S.R. (1987). *Is God a racist? The right wing in Canada.* Toronto: University of Toronto Press.

Barry, H., Child, I., & Bacon, M. (1959).Relation of child training to subsistence economy. *American Anthropologist, 61,* 51–63.

Bartholomew, D., & Horowitz, L.M. (1991) Attachment styles among young adults: A test of a four–category model. *Journal of Personality and Social Psychology, 61,* 226–244.

Bartholomew, K. (1990). Avoidance of intimacy: An attachment perspective. *Journal of Social and Personal Relationships, 7,* 147–178.

Bartholomew, K. (1993). From childhood to adult relationships: Attachment theory and research. In S.W. Duck (Ed.), *Understanding relationship processes 2: Learning about relationships* (pp. 30–32). London: Sage.

Bar–On, D. (1987). Causal attributions and the rehabilitation of myocardial infarction victims. *Journal of Social and Clinical Psychology, 5,* 114–122.

Baugh, S. G., & Parry, L. E. (1991). The relationship between physical attractiveness and grade point average among college women. *Journal of Social Behavior and Personality, 6,* 219–228.

Baumeister, R. F. (1986). *Identity.* New York: Oxford University Press.

Baumeister, R. F., & Covington, N. V. (1985). Self–esteem, persuasion, and retrospective distortion of initial attitudes. *Electronic Social Psychology, 1,* 1–22.

Baumeister, R. F., Chesner, S. P., Sanders, P. S., & Tice, D. M. (1988). Who's in charge here? Group leaders do lend help in emergencies. *Personality and Social Psychology Bulletin, 14,* 17–22.

Baumeister, R. F., Stillwell, A., & Wotman, S. R. (1990). Victim and perpetrator accounts of interpersonal conflict: Autobiographical narratives about anger. *Journal of Personality and Social Psychology, 59,* 994–1003.

Baumeister, R. F., Wotman, S. R., & Stillwell, A. M. (1993). Unrequited love: On heartbreak, anger, guilt, scriptlessness, and humiliation. *Journal of Personality and Social Psychology, 64,* 377–394.

Baxter, L. A. (1990). Dialectical contradictions in relationship development. *Journal of Social and Personal Relationships, 7,* 69–88.

Beaman, A. L. (1991). An empirical comparison of meta–analytic and traditional reviews. *Personality and Social Psychology Bulletin, 17,* 252–257.

Beauvois, J. L., & Dubois, N. (1988). The norm of internality in the explanation of psychological events. *European Journal of Social Psychology, 18,* 299–316.

Beauvois, J. L., & Le Poultier, F. (1986). Norme d'internalite et pouvoir social en psychologie quotidienne. *Psychologie Francaise, 31,* 100–108.

Bell, B. (1991). Loneliness and values. *Journal of Social Behavior and Personality, 6,* 771–778.

Bell, B. E., & Loftus, E. F. (1988). Degree of detail of eyewitness testimony and mock juror judgments. *Journal of Applied Social Psychology, 18,* 1171–1192.

Bell, P. A. (1991). Gender, friendship network density, and loneliness. *Journal of Social Behavior and Personality, 6,* 45–56.

Bell, P. A. (1992). In defense of the negative affect escape model of heat and aggression. *Psychological Bulletin, 111,* 342–346.

Bell, P. A., Fisher, J. D., Baum, A., & Green, T. E. (1990). *Environmental psychology* (3rd ed.). New York: Holt, Rinehart, & Winston.

Benson, P. L., Xarabenick, S. A., & Lerner, R. M. (1976). Pretty pleases: The effects of physical attractiveness, race, and sex on receiving help. *Journal of Experimental Social Psychology, 12,* 409–415.

Berg, J. H., & McQuinn, R. D. (1989). Loneliness and aspects of social support networks. *Journal of Social and Personal Relationships, 6,* 359–372.

Berk, R.A., Berk, S.F., Loseke, D.R. & Rauma, D. (1981). Mutual combat and other family violence myths. In D Finkelhor, R.J. Gelles, G.T. Hotaling, & M.A.Straus (Eds.), *The dark side of families: Current family violence and research.* Beverly Hills, CA: Sage.

Berkowitz, L. (1968, September). Impulse, aggression, and the gun. *Psychology Today,* pp. 18–22.

Berkowitz, L. (1974). Some determinants of impulsive aggression: The role of mediated associations with reinforcements for aggression. *Psychological Review, 81,* 165–176.

Berkowitz, L. (1984). Some effects of thought on anti- and pro-social influence of media events: A cognitive-neoassociation analysis. *Psychological Bulletin, 95,* 410–427.

Berkowitz, L. (1987). Mood, self–awareness, and willingness to help. *Journal of Personality and Social Psychology, 52,* 721–724.

Berkowitz, L. (1988). Frustrations, appraisals, and aversively stimulated aggression. *Aggressive Behavior, 14,* 3–11.

Berkowitz, L. (1989). Frustration-aggression hypothesis: Examination and reformulation. *Psychological Bulletin, 106,* 59–73.

Berkowitz, L. (Ed.) (1969). *Roots of aggression.* New York: Atherton.

Berkowitz, L., & LePage, A. (1967). Weapons as aggression-eliciting stimuli. *Journal of Personality and Social Psychology, 11,* 202–207.

Berndt, T. J. (1992). Friendship and friends' influence in adolescence. *Current Directions in Psychological Science, 1,* 156–159.

Bernstein, W. M., Stephenson, B. O., Snyder, M. L., & Wicklund, R. A. (1983). Causal ambiguity and heterosexual affiliation. *Journal of Experimental Social Psychology, 19,* 78–92.

Berry, D. S., & Brownlow, S. (1989). Were the physiognomists right? Personality correlates of facial babyishness. *Personality and Social Psychology Bulletin, 15,* 266–279.

Berry, D. S., & Zebrowitz-McArthur, L. (1988). What's in a face? Facial maturity and the attribution of legal responsibility. *Personality and Social Psychology Bulletin, 14,* 23–33.

Berry, J.W. (1967). Independence and conformity in subsistence–level societies. *Journal of Personality and Social Psychology, 7,* 415–418.

Berry, J.W. (1969). On cross–cultural comparability. *International Journal of Psychology, 4,* 119–28.

Berry, J.W. (1976). *Human ecology and cognitive style: Comparative studies in cultural and psychological adaptation.* New York: Sage/Halsted.

Berry, J.W. (1978). Social psychology: Comparative, societal and universal. *Canadian Psychogical Review, 19,* 93–104.

Berry, J.W. (1984). Multicultural policy in Canada: A social psychological analysis. *Canadian Journal of Behavioral Science, 16,* 353–370.

Berry, J.W. (1989). Imposed etics—emics—derived etics: the operationalisation of a compelling idea. *International Journal of Psychology, 24,* 721–735.

Berry, J.W., & Annis, R.C. (1974) Ecology, culture and psychological differentiation. *International Journal of Psychology, 9,* 173–193.

Berry, J.W., Kalin, R., & Taylor, D.M. (1977). *Multiculturalism and ethnic attitudes in Canada.* Ottawa: Supply and Services Canada.

Berry, J.W., Kim, U., Minde, T., & Mok, D. (1987). Comparative studies of acculturative stress. *International Migration Review, 21,* 491–551.

Berry, J.W., Poortinga, Y.P., Segal, M.H., & Dasen, P.R. (1992). *Cross-cultural psychology: Research and applications.* New York: Cambridge University Press.

Berscheid, E., Dion, K. K., Walster, E., & Walster, G. W. (1971). Physical attractiveness and dating choice: A test of the matching hypothesis. *Journal of Experimental Social Psychology, 7,* 173–189.

Berscheid, E., Snyder, M., & Omoto, A. M. (1989). The Relationship Closeness Inventory: Assessing the closeness of interpersonal relationships. *Journal of Personality and Social psychology, 57,* 792–807.

Bickman, L. (1972). Social influence and diffusion of responsibility in an emergency. *Journal of Experimental Social Psychology, 8,* 438–445.

Bienert, H., & Schneider, B. H. (1993). Diagnosis-specific social skill is training with peer-nominated aggressive-disruptive and sensitive-isolated preadolescents. *Journal of Applied Developmental Psychology,* in press.

Bierhoff, H. W., Klein, R., & Kramp, P. (1991). Evidence for the altruistic personality from data on accident research. *Journal of Personality, 59,* 263–280.

Birkimer, J. C., Lucas, M., & Birkimer, S. J. (1991). Health locus of control and status of cardiac rehabilitation graduates. *Journal of Social Behavior and Personality, 6,* 629–640.

Birnbaum, M. H., & Sotoodeh, Y. (1991). Measurement of stress: Scaling the magnitudes of life changes. *Psychological Science, 2,* 236–243.

Bishop, G. D. (1987). Lay conceptions in physical symptoms. *Journal of Applied Social Psychology, 17,* 127–146.

Bjorkqvist, K., Lagerspetz, K. M. J., & Kaukiainen, A. (1992). Do girls manipulate and boys fight? Developmental trends in regard to direct and indirect aggression. *Aggressive Behavior, 18,* 117–127.

Black, S. L., & Bevan, S. (1992). At the movies with Buss and Durkee: A natural experiment on film violence. *Aggressive Behavior, 18,* 37–45.

Blankenship, V., Hnat, S. M., Hess, T. G., & Brown, D. R. (1984). Reciprocal interaction and similarity of personality attributes. *Journal of Social and Personal Relationships.*

Bobo, L. (1983). Whites' opposition to busing: Symbolic racism or realistic group conflict? *Journal of Personality and Social Psychology, 45,* 1196–1210.

Bochner, A. P. (1991). On the paradigm that would not die. In J. A. Anderson (Ed.), *Communication yearbook 14* (pp. 44–491). Newbury Park, CA: Sage.

Bodenhausen, G. V. (1988). Stereotypic biases in social decision making and memory: Testing process models of stereotype use. *Journal of Personality and Social Psychology, 55,* 726–737.

Bolger, N., & Schilling, E. A. (1991). Personality and the problems of everyday life: The role of neuroticism in exposure and reactivity to daily stressors. *Journal of Personality, 59,* 355–386.

Bond, C. F. (1982). Social facilitation: A self–presentational view. *Journal of Personality and Social Psychology, 42,* 1042–1050.

Bond, M.H. Leung, K., & Wan, K.C. (1982). The social impact of self effacing attributions: The Chinese case. *Journal of Social Psychology, 118,* 157–166.

Bond, S., & Cash, T. F. (1992). Black beauty: Skin color and body images among African-American college women. *Journal of Applied Social Psychology, 22,* 874–888.

Borrello, G. M., & Thompson, G. (1990). An hierarchical analysis of the Hendrick-Hendrick measure of Lee's typology of love. *Journal of Social Behavior and Personality, 5,* 327–342.

Bossard, J. H. S. (1932). Residential propinquity as a factor in marriage selection. *American Journal of Sociology, 38,* 2l9–224.

Bothwell, R. K., & Jalil, M. (1992). The credibility of nervous witnesses. *Journal of Social Behavior and Personality, 7,* 581–586.

Bothwell, R. K., Brigham, J. C., & Malpass, R. S. (1989). Cross–racial identification. *Personality and Social Psychology Bulletin, 15,* 19–25.

Bothwell, R. K., Deffenbacher, K. A., & Brigham, J. C. (1987). Correlation of eyewitness accuracy and confidence: Optimality hypothesis revisited. *Journal of Applied Psychology, 72,* 691–695.

Bourhis, R.Y. (1979) Language in ethnic interaction: A social psychological approach. In H. Giles & B. Saint–Jacques (Eds.), *Language and ethnic relations.* Oxford: Pergamon.

Bourhis, R.Y. (1984). Cross–cultural communication in Montreal: Two field studies since Bill 101. *International Journal of the Sociology of Language, 46,* 33–47.

Bourhis, R.Y. (1990). Organization communication in bilingual settings: *The linguistic work environment survey. In H. Giles, N. Coupland, & J. Coupland (Eds.), Contexts of accommodation: Developments in applied psycholinguistics.* Cambridge: Cambridge University Press.

Bourhis, R.Y., Giles, H., Leyens, J.P., & Tajfel, H. (1979). Psycholinguistic distinctiveness: Language and divergence in Belgium. In H. Giles & R. St. Clair (Eds.) *Language and social psychology.* Oxford: Blackwell.

Bower, G. H., & Hilgard, E. R. (1981). *Theories of learning* (5th ed.). Englewood Cliffs, NJ: Prentice-Hall.

Bowlby, J. (1973). *Attachment and loss: Vol. 2 Separation: Anxiety and anger.* New York: Basic Books.

Boye, D., & Miller, N. (1968). The reaction of Jews to prejudice. Paper presented at the annual meeting of the Western Psychological Association, San Diego.

Bradbury, T. N., & Fincham, F. D. (1992). Attributions and behavior in marital interaction. *Journal of Personality and Social Psychology, 63,* 613–628.

Branscombe, N. R., & Wann, D. L. (1993). Collective self-esteem consequences of outgroup derogation under identity-threatening and identity-bolstering conditions. *European Journal of Social Psychology,* in press.

Bray, R. M., & Sugarman, R. (1980). Social facilitation among interaction groups: Evidence for the evaluation apprehension hypothesis. *Personality and Social Psychology Bulletin, 6,* 137–142.

Brehm, J. W. (1966). *A theory of psychological reactance.* New York: Academic Press.

Brennan, T. (1982). Loneliness at adolescence. In L. A. Peplau & P. Perlman (Eds.), *Loneliness: A sourcebook of current theory, research, and therapy.* New York: Wiley.

Brewer, M. B. (1989). A dual process model of impression formation. In R. S. Wyer & T. K. Srull (Eds.), *Advances in social cognition* (Vol. 1, pp. 1–36). Hillsdale, NJ: Erlbaum.

Brewer, M. B. (1991). The social self: On being the same and different at the same time. *Personality and Social Psychology Bulletin, 17,* 475–482.

Brewer, M. B., & Caporael, L. R. (1990). Selfish genes vs. selfish people: Sociobiology as origin myth. *Motivation and Emotion, 14,* 237–243.

Brewer, M. B., Ho, H., Lee, J., & Miller, M. (1987). Social identity and social distance among Hong Kong school children. *Personality and Social Psychology Bulletin, 13,* 156–165.

Brewer, M.B. (1986). The role of ethnocentrism in intergroup conflict. In S. Worchel & W.G. Austin (Eds.), *Psychology of intergroup relations* (2nd ed.) (pp. 88-102). Chicago: Nelson–Hall.

Brickner, M., Harkins, S., & Ostrom, T. (1986). Personal involvement: Thought-provoking implications for social loafing. *Journal of Personality and Social Psychology, 51,* 763–769.

Briggs, S. R., & Cheek, J. M. (1988). On the nature of self–monitoring: Problems with assessment, problems with validity. *Journal of Personality and Social Psychology, 54,* 663–678.

Bringle, R. G., & Bagby, G. J. (1992). Self–esteem and perceived quality of romantic and family relationships in young adults. *Journal of Research in Personality, 26,* 340–356.

Bringle, R. G., & Winnick, T. A. (1992, October). *The nature of unrequited love.* Paper presented at the first Asian Conference in Psychology, Singapore.

Brodeur, P. (1992, December 7). The cancer at Slater School. *New Yorker,* pp. 86–94, 96–106, 108–119.

Brody, J. E. (1989, August 24). Boning up on possible mental and physical health needs of children who are bound for college. *New York Times,* p. 912.

Brooks-Gunn, J., & Lewis, M. (1981). Infant social perception: Responses to pictures of parents and strangers. *Developmental Psychology,* 647–649.

Brown, J. D. (1991). Staying fit and staying well: Physical fitness as a moderator of life stress. *Journal of Personality and Social Psychology, 60,* 555–561.

Brown, J. D., & Mankowski, T. A. (1993). Self–esteem, mood, and self–evaluation: Changes in mood and the way you see you. *Journal of Personality and Social Psychology, 64,* 421–430.

Brown, J. D., & Rogers, R. J. (1991). Self–serving attributions: The role of physiological arousal. *Personality and Social Psychology Bulletin, 17,* 501–506.

Brown, J. D., & Siegel, J. M. (1988). Attributions for negative life events and depression: The role of perceived control. *Journal of Personality and Social Psychology, 54,* 316–322.

Brown, J. D., Novick, N. J., Lord, K. A., & Richards, J. M. (1992). When Gulliver travels: Social context, psychological closeness, and self–appraisals. *Journal of Personality and Social Psychology, 62,* 717–727.

Browne, M. W. (1992a, April 14). Biologists tally generosity's rewards. *New York Times,* pp. C1, C8.

Browne, M. W. (1992b, February 25). Cooling with sound: An effort to save ozone shield. *New York Times,* pp. C1, C7.

Bryan, J. H., & Test, M. A. (1967). Models and helping: Naturalistic studies in aiding behavior. *Journal of Personality and Social Psychology, 6,* 400–407.

Burger, J. M. (1986). Temporal effects on attributions: Actor and observer differences. *Social Cognition, 4,* 377–387.

Burger, J. M. (1986a). Increasing compliance by improving the deal: The that's-not-all technique. *Journal of Personality and Social Psychology, 51,* 277–283.

Burger, J. M. (1987). Desire for control and conformity to a perceived norm. *Journal of Personality and Social Psychology 53,* 355–360.

Burger, J. M. (1991). Changes in attributions over time: The ephemeral fundamental attribution error. *Social Cognition, 9,* 182–193.

Burger, J. M. (1992). *Desire for control: Personality, social, and clinical perspectives.* New York :Plenum.

Burger, J. M., & Cooper, H. N. (1979). The desirability of control. *Motivation and Emotion, 3,* 381–393.

Burke, J. P., Hunt, J. P., & Bickford, R. L. (1985). Causal internalization of academic performance as a function of self–esteem and performance satisfaction. *Journal of Research in Personality, 19,* 321–329.

Burn, S. M., & Oskamp, S. (1986). Increasing community recycling with persuasive communication and public commitment. *Journal of Applied Social Psychology, 16,* 29–41.

Burnstein, E. (1983). Persuasion as argument processing. In M. Brandstatter, J. H. Davis, & G. Stocker-Kriechgauer (Eds.), *Human decision processes.* London: Academic Press.

Burnstein, E., & Schul, Y. (1982). The informational basis of social judgments: Operations in forming an impression of another person. *Journal of Experimental Social Psychology, 18,* 217–234.

Bushman, B. J. (1984). Perceived symbols of authority and their influence on compliance. *Journal of Applied Social Psychology, 14,* 501–508.

Bushman, B. J. (1988). The effects of apparel on compliance: A field experiment with a female authority figure. *Personality and Social Psychology Bulletin, 14,* 459–467.

Buss, A. H., Booker, A., & Buss, E. (1972). Firing a weapon and aggression. *Journal of Personality and Social Psychology, 22,* 196–302.

Buss, D. M. (1988). Love acts: The evolutionary biology of love. In R. J. Sternberg & M. L. Barnes (Eds.), *The psychology of love* (pp. 100–118). New Haven, CT: Yale University Press.

Buss, D. M. (1989a). Conflict between the sexes: Strategic interference and the evocation of anger and upset. *Journal of Personality and Social Psychology, 56,* 735–747.

Buss, D. M. (1990). Evolutionary social psychology: Prospects and pitfalls. *Motivation and Emotion, 14,* 265–286.

Buss, D. M. (1991). Evolutionary personality psychology. *Annual Review of Psychology.* Palo Alto, CA: Annual Reviews.

Buss, D. M., Larsen, R. J., Westen, D., & Semmelroth, J. (1992). Sex differences in jealousy: Evolution, physiology, and psychology. *Psychological Science, 3,* 251–255.

Buss, D.M. and 49 others (1990). International preferences in selecting mates: A study of 37 cultures. *Journal of Cross–Cultural Psychology, 21,* 5–47.

Buunk, B., & Hupka, R. B. (1987). Cross-cultural differences in the elicitation of sexual jealousy. *Journal of Sex Research, 23,* 12–22.

Byrne D. (1991). Perspectives on research classics: This ugly duckling has yet to become a swan. *Contemporary Social Psychology, 15,* 84–85.

Byrne, D. (1961). The influence of propinquity and opportunities for interaction on classroom relationships. *Human Relations, 4,* 63–69.

Byrne, D. (1992). The transition from controlled laboratory experimentation to less controlled settings: Surprise! Additional variables are operative. *Communication Monographs,* 190–198.

Byrne, D., & Buehler, R. A. (1955). A note on the influence of propinquity upon acquaintanceships. *Journal of Abnormal and Social Psychology, 51,* 147–148.

Byrne, D., & Clore, G. L. (1970). A reinforcement–affect model of evaluative responses. *Personality: An International Journal, 1,* 103–128.

Byrne, D., & Kelley, K. (1981). *An introduction to personality* (3rd ed.). Englewood Cliffs, NJ: Prentice-Hall.

Byrne, D., & Murnen, S. K. (1988). Maintaining loving relationships. In R. J. Sternberg & M. L. Barnes (Eds.), *The psychology of love* (pp. 293–310). New Haven, CT: Yale University Press.

Byrne, D., & Nelson, D. (1965). Attraction as a linear function of proportion of positive reinforcements. *Journal of Personality and Social Psychology, 1,* 659–663.

Cacioppo, J. T. Martzke, J. S., Petty, R. E., & Tassinary, L. G. (1988). Specific forms of facial EMG response index emotions during an interview: From Darwin to the continuous flow hypothesis of affect-laden information processing. *Journal of Personality and Social Psychology, 54,* 602–604.

Cahoon, D. D., & Edmonds, E. M. (1989). Male-female estimates of opposite-sex first impressions concerning females' clothing styles. *Bulletin of the Psychonomic Society, 27,* 280–281.

Calvert, J. D. (1988). Physical attractiveness: A review and reevaluation of its role in social skill research. *Behavioral Assessment, 10,* 29–42.

Cambell, J.D., Trapnell, P.D., Heine, S.J., Katz, I.M., Lavallee, L.F., & Lehman, D.R. (1994). Personality and Self–Knowledge: Developent of the Self–Concept Confusion Scale and Examination of its Personality Correlates. Unpublished Manuscript, University of British Columbia.

Campbell, D. T., & Specht, J. C. (1985). Altruism: Biology, culture, and religion. *Journal of Social and Clinical Psychology, 3,* 33–42.

Campbell, J. D. (1986). Similarity and uniqueness: The effects of attribute type, relevance, and individual differences in self–esteem and depression. *Journal of Personality and Social Psychology, 50,* 281–294.

Campbell, J. D., Chew, B., & Scratchley, L. S. (1991). Cognitive and emotional reactions to daily events: The effects of self–esteem and self–complexity. *Journal of Personality, 59,* 473–505.

Cann, A., Sherman, S. J., & Elkes, R. (1975). Effects of initial request size and timing of a second request on compliance: The foot-in-the-door and the door-in-the-face.

Journal of Personality and Social Psychology, 32, 774–782.

Cantor, N. (1990). Social psychology and sociobiology: What can we leave to evolution? *Motivation and Emotion, 14,* 245–254.

Cappella, J. N., & Palmer, M. T. (1990). Attitude similarity, relational history, and attraction: The mediating effects of kinesic and vocal behaviors. *Communication Monographs, 57,* 161–183.

Carlson, N., Marcus-Newhall, & Miller, H. (1990). Effects of situational aggression cues: A quantitative review. *Journal of Personality and Social Psychology, 58,* 622–633.

Carroll, S. J., Perkowitz, W. T., Lurigio, A. J., & Waver, F. M. (1987). Sentencing goals, causal attributions, ideology, and personality. *Journal of Personality and Social Psychology, 36,* 107–118.

Carver, C. S., & Scheier, M. F. (1981). *Attention and self-regulation: A control–theory approach to human behavior.* New York: Springer-Verlag.

Carver, C. S., & Scheier, M. F. (1982). *Perspectives on personality* (2nd ed.). Boston: Allyn & Bacon.

Cash, T. F., & Derlega, V. J. (1978). The matching hypothesis: Physical attractiveness among same–sexed friends. *Personality and Social Psychology Bulletin, 4,* 240–243.

Cash, T. F., & Duncan, N. C. (1984). Physical attractiveness stereotyping among black American college students. *Journal of Social Psychology, 122,* 71–77.

Cash, T. F., & Jacobi, L. (1992). Looks aren't everything (to everybody): The strength of ideals of physical appearance. *Journal of Scoial Behavior and Personality, 7,* 621–630.

Cash, T. F., & Kilcullen, R. N. ((1985). The aye of the beholder: Susceptibility to sexism and beautyism in the evaluation of managerial applicants. *Journal of Applied Social Psychology, 15,* 591–605.

Cash, T. F., & Trimer, C. A. (1984). Sexism and beautyism in women's evaluation of peer performance. *Sex Roles, 10,* 87–98.

Caspi, A., & Herbener, E. S. (1990). Continuity and change: Assortative marriage and the consistency of personality in adulthood. *Journal of Personality and Social Psychology, 58,* 250–258.

Caspi, A., Herbener, E. S., & Ozer, D. J. (1992). Shared experiences and the similarity of personalities: A longitudinal study of married couples. *Journal of Personality and Social Psychology, 62,* 281–291.

Castellow, W. A., Wuensch, K. L., & Moore, C. H. (1990). Effects of physical attractiveness of the plaintiff and defendant in sexual harassment judgments. *Journal of Social Behavior and Personality, 5,* 547–562.

Cavoukian, A., & Doob, A. N. (1980). The effect of a judge's charge and subsequent recharge on judgments of guilt. *Basic and Applied Psychology, 1,* 103–114.

Cawte, J. (1972). *Cruel, poor and brutal nations.* Honolulu, HA: University of Hawaii Press.

Chacko, T. I. (1982). Women and equal employment opportunity: Some unintended effects. *Journal of Applied Psychology, 57,* 119–123.

Chance, N. (1960). Culture change and integration: An Eskimo example. *American Anthropologist, 67,* 1028–1044.

Chesek, C. (1992, August). At the American Museum. *Natural History*, p. 64.

Che–Alford, J., Allan, C., & Butlin, G. (1994). *Families in Canada* (Focus on Canada series). Scarborough, Ont.: Statistics Canada and Prentice Hall Canada.

Chidester, T. R. (1986). Problems in the study of interracial aggression: Pseudo-interracial dyad paradigm. *Journal of Personality and Social Psychology, 50,* 74–79.

Christy, P. R., Gelfand, D. N., & Hartmann, D. P. (1971). Effects of competition-induced frustration on two classes of modeled behavior. *Developmental Psychology, 5,* 104–111.

Cialdini, R. B. (1988). *Influence: Science and practice,* (2nd ed.). Glenview, IL: Scott, Foresman.

Cialdini, R. B., & Petty, R. (1979). Anticipatory opinion effects. In R. B. Petty, T. Ostrom, & T. Brock (Eds.), *Cognitive responses in persuasion.* Hillsdale, NJ: Erlbaum.

Cialdini, R. B., Darby, B. L., & Vincent, J. E. (1973). Transgression and altruism: A case for hedonism. *Journal of Experimental Social Psychology, 9,* 502–516.

Cialdini, R. B., Kenrick, D. T., & Bauman, D. J. (1982). Effects of mood on prosocial behavior in children and adults. In N. Eisenberg-Berg (Ed.), *Development of prosocial behavior.* New York: Academic Press.

Cioffi, D., & Holoway, J. (1993). Delayed costs of suppressed pain. *Journal of Personality and Social Psychology, 64,* 274–282.

Clark, L. A., & Watson, D. (1988). Mood and the mundane: Relations between daily life events and self–reported mood. *Journal of Personality and Social Psychology, 54,* 296–308.

Clark, M. S., Ouellette, R., Powel, M. C., & Milberg, S. (1987). Recipient's mood, relationship type, and helping. *Journal of Personality and Social Psychology, 53,* 94–103.

Clark, R. N., Hendee, J. C., & Burgess, R. L. (1972). The experimental control of littering. *Journal of Environmental Education, 4,* 22–28.

Clary, E. G., & Orenstein, L. (1991). The amount and effectiveness of help: The relationship of motives and abilities to helping behavior. *Personality and Social Psychology Bulletin, 17,* 58–64.

Clément, R. (1987). Second language proficiencey and acculturation: an investigation of the effects of language status and individual characteristics. *Journal of Language and Social Psychology, 5,* 271–290.

Clore, G. L., & Byrne, D. (1974). A reinforcement–affect model of attraction. In T. L. Huston (Ed.), *Foundations of interpersonal attraction* (pp. 143–170). New York: Academic Press.

Cohen, A. (1990). *A deal undone: The making and breaking of the Meech Lake Accord.* Toronto: Douglas & McIntyre.

Cohen, S. (1980). Aftereffects of stress on human performance and social behavior: A review of research and theory. *Psychological Bulletin, 81,* 82–108.

Cohen, S., Evans, G. W., Stokols, D., & Krantz, D. (1986). *Behavior, health and environmental stress.* New York: Plenum.

Cohen, S., Glass, D. C., & Singer, J. E. (1973). Apartment noise, auditory discrimination, and reading ability in children. *Journal of Experimental Social Psychology, 9,* 407–422.

Cohen, S., Kaplan, J. R., Cunnick, J. E., Manuck, S. G., & Rabin, G. S. (1992). Chronic social stress, affiliation, and cellular immune response in nonhuman primates. *Psychological Science, 3,* 301–304.

Cohen, S., Tyrrell, D. A. J., & Smith, A. P. (1993). Negative life events, perceived stress, negative affect, and susceptibility to the common cold. *Journal of Personality and Social Psychology, 64,* 131–140.

Cohn, E. G. (1990). Weather and violent crime: A reply to Perry and Simpson, 1987. *Environment and Behavior, 22,* 280–294.

Coleman, L. M., Jussim, L., & Abraham, J. (1987). Students' reactions to teachers' evaluations: The unique impact of negative feedback. *Journal of Applied Social Psychology,* 1051–1070.

Compas, G., Banez, G. A., Malcarne, V., & Worsham, N. (1991). *Journal of Social Issues, 47*(4), 23–34.

Condon, J. W., & Crano, W. D. (1988). Inferred evaluation and the relation between attitude similarity and interpersonal attraction. *Journal of Personality and Social Psychology, 54,* 789–797.

Conger, J. A. (1991). Inspiring others: The language of leadership. *Academy of Management Executives 5*(1), 31–45.

Contrada, R. J. (1989). Type A behavior, personality hardiness, and cardiovascular responses to stress. *Journal of Personality and Social Psychology, 57,* 895–903.

Cook, S. W. (1985). Experimenting on social issues: The case of school desegregation. *American Psychologist, 40,* 452–460.

Cook, S. W., & Pelfrey, M. (1985). Reactions to being helped in cooperating interracial groups: A context effect. *Journal of Personality and Social Psychology, 49,* 1231–1245.

Cooke, P. (1992). Noises out: What it's doing to you. *New York, 25*(4), 28–33.

Cool, L. C. (1991, January). Getting wasted. *Penthouse,* pp. 139, 192.

Cooley, C.H. (1902/1964) *Human nature and the social order.* New York: Schocken Books.

Cooper, J., & Fazio, R. H. (1984). A new look at dissonance theory. In L. Berkowitz (Ed.), *Advances in experimental social psychology* (Vol. 17, pp. 229–266). New York: Academic press.

Cooper, J., & Scher, S. J. (1992). Actions and attitudes: The role of responsibility and aversive consequences in persuasion. In T. Brock & S. Shavitt (Eds.), *The psychology of persuasion.* San Francisco: Freeman.

Costanza, R. S., Derlega, V. J., & Winstead, G. A. (1988). Positive and negative forms of social support: Effects of conversation topics on coping with stress among same–sex friends. *Journal of Experimental Social Psychology, 24,* 182–193.

Cotterell, N., Eisenberger, R., & Speicher, H. (1992). Inhibiting effects of reciprocation wariness on interpersonal relationships. *Journal of Personality and Social Psychology, 62,* 658–668.

Cottrell, H. B., Wack, K. L., Sekerak, G. J., & Rittle, R. (1968). Social facilitation of dominant responses by the presence of an audience and the mere presence of others. *Journal of Personality and Social Psychology, 51,* 245–250.

Cox, M., & Tanford, S. (1989). Effects of evidence and instructions in civil trials: An experimental investigation of rules of admissibility. *Social Behavior, 4,* 31–55.

Cramer, R. E., McMaster, M. R., Bartell, P. A., & Dragna, M.

(1988). Subject competence and minimization of the bystander effect. *Journal of Applied Social Psychology, 18,* 1133–1148.

Crandall, C. S. (1992). Psychophysical scaling of stressful life events. *Psychological Science, 3,* 256–258.

Crouch, A., & Yetton, P. (1987). Manager behavior, leadership style, and subordinate performance: An empirical extension of the Vroom–Yetton conflict rule. *Organizational Behavior and Human Decision Processes, 39,* 384–396.

Crouse, B. B., & Mehrabian, A. (1977). Affiliation of opposite–sexed strangers. *Journal of Research in Personality, 11,* 38–47.

Croyle, R., & Uretsky, M. B. (1987). Effects of mood on self–appraisal of health status. *Health Psychology, 6,* 239–254.

Crusco, A. H., & Wetzel, C. G. (1984). The Midas touch: The effects of interpersonal touch on restaurant tipping. *Personality and Social Psychology Bulletin, 10,* 512–517.

Cruse, D., & Leigh, B. S. (1987). "Adam's Rib" revisited: Legal and non–legal influences on the processing of trial testimony. *Social Behavior, 2,* 221–230.

Cunningham, M. R. (1979). Weather, mood, and helping behavior: Quasi–experiments with the sunshine samaritan. *Journal of Personality and Social Psychology, 37,* 1947–1956.

Cunningham, M. R. (1988). Does happiness mean friendliness? Induced mood and heterosexual self–disclosure. *Personality and Social Psychology Bulletin, 14,* 283–297.

Cunningham, M. R., Shaffer, D. R., Barbee, A. P., Wolff, P. L., & Kelley, D. J. (1990). Separate processes in the relation of elation and depression to helping: Social versus personal concerns. *Journal of Experimental Social Psychology, 26,* 13–33.

Cunningham, M. R., Steinberg, J., & Grev, R. (1980). Wanting to and having to help: Separate motivations for positive mood and guilt–induced helping. *Journal of Personality and Social Psychology, 38,* 181–192.

Curtis, R. S., & Miller, K. (1986). Believing another likes or dislikes you: Behavior making the beliefs come true. *Journal of Personality and Social Psychology, 50,* 284–290.

Cutler, B. L., & Wolfe, R. N. (1989). Self–monitoring and the association between confidence and accuracy. *Journal of Research in Personality, 23,* 410–420.

Cutler, B. L., Moran, G., & Narby, D. J. (1992). Jury selection in insanity defense cases. *Journal of Research in Personality, 26,* 165–182.

Cutler, B. L., Penrod, S. D., & Martens, T. K. (1987). Improving the reliability of eyewitness identification: Putting content into context. *Journal of Applied Psychology, 72,* 629–637.

Dane, F. C. (1992). Applying social psychology in the courtroom: Understanding stereotypes in jury decision making. *Contemporary Social Psychology, 16,* 33–36.

Darley, J. M. (1991). Altruism and prosocial behavior research: Reflections and prospects. In M. S. Clark (Ed.), *Prosocial Behavior* (pp. 312–327). Newbury Park, CA: Sage.

Darley, J. M., & Batson, C. D. (1973). From Jerusalem to Jericho: A study of sitautional and dispositional variables in helping behavior. *Journal of Personality and Social Psychology, 27,* 100–108.

Davidson, A.R., & Thompson, E. (1980). Cross–cultural studies of attitudes and beliefs. In H.C. Triandis & R.N. Brislin (Eds.), *Handbook of cross–cultural psychology* (Vol. 5, pp. 25–71). Boston: Allyn & Bacon.

Davidson, L. M., Hagmann, J., & Baum, A. (1990). An exploration of a possible physiological explanation for stressor aftereffects. *Journal of Applied Social Psychology, 20,* 869–880.

Davie, M. R., & Reeves, R. J. (1939). Propinquity of residence before marriage. *American Journal of Sociology, 44,* 510–517.

Davis, C.G., Lehman, D.R., Wortman, C.B., Silver, R.C., & Thompson, S.C. (in press) Undoing of traumatic life events. *Personality and Social Psychology Bulletin.*

Davis, J. H. (1989). Psychology and the law: The last 15 years. *Journal of Applied Social Psychology, 19,* 119–230.

Davis, J. H., Stasson, M., Ono, K., & Zimmerman, S. (1988). Effects of straw polls on group decision making, sequential voting pattern, timing, and local majorities. *Journal of Personality and Social Psychology, 55,* 918–926.

Davis, J. H., Tindale, R. S., Naggao, D. H., Hinsz, V. B., & Robertson, B. (1984). Order effects in multiple decisions by gruops: A demonstration with mock juries and trial procedures. *Journal of Personality and Social Psychology, 47,* 1003–1012.

Davis, M. H., & Harvey, J. C. (1992). Declines in major league batting performance as a function of game pressure: A drive theory analysis. *Journal of Applied Social Psychology, 22,* 714–735.

Davis, M. H., & Kraus, L. A. (1989). Social contact, loneliness, and mass media use: A test of two hypotheses. *Journal of Applied Social Psychology, 19,* 1100–1124.

Davis, S. F., Miller, K. M., Johnson, D., McAuley, H., & Dinges, D. (1992). The relationship between optimism–pessimism, loneliness, and death anxiety. *Bulletin of the Psychonomic Society, 30,* 135–136.

Dawson, J.L.M. (1963). *Psychological effects of social change in a West African community.* Unpublished D. Phil. Thesis, Oxford.

de Waal, F. (1989). *Peacemaking in primates.* Cambridge, MA: Harvard University Press.

Deaux, K. (1993). Reconstructing social identity. *Personality and Social Psychology Bulletin, 19,* 4–12.

Deaux, K., & Lewis, L. L. (1984). The structure of gender stereotypes: Interrelationships among components and gender label. *Journal of Personality and Social Psychology, 46,* 991–1004.

DeBono, K. G. (1992). Pleasant scents and persuasion: An information processing approach. *Journal of Applied Social Psychology, 22,* 910–919.

DeBono, K. G., & Packer, M. (1991). The effects of advertising appeal on perceptions of product quality. *Personality and Social Psychology Bulletin, 17,* 194–200.

DeJong, W., & Musilli, L. (1982). External pressure to comply: Handicapped versus nonhandicapped requesters and the foot–in–the–door phenomenon. *Personality and Social Psychology Bulletin, 8,* 522–527.

Dellinger, R. W. (1979). Jet roar: Health problems take off near airports. *Human Behavior, 8,* 50–51.

Dengerink, H. A., Schnedler, R. W., & Covey, M. X. (1978). Role of avoidance in aggressive responses to attack and no attack. *Journal of Personality and Social Psychology, 36,* 1044–1053.

Denno, D. J. (1982). *Sex differences in cognition and crime: Early developmental, biological, and social correlates.* Unpublished doctoral dissertation, University of Pennsylvania.

DePaulo, B. M. (1992). Nonverbal behavior and self–presentation. *Psychological Bulletin, 111,* 230–243.

DePaulo, B. M., & Fisher, J. D. (1980). The costs of asking for help. *Basic and Applied Social Psychology, 1,* 23–35.

DePaulo, B. M., Dull, W. R., Greenberg, J. M., & Swaim, G. W. (1989). *Journal of Personality and Social Psychology, 56,* 834–844.

Deutsch, F. M., & Lamberti, D. M. (1986). Does social approval increase helping? *Personality and Social Psychology Bulletin, 12,* 149–157.

Deutsch, F. M., Sullivan, L., Sage, C., & Basile, N. (1991). The relations among talking, liking, and similarity between friends. *Personality and Social Psychology Bulletin, 17,* 406–411.

Deutsch, M., & Collins, M. E. (1951). *Interracial housing.* Minneapolis: University of Minnesota Press.

Devine, P. O. (1989). Stereotypes and prejudice: Their automatic and controlled components. *Journal of Personality and Social Psychology, 56,* 5–18.

Devine, P. O., Monteith, M. J., Zuwerink, R. J., & Elliot, A. J. (1991). Prejudice with and without compunction. *Journal of Personality and Social Psychology, 60,* 817–830.

DiMatteo, M. R., Hays, R. B., & Prince, L. M. (1986). Relationships of physicians' nonverbal communication skill to patient satisfaction, appointment noncompliance, and physician workload. *Health Psychology, 5,* 581–594.

Dion, H. H., & Dion, H. L. (1991). Psychological individualism and romantic love. *Journal of Social Behavior and Personality, 6,* 17–33.

Dion, H. L., & Dion, H. H. (1988). Romantic love: Individual and cultural perspectives. In R. J. Sternberg & M. L. Barnes (Eds.), *The psychology of love* (pp. 264–289). New Haven, CT: Yale University press.

Dion, K. K., Berscheid, E., & Walster, E. (1972). What is beautiful is good. *Journal of Personality and Social Psychology, 24,* 285–290.

Dion, K. L. (1993, March). Personal communication.

Dion, K. L., & Dion, K. K. (1987). Belief in a just world and physical attractiveness stereotyping. *Journal of Personality and Social Psychology, 52,* 775–780.

Dion, K. L., Dion, K. K., & Keelan, J. P. (1990). Appearance anxiety as a dimension of social–evaluative anxiety: Exploring the ugly duckling syndrome. *Contemporary Social Psychology, 14,* 220–224.

Dion, K.L. (1975).Women's reactions to discrimination from members of the same or opposite sex. *Journal of Research in Personality, 9,* 294–306.

Dion, K.L., & Earn, B.M. (1975). The phenomenology of being a target of prejudice. *Journal of Personality and Social Psychology, 32,* 944–950.

Dion, K.L., Earn, B.M., & Yee, P.H.N. (1986). The experience of being a victim of prejudice: an experimental approach. In B. Earn & S. Towson (Eds.), *Readings in social psychology: Classic and Canadian contributions.* Peterborough: Broadview Press.

Dixon, T. M., & Baumeister, R. F. (1991). Escaping the self: The moderating effect of self–complexity. *Personality and Social Psychology Bulletin, 17,* 363–368.

Dodge, K. A., & Coie, J. D. (1987). Social–information–processing factors in reactive and proactive aggression in children's peer groups. *Journal of Personality and Social Psychology, 53,* 1146–1158.

Dodge, K. A., Murphy, R. R., & Buchsbaum, K. (1984). The assessment of intention–cue detection skills in children: Implications for developmental psychopathology. *Child Development, 55,* 163–173.

Dodge, K. A., Price, J. N., Bachorowski, J. A., & Newman, J. P. (1990). Hostile attributional biases in severely aggressive adolescents. *Journal of Abnormal Psychology, 99,* 385–392.

Doktor, R. H. (1990). Asian and American CEOs: A comparative study. *Organizational Dynamics. 18*(3), 46–56.

Dollard, J., Doob, L., Miller, N., Mowrer, O. H., & Sears, R. R. (1939). *Frustration and aggression.* New Haven: Yale University Press.

Doob, A.N. (1976). Evidence, procedure and psychological research. In G. Bermant, C Nemeth & N Vidmar (Eds.), *Psychology and the law.* Lexington, MA: Lexington Books.

Doob, A.N. (1985). The many realities of crime. In A.N. Doob, & E.L. Greenspan (Eds.), *Perspectives in criminal law.* Aurora, Ont.: Canada Law Book.

Doob, A.N., & MacDonald, G.E. (1979). Television viewing and fear of victimization: Is the effect causal? *Journal of Personality and Social Psychology, 37,* 170-179.

Doob, A.N., & Roberts, J.V. (1983). *An analysis of the public's view of sentencing.* Ottawa: Department of Justice, Canada.

Dorian, B. J., Keystone, E., Garfinkel, P. E., & Brown, J. M. (1982). Aberrations in lymphocyte subpopulations and function during psychological stress. *Clinical and Experimental Immunology, 50,* 132–138.

Dovidio, J. F., & Gaertner, S. L. (1993). Stereotypes and evaluative intergroup bias. In D. M. Mackie & D. L. Hamilton (Eds.), *Affect, cognition, and stereotyping: Interactive processes in perception.* Orlando, FL: Academic Press.

Dovidio, J. F., Evans, N., & Tyler, R. B. (1986). Racial stereotypes: The contents of their cognitive representations. *Journal of Experimental Social Psychology, 22,* 22–37.

Downs, A. C., & Lyons, P. M. (1991). Natural observations of the links between attractiveness and initial legal judgments. *Personality and Social Psychology Bulletin, 17,* 541–547.

Drachman, D., DeCarufel, A., & Insko, C. A. (1978). The extra credit effect in interpersonal attraction. *Journal of Experimental Social Psychology, 14,* 458–465.

Drigotas, S. M., & Rusbult, C. E. (1992). Should I stay or should I go? A dependence model of breakups. *Journal of Personality and Social Psychology, 62,* 62–87.

Driscoll, R., Davis, H. E., & Lipetz, M. E. (1972). Parental interference and romantic love: The Romeo and Juliet effect. *Journal of Personality and Social Psychology, 24,* 1–10.

Duck, S., & Barnes, M. H. (1992). Disagreeing about agreement: Reconciling differences about similarity. *Communication Monographs, 59,* 199–208.

Dunn, J. (1992). Siblings and development. *Current Directions in Psychological Science, 1,* 6–11.

Durdan, C. A., Reeder, G. D., & Hecht, P. R. (1985). Litter in a university cafeteria: Demographic data and the use of prompts as an intervention strategy. *Environment and Behavior, 17,* 387–404.

Dutton, D. G., & Aron, A. P. (1974). Some evidence for heightened sexual attraction under conditions of high anxiety. *Journal of Personality and Social Psychology, 30,* 510–517.

Dutton, D. G., & Lake, R. A. (1973). Threat of own prejudice and reverse discrimination in interracial situations. *Journal of Personality and Social Psychology, 28,* 94–100.

Dutton, D.G. (1986a). Wife assaulters' explanations for assault: the neutralization of self–punishment. *Canadian Journal of Behavioral Science, 18,* 381–390.

Dutton, D.G. (1986b). The outcome of court–mandated treatment for wife assault: a quasi–experimental evaluation. *Violence and Victims, 1,* 163–175.

Dutton, D.G. (1987). The criminal justice response to wife assault. *Law and Human Behavior, 11,* 189–206.

Dutton, D.G. (1992). Theoretical and empirical perpectives on the etiology and prevention of wife assault. In R.D. Peters, R.J. McMahon, & V.L. Quinsey (Eds.). *Aggression and violence throughout the life span.* Newbury Park: Sage.

Duval, S., & Wicklund, R. A. (1972). A theory of objective self–awareness. New York: Academic Press.

Eagly, A. H., & Johnson, B. T. (1990). Gender and leadership style: A meta–analysis. *Psychological Bulletin, 108,* 233–256.

Earley, P.C. (1989). Social loafing and collectivism: a comparison of the United States and the People's Republic of China. *Administrative Science Quarterly, 34,* 565–81.

Earn, B., & Towson, S. (Eds.) (1986). *Readings in social psychology: Classic and Canadian contributions.* Peterborough, Ont.: Broadview Press.

Ebbeson, E. B., Kjos, G. L., & Konecni, V. J. (1976). Spatial ecology: Its effects on the choice of friends and enemies. *Journal of Experimental Social Psychology, 12,* 508–518.

Edleson, J.L., & Grusznski, R.J. (1988). Treating men who batter: Four years of outcome data from the domestic Abuse Project. *Journal of Social Science Research, 12,* 3–22.

Edleson, J.L., Syers, M., & Brygger, M.P. (1987). *Comparative effectiveness of group treatment for men who batter.* Paper presented at the Third National Family Violence Conference, Durham, NH.

Eisenberg, N., Cialdini, R. B., McCreath, H., & Shell, R. (1987). Consistency based compliance: When and why do children become vulnerable? *Journal of Personality and Social Psychology, 52,* 1174–1181.

Eisenman, R. (1985). Marijuana use and attraction: Support for Byrne's similarity-attraction concept. *Perceptual and Motor Skills, 61,* 582.

Ekman, P. (1973). Cross–cultural studies of facial expression. In P. Ekman (Ed.), *Darwin and facial expression.* New York: Academic Press.

Ekman, P. (1989). The argument and evidence about universals in facial expressions of emotion. In H. Wagner & A. Manstead (Eds.), *Handbook of psychophysiology: Emotion and social behavior* (pp. 143–164). New York: Wiley.

Ekman, P. (1992). Are there basic emotions? *Psychological Review, 99,* 550–553.

Ekman, P. (in press). An argument for basic emotions. *Cognition and Emotion.*

Ekman, P., & Friesen, W. V. (1975). *Unmasking the face.* Englewood Cliffs, NJ: Prentice–Hall.

Ekman, P., Davidson, R. J., & Friesen, W. V. (1990). The Duchenne smile: Emotional expression and brain physiology II. *Journal of Personality and Social Psychology, 58,* 342–353.

Ellis, R. J. (1988). Self–monitoring and leadership emergence in groups. *Personality and Social Psychology Bulletin, 14,* 681–693.

Ellis, S., Rogoff, B., & Cramer, C. C. (1981). Age segregation in children's social interactions. *Developmental Psychology, 17,* 399–407.

Ellsworth, P. C., & Carlsmith, J. M. (1973). Eye contact and gaze aversion in aggressive encounter. *Journal of Personality and Social Psychology, 33,* 117–122.

Elmer–Dewitt, P. (1992). What's wrong with the weather? *Time, 139*(24), 60–61.

Emmons, R. A. (1992). Abstract versus concrete goals: personal striving level, physical illness, and psychological well–being. *Journal of Personality and Social Psychology, 62,* 292–300.

Epstein, S. (1983). The unconscious, the preconscious, and the self–concept. In J. Suls & A. Greenwald (Eds.), *Psychological perspectives on the self* (Vol. 2, pp. 220–247). Hillsdale, NJ: Erlbaum.

Erber, R. (1991). Affective and semantic priming: Effects of mood on category accessibility and inference. *Journal of Experimental Social Psychology, 27,* 480–498.

Eron, L. B. (1982). Parent–child interaction, television violence, and aggression of children. *American Psychologist, 37,* 197–211.

Esses, V. M. (1989). Mood as a moderator of acceptance of interpersonal feedback. *Journal of Personality and Social Psychology, 57,* 769–781.

Esses, V. M., & Webster, C. D. (1988). Physical attractiveness, dangerousness, and the Canadian criminal code. *Journal of Applied Social Psychology, 18,* 1017–1031.

Evans, G. W., Jacobs, S. V., & Frager, N. (1982). Behavioral responses to air pollution. In A. Baum & J. E. Singer (Eds.), *Advances in environmental psychology* (Vol. 4). Hillsdale, NJ: Erlbaum.

Evans, G. W., Palsane, M. N., & Carrere, S. (1987). Type A behavior and occupational stress: A cross–cultural study of blue–collar workers. *Journal of Personality and Social Psychology, 52,* 1002–1007.

Evans, M. C., & Wilson, M. (1949). Friendship choices of university women students. *Educational and Psychological Measurement, 9,* 307–312.

Fajardo, D. M. (1985). Author race, essay quality, and reverse discrimination. *Journal of Applied Social Psychology, 16,* 255–268.

Fazio, R. H. (1989). On the power and functionality of attitudes: The role of attitude accessibility. In A. R. Pratkanis, S. J. Breckler, & A. G. Greenwald (Eds.), *Attitude structure and function* (pp. 153–179). Hillsdale, NJ: Erlbaum.

Fazio, R. H., & Zanna, N. P. (1981). Direct experience and attitude–behavior consistency. In L. Berkowitz (Ed.),

Advances in experimental social psychology (vol. 14, pp. 161–202). New York: Academic Press.

Fazio, R. H., Chen, J., McDonel, E. C., & Sherman, S. J. (1982). Attitude accessibility and the strength of the object–evaluation association. *Journal of Experimental Social Psychology, 18,* 339–357.

Fazio, R. H., Sanbonmatsu, D. M., Powell, N. C., & Kardes, F. F. (1986). On the automatic activation of attitudes. *Journal of Personality and Social Psychology, 50,* 229–238.

Feingold, A. (1990). Gender differences in the effects of physical attractiveness on romantic attraction: A comparison across five research paradigms. *Journal of Personality and Social Psychology, 59,* 981–993.

Feingold, A. (1992a). Good–looking people are not what we think. *Psychological Bulletin, 111,* 304–341.

Feingold, A. (1992b). Gender differences in mate selection preferences: A test of the parental investment model. *Psychological Bulletin, 112,* 125–139.

Fekken, G. C., & Jakubowski, I. (1990). Effects of stress on the health of Type A students. *Journal of Social Behavior and Personality, 5,* 473–480.

Feldman, D. C. (1984). The development and enforcement of group norms. *Academy of Management Review, 9,* 47–53.

Felson, R. B. (1989). Parents and the reflected appraisal process: A longitudinal analysis. *Journal of Personality and Social Psychology, 56,* 965–971.

Feshbach, S. (1984). The catharsis hypothesis, aggressive drive, and the reduction of aggression. *Aggressive Behavior, 10,* 91–101.

Festinger, L. (1954). A theory of social comparison processes. *Human Relations, 7,* 117–140.

Festinger, L. (1957). *A theory of cognitive dissonance.* Evanston, IL: Row, Peterson.

Festinger, L. (1964). *Conflict, decision and dissonance.* Stanford, CA: Stanford University Press.

Festinger, L., & Carlsmith, J. M. (1959). Cognitive consequences of forced compliance. *Journal of Abnormal and Social Psychology, 38,* 203–210.

Festinger, L., Schachter, S., & Back, K. (1950). *Social pressures in informal groups: A study of a housing community.* New York: Harper.

Fichten, C. S., & Amsel, R. (1986). Trait attributions about college students with a physical disability: Circumplex analyses and methodological issues. *Journal of Applied Social Psychology, 16,* 410–427.

Fiedler, F. E. (1978). Contingency model and the leadership process. In L. Berkowitz (Ed.), *Advances in experimental social psychology* (Vol. 11). New York: Academic Press.

Fiedler, F. E., & Forgas, J. P. (Eds.). (1988). *Affect, cognition, and social behavior.* Toronto: Hogrefe.

Fiedler, F. E., & Garcia, J. E. (1987). *Leadership: Cognitive resources and performance.* New York: Wiley.

Fincham, F. D., & Bradbury, T. N. (1992). Assessing attributions in marriage: The relationship attribution measure. *Journal of Personality and Social Psychology, 62,* 457–468.

Fincham, F. D., & Bradbury, T. N. (1993). Marital satisfaction, depression, and attributions: A longitudinal analysis. *Journal of Personality and Social Psychology, 64,* 442–452.

Fischer, G. (1989). Atmospheric lifetime of carbon dioxide. *Population and Environment, 13,* 177–181.

Fischman, J. (1986, January). Women and divorce: Ten years after. *Psychology Today,* p. 15.

Fisher, H. (1992). Anatomy of love. New York: W. W. Norton.

Fisher, J. D., & Fisher, WI A. (1992). Changing AIDS–risk behavior. *Psychological Bulletin, 111,* 455–474.

Fisher, J. D., Nadler, A., & Whitcher–Alagna, S. (1982). Recipient reactions to aid. *Psychological Bulletin, 91,* 27–54.

Fiske, S. T. (1980). Attention and weight in person perception: The impact of negative and extreme behavior. *Journal of Personality and Social Psychology, 33,* 889–906.

Fiske, S. T. (1989). *Interdependence and stereotyping: From the laboratory to the Supreme Court (and back).* Invited address, American Psychological Association, New Orleans.

Fiske, S. T., & Neuberg, S. L. (1990). A continuum model of impression formation, from category–based to individuating processes: Influence of information and motivation on attention and interpretation. In M. P. Zanna (Ed.), *Advances in experimental social psychology* (Vol. 23). New York: Academic Press.

Fiske, S. T., & Taylor, S. E. (1991). *Social cognition* (2nd ed.). New York: Random House.

Flowers, M. (1977). A laboratory test of some implications of Janis's group think hypothesis. *Journal of Personality and Social Psychology, 55,* 888–896.

Folkman, S., & Lazarus, R. S. (1980). An analysis of coping in a middle–aged community sample. *Journal of Health and Social Behavior, 21,* 219–239.

Forgas, J. P. (1991a). Affective influences on partner choice: Role of mood in social decisions. *Journal of Personality and Social Psychology, 61,* 708–720.

Forgas, J. P. (1991b). Affect and social perception: Research evidence and an integrative theory. In W. Stroebe & M. Newstone (Eds.), *European review of social psychology.* New York: Wiley.

Forgas, J. P. (1992a, in press). Mood and the perception of atypical people: Affect and prototypicality in person memory and impressions. *Journal of Personality and Social Psychology,* in press.

Forgas, J. P. (1993c). On making sense of odd couples: Mood effects on the perception of mismatched relationships. *Personality and Social Psychology Bulletin, 19,* 59–70.

Forgas, J. P. (l993b,). Mood and the perception of unusual people: Affective asymmetry in memory and social judgments. *European Journal of Social Psychology,* in press.

Forgas, J. P., & Bower, G. H. (1988). Affect in social and personal judgments. In K. Fiedler & J. P. Forgas (Eds.), *Affect, cognition, and social behavior.* Toronto: Hogrefe.

Forgas, J.P., Furnham, A., & Frey, D. (1989). Cross–national differences in attributions of wealth and economic success. *Journal of social Psychology, 129,* 643–657.

Forge, K. L., & Phemister, S. (1987). The effect of prosocial cartoons on preschool children. *Child Development Journal, 17,* 83–88.

Forsyth, D. R. (1983). *An introduction to dynamics.* Monterey, CA: Brooks/Cole.

Forsyth, D. R. (1992). *An introduction to group dynamics,* (2nd ed.). Monterey, CA: Brooks/Cole.

Forsythe, S., Drake, M. F., & Cox, C. E. (1985). Influence of applicant's dress on interviewer's selection decisions. *Journal of Applied Psychology, 70,* 374–378.

Fraczek, A., & Kirwil, L. (1992). Living in the family and child aggression: Studies on some socialization conditions of development of aggression. In A. Fraczek & H. Zumkey (Eds.), *Socialization and aggression.* Berlin: Springer–Verlag.

Frank, M. G., & Gilovich, T. (1988). The dark side of self and social perception: Black uniforms and aggression in professional sports. *Journal of Personality and Social Psychology, 54,* 74–85.

Frankel, A., & Prentice–Dunn, S. (1990). Loneliness and the processing of self–relevant information. *Journal of Social and Clinical Psychology, 9,* 303–315.

Freedman, J. L. (1984). Effects of television violence on aggressiveness. *Psychological Bulletin, 96,* 227–246.

Freedman, J. L., & Fraser, S. C. (1966). Compliance without pressure: The foot–in–the–door technique. *Journal of Personality and Social Psychology, 4,* 195–202.

Freedman, J. L., Cunninghman, J. A., & Krismer, K. (1992). Inferred values and the reverse–incentive effect in induced compliance. *Journal of Personality and Social Psychology, 62,* 357–368.

Freudenheim, M. (1992, October 14). Software helps patients make crucial choices. *New York Times,* p. D6.

Friedman, H. S., Riggio, R. E., & Casella, D. F. (1988). Nonverbal skill, personal charisma, and initial attraction. *Personality and Social Psychology Bulletin, 14,* 203–211.

Fry, D. P. (1990). Aggressive interaction among Zapotec children in two different microcultural environments. *Proceedings of the Ninth World Meeting of the International Society for Research on Aggression,* Banff, Canada.

Fry, P.S., & Ghosh, R. (1980). Attributions of success and failure: comparison of cultural differences between Asian and Caucasian children. *Journal of Cross–Cultural Psychology, 11,* 343–363.

Funder, D. C., & Colvin, C. R. (1988). Friends and strangers: Acquaintanceship, agreement, and the accuracy of personality judgment. *Journal of Personality and Social Psychology, 55,* 149–158.

Fussell, S. R., & Krauss, R. M. (1989). Understanding friends and strangers: The effects of audience design on message comprehension. *European Journal of Social Psychology, 19,* 509–525.

Gabrenya, W.K., Wang, Y.E., & Latané, B. (1985). Social loafing on an optimising task: Cross–cultural differences amopng Chinese Americans. *Journal of Cross–Cultural Psychology, 16,* 223–42.

Gaertner, S. L., & Dovidio, J. F. (1986). Prejudice, discrimination, and racism: Problems, progress, and promise. In J. F. Dovidio & S. L. Gaertner (Eds.), *Prejudice, discrimination, and racism* (pp. 315–332). Orlando, FL: Academic Press.

Gaertner, S. L., Mann, J., Murrell, A., & Dovidio, J. F. (1989). Reducing intergroup bias: The benefits of recategorization. *Journal of Personality and Social Psychology, 57,* 239–249.

Gaertner, S. L., Rust, M. C., Dovidio, J. F., Bachman, B. A., & Anastasio, P. A. (1993). The contact hypothesis: The role of a common ingroup identity on reducing intergroup bias. *Small Business Research,* in press.

Galambos, N. I., (1992). Parent–adolescent relations. *Current Directions in Psychological Science, 1,* 146–149.

Gangestad, S., & Snyder, M. (1985). On the nature of self–monitoring: An examination of latent causal structure. In P. Shaver (Ed.), *Review of personality and Social Psychology (Vol. 6,* pp. 65–85). Beverly Hills, CA: Sage.

Ganley, A. (1981). *Participant's manual: Court–mandated therapy for men who batter: A three day workshop for professionals.* Washington, DC:Centre for Women Policy Studies.

Garcia, L. T. (1982). Sex role orientation and stereotypes about male–female sexuality. *Sex Roles, 8,* 863–876.

Garfinkel, H. (1967). *Studies in ethnomethodology.* Englewood Cliffs, NJ: Prentice–Hall.

Gartner, R., & Doob, A.N. (1994). Trends in criminal victimization: 1988 – 1993. *Juristat, 14,* 1–19.

Geen, R. G. (1978). Some effects of observing violence upon the behavior of the observer. In B. A. Maher (Ed.), *Progress in experimental personality research,* (Vol. 8). New York: Academic Press.

Geen, R. G. (1981). Behavioral and physiological reactions to observed violence: Effects of prior exposure to aggressive stimuli. *Journal of Personality and Social Psychology, 40,* 868–875.

Geen, R. G. (1989). Alternative conceptions of social facilitation. In P. B. Paulus (Ed.), *Psychology of group influence* (2nd ed., pp. 1–37). New York: Academic Press.

Geen, R. G. (1991). *Human aggression.* Pacific Grove, CA: Brooks/Cole.

Geen, R. G., & Gange, J. J. (1977). Drive theory of social facilitation: Twelve years of theory and research. *Psychological Bulletin, 8*(3), 1267–1288.

Geertz, C. (1984). "From the native's point of view:" On the nature of anthropological understanding. In R.A.Shweder & R.A.LeVine (Eds.), *Culture theory: Essays on mind, self and emotion.* Cambridge: Cambridge University Press.

Geier, J. G. (1969). A trait approach to the study of leadership in small groups. *Journal of Communication, 17,* 316–323.

Genesee, F. (1984). Beyond bilingualism: Social psychological studies of French immersion programs in Canada. *Canadian Journal of Behavioral Science, 16,* 338–352.

Genesee, F., & Bourhis, R.Y. (1988). Evaluative reactions to language choice strategies:The role of sociostructural factors. *Language and Communication, 8,* 229–250.

George, J. M. (1991). State or trait: Effects of positive mood on prosocial behaviors at work. *Journal of Applied Psychology, 76,* 299–307.

Gerard, H. B., Wilhelmy, R. A., & Conolley, E. S. (1968). Conformity and group size. *Journal of Personality and Social Psychology, 8,* 79–82.

Gilbert, D. T., & Hixon, J. O. (1991). The trouble of thinking: Activation and application of stereotypic beliefs. *Journal of Personality and Social Psychology, 6 ,* 509–517.

Gilbert, D. T., Pelham, B. W., & Rrull, D. S. (1988). On cognitive busyness: When person perceivers meet persons perceived. *Journal of Personality and Social Psychology, 54,* 733–740.

Gilbert, D., & Booker, C. (1993). *The automatization of correction.* Research in progress, University of Texas, Austin.

Gilbert, D., & Jones, E. E. (1986). Perceiver–induced constraint: Interpretations of self–generated reality. *Journal of Personality and Social Psychology, 50,* 269–280.

Giles, H., Mulac, A., Bradac, J., & Johnson, P. (1986). Speech accommodation theory: The first decade and beyond. *Communication Yearbook, 10,* 8–34.

Gillen, B. (1981). Physical attractiveness: A determinant of two types of goodness. *Personality and Social Psychology Bulletin, 7,* 277–281.

Gladue, B. A. (1991). Aggressive behavioral characteristics, hormones, and sexual orientation in men and women. *Aggressive Behavior, 17,* 313–326.

Glass, D. C. (1977). *Behavior patterns, stress, and coronary disease.* Hillsdale, NJ: Erlbaum.

Glass, D. C. (1989). Psychology and health: Obstacles and opportunities. *Journal of Applied Social Psycholoqy, 19,* 1145–1163.

Glass, D. C., Singer, J. E., & Friedman, L. N. (1969). Psychic cost of adaptation to an environmental stressor. *Journal of Personality and Social Psychology, 12,* 200–210.

Glass, S. P., & Wright, T. L. (1992). Justifications for extramarital relationships: The association between attitudes, behaviors, and gender. *Journal of Sex Research, 29,* 361–387.

Godfrey, D. R., Jones, E. E., & Lord, C. C. (1986). Self–promotion is not ingratiating. *Journal of Personality and Social Psychology, 50,* 106–115.

Goethals, G. R. (1986a). Fabricating and ignoring social reality: Self–serving estimates of consensus. In J. Olson, C. P. Herman, & N. P. Zanna (Eds.), *Relative deprivation and social comparison: The Ontario symposium on social cognition IV.* Hillsdale, NJ: Erlbaum.

Goethals, G. R. (1986b). Social comparison theory: Psychology from the lost and found. *Personality and Social Psychology Bulletin, 12,* 261–278.

Goethals, G. R., & Zanna, M. P. (1979). The role of social comparison in choice shifts. *Journal of Personality and Social Psychology, 37,* 1469–1476.

Goethals, G. R., Cooper, J., & Naflicy, A. (1979). Role of foreseen, foreseeable, and unforeseeable behavioral consequences in the arousal of cognitive dissonance. *Journal of Personality and Social Psychology, 37,* 1179–1185.

Gold, J. A., Ryckman, R. M., & Mosley, N. R. (1984). Romantic mood induction and attraction to a dissimilar other: Is love blind? *Personality and Social Psychology Bulletin, 10,* 358–368.

Goldstein, A. G., Chance, J. E., & Schneller, G. R. (1989). Frequency of eyewitness identification in criminal cases: A survey of prosecutors. *Bulletin of the Psychonomic Society, 27,* 71–74.

Goleman, D. (1991, October 15). Happy or sad, a mood can prove contagious. *New York Times,* pp. C1, C8.

Gordin, F. M., Willoughby, A. D., Levine, L. A., Ourel, L., & Neill, K. M. (1987). Knowledge of AIDS among hospital workers: Behavioral correlates and consequences. *AIDS, 1,* 183–188.

Gorman, C. (1992). Danger overhead. *Time, 140*(7), 70.

Gottlieb, B.H. (1985). Social networks and social support: An overview of research, practive, and policy implication. *Health Education Quarterly, 12,* 221–238.

Graham, B., & Folkes, V. (Eds.). *Attribution theory: Applications to achievement, mental health, and interpersonal conflict.* Hillsdale, NJ: Erlbaum.

Graham, J. A., & Argyle, M. (1975). A cross–cultural study of the communication of extra–verbal meaning by gestures. *International Journal of Psychology, 10,* 57–67.

Grant, J. (1988, Winter). Women as managers: What they can offer to organizations. *Organizational Dynamics,* pp. 56–63.

Gray, P. (1993). What is love? Time, 141(7), 46–49.

Green, S. K., Buchanan, D. R., & Heuer, S. K. (1984). Winners, losers, and choosers: A field investigation of dating initiation. *Personality and Social Psychology Bulletin, 10,* 502–511.

Greenbaum, P., & Rosenfield, H. W. (1978). Patterns of avoidance in responses to interpersonal staring and proximity: Effects of bystanders on drivers at a traffic intersection. *Journal of Personality and Social Psychology, 36,* 575–587.

Greenberg, J., Pyszcynski, T., & Solomon, S. (1982). The self–serving attributional bias: Beyond self–presentation. *Journal of Experimental Social Psychology, 18,* 56–67.

Greenberg, M. A., & Stone, A. A. (1992). Emotional disclosure about traumas and its relation to health: Effects of previous disclosure and trauma severity. *Journal of Personality and Social Psychology, 63,* 75–84.

Greenwald, A. G., Bellazza, F. S., & Banaji, M. R. (1988). Is self–esteem a central ingredient of the self–concept? *Personality and Social Psychology Bulletin, 14,* 34–45.

Greenwald, A.G., & Pratkanis, A.R. (1984). The self. In R.S. Wyer & T.K. Srull (Eds.), *The handbook of social cognition* (Vol.3). Hillsdale, NJ: Erlbaum.

Grieshop, J. I., & Stiles, M. C. (1989). Risk and home pesticide users. *Environment and Behavior, 21,* 699–716.

Griffin, D.W., & Bartholomew, K. (1994). The metaphysics of measurement: The case of adult attachment. In D. Perlman & K. Bartholomew (Eds.), *Advances in Personal Relationships, 5,* 17-52.

Griffin, E., & Sparks, G. G. (1990]. Friends forever: A longitudinal exploration of intimacy in same–sex friends and platonic pairs. *Journal of Social and Personal Relationships, 7,* 29–46.

Groff, D. B., Baron, R. S., & Moore, D. L. (1983). Distraction, attentional conflict, and drive like behavior. *Journal of Experimental Social Psychology, 19,* 359–380.

Grondahl, P. (1989, December 5). Trees of life: Reforestation begins in the backyard. *Albany Times Union,* pp. C–l, C–12.

Grover, S. L., & Brockner, J. (1989). Empathy and the relationship between attitudinal similarity and attraction. *Journal of Research in Personality, 23,* 469–479.

Grusec, J. E. (1991). The socialization of altruism. In M. S. Clark (Ed.), *Prosocial behavior* (pp. 9–33). Newbury Park, CA: Sage.

Gudjonsson, G. H., & Clark, N. K. (1986). Suggestibility in police interrogation: A social psychological model. *Social Behaviour, 1,* 83–104.

Gudykunst, W.B., Gao, G., & Franklyn–Stokes, A. (1992) Self–monitoring and concern for social appropriateness in China and England. Fourth Asian regional conference, International Association for Cross–cultural Psychology, Kathmandu, Nepal.

Guidubaldi, J., Perry, J. D., & Nastasi, B. H. (1987). Growing up in a divorced family: Initial and long–term perspectives on children's adjustment. In S. Oskamp (Ed.), *Family processes and problems: Social psychological aspects* (pp. 202–237). Beverly Hills, CA: Sage.

Guimond, S., & Dubé, L. (1989). La représentation des causes de l'infériorité économique des québecois francophones. *Revue Canadienne des Sciences du comportement, 21,* 28–39.

Guimond, S., & Dubé–Simard, L. (1983). Relative deprivation theory and the Quebec nationalist movement: The cognitive–emotion distinction and the personal–group deprivation issue. *Journal of Personality and Social Psychology, 44,* 526–535.

Guimond, S., & Palmer, D. L. (1990). Type of academic training and causal attributions for social problems. *European Journal of Social Psychology, 20,* 61–75.

Guimond, S., Bégin, G., & Palmer, D.L. (1989). Education and causal attributions: The development of "person–blame and "system–blame" ideology. *Social Psychology Quarterly, 52,* 126–140.

Gustafson, R. (1989). Frustration and successful vs. unsuccessful aggression: A test of Berkowitz' completion hypothesis. *Aggressive Behavior, 15,* 5–12.

Halford, W. K., & Sanders, M. R. (1990). The relationship of cognition and behavior during marital interaction. *Journal of Social and Clinical Psychology, 9,* 489–510.

Hall, J. A., & Veccia, E. M. (1990). More "touching" observations: New insights on men, women, and interpersonal touch. *Journal of Personality and Social Psychology, 59,* 1155–1162.

Hallman, W. K., & Wandersman, A. (1992). Attribution of responsibility and individual and collective coping with environmental threats. *Journal of Social Issues, 48*(4), 101–118.

Hamid, P. N. (1990). Optimism and the reporting of flu episodes. *Social Behavior and Personality, 13,* 225–234.

Hamilton, D. L., & Sherman, S. J. (1989). Illusory correlations: Implications for stereotype theory and research. In D. Bar-Tal, C. F. Graumann, A. W. Kruglanski, & W. Stroebe (Eds.), *Stereotyping and prejudice: Changing conceptions* (pp. 59–82). New York: Springer-Verlag.

Hamilton, G. V. (1978). Obedience and responsibility: A jury simulation. *Journal of Personality and Social Psychology, 36,* 126–146.

Hans, V., & Vidmar, N. (1982). Jury selection. In N. L. Kerr & R. M. Bray (Eds.), *The psychology of the courtroom* (pp. 39–82). New York: Academic Press.

Hansen, C. H, & Hansen, R. D. (1988). Finding the face in the crowd: An anger superiority effect. *Journal of Personality and Social Psychology, 54,* 917–924.

Hansen, R. D. (1980). Common sense attribution. *Journal of Personality and Social Psychology, 17,* 398–411.

Harkins, S. (1987). Social loafing and social facilitation. *Journal of Experimental Social Psychology, 23,* 1–18.

Harkins, S., & Petty, R. (1982). Effects of task difficulty and task uniqueness on social loafing. *Journal of Personality and Social Psychology, 43,* 1214–1229.

Harkins, S., & Szymanski, K. (1988). Social loafing and self–evaluation with an objective standard. *Journal of Experimental Social Psychology, 24,* 354–365.

Harkins, S., & Szymanski, K. (1989). Social loafing and group evaluation. *Journal of Personality and Social Psychology, 56,* 934–941.

Harrell, W. A. (1990). Husband's masculinity, wife's power, and marital conflict. *Social Behavior and Personality, 18,* 207–216.

Harré, R., & Secord, P.F. (1972). *The explanation of social behaviour.* Oxford: Blackwell.

Harrigan, J. A. (1985). Self touching as an indicator of underlying affect and language processing. *Social Science and Medicine, 20,* 1161–1168.

Harrigan, J. A., Lucic, K. S., Kay, D., McLaney, A., & Rosenthal, R. (1991). Effect of expresser role and type of self–touching on observers' perceptions. *Journal of Applied Social Psychology, 21,* 585–609.

Harris, M. B., Harris, R. J., & Bochner, S. (1982). Fat, foureyed, and female: Stereotypes of obesity, glasses, and gender. *Journal of Applied Social Psychology, 12,* 503–516.

Harris, M. J., Milich, R., Corbitt, E. M., Hoover, D. W., & Brady, M. (1992). Self–fulfilling effects of stigmatizing information on children's social interactions. *Journal of Personality and Social Psychology, 63,* 41–50.

Harrison, B., & Marmen, L. (1994). *Languages in Canada* (Focus on Canada series). Scarborough Ont.: Statistics Canada and Prentice Hall Canada.

Harvey, J. H., & Weary, G. (Eds.). (1989). *Attribution: Basic issues and applications.* San Diego: Academic Press.

Hastie, R., Penrod, S., & Pennington, N. (1983). *Inside the jury.* Cambridge, MA: Harvard University Press.

Hatfield, E. (1988). Passionate and companionate love. In R. L. Sternberg & M. I. Barnes (Eds.), *The psychology of love* (pp. 191–217). New Haven, CT: Yale University Press.

Hatfield, E., & Rapson, R. L. (1987). Passionate love/sexual desire: Can the same paradigm explain both? *Archives of Sexual Behavior, 16,* 259–278.

Hatfield, E., & Rapson, R. L. (1992a). Similarity and attraction in close relationships. *Communication Monographs, 59,* 209–212.

Hatfield, E., & Rapson, R. L. (1992b, November). *Culture and passionate love.* Paper presented at the meeting of the Society for the Scientific Study of Sex, San Diego.

Hatfield, E., & Rapson, R. L. (1992c). Similarity and attraction in close relationships. *Communication Monographs, 59,* 209–212.

Hatfield, E., & Rapson, R. L. (1993). *Love, sex, and intimacy: Their psychology, biology, and history.* New York: Harper Collins.

Hatfield, E., & Sprecher, S. (1986). *Mirror, mirror. . . The importance of looks in everyday life.* Albany, NY: SUNY Press.

Hatfield, E., & Sprecher, S. (1986a). Measuring passionate love in intimate relations. *Journal of Adolescence, 9,* 383–410.

Hatfield, E., & Walster, G. W. (1981). A new look at love. Reading, MA: Addison–Wesley.

Hau, K., & Salili, F. (1991). Structure and semantic differential placement of specific causes: Academic causal attributions by Chinese students in Hong Kong. *International Journal of Psychology, 26,* 175–193.

Havel, V. (1992, June 3). Rio and the new millennium. *New York Times,* p. A21.

Hayes, S. C., Johnson, S. V., & Cone, J. D. (1975). *The marked item technique: A practical procedure for litter control.* Unpublished manuscript, West Virginia University, Morgantown.

Hays, R. B. (1989). The day–to–day functioning of close versus casual friendships. *Journal of Social and Personal Relationships, 6,* 21–37.

Hays, R. B., & DiMatteo, M. R. (1984). Toward a more therapeutic physician–patient relationship. In S. Duck (Ed.), *Personal relationships: Vol. 5. Repairing personal relationships* (pp. 1–20). New York: Academic Press.

Hazan, C., & Shaver, P. R. (1990). Love and work: An attachment–theoretical perspective. *Journal of Personality and Social Psychology, 59,* 270–280.

Heider, F. (1958). *The psychology of interpersonal relations.* New York: Wiley.

Heilman, M. E., & Herlihy, J. M. (1984). Affirmative action, negative reaction? Some moderating conditions. *Organizational Behavior and Human Performance, 33,* 204–213.

Heilman, M. E., & Martell, R. F. (1986). Exposure to successful women: Antidote to sex discrimination in applicant screening decisions? *Organizational Behavior and Human Decision Processes, 37,* 376–390.

Heilman, M. E., Hornstein, H. A., Cage, J. H., & Herschlag, J. X. (1984). Reactions to prescribed leader behavior as a function of role perspective: The case of the Vroom–Yetton model. *Journal of Applied Psychology, 69,* 50–60.

Heilman, M. E., Martell, R. F., & Simon, M. C. (1988). The vagaries of sex bias: Conditions regulating the undervaluation, equivalation, and overvaluation of female job applicants. *Organizational Behavior and Human Decision Processes, 41,* 98–110.

Heine, S.J., Lehman, D.R., Okugawa, O., & Campbell, J.D. (1992). The effects of culture on self–implicated processes: A comparison of Canadians and Japanese. *Ritsumeikan Review of Social Sciences, 74,* 29–38.

Helgeson, V. S. (1992). Moderators of the relation between perceived control and ajustment to chronic illness. *Journal of Personality and Social Psychology, 63,* 656–666.

Helson, R., & Roberts, B. (1992). The personality of young adult couples and wives' work patterns. *Journal of Personality, 60,* 575–597.

Henderson, J., & Taylor, J. (1985, November 17). Study finds bias in death sentence: Killers of whites risk execution. *Albany Times Union,* p. A–19.

Henderson, M., & Hewstone, M.(1984). Prison inmates' explanations form interpersonal violence: Accounts and attributions. *Journal of Consulting and Clinical Psychology, 52,* 789–794.

Hendrick, C., & Hendrick, S. S. (1986). A theory and method of love. *Journal of Personality and Social Psychology, 50,* 392–402.

Hendrick, S. S., Hendrick, C., & Adler, N. L. (1988). Romantic relationships: Love, satisfaction, and staying together. *Journal of Personality and Social Psychology, 54,* 980–988.

Hendrix, W. H., Steel, R. P., & Schultz, S. A. (1987). Job stress and life stress: Their causes and consequences. *Journal of Social Behavior and Personality, 2,* 291–302.

Henley, N. (1973). Status and sex: Some touching observations. *Bulletin of the Psychonomic Society, 2,* 91–93.

Henry, W. A., III. (1991). The journalist and the murder. *Time 138*(15), 86.

Hepworth, J. T., & West, S. O. (1988). Lynchings and the economy: A time–series reana1ysis of Hovland and Sears (1940). *Journal of Personality and Social Psychology, 55,* 239–247.

Hewstone, M., & Jaspars, J. (1982). Explanations for racial discrimination: The effect of group discussion on intergroup attributions. *European Journal of Social Psychology, 12,* 1–16.

Hewstone, M., Bond, N. . H., & Wan, K. C. (1983). Social factors and social attributions: The explanation of intergroup differences in Hong Kong. *Social Cognition, 2,* 142–157.

Higgins, E. T. (1987). Self–discrepancy: A theory relating self and affect. *Psychological Review, 94,* 319–340.

Higgins, E. T., & Bargh, J. A. (1987). Social cognition and social perception. In M. R. Rosenszweig & L. W. Porter (Eds.), *Annual review of psychology* (Vol. 38, pp. 369–425). Palo Alto, CA: Annual Reviews Inc.

Higgins, E. T., & King, G. (1981). Accessibility of social constructs: Information processing consequences of individual and contextual variability. In N. Cantor & J. Kihlstrom (Eds.), *Personality, cognition, and social interaction* (pp. 69–121). Hillsdale, NJ: Erlbaum.

Higgins, E. T., Rohles, W. S., & Jones, C. R. (1977). Category accessibility and impression formation. *Journal of Experimental Social Psychology, 13,* 141–154.

Hill, C. A. (1987). Affiliation motivation: People who need people but in different ways. *Journal of Personality and Social Psychology, 52,* 1008–1018.

Hill, C. T., Rubin, Z., & Peplau, L. A. (1976). Breakups before marriage: The end of 103 affairs. *Journal of Social Issues, 32,* 147–168.

Hilliard, A. (1985). *Parameters affecting the African-American child.* Paper presented at the Black Psychology Seminar, Duke Unviersity, Durham, NC.

Hinsz, V. B., & Tomhave, J. A. (1991). Smile and (half) the world smiles with you; frown and you frown alone. *Personality and Social Psychology Bulletin, 17,* 586–592.

Hirt, E. R., Zillmann, D., Erickson, G. A., & Kennedy, C. (1992). Costs and benefits of allegiance: Changes in fans' self–ascribed competencies after team victory versus defeat. *Journal of Personality and Social Psychology, 61,* 724–738.

Hoff, T.L. (1992) Psychology in Canada one hundred years ago: James Mark Baldwin at the university of Toronto. *Canadian Psychology, 33,* 683–694.

Hofstede, G. (1980). *Culture's consequences: International differences in work–related values.* Beverly Hills, CA: Sage.

Hofstede, G. (1983). Dimensions of national cultures in fifty countries and three regions. In J. Deregowski, S. Dzuirawiec & R. Annis (Eds.) *Explications in cross–cultural psychology.* Lisse: Swets & Zeitlinger.

Hogan, J. (1989). Personality correlates of physical fitness. *Journal of Personality and Social Psychology, 56,* 284–288. Hokanson, J. E., Burgess, M., & Cohen, M. E. (1963). Effects of displaced aggression on systolic blood pressure. *Journal of Abnormal and Social Psychology, 67,* 214–218.

Holowaty, L. S., Pliner, P., & Flett, G. L. (1990). Social responses to justified and unjustified depression: Evidence for a depression prototype. *Journal of Social Behavior and Personality, 5,* 29–44.

Homer, P.M., & Kahle, L. (1988). A structural equation test of the value–attitude–behavior heirarchy. *Journal of Personality and Social Psychology, 54,* 638–646.

Honigmann, J.J., & Honigmann, I. (1965). *Eskimo townsmen.* Ottawa: Canadian Research Centre for Anthropology.

Hosch, H. M., & Bothwell, R. K. (1990). Arousal, description and identification accuracy of victims and bystanders. *Journal of Social Behavior and Personality, 5,* 481–488.

House, R. J. (1977). A theory of charismatic leadership. In J. G. Hunt & L. L. Larson (Eds.), *Leadership: The cutting edge* (pp. 189–207). Carbondale, IL: Southern Illinois University Press.

House, R. J., Spangler, W. D., & Woycke, J. (1991). Personality and charisma in the U. S. presidency: A psychological theory of leader effectiveness. *Administrative Science Quarterly, 36,* 364–396.

Hovland, C. I., & Sears, R. R. (1940). Minor studies in aggression: VI. Correlation of lynchings with economic indices. *Journal of Psychology, 9,* 301–310.

Hovland, C. I., & Weiss, W. (1951). The influence of source credibility on communication effectiveness. *Public Opinion Quarterly, 1,* 635–650.

Hovland, C. I., Janis, I. L., & Kelley, H. H. (1953). *Communication and persuasion: Psychological studies of one on one.* New Haven, CT: Yale University Press.

Howard, G. S. (1985). The role of values in the science of psychology. *American Psychologist, 40,* 255–265.

Howell, J. M., & Frost, P. J. (1989). A laboratory study of charismatic leadership. *Organizational Behavior and Human Decision Processes, 43,* 243–269.

Hsee, C. K., Hatfield, E., & Chemtob, C. (1992). Assessments of the emotional states of others: Conscious judgments versus emotional contagion. *Journal of Social and Clinical Psychology, 11,* 119–128.

Huesmann, L. R. (1982). Television violence and aggressive behavior. In D. Pearl, L. Bouthilet, & J. Lazar (Eds.), *Television and behavior: Vol., 2. Technical reviews* (pp. 220–256). Washington, DC: National Institute of Mental Health.

Hui, C.H., Triandis, H.C., & Yee, C. (1991). Cultural differences in reward allocation: Is collectivism the explanation? British journal of social Psychology, 30, 145–157.

Humphriss, N. (1989, November 20). Letters. *Time,* p. 12.

Hunter, C. E., & Ross, M. W. (1991). Determinants of health–care workers' attitudes toward people with AIDS. *Journal of Applied Social Psychology, 21,* 947–956.

Hunter, S. MacD., Johnson, C. C., Vizelber, I. A., Webber, L. S., & Berenson, G. S. (1991). Tracking of Type A behavior in children and young adults: The Bogalusa heart study. *Journal of Social Behavior and Personality, 6,* 71–84.

Hutton, D. C., & Baumeister, R. F. (1992). Self–awareness and attitude change: Seeing oneself on the central route to persuasion. *Personality and Social Psychology Bulletin, 18,* 68–75.

Ickes, W., Reidhead, S., & Patterson, M. (1986). Machiavellianism and self-monitoring: As different as "me" and "you." *Social Cognition, 4,* 58–74.

Insko, C. A. (1985). Balance theory, the Jordan paradigm, and the West tetrahedron. In L. Berkowitz (Ed.), *Advances in experimental social psychology.* New York: Academic Press.

Isen, A. M. (1984). Toward understanding the role of affect in cognition. In S. R. Wyer & T. K. Srull (Eds.), *Handbook of social cognition* (Vol. 3, pp. 179–236). Hillsdale, NJ: Erlbaum.

Isen, A. M. (1987). Positive affect, cognitive processes, and social behavior. In L. Berkowitz (Ed.), *Advances in experimental social psychology* (Vol. 20, pp. 203–253. New York: Academic Press.

Isen, A. M., & Baron, R. A. (1991). Affect and organizational behavior. In B. M. Staw & L. L. Cummings (Eds.), *Research in organizational behavior* (vol. 15, pp. 1–53). Greenwich CT: JAI Press.

Isen, A. M., & Daubman, K. A. (1984). The influence of affect on categorization. *Journal of Personality and Social Psychology, 47,* 1206–1217.

Isen, A. M., & Levin, P. A. (1972). Effect of feeling good on helping: Cookies and kindness. *Journal of Personality and Social Psychology, 21,* 384–388.

Isen, A. M., & Shalker, T. E. (1982). Do you "accentuate the positive, eliminate the negative" when you are in a good mood? *Social Psychology Quarterly, 41,* 345–349.

Isen, A. M., Daubman, K. A., & Howicki, G. P. (1987). Positive affect facilitates creative problem solving. *Journal of Personality and Social Psychology, 52,* 1122–1131.

Isen, A. N., Johnson, N. M. S., Merz, E., & Robinson, G. (1985). The influence of positive affect on the unusualness of work association. *Journal of Personality and Social Psychology, 48,* 1413–1426.

Israel, J., & Tajfel, H. (Eds.) (1972). *The context of social psycholgy: A critical assessment.* London: Academic Press.

Istvan, J., Griffitt, W., & Weidner, G. (1983). Sexual arousal and the polarization of perceived sexual attractiveness. *Basic and Applied Social Psychology, 4,* 307–318.

Izard, C. (1991). *Human emotions* (2nd ed.). New York: Plenum.

Izard, C. (1992). Basic emotions, relations among emotions, and emotion–cognition relations. *Psychological Review, 99,* 561–565.

James, W. (1890). *The principles of psychology* (Vols. 1 and 2). New York: Holt.

Janis, I. L. (1954). Personality correlates of susceptablity to persuasion. *Journal of Personality, 22,* 504–518.

Janis, I. L. (1982). *Victims of groupthink* (2nd ed.). Boston: Houghton Mifflin.

Jasnoski, M. L., Cordray, D. S., Houston, G. K., & Osness, W. H. (1987). Modification of Type A behavior through aerobic exercise. *Motivation and Emotion, 111,* 1–17.

Jay, S. M., Ozolins, M., Elliott, C. H., & Caldwell, S. (1983). Assessment of children's distress during painful medical procedures. *Health Psychology, 2,* 133–147.

Jeffries, V. (1987). Love: The five virtues of St. Thomas Aquinas. A factor analysis of love of parents among university students. *Sociology and Social Research, 71,* 174–182.

Jeffries, V. (1990). Adolescent love, perception of parental love, and relationship quality. *Family Perspective, 24,* 175–196.

Jeffries, V. (1993, in press). Virtue and attraction: Validation of a measure of love. *Journal of Social and Personal Relationships, 10,* in press.

Jemmott, J. B., III, & Magloire, K. (1988). Academic stress, social support, and secretory immunoglobulin. *Journal of Personality and Social Psychology, 55,* 803–810.

Jemmott, J. B., III, Ashby, K. L., & Lindenfield, K. (1989). Romantic commitment and the perceived availability of opposite–sex persons: On loving the one you're with. *Journal of Applied Social Psychology, 19,* 1198–1211.

Johnson, B. T., & Eagly, A. H. (1989). Effects of involvement on persuasion: A meta–analysis. *Psychological Bulletin, 106,* 290–314.

Johnson, D. F., & Pittenger, J. B. (1984). Attribution, the attractiveness stereotype, and the elderly. *Developmental Psychology, 20,* 1168–1172.

Johnson, D. J., & Rusbult, C. E. (1989). Resisting temptation: Devaluation of alternative partners as a means of maintaining commitment in close relationships. *Journal of Personality and Social Psychology, 57,* 967–980.

Johnson, H. P., Huston, T. I., Gaines, S. O., Jr., & Levinger, G. (1992). Patterns of married life among young couples. *Journal of Social and Personal Relationships, 9,* 343–364.

Johnson, J. T. (1987). The heart on the sleeve and the secret self: Estimations of hidden emotion in self and acquaintances. *Journal of Personality, 55,* 563–581.

Johnson, K. A., Johnson, J. E., & Petzel, T. P. (1992). Social anxiety, depression, and distorted cognitions in college students. *Journal of Social and Clinical Psychology, 11,* 181–195.

Johnson, R. D., & Downing, L. L. (1979). Deindividuation and valence of cues: Effects on prosocial and antisocial behavior. *Journal of Personality and Social Psychology, 37,* 1532–1538.

Johnson, T. E., & Rule, B. G. (1986). Mitigating circumstance information, censure, and aggression. *Journal of Personality and Social Psychology, 50,* 537–542.

Johnstone, B., Frame, C. L., & Bouman, D. (1992). Physical attractiveness and athletic and academic ability in controversial–aggressive and rejected–aggressive children. *Journal of Social and Clinical Psychology, 11,* 71–79.

Jones, E. E. (1964). *Ingratiation: A social psychological analysis.* New York: Appleton–Century Crofts.

Jones, E. E. (1990). *Interpersonal perception.* New York: W. H. Freeman.

Jones, E. E., & Davis, K. E. (1965). From acts to disposition: The attribution process in person perception. In L. Berkowitz (Ed.), *Advances in experimental social psychology.* (Vol. 2, pp. 219–266). New York: Academic Press.

Jones, E. E., & McGillis, D. (1976). Corresponding inferences and the attribution cube: A comparative reappraisal. In J. H. Harvey, W. J. Ickes, & R. F. Kidd (Eds.), *New directions in attribution research* (Vol. 1). Morristown, NJ: Erlbaum.

Jones, E. E., & Nisbett, R. E. (1971). *The actor and the observer: Divergent perceptions of the causes of behavior.* Morristown, NJ: General Learning Press.

Jones, W. H., Carpenter, B. N., & Quintana, D. (1985). Personality and interpersonal predictors of loneliness in two cultures. *Journal of Personality and Social Psychology, 48,* 1503–1511.

Jones, W. H., Hobbs, S. A., & Hockenbury, D. (1982). Loneliness and social skill deficits. *Journal of Personality and Social Psychology, 42,* 682–689.

Josephson, W. D. (1987). Television violence and children's aggression: Testing the priming, social script, and disinhibition predictions. *Journal of Personality and Social Psychology, 55,* 882–890.

Joy, L.A., Kimball, M., & Zabrack,M.L. (1986). Television and children's aggressive behavior. In T.M. Williams (Ed), *The impact of television: A natural experiment in three communities.* New York: Academic Press.

Judd, C. M., & Krosnick, J. A. (1989). The structural bases of consistency among political attitudes: Effect of political expertise and attitude importance. IN A. R. Pratkanis, S. J. Breckler, & A. G. Greenwald (Eds.), *Attitude structure and function* (pp. 99–128). Hillsdale, NJ: Erlbaum.

Judd, C. M., Drake, R. A., Downing, J. W., & Krosnick, J. A. (1991). Some dynamic properties of attitude structures: Context–induced response facilitation and polarization. *Journal of Personality and Social Psychology, 60,* 193–202.

Judd, C. M., Ryan, C. N., & Parke, B. (1991). Accuracy in the judgment of in–group and out–group variability. *Journal of Personality and Social Psychology, 61,* 366–379.

Jussim, L. (1991). Interpersonal expectations and social reality: A reflection–construction model and reinterpretation of evidence. *Psychological Review, 98,* 54–73.

Kacmar, K. M., Delery, J. E., & Ferris, G. R. (1992). Differential effectiveness of applicant impression management tactics on employment interview decisions. *Journal of Applied Social Psychology, 22,* 1250–1272.

Kagitcibasi, C. (1970). Social norms and authoritarianism: a Turkish–American comparison. *Journal of Cross–Cultural Psychology, 4,* 157–174.

Kahle, L. R., & Beatty, S. E. (1987). Cognitive consequences of legislating post–purchase behavior: Growing up with the bottle bill. *Journal of Applied Social Psychology, 17,* 828–843.

Kahneman, D., & Miller, D. T. (1986). Norm theory: comparing reality to its alternatives. *Psychological Review, 93,* 136–153.

Kahneman, D., & Tversky, A. (1982). The simulation heuristic. In D. Kahneman, P. Slovic, & Tversky, A. (Eds.), *Judgments under uncertainty: Heuristics and biases* (pp. 201–208). New York: Cambridge University Press.

Kalick, S. M. (1988). Physical attractiveness as a status cue. *Journal of Experimental Social Psychology, 24,* 469–489.

Kalick, S. M., & Hamilton, T. E. (1986). The matching hypothesis reexamined. *Journal of Personality and Social Psychology, 51,* 673–682.

Kalin, R., & Berry, J.W. (1982). The social ecology of ethnic attitudes in Canada. *Canadian Journal of Behavioral Science, 14,* 97–109.

Kalmuss, D.S., & Seltzer, J.A. (1986). Continuity of marital behavior in remarriage: The case of spouse abuse. *Journal of Marriage and the Family, 48,* 113–120.

Kameda, T. (1991). Procedural influence in small–group decision making: Deliberation style and assigned decision rule. *Journal of Personality and Social Psychology, 61,* 245–256.

Kandel, D. B. (1978). Similarity in real–life adolescent friendship pairs. *Journal of Personality and Social Psychology, 36,* 306–312.

Kanekar, S., Kolsawalla, M. B., & Nazareth, T. (1988). Occupational prestige as a function of occupant's gender. *Journal of Applied Social Psychology, 19*, 681–688.

Kaniasty, K., & Norris, F. H. (1993). A test of the social support deterioration model in the context of natural disaster. *Journal of Personality and Social Psychology, 64*, 395–408.

Kaplan, H. B., & Pokorny, A. D. (1971). Self–derogation and childhood broken home. *Journal of Marriage and the Family, 33*, 328–337.

Kaplan, M. F., & Miller, C. E. (1987). Group decision making and normative versus informational influence: Effects of type of issue and assigned decision rule. *Journal of Personality and Social Psychology, 59*, 306–313.

Kardiner, A. (1939). *The individual and his society.* New York: Columbia University Press.

Karlins, M., Coffman, T.L., & Walters, G. (1969). On the fading of social stereotypes: Studies in three generations of college students. *Journal of Personality and Social Psychology, 13*, 1–16.

Kashima, Y., & Triandis, H.C. (1986). The self–serving bias in attributions as a coping strategy: a cross–cultural study. *Journal of Cross–Cultural Psychology, 17*, 83–97.

Katz, D., & Braly, K. (1933). Racial stereotypes of one hundred college students. *Journal of Abnormal and Social Psychology, 28*, 280–290.

Katz, I.M., & Campbell, J.D. (1994). Ambivalence over emotional expression *and well–being: Nomothetic and Idiographic tests of the stress–buffering hypothesis. Journal of Personality and Social Psychology, 67*, 513–524.

Keller, L. M., Bouchard, T. J., Jr., Arvey, R. D., Segal, N. L., & Dawis, R. V. (1992). Work values: Genetic and environmental influences. *Journal of Applied Psychology, 77*, 79–88.

Kellerman, J., Lewis, J., & Laird, J. D. (1989). Looking and loving: The effects of mutual gaze on feelings of romantic love. *Journal of Research in Personality, 23*, 145–161.

Kelley, H. H. (1972). Attribution in social interaction. In E. E. Jones et al. (Eds.), *Attribution: Perceiving the causes of behavior.* Morristown, NJ: General Learning Press.

Kelley, H. H., & Michela, J. L. (1980). Attribution theory and research. *Annual Review of Psychology, 31*, 457–501.

Kelman, H. C. (1967). Human use of human subjects: The problem of deception in social psychological experiments. *Psychological Bulletin, 67*, 1–11.

Kenealy, P., Gleeson, K., Frude, N., & Shaw, W. (1991). The importance of the individual in the "causal" relationship between attractiveness and self–esteem. *Journal of Community and Applied Social Psychology, 1*, 45–56.

Kennedy, G. E. (1991). Grandchildren's reasons for closeness with grandparents. *Journal of Social Behavior and Personality, 6*, 697–712.

Kennedy, L.W., & Dutton, D.G. (1989). The incidence of wife assault in Alberta. *Canadian Journal of Behavioral Science, 21*, 40–54.

Kent, D. (1990). A conversation with Claude Steele. *APS Observer, 3*(3), 11–15, 17.

Kent, G. G., Davis, J. D., & Shapiro, D. A. (1981). Effect of mutual acquaintance on the construction of conversation. *Journal of Experimental Social Psychology, 17*, 197–209.

Kenworthy, T. (1993, January 6). Secondhand smoke makes EPA blacklist. *Albany Times Union*, pp. A–I, A–6.

Kerr, D. & Ram, B. (1994). *Population dynamics in Canada* (Focus on Canada series). Scarborough, Ont: Statistics Canada and Prentice Hall Canada.

Kerr, H. L., & Bruun, S. E. (1983). Dispensability of member effort and group motivation losses: Free–rider effects. *Journal of Personality and Social Psychology, 45*, 78–94.

Kerr, H. L., & MacCoun, R. J. (1985). The effects of jury size and polling method on the process and product of jury deliberations. *Journal of Personality and Social Psychology, 48*, 349–363.

Kessler, R. C., Kendler, K. S., Heath, A., Neale, M. C., & Eaves, L. J. (1992). Social support, depressed mood, and adjustment to stress: A genetic epidemiologic investigation. *Journal of Personality and Social Psychology, 62*, 257–272.

Kidwell, J. S. (1982). The neglected birth order: Middleborns. *Journal of Marriage and the Family, 44*, 225.

Kiesler, A., Reber, G., & Wunderer, R. (Eds.), *Encyclopedia of leadership* (pp. 378–390). Kernerstrasse, FRG: C. E. Paeschel Verlag.

Kiesler, C. A., & Kiesler, S. B. (1969). *Conformity.* Reading, MA: Addison–Wesley.

Kilham, W., & Mann, L. (1974). Level of destructive obedience as a function of transmitter and executant roles in the Milgram obedience paradigm. *Journal of Personality and Social Psychology, 29*, 696–702.

King, L.A., & Emmons, R.A. (1990). Conflict over emotional expression: Psychological and physical correlates. *Journal of Personality and Social Psychology, 58*, 864–877.

King, L.A., & Emmons, R.A. (1991). Psychological, physical, and interpersonal correlates of emotional expressiveness, conflict and control. *European Journal of Personality, 5*, 131-150.

Kipnis, D., & Schmidt, S. M. (1988). Upward influence styles: Relationship with performance evaluation, salary, and stress. *Administrative Science Quarterly, 33*, 528–542.

Kirchler, E., & Davis, J. H. (1986). The influence of member status differences and task type on group consensus and member position change. *Journal of Personality and Social Psychology, 51*, 83–91.

Kirkpatrick, S. A., & Locke, E. A. (1991). Leadership: Do traits matter? *Academy of Management Executive, 5*(2), 48–60.

Klagsbrun, F. (1992). *Mixed feelings: Love, hate, rivalry, and reconciliation in brothers and sisters.* New York: Bantam.

Klein, S. B., & Loftus, J. (1988). The nature of self–referent encoding: The contributions of elaborative and organizational processes. *Journal of Personality and Social Psychology, 55*, 5–11.

Klein, S. B., Loftus, J., & Burton, H. A. (1989). Two self–reference effects: The importance of distinguishing between self–descriptiveness judgments and autobiographical retrieval in self–referent encoding. *Journal of Personality and Social Psychology, 56*, 853–865.

Kleinke, C. L. (1986). Gaze and eye contact: A research review. *Psychological Bulletin, 100*, 78–100.

Knapp, M. L. (1978). *Nonverbal communication in human interaction.* New York: Holt, Rinehart, & Winston.

Knox, R. E., & Safford, R. K. (1976). Group caution at the race track. *Journal of Experimental Social Psychology, 12,* 317–324.

Knox, R.E., & Inkster, J.A. (1968). Postdecision dissonance at post time. *Journal of Personality and Social Psychology, 8,* 319–323.

Kobasa, S. C. (1979). Stressful life events, personality, and health: An inquiry into hardiness. *Journal of Personality and Social Psychology, 37,* 1–11.

Koestner, R., Bernieri, F., & Zuckerman, M. (1992). Self–regulation and consistency between attitudes, traits, and behaviors. *Personality and Social Psychology Bulletin, 18,* 52–59.

Korte, C., & Kerr, N. (1975). Responses to altruistic opportunities under urban and rural conditions. *Journal of Psychology, 95,* 183–189.

Korten, F. F., (1974). The influence of culture and sex on the perception of persons. *International Journal of Psychology, 9,* 31–44.

Kotter, J. (1982). *The general managers.* New York: Free Press.

Krauss, R. M., Morrel–Samuels, P., & Colasante, C. (1991). Do conversational hand gestures communicate? *Journal of Personality and Social Psychology, 61,* 743–754.

Kremer, J. F., & Stephens, L. (1983). Attributions and arousal as mediators of mitigation's effects on retaliation. *Journal of Personality and Social Psychology, 45,* 335–343.

Krosnick, J. A. (1989). Attitude importance and attitude accessibility. *Personality and Social Psychology Bulletin, 15,* 297–308.

Krosnick, J. A., & Alwin, D. F. (1989). Aging and susceptibility to attitude change. *Journal of Personality and Social Psychology, 57,* 416–425.

Krosnick, J. A., Betz, A. L., Jussim, L. J., & Lynn, A. R. (1992). Subliminal conditioning of attitudes. *Personality and Social Psychology Bulletin, 18,* 152–162.

Krupat, E. (1975). *Psychology is social.* Glenview, IL: Scott, Foresman.

Kudrle, R.T., & Marmor, T.R. (1981) The development of welfare states in North America. In P. Flora & A.J. Heidenheimer (Eds.). *The development of welfare states in Europe and America.* New Brunswick, NJ: Transaction Books.

Kulik, J. A., & Mahler, H. I. M. (1987). Effects of preoperative roommate assigment on preoperative anxiety and recovery from coronary–bypass surgery. *Health Psychology, 6,* 525–544.

Kulik, J. A., & Mahler, H. I. M. (1989). Stress and affiliation in a hospital setting: Preoperative roommate preferences. *Personality and Social Psychology Bulletin, 15,* 183–193.

Kunda, Z., Fong, G. T., Sanitioso, R., & Reber, E. (1993). Directional questions direct self–conceptions. *Journal of Experimental Social Psychology, 29,* 63–86.

Kurdek, L. A. (1993). Predicting marital dissolution: A 5–year longitudinal study of newlywed couples. *Journal of Personality and Social Psychology, 64,* 221–242.

LaCroix, J.M., & Rioux, Y. (1978). La communication non–verbale chez les bilingues. *Canadian Journal of Behaviour Science, 10,* 130–140.

Lakey, G., Moineau, S., & Drew, J. (1992). Perceived social support and individual differences in the interpretation and recall of supportive behaviors. *Journal of Social and Clinical Psychology, 11,* 336– 348.

Lambert, W.E. (1967). A social psychology of bilingualism. *Journal of Social Issues, 23,* 91–109.

Lambert, W.E. (1974). The St. Lambert project. In S.T. Carey (Ed.), *Bilingualism, biculturalism and education.* Edmonton: University of Alberta.

Lambert, W.E. (1978). Some cognitive and sociocultural aspects of being bilingual. In J.P. Alatis (Ed.), *International dimensions of bilingual education.* Washington, DC: Georgetown University Press.

Lambert, W.E., & Taylor, D. M. (1984). Language and the education of ethnic minority children in Canada. In R.J. Samuda, J.W. Berry, & M. Laferriere (Eds.), *Multiculturalism in Canada.* Toronto: Allyn & Bacon.

Lambert, W.E., & Tucker, G.R. (1972). *Bilingual education in children: The St. Lambert experiment.* Rowley, MA: Newbury House.

Lambert, W.E., Gardner, R.C., Barik, H.C., & Tunstall, K. (1963). Attitudinal and cognitive aspects of intensive study of a second language. *Journal of Abnormal and Social Psychology, 66,* 358–368.

Lambert, W.E., Mermigis, L., & Taylor, D.M. (1986). Greek Canadians' attitudes toward own group and other Canadian ethnic groups: A test of the multiculturalism hypothesis. *Canadian Journal of Behavioral Science, 18,* 35–51.

Lamm, H. & Myers, D. C. (1978). Group–induced polarization of attitudes and behavior. In L. Berkowitz (Ed.), *Advances in experimental social psychology.* New York: Academic Press.

Langley, T., O'Neal, E. C., Craig, K. M., & Yost, E. A. (1992). Aggression–consistent, –inconsistent, and –irrelevant priming effects on selective exposure to media violence. *Aggressive Behavior, 18,* 349–356.

Langston, C. A., & Cantor, N. (1989). Social anxiety and social constraint: When making friends is hard. *Journal of Personality and Social Psychology, 56,* 649–661.

LaPiere, R. T. (1934). Attitude and actions. *Social Forces, 13,* 230–237.

LaPrelle, J., Hoyle, R. H., Insko, C. A., & Bernthal, P. (1990). Interpersonal attraction and descriptions of the traits of others: Ideal similarity, self similarity, and liking. *Journal of Research in Personality, 24,* 216–240.

Larsen, R. J., & Kasimatis, M. (1991). Day–to–day physical symptoms: Individual differences in the occurrence, duration, and emotional concomitants of minor daily illnesses. *Journal of Personality, 59,* 387–423.

Larson, D. G., & Chastain, R. L. (1990). Self–concealment: Conceptualization, measurement, and health implications. *Journal of Social and Clinical Psychology, 9,* 439–455.

Larson, J. H., & Bell, N. J. (1988). Need for privacy and its effects upon interpersonal attraction and interaction. *Journal of Social and Clinical Psychology, 6,* 1–10.

Lasswell, M. E., & Lobsenz, N. M. (1980). *Styles of loving.* New York: Ballantine.

Latané, B., & Darley, J. M. (1968). Group inhibition of bystander intervention in emergencies. *Journal of Personality and Social Psychology, 10,* 215–221.

Latané, B., & Darley, J. M. (1970). *The unresponsive bystander: Why doesn't he help?* New York: Appleton-Century-Crofts.

Latané, B., Williams, K., & Harkins, S. (1979). Many hands make light the work: The causes and consequences of social loafing. *Journal of Personality and Social Psychology, 37,* 822–832.

Lau, S., & Gruen, G. E. (1992). The social stigma of loneliness: Effect of target person's and perceiver's sex. *Personality and Social Psychology Bulletin, 18,* 182–189.

Lauer, J., & Lauer, R. (1985, June). Marriages made to last. *Psychology Today,* pp. 22–26.

Lazarus, R. S. (1966). *Psychological stress and the coping process.* New York: McGraw–Hill.

Lazarus, R. S. (1993). From psychological stress to the emotions: A history of changing outlooks. In L. W. Porter & M. R. Rosenzweig (Eds.), *Annual review of psychology* (Vol. 44, pp. 1–21). Palo Alto, CA: Annual Reviews, Inc.

Le Vine, R.A., & Campbell, D.T. (1972). *Ethnocentrism: Theories of conflict, ethnic attitudes and group behavior.* Toronto: Wiley.

Leary, M. R., Kowalski, R. M., & Bergen, D. J. (1988). Interpersonal information acquisition and confidence in first encounters. *Personality and Social Psychology Bulletin, 14,* 68–77.

Leary, W. E. (1988, November 15). Novel methods unlock witnesses' memories. *New York Times,* pp. C1, C15.

Leippe, M. R., Manion, A. P., & Romanczyk, A. (1992). Eyewitness persuasion: How and how well do fact finders judge the accuracy of adults' and children's memory reports? *Journal of Personality and Social Psychology, 63,* 181–197.

Lemonick, M. D. (1992). The ozone vanishes. *Time,* 139(7), 60–63.

Lerner, M.J. (1974). The justice motive: Equity and parity among children. *Journal of Personality and Social Psychology, 29,* 539-550.

Lerner, M.J. (1981). The justice motive in human relations: some thoughts on what we know and need to know about justice. In M.J. Lerner & S.C. Lerner (Eds.), *The justice motive in social behavior: Adapting to times of scarcity and change.* New York: Plenum Press.

Lerner, M.J. (1982). The justice motive in human relations and the economic model of man: A radical analysis of facts and fictions. In V.J. Derlega & J. Grzelak (Eds.), *Cooperation and helping behavior:Theories and research* (pp. 249–278). New York: Academic Press.

Leung, K & Iwawaki, S. (1988). Cultural collectivism and distributive behavior: A cross–cultural study. *Journal of Cross–Cultural Psychology, 19,* 35–49.

Leung, K., & Bond, M.H. (1984). The impact of cultural collectivism on reward allocation. *Journal of Personality and Social Psychology, 47,* 793–804.

Leung, K., & Park, H.J. (1986). Effects of interactional goal on choice of allocation rules: A cross–national study. *Organizational Behavior and Human Decision Processes, 37,* 111–120.

Levenson, R. W., Ekman, P., & Friesen, W. V. (1990). Voluntary facial action generates emotion–specific autonomic nervous system activity. *Psychophysiology, 27,* 363–384.

Levenson, R. W., Ekman, P., Heider, K., & Friesen, W. V. (1992). Emotion and autonomic nervous system activity in the Minangkabau of West Sumatra. *Journal of Personality and Social Psychology, 62,* 972–988.

Leventhal, A., Nerenz, D. R., & Steele, D. J. (1984). Illness representations and coping with health threats. In A. Baum & J. Singer (Eds.), *Handbook of psychology and health* (pp. 219–252). Hillsdale, NJ: Erlbaum.

Leventhal, G.S. (1976) The distribution of rewards and resources in groups and organizations. in L Berkowitz & E. Walster (Eds.), *Advances in experimental social psychology* (Vol. 9). New York: Academic Press.

Leventhal, G.S., Michaels, J.W., & Sanford, C. (1972). Inequity and interpersonal conflict: Reward allocation and secrecy about reward as methods of preventing conflict. *Journal of Personality and Social Psychology, 23,* 753–763.

Leventhal, H., Singer, R., & Jones, S. (1965). The effects of fear and specificity of recommendation upon attitudes and behavior. *Journal of Personality and Social Psychology, 2,* 20–29.

Levinger, G. (1980). Toward the analysis of close relationships. *Journal of Experimental Social Psychology, 16,* 510–544.

Levinger, G. (1988). Can we picture "love"? In R. J. Sternberg & M. L. Barnes (Eds.), *The psychology of love* (pp. 139–158). New Haven, CT: Yale University Press.

Lewin, K. (1948). *Resolving social conflicts: Selected papers on group dynamics.* New York: Harper & Row.

Lewin, K., Lippitt, R., & White, R. R. (1939). Patterns of aggressive behavior in experimentally created "social climates." *Journal of Social Psychology, 10,* 271–299.

Leyens, J. P., Camino, L., Parke, R. D., & Berkowitz, L. (1975). Effects of movie violence on aggression in a field setting as a function of group dominance and cohesion. *Journal of Personality and Social Psychology, 32,* 346–360.

Liden, R. C., & Mitchell, T. R. (1988). Ingratiatory behaviors in organizational settings. *Academy of Management Review, 13,* 572–587.

Liebert, R. N., & Baron, R. A. (1972). Some immediate effects of televised violence on children's behavior. *Developmental Psychology, 6,* 469–47S.

Liebert, R. N., Sprafkin, J. H., & Davidson, E. S. (1989). *The early window: Effects of television on children and youth,* (3rd ed.). New York: Pergamon.

Linville, P. W., Fischer, O. W., & Salovey, P. (1989). Perceived distributions of the characteristics of in–group and out–group members: Empirical evidence and a computer simulation. *Journal of Personality and Social Psychology, 57,* 165–188.

Lippa, R., & Donaldson, S. I. (1990). Self–monitoring and idiographic measures of behavioral variability across interpersonal relationships. *Journal of Personality, 58,* 465–479.

Lipset, S.M. (1989). Voluntary activities: More Canadian comparisons—a reply. *Canadian Journal of Sociology, 14,* 377–382.

Lipset, S.M. (1990a). *Continental divide: The values and institutions of the United States and Canada.* New York: Routledge.

Lipset, S.M. (1990b). *North American cultures: Values and institutions in Canada and the United States.* Orona, ME: Borderlands.

Littlepage, G. E. (1991). Effects of group size and task characteristics on group performance: A test of Steiner's model. *Personality and Social Psychology Bulletin, 17,* 449–456.

Lord, R. G., DeVader, C. L., & Alliger, G. M. (1986). A meta–analysis of the relationship between personality traits and leadership perceptions: An application of validity generalization procedures. *Journal of Applied Psychology, 17,* 401–410.

Lorenz, K. (1966). *On aggression.* New York: Harcourt, Brace, & World.

Lorenz, K. (1974). *Civilized man's eight deadly sins.* New York: Harcourt, Brace, Jovanovich.

Luginbuhl, J., & Palmer, R. (1991). Impression management aspects of self–handicapping: Positive and negative effects. *Personality and Social Psychology Bulletin, 17,* 655–662.

Luhtanen, R., & Crocker, J. (1992). A collective self–esteem scale: Self–evaluation of one's social identity. *Personality and Social Psychology Bulletin, 18,* 302–318.

Lupfer, M. B., Clark, L. F., & Hutcherson, H. W. (1990). Impact of context on spontaneous trait and situational attributions. *Journal of Personality and Social Psychology, 58,* 239–249.

Maas, A., & Clark, R. D. III. (1984). Hidden impact of minorities: Fifteen years of minority influence research. *Psychological Bulletin, 95,* 233–243.

Macaulay, J. (1970). A shill for charity. In J. Macaulay & L. Berkowitz (Eds.), *Altruism and helping behavior* (pp. 43–59). New York: Academic Press.

Mack, D., & Rainey, D. (1990). Female applicants' grooming and personnel selection. *Journal of Social Behavior and Personality, 5,* 399–407.

Macrae, C. N., & Milne, A. B. (1992). A curry for your thoughts: Empathic effects on counterfactual thinking. *Personality and Social Psychology Bulletin, 18,* 625–630.

Maisonneuve, J., Palmade, G., & Fourment, C. (1952). Selective choices and propinquity. *Sociometry, 15,* 135–140.

Major, B., Carrington, P. I., & Carnevale, P. J. D. (1984). Physical attractiveness and self–esteem: Attributions for praise from an other–sex evaluator. *Personality and Social Psychology Bulletin, 10,* 43–50.

Major, B., Schmidlin, A. M., & Williams, L. (1990). Gender patterns in social touch: The impact of setting and age. *Journal of Personality and Social Psychology, 58,* 634–643.

Mallick, S. K., & McCandless, B. R. (1966). A study of catharsis of aggression. *Journal of Personality and Social Psychology, 4,* 591–596.

Mann, L., Radford, M.,& Kanagawa, C. (1985). Cross–cultural differences in children's use of decision rules: a comparison of Japan and Australia. *Journal of Personality and Social Psychology, 49,* 1557–1564.

Marangoni, C., & Ickes, W. (1989). Loneliness: A theoretical review with implications for measurement. *Journal of Social and Personal Relationships, 6,* 93–128.

Margolin, G., John, R. S., & O'Brien, M. (1989). Sequential affective patterns as a function of marital conflict style. *Journal of Social and Clinical Psychology, 8,* 45–61.

Markman, H. J. (1981). Prediction of marital distress: A 5–year follow–up. *Journal of Consulting and Clinical Psychology, 49,* 760–762.

Marks, G., & Miller, N. (1982). Target attractiveness as a mediator of assumed attitude similarity. *Personality and Social Psychology Bulletin, 8,* 728–735.

Markus, H. (1978). The effects of mere presence on social facilitation: An unobtrusive test. *Journal of Experimental Social Psychology, 14,* 389–397.

Markus, H., & Nurius, P. (1986). Possible selves. *American Psychologist, 41,* 954–969.

Markus, H., & Wurf, E. (1987). The dynamic self–concept: A social psychological perspective. In M. R. Rosenszweig & L. W. Porter (Eds.), *Annual review of psychology* (Vol. 38, pp. 299–377). Palo Alto, CA: Annual Reviews Inc.

Markus, H.R., & Kitayama, S. (1991a). Culture and the self: Implication for cognition, emotion, and motivation. *Psychological Review, 98,* 224–253.

Markus, H.R., & Kitayama, S. (1991b) Cultural variation in the self–concept. In G.R. Goethals & J. Strauss (Eds.), *Multidisciplinary perspectives on the self* (pp. 18–48). New York: Springer–Verlag.

Marshall, G. D., & Zimbardo, P. (1979). Affective consequences of inadequately explained physiological arousal. *Journal of Personality and Social Psychology, 37,* 970–988.

Maslach, C., Santee, R. T., & Wade, C. (1987). Individuation, gender role, and dissent: Personality mediators of situational forces. *Journal of Personality and Social Psychology, 53,* 1088–1094.

Mathes, E. W., Adams, H. E., & Davies, R. M. (1985). Jealousy: Loss of relationship rewards, loss of self–esteem, depression, anxiety, and anger. *Journal of Personality and Social Psychology, 48,* 1552–1561.

Matlin, M. W., & Zajonc, R. B. (1968). Social facilitation of word associations. *Journal of Personality and Social Psychology, 10,* 455–460.

Matsui, T., Kakuyama, T., & Onglatco, M.L. (1987). Effects of goals and feedback on performance in groups. *Journal of Applied Psychology, 72,* 407–415.

Matsumoto, D. (1994). *People: Psychology from a cultural perspective.* Pacific Grove, CA: Brooks/Cole.

May, J. L., & Hamilton, P. A. (1980). Effects of musically evoked affect on women's interpersonal attraction and perceptual judgments of physical attractiveness of men. *Motivation and Emotion, 4,* 217–228.

McAdams, D. P., & Constantian, C. A. (1983). Intimacy and affiliation motives in daily living: An experience sampling analysis. *Journal of Personality and Social Psychology, 45,* 851–861.

McAdams, D. P., & Losoff, M. (1984). Friendship motivation in fourth and sixth graders: A thematic analysis. *Journal of Social and Persnal Relationships, 1,* 11–27.

McArthur, L. A. (1972). The how and what of why: Some determinants and consequences of causal attribution. *Journal of Personality and Social Psychology, 22,* 171–193.

McCanne, T. R., & Anderson, J. A. (1987). Emotional responding following experimental manipulation of facial electromyographic activity. *Journal of Personality and Social Psychology, 52,* 759–768.

McCauley, C. (1989). The nature of social influence in groupthink: Compliance and internalization. *Journal of Personality and Social Psychology, 57,* 250–260.

McClintock, C. G., & Allison, S. T. (1989). Social value orientation and helping behavior. *Journal of Applied Social Psychology, 19,* 353–362.

McDougall, W. (1908). *Introduction to social psychology.* London: Methuen.

McFarlane, A. H., Norman, G. R., Streiner, D. L., & Roy, R. G. (1983). The process of social stress: Stable, reciprocal, and mediating relationships. *Journal of Health and Social Behavior, 24,* 160–173.

McGaughey, K. J., & Stiles, W. B. (1983). Courtroom interrogation of rape victims: Verbal response mode use by attorneys and witnesses during direct examination vs. cross–examination. *Journal of Applied Social Psychology, 13*, 78–87.

McGonagle, K. A., Kessler, R. C., & Schilling, E. A. (1992). The frequency and determinants of marital disagreements in a community sample. *Journal of Social and Personal Relationships, 9*, 507–524.

McGue, M., & Lykken, D. T. (1992). Genetic influence on risk of divorce. *Psychological Science, 3*, 368–373.

McIntyre, C. W., Watson, D., Clark, L. A., & Cross, S. A. (1991). The effect of induced social interaction on positive and negative affect. *Bulletin of the Psychonomic Society, 29*, 67–70.

McKillip, J., & Reidel, S. L. (1983). External validity of matching on physical attractiveness for same and opposite sex couples. *Journal of Applied Social Psychology, 13*, 328–337.

McPhail, C. *The myth of the madding crowd.*

Mead, G.H. (1934). *Mind, self and society.* (C.W. Morris, Ed.). Chicago: University of Chicago Press.

Mechanic, D. (1983). Adolescent health and illness behavior: Hypotheses for the study of distress in youth. *Journal of Human Stress, 9*, 4–13.

Mednick, S. A., Brennan, P., & Kandel, E. (1988). Predispositions to violence. *Aggressive Behavior, 14*, 25–33.

Meecham, W. C., & Smith, H. G. (1977, June). (*British Journal of Audiology.*) Quoted in N. Napp, Noise drives you crazy—jets and mental hospitals. *Psychology Today*, p. 33.

Mehrabian, A., & Weiner, M. (1967). Decoding of inconsistent communications. *Journal of Personality and Social Psychology, 6*, 109–114.

Meindl, J. R., & Lerner, M. J. (1985). Exacerlation of extreme responses to an out-group. *Journal of Personality and Social Psychology, 47*, 71–84.

Mellers, B. A., Richards, V., & Birnbaum, M. H. (1992). Distributional theories of impression formation. *Organizational Behavior and Human Decision Processes, 51*, 313–343.

Meyer, D., Leventhal, H., & Gutman, M. (1985). Common–sense models of illness: The example of hypertension. *Health Psychology, 4*, 115–135.

Milestones. (1989, September 18). *Time*, p. 75.

Milgram, S. (1963). Behavioral study of obedience. *Journal of Abnormal and Social Psychology, 67*, 371–378.

Milgram, S. (1965a). Liberating effects of group pressure. *Journal of Personality and Social Psychology, 1*, 127–134.

Milgram, S. (1965b). Some conditions of obedience and disobedience to authority. *Human Relations, 18*, 57–76.

Milgram, S. (1974). *Obedience to authority.* New York: Harper.

Millar, M. G., & Tesser, A. (1989). The effects of affective–cognitive consistency and thought on the attitude–behavior relation. *Journal of Experimental Social Psychology, 25*, 189–202.

Miller, D. T., & McFarland, C. (1986). Counterfactual thinking and victim compensation: A test of norm theory. *Personality and Social Psychology Bulletin, 12*, 513–519.

Miller, D. T., & Ross, M. (1975). Self–serving biases in attribution of causality: Fact or fiction? *Psychological Bulletin, 82*, 313–325.

Miller, D. T., Turnbull, W., & McFarland, C. (1990). Counterfactual thinking and social perception: Thinking about what might have been. In M. P. Zanna (Ed.), *Advances in experimental social psychology* (Vol. 23, pp. 305–331). Orlando FL: Academic Press.

Miller, J. (1984). Culture and the development of everyday social explanation. *Journal of Personality and Social Psychology, 46*, 961–978.

Miller, M. L., & Thayer, J. F. (1989). On the existence of discrete classes in personality: Is self–monitoring the correct joint to carve? *Journal of Personality and Social Psychology, 57*, 143–155.

Miller, N., Boye, D., & Gerard, H.B. (1968). When failure can be attributed to others' prejudice: Self–evaluation and subsequent performance. Paper presented at the annual meeting of the Western Psychological Association, San Diego.

Miller, N., Maruyama, G., Beaber, R. J., & Valone, K. (1976). Speed of speech and persuasion. *Journal of Personality and Social Psychology, 34*, 615–624.

Miller, R. S. (1991). On decorum in close relationships: Why aren't we polite to those we love? *Contemporary Social Psychology, 15*, 63–65.

Miller, S. N., Brody, D. S., & Summerton, J. (1988). Styles of coping with threat: Implications for health. *Journal of Personality and Social Psychology, 54*, 142–148.

Milliman, R. (1982). Using background music to affect the behavior of supermarket shoppers. *Journal of Marketing, 46*, 86–91.

Moghaddam, F.M. (1987). Psychology in the three worlds: As reflected by the crisis in social psychology and the move toward indigenous Third World psychology. *American Psychologist, 42*, 912–920.

Moghaddam, F.M. (1990). Modulative and generative orientations in psychology: Implications for Psychology in the three worlds. *Journal of Social Issues, 46*, 21-41.

Moghaddam, F.M., Ditto, B., & Taylor, D.M. (1990). Attitudes and attributions related to psychological symptomatology in Indian immigrant women. *Journal of Cross–Cultural Psychology, 21*, 335–350.

Moghaddam, F.M., Taylor, D.M., & Wright, S.C. (1993). *Social psychology in cross–cultural perspective.* NewYork: W.H. Freeman.

Monsour, M. (1992). Meanings of intimacy in cross– and same–sex friendships. *Journal of Social and Personal Relationships, 9*, 277–295.

Montag, I., & Levin, J. (1990). The location of the Self–Monitoring Scale in the factor space of the EPQ and the IGPF. *Journal of Research in Personality, 24*, 45–56.

Montepare, J. M., & Zebrowitz–McArthur, L. (1987). Perceptions of adults with childlike voices in two cultures. *Journal of Experimental Social Psychology, 23*, 331–349.

Montepare, J. M., & Zebrowitz–McArthur, L. (1988). Impressions of people created by age–related qualities of their gaits. *Journal of Personality and Social Psychology, 54*, 547–556.

Moore, J. S., Graziano, W. G., Miller, M. G. (1987). Physical attractiveness, sex role orientation, and the evaluation of adults and children. *Personality and Social Psychology Bulletin, 13*, 95–102.

Moorhead, G., & Montanari, J. R. (1986). An empirical investigation of the groupthink phenomenon. *Human Relations, 39,* 399–410.

Moran, G., & Cutler, B. L. (1991). The prejudicial impact of pretrial publicity. *Journal of Applied Social Psychology, 21,* 345–367.

Moreland, R. L. (1987). The formation of small groups. In C. Hendrick (Ed.), *Review of personality and social psychology,* (Vol. 8, pp. 80–110). Newbury Park, CA: Sage.

Moreland, R. L., & Beach, S. R. (1992). Exposure effects in the classroom: The development of affinity among students. *Journal of Experimental Social Psychology, 28,* 255–276.

Moreland, R. L., & Levine, J. M. (1992a). The composition of small groups. *Advances in Group Processes, 9,* 237–280.

Moreland, R. L., & Zajonc, R. B. (1982). Exposure effects in person perception: Familiarity, similarity, and attraction. *Journal of Experimental Social Psychology, 18,* 395–415.

Morell, M. A., Twillman, R. K., & Sullaway, M. E. (1989). Would a Type A date another Type A?: Influence of behavior type and personal attributes in the selection of dating partners. *Journal of Applied Social Psychology, 19,* 918–931.

Morgan, D. L., & White, R. L. (1993). The structure of the field of personal relationships: Part I. Disciplines. *Personal Relationships Issues, 1,* 2–5.

Mori, D. A., Chaiken, S., & Pliner, P. (1987). "Eating lightly" and the self–presentation of femininity, *Journal of Personality and Social Psychology, 53,* 693–702.

Morris, D., Collett, P., Marsh, P., & O'Shaughnessy, M. (1979). *Gestures: Their origins and distribution.* London: Jonathan Cape.

Morris, W. N., & Miller, R. S. (1975). The effects of consensus–breaking and consensus–preempting partners on reduction of conformity. *Journal of Personality and Social Psychology, 11,* 215–223.

Morris, W. N., Miller, R. S., & Spangenberg, S. (1977). The effects of dissenter position and task difficulty on conformity and response to conflict. *Journal of Personality, 45,* 251–266.

Morris, W. N., Worchel, S., Bois, J. L., Pearson, J. A., Rountree, C. A., Samaha, G. M., Wachtler, J., & Wright, S. I. (1976). Collective coping with stress: Group reactions to fear, anxiety, and ambiguity. *Journal of Personality and Social Psychology, 33,* 674–679.

Morrison, E. W., & Bies, R. J. (1991). Impression management in the feedback–seeking process: A literature review and research agenda. *Academy of Management Review, 16,* 322–341.

Moscovici, S. (1972). Society and theory in social psychology. In J. Israel & H. Tajfel (Eds.), *The context of social psychology.* London: Academic Press.

Moscovici, S. (1985). Social influence and conformity. In G. Lindzey & E. Aronson (Eds.), *Handbook of social psychology.* 3rd ed. New York: Random House.

Moser, C. G., & Dyck, D. G. (1989). Type A behavior, uncontrollability, and the activation of hostile self–schema. *Journal of Research in Personality, 23,* 248–267.

Muecher, H., & Ungeheuer, H. (1961). Meterological influence on reaction time, flicker–fusion frequency, job accidents, and medical treatment. *Perceptual and Motor Skills, 12,* 163–168.

Mugny, G. (1975). Negotiations, image of the other and the process of minority influence. *European Journal of Social Psychology, 5,* 209–229.

Mullen, B., & Johnson, C. (1990). Distinctiveness-based illusory correlations and stereotyping: A meta-analytic integration. *British Journal of Social Psychology, 29,* 11–28.

Mumford, M. D., O'Connor, J., Clifton, T. C., Connelly, M. S., & Zaccaro, S. D. (in press). Background data constructs as predictors of leadership behavior. *Human Performance.*

Murphy–Berman, V., Berman, J.J., Singh, P., Pachauri, A., & Kumar, P. (1984). Factors affecting allocation to needy and meritorious recipients: A cross–cultural comparison. *Journal of Personality and Social Psychology. 46,* 1267–1272.

Murray, H. A. (1938/1962). *Explorations in personality.* New York: Science Editions.

Murstein, B. I., Merighi, J. R., & Vyse, S. A. (1991). Love styles in the United States and France: A cross–cultural comparison. *Journal of Social and Clinical Psychology, 10,* 37–46.

Nadler, A. (1986). Help seeking as a cultural phenomenon: Differences between city and kibbutz dwellers. *Journal of Personality and Social Psychology, 51,* 976–982.

Nadler, A. (1987). Determinants of help-seeking behaviour: The effects of helper's similarity, task centrality and recipient's self esteem. *European Journal of Social Psychology, 17,* 57–67.

Nadler, A. (1991). Help-seeking behavior: Psychological costs and instrumental benefits. In M. S. Clark (Ed.), *Prosocial behavior* (pp. 290–311). Newbury Park, CA: Sage.

Nadler, A. (1993, March). Personal communication as a function of the channel of communication. *Social.Behaviour 1,* 135–142.

Nadler, A., & Fisher, J. D. (1986). The role of threat to self-esteem and perceived control in recipient reactions to aid: Theory development and empirical validation. In L. Berkowitz (Ed.), *Advances in experimental social psychology* (Vol. 17, pp. 81–123). New York: Academic Press.

Nadler, A., Fisher, J. D., & Itzhak, S. B. (1983). With a little help from my friend: Effect of a single or multiple act of aid as a function of donor and task characteristics. *Journal of Personality and Social Psychology, 44,* 310–321.

Nahemow, L., & Lawton, M. P. (1975). Similarity and propinquity in friendship formation. *Journal of Personality and Social Psychology, 32,* 205–213.

Narby, D. J., Cutler, B. L., & Moran, G. (1993). A meta–analysis of the association between authoritarianism and jurors' perceptions of defendant culpability. *Journal of Applied Psychology, 78,* 34–42.

Nasar, S. (1992, May 31). Cooling the globe would be nice, but saving lives now may cost less. *New York Times,* p. E6.

Nemeth, C. J. (1986). Differential contributions of majority and minority influence. *Psychological Review, 93,* 23–32.

Neto, F. (1992). Loneliness among Portuguese adolescents. *Social Behavior and Personality, 20,* 15–22.

Neuberg, S. L. (1989). The goal of forming accurate impressions during social interactions: Attenuating the impact of negative expectancies. *Journal of Personality and Social Psychology, 56,* 374–386.

Newcomb, M. D., Rabow, J., & Hernandez, A. C. R. (1992). A cross–national study of nuclear attitudes, normative support, and activist behavior: Additive and interactive effects. *Journal of Applied Social Psychology, 22,* 780–800.

Newcomb, T. M. (1961). *The acquaintance process.* New York: Holt, Rinehart, & Winston.

Nicola, J. A. S., & Hawkes, G. R. (1986). Marital satisfaction of dual–career couples: Does sharing increase happiness? *Journal of Social Behavior and Personality, 1,* 47–60.

Niedenthal, P. M., Setterlund, M. B., & Wherry, M. B. (1992). Possible self–complexity and affective reactions to goal–relevant evaluation. *Journal of Personality and Social Psychology, 63,* 5–16.

Nisbett, R. E. (1990). Evolutionary psychology, biology, and cultural evolution. *Motivation and Emotion, 14,* 255–264.

Nisbett, R.E., & Kunda, Z. (1985). Perception of social distributions. *Journal of Personality and Social Psychology, 48,* 297–311.

Nowicki, S., Jr., & Manheim, S. (1991). Interpersonal complementarity and time of interaction in female relationships. *Journal of Research in Personality, 25,* 322–333.

Nuttin, J. M., Jr. (1987). Affective consequences of mere ownership: The name letter effect in twelve European languages. *European Journal of Social Psychology, 17,* 381–402.

O'Connell, P. D. (1988). Pretrial publicity, change of venue, public opinion polls—A theory of procedural justice. *University of Detroit Law Review, 65,* 169–197.

O'Grady, K. E. (1989). Physical attractiveness, need for approval, social self–esteem, and maladjustment. *Journal of Social and Clinical Psychology, 8,* 62–69.

O'Sullivan, C. S., & Durso, F. T. (1984). Effects of schema–incongruent information on memory for stereotypical attributes. *Journal of Personality and Social Psychology, 47,* 55–70.

Oberg, K. (1960). Culture shock: adjustment to a new cultural environment. *Practical Anthropology, 7,* 177–182.

Ohbuchi, K. I., & Ogura, S. (1984). The experience of anger (1): The survey for adults and university students with Averill's questionnaire (Japanese). *Japanese Journal of Criminal Psychology, 22,* 15–35.

Ohbuchi, K. I., Kameda, M., & Agarie, N. (1989). Apology as aggression control: Its role in mediating appraisal of and response to harm. *Journal of Personality and Social Psychology, 56,* 219–227.

Olczak, P. V., Kaplan, M. F., & Penrod, S. (1991). Attorneys' lay psychology and its effectiveness in selecting jurors: Three empirical studies. *Journal of Social Behavior and Personality, 6,* 431–452.

Oliner, S. P., & Oliner, P. M. (1988). *The altruistic personality: Rescuers of Jews in Nazi Europe.* New York: Free Press.

Olivenstein, L. (1992). Cold comfort. *Discover, 13*(8), 18, 20–21.

Olmstead, R. E., Guy, S. M., O'Malley, P. M., & Bentler, P. M. (1991). Longitudinal assessment of the relationship between self–esteem, fatalism, loneliness, and substance use. *Journal of Social Behavior and Personality, 6,* 749–770.

Olson, J. N., & Ross, N. (1988). False feedback about placebo effectiveness: Consequences for the misattribution of speech anxiety. *Journal of Experimental Social Psychology, 24,* 275–291.

Orive, R. (1988). Social projection and social comparison of opinions. *Journal of Personality and Social Psychology, 54,* 953–964.

Osterwell, Z., & Nagano–Hakamura, K. (1992). Maternal views on aggression: Japan and Israel. *Aggressive Behavior, 18,* 263–270.

Page, N. M., & Kahle, L. R. (1976). Demand characteristics in the satiation–deprivation effect on attitude conditioning. *Journal of Personality and Social Psychology, 33,* 553–562.

Page, R. M. (1991). Loneliness as a risk factor in adolescent hopelessness. *Journal of Research in Personality, 25,* 189–195.

Pan, S. (1993). China: Acceptability and effect of three kinds of sexual publication. *Archives of Sexual Behavior, 22,* 59–71.

Parke, R. D., Berkowitz, L., Leyens, J. P., West, S. G., & Sebastian, R. J. (1977). Some effects of violent and non-violent movies on the behavior of juvenile delinquents. In L. Berkowitz (Ed.), *Advances in experimental social psychology* (Vol. 10). New York: Academic Press.

Patch, M. E. (1986). The role of source legitimacy in sequential request strategies of compliance. *Personality and Social Psychology Bulletin, 12,* 199–205.

Paulhus, D. L., & Bruce, M. N. (1992). The effect of acquaintanceship on the validity of personality impressions: A longitudinal study. *Journal of Personality and Social Psychology, 63,* 816–824.

Paulus, P. B. (ed.) (1989). *Psychology of influence* (2nd ed.). Hillsdale, NJ: Erlbaum.

Pear, R. (1993, January 15). Poverty erodes family, study finds. *Albany Times Union,* pp. A–I, A–8.

Pearson, K., & Lee, A. (1903). On the laws of inheritance in man: I. Inheritance of physical characters. *Biometrika, 2,* 357–462.

Pendleton, M. G., & Batson, C. D. (1979). Self– presentation and the door–in–the–face technique for inducing compliance. *Personality and Social Psychology Bulletin, 5,* 77–81.

Pennebaker, J. W., & Beall, S. (1986). Confronting a traumatic event: Toward an understanding of inhibition and disease. *Journal of Abnormal Psychology, 95,* 274–281.

Pennebaker, J. W., Hughes, C. F., & O'Heron, R. C. (1987). The psychophysiology of confession: Linking inhibitory and psychosomatic processes. *Journal of Personality and Social Psychology, 52,* 781–793.

Peplau, L. A., & Perlman, D. (1982). Perspective on loneliness. In L. A. Peplau & D. Perlman (Eds.), *Loneliness: A sourcebook of current theory, research, and therapy.* New York: Wiley.

Perdue, C. W., & Gurtman, M. B. (1990). Evidence for the automaticity of ageism. *Journal of Experimental Social Psychology, 26,* 199–216.

Perlman, D. (1986). An interview with Dan Perlman. In B. Earn & S. Towson (Eds.) *Readings in social psychology: Classic and Canadian contributions.* Peterborough: Broadview Press.

Perlman, D., & Peplau, L.A. (1981). Toward a social psychology of loneliness. In S. Duck & R. Gilmour (Eds.), *Personal relationships 3: Personal relationships in disorder.* London: Academic Press.

Perrewe, P. L., & Anthony, W. P. (1990). Stress in a steel pipe mill: The impact of job demands, personal control, and employee age on somatic complaints. *Journal of Social Behavior and Personality, 5,* 77–90.

Peters, L. H., Hartke, D. D., & Pohlman, J. R. (1985). Fiedler's contingency theory of leadership: An application of the meta–analysis procedures of Schmidt and Hunter. *Psychological Bulletin, 97,* 274–285.

Petersen, J., & Brooks–Gunn, Jr. (Eds.). *The encyclopedia of adolescence.* New York: Garland.

Peterson, C., Seligman, M. E. P., & Vaillant, G. (1988). Pessimistic explanatory style as a risk factor for physical illness: A thirty–five–year longitudinal study. *Journal of Personality and Social Psychology, 55,* 23–27.

Pettigrew, M. (1987, May 12). "Useful" modes of thought contribute to prejudice. *New York Times,* pp. 17–20.

Pettigrew, T. (1958). Personality and sociocultural factors in intergroup attitudes: A cross–national comparison. *Journal of Conflict Resolution, 2,* 29–42.

Pettigrew, T. F. (1969). Racially separate or together? *Journal of Social Issues, 25,* 43–69.

Pettigrew, T. F. (1979). The ultimate attribution error: Extending Allport's cognitive analysis of prejudice. *Personality and Social Psychology Bulletin, 5,* 461–476.

Pettigrew, T. F. (1981). Extending the stereotype concept. In D. L. Hamilton (Ed.), *Coganitive processes in stereotyping and intergroup behavior* (pp. 303–331). Hillsdale, NJ: Erlbaum.

Petty, R. E., & Cacioppo, J. P. (1979). Issue involvement can increase or decrease persuasion by enhancing message–relevant cognitive responses. *Journal of Personality and Social Psychology, 37,* 1915–1926.

Petty, R. E., & Cacioppo, J. T. (1986). The elaboration likelihood model of persuasion. In L. Berkowitz (Ed.), *Advances in experimental social psychology* (Vol. 19, pp. 123–205). New York: Academic Press.

Petty, R. E., Ostrom, T. N., & Brock, T. C. (Eds.). (1981). *Cognitive responses in persuasion.* Hillsdale, NJ: Erlbaum.

Petty, R. E., Wells, G. L., & Brock, T. C. (1976). Distraction can enhance or reduce yielding to propaganda: Thought disruption versus effort justification. *Journal of Personality and Social Psychology, 34,* 874–884.

Pierce, C. A. (1992). *The effects of physical attractiveness and height on dating choice: A meta–analysis.* Unpublished masters thesis, University at Albany, State University of New York.

Pilisuk, M., & Acredolo, C. (1988). Fear of technological hazards: One concern or many? *Social Behavior, 3,* 17–24.

Pilisuk, M., Boylan, R., & Acredolo, C. (1987). Social support, life stress, and subsequent medical care utilization. *Health Psychology, 6,* 273–288.

Pillow, D. R., West, S. G., & Reich, J. W. (1991). Attributional style in relation to self-esteem and depression: Mediational and interactive models. *Journal of Research in Personality, 25,* 57–69.

Pines, A., & Aronson, E. (1983). Antecedents, correlates, and consequences of sexual jealousy. *Journal of Personality, 51,* 108–136.

Pittenger, J. B., Mark, L. S., & Johnson, D. F. (1989). Longitudinal stability of facial attractiveness. *Bulletin of the Psychonomic Society, 27,* 171–174.

Planalp, S., & Benson, A. (1992). Friends' and acquaintances' conversations I: Perceived differences. *Journal of Social and Personal Relationships, 9,* 483–506.

Platz, S. G., & Hosch, H. M. (1988). Cross–racial/ethnic eyewitness identification: A field study. *Journal of Applied Social Psychology, 13,* 972–984.

Pliner, P., & Chaiken, S. (1990). Eating, social motives, and self–presentation in women and men. *Journal of Experimental Social Psychology, 26,* 240–254.

Pliner, P., Hart, H., Kohl, J., & Saari, D. (1974). Compliance without pressure: Some further data on the foot–in–the–door technique. *Journal of Experimental Social Psychology, 10,* 17–22.

Popper, K. (1959). *The logic of scientific discovery.* London: Hutchinson.

Porter, C., Markus, H., & Nurius, P. S. (1984). *Conceptions of possibility among people in crisis.* Unpublished manuscript, University of Michigan, Ann Arbor.

Powell, G. N. (1990). One more time: Do female and male managers differ? *Academy of Management Executive, 4*(3), 68–75.

Powers, P. C., & Geen, R. G. (1972). Effects of the behavior and perceived arousal of a model on instrumental aggression. *Journal of Personality and Social Psychology, 23,* 175–184.

Pratkanis, A. R., Breckler S. J., & Greenwald, A. G. (Eds.). (1989). *Attitude structure and function.* Hillsdale, NJ: Erlbaum.

Prentice-Dunn, S., & Rogers, R. (1983). Deindividuation in aggression. In R. G. Geen & E. I. Donnerstein (Eds.), *Aggression: Theoretical and empirical reviews* (Vol. 2, pp. 155–171). New York: Academic Press.

Price, K. H., & Vandenberg, S. G. (1979). Matching for physical attractiveness in married couples. *Personality and Social Psychology Bulletin, 5,* 398–400.

Prohaska, T. R., Keller, M. L., Leventhal, E. A., & Leventhal, H. (1987). Impact of symptoms and aging attribution on emotions and coping. *Health Psychology, 6,* 495–514.

Provine, R. R. (1992). Contagious laughter: Laughter is a sufficient stimulus for laughs and smiles. *Bulletin of the Psychonomic Society, 30,* 1–4.

Pryor, J. B., Biggons, F. X., Wicklund, R. A., Fazio, R. H., & Hood, R. (1977). Self–focused attention and self–report validity. *Journal of Personality, 45,* 514–527.

Ptacek, J. T., Smith, R. E., & Zanas, J. (1992). Gender, appraisal, and coping: A longitudinal analysis. *Journal of Personality, 60,* 747–770.

Quadrel, M. J., & Lau, R. R. (1989). Health promotion, health locus of control, and health behavior: Two field experiments. *Journal of Applied Social Psychology, 19,* 1497–1521.

Rathje, W. L. (1991). Once and future landfills. *National Geographic, 179*(5), 116–134.

Rawls, J. (1970). *A theory of justice.* Oxford: Oxford University Press.

Redfield, R., Linton, R., & Herskovits (1936) Memorandum on the study of acculturation. *American Anthropologist, 38,* 149–152.

Reifman, A. S., Larrick, R. P., & Fein, S. (1991). Temper and temperature on the diamond: The heat–aggression relationship in major league baseball. *Personality and Social Psychology Bulletin, 17,* 580–585.

Reis, H. T., Nezlek, J., & Wheeler, L. (1980). Physical attractiveness in social interaction. *Journal of Personality and Social Psychology, 38,* 604–617.

Reis, T. J., Gerrard, M. & Gibbons, F. X. (1993). Social comparison and the pill: Reactions to upward and downward comparison of contraceptive behavior. *Personality and Social Psychology Bulletin, 19,* 13–20.

Reisenzein, R. (1983). The Schachter theory of emotion: Two decades later. *Psychological Bulletin, 94,* 239–264.

Reisman, J. M. (1984). Friendliness and its correlates. *Journal of Social and Clinical Psychology, 2,* 143–155.

Reiss, I. L. (1990). *An end to shame: Shaping our next sexual revolution.* Buffalo, NY: Prometheus.

Revenson, T. A. (1981). Coping with loneliness: The impact of causal attributions. *Personality and Social Psychology Bulletin, 7,* 565–571.

Rhodewalt, F., & Davison, J., Jr. (1983). Reactance and the coronary–prone behavior pattern: The role of self–attribution in response to reduced behavioral freedom. *Journal of Personality and Social Psychology, 44,* 220–228.

Riess, M., & Schlenker, B. R. (1977). Attitude change and responsibility avoidance as modes of dilemma resolution in forced–compliance situations. *Journal of Personality and Social Psychology, 35,* 21–30.

Riordan, C. A. (1978). Equal–status interracial contact: A review and revision of a concept. *International Journal of Intercultural Relations, 2,* 161–185.

Rittle, R. H. (1981). Changes in helping behavior: Self–versus situational perceptions as mediators of the foot–in–the–door effect. *Personality and Social Psychology Bulletin, 7,* 431–437.

Roballey, T. C., McGreevy, C., Rongo, R. R., Schwantes, M. L., Steger, P. J., Wininger, M. A., & Gardner, E. B. (1985). The effect of music on eating behavior. *Bulletin of the Psychonomic Society, 23,* 221–222.

Robberson, N. R., & Rogers, R. W. (1988). Beyond fear appeals: Negative and positive persuasive appeals to health and self–esteem. *Journal of Applied Social Psychology, 18,* 277–287.

Roberts, J. E., & Monroe, S. M. (1992). Vulnerable self–esteem and depressive symptoms: Prospective findings comparing three alternative conceptualizations. *Journal of Personality and Social Psychology, 62,* 804–812.

Roberts, J. V., & Edwards, D. (1989). Contextual effects in judgments of crimes, criminals, and the purposes of sentencing. *Journal of Applied Social Psychology, 19,* 902–917.

Roberts, J.V., & Doob, A.N. (1990). News media influences on public views of sentencing. *Law and Human Behavior, 14,* 451–468.

Rodgers, J. L., Billy, J. O. B., & Udry, J. R. (1984). A model of friendship similarity in mildly deviant behaviors. *Journal of Applied Social Psychology, 14,* 413–425.

Rodin, J., & Salovey, P. (1989). Health psychology. In M. R. Rosenzweig & L. W. Porter (Eds.), *Annual review of psychology* (Vol. 40, pp. 533–579). Palo Alto, CA: Annual Reviews.

Rodin, M. J. (1987). Who is memorable to whom: A study of cognitive disregard. *Social Cognition, 5,* 144–165.

Rogers, M., Miller, N., Mayer, F. S., & Duvall, S. (1982). Personal responsibility and salience of the request for help: Determinants of the relations between negative affect and helping behavior. *Journal of Personality and Social Psychology, 43,* 956–970.

Rogers, R. W. (1980). *Subjects' reactions to experimental deception.* Unpublished manuscript, University of Alabama, Tuscaloosa.

Rogers, R. W., & Ketcher, C. M. (1979). Effects of anonymity and arousal on aggression. *Journal of Psychology, 102,* 13–19.

Roscoe, B., & Kruger, T. L. (1990). AIDS, late adolescents' knowledge and its influence on sexual behaviour. *Adolescence, 25,* 39–48.

Rose, S. M. (1984). How friendships end: Patterns among young adults. *Journal of Social and Personal Relationships, 1,* 267–277.

Rosenbaum, M. E. (1986). The repulsion hypothesis: On the nondevelopment of relationships. *Journal of Personality and Social Psychology, 51,* 1156–1166.

Rosenbaum, M. E., & Levin, I. P. (1969). Impression formation as a function of source credibility and the polarity of information. *Journal of Personality and Social Psychology, 12,* 34–37.

Rosenblatt, A., & Greenberg, J. (1988). Depression and interpersonal attraction: The role of perceived similarity. *Journal of Personality and Social Psychology, 54,* 112–119.

Rosenfield, D., Greenberg, J., Folger, R., & Borys, R. (1982). Effect of an encounter with a black panhandler on subsequent helping for blacks: Tokenism or conforming to a negative stereotype? *Personality and Social Psychology Bulletin, 8,* 664–671.

Rosenhan, D. L., Salovey, P., & Hargis, K. (1981). The joys of helping: Focus of attention mediates the impact of positive affect on altruism. *Journal of Personality and Social Psychology, 40,* 899–905.

Rosenthal, A. M. (1964). *Thirty–eight witnesses.* New York: McGraw–Hill.

Rosenthal, E. (1992, August 18). Troubled marriage? Sibling relations may be at fault. *New York Times,* pp. C1, C9.

Rosenzweig, J. M., & Daley, D. M. (1989). Dyadic adjustment/sexual satisfaction in women and men as a function of psychological sex role self–perception. *Journal of Sex and Marital Therapy, 15,* 42–56.

Roskos–Ewoldsen, D. R., & Fazio, R. H. (1992). The accessibility of source likability as a determinant of persuasion. *Personality and Social Psychology Bulletin, 18,* 19–25.

Ross, L. D. (1977). Problems in the interpretation of 'self–serving' assymetries in causal attribution: Comments on the Stephan et al. paper. *Sociometry, 40,* 112–114.

Rotenberg, K. J., & Kmill, J (1992). Perception of lonely and non–lonely persons as a function of individual differences in loneliness. *Journal of Social and Personal Relationships, 9,* 325–330.

Roter, D. L. (1984). Patient question asking in physician–patient interaction. *Health Psychology, 3,* 395–409.

Roth, D. L., Wiebe, D. J., Fillingim, R. G., & Shay, K. A. (1989). Life events, fitness, hardiness, and health: A simultaneous analysis of proposed stress–resistance effects. *Journal of Personality and Social Psychology, 57,* 136–142.

Rotton, J., & Frey, J. (1985). Psychological costs of air pollution: Atmospheric conditions, seasonal trends, and psychiatric emergencies. *Population and Environment, 7,* 3–16.

Rotton, J., & Kelley, I. W. (1985). Much ado about the full moon: A meta-analysis of lunar-lunacy research. *Psychological Bulletin, 97,* 286–306.

Rotton, J., Frey, J., Barry, T., Milligan, M., & Fitzpatrick, M. (1979). The air pollution experience and physical aggression. *Journal of Applied Social Psychology, 9*, 397–412.

Routh, D. K., & Ernst, A. R. (1984). Somatization disorder in relatives of children and adolescents with functional abdominal pain. *Journal of Pediatric Psychology, 50*, 427–437.

Rozin, P., Millman, L., & Nemeroff, C. (1986). Operation of the laws of sympathetic magic in disgust and other domains. *Journal of Personality and Social Psychology, 50*, 703–712.

Rubin, J. Z. (1985). Deceiving ourselves about deception: Comment on Smith and Richardson's "Amelioration of deception and harm in psychological research." *Journal of Personality and Social Psychology, 48*, 252–253.

Rubin, Z. (1982). Children without friends. In L. A. Peplau & D. Perlman (Eds.), *Loneliness: A sourcebook of current theory, research, and therapy.* New York: Wiley.

Rule, B. G., Taylor, B. R., & Dobbs, A. R. (1987). Priming effects of heat on aggressive thoughts. *Social Cognition, 5*, 131–143.

Rule, B.G., & Ferguson, T.J. (1986). The effects of media violence on attitudes, emotions and cognitions. Journal of Social Issues, *2*, 29–50.

Rule, B.G., & Nesdale, A.R. (1976). Emotional arousal and aggressive behavior. *Psychological Bulletin, 83*, 851–863.

Rule, B.G., & Well, G. L. (1981). Experimental social psychology in Canada: A look at the seventies. *Canadian Psychology, 22*, 69–84.

Rusbult, C. E. (1983). A longitudinal test of the investment model: The development (and deterioration) of satisfaction and commitment in heterosexual involvements. *Journal of Personality and Social Psychology, 45*, 101–117.

Rusbult, C. E., & Zembrodt, I. M. (1983). Responses to dissatisfaction in romantic involvements: A multidimensional scaling analysis. *Journal of Experimental Social Psychology, 19*, 274–293.

Rusbult, C. E., Morrow, G. D., & Johnson, D. J. (1990). Self–esteem and problem–solving behavior in close relationships. *British Journal of Social Psychology.*

Rushton, J. P. (1989a). Genetic similarity, human altruism, and group selection. *Behavioral and Brain Sciences, 12*, 503–559.

Rushton, J. P. (1989b). Genetic similarity in male friendships. *Ethology and Sociobiology, 10*, 361–373

Rushton, J. P. (1990). Sir Francis Galton, epigenetic rules, genetic similarity theory, and human life–history analysis. Journal of Personality, *58*, 117–140.

Rushton, J. P., & Nicholson, I. R. (1988). Genetic similarity theory, intelligence, and human mate choice. *Ethology and Sociobiology, 9*, 45–57.

Rushton, J.P. (1978). Urban density and altruism: Helping strangers in a Canadian city, suburb, and small town. *Psychological Reports, 43*, 987–990.

Russell, D., Peplau, L. A., & Cutrona, C. E. (1980). The revised UCLA Loneliness Scale: Concurrent and discriminant validity evidence. *Journal of Personality and Social Psychology, 39*, 472–480.

Russell, G. W. (1981). Aggression in sport. In P. F. Brain & D. Benton (Eds.), *Multidisciplinary approaches to aggression research* (pp. 431–446). Amsterdam: Elsevier/North Holland.

Russell, J. A., Weiss, A., & Mendelsohn, C. A. (1989). Affect grid: A single-item scale of pleasure and arousal. *Journal of Personality and Social Psychology, 57*, 493–502.

Rutkowski, G. K., Gruder, C. L., & Romer, D. (1983). Group cohesiveness, social norms, and bystander intervention. *Journal of Personality and Social Psychology, 44*, 545–552.

Ryan, R. H., & Geiselman, R. E. (1991). Effects of biased information on the relationship between eyewitness confidence and accuracy. *Bulletin of the Psychonomic Society, 29*, 7–9.

Sadalla, E. K., Kenrick, D. T., & Vershure, B. (1987). Dominance and heterosexual attraction. *Journal of Personality and Social Psychology, 52*, 730–738.

Salovey, P. (1992). Mood-induced self–focused attention. *Journal of Personality and Social Psychology, 62*, 699–707.

Salovey, P., & Rodin, J. (1991). Provoking jealousy and envy: Domain relevance and self–esteem threat. *Journal of Social and Clinical Psychology, 10*, 395–413.

Salovey, P., Mayer, J. D., & Rosenhan, D. L. (1991). Mood and helping: Mood as a motivator of helping and helping as a regulator of mood. In M. S. Clark (Ed.), *Prosocial behavior* (pp. 215–237). Newbury Park, CA: Sage.

Sampson, E. E. (1978). Scientific paradigms and social values: Wanted a scientific revolution. *Journal of Personality and Social Psychology, 36*, 1332–1343.

Sampson, E. E. (1991). *Social worlds, personal lives.* New York: Harcourt Brace Jovanovich.

Sanbonmatsu, D. M., Shavitt, S., & Sherman, S. J. (1991). The role of personal relevance in the formation of distinctiveness–based illusory correlations. *Personality and Social Psychology Bulletin, 17*, 124–132.

Sanchez, E., & Wiesenfeld, E. (1987). Environmental psychology: A new field of application in psychology and a new professional role for the psychologist. *Interamerican Journal of Psychology, 21*, 90–100.

Sanders Thompson, V. L. (1988). *A multi–faceted approach to racial identification.* Unpublished doctoral dissert at ion, Duke University, Durham, NC.

Sanders Thompson, V. L. (1990). Factors affecting the level of African American identification. *Journal of Black Psychology, 17*, 14–23.

Sanders Thompson, V. L. (1991). Perceptions of race and race relations which affect African American identification. *Journal of Applied Social Psychology, 21*, 1502–1516.

Sanders, G. S. (1983). An attentional process model of social facilitation. In A. Hare, H. Blumberg, V. Kent, and M. Davies (Eds.), *Small groups.* London: Wiley.

Sanders, G. S. (1984). Effects of context cues on eyewitness identification responses. *Journal of Applied Social Psychology, 14*, 386–397.

Sanders, G. S., & Chiu, W. (1988). Eyewitness errors in the free recall of actions. *Journal of Applied Social Psychology, 18*, 1241–1259.

Schachter, S. (1951). Deviation, rejection, and communication. *Journal of Abnormal and Social Psychology, 46*, 190–207.

Schachter, S. (1959). *The psychology of affiliation.* Stanford, CA: Stanford University Press.

Schachter, S., & Singer, J. E. (1962). Cognitive, social and physiological determinants of emotional states.

Psychological Review, 69, 379–399.

Schaller, M. (1992). In–group favoritism and statistical reasoning in social inference: Implications for formation and maintenance of group stereotypes. *Journal of Personality and Social Psychology, 63,* 61–74.

Schaller, M., & Maas, A. (1989). Illusory correlation and social categorization: Toward an integration of motivational and cognitive factors in stereotype formation. *Journal of Personality and Social Psychology, 56,* 709–721.

Scheier, M. F., & Carver, C. S. (1987). Dispositional optimism and physical well–being: The influence of generalized outcome expectancies in health. *Journal of Personality, 55,* 169–210.

Scheier, M. F., Matthews, K. A., Owens, J. F., Magovern, G. J., Sr., Lefebvre, R. C., Abbott, R. A., & Carver, C. S. (1989). Dispositional optimism and recovery from coronary artery bypass surgery: The beneficial effects on physical and psychological well–being. *Journal of Personality and Social Psychology, 57,* 1024–1040.

Scher, S. J., & Cooper, J. (1989). Motivational basis of dissonance: The singular role of behavioral consequences. *Journal of Personality and Social Psychology, 56,* 899–906.

Schiller, B. (1932). A quantitative analysis of marriage selection in a small group. *Journal of Social Psychology, 3,* 297–319.

Schleifer, S. J., Keller, S. E., Camerino, M., Thornton, J. C., & Stein, M. (1983). Suppression of lymphocyte function following bereavement. *Journal of the American Medical Association, 250,* 374–377.

Schlenker, B. R. (1980). *Impression management: The self–concept, social identity, and interpersonal relations.* Belmont, CA: Brooks/Cole.

Schmidt, G., & Weiner, B. (1988). An attributional affectation theory of behavior: Replications of judgments of helping. *Personality and Social Psychology Bulletin, 14,* 610–621.

Schmitt, B., Gilovich, T., Goore, H., & Joseph, L. (1986). Mere presence and social facilitation: One more time. *Journal of Experimental Social Psychology, 22,* 242–248.

Schneider, K. (1991, August 13). Ranges of animals and plants head north. *New York Times,* pp. C1, C9.

Schneider, S. H. (1989). *Global warming.* San Francisco: Sierra Club.

Schoenrade, P. A., Batson, C. D., Brandt, J. R., & Loud, R. E. (1986). Attachment, accountability, and motivation to benefit another not in distress. *Journal of Personality and Social Psychology, 51,* 557–563.

Schooler, J. W., & Engstler–Schooler, T. Y. (1990). Verbal overshadowing of visual memories: Some things are better left unsaid. *Cognitive Psychology, 22,* 36–71.

Schooler, J. W., & Loftus, E. F. (1986). Individual differences and experimentation: Complementary approaches to interrogative suggestibility. *Social Behaviour, 1,* 105–112.

Schullo, S. A., & Alperson, B. I. (1984). Interpersonal phenomenology as a function of sexual orientation, sex, sentiment, and trait categories in long–term dyadic relationships. *Journal of Personality and Social Psychology, 47,* 983–1002.

Schuster, E., & Elderton, E. M. (1906). The inheritance of psychical characters. *Biometrika, 5,* 460–469.

Schwalbe, M. L. (1991). Role–taking, self–monitoring, and the alignment of conduct with others. *Personality and Social Psychology Bulletin, 17,* 51–57.

Schwartz, S. H., & Gottlieb, A. (1980). Bystander anonymity and reaction to emergencies. *Journal of Personality and Social Psychology, 39,* 418–430.

Schwartz, S.H. & Bilsky, W. (1987). Towards a psychological structure of human values. *Journal of Personality and Social Psychology, 53,* 550–562.

Schwartz, S.H. (1992). The universal content and structure of values: Theoretical advances and empirical tests in 20 countries. In M. Zanna (Ed.), *Advances in experimental social psychology* (Vol. 25, pp. 1–65). New York: Academic Press.

Schwarz, N. (1990). Feelings as information: Informational and motivational functions of affective states. In R. Sorrentino & E. T. Higgins (Eds.), *Handbook of motivation and cognition: Foundations of social behavior* (Vol. 2, pp. 527–561). New York: Guilford.

Schwarz, N., & Bless, H. (1992). Scandals and the public's trust in politicians: Assimilation and contrast effects. *Personality and Social Psychology Bulletin, 13,* 574–579.

Schwarz, N., Bless, H., Strack, F., Klumpp, G., Rittenauer–Schatka, G., & Simons, A. (1991). Ease of retrieval as information: Another look at the availability heuristic. *Journal of Personality and Social Psychology, 61,* 195–202.

Schwarzwald, J., Amir, Y,., & Crain, R. L. (1992). Long–term effects of school desegregation experiences on interpersonal relations in the Israeli defense forces. *Personality and Social Psychology Bulletin, 18,* 357–368.

Scott, J. P. (1992). Aggression: Functions and control in social systems. *Aggressive Behavior, 18,* 1–20.

Sears, D. O., & Allen, H. M., Jr. (1984). The trajectory of local desegregation controversies and whites' opposition to busing. In N. Miller & M. Brewer (Eds.), *Groups in contact: The psychology of desegregation.* (pp. 123–151). Orlando, FL: Academic Press.

Sears, D. O., & Kinder, D. R. (1985). Whites' opposition to busing: On conceptualizing and operationalizing group conflict. *Journal of Personality and Social Psychology, 48,* 1141–1147.

Sears, D.O. (1986). College sophomores in the laboratory: Influences of a narrow data base on social psychology's view of human nature. *Journal of Personality and Social Psychology, 51,* 515-530.

Sedikides, C. (1992). Attentional effects on mood are moderated by chronic self–conception valence. *Personality and Social Psychology Bulletin, 18,* 580–584.

Segal, M. M. (1974). Alphabet and attraction: An unobtrusive measure of the effect of propinquity in a field setting. *Journal of Personality and Social Psychology, 30,* 654–657.

Seligman, M. E. P. (1975). *On depression, development, and death.* San Francisco: Freeman.

Selye, H. (1956). *The stress of life.* New York: McGraw–Hill.

Seta, J. J., Seta, C. E., & Wang, M. A. (1991). Feelings of negativity and stress: An averaging summation analysis of impressions of negative life experiences. *Personality and Social Psychology Bulletin, 17,* 376–384.

Shaffer, D. R., & Graziano, W. G. (1983). Effects of positive and negative moods on helping tasks having pleasant or unpleasant consequences. *Motivation and Emotion, 7,* 269–278.

Shanab, N. E., & Yahya, K. A. (1977). A behavioral study of obedience in children. *Journal of Personality and Social Psychology, 35,* 530–536.

Shapiro, D. L., Buttner, E. H., & Barry, B. (1992). Explanations: What factors enhance their perceived adequacy? *Organizational Behavior and Human Decision Processes.*

Shapiro, D.M., & Stelcner, M. (1987). Earning disparities among linguistic groups in Quebec, 1970–1980. *Analyse de politique, 13,* 97–104.

Shapiro, J. P. (1988). Relationships between dimensions of depressive experience and evaluative beliefs about people in general. *Personality and Social Psychology Bulletin, 14,* 388–400.

Shaver, P. R., & Brennan, K. A. (1992). Attachment styles and the "big five" personality traits: Their connections with each other and with romantic relationship outcomes. *Personality and Social Psychology Bulletin, 18,* 536–545.

Shavitt, S. (1989). Operationalizing functional theories of attitudes. In A. R. Pratkanis, S. J. Breckler, & A. G. Greenwald (Eds.), *Attitude structure and function* (pp. 311–337). Hillsdale, NJ: Erlbaum.

Shavitt, S. (1990). the role of attitude objects in attitude functions. Journal of Experimental Social Psychology, *26,* 124–148.

Shepard, M. (1987). *Interventions withmen who batter: An evaluation of a domestic abuse program.* Paper presented at the Third National Family Violence Research Conference. Durham, NH.

Sheppard, B. H., Bazerman, M. H., & Lewicki, R. J. (Eds.). (1990). *Research in negotiation in organizations* (Vol. 2). Greenwich, CT: JAI Press.

Shepperd, J. A., & Kashani, J. H. (1991). The relationship of hardiness, gender, and stress to health outcomes in adolescents. *Journal of Personality, 59,* 747–768.

Sher, J. (1983). *White hoods: Canada's Ku Klux Klan.* Vancouver: New Star Books.

Sherif, M. (1935). A study of some social factors in perception. *Archives of Psychology,* No. 187.

Sherif, M., Harvey, O. J., White, B. J., Hood, W. E., & Sherif, C. W. (1961). *Intergroup conflict and cooperation: The Robbers Cave experiment.* Norman, OK: Institute of Group Relations.

Sherman, S. J., Presson, C. C., & Chassin, L. (1984). Mechanisms underlying the false consensus effect: The special role of threats to the self. *Personality and Social Psychology Bulletin, 10,* 127–138.

Sherman, S. S. (1980). On the self–erasing nature of errors of prediction. *Journal of Personality and Social Psychology, 16,* 388–403.

Shields, N.M., & Hanneke, C.R. (1983). Attribution processes in violent relationships: Perceptions of violent husbands and thei wives. *Journal of Applied Social Psychology, 13,* 515–517.

Shotland, R. I., & Strau, M. K. (1976). Bystander response to an assault: When a man attacks a woman. *Journal of Personality and Social Psychology, 34,* 990–999.

Showers, C. (1992a). Compartmentalization of positive and negative self–knowledge: Keeping bad apples out of the bunch. *Journal of Personality and Social Psychology, 62,* 1036–1049.

Showers, C. (1992b). Evaluative integrative thinking about characteristics of the self. *Personality and Social Psychology Bulletin, 18,* 719–729.

Shweder, R. & Bourne, E.J., (1982). Does the concept of the person vary cross–culturally ? In A.J. Marsella & G.M. White (Eds.), *Cultural conceptions of mental health and therapy.* Dordrecht, Holland: D. Riedel.

Sigelman, C. K., Thomas, D. B., Sigelman, L., & Ribich, F. D. (1986). Gender, physical attractiveness, and electability: An experimental invesigation of voter biases. *Journal of Applied Social Psychology, 16,* 229–248.

Sigelman, C.K., Berry, C.J., & Wiles, K.A. (1984). Violence in college students' dating relationships. *Journal of Applied Social Psychology, 5,* 530–548.

Simmons, C. H., vom Kolke, A., & Shimizu, H. (1986). Attitudes toward romantic love among American, German, and Japanese students. *Journal of Social Psychology, 126,* 327–336.

Simmons, D. D., Binney, S. E., & Dodd, B. (1992). Valuing "a clean environment": Factor location, norms, and relation to risks. *Journal of Social Behavior and Personality, 7,* 649–658.

Simpson, J. A. (1987). The dissolution of romantic relationships: Factors involved in relationship stability and emotional stress. *Journal of Personality and Social Psychology, 53,* 683–692.

Simpson, M., & Perry, J. D. (1990). Crime and climate: A reconsideration. *Environment and Behavior, 22,* 295–300.

Sinha, D. (1986). *Psychology in a Third World country: The Indian experience.* New Delhi: Sage.

Sivacek, J., & Crano, W. D. (1982). Vested interest as a moderator of attitude–behavior consistency. *Journal of Personality and Social Psychology, 43,* 210–221.

Skelton, J. A., & Strohmetz, D. (1990). Priming symptom reports with health–related cognitive activity. *Personality and Social Psychology Bulletin, 16,* 449–464.

Skinner, B. F. (1986). What is wrong with daily life in the Western world? *American Psychologist, 41,* 568–574.

Slater, E. J., & Calhoun, K. S. (1988). Familial conflict and marital dissolution: Effects on the social functioning of college students. *Journal of Social and Clinical Psychology. 65,* 118–126.

Smith, A., & Stansfeld, S. (1986). Aircraft noise exposure, noise sensitivity, and everyday errors. *Environment and Behavior, 18,* 214–226.

Smith, D. E., Gier, J. A., & Willis, F. N. (1982). Interpersonal touch and compliance with a marketing request. *Basic and Applied Social Psychology, 3,* 35–38.

Smith, E. R. (1989). *Interpersonal attraction as a function of similarity and assumed similarity in traditional gender role adherence.* Unpublished doctoral dissertation, University at Albany, State University of New York.

Smith, K. D., Keating, J. P., & Stotland, E. (1989). Altruism reconsidered: The effect of denying feedback on a victim's status to empathetic witnesses. *Journal of Personality and Social Psychology, 57,* 641–650.

Smith, P. B., & Bond, N. H. (1993). *Social psychology across cultures.* Boston: Allyn & Bacon.

Smith, R. E., Smoll, F. L., & Ptacek, J. T. (1990). Conjunctive moderator variables in vulnerability and resiliency research: Life stress, social support and coping skills, and adolescent sport injuries. *Journal of Personality and Social Psychology, 58,* 360–370.

Smith, R. H., Kim, S. H., & Parrott, W. G. (1988). Envy and jealousy: Semantic problems and experiential distinctions. *Personality and Social Psychology Bulletin, 14*, 401–409.

Smith, S. M., & Shaffer, D. R. (1991). Celerity and cajolery: Rapid speech may promote or inhibit persuasion through its impact on message elaboration. *Personality and Social Psychology Bulletin, 17*, 663–669.

Smith, S. S., & Richardson, D. (1985). On deceiving ourselves about deception: Reply to Rubin. *Journal of Personality and Social Psychology, 48*, 254–255.

Smith, T. W., & Christensen, A. J. (1992). Cardiovascular reactivity and interpersonal relations: Psychosomatic processes in social context. *Journal of Social and Clinical Psychology, 11*, 279–301.

Smith, T. W., & Pope, M. K. (1990). Cynical hostility as a health risk: Current status and future directions. *Journal of Social Behavior and Personality, 5*, 77–88.

Smith, T. W., & Williams, P. G. (1992). Personality and health: Advantages and limitations of the five–factor model. *Journal of Personality, 60*, 395–423.

Smith, V. I., & Ellsworth, P. C. (1987). The social psychology of eyewitness accuracy: Misleading questions and communicator expertise. *Journal of Applied Psychology, 72*, 294–300.

Sniffen, M. J. (1991, September 30). Blacks make up 40% of death row. *Albany Times Union,* p. A–3.

Snyder, C. R., & Endelman, J. R. (1979). Effects of degree of interpersonal similarity on physical distance and self–reported attraction: A comparison of uniqueness and reinforcement theory predictions. *Journal of Personality, 47*, 492–505.

Snyder, C. R., & Fromkin, H. L. (1980). *Uniqueness: The human pursuit of difference.* New York: Plenum.

Snyder, M. (1974). Self-monitoring of expressive behavior. *Journal of Personality and Social Psychology, 30*, 526–537.

Snyder, M., & Ickes, W. (1985). Personality and social behavior. In G. Lindzey & E. Aronson (Eds.), *The handbook of social psychology* (Vol. 1, 3rd ed., pp. 883–947). New York: Random House.

Snyder, M., & Simpson, J. A. (1984). Self–monitoring and dating relationships. *Journal of Personality and Social Psychology, 47*, 1281–1291.

Snyder, M., & Swann, W. B., Jr. (1978) Behavioral confirmation in social interaction: From social perception to social reality. *Journal of Experimental Social Psychology, 14*, 148–162.

Snyder, M., Gangestad, S., & Simpson, J. A. (1983). Choosing friends as activity partners: The role of self–monitoring. *Journal of Personality and Social Psychology, 45*, 1061–1072.

Sogin, S. R., & Pallak, M. S. (1976). Bad decisions, responsibility, and attitude change: Effects of violation, foreseeability, and locus of causality of negative consequences. *Journal of Personality and Social Psychology, 33*, 300–306.

Solano, C. H., & Koester, N. H. (1989). Loneliness and communication problems: Subjective anxiety or objective skills? *Personality and Social Psychology Bulletin, 15*, 126–133.

Solano, C. H., Barren, P. G., & Parish, E. A. (1982). Loneliness and patterns of self–disclosure. *Journal of Personality and Social Psychology, 43*, 524–531.

Solomon, R. C. (1981, October). The love lost in cliches. *Psychology Today,* pp. 83–85, 87–88.

Sonkin, D.J., Martin, D., & Walker, L.E.A. (1986). *The male batterer: A treatment approach.* New York: Springer.

Spencer, J. (1990). Collective violence and everyday practice in Sri Lanka. *Journal of Asian Studies, 24*, 603–623.

Srull, T. K., & Wyer, R. S. (1989). Person memory and judgment. *Psychological Review, 96*, 58–83.

Staats, A. W., & Staats, C. K. (1958). Attitudes established by classical conditioning. *Journal of Abnormal and Social Psychology, 15*, 37–40.

Staats, A. W., Staats, C. K., & Crawford, H. L. (1962). First–order conditioning of meaning and the parallel conditioning of GSR. *Journal of General Psychology, 67*, 159–167.

Stalling, R. (1992). Mood and pain: The influence of positive and negative affect on reported body aches. *Journal of Social Behavior and Personality, 7*, 323–334.

Standing, L., Lynn, D., & Moxness, K. (1990). Effects of noise upon introverts and extraverts. *Bulletin of the Psychonomic Society, 28*, 138–140.

Stasser, G. (1992). Pooling of unshared information during group discussion. In S. Worchel, W. Wood, & J. H. Simpson (Eds.), *Process and productivity* (pp. 48–67). Newbury Park, CA: Sage.

Stasser, G., & Stewart, D. (1992). Discovery of hidden profiles by decision–making groups: Solving a problem versus making a judgment. *Journal of Personality and Social Psychology, 63*, 426–434.

Stasser, G., & Titus, W. (1985). Pooling of unshared information in group decision making: Biased information sampling during discussion. *Journal of Personality and Social Psychology, 48*, 1467–1478.

Stasser, G., & Titus, W. (1987). Effects of information load and percentage of shared information on the dissemination of unshared information during group discussion. *Journal of Personality and Social Psychology, 55*, 81–93.

Stasser, G., Kerr, N. L., & Davis, J. H. (1989). Influence processes and consensus models in decision–making groups. In P. B. Paulus (Ed.), *Psychology of influence* (2nd ed.). Hillsdale, NJ: Erlbaum.

Stasser, G., Taylor, L. A., & Hanna, C. (1989). Information sampling in structured and unstructured discussions of three- and six-person groups. *Journal of Personality and Social Psychology, 57*, 67–78.

Steele, C. M., Critchlow, B., & Liu, T. J. (1985). Alcohol and social behavior: The helpful drunkard. *Journal of Personality and Social Psychology, 48*, 35–46.

Steinberg, R., & Shapiro, S. (1982). Sex differences in personality traits of female and male master of business administration students. *Journal of Applied Psychology, 67*, 306–310.

Steiner, I. D. (1972). *Process and productivity.* New York: Academic Press.

Steiner, I. D. (1976). Task–performing groups. In J. W. Thibaut, J. T. Spence, & R. C. Carson (Eds.), *Contemporary topics in social psychology.* Morristown, NJ: General Learning Press.

Steiner, I.D. (1974). Whatever happened to the group in social psychology? *Journal of Experimental Social Psychology, 10*, 94–108.

Steinfels, P. (1992, January 20). Apathy is seen toward agony of the homeless. *New York Times,* pp. Al, B7.

Stephan, W. G. (1985). Intergroup relations. In G. Lindzey & E. Aronson (Eds.), *Handbook of social psychology* (Vol. 2, pp. 599–658). New York: Random House.

Stephan, W. G., & Stephan, C. W. (1988). Emotional reactions to interracial achievement outcomes. *Journal of Applied Social Psychology, 19,* 608–621.

Stern, P. C. (1992). Psychological dimensions of global environmental change. In M. R. Rosenzweig & L. W. Porter (Eds.), *Annual review of psychology* (Vol. 43, pp. 269–302). Palo Alto, CA: Annual Reviews, Inc.

Sternberg, R. J. (1986). A triangular theory of love. *Psychological Review, 93,* 119–135.

Sternberg, R. J. (1988). Triangulating love. In R. J. Sternberg & M. L. Barnes (Eds.), *The psychology of love* (pp. 119–138). New Haven, CT: Yale University Press.

Stevens, W. K. (1992, February 25). Global warming threatens to undo decades of conservation efforts. *New York Times,* p. C4.

Stevens, W. K. (1991b, February 19). Warming of globe could build on itself, some scientists say. *New York Times,* p. C4.

Stewart, J. E. (1980). Defendant's attractiveness as a factor in the outcome of criminal trials: An observational study. *Journal of Applied Social Psychology, 10,* 348–361.

Stier, D. S., & Hall, J. A. (1984). Gender differences in touch: An empirical and theoretical review. *Journal of Personality and Social Psychology, 47,* 440–459.

Stiles, W. B., Shuster, P. L., & Harrigan, J. A. (1992). Disclosure and anxiety: A test of the fever model. *Journal of Personality and Social Psychology, 63,* 980–988.

Stinson, L., & Ickes, W. (1992). Empathic accuracy in the interactions of male friends versus male strangers. *Journal of Personality and Social Psychology, 62,* 787–797.

Stone, A. A., Cox, D., Valdimarsdotti, H., Jandorf, L., & Neale, J. M. (1987). Evidence that secretory IGA antibody is associated with daily mood. *Journal of Personality and Social Psychology, 52,* 988–993.

Stoner, J. A. F. (1961). *A comparison of individual and group decisions involving risk.* Unpublished master's thesis, School of Industrial Management, MIT.

Straus, M.A., & Gelles, R.J. (1985). *Is family violence increasing? A comparison of 1975 and 1985 national survey rates.* Paper presented at the American Society of Criminology, San Diego, CA.

Straus, M.A., Gelles, R.J., & Steinmetz, S. (1980). *Behind closed doors: Violence in the American family.* Garden City, NY: Doubleday.

Street, R. L., Jr., & Buller, D. G. (1987). Nonverbal response patterns in physician–patient interactions: A functional analysis. *Journal of Nonverbal Behavior, 11,* 234–253.

Strentz, T., & Auerbach, S. M. (1988). Adjustment to the stress of simulated captivity: Effects of emotion–focused versus problem–focused preparation on hostages differing in locus of control. *Journal of Personality and Social Psychology, 55,* 652–660.

Strickland, L.H., Aboud, F.E., & Gergen, K.J. (Eds.). (1974). *Social psychology in transition.* New York: Plenum Press.

Stroessner, S. J., Hamilton, D. L., & Mackie, D. M. (1992). Affect and stereotyping: The effect of induced mood on distinctiveness–based illusory correlations. *Journal of Personality and Social Psychology, 62,* 564–576.

Strube, M. J., & Garcia, J. E. (1981). A meta-analytic investigation of Fiedler's contingency model of leadership effectiveness. *Psychological Bulletin, 90,* 307–321.

Sullins, E. S. (1991). Emotional contagion revisited: Effects of social comparison and expressive style on mood convergence. *Personality and Social Psychology Bulletin, 17,* 166–174.

Sulman, F. G., Levy, D., Levy, A., Pfeifer, Y., Saperstein, E., & Tal, E. (1974). Ionometry of hot, dry desert winds (*sharav*) and application of ionizing treatment to weather–sensitive patients. *International Journal of Biometeorology, 13,* 393.

Suls, J., & Fletcher, B. (1985). The relative efficacy of avoidant and nonavoidant coping strategies: A meta–analysis. *Health Psychology, 4,* 249–288.

Suls, J., & Greenwald, A. G. (Eds.). (1986). *Psychological perspectives on the self* (Vol. 3). Hillsdale, NJ: Erlbaum.

Suls, J., & Rosnow, J. (1988). Concerns about artifacts in behavioral research. In M. Morawski (Ed.), *The rise of experimentation in American psychology* (pp. 163–187). New Haven, CT: Yale University Press.

Suls, J., & Wan, C. K. (1987). In search of the false uniqueness phenomenon: Fear and estimates of social consensus. *Journal of Personality and Social Psychology, 52,* 211–217.

Suls, J., & Wan, C. K. (1989). The effects of sensory and procedural information on coping with stressful medical procedures and pain: A meta–analysis. *Journal of Consulting and Clinical Psychology, 57,* 372–379.

Suls, J., Wan, C. K., & Sanders, G. S. (1988). False consensus and false uniqueness in estimating the prevalence of health–protective behaviors. *Journal of Applied Social Psychology, 19,* 66–79.

Summers, R. J. (1991). The influence of affirmative action on perceptions of a beneficiary's qualifications. *Journal of Applied Social Psychology, 21,* 1265–1276.

Sunnafrank, M. (1992). On debunking the attitude similarity myth. *Communication Monographs, 59,* 165–179.

Sunstein, C. R. (1993). Valuing life. *New Republic, 208*(7), 36–40.

Swallow, S. R., & Kuiper, N. A. (1987). The effects of depression and cognitive vulnerability to depression on judgments of similarity between self and other. *Motivation and Emotion, 11,* 157–167.

Swann, W. B., Jr., Griffin, J. J., Jr., Predmore, S. C., & Gaines, B. (1987). Cognitive-affective crossfire: When self-consistency meets self–enhancement. *Journal of Personality and Social Psychology, 52,* 881–889.

Swann, W. B., Jr., Hixon, J. G., & De La Ronde, C. (1992). Embracing the bitter "truth": Negative self-concepts and marital commitment. *Psychological Science, 3,* 118–121.

Swann, W. B., Jr., Stein-Seroussi, A., & Giesler, R. B. (1992). Why people self–verify. *Journal of Personality and Social Psychology, 62,* 392–401.

Swap, W. C. (1977). Interpersonal attraction and repeated exposure to rewarders and punishers. *Personality and Social Psychology Bulletin, 3,* 248–251.

Szymanski, K., & Harkins, S. (1987). Social loafing and self–evaluation with a social standard. *Journal of Personality and Social Psychology, 55,* 891–897.

Tajfel, H. (1970). Experiments in intergroup discrimination. *Scientific American, 223* (5), 96–102.

Tajfel, H. (1978). *Differentiation between social groups: Studies in the social psychology of intergroup relations.* London: Academic Press.

Tajfel, H. (1982). *Social identity and intergroup relations.* Cambridge: Cambridge University Press.

Tajfel, H., & Turner, J.C. (1979). An integrative theory of intergroup conflict. In W.G. Austin & S. Worchel (Eds.), *The social psychology of intergroup relations* (pp. 33–47). Monterey, CA: Brooks/Cole.

Takahashi, T. (1991). A comparative study of Japanese and American group dynamics. *Psychoanalytic Review, 78*(1), 49–62.

Tanford, S., & Penrod, S. (1984). Social influence model: A formal integration of research on majority and minority influence processes. *Psychological Bulletin, 95,* 189–225.

Taylor, D.M. (1981). Stereotypes and intergroup relations. In R.C. Gardner & R. Kalin (Eds.), *A Canadian social psychology of ethnic relations* (pp. 151–171). Toronto: Methuen.

Taylor, D.M., & Brown, R.J. (1979). Towards a more social social psychology? *British Journal of Social and Clinical Psychology, 18,* 173–180.

Taylor, D.M., & Gardner, R.C. (1969). Ethnic stereotypes: Their effects on the perception of communicators of varying credibility. *Canadian Journal of Psychology, 23,* 161-173.

Taylor, D.M., & Jaggi, V. (1974). Ethnocentrism in a south Indian context. *Journal of Cross–Cultural Psychology, 5,* 162–172.

Taylor, D.M., & McKirnan, D.J. (1984). A five-stage model of intergroup relations. *British Journal of Social Psychology, 23,* 291–300.

Taylor, D.M., & Moghaddam, F.M. (1987). *Theories of intergroup relations: International social psychological perspectives.* New York: Praeger.

Taylor, D.M., Doria, J.R., & Tyler, K. (1983). Group performance and cohesiveness: An attributional analysis. *Journal of Social Psychology, 119,* 187–198.

Taylor, D.M., Wong–Rieger, D., McKirnan, D.J., & Bercusson, T. (1982). Social comparison in a group context. *Journal of Social Psychology, 117,* 257–259.

Taylor, D.M., Wright, S.C., Moghaddam, F.M., & Lalonde, R.N. (1990). *Personality and Social Psychology Bulletin, 16,* 254–262.

Taylor, S. E., Buunk, B. P., & Aspinwall, L. G. (1990). Social comparison, stress, and coping. *Personality and Social Psychology Bulletin, 16,* 74–89.

Taylor, S. E., Helgeson, V. S., Reed, G. M., & Skokan, L. A. (1991). Self–generated feelings of control and adjustment to physical illness. *Journal of Social Issues, 47,* 91–109.

Taylor, S.E. (1989) *Positive illusions: Creative self–deception and the healthy mind.* New York: Basic Books.

Tedeschi, J. T., & Melburg, V. (1984). Impression management and influence in organizations. In S. B. Bacharach & E. J. Lawler (Eds.), *Research in the sociology of organizations* (Vol 3., pp. 31–58). Greenwich, CT: JAI Press.

Terry, R. L., & Macy, R. J. (1991). Children's social judgments of other children who wear eyeglasses. *Journal of Social Behavior and Personality, 6,* 965–974.

Tetlock, P. E., & Boettger, R. (1989). Accountability: A social magnifier of the dilution effect. *Journal of Personality and Social Psychology, 57,* 388–398.

Tetlock, P. E., Peterson, R. S., McGuire, C., Change, S., & Feld,

P. (1992). Assessing political group dynamics: A test of the groupthink model. *Journal of Personality and Social Psychology, 63,* 403–425.

Thomas, W. K. (1992). Conflict and negotiation processes. In M. Dunnette (Ed.), *Handbook of industrial and organizational psychology* (2nd ed.). Chicago: Rand McNally.

Thompson, L., Brodt, S. E., & Peterson, E. (1993). *Team versus solo negotiations: Are two heads better than one?* Unpublished manuscript, University of Washington, Seattle, WA.

Thompson, S. C., Sobolew–Shubin, A., Galbraith, M. E., Schwankovsky, L., & Cruzen, D. (1993). Maintaining perceptions of control: Finding perceived control in low–control circumstances. *Journal of Personality and Social Psychology, 64,* 293–304.

Thompson, W. C., Cowan, C. L., & Rosenhan, D. L. (1980). Focus of attention mediates the impact of negative affect on altruism. *Journal of Personality and Social Psychology, 38,* 291–300.

Thorne, A. (1987). The press of personality: A study of conversations between introverts and extraverts. *Journal of Personality and Social Psychology, 53,* 718–726.

Ting–Toomey, S. (1988). Intercultural conflict styles: A face–negotiation theory. In Y. Kim & W. Gudykunst (Eds.), *Theories in intercultural communication* (pp. 313–235). Newbury Park, Ca: Sage.

Ting–Toomey, S. (1991). Intimacy expressions in three cultures: France, Japan, and the United States. *International Journal of Intercultural Relations, 15,* 29–46.

Ting–Toomey, S., Gao, G., Trubisky, P., Yang, Z., Kim, H. S., Lin, S. L., & Nishida, T. (1991). Culture, face maintenance, and styles of handling interpersonal conflict: A study in five cultures. *International Journal of Conflict Management, 2,* 275–296.

Tooley, V., Brigham, J. C., Maass, A., & Bothwell, R. K. (1987). Facial recognition: Weapon effect and attentional focus. *Journal of Applied Social Psychology, 17,* 845–859.

Topf, M. (1989). Sensitivity to noise, personality hardiness, and noise–induced stress in critical care nurses. *Environment and Behavior, 21,* 717–733.

Torestad, B. (1990). What is anger provoking: A psychophysical study of perceived causes of anger. *Aggressive Behavior, 16,* 9–26.

Toufexis, A. (1989, July 17). Panic over power lines. *Time,* p. 71.

Toufexis, A. (1993). The right chemistry. *Time, 141*(7), 49–51.

Triandis, H.C. (1980). Introduction. In. H.C. Triandis & W.W. Lambert (Eds.) *Handbook of cross–cultural psychology, 1, Perspectives.* Boston: Allyn & Bacon.

Triandis, H.C. (1989) The self and social behavior in different cultural contexts. *Psychological Review, 96,* 506–20.

Triplett, H. (1898). The dynamogenic factors in pace making and competition. *American Journal of Psychology, 9,* 507–533.

Trope, Y. (1986). Identification and inferential processes in dispositional attribution. *Psychological Review, 93,* 239–257.

Turner, J. C., Hogg, M. A., Oakes, P. J., Reicher, S. D., & Wetherell, M. S. (1987). *Rediscovering the social group: A self–categorization theory.* Oxford, England: Blackwell.

Tversky, A., & Kahneman, D. (1973). Availability: A heuristic for judging frequency and probability. *Cognitive Psychology, 5,* 207–232.

Tversky, A., & Kahneman, D. (1982). Judgment under uncertainty: Heuristics and biases. In D. Kahnamen, P. Slovic, & A. Tversky (Eds.), *Judgment under uncertainty* (pp. 3–20). New York: Cambridge University Press.

Tyler, T. R., & Schuller, R. A. (1991). Aging and attitude change. *Journal of Personality and Social Psychology, 61,* 689–697.

Type A's lack cholesterol aid, study says. (1992, November 18). *Albany Times Union,* p. A–5.

Uchino, G. N., Kiecolt–Glaser, J. K., & Cacioppo, J. T. (1992). Age–related changes in cardiovascular response as a function of a chronic stressor and social support. *Journal of Personality and Social Psychology, 63,* 839–846.

Ullman, C. (1987). From sincerity to authenticity: Adolescents' view of the "true self. " *Journal of Personality, 55,* 583–595.

Urbanski, L. (1992, May 21). Study uncovers traits people seek in friends. *The Evangelist,* p. 41

Van Hook, E., & Higgins, E. T. (1988). Self–related problems beyond the self–concept: Motivational consequences of discrepant self–guides. *Journal of Personality and Social Psychology, 55,* 625–633.

Van Vianen, A. E. M., & Willemsen, T. M. (1992). The employment interview: The role of sex stereotypes in the evaluation of male and female job applicants in the Netherlands. *Journal of Applied Social Psychology, 22,* 471–491.

Vanbeselaere, N. (1987). The effects of dichotomous and crossed social categorization upon intergroup discrimination. *European Journal of Social Psychology, 17,* 143–156.

Vecchio, R. P. (1987). Situational leadership theory: An examination of a prescriptive theory. *Journal of Applied Psychology, 72,* 444–451.

Vining, J., & Ebreo, A. (1990). What makes a recycler? A comparison of recyclers and nonrecyclers. *Environment and Behavior, 22,* 55–73.

Vinokur, A., & Burnstein, E. (1974). Effects of partially shared persuasive arguments on group–induced shifts: A group problem–solving approach. *Journal of Personality and Social Psychology, 29,* 305–315.

Vitaliano, P. P. (1985). The Ways of Coping Checklist: Revision and psychometric properties. *Multivariate Behavioral Research, 20,* 3–26.

Vroom, V. H., & Jago, A. G. (1978). On the validity of the Vroom–Yetton model. *Journal of Applied Psychology, 63,* 151–26.

Vroom, V. H., & Yetton, P. W. (1973). *Leadership and decision–making.* Pittsburgh: University of Pittsburgh Press.

Wagner, P. J., & Curran, P. (1984). Health beliefs and physician identified "worried well. : *Health Psychology, 3,* 459–474.

Waller, N. G., Koietin, B. A., Bouchard, T. J., Jr., Lykken, D. T., & Tellegen, A. (1990). Genetic and environmental influences on religious interests, attitudes, and values: A study of twins reared apart and together. *Psychological Science, 1,* 138–142.

Walster, E., & Festinger, L. (1962). The effectiveness of "overheard" persuasive communication. *Journal of Abnormal and Social Psychology, 65,* 395–402.

Walster, E., Walster, G.W., & Berscheid, E. (1978) *Equity theory and research.* Boston: Allyn and Bacon.

Wann, D. L., & Branscombe, N. R. (1990). Person perception when aggressive or nonaggressive sports are primed. *Aggressive Behavior, 16,* 27–32.

Watson, D., & Clark, L. A. (1992). Affects separable and inseparable: On the hierarchical arrangement of the negative affects. *Journal of Personality and Social Psychology, 62,* 489–505.

Watson, O.M. (1970). *Proxemic behavior: A cross–cultural study.* The Hague: Mouton.

Watts, B. L. (1982). Individual differences in circadian activity rhythms and their effects on roommate relationships. *Journal of Personality, 50,* 374–384.

Wayne, S. J., & Kacmar, K. M. (1991). The effects of impression management on the performance appraisal process. *Organizational Behavior and Human Decision Processes, 48,* 70–88.

Wedell, D. H., Parducci, A., & Geiselman, R. E. (1987). A formal analysis of ratings of physical attractiveness: Successive contrast and simultaneous assimilation. *Journal of Experimental Social Psychology, 23,* 230–249.

Weenig, M. W. H., & Midden, C. J. H. (1991). Communication network influences on information diffusion and persuasion. *Journal of Personality and Social Psychology, 54,* 734–742.

Wegner, D. M., Short, J. W., Blake, A. W., & Page, M. S. (1990). The suppression of exciting thoughts. *Journal of Personality and Social Psychology, 58,* 409–418.

Weidner, G., Istvan, J., & McKnight, J. D. (1989). Clusters of behavioral coronary risk factors in employed women and men. *Journal of Applied Social Psychology, 19,* 468–480.

Weinberger, M., Hiner, S. L., & Tierney, W. M. (1987). In support of hassles as a measure of stress in predicting health outcomes. *Journal of Behavioral Medicine, 16,* 19–32.

Weiner, B. (1980). A cognitive (attribution) emotion–action model of motivated behavior: An analysis of judgments of helpgiving. *Journal of Personality and Social Psychology, 39,* 186–200.

Weiner, B., Amirkhan, J., Folkes, V. S., & Verette, J. A. (1987). An attributional analysis of excuse giving: Studies of a naive theory of emotion. *Journal of Personality and Social Psychology, 52,* 316–324.

Weldon, E., & Mustari, L. (1988). Felt dispensability in groups of coactors: The effects of shared responsibility and explicit anonymity on cognitive effort. *Organizational Behavior and Human Decision Processes, 41,* 330–351.

Wells, G. L. (1984). The psychology of lineup identification. *Journal of Applied Social Psychology, 14,* 89–103.

Wells, G. L., & Luus C. A. E. (1990). Police lineups as experiments: Social methodology as a framework for properly conducted lineups. *Personality and Social Psychology Bulletin, 16,* 106–117.

Wells, G. L., Wrightsman, L. S., & Miene, P. K. (1985). The timing of the defense opening statement: Don't wait until the evidence is in. *Journal of Applied Social Psychology, 15,* 758–772.

Werner, C. M., Altman, I., & Brown, B. B. (1992). A transactional approach to interpersonal relations: Physical environment, social context, and temporal qualities. *Journal of Social and Personal Relationships, 9,* 297–323.

Werner, C. M., Strube, M. J., Cole, A. M., & Kagehiro, D. K. (1985). The impact of case characteristics and prior jury experience on jury verdicts. *Journal of Applied Social Psychology, 15,* 409–427.

Weyant, J. M. (1986). *Applied social psychology.* New York: Oxford University Press.

White, G. L. (1980). Inducing jealousy: A power perspective. *Personality and Social Psychology Bulletin, 6,* 222–227.

White, G. L., & Mullen, P. E. (1990). *Jealousy: Theory, research, and clinical strategies.* New York: Guilford.

White, J. L. & Parham, T. (1990). *The psychology of blacks: An African-American perspective.* Englewood Cliffs, NJ: Prentice Hall.

White, R. K. (1977). Misperception in the Arab-Israeli conflict. *Journal of Social Issues, 33,* 190–221.

Whitley, G. E., & Greenberg, M. S. (1986). The role of eyewitness confidence in juror perceptions of credibility. *Journal of Applied Social Psychology, 16,* 387–409.

Whyte, W. W., Jr. (1956). *The organization man.* New York: Simon and Schuster.

Wicker, A. W. (1969). Attitudes versus actions: The relationship of verbal and overt behavioral responses to attitude objects. *Journal of Social Issues, 25,* 41–78.

Wiebe, D. J., & McCallum, D. M. (1986). Health practices and hardiness as mediators in the stress–illness relationship. *Health Psychology, 5,* 425–438.

Wiegele, T. C., & Oots, K. L. (1990). Type A behavior and local government elites. *Political Psychology, 11,* 721–737.

Wilder, D. A. (1977). Perception of groups, size of opposition, and social influence. *Journal of Experimental Social Psychology, 13,* 253–268.

Wilder, D. A. (1984). Intergroup contact: The typical member and the exception to the rule. *Journal of Experimental Social Psychology, 20,* 177–194.

Williams, J. G., & Solano, C. H. (1983). The social reality of feeling lonely: Friendship and reciprocation. *Personality and Social Psychology Bulletin, 9,* 237–242.

Williams, K. D., & Karau, S. J. (1991). Social loafing and social compensation: The effects of expectations of co–worker performance. *Journal of Personality and Social Psychology, 61,* 570–581.

Williams, K., Harkins, S., & Latane, B. (1981). Identifiability as a deterrent to social loafing: Two cheering experiments. *Journal of Personality and Social Psychology, 40,* 303–311.

Williams, R. L. (1976). *Manual of directions for Williams awareness sentence completion.* St. Louis, MO: Robert L. Williams & Associates, Inc.

Williams, T.M. (Ed.) (1986). *The impact of television: a natural experiment in three communities.* New York: Academic Press.

Wilson, D. K., Kaplan, R. M., & Schneiderman, L. J. (1987). Framing of decisions and selections of alternatives in health care. *Social Behavior, 2,* 51–59.

Wilson, D. W. (1981). Is helping a laughing matter? *Psychology, 18,* 6–9.

Wilson, J. P., & Petruska, R. (1984). Motivation, model attributes, and prosocial behavior. *Journal of Personality and Social Psychology, 46,* 458–468.

Winn, K. I., Crawford, D. W., & Fischer, J. (1991). Equity and commitment in romance versus friendship. *Journal of Social Behavior and Personality, 6,* 301–314.

Wolf, S., & Bugaj, A. M. (1990). The social impact of courtroom witnesses. *Social Behaviour, 5,* 1–13.

Wolfe, S. (1985). Manifest and latent influence of majorities and minorities. *Journal of Personality and Social Psychology, 48,* 899–908.

Wood, W. (1982). Retrieval of attitude–relevant information from memory: Effects on susceptibility to persuasion on intrinsic motivation. *Journal of Personality and Social Psychology, 42,* 798–810.

Wood, W., Wong, F. Y., & Chachere, J. G. (1991). Effects of media violence on viewers' aggression in unconstrained social interaction. *Psychological Bulletin, 109,* 371–383.

Woodall, W. G., & Burgoon, J. R. (1984). Talking fast and changing attitudes: A critique and clarification. *Journal of Nonverbal Behavior, 8,* 126–142.

Wortman, C. B., & Linsenmeier, J. A. W. (1977). Interpersonal attraction and techniques of ingratiation in organizational settings. In B. N. Staw & G. R. Salancik (Eds.), *New directions in organizational behavior* (pp. 133–178). Chicago: St. Clair Press.

Wright, M.J., & Myers, C.R. (Eds.) (1982). History of academic psychology in Canada. Toronto: Hogrefe.

Wright, P. H. (1984). Selfreferent motivation and the intrinsic quality of friendship. *Journal of Social and Personal Relationships, 1,* 115–130.

Wu, C., & Shaffer, D. R. (1987). Susceptibility to persuasive appeals as a function of source credibility and prior experience with the attitude object. *Journal of Personality and Social Psychology, 52,* 677–688.

Wuensch, K. L., Castellow, W. A., & Moore, C. H. (1991). Effects of defendant attractiveness and type of crime on juridic judgment. *Journal of Social Behavior and Personality, 6,* 713–724.

Wyer, R. S. (1988). Social memory and social judgment. In P. R. Solomon, G. R. Goethals, C. M. Kelley, & B. R. Stephens (Eds.), *Perspectives on the research.* New York: Springer–Verlag.

Wyer, R. W., & Srull, T. K. (1984). Human cognition in its social context. *Psychological Review, 93,* 322–359.

Wyer, R. W., & Srull, T. X. (1980). Category accessibility and social perception: Some implications for the study of person memory and interpersonal judgments. *Journal of Personality and Social Psychology, 28,* 841–856.

Yamagishi, T. (1988). Exit from the group as an individualistic solution to free rider problem in the United States and Japan. *Journal of Experimental Social Psychology, 24,* 530–542.

Yamagishi, T. (1988). Exit from the group as an individualistic solution to free rider problems in the United States and Japan. *Journal of Experimental Social Psychology, 24,* 530–542.

Yates, S. (1992). Lay attributions about distress after a natural disaster. *Personality and Social Psychology Bulletin, 18,* 217–222.

Young, J. E. (1982). Loneliness, depression, and cognitive therapy: Theory and application. In L. A. Peplau & D. Perlman (Eds.), *Loneliness: A sourcebook of current theory, research, and therapy.* New York: Wiley.

Young, M.Y., & Gardner, R.C. (1990). Modes of acculturation and second language proficiency. *Canadian Journal of Behavioral Science, 22,* 59–71.

Yuille, J. (1993) *American Psychologist, 48.*

Yuille, J. C., & Cutshall, J. L. (1986). A case study of eyewitness memory of a crime. *Journal of Applied Psychology, 71,* 291–301.

Yuille, J. C., & McEwan, N. H. (1985). Use of hypnosis as an aid to eyewitness memory. *Journal of Applied Psychology, 70,* 389–400.

Yuille, J. C., & Tollestrup, P. A. (1990). Some effects of alcohol on eyewitness memory. *Journal of Applied Psychology, 75,* 268–273.

Yukl, G. (1981). *Leadership in organizations.* Englewood Cliffs, NJ: Prentice–Hall.

Yukl, G. (1989). *Leadership in organizations* (2nd ed.). Englewood Cliffs, NJ: Prentice–Hall.

Yukl, G., & Falbe, C. M. (1990). Influence tactics and objectives in upward, downward, and lateral influence attempts. *Journal of Applied Psychology, 75,* 132–140.

Yukl, G., & Falbe, C. M. (1991). Importance of different power sources in downward and lateral relations. *Journal of Applied Psychology, 76,* 416–423.

Yukl, G., & Tracey, J. B. (1992). Consequences of influence tactics used with subordinates, peers, and the boss. *Journal of Applied Psychology, 77,* 525–535

Zaccaro, S. J., & McCoy, M. C. (1988). The effects of task and interpersonal cohesiveness on performance of a disjunctive group task. *Journal of Applied Social Psychology, 18,* 837–851.

Zaccaro, S. J., Foti, R. J., & Kenny, D. A. (1991). Self–monitoring and trait–based variance in leadership: An investigation of leader flexibility across multiple group situations. *Journal of Applied Psychology, 76,* 308–315.

Zajonc, R. B. (1965). Social facilitation. *Science, 149,* 269–274.

Zajonc, R. B. (1968). Attitudinal effects of mere exposure. *Journal of Personality and Social Psychology Monograph Supplement, 9,* 1–27.

Zajonc, R. B., & McIntosh, D. N. (1992). Emotions research: Some promising questions and some questionable promises. *Psychological Science, 3,* 70–74.

Zajonc, R. B., & Sales, S. H. (1966). Social facilitation of dominant and subordinate responses. *Journal of Experimental Social Psychology, 2,* 160–168.

Zajonc, R. B., Adelmann, P. K., Murphy, S. T., & Niedenthal, P. M. (1987). Convergence in the physical appearance of spouses. *Motivation and Emotion, 11,* 335–346.

Zajonc, R. B., Heingartner, A., & Herman, E. M. (1969). Social enhancement and impairment of performance in the cockroach. *Journal of Personality and Social Psychology, 13,* 83–92.

Zillmann, D. (1979). *Hostility and aggression.* Hillsdale, NJ: Erlbaum.

Zillmann, D. (1983). Transfer of excitation in emotional behavior. In J. T. Cacioppo & R. E. Petty (Eds.), *Social psychophysiology: A sourcebook* (pp. 215–240). New York: Guilford Press.

Zillmann, D. (1988). Cognition–excitation interdependencies in aggressive behavior. *Aggressive Behavior, 14,* 51–64.

Zimbardo, P. G. (1977). *Shyness: What it is and what we can do about it.* Reading, MA: Addison–Wesley.

Zimmerman, M. A. (1990). Toward a theory of learned hopefulness: A structural model and analysis of participation and empowerment. *Journal of Research in Personality, 24,* 71–86.

Zuber, J. A., Crott, H. W., & Werner, J. (1992). Choice shift and group polarization: An analysis of the status of arguments and social decision schemes. *Journal of Personality and Social Psychology, 62,* 50–61.

Zuckerman, M., & Driver, R. E. (1989). What sounds beautiful is good: The vocal attractiveness stereotype. *Journal of Nonverbal Behavior, 13,* 67–82.

Name Index

Threat, two-level response to, 355, 356

Tokenism, 171

Touching, and age, 45-46

 cultural differences in, 48

 gender differences in, 45-46

 as nonverbal cue, 45-46

Transformational leadership, 344-46

Triangular model of love, 208, 210

Truth-wins rule, 328

Twin studies, 83-84

Two-factor theory (Schachter), 70

Two-thirds majority rule, 328

Type A personality, 357, 358

Type B personality, 357

U

UCLA Loneliness Scale, 227

Ultimate attribution error, 60-61

Us-versus-them effect, 156-57, 179-80

V

Values, 82-84

 of Canadians and Americans, 82-83, 84

cross-cultural comparison, 132

 of English-Canadians and French-Canadians, 83, 84

Variables, 22

 confounding of, 25, 28

 dependent, 23

 independent, 23

Variable self-esteem, 114

Verdict-driven deliberation, 329

Vested interest, 86-87

Vicarious control, 363

Victims, asking for help, 283-84

 characteristics of, and altruism, 282-84

 reactions to being helped, 284

 responsibility of, 282

 self-esteem, 284

Violence, in Canada, 12-13

 effect of temperature on, 366

 in the media, 297-300, 302-3

 newspaper reportage of violent crime, 375

 punishment as a deterrent to, 304-5

 see also Aggression

Voir dire process, 379, 380

W

Waste products, 370-71

Weapons effect, 301-2

Wishful thinking, 365

Witnesses, *see* Eyewitnesses

Women, abuse by husbands, 306-8

 discrimination against, 160-62

 effect of gender stereotypes on, 160-62, 382

 as leaders, 340

Working self-concept, 112

Writing about stressful events, health benefits of, 359-60

Y

Yale Approach, 89

Chapter 1

1.3a, Rokuo Kawakami/The Image Bank; 1.3b, David de Lossy/The Image Bank; 1.5a, Janeart, Ltd./The Image Bank; 1.5b, Frank Siteman/Stock, Boston; 1.6, CanadaWide; 1.7, CanadaWide; 1.8, Jeff Greenberg/The Picture Cube; 1.10, Al Harvey.

Chapter 2

2.2a, Carol Lee/The Picture Cube; 2.2b, C.J. Allen/Stock, Boston; 2.2c, Sarah Putnam/The Picture Cube; 2.2d, Lynn McLaren/The Picture Cube; 2.2e, Ellis Herwig/The Picture Cube; 2.2f, Dag Sundberg/The Image Bank; 2.3, Copyright Paul Ekman; 2.6, CanadaWide; 2.7, Don Smetzer/Tony Stone Worldwide; 2.10, CanadaWide; 2.11, CanadaWide; 2.12, Uniphoto; 2.13, Rock Browne/Stock, Boston; 2.14, Michael Keller/Uniphoto.

Chapter 3

3.3, Dick Hemingway; 3.8, CanadaWide.

Chapter 4

4.3, H. Sund/The Image Bank; 4.5, Jack McConnell/McConnell, McNamara & Company; 4.9, CanadaWide.

Chapter 5

5.1, CanadaWide; 5.11a, Nancy Brown/The Image Bank; 5.11b, Jack McConnell/McConnell, McNamara & Company; 5.11c, David de Lossy/The Image Bank; 5.11d, Kevin Forest/The Image Bank; 5.11e, Tim Bieber/The Image Bank; 5.11f, André Gallant/The Image Bank; 5.15, Paula Gross/The Picture Cube.

Chapter 6

6.2, Robyn Craig; 6.4, Paul Mozell/Stock, Boston; 6.7, Canapress; 6.9, The Bettmann Archive.

Chapter 7

7.2a, Nancy Brown/the Image Bank; 7.2b, Don Smetzer/TSW/Click/Chicago; 7.5, Michael Melford/The Image Bank; 7.8a, Peter Menzel/Stock, Boston; 7.8b, Theresee Frare/The Picture Cube; 7.8c, Lawrence Berman/The Image Bank; 7.11, Andrew Holbrooke/Black Star; 7.13, Wide World Photos; 7.14, From the film *Obedience*, distributed by Pennsylvania State University Film Library, Copyright 1965 by Stanley Milgram; 7.16, Superstock.

Chapter 8

8.1a, Scott Photo Service and Susan Van Etten; 8.1b, Rhoda Sidney/Southern Light; 8.6, Anthony Boccaccio/The Image Bank; 8.8, Lynn Johnson/Black Star; 8.11, The Bettmann Archive; 8.14a, Ted Spiegel/Black Star; 8.14b, Steve Stone/The Picture Cube; 8.22, CNN.

Chapter 9

9.1a, Robert Daemmrich/Stock, Boston; 9.1b, André Gallant/The Image Bank; 9.1c, John Coletti/Stock, Boston; 9.2, Canapress; 9.5a, Gerard Champlong/the Image Bank; 9.5b, Nubar Alexanian/Stock, Boston; 9.11, Canapress; 9.13a, CanadaWide; 9.13b, Wide World Photos.

Chapter 10

10.8, Marko Shark; 10.11, Stacy Pick/Stock, Boston.